TABLE OF CONTENTS

INTRODUCTION: QUICK REFERENCE & GLOSSARY 2
GAME MODES 14
SYSTEM & GAMEPLAY 24
CHARACTER STRATEGY

MARVEL:

CAPTAIN AMERICA 59
DEADPOOL 67
DOCTOR DOOM 75
DORMAMMU 83
HULK 93
IRON MAN 101
MAGNETO 111
M.O.D.O.K. 119
PHOENIX 127
SHE-HULK 137
SPIDER-MAN 145
STORM 153
SUPER-SKRULL 161
THOR 169
WOLVERINE 177
X-23 187

CAPCOM:

AMATERASU 197
ARTHUR 207
CHRIS REDFIELD 217
CHUN-LI 227
C. VIPER 237
DANTE 247
FELICIA 257
HAGGAR 265
MORRIGAN 275
RYU 283
SPENCER 293
TRISH 301
TRON 307
WESKER 315
VIEWTIFUL JOE 325
ZERO 333

HIDDEN CHARACTERS

SENTINEL 345
TASKMASTER 353

HIDDEN CHARACTERS

AKUMA 361
HSIEN-KO 371

DLC CHARACTER

SHUMA-GORATH 379

DLC CHARACTER

JILL 385

TROPHIES, ACHIEVEMENTS, ICONS, & TITLES 391

The contents of this strategy guide are based solely on the research of BradyGAMES.

INTRODUCTION

FATE OF TWO WORLDS

Victor Von Doom has assembled the greatest villains his world has to offer. But there are other worlds than theirs...

Together with the diabolical Albert Wesker, a villain from another such world, this unholy alliance will join their respective universes in an effort to conquer both.

But doing so has come with a terrible price. A great and powerful threat has been awakened...a threat that will set into motion a battle the likes of which neither world has ever known.

A battle that will decide the fate of two worlds!

USING THIS GUIDE

Marvel® vs. Capcom® 3: Fate of Two Worlds is an extremely complex game. While hardened veterans of *Marvel vs. Capcom 2: New Age of Heroes* will have little trouble jumping in and feeling at home, fans of other fighting games—or Marvel® Comics and Capcom fans new to fighters in general—will require an acclimation period. Consider this guide your indoctrination. The authors of this guide have attempted to create a guide that will be all things to all people. This chapter serves as an introduction and quick reference. Included are basic controls and a glossary of terms, so that any general questions can hopefully be answered as quickly as possible. Following this chapter are sections that break down the various modes in the game, as well as the game systems that churn under the action. We assume you are completely green in these sections—if you're new to fighters, or even just the *MvC* series, it's here you'll want to start. Later on, our character-specific strategic chapters assume that you have a fairly decent handle on game mechanics, and delve into thorough depth discussing match strategies for each character, both individually and in a team context. It's here that a comfortable or experienced player will find the most value—our character-specific sections contain frame data for each character's move set, along with powerful combos and winning strategies.

Many players, whether casual fighting fans or avid comic readers, are most interested in *MvC3* because of its pedigree. Few creative houses can boast the rich characters and history of Marvel® Comics or Capcom, after all. If this is you, we hope you enjoy this book as a collector's piece to accompany the game. It's replete with art, quotes, and biographical details for all the heroes. (We also secretly hope that we can make a light bulb go off over your head, and help you to appreciate this game, and the fighting genre in general, at a greater depth!)

For the novice looking to get into fighters, or the intermediate-level player looking to improve, we hope to make that light bulb shine brighter—perhaps replacing that old, flickering incandescent with a nice, long-lasting compact fluorescent? Sorry about that analogy; we simply hope to encourage your passion. On this note, if you are new, ***do not get discouraged*** if you go online, or to a friend's place, or wherever, and have your you-know-what handed to you for a while! Everyone has to start somewhere, and you must learn to walk before you can learn to ~~run~~ wavedash. Do not get upset when you lose (and you *will* lose, especially if you're relatively new). Instead, view every match as a learning opportunity, rather than a test. This is good advice even for very experienced players—any player can win any given match, but what does it matter if you didn't learn anything? The complexity of the game may seem overwhelming at times, but again, don't get discouraged. Take it a little bit at a time, working on one or two concepts at a time until you've totally internalized them before you incorporate more tactics and strategies.

For the pros, our frame data and combos should give you an excellent jumping-off point to develop and refine your own combos and strategies. You might not even think we can help you, but we beg to differ—you'll find this book useful as a data reference, and as a place to start when exploring new characters.

QUICK REFERENCE

ALL COMMANDS IN THIS GUIDE ASSUME YOUR CHARACTER IS STANDING TOWARD THE LEFT, ON THE PLAYER 1 SIDE, FACING RIGHT TOWARD THE PLAYER 2 SIDE. FORWARD IS THUS EXPRESSED AS →, BACKWARD AS ←. FOR A CHARACTER ON THE RIGHT, FACING LEFT TOWARD THE PLAYER 1 SIDE, REVERSE ANY DIRECTIONAL INPUTS.

MvC3 can be played with a variety of gamepads and joysticks. To accommodate many kinds of potential input devices, you can customize your control scheme from within the options menu.

DEFAULT BUTTON CONFIGURATIONS

The default control schemes on both PlayStation 3 and Xbox 360 assign the buttons to similar locations.

To simulate the arcade experience, many players prefer using a joystick. Having a truly great home stick used to mean going the custom route, but now there are excellent, widely-available joysticks for each console, most notably variations of the MadCatz Tournament Edition joystick, which uses high-quality arcade parts and is extremely durable and accurate. The manufacturer Hori also produces high-quality console joysticks, such as the Real Arcade Pro.

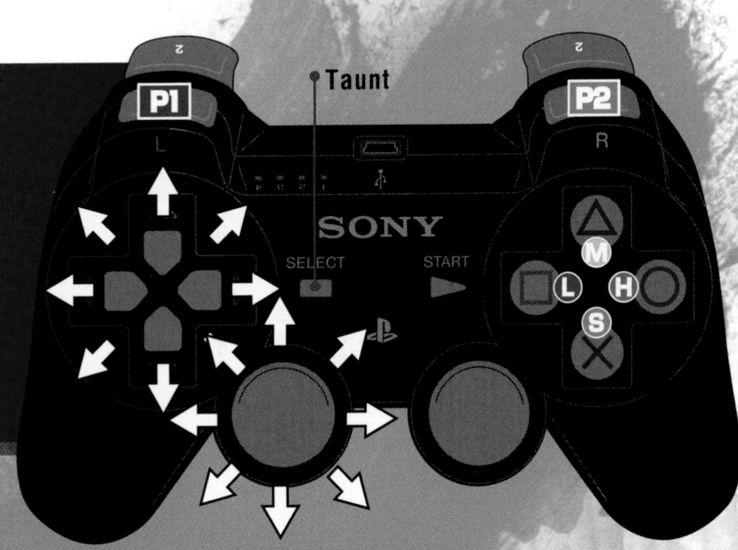

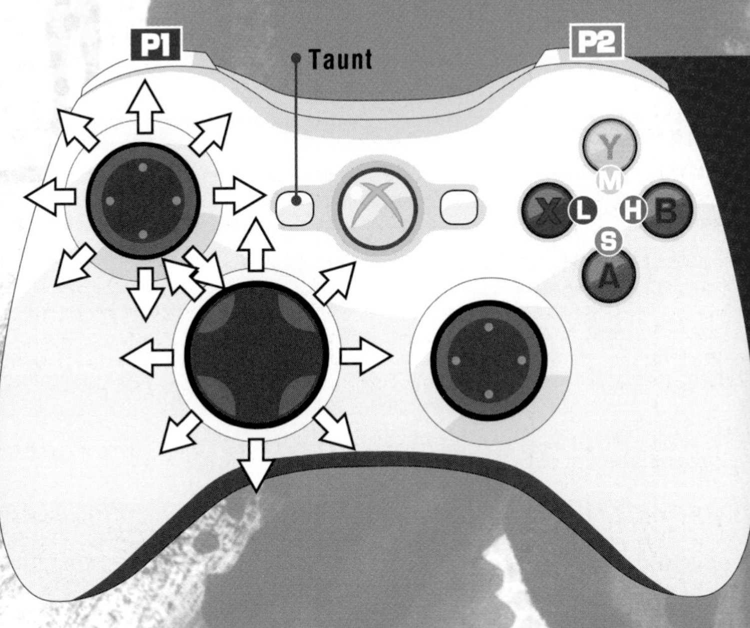

The use of a gamepad or joystick comes down to preference. When almost all tournaments were in arcades, players had little choice. But now, with the preeminence of console and online play, there is no forced specialization. PlayStation joypads have been competent for fighting games since their inception, and Xbox 360 has a recently-released special edition gamepad available with an improved, adjustable D-pad, specifically to better cater to finely-tuned games like fighters.

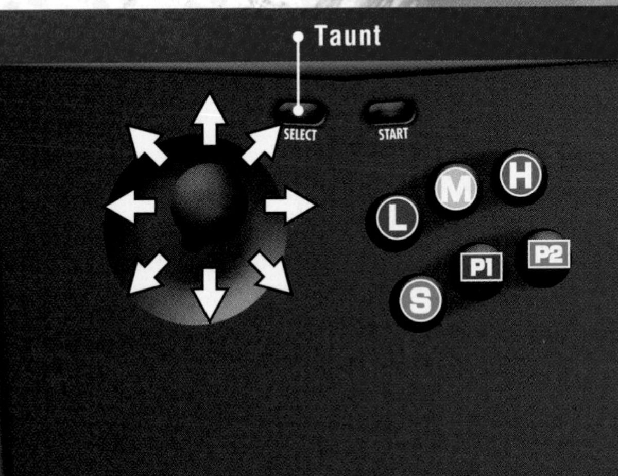

The intended, default configuration for a six-button joystick. Depending on your joystick, this is almost certainly not the default mapping. Check in the options, and customize as needed. For a Madcatz, it's as easy as setting controller type to β. For any Hori joystick, you'll need configure a custom controller setup. Of course, for online play you can map your buttons however you like, and most tournaments will also allow button mapping. Some players frown on multiple inputs mapped to one button, but others view concern as much ado about nothing. However, most players seriously frown on the use of turbo or macro functions on controllers, and just about every tournament bans them as well, for good reason in a game that relies so heavily on dexterous execution.

SIMPLE PLAY

A simplified control scheme is also available. This scheme allows special moves and hyper combos to be performed simply by pressing single buttons, and chain combos can be executed by repetitiously pressing the same button, but Simple Play mode does not grant access to the full arsenal of each character. The button configuration in simple play mode is not customizable, so your results on a non-standard controller may be very mixed. This guide assumes the player is using normal play mode, for maximum potential. The same strategies described for normal play will work for simple play too, within the limitations of simple play's diminished movelist.

SIMPLE PLAY BUTTON CONFIGURATION

PlayStation 3	Xbox 360	Function	Limitations versus normal mode
■ (■■■ for chain combo)	Ⓧ (ⓍⓍⓍ for chain combo)	Basic attack (press repeatedly for a chain combo emulating normal play mode Ⓛ, Ⓜ, Ⓗ)	Initial press is always Ⓛ; no access to Ⓜ or Ⓗ attacks for use outside of combos. No access to chains other than Ⓛ, Ⓜ, Ⓗ. Some command attacks missing.
▲	Ⓨ	Special move	Cannot choose special move strength. Many special moves are missing (though some can be accessed by holding a direction while pressing the special move button).
●	Ⓑ	Hyper combo	Not all hyper combos are available.
✕	Ⓐ	Special attack (press repeatedly to launch then super jump automatically)	—
L1	LB	[P1] Partner 1	—
L2	LT	[P1+P2] Partner 1 + Partner 2	—
R1	RB	[P2] Partner 2	—
R2	RT	Ⓛ + Ⓜ + Ⓗ	—

NOTATIONS

Many icons are used throughout this guide to indicate button presses and techniques. Directions assume a character facing right. Guarding is always relative to the other team's point character—the enemy's partner behind you doesn't alter how you guard.

Icon	Description	May Also Be Called
⇨	Indicates forward. Hold ⇨ to walk forward, tap ⇨⇨ to forward dash.	—
⇘	Diagonally down-forward.	Offensive crouch.
⇩	Down. Hold ⇩ to crouch. You must also tap ⇩ before tapping any upward direction for a super jump.	Crouch.
⇙	Diagonally down-back. Hold ⇙ for crouching guard when low attacks are incoming.	Defensive crouch.
⇦	Back. Hold ⇦ to walk backward, or for standing guard against high and mid attacks. Tap ⇦⇦ to backward dash.	—
⇖	Up-back. Starts a backward jump. Hold any backward direction to guard while airborne.	Defensive jump.
⇧	Up. Starts a jump. Tap ⇩ first before any upward direction for a super jump. After actions that are cancelable with jumps or super jumps, like Ⓢ launchers, simply hold any upward direction to cancel to a jump or super jump (the result is move-dependent).	Jump.
⇗	Up-forward. Starts a forward jump.	Offensive jump.
Ⓛ	Light attack, or L.	1 or A, as a holdover from *Tatsunoko vs. Capcom All-Stars*; jab or short, as a holdover from *Street Fighter*.
Ⓜ	Medium attack, or M.	2 or B, as a holdover from *Tatsunoko vs. Capcom All-Stars*; strong or forward, as a holdover from *Street Fighter*.
Ⓗ	Hard attack, or H.	3 or C, as a holdover from *Tatsunoko vs. Capcom All-Stars*; fierce or roundhouse, as a holdover from *Street Fighter*.
ATK	Attack icon. Indicates any of Ⓛ, Ⓜ, or Ⓗ may be used. Most hyper combos require ATK ATK for button inputs following the right motion, and dashes can also be performed with ATK ATK.	Basic attacks, normal moves.
Ⓢ	Special attack, or S.	Exchange, as a holdover from *MvC3*'s pre-final development.
[P1]	Partner 1. Partners can be called while standing or crouching, and during normal jumps, flight modes starting from normal jumps, and during basic attacks starting from any of those positions.	Assist 1.
[P2]	Partner 2. Partners cannot be called while guarding, nor while executing special moves or hyper combos, nor during super jumps or flight modes originating from super jumps.	Assist 2.
[P1 or P2]	Partner 1 *or* 2 (but not both!). This is used often in our notation of combos, as the right assist for a combo or tactic may be in a different slot depending on your overall team makeup and the flow of the match.	—
[P1+P2]	Partner 1 + Partner 2, resulting in a crossover combination if the hyper combo gauge has at least 1 level.	Team hyper combo, as a holdover from *MvC2*. Here, team hyper combo means what delayed hyper combo, or DHC, used to mean in *MvC2*.
CANCEL ➔	Cancel icon. Indicates the action preceding CANCEL ➔ is interrupted with the following action, e.g. crouching Ⓜ CANCEL ➔ ⇩⇘⇨ + Ⓗ	Buffer.
Ⓛ)), Ⓜ)), Ⓗ)), ATK))	Icon indicating a move that requires at least three rapid inputs to activate. Some of these moves are sustainable, given continued inputs.	Pressing an input rapidly is often called "mashing."
X-Factor icon	X-Factor. Executed by pressing Ⓛ+Ⓜ+Ⓗ+Ⓢ all together while standing. The activation of X-Factor cancels any action, even hyper combos or guarding, and X-Factor itself increases speed and power for a limited time. Can only be used once per match.	—

GLOSSARY OF TERMS

The lexicon of fighting game terms has roots stretching as far back as 1991, the year that *Street Fighter 2: The World Warrior* took the arcade world by storm and essentially created the competitive fighting game. The popularity of this then-fledgling genre was instrumental in ushering in more complex video games in general, yet fighting games remain among the most complicated. A lot of information must be internalized in order to be successful. If you're new to fighting games, or maybe just *Marvel Vs. Capcom* and the larger "*Vs.*" series, this section is designed to clear up any questions on terms and concepts as quickly as possible. For more in-depth discussion, check out the **System & Gameplay** chapter, or sections for individual characters. It is important to note that many terms included here match official in-game terms, but some non-standard definitions are included. These are appropriated from other games, or from the consensus of the competitive community, in the interests of thoroughness and clarity.

active	Refers to "active frames," or the period during which an attack can strike an opponent. After this period, a move enters its **recovery** phase.
advancing guard	Perform by pressing ATK ATK while **guarding** an opponent's attack. Creates separation from the opponent, which is invaluable for breathing room. Can also be called **pushblock**.
advantage	The opportunity to act first, between two combatants acting as soon as possible after some sort of interaction. Converse – **Disadvantage**. See **frame advantage/frame disadvantage**.
aerial rave	Synonym for **air combo**; a holdover from *MvC1*.
air combo	Can simply refer to a combo that occurs in mid-air. Can also refer to a **combo** performed after **launching** with S **special attack**, then **canceling** into a **super jump** by holding any upward direction. During a super jump, all characters are capable of the full air **chain** L L M M H S. Positioning usually makes that full chain hard to actually accomplish, and **damage scaling** and **hitstun deterioration** make the repeated use of low-damage L attacks imprudent anyway. During an air combo following a launcher, air S will cause **flying screen**, while directional input + S will start a **team aerial combo**, or **TAC**. For almost all characters, air M, M, H, S is a reliable air combo that leads to an **OTG** opportunity. As an alternative to flying screen, you can end an air combo with a **special move, hyper combo,** or **reset** attempt.
air control	The degree to which you can, or cannot, influence the trajectory of your character's airborne jump arc with ← or → controller input.
airdash	A dash performed in mid-air. Having extra mobility is never a bad thing. Some characters can airdash in any direction, but others can only airdash backward, or forward, or both. Characters like Morrigan and Amaterasu have peculiar airdashes.
air recovery	**Hitstun** that ends such that the victim is airborne results in air recovery. Air recovery occurs in place automatically, or → or ← can be held to choose a direction in which to recover. After air recovery, a character is considered to be in a **normal jump** state.
air throw	**Throw** performed air-to-air. Accomplished with air ← or → + H. Some characters have mid-air **command throws**. Usually leads to an **unrecoverable knockdown** and thus an **OTG** opportunity.
anti-air	Any attack or action used to stop a **jump-in** or otherwise counter an airborne opponent.
assist type	Assist types are organized by the first three letters of the Greek alphabet—α (alpha), β (beta), γ (gamma). Assist types are further described by their characteristics. Shot type means that the character fires a **projectile** or **beam**, while direct type means they attack using their body, for example.
backward	Action, movement, or directional input away from an opponent.
backward dash	A quick backward movement, accomplished with ← ← or ← + ATK ATK. Usually just called **backdash**.
backward jump	A defensive leap away from the enemy. Tap ↙ to jump backward. Tap ↓ first for a backward **super jump**.
basic attack	An attack performed with just L, M, or H. Differs depending on whether **standing**, **crouching**, or airborne. Basic attacks can be **canceled** into one another with **chain combos**. Can also be called **normal moves.**
battery	A character whose primary purpose on a team is to build up the **hyper combo gauge**.
beam	**Projectile**-like blast of energy that behaves a bit differently than standard projectiles. Beams usually hit many more times than projectiles, and will disappear instantly if the beamer is **counterhit** in the act of firing the beam. When beams clash with other beams or projectiles, they'll exchange **durability points** from the opposing beam or projectile every **frame** for a certain number of frames, until one or the other is depleted of durability points and thus destroyed.
block	Synonymous with **guard**.
block damage	Damage taken from an attack even if **guarded**. Most **special moves** and **hyper combos**, and even a few **basic attacks**, inflict block damage. Block damage is sometimes also called **chip**. This damage is 30% that of an actual hit.
blockstun	Synonymous with **guardstun**.
break away	A break away is a **throw** escape (sometimes called a "tech throw"). A throw can be broken by inputting ← or → + H within 7 **frames** of being thrown. Note that **command throws** cannot be escaped! After a break away both characters end up next to each other, ready to act, with the throw initiator having +1 **frame advantage** (conversely, the character who broke the throw is at -1 **frame disadvantage**).
buffering	Multiple definitions. Can refer to using the commands or motion for one action to also count for another; used often in **cancels** and **combos**. Buffering can also refer to entering the command for your next action while a current action is still underway. In both instances, you're taking advantage of a game engine feature that allows inputs to account for multiple actions.
bug	Unintended game feature. Synonymous with **glitch**. Sometimes enhances or detracts from gameplay.
cancel	Interrupting one action before its normal recovery period ends by starting another action. This is key to lots of advanced gameplay, and **combos** in general. "Cancelable" is often used as a characteristic of important attacks; for example a move that is "jump-cancelable" can be interrupted with a jump.
chain combo	A string of **basic attacks,** canceled into one another. The ultimate rules are character-dependent and fall under a few archetypes, but generally attacks can always be chained upward in strength, and can almost always chain to S **special attack**. Chain combos are accomplished simply by pressing the button for the next basic attack while the current one is in progress. Usually just called **chains**.
chip damage	Synonymous with **block damage**. Usually just called **chip**.
close range	Characters right next to each other, in range of each others' **launchers** and **throws**, are at close range. Close range combat is usually focused on **mix-ups** between **overheads**, **low** attacks, and **throws**, each of which must be dealt with differently.
combo	A sequence of attacks that is guaranteed if the first attack is not **guarded**. Works because of **hitstun**.
command throw	**Throw** that requires a motion to accomplish, like a **special move**. **Command throws** cannot be escaped, and sometimes have other properties that distinguish them from normal throws, such as increased range, damage, or follow-up opportunities . Normal throws grab on the 1st frame, however, while many—but not all—command throws are slower to activate. Some command throws (like Thor's Mighty Hurricane H, or Wesker's Mustang Kick) grab on the first frame!
corner	The side of a stage. Cornering an enemy usually grants a huge advantage; cornered opponents can no longer move backward, are usually susceptible to larger combos, and have limited, predictable options for escaping the corner. **Advancing guard**, normally a cornerstone of defense, is also much less effective when cornered. Being cornered is generally bad, unless you are intentionally attempting something like a backward **throw** into a corner-only **combo**.
corner-only	Refers to a **combo** or tactic that only works with the foe pushed against into a corner.
counter	Counter can refer generally to any action that is used to **reverse** the opponent's intentions, or specifically to refer to **special moves** that deflect incoming attacks, such as Wesker's Tiger Uppercut or Amaterasu's Solar Flare.
counterhit	Striking the opponent while they try to attack results in a counterhit. Counterhits do not have an across-the-board damage increase in *MvC3* like they do in most fighting games; rather, counterhits create 2 additional frames of **hitstun,** and occasionally cause special **hit states** on a case-by-case basis, based on a given move.

crossover assist — Call for help from a partner by tapping [P1 or P2]. Every character has three assist types, which dictate the attack they will perform when called. Assist type also dictates which **hyper combo** they will perform during a **crossover combination**. This is usually a **special move** or **command attack** from their arsenal, though a few crossover assists are unique actions. Usually just called **assists.**

crossover attack — Accomplished by holding [P1 or P2]. If available, the requested partner will tag in with a quick **overhead** attack, before becoming the **point character**.

crossover combination — Performed by pressing [P1+P2]. Requires one bar of **hyper combo gauge** for every partner participating. Depending on how many characters remain, and how much hyper combo gauge is available, 1~3 characters come onscreen simultaneously to perform **hyper combos** together. The hyper combo each character executes is dictated by their **crossover assist** type.

crossover counter — Accomplished by **blocking**, then inputting → + [P1 or P2]. One level of **hyper combo gauge** is consumed, and the chosen hero tags in with a **crossover assist**.

cross-up — An attack that must be guarded in the opposite direction than expected. **Cross-ups** are usually set up by **jumping** just over an opponent's head, so that you cross over at the last second. Cross-ups are particularly effective when used against an opponent pinned by a **crossover assist**, or recovering from a **knockdown**.

crouch — A ducking position accomplished by holding any downward direction. A crouching character is a shorter target than a standing one, but is susceptible to **overheads,** and certain "pass-through" tricks which don't work on standing characters (for example, Hulk's forward **dash** will actually pass *over* many crouching characters). "Cr." is used in the combo strings of this guide as shorthand for crouching.

crouching guard — A defensive stance that guards against incoming **low** and **mid** attacks. Vulnerable to **throws** and **overheads**.

crumple — Special hit effect caused by certain attacks, like C. Viper's EX Thunder Knuckle, or her Focus Attack. The victim slumps slowly to the floor, and is vulnerable to continued punishment on the way down. Victims hit during a crumple will be **juggled** into aerial **hitstun**.

damage scaling — A safety feature innate to **combos** in which successive hits deal a dwindling percentage of base damage. Prevents combos from being totally overpowering. Damage scaling is considerably lessened with **X-Factor** active, and doesn't apply to **level 3 hyper combos** at all.

dash — A quick movement. Dashes are vital to covering distance quickly, regaining positioning after being pushed back with advancing guard, and keeping the enemy on their toes. Can be accomplished either by tapping ← ← or → →, or by pressing ← or → + [ATK][ATK].

delay — Delaying move execution either to **hit-confirm** before continuing a **chain combo**, or to bait the opponent into attempting to attack. Coaxing the opponent to stick out attacks when they don't really have time to do so is called a **frame trap**, and is a prime way to cause **counterhits**. For example, if your opponent **guards** your opening of crouching (L), crouching (M), yet they do not use **advancing guard** to push you out, you can recognize this and wait longer than usual before **chaining** into (H) very late. Opponents who see the small gap and attempt to take the initiative back with a **poke** of their own will eat the late chained (H) as a counterhit.

disadvantage — Refers to a situation in which your earliest possible action will occur after your opponent's. The opposite of **advantage**. See also **frame advantage/frame disadvantage**. Usually expressed as a number; for example a disadvantage of -4 means the opponent can act four frames before you.

dizzy — A hit effect created by certain moves, such as Haggar's air ↑ + (H) that **counterhits** a standing opponent. The victim reels, stunned, unable to act until dizzy ends.

draw — The result if both teams have an equal percentage of life remaining when the timer runs out. Neither team wins.

durability points & projectile priority — When **projectiles** or **beams** (or attacks that can destroy projectiles, such as some of Dormammu's or Sentinel's **basic attacks**) strike each other, hidden properties dictate which projectile will win. The first check is **projectile priority**. Projectiles have either low, medium, or high priority against other projectiles or projectile-like attacks. Higher-priority projectiles will destroy lower-priority projectiles outright. When equal-priority projectiles or projectile-like attacks collide, **durability points** come into play. Equal-priority projectiles will mutually deplete each other's durability points frame after frame (by a set amount per frame—the actual durability points value[md]that varies per projectile), until the loser projectile is destroyed and the victor projectile continues forward as normal, but with a depleted reserve of remaining durability points, which becomes relevant if another projectile is encountered.

empty jump — A **jump** performed without any attack. Usually followed by a fast **low** attack upon landing. Since most jumping attacks are **overheads** (meaning they must be **guarded** while standing), an opponent's defensive reaction to recognizing a jump should be to guard standing, which makes them susceptible to low attacks.

fireball — Generic term that applies to **projectiles** and **beams**.

Flight — The power of Flight is possessed by many heroes here. Flight modes are both started and stopped with ↓ ↙ ← + (S). The properties of Flight are slightly different depending on when it was initiated. In short, there is "super jump flight," when activating flight during a super jump, and "normal jump flight," when starting flight from a normal jump or a standing position. Mobility is increased during Flight, at the cost of not being able to **guard**. Flight will end naturally after roughly two seconds (character depending), after using air (S), after receiving a hit, after particular moves, or after another input of ↓ ↙ ← + (S). The **startup** of Flight, or its manual **cancelation**, can both be used to cancel **basic attacks**.

Flight cancel — **Canceling** a **basic attack** into **flight**, or using the manual cancelation of flight to cancel a basic attack. Some characters can use Flight-canceling to prolong **air combos**, or to suddenly switch from ground attacks that can be guarded crouching to air attacks that must be guarded standing.

float — Ability possessed only by Storm. Hold ↑ in mid-air to slow her descent. As perhaps an unintended consequence of this ability, Storm can execute extremely fast air **overhead** attacks just off the ground; see Storm's character chapter for details.

flying screen — The unique event that occurs after **launching** the opponent with (S), then ending the subsequent **air combo** with air (S). The character struck by the combo is hurtled quickly to the ground, and the screen flies violently as the aggressive character falls downward to catch up. Flying screen leaves the victim in an **unrecoverable knockdown**, so **OTG**s are possible.

footsies — Refers to positional game that usually takes place at the edge of each characters' range, in which players try to **poke**, counter-**poke**, and score **knockdowns**. The *Vs.* games are unique among fighters in how much this takes place in the air as much as on the ground, thanks to the aerial mobility exhibited by so much of the cast, and because of the flexibility offered by team dynamics and **crossover assists**.

"for free" — A catch-all fighting game term that indicates an action is guaranteed and risk-free, e.g. "after guarding X move, you can land Y combo for free."

forward — Refers to directions toward your opponent. This guide assumes your character is on the left side of the screen (often called the 1P side), facing your opponent on the right, for forward is represented as →.

forward dash — An aggressive movement toward the opponent. Accomplished with → → or → + [ATK][ATK]. Most characters can cancel their dash at any time with most actions, but a few characters can only cancel their dash after a certain point, and some characters can't cancel their dashes at all.

forward jump — Sometimes called offensive jump. Tap ↗ to jump forward. Tap ↓ first for a forward **super jump**.

frame — The game's unit of time measurement. 60 frames is equal to one second.

frame advantage / frame disadvantage — Most encounters in the game result in one character ready to act slightly before the other. Being able to act before an opponent is called frame advantage, or simply advantage. When your opponent can act first, you are at a frame disadvantage, or simply disadvantage. The concept of frame advantage or disadvantage can be expressed with a number—for example, +6 would indicate a frame advantage of +6, meaning you can act six frames before the opposition.

frame trap — Intentionally placing very small, educated gaps in an offense so an opponent has time to stick out an attack, just in time to be **counterhit**. You want these gaps to be very small, just a few frames; long enough for the opponent's attack to **startup**, but not long enough for it to be **active**.

glitch — Synonymous with **bug**.

ground bounce — Hit effect in which a character is ricocheted forcibly off the ground. Victim is vulnerable to further punishment. Only one ground bounce is normally allowed per **combo,** but exceptions to this rule exist.

ground recovery — After most **knockdowns**, the victim will spring up instantly off the ground. By holding ← or →, this recovery can be directed. Victims are momentarily invincible while recovering from the floor.

FRAME DATA: A BRIEF PRIMER

Throughout this guide we refer specifically to frame data figures that illustrate the actual period of time taken up by attacks and actions. This information may seem daunting at first, if you're unfamiliar with frame data up until now, but as you play the game while referring to this guide you'll quickly grasp the ideas involved, and the usefulness of the data.

Startup frames always include the first active frame, for ease of reading to find possible links. For example, a character with a +8 advantage will be able to link any move with 8 or fewer startup frames, thus creating or perpetuating a combo.

Active frames represent the number of frames in which an attack can actually contact the opponent.

Recovery frames start 1 frame after the last active frame of non-projectile moves, and end the frame before the character returns to a neutral state. Once recovery is complete, the character is free to perform another action.

Projectile recovery starts one frame after the last projectile released becomes active, and ends the frame before the character can perform another action. For example, if Ryu's Hadoken has a 10 frame startup, recovery starts on frame 11.

Frame advantage is always shown assuming that the *first* active frame is the one to make contact with an opposing character. In effect, this makes the remaining active frames a part of recovery, as well. Timing attacks to strike during the end of active frames (a "meaty" attack) results in more frame advantage, but is not always feasible.

Frame advantage usually (but not always!) differs depending on whether the opponent eats an attack, or guards it. If the opponent guards properly and pushes you away with advancing guard, the issue of frame advantage or disadvantage is usually rendered irrelevant due to the separation created; however, some characters have methods to keep advantage even when pushed out with advancing guard.

SPECIFIC NOTATIONS USED IN HIT, DAMAGE, AND FRAME DATA.

Parentheses indicate inactive frames in the active frame column. For example, 5(3)5 would indicate that there are 5 active frames, then 3 inactive frames that cannot interact with the opposing character, and then 5 more active frames.

When the tilde (~) is used, it means that the values can be either one of the listed values, or somewhere in between, depending on the move and situation. A common example is for moves that can be charged. Other examples include moves that can require repeated button presses to increase the number of hits by a limited amount, or have some other mechanic that can cause any of the data to be variable within a fixed range of values.

Similarly, when / is used it indicates values for different states of the same move. For example, charge moves that have multiple stages that increase the power in each stage, such as Zero's Hyper Zero Blaster. When a character is in a powered-up state that drastically alters a majority of a character's data, such as Wolverine's Berserker Charge, *italics* are used to indicate the altered data while that character is in the powered-up state.

Finally, frame data for hyper combo startup is depicted just a little bit differently. Hyper combos have a "cutscene" right at the beginning that shows the character close-up. During this cutscene, all other action stops briefly. Therefore, hyper combo startup involves both the period leading up to that cutscene, and the period after the cutscene until the hyper combo is actually active. We depict these two periods with a + sign. For example, a hyper combo startup of 10+4 indicates there are 10 frames before the cutscene, then 4 frames after the cutscene, until the hyper combo can actually strike the enemy.

*The contents of this strategy guide are based solely on the research of BradyGames

guard	A critical defensive action that negates some or all of the damage sustained from incoming attacks. In the air, guarding is accomplished simply by holding any backward direction, relative the opponent's **point character**—⇙, ⇐, or ⇖, it doesn't matter. On the ground, you must choose to guard either standing, by holding ⇐, or crouching, by holding ⇙. **Standing guard** will block incoming high and mid attacks, while **crouching guard** will block incoming mid and low attacks. Guarding is not impenetrable—**unguardable** attacks and **throws** ignore guard. Also called **blocking.**
guard break	In previous *Vs.* series titles, and speaking here very generally, characters could only act once per normal jump. This meant that characters who attacked while normal jumping were then unable to guard until landing; more significantly it meant characters who guarded something in the air, and then stopped guarding, *could not guard again until landing.* It turned out to be very easy to create situations where this was exploitable—take every single time a partner character fell in to replace a knocked out point, for example. However, in *MvC3* normal jumps are not restricted in the same way, and guard breaks are no longer a threat.
guardstun	The period of time a character spends stuck in a defensive animation while successfully **guarding**. While engaged in guardstun, the only actions possible are **crossover counters**, **advancing guard**, and **X-Factor**. Characters stuck in guardstun cannot be **thrown** until 4 frames after guardstun ends.
guessing game	Any situation where you cannot be sure what will happen, and are forced to take a guess. It is beneficial to set these situations up in your favor, and avoid them yourself.
high attack	An attack that will strike crouching opponents, and must be **blocked** standing. Commonly called **overheads**. Most air attacks are overheads, along with some **command attacks**, some **special moves,** and Akuma—γ and C. Viper—γ **assists**.
hitbox	Hitboxes are hidden engine mechanics that dictate how interactions between characters play out. There are three types—attacking hitboxes, which dictate the area of an attack that can actually impact the opponent; defending hitboxes, which dictate the areas of a character's body that can actually be struck; and push hitboxes, which dictate how characters will push against or pass around one another in physical space. Hitboxes are not visible to the player, and not necessarily tied directly to the animation of a given attack, or the posture of a character.
hit confirmation	Visually confirming that an attack is successful before initiating follow-up attacks. Crucial to avoid putting yourself at too much risk when attacking, and to avoid wasting opportunities.
hitstun	The period of time a character reels after being struck by an attack. No actions are possible during hitstun. Being struck again during hitstun creates or perpetuates a **combo**. Also called **hitreel.**
hitstun deterioration	Safety mechanism in place to prevent the **infinites** that have, to a degree, characterized the *Vs.* series up to this point. As hits pile up in a combo, eventually a threshold is crossed where the length of time that hitstun lasts begins to degrade (character and situation depending, this usually begins after 6~12 hits, with less leeway for ground and **normal jump combos** than **super jump air combos**). This dwindling hitstun naturally makes combos harder as they go on, and eventually makes it impossible to continue. Works hand-in-hand with **damage scaling** to somewhat limit the potential of **combos**.
hyper armor	Property innate to Sentinel's Ⓢ **launcher** and Hsien-Ko's Rimoukon **hyper combo**. Any number of attacks will be absorbed without interrupting the attack while hyper armor is active. Sentinel's hyper armor also prevents him from taking damage, while Hsien-Ko's does not.
hyper combo	The apex of a hero's power is deployed during a hyper combo. Hyper combos require bars from the hyper combo gauge—most hyper combos cost one level, though some characters have more powerful **level 3 hyper combos**. Phoenix has a unique hyper combo that activates automatically if she is knocked out while possessing 5 bars. As holdovers from *Street Fighter*, sometimes also called supers or ultras. Most hyper combos deal direct damage to the enemy, though some hyper combos are intended to enhance abilities for a limited period of time, or activate other special effects. Team members can chain hyper combos together with **team hyper combos**, or perform hyper combos simultaneously during a **crossover combination.**
hyper combo gauge	Meter at the bottom of the screen that displays how many levels of energy you have available for use on powerful techniques. Built up primarily by interacting with the opponent, with hit or blocked attacks. The hyper combo gauge powers **hyper combos**, **level 3 hyper combos**, **crossover counters**, **snap backs**, **team hyper combos**, **crossover combinations**, C. Viper's EX **special moves**, and Phoenix's Dark Phoenix Rising.

hyper meter	A common shorthand for **hyper combo gauge**. Also **super meter**.
incapacitation	**Hit state** caused by certain attacks, in which the victim is unable to act or guard for several seconds, and is thus vulnerable to a **combo**. Examples of moves that induce this state include Spider-Man's Web Ball, Magneto's throw, and Magneto's Hyper Gravitation.
infinite	A never-ending **combo**. **Hitstun deterioration** in *MvC3* prevents most infinites in the traditional sense, but some infinites are still possible during **X-Factor**, using **special moves** that ignore hitstun deterioration.
judgment	When a match ends by time-out, with neither side winning outright, the winner is determined by remaining **vitality**. This is called judgment.
juggle	Jargon referring to a character striking an opponent who is in the air, stuck in aerial **hitstun**. Used in very many, if not most, **combos**.
jump	An upward leap into the air, accomplished by tapping any upward direction. Sometimes called normal jump, to distinguish from **super jump**, the latter of which is accomplished by tapping ↓ just before any upward direction.
jump cancel / super jump cancel	Refers to canceling an attack with a jump of some sort. Everyone can super jump cancel (S) on hit (but not on block) simply by holding any upward direction. Some characters have basic attacks that can be canceled with a jump simply by tapping any upward direction.
jump-in	An air attack performed while jumping or flying at a grounded opponent. Useful for pressure, beginning **combos**, and setting up **throws**.
kara cancel	The Japanese term for **canceling** a move very quickly after activation, within a fraction of a second. Often this is done before a move even perceptibly animates. Properties of the move **canceled** can sometimes be transferred to the follow-up move, such as forward movement.
knockdown	Refers to knocking your opponent to the floor or off their feet, or of being knocked down. After a **knockdown** a character is sometimes referred to as being "**floored**." Characters rise automatically in place from knockdowns, and can also be directed with ← or →. After an **unrecoverable knockdown**, however, a character stays prone for longer and is susceptible to **OTG**s. Guessing games employed against **floored** opponents are sometimes called **okizeme**.
knockdown followup	Synonymous with **OTG**.
knockdown recovery	Hold ← or → while being knocked down to use knockdown recovery to rise from the floor in the desired direction. Without directional input, characters will recover in place. Characters are invincible during knockdown recovery, and **crossover assists** can be called.
launcher combo	A ground combo that leads to (S), which launches the opponent. From here, you can hold any upward direction to **super jump cancel** (S), then you can continue with an **air combo**. Air combos that start with (S) **launcher** and end with air (S) cause **flying screen**. Air combos that start with (S) launcher then proceed to a directional input + (S) lead into **team aerial combos**.
level 3 hyper combo	A powerful **hyper combo** that requires 3 bars of **hyper combo gauge** to use. A big reason that these hyper combos are so strong is that they are unaffected by **damage scaling,** so they make ideal **combo** enders. You can **THC** *to*, but not *from*, a lv.3 hyper combo, and lv.3 hyper combos cannot be **canceled** with **X-Factor**.
link	Perpetuating a **combo** using moves that have completely recovered rather than **canceling** or **chaining** moves.
long range	All the way across the screen, out of the immediate range of any opposing attacks. Combat at this distance is based on either **zoning** the opponent out or trying to find a way back in. The quickest threat from this distance is a fast **beam hyper combo** like Akuma's ↓↘→ + (ATK)(ATK), hold (H).
low attack	An attack that must be guarded **crouching**. Many crouching attacks hit low, along with a handful of **crossover assists** (Felicia—α, She-Hulk—α, Wesker—β, X-23—β).
magic series	The combination of basic attacks a character can use to **chain combo**. Also called **chain combo archetype.**
mashing	Several definitions; can refer to pressing button inputs rapidly. Can also refer to unseasoned play that does not involve premeditation, thinking, or **guarding**. Also slang to refer to repetitive tactics, e.g. "mashing out fireballs."
meaty	An attack performed so that it hits very late during its **active** period. Sometimes allows for greater **frame advantage** and follow-ups/ **combos** not normally possible.
mid attack	An attack that can be guarded either **standing** or **crouching**. Most standing **basic attacks** are mids.
mid range	Refers to where characters stand on the edge of each others' **poke** range. Not as far apart as **long range**, but neither is it fighting in a phone booth at **close range**.
mid-screen only	Refers to a tactic which only works mid-screen, and doesn't function properly in a corner. Usually this is due to reasons of spacing, like an **assist** behaving differently in a combo in the corner rather than mid-screen, or Captain America's shield having varied travel time depending on screen position.
mix-up	Presenting the opponent with a situation where they have to guess between oncoming threats. A good mix-up demands that options be defended against differently, such as deciding between **guarding low**, **high** or breaking a **throw**.
negative edge	Button presses in *Street Fighter* register on release as well as the initial press, for purposes of **special moves**. **Negative Edge** refers to using the release to activate special moves. Negative edge is *NOT* an engine feature in *MvC3*.
normal attack	An attack performed by pressing (L), (M), or (H). The resulting normal attack will be different depending on whether you are crouching, standing, or airborne. Synonymous with **basic attack**.
O.C.V.	Initials meaning **o**ne-**c**haracter **v**ictory. Refers to winning without swapping out the first point character. Typically quite embarrassing for the victim! The only fate worse is getting **perfected**...
option select	An advanced fighting game concept, critical to successfully employing and defending against **mix-ups** and **guessing games**. An **option select** is a combination of inputs or actions that will defeat or defend against multiple options at once, removing some of the guesswork from playing. An example would be always performing (H) **heavy attacks** as ← or → + (H). Doing this means that you will sometimes score **throws** or **break away** just because you happened to be doing the throw input also. Without being in position to throw, or without a throw incoming to break, you'll simply perform a heavy attack, which is what you wanted to do anyway—"accidentally" scoring a throw, or breaking one, is just icing on the cake.
O.T.G.	Initials meaning **off the ground**. While opponents are floored from an **unrecoverable knockdown**, they are invincible to all attacks that are not OTG-capable. It is possible to OTG repeatedly in the same combo. Situations where **OTGs** are possible occur after **flying screen**, most **throws,** and some **crossover assists, special moves** and **hyper combos**. While some characters are capable of OTG combos on their own (an extremely valuable ability), other characters require the services of certain assists.
overhead	Synonymous with **high attack**. Most air attacks are overheads, as well as some **command attacks, special moves**, and **crossover assists** (Akuma—γ and C. Viper—γ).
partner	A hero waiting in the wings, ready to assist. Call them in for a **crossover assist** with (P1 or P2). Hold (P1 or P2) for a **crossover attack**, an **overhead** strike which will also make the chosen partner the point character. While **guarding** on the ground, tap → + (P1 or P2) for a **crossover counter**, which also swaps control to the partner. **Team aerial combos** also employ partners, as well as **team hyper combos** and **crossover combinations**.
partner's vitality gauge	The **vitality gauges** for partners waiting in the wings are displayed under the vitality gauge for the current **point character**. Also displayed are the buttons required to call each partner. "ASSIST OK!!" is displayed on this gauge whenever a partner is ready to be called again, though assists can actually be summoned again a few frames before ASSIST OK!! actually appears.
perfect	A win achieved without sustaining *any* damage (or by sustaining **red damage**, but having it regenerate before the match ends). The chaotic team-based nature of *MvC3* makes perfects *exceedingly* rare compared to other fighting games—the vast majority of players will never score a perfect in *MvC* titles! As with **O.C.V.**, it's pretty humiliating to be on the receiving end!
point character	The character currently being directly controlled on-screen. **Partners** wait in the background, ready to be summoned as **crossover assists** with (P1 or P2).
poke	An attack that, due to speed, priority, or range, is relatively safe to use for pressuring or **zoning** your opponent.
primary assist	A character whose primary purpose on your team is to provide the main **crossover assist**.
primary user	A character whose primary purpose on your team is to expend **hyper combo gauge**.
priority	The likelihood that one attack will beat another.

projectile — A ranged attack that is a distinct object, separate from the character who produces it. Many characters have **projectiles**, which are valuable for both **long range** tactics and **close range** pressure. **Beams** have similar function, but work slightly differently. When projectiles clash with other projectiles or beams, the projectile that wins the exchange and continues forward is determined by a hidden value called **durability points.**

pushblock — Another term for **advancing guard**.

recovery — The period during which a move is still animating, but is no longer **active**. Characters are vulnerable during this period. **Canceling** moves avoids this period altogether.

red damage — Damage that has been sustained, but is not yet permanent. Half of initial damage on **point characters**, and all damage on **partner characters**, is inflicted as red damage. Partner characters recover red damage over time, and point characters recover red damage during **X-Factor**. A partner's red damage becomes permanent if they become the new point character via: a crossover attack (hold P1⇔P2); the previous character is knocked out; the opponent forces them in with a **snap back** (⇩ ⇘ ⇨ + P1⇔P2).

reset — Intentionally ending a **combo** in a confusing manner, such that another **combo** or **mix-up** can be started up. Often attempted in order to circumvent **damage scaling**, since starting a new combo resets the combo meter, and thus the scaling.

reversal — Performing a move at the first possible frame following the end of **guardstun/hitstun/knockdown** states. Moves that are invincible on the first frame make the best reversals, since nothing will beat them out. Reversal is also used as a generic term describing any situation in which you thwart (or reverse) the opponent's intentions.

roll — After a **knockdown**, characters can be made to roll up to their feet by holding either ⇦ or ⇨ . Rolling to one side or the other keeps the waiting opponent on their toes, and forces them to act differently than if they could be sure of where you'd stand. Also called **knockdown recovery**. Characters rolling to their feet are invulnerable, and **crossover assists** can be called while rolling!

safe on guard — Refers to attacks that do not leave the user open to guaranteed punishment if **guarded**.

simple mode — A simplified control scheme that can be selected instead of normal mode. **Special moves** and **hyper combos** do not require motions, and can instead be activated with the press of a button. Not all attacks and tactics are available in simple mode, however. This guide assumes the use of normal mode, but tactics will translate to simple mode, as long as the recommended options are actually available. Simple mode is detailed more thoroughly earlier in this chapter.

special attack — An attack performed with Ⓢ. Differs depending on whether you are grounded or airborne. Ⓢ can be chained into from almost any **basic attack**. Grounded Ⓢ will **launch** the opponent, while air Ⓢ causes **flying screen** when used in **air combos** that follow Ⓢ launcher. The special attack button is also used for some **special moves**, such as **Flight,** and command movements like Felicia's Ⓢ + ATK Foreground Dash.

special move — An attack or action performed with a sequence of commands, ending in an attack button press.

square jump — Refers to using lateral **airdashes** performed very low to the ground. Can also be called an **instant airdash, squaredash**, or **box jump**. Square jumps are used to strike the enemy with a fast **overhead** attack, to pass just over their heads with a **cross-up**, or to pass clean over the opponent, hopefully after having called a **crossover assist** that lands on the side you just vacated.

stagger — Special hit effect caused by certain attacks, like Amaterasu's Thunder Edge ⇨ ⇨ + Ⓗ (hold). Victim staggers on their feet, and is vulnerable to further punishment.

Standing — A character idling, walking, or **dashing** on the ground is in a standing state. This is distinct from **crouching** or **jumping**. **Basic attacks** performed will be the standing variants, and any **Flight** mode initiated will follow **normal jump** rules. Characters must **guard** while standing to block **overhead** attacks; **low** attacks will crush the guard of standing characters. When standing basic attacks are required for combos in our combo transcriptions, we will preface these attacks with "standing," or the abbreviation "St."

standing guard — Accomplished by holding ⇦ . **High** and **mid** attacks can be guarded standing.

startup — The length of time a move takes to become **active** and capable of connecting, assuming it strikes on the first possible active **frame**. The fastest attacks are active in as few as 2 to 4 frames!

super armor — Property innate to certain moves, in which one incoming hit will be absorbed, without interrupting the attack.

super jump — Performed by quickly tapping down, then any upward direction within 9 frames. Super jumps go much higher and travel further than normal jumps. **Chain combos** and **command attack** use are unrestricted during super jumps. **Crossover assists** cannot be called during a super jump, however. **Flight** activated during a super jump will inherit the properties of a super jump.

taunt — Activated by pressing Select or Back, this is a humorous action designed to rile your opponent. No other effect. Cannot be **canceled** with other actions, except **X-Factor** activation.

team aerial combo (TAC) — An **air combo** in which the next partner is swapped in to continue the aerial assault. Accomplished by **chaining** into ⇧ or ⇩ or ⇦ or ⇨ + Ⓢ after **launching** an opponent. Often called **air tags.** ⇩ + Ⓢ builds an entire bar of **hyper combo gauge**, while ⇨ or ⇦ + Ⓢ builds half a bar. ⇧ + Ⓢ does slightly more damage, and puts an opponent into better **juggle** position. For each character that tags in during a **TAC**, **hitstun deterioration** is diminished, to allow extended **air combos** that are otherwise impossible.

team aerial counter — **Team aerial combo** (TAC) attempts can be thwarted by pressing the same command your opponent used to execute the combo within 15 frames: either ⇧ + Ⓢ, ⇩ + Ⓢ, or ⇦ or ⇨ + Ⓢ (the game does not differentiate between ⇦ or ⇨ + Ⓢ in air combos). You are only allowed one escape "guess" per TAC break window, and inputting neutral Ⓢ (which itself does not count as a potential team aerial counter command) prevents a correct direction + Ⓢ input afterward!

team hyper combo (THC) — While a **hyper combo** is in progress, input a hyper combo command for the next character in the team order and that character will tag in with that hyper combo. This is called a team hyper combo. You can continue to team hyper combo until you either run out of **hyper combo gauge**, or until all three characters have participated.

tech — Generic term referring to an escape action, such as "tech throws" or "tech rolls."

throw — An **unguardable** attack performed with ⇨ or ⇦ + Ⓗ at close range. Throws are possible both on the ground and airborne, and are active in 1 frame. Almost all throws result in an **unrecoverable knockdown** that an opponent can't quickly recover from, which often allows an OTG follow-up depending on character and position. Normal throws can be escaped if the victim inputs ⇨ or ⇦ + Ⓗ within 7 frames of the start of the throw. **Special move** throws, often called **command throws**, are executed with directional sequences followed by a button press, and are not escapable.

tick — A quick move used to incite a particular reaction. For example, most crouching **light attacks** give an opponent the expectation that more crouching light attacks are coming. This presents an ideal opening to step forward and **throw**. Unsurprisingly, this common tactic is called a "**tick-throw**." Once the opponent is conditioned to expect a throw after the tick, you can then chain into **delayed** attacks after the tick to potentially **counterhit** their throw **reversal** attempt—this kind of layered baiting, with small intentional gaps, is called a **frame trap**.

timer — The clock ticking away remaining match time at the top-center of the screen. When this hits 0, the team with the most vitality remaining is declared the winner. If both teams have the same exact amount of life left (based on percentage of **vitality gauges** still full), the match is declared a **draw**.

triangle jump — Refers to using angled **airdashes** immediately after a jump to return to the ground quickly, potentially with a **high**-hitting air attack. Fast **mix-ups** between triangle jump air hits and **low** attacks are very hard to **guard** consistently.

unfly — Generically, simply refers to cease **Flight** by re-inputting the command (⇩ ⇙ ⇦ + Ⓢ). Unfly can also refer to using the manual cancelation of Flight to **cancel** the **recovery** of an air **basic attack**. Unfly allows for extended **air combos** after Flight expires. Characters can also unfly and **guard** in mid-air while falling to the ground, to block incoming attacks.

unguardable — Also called **unblockable.** An attack that cannot be guarded. **Throws** are unblockable, as are some moves like C. Viper's fully-charged Focus Attack. Situations that are unblockable, or close enough to be indistinguishable, can also be created by striking simultaneously with **overhead** attacks along with a **low**-hitting **crossover assist,** or vice-versa (Felicia—α, She-Hulk—α, Wesker—β, and X-23—β hit low; Akuma—γ and C. Viper—γ are overheads).

unrecoverable knockdown	A hard knockdown that prevents the victim from recovering for a second, and thus creates an **OTG** opportunity. Unrecoverable knockdowns occur after most **throws**, some **special moves** and **hyper combos**, and after Ⓢ **launcher combos** that end with Ⓢ **special attack**. Victims of unrecoverable knockdowns should almost always opt to recover earlier by holding forward or backward to roll to their feet, to avoid staying sprawled on the ground any longer than is necessary.
unsafe on guard	Refers to attacks that are risky when blocked because an alert opponent is assured an opportunity to punish you.
verification	Refers to insuring that an action is successful before performing desired follow-ups. Success is dependent upon the speed of the attacks and the reaction time of the player. Also called **hit confirmation**. Verification is a vital skill, to avoid needlessly using resources or putting yourself at unnecessary risk.
vitality gauge	The meter at the top of the screen that displays remaining health.
wakeup	This refers to the frequent situation where one character is standing and another is floored, waiting to rise with **ground recovery**. The standing character has a large advantage here, since mix-ups can be staged against a floored foe as they recover from the ground. The Japanese term for mix-ups staged against a rising foe is **okizeme.**
wall bounce	Hit effect in which a character is ricocheted forcibly off the wall. Victim is vulnerable to further punishment. Only one wall bounce is allowed per **combo**.
wavedash	**Canceling** one **dash** into another, to cover space more quickly. With perfect timing, this can be accomplished simply by inputting ⇨⇨ or ATK ATK *very* quickly. If precision is a problem, you may find it easier to accomplish by tapping ⇩ briefly to crouch-cancel each dash before starting the next one.
whiff	Missed attacks, whether intentional or not.
X-Factor	System new to *MvC3* in which, once per match, a team can unleash its true potential for a brief period. Activated with Ⓛ + Ⓜ + Ⓗ + Ⓢ. Speed and damage output are increased, and **red damage** recovers more quickly. The effect is more substantial with fewer characters still standing.
X-Factor cancel	**X-Factor** can be activated on the ground at any time except during **hitstun** or **throws**. X-Factor can therefore be used to create otherwise-impossible **combos** and setups. **Canceling** other actions with X-Factor is indicated in our combo transcriptions with .
zoning	Refers to keeping your opponent in a particular range that is beneficial to your characters and gameplan, and detrimental to theirs.

GONNA TAKE YOU FOR A RIDE: THE HISTORY OF MARVEL VS. CAPCOM

1994: *X-MEN: CHILDREN OF THE ATOM*

1995: *MARVEL SUPER HEROES*

1996: *X-MEN VS. STREET FIGHTER*

1997: *MARVEL SUPER HEROES VS. STREET FIGHTER*

1998: *MARVEL VS. CAPCOM: CLASH OF SUPER HEROES*

2000: *MARVEL VS. CAPCOM 2: NEW AGE OF HEROES*

NOW: *MARVEL VS. CAPCOM 3: FATE OF TWO WORLDS*

Video games haven't been around for very long. Their tenure as an accepted and important part of modern culture is even shorter. Their utility as a forum for recognized, skilled competition, briefer still. This is easy to take for granted now, in the days of photo-realistic blockbuster games that reproduce settings real and imagined to finest detail, which foster and support international competitive scenes and tournaments, while sometimes out-grossing Hollywood films. Where games started as rudimentary text interfaces, or a paddle wheel, or a directional control and a single button, we now have controls sometimes approaching the nuance of a musical instrument.

Of course, things didn't start out that way. During its infancy, gaming was regarded as a single-player diversion for children. Controls were simple, by and large. Direct competition between players was non-existent outside of competing for high scores, which themselves were attained mostly through memorization, pattern recognition, and sheer endurance. Dallas-based id had not yet essentially created both online competitive play and catapulted the fledgling FPS genre with *DOOM*. Midway's *NBA Jam* had not yet saturated every place it would fit into. Blizzard's monster franchises *Diablo* and *Starcraft* were years away, *World of Warcraft* further still. Arcades existed to inhale quarters with punishing games like *Double Dragon*, *Final Fight*, *Shinobi*, and *TMNT*.

But then, in 1991, Capcom released *Street Fighter 2: The World Warrior*. The "*2*" in the title may as well be apocryphal; *Street Fighter* the first bears little resemblance to its revolutionary sequel. Most games used a button or three (the original *Street Fighter* famously had arcade cabinets with only one large pressure-sensitive button, the primary purpose of which seemed to be to break). This game used *six*, all of which had many different contextual results (jumping, standing, crouching). Does that seem quaint now? It wasn't, then. In action games at the time, player-controlled characters had an arsenal of actions numbering in the single-digits. In *Street Fighter 2*, every single character had dozens of moves, and there were a dozen distinct characters. With a few exceptions, most characters were decidedly different, creating an interlocking web made of dozens of different matchups, each with their own ins and outs.

SF2 was, simply put, the quickest and most complex video game yet seen for head-to-head competition, requiring for success the highest dexterity, and the most practice and foreknowledge. A new genre was born, and the purpose of arcades (and gas stations, and convenience stores, and pizza places, and bus stops, and bowling alleys) changed entirely. If you wanted to play Pop-A-Shot, ski-ball, a skill crane, or pinball, you'd have to shoulder past dozens of players crowded around *SF2* cabinets, players clutching their dot-matrix-printed move sheets, or their now-ancient issues of *GamePro* filled with movelists and ProTips; players unbridled in their enthusiasm to see who was the best.

Arcade machines then still represented the cutting edge; not until the Sega Dreamcast and Sony PlayStation 2 did consoles start to catch up to the experience of the best arcade titles, and not until the Xbox 360 did the online experience begin to catch up to the social feel of the arcade. For a time, arcades were not the fringe establishment they are now: absent in most places, usually corporate or gimmick-driven where they remain. Instead, arcades were *the* definitive gaming experience. Only a few bastions remain in North America to remind us of what once was…Game Galaxy in Nashville, or Arcade UFO in Austin, or Chinatown Fair in NYC, or Family Fun Arcade in Los Angeles, to name a few that hold out, against the proverbial dying of the light.

But, while traditional arcades are largely a relic today, those players are still around, still huddled, still boisterous in their passion and razor-sharp in their skill. The difference is that now you'll find them online, or at tournaments, or at your cousin's house, or you'll invite them over, or meet up with them at websites like shoryuken.com. And *SF2* is now not the only game in town (though, amazingly, it's still around—see the recent success *Super Street Fighter 2: HD Remix!*). Competitors from other developers sprang up more or less immediately, and *SF2* itself directly spawned dozens more fighting games from Capcom. The core of most of these games is not so different—controls are generally still rooted in the fundamentals laid down by *SF2*—but the important aspects of gameplay in each title and series differ greatly.

Almost all of these titles, even today, feature one-on-one battles, with mechanics and pacing that resemble *SF2*. But in 1994, Capcom went for something a little looser, less rigid and disciplined than the *SF2* series. Drawing on the massive treasure trove of beloved Marvel Comics creations, Capcom released ***X-Men: Children of the Atom*** (usually referred to in fighting game circles as, simply, ***COTA***). This was the first game in a string of beefed-up fighters that kept the bedrock concepts of *SF2*, but, in the details, spun off in a new direction entirely. This was the beginning of what is now known as the "***Vs.***" series, the fighting game taxonomy that leads directly to ***Marvel vs. Capcom 3: Fate of Two Worlds***. Foreshadowing the fully-fledged crossover games that later defined the *Vs.* series, Capcom's Akuma was even present as a secret character!

X-MEN: CHILDREN OF THE ATOM ROSTER

- Akuma (secret character)
- Colossus
- Cyclops
- Iceman
- Juggernaut (sub-boss)
- Magneto (boss)
- Omega Red
- Psylocke
- Sentinel
- Silver Samurai
- Spiral
- Storm
- Wolverine

The next year, in 1995, *COTA* would get an indirect sequel in the form of ***Marvel Super Heroes*** (or ***MSH***). New heroes and villains appeared, and gameplay was spiced up further with the introduction of Infinity Gems, Thanos-related power-ups which could be picked up to enhance the power of your character.

MARVEL SUPER HEROES ROSTER

- Blackheart
- Captain America
- Doctor Doom (sub-boss)
- Hulk
- Iron Man
- Juggernaut
- Magneto
- Psylocke
- Shuma-Gorath
- Spider-Man
- Thanos (boss)
- Wolverine

Another year brought another update, and ***X-Men vs. Street Fighter*** released in 1996. Now, things were heating up! Fulfilling the potential hinted at with secret Akuma in *COTA*, *X-Men vs. Street Fighter* (predictably usually just called ***XvSF***) was a full crossover battle between Capcom and Marvel characters! Not only was this the first crossover fighting game, but it was also the first game to forgo one-on-one fighting for team combat. As the first team-based fighter, it also blazed a trail in the sense that characters fought together, rather than simply one after the other (as is the case in most team-based fighting games since). Battles were fast and fluid, and deep team dynamics emerged—with two characters to your team, you may have some match-ups that are bad for one hero, but good for the other; you may have one character that you preferred to use hyper combo gauge with, while the other primarily built it up; and so on. *XvSF* was very popular, but this popularity underscored the disparity that then existed between arcades and consoles—the eventual PlayStation 1 version was stripped down, removing the tag battle feature that made *XvSF* stand out. Home consoles at the time simply lacked the memory to handle all the action and characters! However, the Japanese release of the Sega Saturn version actually came with a RAM cartridge that upped the system's capabilities specifically to run *XvSF* at full potential. Fighting games would not just increase the complexity of gaming—they pushed the envelope for hardware requirements as well!

X-MEN VS. STREET FIGHTER ROSTER

Marvel

- Apocalypse (boss)
- Cyclops
- Gambit
- Juggernaut
- Magneto
- Rogue
- Sabretooth
- Storm
- Wolverine

Capcom

- Akuma
- Cammy
- Charlie
- Chun-Li
- Dhalsim
- Ken
- M. Bison
- Ryu
- Zangief

XvSF earned the first direct sequel in the *Vs.* series, with 1997's ***Marvel Super Heroes vs. Street Fighter***. This title retained the tag-team fighting of its progenitor, while adding the ability to directly call your off-screen teammate to briefly assist in battle—apart from the initial tag-team concept in the first place, this would become *the* defining trait of the then-forthcoming *MvC* series. Like *XvSF*, ***MSHvSF*** would require the services of the Sega Saturn's RAM cart for a faithful home version, and even then only in Japan, as the PlayStation 1 port again excised features. Happily, with the release of the Sega Dreamcast around the corner, this kind of feature-stripping to squeeze arcade games onto home ports was close to being a thing of the past.

MARVEL SUPER HEROES VS. STREET FIGHTER ROSTER

Marvel

- Apocalypse (sub-boss)
- Blackheart (secret version: Mephisto)
- Captain America (secret version: U.S. Agent)
- Cyclops
- Hulk
- Omega Red
- Shuma-Gorath
- Spider-Man (secret version: Armored Spider-Man)
- Wolverine

Capcom

- Akuma
- Chun-Li
- Dan
- Dhalsim
- Ken
- M. Bison
- Ryu
- Sakura (secret version: Evil Sakura)
- Shadow (Evil Charlie)
- Zangief (secret version: Mecha-Zangief)
- Cyber-Akuma (boss)

The full promise and breadth of ideas attempted in *COTA, MSH, XvSF, and MSHvSF* were then synthesized into the first of a new series that would become a sensation. ***Marvel vs. Capcom: Clash of Super Heroes*** released in early 1998, with a Dreamcast port following around a year later that was, for the first time, virtually indistinguishable from the arcade version. ***MvC1*** retained the tag combat of *XvSF* and *MSHvSF*, while casting the Capcom net wider, to include characters from throughout Capcom's franchises rather than just *Street Fighter*. Assists, first present in *MSHvSF*, returned, though tweaked—rather than use the off-screen partner as an assist, an assist-only helper character was selected along with the two actual point characters for a team. This helper was selected from a random reel, though secret codes allowed precise selection of a desired assist. Assists could only be used a limited number of times per match; a limitation that did not apply to *MSHvSF* or subsequent titles in the *MvC* series. *MvC1* also introduced Duo Attacks—tremendous displays of power in which both characters on a team came onscreen simultaneously, both controlled by the player at once, both capable of infinite hyper combos for the duration of the Duo Attack!

Marvel vs. Capcom: Clash of Super Heroes Roster

Marvel point characters
- Captain America
- Gambit
- Gold War Machine (secret character)
- Hulk
- Onslaught (boss)
- Orange Hulk (secret character)
- Red Venom (secret character)
- Spider-Man
- Venom
- War Machine
- Wolverine

Marvel assist characters (not available as point characters)
- Colossus
- Cyclops
- Iceman
- Jubilee
- Juggernaut
- Magneto
- Psylocke
- Rogue
- Sentinel
- Storm
- Thor
- U.S. Agent

Capcom point characters
- Captain Commando
- Chun-Li
- Jin
- Lilith (secret character)
- Mega Man
- Morrigan
- Roll (secret character)
- Ryu
- Shadow Lady (secret character)
- Strider Hiryu
- Zangief

Capcom assist characters (not available as point characters)
- Anita
- Arthur
- Devilotte
- Lou & Siva
- Michelle Heart
- Pure & Fur
- Saki Omokane
- Shadow
- Ton Pooh
- Unknown Soldier

For most gamers, the Sega Dreamcast represents a quirky footnote in console gaming history. In both chronology and horsepower it was sandwiched ahead of the original PlayStation, N64, and Sega's own Saturn, and behind the PlayStation 2. The PlayStation 2 did the Dreamcast no favors by releasing not very long into the Dreamcast's abbreviated lifecycle. By the time the original Xbox rose to compete with the PlayStation 2, the Dreamcast was already becoming a memory—to be sure, the home of some truly memorable titles like *Seaman* and *Shenmue,* but ultimately proof of the growing pains of nascent high-fidelity console gaming.

For fighting game enthusiasts, though, the Dreamcast was the most important console yet produced; it might still be. Finally, compromises did not have to be made when bringing arcade fighting games into the living room, and a veritable deluge of Capcom titles followed, to say nothing of offerings from other developers. From Capcom alone, the Dreamcast hosted *MvC1, Street Fighter Alpha 3,* every version of *Street Fighter 3* (*New Generation, 2nd Impact,* and *3rd Strike*), *Power Stone* and *Power Stone 2, Plasma Sword, Rival Schools: Project Justice*, and both *Capcom vs. SNK: Millenium Fight 2000* and *Capcom vs. SNK 2: Mark of the Millenium.* To this day, some gamers maintain working Dreamcast consoles to play the best versions of some fighting titles. Nowhere else is this more the case than with ***Marvel vs. Capcom 2: New Age of Heroes*** (or, simply, ***MvC2***). This sequel to *MvC1* released in 2000 with an *enormous* roster and greatly expanded mechanics over its predecessors. Teams were three characters instead of two; the hyper combo gauge topped out at 5 bars; the entire team could attack at once with what were then called team hyper combos (in *MvC3*, this has become the crossover combination); assist calls were potentially limitless and performed directly by the point character's teammates. In general the team dynamics introduced in earlier *Vs.* titles were emphasized even further, while the over-the-top nature of the combat itself was highlighted as well.

MARVEL VS. CAPCOM 2: NEW AGE OF HEROES ROSTER

Marvel

- **Blackheart**
- **Cable**
- **Captain America**
- **Colossus**
- **Cyclops**
- **Doctor Doom**
- **Gambit**
- **Hulk**
- **Iceman**
- **Iron Man**
- **Juggernaut**
- **Magneto**
- **Marrow**
- **Omega Red**
- **Psylocke**
- **Rogue**
- **Sabretooth**
- **Sentinel**
- **Shuma-Gorath**
- **Silver Samurai**
- **Spider-Man**
- **Spiral**
- **Storm**
- **Thanos**
- **Venom**
- **War Machine**
- **Wolverine (Adamantium claws)**
- **Wolverine (Bone claws)**

Capcom

- **Abyss (boss)**
- **Akuma**
- **Amingo**
- **Anakaris**
- **B.B. Hood**
- **Cammy**
- **Captain Commando**
- **Charlie**
- **Chun-Li**
- **Dan**
- **Dhalsim**
- **Felicia**
- **Guile**
- **Hayato**
- **Jill Valentine**
- **Jin**
- **Ken**
- **M. Bison**
- **Mega Man**
- **Morrigan**
- **Roll**
- **Ruby Heart**
- **Ryu**
- **Sakura**
- **Servbot**
- **SonSon**
- **Strider Hiryu**
- **Tron Bonne**
- **Zangief**

Somewhat simultaneously, several things happened. The internet came truly into form in the late 1990s and early 'aughts, leaving behind the detritus of bulletin board systems, usenet groups, and IRC channels for fully-formed websites and forums. Two brothers from California, fans of fighting games, started the seminal website shoryuken.com, the natural and more concrete extension of usenet's alt.games.sf2, where serious fighters gathered for mutual discussion, debate, and derision. The rise of SRK (the shorthand by which readers refer to shoryuken.com) as a meeting place made *MvC2* the first, and most important, competitive fighting game of the online era. Never before had detailed information been available so readily, and never before had match videos been so easily attainable. The eventual inception of YouTube only enhanced this synergy. Fighting games had flagged somewhat in the face of burgeoning online play, drifting arcade revenue, and home consoles that finally matched the capabilities of dedicated arcade boards. *Marvel vs. Capcom 2* re-energized the scene, while elevating the general level of play, and the number of skilled players, to previously-unseen heights.

But it was not just this synergy that propelled *MvC2* to a decade of competitive and commercial success. The game is astounding in its own right. Unrestrained in its action, polarizing in its immense and heavily stratified roster, seemingly accessible on the surface but with a gameplay rabbit hole that goes down further than the Challenger Deep, everyone knew about *Marvel vs. Capcom 2*. It became the reason to own a Dreamcast long after the Dreamcast presses stopped, whether you were a casual gamer who wanted to mash out fun with your friends, or a hardcore tournament "head" looking to perfect your Magneto resets and Sentinel fast flies at home. Upon its triumphant re-release on Xbox Live Arcade and PlayStation Network in 2009, *MvC2* immediately shot up the charts as one of the most-bought and most-played titles…*ten years after its initial release*, and in direct competition with ridiculously successful modern online franchises like *Halo* and *Call of Duty*.

While *Street Fighter 2* has its following and its tournament players to this day, and now *Street Fighter 4* has performed its own trick of revitalizing the scene yet again, there is something of a public relations problem with the keystone fighting game franchise. It can be hard, or impossible, for a casual fan to tell the difference between two pros engaging in an intense, measured zoning war, versus just two players who happen to know how to throw fireballs at each other. Apart from the happy happenstance of the release of *MvC2*, the rise of the internet, and the start of shoryuken.com, the mark of the *Vs.* franchise, *Marvel vs. Capcom 2* in particular, and now *Marvel vs. Capcom 3*, is that there is nothing subtle about it. It is blatantly obvious, and in the most excessive, wonderful, outrageous way possible, when someone knows what they are doing. Using the most open movement and combo systems of any fighting game to date, some players truly reach for the heights of artistry with their play, elevating as far above and beyond average players as professional musicians and athletes do beyond the amateur hobbyist. *Marvel vs. Capcom* is not Kurt Rambis doing the small things to win basketball games…it is Michael Jordan issuing a clarion call, making the gulf obvious beyond a shadow of a doubt, and making it seem effortless in the process.

That is the ultimate legacy of *Marvel vs. Capcom*—combat unmatched in excess, unquestionable in depth, unrivaled in breadth. If *Street Fighter 1* was klondike, and *Street Fighter 2* is poker (a comparison we are hardly the first to make; incidentally, many tournament *SF* players make great cardslingers!), *Marvel vs. Capcom* is a wild variant—let's say pineapple with 4s, 8s, and queens wild.

You didn't think it could happen, we didn't think it could happen, but here we are. A decade later, beyond the death of arcades and the predominance of online play, after three console generations and legal wrangling unimaginable between juggernaut intellectual properties, no one is happier than your humble authors to say:

Welcome to Marvel vs. Capcom 3!

GAME MODES

PLAYER POINTS & UNLOCKABLE REWARDS

You'll accumulate about 2000~3000 PP for completing all of a single character's Missions, or for completing Arcade Mode once. An hour or two in Training Mode can net you far more!

Playing any Game Mode will garner Player Points, or PP. PP serves as a general indicator of how much you've played *Marvel vs. Capcom 3*, and its accumulation also determines when many in-game rewards are unlocked. Most significantly, this includes four extra playable heroes, but there are also extra opening cinemas, art pieces, titles, and icons to unlock. Whenever you're done with a session of *MvC3,* be sure to back out all the way back out to the main menu to insure that PP saves before shutting the console down!

You can see how many Player Points you have by checking out your License Card. Here, you can also set your current icon and title, as well as browse stats tracking various aspects of your performance. The License Card is also where you may set up Reserve Units, if desired—these are pre-sets that allow for quick selection of up to three favorite teams at the character select screen.

If you're interested in getting all the unlockables, simply playing through Arcade Mode to see every character's ending will take care of most. The rest can easily come by using Training and Mission Modes to brush up on combos and tactics, and Online Modes to get practice against human opponents. In other words, rewards will come as a matter of course while playing *MvC3*.

Playable Character Unlock	Condition
AKUMA	Get 2,000 PP (Play Points)
SENTINEL	Get 4,000 PP (Play Points)
HSIEN-KO	Get 6,000 PP (Play Points)
TASKMASTER	Get 8,000 PP (Play Points)

Cinema Unlock	Condition
Opening 1	Available initially
Opening 2	Get 15,000 PP (Play Points)
Opening 3	Get 30,000 PP (Play Points)
Opening 4	Get 60,000 PP (Play Points)
Credits	Beat the game.

Special Art Unlock	Condition
Special Art 1	Get 10,000 PP (Play Points)
Special Art 2	Get 15,000 PP (Play Points)
Special Art 3	Get 20,000 PP (Play Points)
Special Art 4	Get 25,000 PP (Play Points)
Special Art 5	Get 30,000 PP (Play Points)

Character Art Unlock	Condition
Character ending	Land final blow in Arcade Mode with a given character on any difficulty
Character bio	Land final blow in Arcade Mode with a given character on any difficulty
Character 3-D model	Land final blow in Arcade Mode with a given character on any difficulty
Special ending	Lose final stage of Arcade Mode.
Special bio	Beat Arcade Mode with every character.
Special 3-D model	Beat Arcade Mode with every character.
First piece of character art	Complete any Mission Mode assignment with a given character
Second piece of character art	Land final blow in Arcade Mode with a given character on any difficulty
Third piece of character art	Land final blow in Arcade Mode with a given character on any difficulty

Stage Art Unlock	Condition	
Stage 01	Complete Arcade Mode once.	Danger Room (Training Stage)
Stage 02	Complete Arcade Mode twice.	The Daily Bugle
Stage 03	Complete Arcade Mode three times.	Metro City
Stage 04	Complete Arcade Mode four times.	Demon Village
Stage 05	Complete Arcade Mode five times.	Kattelox Island
Stage 06	Complete Arcade Mode six times.	Hand Hideout
Stage 07	Complete Arcade Mode seven times.	S.H.I.E.L.D. Helicarrier
Stage 08	Complete Arcade Mode eight times.	Asgard
Stage 09	Complete Arcade Mode nine times.	Tricell Laboratory
Stage 10	Complete Arcade Mode ten times.	Fate Of The Earth

STAGES

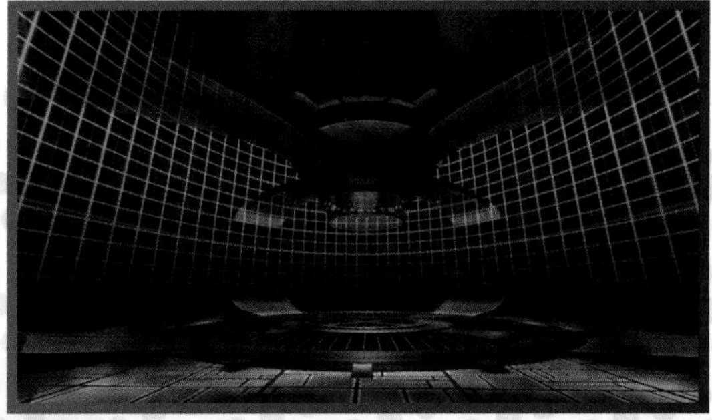
Danger Room (Training/Versus/Mission Mode only)

Hand Hideout

The Daily Bugle

S.H.I.E.L.D. Helicarrier

Metro City

Asgard

Demon Village

Tricell Laboratory

Kattelox Island

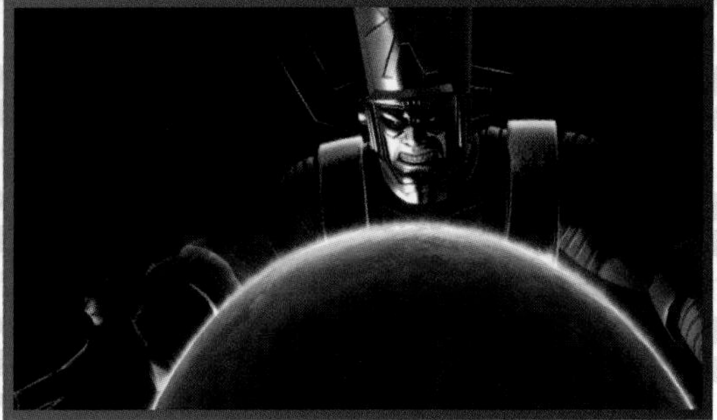
Fate of the Earth (Galactus only)

GAME MODES

OFFLINE MODES

ARCADE

In Arcade Mode, you'll choose your difficulty, time limit, damage level, Fight Request status, and team, before embarking on a seven-stage quest with a goal no less noble than saving the world! Only one character at a time gains credit for completing Arcade Mode—the point character on the screen when Galactus is defeated is declared the winner.

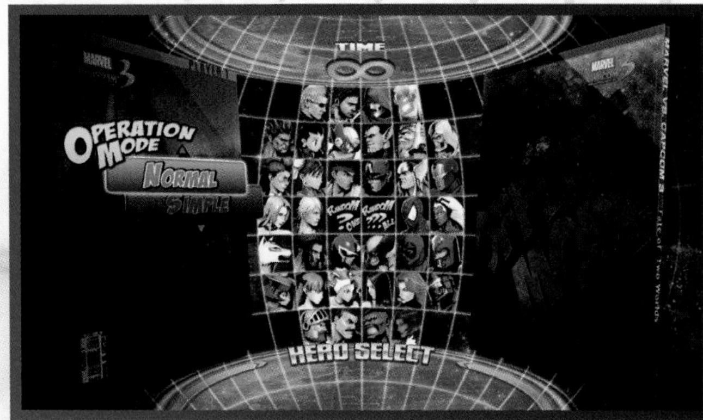

Battles are waged against randomized teams controlled by the CPU. At lower difficulties, the CPU is fairly passive and hapless, and can be cowed by repetitive, relatively safe tactics. At the highest difficulty, the CPU will react and punish with inhuman speed and accuracy, almost to a frustrating degree! You'll need airtight offense and solid defense to make headway against the CPU on Very Hard.

If your team is knocked out, you can continue and try again without penalty. You can even switch teams, if desired.

With Fight Request on, online opponents may interrupt your Arcade Mode bouts with a match challenge.

After six successful stages of pushing aside other trios of CPU-controlled heroes, you'll face down Galactus himself, amongst debris in Earth orbit.

GALACTUS

"NO AMOUNT OF TRAINING CAN PREPARE YOU FOR GALACTUS."

After successfully clearing six stages in Arcade Mode, you'll be face-to-face (or, face-to-chest, really) against this colossal entity. Your team of three will have to topple almighty Galactus to save the Earth!

As the only survivor of the universe previous to ours, and wielding the Power Cosmic, Galactus stands on even keel with the deities. The machinations of Doctor Doom and Albert Wesker to control the fates of their parallel Earths have inadvertently drawn the attention of this towering, unfathomable being, who, for his nourishment, consumes entire worlds filled with sentient beings. For Galactus, there is not necessarily malice, only need...though that's little consolation to his scores of victims.

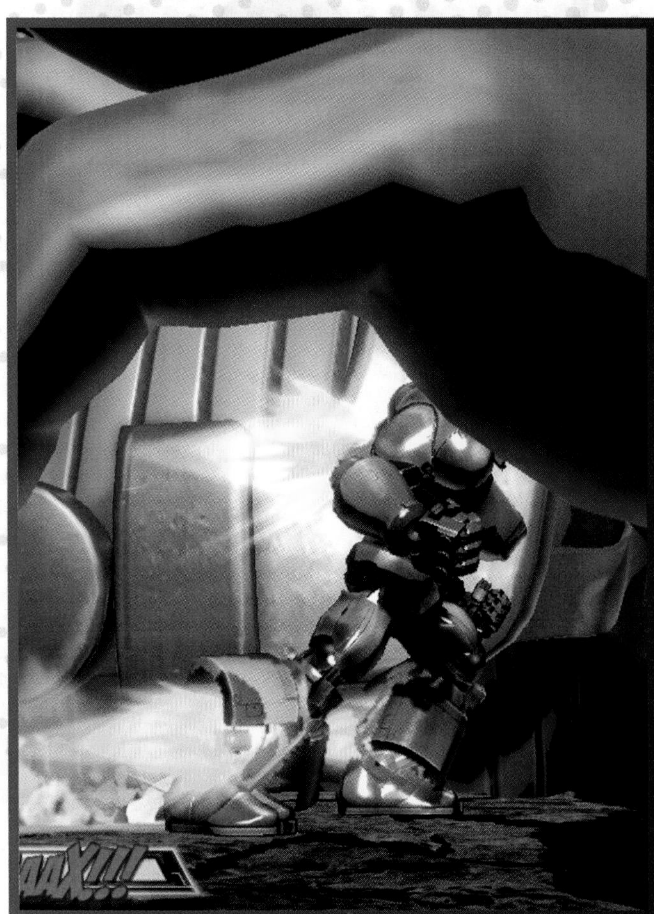

Technically, Galactus can manifest himself at any size he likes. Clearly, he's thinking big in *Marvel vs. Capcom 3.*

PHASE 1

"YOUR PLANET WILL PROVIDE ME WITH SOME MUCH-NEEDED NOURISHMENT."

During phase 1, Galactus will summon his Heralds—evil game characters now looking a bit more "Silver"—to fight in his stead, as he glowers over Earth in the background. Galactus can summon Akuma, Doctor Doom, Dormammu, Super-Skrull, or Wesker to slow you down. At first, he'll only summon one of this evil quintet to aid him. After nine ticks off the timer (or about 17 seconds), he'll summon a second Herald. Once both of Galactus's minions are drawn out, they'll attack in tandem—veterans of Capcom fighting games will be reminded of the "Dramatic Battle" modes present in Street Fighter Alpha and some versions of Street Fighter Alpha 3.

If you manage to deplete the vitality gauge of the first summoned Herald before about 17 seconds have elapsed, you won't have to deal with a second Galactus Herald at all.

Try to stay out from between the two characters, since it can be tricky trying to block when standing between two foes who are both considered point characters!

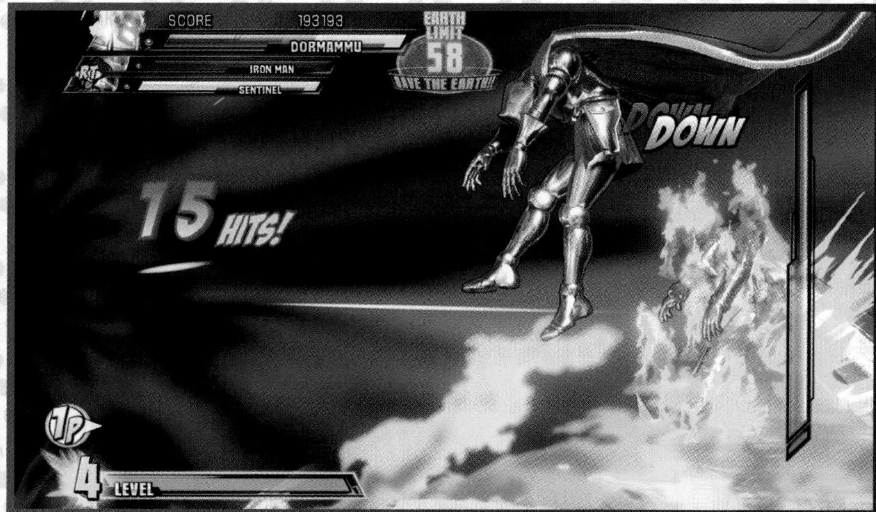

Catch both Galactus Heralds at once with a combo or hyper combo and you'll destroy them very quickly on any difficulty. Save X-Factor for Galactus!

These Heralds share one vitality gauge, which is visible on the right edge of the screen. Once this gauge is depleted, these Heralds return to dust and Galactus takes a moment from his coveting of Earth to step to the fore and personally dispense with your pesky team.

PHASE 2

"ONLY THE ULTIMATE NULLIFIER WOULD GIVE ME PAUSE."

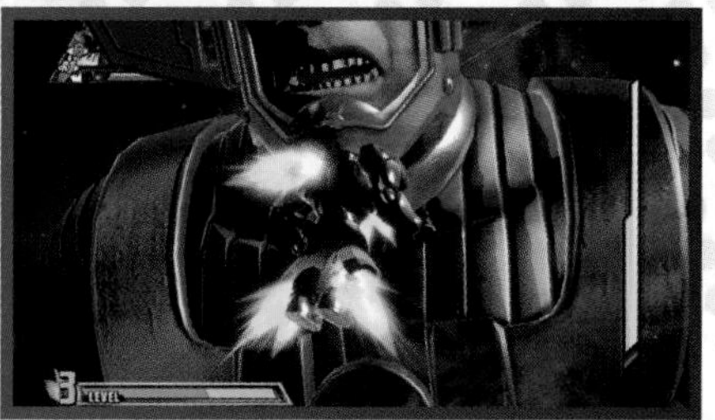

Want something done right; you have to do it yourself. Galactus shifts his attention from his celestial meal to your team. Galactus takes up the entire right half of the playing field. Like his summoned Heralds, his vitality gauge occupies the right edge of the screen.

The higher the difficulty, the more frequently Galactus will attack, and the less damage he'll take. Any part of Galactus is a viable target, with his chest and head being the most convenient area to strike. Galactus cannot guard! Any attack that touches him will deal damage.

You shouldn't just attack with abandon, however. Galactus has some incredibly powerful attacks, some of which can annihilate a hero with a single stroke. Luckily, most of his attacks are heavily telegraphed, either with visual or audio cues. This allows you to hold off on your offense for a moment, to guard or dodge as necessary. Because of the high power of his entire arsenal, and the damage penalty crossover assists sustain when hit, you should not call assists at all during this battle. Some of his attacks will one-shot full-vitality assists!

Galactus attacks with a limited arsenal while he retains more than about half of his vitality:

Stand on the ground against Galactus's torso, and he'll strike with two attacks for which he gives little or no warning—a backhand swat with his left arm, or a dismissive finger-flick snap back. Striking his torso is easy, but don't commit to any lengthy attacks. Stick to short chain combos and be ready to guard if you see him shift his hand or arm forward.

"INSOLENT WELP."
"FALL."
"SUBMIT."

Stand a little bit further back, or take to the skies, and Galactus will attack primarily with hammer punches downward. Depending on where he brings his fist down, his blows can sometimes be avoided by either super jumping up and away, or dashing in close to his torso. There is not really enough time to tell where he'll strike, however, so the safest bet is to guard. He will usually only strike with one or two smashes at a time, but occasionally he'll unleash a flurry of four or five blows in a row! Be sure to watch if he's still winding up more hammer punches before attacking again.

"ENOUGH!"

Galactus's hyper combo while he's still healthy is a powered-up version of one of his hammer blows. It's easy to see coming—while there's no hyper combo screen freeze, there is a hyper combo activation sound, and Galactus's fist glows electric blue before the strike. You can't miss it. Guard accordingly.

"INSIGNIFICANT!"
"YIELD!"
"I AM A FORCE OF NATURE."

Occasionally, rather than bringing his fists down from above or using a quick backhand blow or finger flick, Galactus will wind up a tremendous, quick haymaker with his right arm. Galactus announces this attack with one of several quotes, and it can be avoided by super jumping on reaction. Use the opportunity to hit him in the face for free while he recovers.

"FEEL MY WRATH."
"YOU WILL KNOW PAIN."

The most dangerous attack during this phase is Galactus's throw. He will shift into the background and bring his hands together with tremendous force at ground level. Any character standing on the ground, or airborne at normal jump height, will be snared and smashed, taking tremendous damage. Wait until Galactus is positioned roughly as depicted in this screenshot, then super jump! The timing can be rough for characters who lack air mobility options—for heroes who can airdash or fly, simply super jump then airdash upward, or activate Flight. If Galactus misses his grab, you are free to hit him without fear of reprisal until he returns to his original position. He can be struck as normal even while he stands in the background.

PHASE 3

"YOU ARE LIKE AN ANT, FIGHTING THE SUN."

Take Galactus below half vitality and he will stagger briefly. Apparently, he's underestimated your team! He'll be far more aggressive afterward, and unleash some deadly new attacks.

Galactus's attack grows more urgent as he nears the unimaginable prospect of defeat. Continue to strike whenever it's safe to do so, but err on the side of caution—Galactus can hurt you a lot faster than you can hurt him, so don't get greedy. Don't use laggy attacks, and cut chain combos short if it seems like he's about to attack. Desperate Galactus reveals the full extent of his power; he'll continue using the attacks he deployed in phase 2, but he will also use several new, terrifying attacks.

"DIE."
"YOU MAY DIE NOW."

Galactus replaces most of his assaults against a grounded character with a very quick, full-screen beam projected from his finger. The attack itself is fast, but Galactus always announces it with a stern directive urging you not to be alive anymore. Don't heed his command; super jump on reaction to his morbid advice. If you are using a Flight-capable character, or a hero with aerial special moves or hyper combos that hold them in place in mid-air, unload on Galactus's face while the beam passes harmlessly underneath.

"ENOUGH! YOU WILL RUE THIS DAY."

The hyper combo version of Galactus's ground-level beam. As before, if you have time, super jump over the top and hit Galactus in the face while he's busy firing at nothing. If you get caught blocking, use advancing guard repeatedly to potentially reduce a bit of the chip damage.

"AWAY WITH YOU!" "YOU CANNOT HIDE FROM ME!"

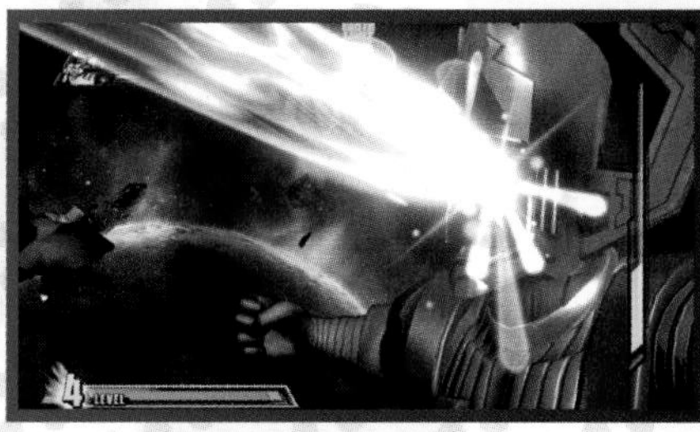

Galactus can use lasers from his eyes to sweep the entire playing field. The beam starts at the ground by his torso before sweeping clockwise to the sky. If you're feeling saucy and piloting an appropriate character, you can attempt to teleport around the beam just before it reaches you, but the safe bet is to simply guard it at ground level, then dash in and hit Galactus while he fires the rest of the beam worthlessly skyward. If you block, this beam isn't a big deal; it passes over your character soon enough. If you DON'T block, you have probably lost a team member, especially if he catches you early on in the beam's path.

"YIELD TO ME...YOU ARE BROKEN."

One of Galactus's two most powerful attacks. He steps into the background much more quickly than during his throw, and unleashes an astonishing maelstrom of beams that saturates the entire playing field. If this hits your hero, kiss that hero good-bye. Even if guarded, this ferocious projection of energy deals tons of chip damage. The only way around taking damage is to stay grounded and activate X-Factor on reaction to Galactus winding up his lasers while stepping into the background. Happily, now's the time to activate X-Factor anyway—use all the firepower you can to diminish the second half of Galactus's vitality quickly. By now, time may be winding down, and a time out is never in your favor here, even if your team is healthy and Galactus is near defeat.

"THERE IS NO HOPE FOR YOU...THIS CHARADE IS OVER."

He isn't kidding. For his most powerful onslaught, Galactus raises his right hand aloft and begins gathering incredible energy. As he gathers the Power Cosmic, he'll slowly raise his right hand up higher. Once this attack is fully charged, he'll bring his hand down with unspeakable force, instantly knocking out ***any*** character in the way...whether or not you're guarding, and whether or not you have X-Factor active! The ***only*** way to avoid certain doom is to hit Galactus over and over again while he charges up this attack. Hit him enough, and you can cause him to stagger out of the charge, interrupting the move.

X-Factor boosts damage considerably against Galactus, especially with only one character left. As mentioned, X-Factor can also be used to negate the extreme chip damage dealt if you're caught in his late-stage, beam hyper combos. When Galactus is defeated, the current point character is declared the winner. The winning hero's ending will play, and several cool items in Gallery Mode will unlock for that character.

Since only one character can earn an ending per playthrough, don't fret if you lose a character or two, unless you're going for a high score. Instead, decide whose ending you're after, then consider the other two characters expendable; use them to push aside Galactus's minions and get a start on Galactus himself, but don't be too careful with them—let them fall to Galactus so the character whose ending you'd like can come in, hulk up (so to speak) with lv.3 X-Factor, then finish Galactus off easily with a flurry of hyper combos built up by the expendable partners.

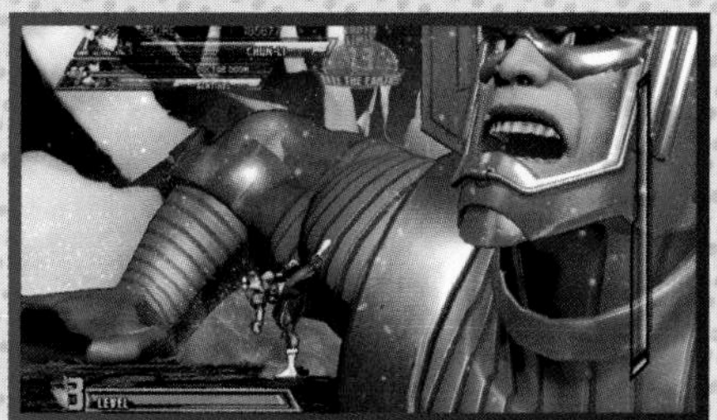

What's that saying about hubris? You don't need the Ultimate Nullifier to defeat Galactus after all. Sorry, big guy. Legend of Chun-Li, indeed.

There are rewards both for beating Arcade Mode with every character, and for getting to Galactus, but *losing!* After all, Galactus himself has an ending, but the residents of the respective worlds of Marvel and Capcom aren't going to like it too much...

VERSUS

Here, you can play local matches against friends offline. Of course you'll need two controllers. After each match, you can opt to rematch immediately with the same teams and assists, with no need to revisit the character select screen or reload the stage. Of course, you can also opt to re-select teams as well. Like any other mode, playing in Versus garners PP, so be sure to exit all the way out when you're done with your session.

TRAINING

If you're going to get good at *MvC3,* you're going to spend some time in Training Mode. Rugby it is not, but playing video games is still a physical endeavor, one which requires mild to heavy dexterity and hand-eye coordination. Like Capcom's recent fighters *Street Fighter 4* and *Super Street Fighter 4, MvC3* features a few concessions to new players (such as Simple Play Mode, and generally less complicated input requirements for individual moves than the *SF* series). Still, *MvC3* at a proficient level of play remains in the upper echelon of games when it comes to the finger gymnastics required. Spending some time honing muscle memory is, at least to a certain extent, required rather than optional. Additionally, beyond the athletic question of execution, there is the more cerebral aspect—more than any other fighting game, in addition to the action onscreen at any given time, there are resources to be monitored and considered, and all sorts of situations to be watchful for. Issues of general strategy, as well as matchup and character specific tactics, will have to be explored at some point outside of matches, and continuously throughout a player's career. Happily, *Marvel vs. Capcom 3* has a fantastic training mode, one that should suit your purposes, whatever they are, quite well.

To begin, you'll choose an operation mode, teams for both sides, the CPU's difficulty level, the timer setting, the damage setting, and the stage.

Once in Training Mode, the first thing you should do (the first thing!) is to visit Controller Settings in the Pause Menu. As in the Controller Menu in other modes, you can assign the six main buttons (L, M, H, S, P1, and P2) however you like. Training Mode has a few control options not available in other modes to add to these. On either console controller this leaves four buttons free for other tasks—two shoulder buttons, and the buttons registered by pushing in each analog stick. If you are using a joystick instead (depending on your joystick whether commercially available or custom-made), you may only have two extra buttons to assign, or none at all. In Training Mode, these buttons can (and should!) be assigned to control the training dummy on the fly in specific ways:

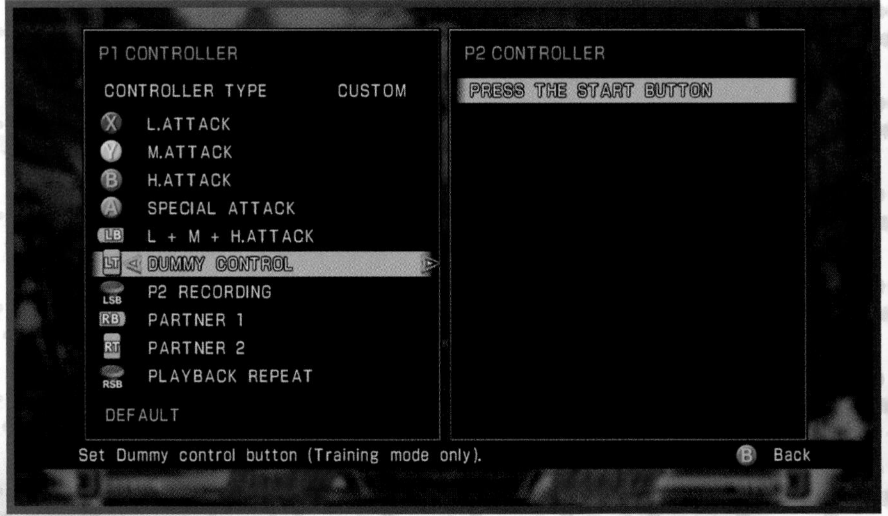

DUMMY CONTROL Assign this button, and you can hold it at any time to take total control of the dummy. This is extremely useful; if your controller or joystick makes it so you can comfortably just hold that button down (easy to do assigning it to, say, one of the left shoulder buttons on a gamepad; equally easy to do using a pinkie finger on a joystick, or using a small, sufficiently-heavy object), you can play the dummy team just like your own. This effectively means you can train two teams, six characters, and eighteen crossover assists at a time in Training Mode! It's also helpful to briefly take control of the dummy to move them slightly when practicing position-specific stuff, or to make them jump out of the corner when you want to practice mid-screen, rather than corner-only, combos and tactics. Moving the dummy yourself is much faster than using the point character on your team to throw or hit the opposing character into position, or by resetting Training Mode itself by holding Back or Select, then pressing Start.

P1 / P2 RECORDING These buttons refer to Player 1 or Player 2, not partner 1 or partner 2. By assigning and pressing this button, you can then record up to 10 seconds of input to either team. This input can then be played back, either once or on a loop, while you control either team. The recording feature is the best feature of Training Mode. If you find yourself having trouble against a particular tactic—like say a teleport or square jump backed by a crossover assist, or a sudden hyper combo, or a zoning, trapping projectile pattern, and so on—record the tactic that's driving you mad. Play it back and learn how to guard properly, and look for holes. The same can be done to hone your own tactics—if you wonder about the effectiveness of your offense, record your sequences with the dummy team, then play them back against yourself and see how hard it is to counter. Remember, the recording feature is simply playing back inputs, exactly as you first performed them. Depending on the position and situation, this playback may not be as you intended. For this reason it's usually best to keep recording clips as brief and disciplined as possible.

PLAYBACK / PLAYBACK REPEAT A button to set for playback repetition. There is little reason not to assign Playback Repeat as your only playback button, as you can simply press the button again to cancel the looped playback whenever you like. If you would like more time between playback loops, simply have the training dummy stand around doing nothing for a few moments after recording the desired sequence.

DUMMY FORWARD / DUMMY JUMP Sets a button to either make the dummy jump, or walk forward. The Dummy Control setting is more of a comprehensive catch-all, largely negating the need to assign these functions. Using Dummy Control instead means if you want the dummy to walk forward or jump you can, but you can also make them do anything else, too. That said, while holding a button to trigger Dummy Control you *cannot* control your own team, so these functions can be useful for testing situations where you want the dummy to jump or move while still controlling your character, too.

After setting dummy control of some kind (Dummy Control, P2 Recording, and Playback Repeat availed us most of the time), check out the second page of the Training Mode Pause Menu. Here, you can set the parameters for the training dummy. This is important too. Remember that practice doesn't make perfect; *perfect* practice makes perfect. You won't run into many players (or even CPU-controlled teams) who stand stock-still and never guard, so it doesn't make much sense to practice that way either. At the very least, the following settings are recommended.

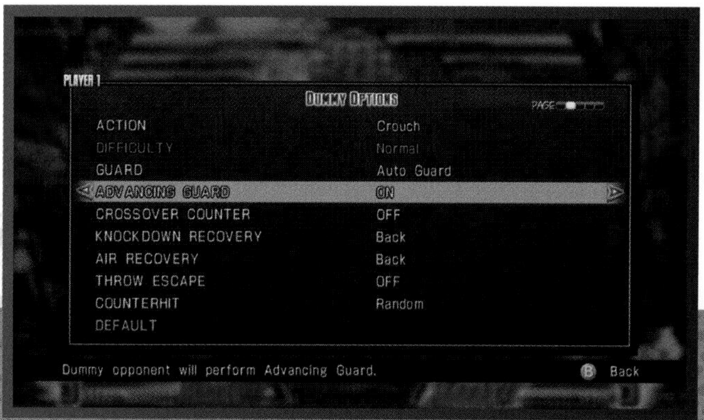

ACTION This varies. Set the dummy to stand when you are practicing combos you expect to land on a standing opponent. These kind of situations include against opponents dashing, attempting a throw, or trying to anti-air from the ground. Set the dummy to crouch when practicing combos for other situations, like when pinning the foe with an assist, or after using a fast overhead (such as a triangle jump or instant overhead jumping attack). Set the dummy to jump or super jump when practicing air throw combos or anti-air combos.

DIFFICULTY This is only relevant if you choose to set the dummy to CPU control, which allows you to spar against a moving target. This can be useful for exactly that reason—to practice versus a moving target, rather than a motionless mannequin—but human competition and a CPU that runs off of patterns and reacting inhumanly to your inputs are two very, very different things. Focus on combo execution and confident movement against computer opponents, but do not rely on CPU sparring to make you a better strategist. An over-reliance on playing the CPU can actually be detrimental when you do get around to playing human opponents, because you will unconsciously train tactics that just work on the CPU, rather than being deliberate about each action that you take while actively attempting to read a thinking opponent.

GUARD This setting will differ depending on your aim. At the very least, set this to Auto Guard. This means the dummy will block in any circumstance where you start hitting them, but then do not perpetuate a combo. This is useful for perfecting your execution of basic ground chains. Later, when you're practicing tactics instead of just execution, set this to Random Guard. This will help you train yourself to cut offensive sequences short when the enemy guards properly.

ADVANCING GUARD Advancing guard is a huge deal for defense in *MvC3*. Mid-screen, the defending character pushes back the aggressor almost a full screen away! As such, it's important to be ready to react when your opponent blocks and pushes you out, which will inevitably happen often. Some characters have means to get right back in after advancing guard pushes them away, such as a teleport or fast lateral move, while other characters essentially lose all momentum. Between having the dummy set to some kind of guard (usually Auto Guard or Random Guard) and turning advancing guard on, you can work on regaining lost momentum quickly, or bypassing advancing guard in the first place by timing attacks and assists to strike your opponent simultaneously. It's important to note that the training dummy will always use advancing guard with the fastest possible timing. This may produce results that differ from what usually happens in actual match play. This setting should stay set to "on" as a default.

CROSSOVER COUNTER With this setting on, the dummy will crossover counter to the next character in line whenever the dummy's team has at least 1 bar of hyper combo gauge available. For general training purposes, it will actually be more annoying than helpful to turn on this setting—opponents who aren't just mashing simply won't be using crossover counters that much, and most assists don't make great crossover counters against a point-blank, aggressive character anyway (though certainly some do). Instead, turn this on periodically when you want to specifically check how vulnerable your close-range tactics are to some of the better crossover counters, such as Haggar—α or Chun-Li—γ. If you're practicing zoning patterns, you can also turn this on to see what happens when the opponent uses your full-screen attacks as an opportunity to crossover counter and switch characters safely—perhaps you have some way to punish them for that on reaction, like with a quick beam hyper combo.

KNOCKDOWN RECOVERY / AIR RECOVERY Both of these settings should be set to either forward or back, or at the very least to random. This setting should *never* be set to "off." When opponents are knocked to the turf or flip out in mid-air, they will recover in one direction or the other almost all the time—and usually backward, unless they're intentionally trying to mix things up. Recovering characters are briefly invincible, and less vulnerable to continued aerial juggles or OTG hits when on the floor. Opponents may sometimes opt simply not to recover in either direction, however, making it important to be ready to react appropriately—hence the utility of the "Random" setting. Note that there is a Training Mode quirk with this function: training dummies launched with Ⓢ will *not* perform aerial recovery, even when it's turned on.

THROW ESCAPE Normal throws (accomplished with ➡ or ⬅ + Ⓗ, whether on the ground or in the air) are very quick in *MvC3* (grabbing on the 2nd frame after input), and create OTG openings for most characters. This means, naturally, that throws are pretty good, and a more or less required part of any decent offense. Throws can be broken, however, which leads to a situation where both characters are standing next to each other and ready to act, with nothing having actually happened. It's important to be able to react to throw breaks—they happen *extremely* quickly, faster than in any other fighting game—so turn this on periodically to train yourself to be ready with instant follow-ups or evasive actions when your throws are escaped.

COUNTERHIT Hits against characters who are themselves winding up an attack are counterhits, and will cause a distinctive red hit spark. +2 frames are added to the hitstun created, and for certain moves an entirely different effect than normal hitstun will occur, such as causing the opponent to stagger. Certain combos and links are only possible after a successful counterhit, so turn this on when practicing such tactics. You can even set this to random, which you should probably do eventually, so you actually get a feel for trying to react to the red spark rather than just doing a counterhit setup on auto-pilot. This is difficult, but possible.

Apart from dummy action settings, there are general settings that can be adjusted which apply to training "matches," and to both the player's team and the dummy's.

PLAYER 1

PLAYER SETTINGS

LIFE RECOVERY	ON
LIFE GAUGE	100%
H.C. GAUGE RECOVERY	ON
H.C. GAUGE	1
X-FACTOR	Infinity
X-FACTOR LEVEL	Normal
CHARACTER 1 ASSIST TYPE	α
CHARACTER 2 ASSIST TYPE	β
CHARACTER 3 ASSIST TYPE	γ
DEFAULT	

Can be used multiple times without restarting. B Back

LIFE RECOVERY Determines whether characters will regenerate health. With this on, characters in Training Mode cannot be knocked out. Usually you'll want this on, unless you're trying to simulate real matches, or practice with Dark Phoenix (who is activated by having Phoenix knocked out with 5 hyper combo gauge bars in reserve).

H.C. GAUGE RECOVERY Determines whether the hyper combo gauge will automatically refill whenever bar is expended. When simply training execution, you'll want this on. If you're trying to get a sense of how quickly you actually build hyper combo gauge when attacking, turn this off. You'll also want this off if you're trying to simulate match settings.

X-FACTOR SETTINGS You can adjust both whether X-Factor can be used repeatedly in Training Mode, and what level it will register as when it is activated. With both settings on normal, X-Factor will behave as it does in matches—only one use per session (unless Training Mode is reset by holding Back or Select, then pressing Start), with X-Factor strength determined by how many characters are left on your team (with Life Recovery set to on, X-Factor will always registered as level 1, since none of your characters will ever be knocked out). When practicing X-Factor setups and hit-confirm combos, set X-Factor use to infinity. When trying to simulate real matches in Training Mode, set it to normal.

ASSIST TYPES Beautifully, and unlike previous *Vs.* titles, you do not have to back all the way out to the character select screen to try out different assist types! Simply change the assist types for each character on either team here. Very useful!

When simply training execution (practicing inputs and combos) or matchup difficulties (using record and dummy control functions to simulate troublesome situations), you'll probably want the timer set to infinite. You'll likely also want hyper combo gauge recovery on, along with vitality gauge recovery. Attack Data is an extremely useful tool—with this window active, you'll see how much damage your combos do in real-time. This can help you gauge how useful combos and tactics are when practicing. Turning Input Display on can also be very helpful to troubleshoot your move execution when you're having difficulty performing complicated techniques.

With a sparring partner, however, it can be interesting to set training mode to 99 seconds. You can pick the teams both of you want, then assign dummy control to 2P. Turn vitality gauge and hyper combo gauge recovery off for both player and dummy, and set X-Factor use to normal. With these settings, you can play sparring matches back-to-back much more quickly than using Versus Mode, even selecting Rematch! The instant a "match" ends, either through three characters on a side being knocked out or the timer running out, another "match" starts immediately! This grants the added flexibility of stopping a "match" to check a specific situation out; you can then reset Training Mode, and thus the "match," by holding Back or Select then pressing Start. Nothing in Training Mode counts towards Trophies or Achievements, and wins/losses aren't tabulated as in Versus mode, but if you exit properly (instead of simply shutting off the console) after a session, tons of Player Points will be earned. And if you're playing enough to spar, you're probably playing a lot of *MvC3* anyway, so those things are already taken care of.

TRAINING MODE RESET Training mode can be reset at any time by holding Select or Back, then pressing Start. If you hold left or right while resetting Training mode, Training mode will reset with characters standing near either corner.

MISSION MODE

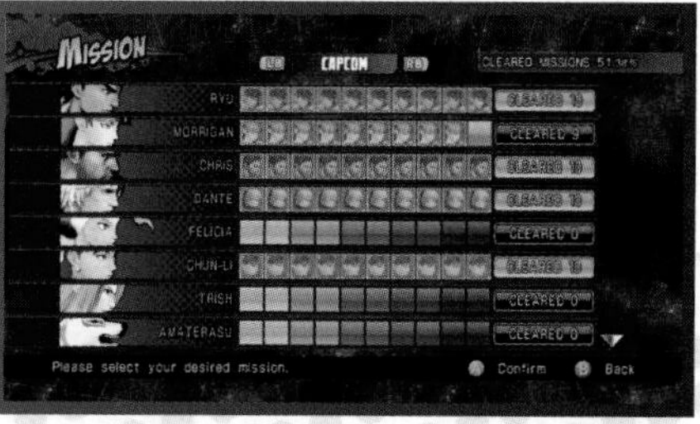

Mission Mode is similar to the Trials of *Street Fighter 4* and *Super Street Fighter 4*. Each character has 10 Missions to complete, each of which highlight a particular combo that character is capable of. The combos start out simply enough, before progressing to harder combos that require the use of special hit states, assists, OTGs, and generally more advanced setups. Even the high-level Missions for each character don't represent the best possible combos—in our character sections you'll find more damaging combos for everyone—but completion of Missions can help you a lot when growing accustomed to using a hero you're unfamiliar with. Completing Missions also earns a lot of Player Points, and some special titles you can apply to your license card! Missions are not initially available for Akuma, Hsien-Ko, Sentinel, or Taskmaster, but once these characters are unlocked their Missions will appear as well. Forthcoming DLC characters Shuma-Gorath and Jill will have Missions available too, though of course not until they're actually released!

ONLINE MODE

MvC3 has several Online Modes you can enter to test your mettle against other fans of Marvel® Comics and Capcom. Whether engaging in Player Matches for fun, or Ranked Matches that go toward your overall record and ranking, we expect this is where most players will spend the majority of their time.

By participating in Ranked Matches, you'll have a chance to jockey for position on the leaderboards across several metrics. There are separate leaderboards for win streaks, win/loss record, and overall ranking. There is also a leaderboard for Arcade Mode high score, though of course that's not an online mode.

GALLERY

As indicated earlier in this chapter, a great many fan-friendly unlockables are available for your perusal. These include intro cinemas, art pieces, sound effects and background music, and a model viewer to check out various characters up close.

OPTIONS

General settings can be tailored to your preference here.

CONTROLLER Command inputs can be customized here. Note that Training Mode has more controller options than other modes, and these controls can only be set while in Training Mode.

OPERATION MODE Here you can select whether you'll always be in either Normal or Simple Mode, and whether this choice will appear before every match. As stated in the introductory chapter, it is recommended that you play in Normal Mode. Simple Mode cuts away much of each characters' arsenal, and diminishes a lot of what makes combat interesting and varied—which is not to mention that it doesn't actually make certain aspects of the game any simpler, such as assist calling and team dynamics in general. Only the most casual fans should stick to Simple Mode for very long.

HUD POSITION Here you can adjust the position of the vitality gauges and timer, and the hyper combo gauges. You can even position them both entirely offscreen, if you want to enjoy the visuals unfettered by UI elements.

SOUND Here you can adjust various sound options. With Classic BGM selected, theme music for various characters will play when they appear!

CHARACTER VOICE Here, you can choose between Japanese or English voiceovers for several characters, as you like.

SYSTEM Turn notifications on or off. You may want to set this to off if you'd prefer no distractions while playing matches online; but then you won't see match invites from friends, either!

System & Gameplay

Getting the hang of *MvC3* requires understanding the display, the basic concepts, and the flow of a match.

A match is a showdown between two teams comprised of three heroes each.

The first team to deplete the vitality gauges of all three opposing characters wins.

Wins can also come by having more vitality left than the other team when the timer expires.

During combat, one character on each team is considered the "point" character. This character is directly controlled by a player or the CPU. The other two partners on a team wait in the wings, available to perform **crossover assists**, where they leap on screen briefly to aid the **point character**. Partner characters take damage if interrupted during assists—50% more damage than point characters, in fact! Partner characters can also be subbed in for the point character in a number of different ways—by tagging in with a **crossover attack**, by launching into a **team aerial combo**, or by burning one bar of the hyper combo gauge for either a **team hyper combo** or a **crossover counter**. The next character in line also subs in automatically if the current point character is knocked out.

In addition to getting used to the actions of simply playing the game, success in *MvC3* is reliant on planning. It helps to think of a team in aggregate as a character, rather than a collection of three distinct heroes. Characters don't just fight one after another; they fight together, and they share resources. As such, they should also have roles, and your team should have a purpose.

Do you want to rush and pressure your opponent, or run away and chip at them with damage? Bulldog an opponent, or run the clock down and punish assist calls? Which hero will build hyper combo gauge, and who will use it? Who has the most important crossover assist, or crossover counter? Who is likely to be around in last-hero-standing situations—are they fragile? Will they have solid options to mount a comeback without the aid of assists? Are they particularly good with X-Factor?

This combination of managing blazing quick combat, along with team resources, and an overall strategy on the fly gives the *MvC* series a unique flavor among fighting games.

Time, Vitality, and X-Factor

The Timer

The game clock is displayed between the vitality gauges. If this timer hits 0 with both teams still standing, the team with more vitality overall wins the match. The vitality measured for a judgment victory is based on the percentage of max vitality available, not actual numeric vitality. So, for example, if time expires and only full-vitality Sentinel and full-vitality Phoenix are left against each other, the match is a draw—although, in absolute terms, Sentinel has over *three times* more vitality than Phoenix.

With the default timer setting of 99, a time out match takes 3 minutes.

It is recommended that you play with the timer on the default setting of 99. Not only will most, if not all, tournaments use this setting, but this is also the setting most experienced players will favor online. The timer serves a useful purpose within gameplay—most matches between competent players will not actually go the distance, but the very threat of a time over victory forces players to take action eventually, and prevents eternal standoff contests.

Team Vitality Gauges & Team Order

The vitality gauges for each team member are displayed at the top of the screen. These gauges also indicate the order of team members—the top vitality gauge is for the current point character, the second gauge is for partner 1, and the third vitality gauge is for partner 2. This order determines who will come in next if the current point character is knocked out, along with which partner is called by the P1 and P2 buttons. It is important to note that the assignments for the buttons P1 and P2 are actually shown. "ASSIST OK!!" indicators also appear over a given character's vitality gauge when their **crossover assist** has recovered, and is ready to be called again.

Actions that change team order:
Crossover attack (red damage becomes permanent)
Crossover counter
Point character knocked out (red damage becomes permanent)
Struck with opponent's snap back (red damage becomes permanent)
Team aerial combo
Team hyper combo

Characters are not created equal where vitality is concerned—some of these heroes can stand up to more withering punishment than others. The mutant-killing robot Sentinel repeats its turn as the sturdiest character from *MvC2*, with Hulk and Thor close behind—Haggar and Tron round out the heavies on the Capcom side. These bruisers all have 1,200,000 or more vitality (as compared to the damage values in this guide, or by turning on attack data in training options). A few diminutive characters have comparatively low vitality—Akuma, Amaterasu, Arthur, and Zero all possess 800,000. For fragility, Phoenix easily trumps all—this possessed version of Jean Grey has only 420,000 vitality! However, this is somewhat balanced by her unique ability to resurrect as the ferocious Dark Phoenix if she is K.O.ed with 5 bars of hyper combo gauge in reserve...

Throughout this guide, we'll transcribe and make frequent reference to combos and sequences that routinely deal hundreds of thousands of points of damage, and often over a million. And this is not always taking into account the effects of **X-Factor**, a feature new to *MvC3*, where an entire team's damage output is temporarily increased by 130~230%! The point is, although some characters have a bit more vitality than others, in the right situation every one of them can be taken down, even with max vitality—level 3 X-Factor essentially makes *any* solid combo a knockout blow! A glowing red opponent means *be careful*!

THAT LAST LITTLE BIT...

DANGER! will flash on screen when a character nears defeat.

The last pixel of damage is sturdier than preceding pixels.

THE VITALITY POINT TOTALS LISTED HERE FOR EACH CHARACTER ARE DISTRIBUTED EVENLY ACROSS MOST OF A VITALITY GAUGE, BUT THE VERY LAST LITTLE BIT OF THE GAUGE PACKS IN A DISPROPORTIONATE AMOUNT OF VITALITY POINTS. THIS IS WHY CONTINUOUS DAMAGE ACCRUED ON THE VITALITY GAUGE WILL SOMETIMES SEEM TO "FREEZE" ON THAT VERY LAST PIXEL, JUST BEFORE A CHARACTER IS KNOCKED OUT. NOTHING ODD IS GOING ON—THE OPPONENT IS STILL TAKING DAMAGE NORMALLY. IF THEY SURVIVE AT A PIXEL OF HEALTH, THEY JUST HAVE A LITTLE MORE LEFT.

MARVEL CHARACTER VITALITY

Name	Max Vitality
Sentinel	1,300,000
Thor	1,250,000
Hulk	1,200,000
She-Hulk	1,150,000
TaskMaster	1,100,000
Captain America	1,050,000
Doctor Doom	1,000,000
Dormammu	1,000,000
Super-Skrull	1,000,000
Iron Man	950,000
M.O.D.O.K.	950,000
Shuma-Gorath (DLC)	950,000
Wolverine	950,000
Deadpool	900,000
Spider-Man	900,000
Magneto	850,000
Storm	850,000
X-23	830,000
Phoenix / Dark Phoenix	420,000

CAPCOM CHARACTER VITALITY

Name	Max Vitality
Haggar	1,200,000
Tron	1,200,000
Chris	1,100,000
Wesker	1,100,000
Spencer	1,050,000
Ryu	1,000,000
Morrigan	950,000
Viewtiful Joe	950,000
C. Viper	900,000
Dante	900,000
Hsien-Ko	900,000
Felicia	880,000
Chun-Li	850,000
Jill (DLC)	850,000
Trish	850,000
Akuma	800,000
Amaterasu	800,000
Arthur	800,000
Zero	800,000

RED DAMAGE

INITIALLY, HALF OF THE DAMAGE RECEIVED AGAINST POINT CHARACTERS, AND *ANY* DAMAGE INFLICTED AGAINST ASSISTS, IS RED DAMAGE. RED DAMAGE IS NOT PERMANENT! PARTNERS WILL RECOVER RED DAMAGE SLOWLY OVER TIME, WHENEVER THEY ARE NOT ACTIVELY PERFORMING A ***CROSSOVER ASSIST***. UNDER THE INFLUENCE OF X-FACTOR, POINT CHARACTERS RECOVER RED DAMAGE AS WELL (EXCEPT WHEN BEING HIT), AND PARTNER CHARACTERS RECOVER RED DAMAGE FASTER THAN NORMAL.

THE RATE OF RECOVERY FOR RED DAMAGE ON PARTNER CHARACTERS IS BASED ON MAXIMUM NUMERIC VITALITY, RATHER THAN THE VITALITY GAUGE PERCENTAGE. THIS MEANS THAT PARTNER CHARACTERS WITH LOWER MAXIMUM HEALTH WILL REFILL RED DAMAGE MUCH MORE QUICKLY. LET'S SAY YOU HAVE A THIRD CHARACTER THAT YOU'RE USING PRIMARILY FOR THEIR CROSSOVER ASSIST, BUT A COUPLE ASSIST CALLS ARE HARSHLY PUNISHED AND THE PARTNER CHARACTER TAKES 99% RED DAMAGE—LEFT STANDING AND 1 PIXEL AWAY FROM DEFEAT. PRUDENTLY, YOU DECIDE NOT TO CALL THAT CHARACTER AGAIN, NOR SWAP TO THEM, UNTIL THEIR RED DAMAGE HAS COMPLETELY REGENERATED. FOR SENTINEL, THIS TAKES ROUGHLY 1 MINUTE AND 50 SECONDS, WHILE PHOENIX REGAINS ALL RED DAMAGE IN ROUGHLY 35 SECONDS!

RED DAMAGE BECOMES PERMANENT WHEN A PARTNER CHARACTER IS TAGGED IN VIA A CROSSOVER ATTACK (HOLD P1=P2), WHEN A CHARACTER COMES IN TO REPLACE A KNOCKED OUT PARTNER, OR WHEN A CHARACTER IS FORCED IN WITH AN OPPONENT'S SNAP BACK (↓ ↘ → + P1=P2, REQUIRES 1 BAR). THIS IS WHERE ***SNAP BACKS*** COME IN MOST HANDY STRATEGICALLY—IF YOU INFLICT HEAVY RED DAMAGE TO ONE OF YOUR OPPONENT'S ASSIST CHARACTERS, LOOK FOR OPPORTUNITIES TO SNAP THAT CHARACTER IN AND MAKE IT ALL PERMANENT! THIS IS OFTEN THE MOST EFFICIENT USE OF HYPER COMBO GAUGE—SNAPPING IN A CHARACTER THAT HAS 90% RED DAMAGE DOES A LOT MORE THAN A HYPER COMBO THAT DOES 15-30% DAMAGE TO THE OPPOSING POINT CHARACTER, AND NOT ALL OF THAT DAMAGE IS PERMANENT. SIMILARLY, BE WARY WHEN YOU HAVE PARTNER CHARACTERS WHO'VE SUSTAINED SEVERE RED DAMAGE, ESPECIALLY IF IT'S PARTNER 1. THAT RED DAMAGE IS ONLY A SNAP BACK AWAY FROM BECOMING PERMANENT. YOUR POINT CHARACTER MAY SUCCUMB IN THE MEANTIME AS WELL, FORCING PARTNER 1 TO REPLACE THEM.

When partner 1 has sustained severe red damage, don't use their ***crossover assist*** (tap P1) or tag them in with ***crossover attack*** (hold P1). Also, be extra cautious to avoid having your point character knocked out. This forces partner 1 to replace that character and makes the red damage permanent. If your point character's vitality is low (in addition to significant red damage on partner 1), you should look for ways to bring in partner 2 safely, which will buy time for both ailing characters to heal the red damage, and lessen your immediate risk of having two low-health characters in jeopardy. The fastest method is a crossover attack to partner 2 (hold P2), but your opponent may expect this and wait for it, eager to punish your new point character while they pose after the tag-in. A 3-stage ***team hyper combo*** all the way to partner 2, or a ***team aerial combo*** involving all three characters, are better ways to get partner 2 in safely. You can also guard your opponent's attack and use a ***crossover counter*** (tap ⇨ + P2 while guarding, requires 1 bar).

When partner 2 has sustained severe red damage, refrain from further P2 assist calls. At least partner 2 isn't in imminent danger of having all that red damage become permanent yet (due to filling in for an expired point character), so as long as you lay off that ***crossover assist*** for a while, you should be fine. Beware of accidentally hitting ⇨ + P2 while blocking, since this will cause an inadvertent ***crossover counter*** that swaps in partner 2, which is the last thing you want. This won't make the red damage permanent, but it will put the character in further jeopardy because knock outs are dependent on depleting regular vitality, not red damage. You shouldn't be calling an assist that is this battered anyway, so just consider the P2 button off-limits for a while.

If both partner 1 and 2 are in bad shape, with deep red damage, then you could be in trouble. Any poorly-timed partner call could just get them knocked out, but your point character can't afford to get knocked out either. You also cannot afford to tag either character in with a ***crossover attack***, since this will just make a lot of red damage permanent and compound a difficult situation. Furthermore, playing sheepishly without assists is usually just delaying the inevitable, unless your capacity for stalling is confident and immaculate. Although ***X-Factor*** is at its least potent with three characters still standing, consider using at this point. Getting health back for all three ailing characters, and thus breathing room, can help right the ship in a match that has gone wrong early. Be aware that later on in the match, as characters start to fall on both sides and the stakes and risks rise, your opponent may still have X-Factor available, while you may not.

X-FACTOR

Ⓛ + Ⓜ + Ⓗ + Ⓢ (ONCE PER MATCH; NOTATED THROUGHOUT GUIDE IN COMBOS AND SEQUENCES AS X-Factor icon)

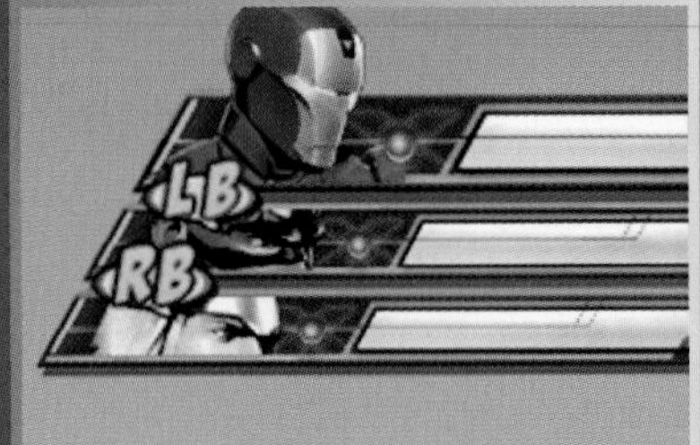

X-Factor available; press Ⓛ + Ⓜ + Ⓗ + Ⓢ (X-Factor icon) while grounded to activate.

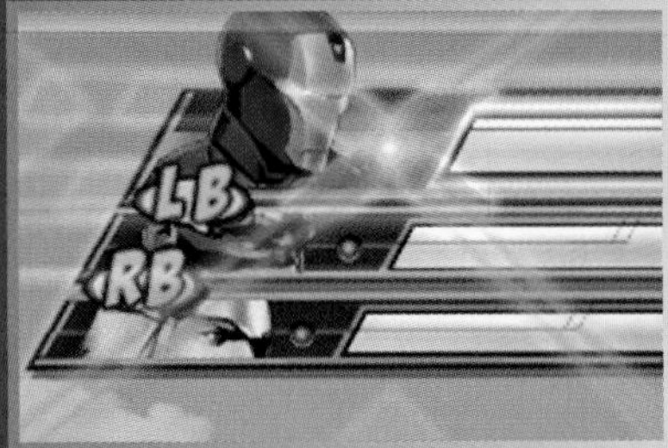

X-Factor activated!

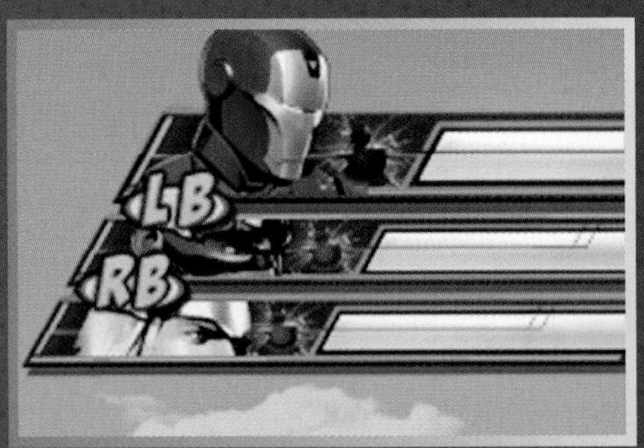

X-Factor unavailable. X-Factor can only be used once per match. The potential and duration of X-Factor is greater the fewer partners you have remaining, and the X-Factor indicator itself will become more pronounced if you haven't yet used X-Factor with only one hero left.

Tucked between the portrait of each character and his or her (or its... Sentinel doesn't really have a gender, after all) vitality gauge is the X-Factor indicator. This ruby-like symbol indicates whether X-Factor is available. X-Factor cannot be activated while airborne, while knocked down, while stuck in hitstun, nor during level 3 hyper combos or throws. Otherwise, X-Factor can be activated at any time on the ground.

Ground actions cancelable with X-Factor activation:
Basic Attacks (Ⓛ, Ⓜ, Ⓗ)
Special Attacks (Ⓢ)
Command Attacks (⇨ + Ⓗ, etc.)
Special Moves (⇩ ⬂ ⇨ + ATK, etc.)
Hyper Combos (⇩ ⬂ ⇨ + ATK ATK, etc.; not including lv.3 hyper combos)
Guardstun

New to *MvC3*, X-Factor adds a wild new wrinkle to combat. X-Factor can be used once per match, and applies to an entire team at a time, including crossover assists. During X-Factor's duration, characters for that team will be encased in a furious red glow. The strength and speed of the point character, and the strength of assists, are greatly increased during X-Factor. The speed boost means that attacks used during X-Factor have shorter startup and faster recovery than outside of X-Factor. This leads to opportunities for link combos which are impossible otherwise. Both the strength and speed boosts innate to X-Factor vary from character to character—depending on the character using X-Factor, and the number of teammates they have left, speed and attack recovery are enhanced by 6-25%, and normal damage is buffed to 120-230%! Partner characters will recover red vitality more quickly than normal, and the point character will also recover red vitality whenever not actively occupied by hitstun or guardstun. Finally, no chip damage is received during X-Factor.

The remaining duration of X-Factor is indicated by a glowing, shrinking red border around the vitality gauge.

X-Factor potential	X-Factor level	Duration	Damage increase (character dependent)	Speed increase (character dependent)
Three characters standing	X-Factor level 1	10 seconds	120~160%	100~125%
Two characters standing	X-Factor level 2	15 seconds	135~180%	100~150%
One character standing	X-Factor level 3	20 seconds	150~230%	100~175%

In addition to significantly boosting damage, X-Factor also reduces the effect of ***damage scaling***, increasing damage even further in general, and upping the damage of multi-hit moves disproportionately!

X-Factor's purpose and potential uses are multifaceted:

Since X-Factor activation can cancel any action, you can hit-confirm an attack into X-Factor from the beginning of any ground combo. The ideal application for a hit-confirmed X-Factor combo is when you recognize that you've nailed both the opponent's point and partner character at once—a solid X-Factor combo, even at X-Factor level 1, will easily knock out any full-vitality assist, and most full-vitality point characters! Two-for-one is just about the best deal you'll find in *MvC3*.

The ability to X-Factor cancel any ground action also means that you can create aggressive setups that aren't normally possible, by canceling the recovery of certain projectiles and hyper combos with X-Factor. This is analogous to using FADC (focus attack dash cancel) in *Super Street Fighter 4* (or "roman canceling" in *Guilty Gear XX* and its sequels) to throw a fireball, then dash immediately behind it.

Similarly, you can use X-Factor to achieve otherwise impossible, outrageous combos, by canceling a ground hyper combo partway through into another hyper combo. This is great when you want to insure that a combo results in a knock out, rather than simply a severely damaged foe.

You can also use X-Factor to cut guardstun short after blocking a recovery-heavy attack—your punishment will be much stronger with X-Factor active, and you can get to it sooner without waiting for guardstun to decay naturally. This can be good to harshly punish some crossover assists, which are vulnerable only very briefly (if at all) after being blocked.

X-Factor can also be used during guardstun to avoid a chip damage knock out, for example while blocking a beam like Iron Man's Proton Cannon. Depending on the situation, this can be a lot more palatable than using a crossover counter out of desperation, which wastes a bar of meter and often just means that you trade the knockout of one character for another.

Expanding on this medical role, if your point character and partners have banged-up vitality gauges filled with red damage, you can activate X-Factor and run away from your opponent for a bit while red damage replenishes more quickly than normal.

Finally, you can simply keep X-Factor in reserve, to deploy in last-man-standing scenarios. X-Factor is tremendously powerful when it is used by a single, unassisted character. It can greatly increase comeback potential if you find yourself sliding down the slippery slope of dwindling numbers!

It's easy to recommend knocking out two characters at once—both a point character and an assist—as the most efficient and proactive use of X-Factor. In effect, this resembles the "double snap back" assist infinites that became one of the most deadly high-level tactics in *MvC2*—you receive an outsized reward for an incidental, or even *accidental*, hit. And, in some ways, this is even *more* powerful. Here, you don't just knock out one character and gain tremendous momentum against the next. Instead, you just outright demolish two characters! (Consult the combo section later in this chapter for a brutal example.) However, that situation may not come up in a given match, or you may not have time to react to glancing blows that strike two opposing characters. How you use X-Factor each match will be a judgment call, and the factors for that judgment will differ from bout to bout and opponent to opponent. The only sure thing regarding X-Factor is that it's far too powerful to overlook. So, at the very least, don't neglect to use it if you're down to your last hero. There is no reason not to, at that point. But you should also look for efficient opportunities to use X-Factor, rather than just a last-ditch, comeback effort!

Solo Wolverine has caught and K.O.ed an assist with just a few hits. One versus three is a tall order, but the playing field is somewhat leveled by the boost, especially since X-Factor is much more potent when activated solo, rather than with a full team.

Hulk has followed up an air combo on two opposing characters with OTG Gamma Quake, before using X-Factor to hyper combo cancel and also land Gamma Crush. Both of those characters are gone now... Since X-Factor allows the cancelation of ground-based special moves and hyper combos, It also allows for very damaging combos and extremely devious setups that are not possible otherwise. This also means you can hit-confirm X-Factor, verifying that you've actually started a combo before activating this once-per-match boost, rather than simply using it cold and watching your opponent clam up and run away until your X-Factor expires.

X-Factor Sentinel catches two characters with a launcher together. One Hyper Sentinel Force OTG combo later—they're both dust. With fast reactions, you may realize you've caught both the opposing point character and their assist partner in a combo. This is an ideal time to activate X-Factor, so you can finish the combo strong and take out two characters with one stroke! Between X-Factor's considerable damage boost and the 50% extra damage taken by assists, you can knock out your opponent's partner character in seconds flat!

HYPER COMBO GAUGE

While team members have individual **vitality gauges**, they all share the hyper combo gauge. The hyper combo gauge is built up by interacting with opposing characters. Building and using hyper combo gauge effectively is a key aspect of team management. With three characters on a team, there's rarely enough hyper combo gauge to go around for everyone. But a team isn't created just by slapping together three characters that will operate in individual vacuums. Consideration should be paid to the facts about each character in the team. Who builds bar well? Who needs to expend bar to be effective? Who is present mostly for their assist? Who is a good **THC** (team hyper combo) partner? These questions will help you decide the general roles of each member of your team ahead of time. Will one character primarily serve as a battery, building hyper combo gauge early on without needing to use much? Which character makes the best use of hyper combo gauge? Are any of your characters utterly dependent on using the hyper combo gauge to be effective? Should one character be considered a primary hyper combo gauge user? What tactics do you have available for building bar—will you rush the enemy and rely on melee hits to build gauge? Or, will you try to whittle away at your foe from afar with blocked attacks, slowly but safely stockpiling? You can also be aggressive and go for **team aerial combos** with air ⇩ + Ⓢ (or, though less fruitful, air ⇨ or ⇦ + Ⓢ), or construct a team around point Felicia or Thor (who possess special moves that build hyper combo gauge at will), or use a bar-building crossover assist (Morrigan—γ or Amaterasu—γ).

The most effective way to build hyper combo gauge is with a downward-aimed ***team air combo*** (launch an opponent with Ⓢ, then super jump and air combo into ⇩ + Ⓢ; this tags in your next character while granting one full bar of the hyper combo gauge!

Building hyper combo gauge is inevitable—just about any interaction generates bar. So, plan for it or not, you'll have bar to burn. With just a little forethought as to where that hyper combo gauge will come from, and where it will ultimately actually go, you'll gain a slightly more firm grip on the match. The various uses of hyper combo gauge are covered in further depth later on in this chapter, and throughout the chapters on character strategy, as appropriate.

Building hyper combo gauge (in order of effectiveness):
Perform a team aerial combo by launching with Ⓢ, then chaining into air ⇩ + Ⓢ
Perform a team aerial combo by launching with Ⓢ, then chaining into air ⇨ or ⇦ + Ⓢ
Call Morrigan—γ or Amaterasu—γ
Use ⇩ ⇩ + Ⓗ (hold) with Felicia or Thor
Hit an opponent
Receive an attack from an opponent
Hit an opponent (guarded)
Guard an opponent's attack
Hyper combo gauge usage

HYPER COMBO GAUGE USAGE

Ability	Hyper combo gauge bar cost	Purpose
C. Viper EX moves	1	Special properties
Crossover combination	1~3	Damage, combo extension
Crossover counter	1	Safely swap partners, retaliate against blocked attacks, avoid chip damage K.O.
Hyper combo	1~3, 5 for Dark Phoenix Rising	Damage, combo extension, enhancement
Snap back	1	Mess up opposing team order, force in an opposing character who has low vitality or significant red damage
Team hyper combo	2~5 (lv.3 hyper combos can finish THCs)	Damage, combo extension, safely swap partners

Users of Amaterasu—γ and Morrigan—γ should try to stick those assists into combos whenever possible. For example, there is no reason not to call them just as you use Ⓢ special attack to launch and start an air combo!

THE FOUNDATION: GUARDING, MOVING, & ATTACKING

GUARDING

⇦ (STANDING GUARD) OR ⬃ (CROUCHING GUARD)

Let's be clear—the most important thing you can do to improve at any fighting game (*any fighting game)* is to understand how to guard properly. The number one thing that novice and intermediate players neglect to develop is defense. For the most part, whenever you are in doubt in *MvC3*, the prime directive is to rely on solid guarding, while staying calm and looking for a way to turn momentum to your favor. None of that works if you didn't block correctly in the first place, however. Guarding an attack negates most or all of its damage, and allows you to push ATK ATK to push the attacker away with **advancing guard**. Many attacks, including most **special moves** and **hyper combos**, will deal damage even when guarded—this is called **chip**, or block damage. Chip damage amounts to 30% of the damage that an attack would have caused if it wasn't blocked. Guarding is accomplished by holding a backward direction.

Defensive input	Result without incoming attack	Result with incoming attack
⬁	Backward jump	Standing guard during 3 pre-jump frames / air guard after 4th frame
⇦	Backward walk	Standing guard
⬃	Crouch	Crouching guard

The speed of the action in the *MvC* series is unsurpassed among fighting games, and many offensive tactics are based on creating situations where it's difficult, or close to impossible, for a player to guard properly. This makes guarding under pressure an absolutely crucial skill. Because of the nature of *MvC*, some of the time your success will be based on sheer reactions and skill, but much of the time it will be based on solid guesswork and knowledge of your opponent. Sure, understanding how to block is key in any fighting game, but few games will demand such a heavy price for getting it wrong.

NO PROXIMITY BLOCKING!

MVC3 DOES NOT HAVE "PROXIMITY BLOCKING," A FEATURE FOUND IN MANY CAPCOM FIGHTING GAMES WHERE NEARBY WHIFFED ATTACKS WILL FORCE YOU INTO A ***GUARD ANIMATION***, PREVENTING YOU FROM WALKING BACKWARDS. HERE, CHARACTERS ONLY ENTER GUARD ANIMATION WHEN THEY ARE ACTUALLY GUARDING AN ATTACK.

Guard type	Guards against	Vulnerable to	Actions available during guardstun
Standing Guard	High, mid	Low, throw	Advancing guard, crossover counter, X-Factor
Crouching Guard	Low, mid	High, throw	Advancing guard, crossover counter, X-Factor
Air Guard	—	Air throw, anti-air special throw	Advancing guard

ACTIVE BLOCKING / ABSOLUTE GUARD

ATTACKS THAT STRIKE QUICKLY ENOUGH TO LEAVE NO GAPS FOR THE DEFENDER TO MOVE OR ACT WILL ALL BE GUARDED AUTOMATICALLY IF THE FIRST ATTACK IS BLOCKED CORRECTLY, BECAUSE THE DEFENDING CHARACTER IS STUCK IN ***GUARDSTUN***. THESE GAPLESS SEQUENCES, WHICH PREVENT THE DEFENDER FROM SURPRISING THE AGGRESSOR WITH A ***REVERSAL*** OR SIMILAR ESCAPE TACTIC, ARE OFTEN CALLED ***TRUE BLOCKSTRINGS***. AS AN EXAMPLE, BLOCK THE BEGINNING OF IRON MAN'S PROTON CANNON ***HYPER COMBO***, THEN STOP HOLDING BACK. YOUR CHARACTER WILL STILL GUARD THE ENTIRE HYPER COMBO. THIS IS CALLED ***ACTIVE BLOCKING***, OR ***ABSOLUTE GUARD***. DON'T RELY ON ACTIVE BLOCKING, HOWEVER—THIS CAN GET YOU INTO TROUBLE IF OPPONENTS SWITCH FROM LOW TO HIGH (OR VICE-VERSA) IN A SERIES OF ATTACKS, OR IF ATTACKS ARE DELAYED.

Wrong.

Right! ***Low*** attacks must be guarded crouching. Many crouching basic attacks are low attacks, along with certain crossover assists and other moves.

Low-hitting crossover assists / crossover counters (must be guarded crouching)
Felicia—α
She-Hulk—α
Wesker—β
X-23—β

Crouching guard is executed by holding ⬃. The main purpose of crouching guard is to repel **low** attacks, but it will block mid attacks as well. **Overheads**, however, will crush crouching guard.

Many attacks can be guarded standing or crouching. These are sometimes called ***mid*** attacks. Most (but not all!) standing basic attacks, assists, special moves, and hyper combos are mid attacks.

Wrong.

Right! ***High*** attacks must be guarded standing. Also called ***overheads***. Most air basic attacks are overheads, as are some command attacks and special moves. Crossover attacks, accomplished by holding P1⇔P2 to switch characters, are overheads.

Overhead crossover assists / crossover counters (must be guarded standing)
Akuma—γ
C. Viper—γ

Standing guard is executed by holding ⇦. Standing guard will repel incoming **overheads** and mid attacks, but is susceptible to **low** attacks.

CROSSOVER COUNTER

➡ + P1 or P2 DURING GUARDSTUN (REQUIRES 1 BAR OF HYPER COMBO GAUGE AND AN AVAILABLE PARTNER)

Crossover counters can be used just like variable counters from *MvC2*, to block and hit back opponents, or to escape chip damage knockouts.

When guarding on the ground, you can perform a crossover counter by pressing ➡ + P1 or P2. If a partner is present and hyper combo gauge is available, the chosen character will tag in and perform their crossover assist. The incoming character becomes the point character immediately, and the move performed adopts the characteristics of a special move rather than a crossover assist. This means that it can be hyper combo canceled, or interrupted with X-Factor. C. Viper's crossover counters can be canceled with a feint by pressing S, just like her special moves.

The most obvious use of crossover counters is in desperation—you can crossover counter to avoid a chip damage knockout. You have to weigh whether it's worth eating some guaranteed damage on the character coming in, versus letting the low-health character expire. This will be a case-by-case decision, since countering in a character to eat the end of a hyper combo for someone else may just lead to them getting knocked out instead.

Crossover counters can also be used more proactively on defense, timing the tag in to hit an opponent while they're still recovering from their blocked attack. If you used a good crossover assist for this, you'll have the chance to hit-confirm and cancel into the new character's hyper combo!

Crossover counters can be performed during guardstun, whether standing or crouching.

Input ➡ + P1 or P2, and the new character tags in with their crossover assist! They become your new point character immediately.

Character-depending, you have follow-up options if this crossover assist hits... For example, canceling into a hyper combo!

AIR GUARD

⇦ IN AIR

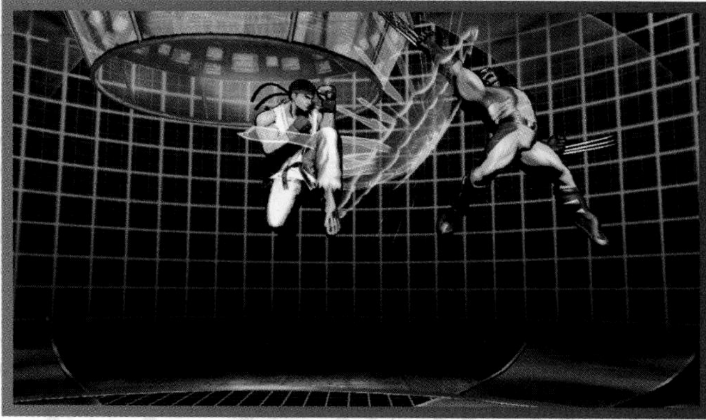

High or low doesn't matter with air blocking; only holding backward matters.

Guarding is possible in the air as well, by holding any backward direction. You don't have to worry about high or low attacks when guarding in mid-air. You can use this to your advantage, jumping defensively to reduce the number of blocking variables from four to two. Jump defensively with caution, though. Before jumping you risk being hit by a low attack during the 3 pre-jump frames, and once off the ground you risk eating an **air throw**. As with guarding on the ground, guarding in mid-air puts you into **guardstun**—your character's blocking animation. During aerial guardstun, the *only* thing you can do is press ATK ATK to push your foe away with **advancing guard**.

Flying characters cannot guard. Guarding is possible the rest of the time while airborne, but using some moves means you can't guard (or act in general) until landing on the ground again. Examples include Storm's S + ATK Lightning Attack (used outside of Flight) and Wolverine's S + ATK Drill Claw. Do not use these moves carelessly. Watchful opponents will recognize that you are vulnerable all the way down; all they have to do is launch you or start a hyper combo before you land.

ADVANCING GUARD

ATK ATK DURING GUARDSTUN

Advancing guard pushes both the aggressive and defensive characters apart. When cornered, advancing guard is less effective, because only the aggressor character is pushed back—the defensive character has nowhere to go!

Advancing guard (sometimes also called pushblock) can be performed at any time during **guardstun** by pressing ATK ATK. Against multi-hit attacks, advancing guard can be performed many times successively. Advancing guard pushes the defender and the attacker away from each other, and may reduce some of the **chip damage** received from blocked attacks, depending on positioning. *MvC3* is full of fast characters, equipped with devious options, to compromise your blocking and score a hit. So, when you do block correctly, it's almost always crucial to buy yourself some space with advancing guard. The only reason you wouldn't want to use advancing guard is if your opponent has let you guard something that has enough recovery for you to punish it for free. In these instances, advancing guard is actually detrimental—you waste an opportunity to punish your foe! Savvy opponents won't hand it over for free very frequently, so err on the side of using advancing guard to repel any enemy offensive, and always use advancing guard repeatedly when guarding a continual attack like a beam hyper combo.

COUNTERS TO ADVANCING GUARD

Advancing guard doesn't work against certain moves, and is less effective against some tactics that force you to block separate attacks simultaneously.

Advancing guard does not represent an unassailable wall. Advancing guard is far less potent when cornered.

If you are made to guard against attacks from both a point character and assist at the same time, advancing guard is diminished in effect. This is especially troublesome if the opposing point character manages to drop an assist on one side and attacks from the other—a situation some **teleport** and **square jump** capable characters can create at will.

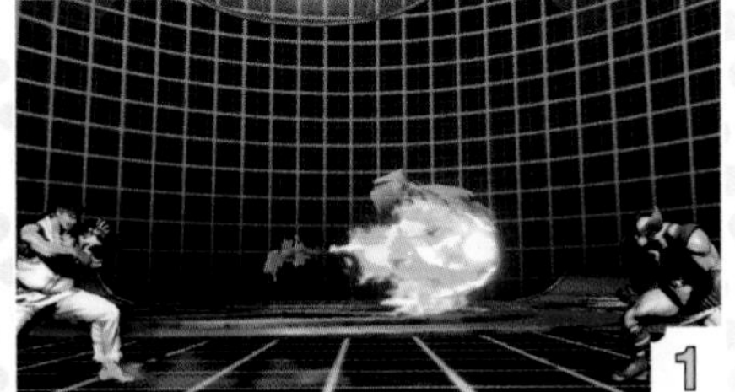

Input a dash JUST as the opponent's advancing guard animation begins.

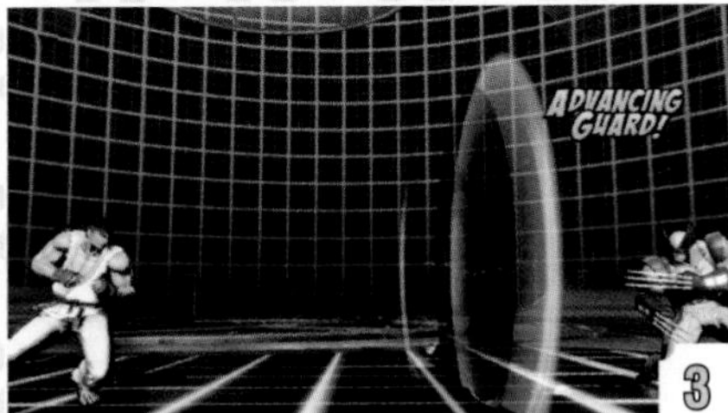

Projectile characters can ignore advancing guard entirely by dashing just as the opponent initiates advancing guard against a projectile.

Characters that have thrown a projectile and have fully recovered can negate advancing guard with precise timing. Wait until just as the opponent guards and begins to advancing guard a projectile, then dash forward. If you dash a little early, you'll just get pushed back as normal. With perfect timing, your character will simply appear to dash forward, as if advancing guard had no effect at all! With slightly late timing, you'll get pushed backward for a split-second before initiating the forward dash, which means you'll probably keep roughly the same overall position.

Take care not to simply mash on ATK ATK when you expect to block an attack. In other words, try very hard to react to attacks before using advancing guard, rather than anticipating attacks and pressing ATK ATK on autopilot. If your opponent doesn't actually produce an attack for you to guard, you will accidentally trigger either a dash, or an unintentional attack. Either result can be disastrous against an attentive foe.

THE THEORY OF RELATIVITY (FOR GUARDING, AT LEAST)

No matter where an opponent's assist is, block away from their point character. Assist characters have PLAYER 1 or PLAYER 2 above their heads, depending on the team they belong to.

If your opponent manages to place their crossover assist far behind you, you must block both the assist's attack and anything from the point character by holding ***away from the point character***. Do not be confused by the crossover assist!

With all the mayhem that is possible in a match, with up to six characters on screen amidst effects and explosions innumerable, it's important to keep yourself oriented. No matter where characters are positioned, no matter where crossover assists are being called, no matter what's going on, guarding is *always* relative the opposing team's **point character**. So if the opposing point character is to the right, block with ⇦ or ⬃. To the left, block with ⇨ or ⬂.

Many tactics are devised to be confusing, specifically to put the onus on the defensive player to block properly. For example, say a teleport-capable character calls a pinning crossover assist on one side of an opponent, then teleports to the other side. The defensive player not only has to process that the teleporting point character swapped sides, and that the crossover assist now stuck to their character's back is irrelevant (though it still must be guarded!), but they also have to be watchful for that point character to mix-up between overheads and low attacks, or maybe even another side switch. Often in these kinds of situations, the presence of a pinning assist disables advancing guard, so it's important to have good guarding fundamentals when this issue is forced upon you. Don't panic or worry about chip damage. Just try to react to what the offense executes, and guard accordingly until you have an opportunity to use advancing guard to begin an escape. Keep in mind that if you are set up for solid **crossover counters**, an opponent trying to pin you with an assist from the front while also attacking represents the best time to counter—catching two characters is better than one, and can turn the tide of a match instantly!

ADVANCING GUARD TIDBITS:

- **Can be activated at any time during guardstun, even the last frame of guardstun.**
- **Once the "push" actually happens, advancing guard recovers from guardstun after 21 frames, independent of the attack being guarded.**
- **The earliest time a "push" happens is after one-third of the attack's guardstun has passed. You can input the advancing guard and it will accept it, but the push just won't happen until this timeframe has passed.**
- **Advancing guard almost always results in more guardstun than normal blocking, unless the move guarded has an abnormally high amount of guardstun: like 35 or more.**
- **Both characters get pushed back after advancing guard, though the attacker gets pushed back farther. This is why advancing guard in the corner means less.**

MOVEMENT

The *Vs.* series is, among other things, characterized by its huge freedom of movement for most characters. This is an aspect that is only (perhaps) rivaled elsewhere by the *Guilty Gear* titles. With such fast action, an emphasis on the importance of space control, and an enormous playing field, it's vital that a player becomes comfortable with moving about the place.

ON THE GROUND

WALKING

HOLD ⇦ OR ⇨

The most basic way to move. Holding ⇦ also doubles as standing guard if a foe decides to attack. Apart from fine positioning, or using Arthur on point, you probably won't be doing a lot of sustained walking. The pace of the game is simply too fast for this to be a viable primary method of locomotion.

DASHING

⇨⇨ OR ⇦⇦ (WITH NO MORE THAN 9 FRAMES SEPARATING THE INPUTS); ATK ATK OR ⇦ + ATK ATK (WITH NO MORE THAN 1 FRAME SEPARATING THE BUTTON PRESSES; REFERRED TO AS "COMMAND DASH")

A dash on the ground is a fast movement either backward or forward. This is probably how your characters will travel most of the time on the ground, unless you plan to focus on Arthur and Hsien-Ko (Arthur cannot dash, and Hsien-Ko warps forward rather than a dash). Dashing allows you to either close distance with a foe or retreat very quickly. Most characters can **cancel** a dash with other actions, and you should get in the habit of being ready to guard, jump, or attack *immediately* after starting a dash. Dashing forward then guarding immediately is one of the best ways to cautiously gain ground and test an opponent's defensive reactions, without running into enemy assists or attacks carelessly.

WAVEDASHING

WAVEDASHING REFERS TO CANCELING A DASH INTO ANOTHER DASH. THERE ARE TWO WAYS TO DO THIS. FOR THE MORE DIFFICULT, BUT FASTER, METHOD, SIMPLY INPUT A DASH COMMAND OVER AND OVER EXTREMELY QUICKLY, WITH PRECISE TIMING. THIS CANCELS DASHES DIRECTLY INTO ONE ANOTHER, BUT IS QUITE HARD. FOR A MORE LENIENT VERSION, CROUCH-CANCEL EACH DASH INDIVIDUALLY BY TAPPING DOWN BEFORE INPUTTING ANOTHER DASH COMMAND (ATK ATK, ↓, ATK ATK, ↓, ETC. OR →→, ↓, →→, ↓, ETC.). BE SURE TO RETURN THE CONTROLLER TO NEUTRAL IN BETWEEN INPUTS. FOR THE CROUCH-CANCEL METHOD, YOU MUST BE CAREFUL NOT TO ACCIDENTALLY INPUT ↓↘→ WHILE CROUCH-CANCELING A DASH, AS YOU MAY END UP WITH AN ERRANT SPECIAL MOVE OR HYPER COMBO INSTEAD!

MASTERY OF WAVEDASHING WILL ALLOW YOUR CHARACTER TO CROSS THE GROUND MUCH MORE QUICKLY—USEFUL IF AN ENEMY IS TRYING TO RUN AWAY OR ZONE FROM THE AIR, OR IF THEY LEAVE THEMSELVES VULNERABLE FROM FAR AWAY. IT CAN ALSO OPEN UP EXTRA COMBO AND OTG POSSIBILITIES FROM FURTHER OUT THAN WHAT IS USUALLY POSSIBLE WITH A NORMAL DASH.

CHARACTERS WHO CANNOT CANCEL A DASH ALSO CANNOT WAVEDASH; CHARACTERS WHO CAN ONLY CANCEL A DASH MIDWAY THROUGH CANNOT WAVEDASH AS QUICKLY AS THE REST OF THE CAST. THE OPTIMAL TIME TO DASH VARIES FROM CHARACTER TO CHARACTER.

While most characters can cancel a dash with any other action, some characters can't cancel a dash for a brief period at the beginning, and a handful of characters can't cancel a dash at all! Players of these characters must be more careful with their use of dashes than with the rest of the cast, who have the luxury of being able to cancel their dashes with attacks, or more importantly by guarding, at any time. Characters that cannot cancel their dashes early, or at all, will also occasionally run into problems with jump-in combos. Other characters may land a jump-in hit from far away, then land, dash, and immediately cancel the dash with an attack to hit an opponent point-blank and continue into a full combo. Characters that can't interrupt dashes can't do this. However, by the time their dash is cancelable (or ended), the defensive character will be able to guard. Thus, in addition to taking extra care with movement, players of these characters must be more precise with their air-to-ground offense.

Dashes not cancelable
Doctor Doom
Dormammu
Hulk

Dashes cancelable midway through
Chris
Iron Man
Ryu
Tron

Irregular Dashes	
Arthur	Cannot dash.
Hsien-Ko	Backdash is normal; forward warp replaces forward dash.
Morrigan	Has no ground dash; goes airborne with airdash instead.

Ground command movements	
Captain America	S + ATK Backflip
Felicia	S + ATK Foreground dash
Spider-Man	direction + S + ATK 2-way Web Glide
Spencer	direction + S + ATK 5-way bionic grappling hook

DASH INPUT LENIENCY, AND BACKDASH FEINTS

When dashing using tap commands, you must leave a gap of no more than 9 frames between → or ← inputs. With a gap of 10 frames, no dash is produced. This is true of airdashes as well.

When dashing using attack button presses (L, M, and H—when any of these will do, ATK is notated throughout this guide), things work differently. To simply dash forward, press any two basic attack buttons together (this does not include S). There is *very* slight leniency here—the inputs are intended to be simultaneous, but they do not have to be, exactly. Press one attack button, then another attack button on the *very next frame*, and a dash is still produced.

To backdash with attack buttons, press ← + ATK ATK. You MUST hit ← at the same time as at least one attack button, and the same tiny leniency applies for the other attack button press—a gap of one frame is allowed, and the dash will still register.

However, if you tap ←, then wait at least 1 frame, but up to 8 frames, before inputting ATK ATK, something strange will happen: your character will backdash for 4 frames, then automatically cancel into a forward dash! This can be useful as a visual feint when you want to dash forward anyway—if your character has a particularly distinctive backward dash animation (such as Haggar's, or M.O.D.O.K.'s, or Sentinel's) this trick may incite reactions from an opponent who expects a backdash. For characters without distinctive animations at the beginning of a backdash, this is not useful, however.

Note that this backdash feint trick does not work for the characters who cannot cancel dashes immediately (Chris, Doctor Doom, Dormammu, Hulk, Iron Man, Ryu, and Tron). For them, tapping ← then ATK ATK within 8 frames simply results in a backdash. With a gap of 9 frames or larger, a forward dash is produced.

UP IN THE AIR

In most fighting series, it's imprudent to spend too much time in the air. That's definitely not the case here. *MvC3* battles can take place as much in the air as they do on the ground. Characters vary wildly in their aerial capabilities; some may be best used in the air almost the entire time, while others may be used to the best capacity while they are grounded. Check out the character-specific chapters for details on aerial combat with any given hero.

The screen is capable of shifting the focus of the match up to the sky, so that the ground is not visible. Point characters that are still grounded will be represented by "1P" and "2P" indicators, and can still move around and act as normal. Assist characters are ***not indicated*** from super jump height! The only way to know if an assist was called is by audio cues and the disappearance of assist button icons over vitality gauges.

In a departure from previous *Vs.* titles, characters *do not* turn around on their own when **jumping**! That is to say, if you jump over an opposing **point character**, you will *not* automatically turn back to face them involuntarily until landing again. While you can still air **guard**, or air **throw** an opponent with ⇨ or ⇦ + Ⓗ if close enough, this does mean aerial **basic attacks** will whiff in the wrong direction! The only way around this is to use a **special move** after you've crossed over a foe—this will re-orient your character properly. Like guarding, the commands for special moves are *always* relative the opponent's character, no matter which direction your character is actually facing.

Flight characters have it best here, since activating Flight will re-orient them with more freedom to maneuver. Additionally, passing over an opponent during Flight will automatically auto-correct a character's orientation.

Watch out for teleport-capable characters, which may teleport behind your character on reaction to your jumps and super jumps, putting you at a disadvantage every time.

While airborne, you won't need to worry about whether to guard **high** or **low**; only holding backward, away from the opposing point character, matters. You are still susceptible to air throws, though, most of which lead to **OTG** opportunities. Also, flying characters cannot block, and certain characters cannot block until landing after using certain attacks.

LIMITATION ON SPECIAL MOVES DURING AIRBORNE PERIODS

IN A GIVEN AIRBORNE PERIOD, WHICH IS DEFINED AS THE TIME BETWEEN WHEN YOUR CHARACTER LEAVES THE GROUND AND WHEN THEY LAND AGAIN, NO MORE THAN THREE ***SPECIAL MOVES*** CAN BE USED. THERE IS ONE WAY AROUND THIS—FLIGHT-CAPABLE CHARACTERS CAN USE AS MANY SPECIAL MOVES AS THEY WANT WHILE FLYING, PROVIDED THEY ACTUALLY ACTIVATE FLIGHT BEFORE *ALREADY* USING THREE SPECIAL MOVES. FLIGHT ACTIVATION ACTUALLY COUNTS AS A SPECIAL MOVE, SO YOU CAN'T START FLYING IF YOU'VE ALREADY USED THREE SPECIALS! ONCE ACTIVATED, FLIGHT IS ITS OWN DISTINCT STATE, WHICH ALLOWS THE USE OF AS MANY SPECIAL MOVES AS YOU CAN PERFORM. ONCE FLIGHT EXPIRES, YOU'LL ONLY BE ABLE TO USE A SPECIAL MOVE AGAIN IF YOU HAVEN'T USED MORE THAN TWO SPECIAL MOVES ALREADY, INCLUDING THE FLIGHT ACTIVATION, AND ANY SPECIALS USED DURING FLIGHT.

NORMAL AND SUPER JUMPING

NORMAL JUMP: TAP ANY UPWARD DIRECTION

SUPER JUMP: TAP DOWN, THEN ANY UPWARD DIRECTION WITHIN 9 FRAMES

(SOME ATTACKS CAN ALSO BE CANCELED INTO A NORMAL OR SUPER JUMP SIMPLY BY HOLDING ANY UPWARD DIRECTION; FOR EXAMPLE EVERY CHARACTER'S Ⓢ SPECIAL ATTACK LAUNCHER ON HIT)

The most direct way to get airborne is through jumping. There are two kinds of jumps: normal jumps, and super jumps. Both types of jumps have 3 pre-jump frames after input, before they actually leave the ground on the 4th frame. Input the command for a basic attack during pre-jump frames, and the command will be buffered and executed as early as possible during the jump. However, if the command for a ground-based special move or hyper combo is finished during pre-jump frames, the jump will be canceled into the ground-based action, and never even animate!

Normal jumps keep the battle at "normal jump height," and do not shift the playing field upward. Assists can be called.

A normal jump keeps the screen focused on ground level, and doesn't travel as fast or as far as a super jump (though both leave the ground at the same speed, on the 4th frame after the upward input). The following rules apply to normal jumps:

Chain combos are restricted for certain characters—while every character can chain air Ⓛ, Ⓛ, Ⓜ, Ⓜ, Ⓗ, Ⓢ during a super jump, some characters are only allowed to perform three hits of that chain during a normal jump before further basic attacks are prevented.

Normal jumps have a great advantage over super jumps in a rather important area: crossover assists can be called during a normal jump!

Some ground attacks can be canceled into a normal jump by simply holding any upward direction as the attack connects. Examples include Chun-Li's standing or crouching Ⓗ, Storm's standing Ⓜ and crouching Ⓗ, Dante's ⇨⇩⇘ + Ⓜ Volcano, and Morrigan's ⇨ + Ⓗ.

Hitstun produced by a successful air attack is less during a normal jump than the hitstun produced by that exact same attack during a super jump. In effect, this makes some air combos harder, if not impossible, during a normal jump state.

Flight modes started while either standing or normal jumping will follow the rules of a normal jump. That is, assists can be called, but certain characters have limited chain combos, and hitstun produced by attacks is shorter.

AIR RECOVERY

AIR RECOVERY HAPPENS WHEN A CHARACTER RECOVERS FROM HITSTUN WHILE IN THE AIR. AIR RECOVERY OCCURS AUTOMATICALLY WHEN APPLICABLE, BUT CHARACTERS CAN ALSO BE DIRECTED TO RECOVER IN A DESIRED DIRECTION BY HOLDING FORWARD OR BACKWARD. NO MATTER THE DIRECTION, AIR RECOVERY TAKES 12 FRAMES, AND CHARACTERS ARE INVINCIBLE AND INCAPABLE OF ACTION DURING AIR RECOVERY. AFTER AIR RECOVERY, A CHARACTER IS CONSIDERED TO BE NORMAL JUMPING—EVEN IF AIR RECOVERY LEAVES THEM AT THE TOP OF THE PLAYING FIELD! BEING IN A NORMAL JUMP STATE AFTER AIR RECOVERY MEANS CROSSOVER ASSISTS CAN BE CALLED TO HELP REGAIN MOMENTUM.

M.O.D.O.K. AND NORMAL JUMP FLIGHT

The diabolical M.O.D.O.K. doesn't have a normal jump. Instead, tapping any upward direction while grounded will cause M.O.D.O.K. to shift into a normal jump Flight state. This special Flight mode, available only to M.O.D.O.K., is the fastest way to get from the ground to the air *in the game*—M.O.D.O.K. is airborne and ready to act the *next frame* after input! To contrast, normal and super jumps are not airborne until the 4th frame after input, and activating Flight from the ground for other Flight-capable characters still leaves 15 or more frames before they can act.

M.O.D.O.K.'s normal jump Flight shares the rules of any normal jump state, with two exceptions: M.O.D.O.K.'s Flight lasts much longer than for other Flight characters (5 seconds, compared to 2 for other Flight characters, and 3 for Devil Trigger Dante), and M.O.D.O.K. is the only character who can fly twice in one airborne period (start with normal jump Flight by tapping up from the ground, then activate special move ↓ ↙ ← + Ⓢ Flight after the first Flight period ends).

SUPER JUMPS

During a super jump, a character soars to the top of the playing field, and the screen shifts to follow. Super jumping characters can alter their airborne trajectory in a way that normal jumping characters cannot via **air control**. Simply hold left or right to influence the jump arc (different characters can exert different degrees of air control). Grounded point characters aren't shown while the screen is following super jumping characters, and will instead have their positions marked with "1P" or "2P" indicators.

Super jumps take the fight to the skies. The screen drags upward to "super jump height," and assists cannot be called.

The full air chain combo is possible for every character during a super jump.

Crossover assists *cannot* be called during super jumps.

Some attacks can be canceled into a super jump simply by holding any upward direction.

Super jumps for most characters can be "steered" with air control by holding ⇦ or ⇨.

Hitstun produced by a successful attack during a super jump is longer than hitstun from the same attack during a normal jump. This means many air combos are easier, or only possible, during a super jump. This includes super jump Flight mode!

Flight modes started during a super jump will follow super jump rules. That is, assists cannot be called, but full chain combos are allowed for every character, and hitstun produced by attacks is longer.

DOUBLE JUMPS, TRIPLE JUMPS, & WALL JUMPS

DOUBLE AND TRIPLE JUMPS: TAP ANY UPWARD DIRECTION WHILE AIRBORNE

WALL JUMPS: NORMAL JUMP BACKWARDS ALONG THE SCREEN EDGE AND PRESS DIAGONALLY UP-FORWARD

1 Viewtiful Joe jumps with instant overhead air Ⓗ while calling She-Hulk—α, but Thor guards successfully

2 Viewtiful Joe cancels air Ⓗ into a double jump...

3 ...then cancels the double jump into a forward airdash that negates advancing guard.

4 Viewtiful Joe comes down on Thor with overhead air Ⓗ as She-Hulk—α hits low!

Some characters, having left the ground with a jump already, can then jump one or two more times from mid-air. Double and triple jumps follow the rules of the jump they started from, just as Flight does. Most significantly, this means you can normal jump, then double or triple jump to achieve great height, while still being capable of calling assists!

Double and triple jumps add air mobility, and increase the potential of both combos and mix-ups. Many air basic attacks can be canceled by a double jump, leading to devious tactics like late, second-chance overheads, or overheads canceled into a double jump over an opponent while your assist arrives on the original side.

Double jump characters
Arthur
C.Viper
Dante
Deadpool
Iron Man
Sentinel
Trish

Triple jump characters
Chun-Li
Viewtiful Joe

For each double or triple jump capable character, some air basic attacks are cancelable by double or triple jumps. Simply tap an upward direction during one such move and the character will immediately cancel the attack with the double or triple jump. This gives double and triple jump characters great potential during air combos (particularly **team air combos**, where they shine), but also allows for unorthodox mix-ups. For example, against a standing opponent, you can jump-in with an attack, then double jump cancel it on impact. Normally, opponents expect a character falling in with an attack to land, so this may throw them off. Depending on whether you double jump straight up or forward over an opponent (and whether they use advancing guard against your initial assault), you can either go for another overhead attack, or call an assist to land on the side you started from, while you land behind your foe!

Be careful with upward inputs on these characters: double jumping can be accomplished on the first frame a jump is airborne, so if you get an extraneous double jump input in early, you may use up a double jump immediately and not even realize it until you need it later!

1

This "touchiness" actually does come in handy in certain instances, since you can double jump on the very first frame after canceling Flight—so long as you didn't use your double jump before activating Flight.

2

Flying basic attack recovery is canceled with Flight deactivation; Morrigan can Flight cancel special moves, too!

3

A character begins falling immediately. Attack or double jump right away, if you're going to.

4

Some characters can jump forward off of the edge of the screen during a normal jump. To accomplish this, simply normal jump backward (↖) along a screen edge, then press up-forward (↗). Jumping straight up won't work, even in a corner; you *must* jump diagonally backward. Felicia works slightly differently—first, normal jump diagonally backward against a screen edge, then tap ← to initiate her wall cling. From here, simply release ← to wall jump. Wall jumps aren't possible during super jumps, but characters with double jumps can normal jump (in any direction), then double jump backward against a screen edge in order to wall jump at higher altitude. In general, wall jumps are useful for these characters for surprise maneuvering, and for escaping corners. Since wall jumps occur during normal jumps only, it's also always possible to call **crossover assists**! However, you can also super jump, double jump, and then wall jump; in this case, assists aren't available.

Wall jump characters
Chun-Li
Deadpool
Felicia (after wall cling)

Wall jump characters
She-Hulk
Spider-Man
Wolverine

Wall jump characters
X-23

AIRDASHING

DIRECTION + ATK ATK OR DOUBLE-TAP A DIRECTION; DIRECTIONS AVAILABLE AND AIRDASH BEHAVIOR VARIES PER CHARACTER

The ability to airdash is a great boon to characters that possess this power. Airdashes are what they sound like—dashes in mid-air! Airdashes are accomplished like ground dashes. To airdash in a particular direction, hold that direction while pressing ATK ATK. Alternatively, you can double-tap the desired direction. Use whichever is easier and more consistent for you, but note that double-tapping a diagonal input is much less consistent than simply pressing that diagonal plus ATK ATK. Airdashing has myriad applications:

Some air basic attacks can be canceled with an airdash. This allows for combo extension, and for enhanced air zoning tactics.

Airdashes allow quick retreat from the opposition by jumping and airdashing back, up-back, or up. Like double jumps and Flight, airdashes keep the properties of the jump they originated from, so if you retreat with an airdash from a normal jump, you can also call a crossover assist to cover your tracks. Similarly, if you normal jump, then airdash upward, you'll achieve super jump height while remaining in a normal jump state.

Airdashes allow you to advance laterally from long or mid range at a safer trajectory than a ground dash.

Flight characters can airdash repeatedly while Flight is active, allowing for even faster retreats or advances.

Airdashes can be used to return to the ground as quickly as possible after jumping at close range, usually with a quick overhead attack—this is usually called a triangle jump. Strong mix-ups between low-hitting combos, triangle jump overheads, and cross-ups can be essentially impossible to block consistently. Opponents will often have to rely at least in part on luck and guesswork to resist a truly furious and varied offensive fusillade.

Lateral airdashes just after jumping near an opponent, going over their heads, can be used to "square jump" over them, while placing an assist on the side you just vacated. Do this a little bit lower with an air attack, so you don't actually pass over the opposing character's head, and the effect is a very fast overhead just like a triangle jump. This is sometimes also called an instant airdash, box jump, square jump, or squaredash (angle-oriented terms, like triangle jump).

8-way airdash
C. Viper
Doctor Doom
Dormammu
Iron Man

8-way airdash
Magneto
M.O.D.O.K.
Phoenix
Storm

8-way airdash
Thor
Trish

6-way S + ATK air grappling hook
Spencer

Up-forward airdash
Super-Skrull

4-way S + ATK Web Glide in air
Spider-Man (can also swing forward on webbing with → →)

Forward or backward airdash
Dante
Hsien-Ko
Morrigan (hold direction to airdash longer)
Tron
Zero

Parabolic upward and downward airdash
Morrigan

3-way forward airdash
Amaterasu

2x forward airdash
Chun-Li

2x forward or backward airdash
Viewtiful Joe

Lateral airdashes at normal jump height allow you to advance while calling an assist along a different horizontal plane. The opponent is unlikely to be capable of attacks that hit both of your characters cleanly.

Characters *cannot* air guard while airdashing, and neither can airdashes be canceled by air guarding, but airdashes can be canceled with any air attacks. This includes throws, basic attacks, special moves, and hyper combos. Moves executed during an airdash will often adopt the inertia of the airdash.

Air attacks from low altitude, lateral airdashes make great overheads. Some airdash attacks can cross up, if you dash over the opposing character's head. Low lateral dashes are often called instant airdashes, square jumps, or box jumps.

An airdash-capable character that can also fly, falling after Flight expires naturally, can only airdash if they didn't airdash previously in the airborne period; if they airdashed at all either before or during Flight, attempting to airdash after flight expires won't work.

Additionally, characters that can both double jump and airdash can only do one or the other per airborne period. The exceptions are Chun-Li and Viewtiful Joe, the triple jump characters—they can both airdash and double jump in the same airborne period (or do a double jump and triple jump, or two airdashes).

TRIANGLE JUMPING

Airdashes are perhaps most useful, and most infamous, in their capacity for driving ultrafast overhead attacks. By jumping near a character, then immediately airdashing straight down or down-forward at a 45 degree angle, you can leave the ground and return almost immediately. Remember that most attacks used while airborne are overheads—if you can get an attack out before landing, it's impossible for most people to guard standing on reaction. This is a problem for any player on defense (that includes you and the authors of this guide), but here's a tip: when faced with an opponent who triangle jumps aggressively, watch for the dust that explodes up when a character jumps. With a little practice looking for it, that dust can be an extra visual cue that alerts you that a triangle jump overhead is coming. This isn't foolproof, since some other moves make dust puffs too, some characters (like Magneto, and Storm) do not produce dust effects when they leave the ground, and opponents may mix it up by landing without attacking then striking low, but it's better than nothing.

Diagonal triangle jumps have the most notoriety, but lateral airdashes have just as much use. Super jumping into a quick lateral airdash is one of the safest ways to gain a little ground on an opponent. You only have to watch out for a few assists, like Dante—α or Dormammu—β, and you'll be done with the airdash and able to air block long before most characters can do anything about it on reaction. The biggest worry is that an opponent will use an anti-air command throw, or simply jump and air throw you. The problem of being air thrown can be somewhat obviated by trying to make air → + Ⓗ your primary airborne attack, if that's at all workable for your characters of choice. Using this command will produce a heavy air attack under most circumstances, but if a foe happens to be in throw range it will instead produce an air throw. As a bonus, you may happen to break away from foes who air throw you first, essentially on accident. Using one input to cover several options, as is the case here, is called an option select.

Lateral airdashes can also be used just off the ground right in an opponent's face, as overheads with the same purpose as triangle jumps. Use air → + Ⓗ when possible; this can result in either an attack, or an air throw.

Used from a slightly higher altitude, a lateral airdash can make you pass just over an opposing character's head. This forces an opponent to switch the direction they're blocking in. You can take advantage of this by creating confusing situations—get near the opposition, jump straight up or up-forward near their head, then call an assist before airdashing to the other side. Depending which assist you call, when you airdash, and what you do during the airdash, this can force the opponent to have to block more or less at random, if you vary how you approach the setup.

Utilizing airdashes effectively is incredibly powerful. Offensive tactics that are this good essentially means that the trick is to never be put into bad defensive situations in the first place, rather than getting out of them consistently once you're trapped.

AIRDASHES HAVE HEIGHT RESTRICTIONS—THEY CAN ONLY BE PERFORMED ONCE YOUR CHARACTER HAS TRAVELED A CERTAIN DISTANCE FROM THE GROUND. IT'S FASTER TO GET TO THIS ALTITUDE WITH SUPER JUMPING THAN NORMAL JUMPING. DIFFERENT CHARACTERS HAVE DIFFERENT HEIGHT RESTRICTIONS FOR AIRDASHES, MAKING THEIR REQUIRED TIMING DIFFERENT FOR TRIANGLE JUMPS.

FLIGHT

⇩ ⇙ ⇦ + Ⓢ (IN AIR OK)

One-third of the cast is capable of the grand human dream of unassisted flight. This Flight mode is activated by inputting ⇩ ⇙ ⇦ + Ⓢ. Flight can be started on the ground or in the air, and the activation (or manual cancelation) of Flight can be used to cancel basic attacks. There is a brief dead period of 14~30 frames (character dependent) during which no inputs are accepted while the Flight animation begins, but afterward characters can act as they normally can in mid-air.

All Flight modes are both activated and canceled with ⇩ ⇙ ⇦ + Ⓢ. (M.O.D.O.K. can also activate Flight with ⇧ from the ground)

Flight
Dante (during Devil Trigger)
Doctor Doom
Dormammu
Iron Man

Flight
M.O.D.O.K.
Magneto
Morrigan
Phoenix

Flight
Sentinel
Storm
Thor
Trish

Movement during Flight is enhanced—characters can be made to simply flit about as you please, in any direction. You can use as many **special moves** as you can manage while Flight is active—the normal limit of three special moves per airborne period doesn't apply during Flight. This applies to **airdashes** too—Flight-capable characters can airdash over and over during Flight. Flight ends after any of a handful of things happens:

- **Receiving the enemy's attack (characters cannot block while in Flight)**
- **Inputting ⇩ ⇙ ⇦ + Ⓢ again (Flight canceling—can be used to cancel basic attack recovery, and Morrigan special move recovery)**
- **Attacking with air Ⓢ during Flight**
- **Certain attacks are used (for example, M.O.D.O.K.'s Ⓢ + ATK Body Attack)**
- **Flight expires naturally (occurs after about two seconds for most characters, three seconds for Devil Trigger Dante, five seconds for M.O.D.O.K.)**

Flight can only be activated once per airborne period. The exception here, once again, is M.O.D.O.K., whose "normal jump" flight (activated simply by tapping any upward direction while grounded; M.O.D.O.K. does not have a normal jump!) does not preclude him from using special move Flight later in the same airborne period. M.O.D.O.K. is another exception in the duration of his Flight states—Flight for most characters ends naturally after two seconds, but for M.O.D.O.K. it lasts five seconds!

It's not as big a deal as it sounds that you cannot guard during Flight—after all, the point of Flight is to be unpredictable and evade attacks in the first place.

Flight and airdash characters are able to airdash after flight expires only if they didn't airdash at all before *or during* Flight mode. Likewise, Flight and double jump characters retain their double jump after flight only if they didn't double jump before. Characters that can both airdash *and* double jump can do one or the other after Flight expires, only if they used neither during the airborne period prior to Flight ending. These details of what's left after Flight ends are most important when using Flight in air combos, but are also useful to know for positioning and zoning reasons.

Normal jump Flight can be used to place crossover assists behind foes while flying or airdashing over them. Flying characters correct their orientation after switching sides, allowing you to sandwich a foe between the point character and the assist.

The properties of Flight are different depending on when Flight was activated. Flight that begins during a normal jump, while a character is grounded, or after air recovery, can be thought of as "normal jump Flight." Flight that begins during a super jump can be thought of as "super jump Flight." The differences between normal jump Flight and super jump Flight are similar to the differences between normal and super jumps themselves. During normal jump Flight, crossover assists can be called, and certain characters (Doctor Doom, Dormammu, Magneto, M.O.D.O.K., Sentinel, and Thor) are restricted to 3-hit air chain combos. The hitstun produced by successful attacks is also shorter than during super jump Flight. During super jump Flight, crossover assists *cannot* be called, but the full air chain combo is available for all Flight characters, and the hitstun produced by attacks is longer than during normal jump Flight.

ATTACKING

So we come to the proverbial meat-and-potatoes of combat, the actual fighting. There are numerous ways to attack in *MvC3*, and this section aims to help you understand how it all works.

HITSTUN

Hitstun is the counterpoint to **guardstun**. As guardstun is the state in which defending characters are actually blocking, hitstun is the state in which the victim on the receiving end of an attack is actually reeling. At least during guardstun, the defensive character still has some ability; during hitstun, victimized characters cannot do *anything*. The length and nature of hitstun depends on the attack that caused it. Generally, heavier attacks cause more hitstun than lighter ones. Strike a character again while they're still in hitstun, and you'll create a **combo**.

NORMAL HITS AND COUNTERHITS

Our frame data figures assume a normal hit.

Normal hits occur when a character is struck while standing, crouching, moving, but not performing an attack. Throughout this book, you'll find references to the frame advantage created "on hit"—in all cases, unless otherwise noted, the frame advantage referenced describes a normal hit.

Counterhits are indicated by a special red spark, grant +2 frame advantage. Some counterhits result in special hit states.

A counterhit occurs when a character is struck during their own attack, whether during startup, active, or recovery frames. A counterhit is visually indicated by a red hit effect. Counterhits sometimes create hit states that normal hits don't, such as **crumples** or **knockdowns** where a normal hit would just cause standard hitstun. Counterhits—all counterhits—also add +2 to the frame advantage that is conferred on hit. This means that landing a counterhit can lead to **link** combo opportunities that are not available with normal hits.

SPECIAL HIT STATES

Most attacks just cause characters to reel, whether on normal or counterhit. Some attacks cause special hit states that do different things.

KNOCKDOWN (GROUND OR AIR)

Nothing is guaranteed after a knockdown, but if you guess right on which way your foe recovers, you can keep offensive momentum going.

The idea of a "knockdown" is a little different in *MvC3* than in other fighting games. Most knockdown-capable moves result in the victim recovering more or less immediately, and automatically. With no controller input, characters that are knocked down will simply rise in place right away. Characters can be made to recover in a desired direction by holding ⇦ or ⇨ as they recover. This is called **ground recovery** or **air recovery**, depending on where it takes place—not all knockdowns in *MvC3* knock an opponent to the turf! Very many attacks will cause victims to be "knocked down" into aerial hitstun, after which they will perform an air recovery. After an air recovery, the airborne character is considered to be normal jumping, with all the attendant benefits (crossover assist calls allowed) and limitations (chain combos may be limited; hitstun from attacks is shorter) that this entails.

During ground or air recovery, your point character is invulnerable, and assists can be called. Be wary of mix-ups intentionally designed to be confusing or difficult to defend against just as you become vulnerable after recovery ends. Getting an assist out can help run interference, but if you're careless it can just result in two characters getting hit instead of one.

UNRECOVERABLE KNOCKDOWN

Spencer ends an air combo with air (S), causing flying screen.

Immediately upon landing he dashes forward, then performs Wire Grapple H just off the ground, to OTG the enemy.

The universal way to cause an unrecoverable knockdown is flying screen—start a launcher combo with (S), then chain to air (S). Most throws also cause unrecoverable knockdowns, and some other attacks. OTG-capable attacks will hit opponents stuck in an unrecoverable knockdown.

After most knockdowns, the leveled character leaps back up right away, and can even be directed to roll for positioning before regaining footing by holding ⇦ or ⇨. Some knockdowns, however, prevent immediate ground or air recovery, and instead leave the victim laid out on the floor, unable to move, for several seconds. During this period, the floored victim of the unrecoverable knockdown is vulnerable to **off the ground** (**OTG**) hits. After an unrecoverable knockdown ends, players can ground recover left, right, or get up neutral. Left or right ground recovers finish in 34 frames, while neutral recover takes 20 frames. All recoveries are invincible, and the lateral recoveries can pass through opponents—useful for escaping the corner!

Technically, there is no limit on the number of unrecoverable knockdowns and OTG hits that can be used in a single combo—the limiting factors are player creativity, and **hitstun deterioration**.

OTG-Capable Crossover Assists
Akuma—γ
Arthur—γ (delayed)
Chris—γ (delayed)
C. Viper—β
Dante—β
Deadpool—β
Dormammu—β
Hulk—α
Iron Man—γ

OTG-Capable Crossover Assists
Sentinel—β (delayed)
Sentinel—γ
She-Hulk—α
Shuma-Gorath—α (DLC)
Storm—β (delayed)
Viewtiful Joe—γ (delayed)
Wesker—β
X-23—β

GROUND BOUNCE

Some attacks cause the victim to bounce off the floor forcibly. Before the victim lands on the ground a second time, they are vulnerable to continued attacks. For the most part, only one ground bounce is possible per combo, but there are exceptions to this rule during ⇩ + (S) team aerial combos.

One ground bounce can be used per combo. Exception applies when using ground bounce in a combo before a team aerial combo (air ⇩ + (S)) ground bounce tag.

Crossover Assists That Cause Ground Bounce
Akuma—γ (air hit only)
Deadpool—β
Felicia—γ (air hit only)
Haggar—γ
Jill—α (DLC)
Spider-Man—γ

WALL BOUNCE

One wall bounce can be used per combo. Subsequent wall bounce moves will simply cause a knockdown.

Some attacks cause the victim to bounce forcibly off the side of the screen, rather than the floor. This is a wall bounce. Characters subjected to a wall bounce are vulnerable until they hit the ground.

Crossover Assists That Cause Wall Bounce
Spencer—γ
Super-Skrull—α
Jill—β (DLC)

SPINNING KNOCKDOWN

Some attacks cause a violent spinning knockdown, which hurls the victim across the screen. Spinning characters cannot do anything or recover until they hit the ground. So, as with both types of bounces, these victims are open to more punishment. The difference is that there is no innate limit on the number of spinning knockdowns allowed during a combo.

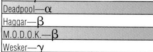

The spinning knockdown effect usually causes a ton of hitstun, depending on the move, so you can usually find a way to combo afterward.

Crossover Assists That Cause Spinning Knockdown
Chris—γ
Deadpool—α
Haggar—β
M.O.D.O.K.—β
Wesker—γ

STAGGER

Some attacks, like Amaterasu's Thunder Edge—⇨ + (H) (hold), cause a lengthy stagger rather than regular hitstun. This stagger lasts a set length of time, allowing further ground hits. Multiple staggers can be used in the same combo without diminishing the effect.

A stagger is just a rare, move-specific, lengthy hitstun. Technically, staggers can be linked in perpetuity; the victim stays grounded.

CRUMPLE

When a character eats an attack like C. Viper's (S) + (ATK) Focus Attack, they will crumple slowly to the ground, vulnerable on the way down. Hitting an opponent during this time will juggle them into the air. Like with ground and wall bounces, only one crumple is possible per combo.

Certain attacks cause a crumple. Characters hit during crumples are juggled into the air.

INCAPACITATION & DIZZY

As many incapacitation and dizzy moves can be used in the same combo as you can manage. Victims cannot mash inputs to escape more quickly!

Incapacitation is a state created by certain moves, like Spider-Man's Web Ball. During incapacitation, the victim is tied up one way or another and cannot act for a set period of time. After this time has elapsed, the victim recovers normally, but in the meantime they are completely vulnerable. Dizzy is similar—the victim reels for a set period of time before recovering.

PARTNERS

Partner characters, usually just called **partners** or **assists**, are a huge part of what makes *MvC3* the unique beast it is. In this game, teammates are active participants in a battle, and can contribute their efforts, or tag in and become the point character, in a variety of ways.

Each teammate has his or her (or its) own vitality gauge, visible at the top of the screen. Partners not actively performing an action will slowly regenerate **red damage**. Red damage regeneration speeds up during **X-Factor**.

The basis of partner gameplay is the **crossover assist**, usually just called assist. For each of the three characters you select, you'll also have to pick one of three assist types—either α, β, or γ. The type you select determines the attack that character will use when called upon to perform a crossover assist (tap P1orP2), or crossover counter (during guardstun, tap ⇨ + P1orP2 with at least one bar of hyper combo gauge available). Assist type also determines which **hyper combo** will be used within a **crossover combination** (P1+P2).

Assist Type	Description
Direct	Character attempts a direct attack.
Shot	Character produces a projectile or beam of some sort.
Extra	Irregular effects.
Instant	Action occurs immediately.
Front	Attack is directed laterally.
Tilt Dw	Attack is aimed at the ground, is likely OTG-capable.
Tilt Up	Attack is aimed up in the air.
Upward	Attack is aimed straight up; likely comes right back down.

ASSISTS AND SCREEN POSITION

ASSISTS FOLLOW THE SAME HITSTUN RULES AS POINT CHARACTERS. ASSISTS CANNOT BLOCK.

ASSISTS ARE *NOT* RESTRICTED TO REMAIN WITHIN THE LATERAL BOUNDS OF THE SCREEN AND ON THE PLAYING FIELD, LIKE POINT CHARACTERS. CALL AN ASSIST THAT NORMALLY COMES OUT FAR BEHIND YOUR POINT CHARACTER (MOST PROMINENTLY PHOENIX—α WHILE BACKED AGAINST A SCREEN EDGE, AND THE ASSIST WILL STILL TOSS THEIR ATTACK ON SCREEN, BUT NEVER BE ON THE SCREEN OR VULNERABLE THEMSELVES!

SIMILARLY, IF A CROSSOVER ASSIST IS HIT HARD BY AN ATTACK THAT TOSSES THEM OFF THE SCREEN, FOLLOW-UP ATTACKS WON'T CONTINUE PUNISHING THE ASSIST (EVEN FULL-SCREEN ATTACKS LIKE STORM'S HAIL STORM OR AMATERASU'S OKAMI SHUFFLE).

CROSSOVER ASSIST

TAP P1orP2 (P1 FOR PARTNER 1; P2 FOR PARTNER 2)

Pressing P1orP2 "calls" an assist. The chosen partner character will leap onto the playing field and perform the crossover assist that was selected before the match. While some assists are invulnerable for small periods of time, all assists can be struck at some point (most assists are vulnerable the entire time that they are attacking). For almost all assists, being hit will stop whatever action they had in progress. If a point character gets hit after calling an assist, but before the assist performs their attack, the assist will attack anyway—striking the point character doesn't stop an assist the way it did in *MvC2*!

Assist characters take 50% more damage than point characters. Furthermore, if the point character that called an assist blocks repeated attacks while they strike that assist, the assist eats the damage of each hit unscaled! A blocking point character prevents the game from recognizing hits on an assist as being part of a combo, and so **damage scaling** never kicks in!

Assists **can** be called:

- **When standing, crouching, or normal jumping.**
- **During flight, dashes, or airdashes that began while standing or performing a normal jump.**
- **With basic attacks performed during any of the preceding states.**
- **During ground or air recovery.**

Assists **cannot** be called:

- **When stuck in hitstun or guardstun.**
- **When performing a special move, hyper combo, or throw (though there are exceptions, such as during Wolverine's ⇦ + (H) throw).**
- **During a super jump, nor during any airdash or flight mode that starts from a super jump.**
- **When assist characters are not ready, due to other assists or partner actions. "ASSIST READY!!" displays momentarily across each team member's vitality gauge to indicate when they are ready for action.**

The safeguard preventing assists from being called during special moves or hyper combos is very thorough—if you hit an assist button while performing a move motion, then hit the button to finish the move, but the assist is not yet on screen, then the assist will never come out! Thus, if you plan to call assists before using special moves or hyper combos, make sure your inputs are very clean, and insure you've pushed P1orP2 a little early, to insure your special move motion doesn't eat up the input.

CROSSOVER ATTACK

HOLD P1orP2 FOR 15 FRAMES (P1 FOR PARTNER 1; P2 FOR PARTNER 2), 27,000 DAMAGE

Crossover attacks are air overheads that swoop in and send victims into a small spinning knockdown. Incoming characters pose briefly after a crossover attack, making them vulnerable if the attack whiffs.

A crossover attack is the most direct way to swap a partner character in for the current point character. In order to accomplish a crossover attack, you must hold down P1orP2 for 15 frames. This can be buffered behind other actions to mask your intention, but it does require that the decision to swap be at least somewhat premeditated. **If incoming characters have any red damage, it becomes permanent after a crossover attack.** The previous point character, now leaving, is invincible from the first frame. The incoming, new point character isn't invincible at all. Crossover attack guardstun is character-specific, but ranges between 29-33 frames. The pose after crossover attacks is character-specific also, but ranges between 31-34. Due to crossover attacks generally not hitting as late as possible, resultant frame disadvantage is usually between -15 and -20.

During a crossover attack, the incoming partner strikes with an **overhead** attack that soars out to mid-screen, deals 27,000 damage, and causes a **spinning knockdown** on hit. Victims are vulnerable until they hit the ground during a spinning knockdown, but because characters pose briefly at the end of a crossover attack, this knockdown is sometimes hard or impossible to take advantage of.

Novice players almost always make the mistake of using crossover attacks too often. Switching characters too often takes away cohesion and momentum from your team. Not to mention that you are taking a risk every time you perform a crossover attack. Yes, it's an overhead, but it's a remarkably weak one, and you are always vulnerable for at least a little bit at the end. If an opponent anticipates a crossover attack, they may wait and simply look to punish one. Find another way to swap a character in if you really must, or surprise your foe by dashing in with a low attack.

However, used sparingly, or from far away, it's pretty safe to tag a character in with a crossover attack. Some characters have moves that can cover the vanity of a posing character. Phoenix's homing TK Shot H is an example. You can also wait until the opponent super jumps, and tag in as soon as possible—their upward trajectory will not only visually mask your tag, but it will also (more or less) guarantee that they don't have an angle to punish. Finally, if your opponent is all over you, it can sometimes pay off to use crossover attacks as a kind of high-risk reversal, but this should be done very sparingly.

Team Position	Initial Order	After crossover attack by holding P1	After crossover attack by holding P2
Point Character	Member A	B	C
Partner 1	Member B	A	B
Partner 2	Member C	C	A

CROSSOVER COMBINATION

P1+P2

During a crossover combination, as many heroes as possible join their efforts to generate a tremendous attack. Each character performs the hyper combo dictated by the assist type you chose for them. One bar of hyper combo gauge is expended for each character participating.

With at least 3 hyper combo gauge bars and three heroes, your whole team will join in. With only 2 bars or two heroes, only two will join in. With only 1 bar or hero, your hero will still perform their crossover combination hyper combo, but no one else will join in.

The startup, damage, and other characteristics of your crossover combination are dictated by the hyper combos of the characters on your team. So, for example, if you have a character like Iron Man or Spencer, whose hyper combos hit faster than most, or a hyper combo that returns control of the point character early, your crossover combination will share that advantage.

As is true elsewhere in combos, keeping the number of hits low helps boost combo damage by virtue of smaller combos having less damage scaling. A crossover combination featuring Spencer, Hulk—γ, and Viewtiful Joe—α or γ will deal extremely heavy damage without many hits!

You can cancel into a crossover combination from grounded basic attacks, but not from special moves or hyper combos (unless you use X-Factor canceling as a bridge). Amazingly, you can use X-Factor to cancel your point character's hyper combo during a crossover combination—the other two characters keep performing theirs, while your point is free to move!

Trish—α or β on point starting a crossover combination will still be able to move as normal and mix it up during Round Harvest, while her partners help hold a foe in place and deal chip damage with their hyper combos.

CROSSOVER COUNTER

DURING GUARDSTUN, ⇨ + P1 or P2 WITH AT LEAST ONE BAR OF HYPER COMBO GAUGE AVAILABLE

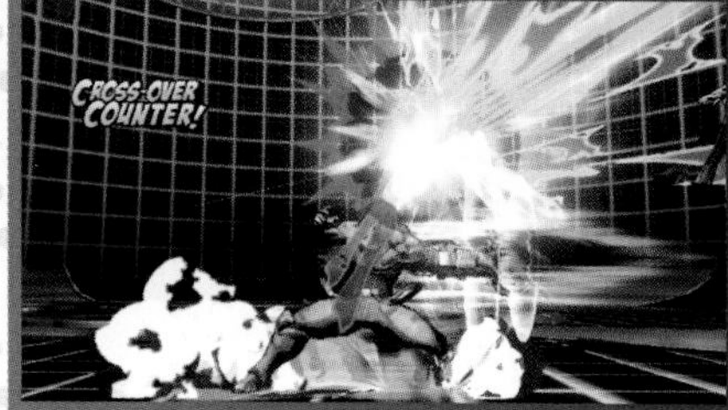

Crossover counters allow you to turn the tables on aggressors.

Crossover counters allow you to take advantage of guardstun by tagging in a partner, who then immediately performs their crossover assist while becoming the point character. Crossover counters can be good for avoiding chip damage knockouts, or for surprising aggressive foes with strong reversal crossover assists like Haggar—α or Magneto—γ. Crossover counters can be canceled into hyper combos, or character-specific actions. For example, C. Viper crossover counters can be made into feints by pressing S, same as her special move versions of those attacks. More on crossover counters can be found earlier in this chapter, in the section on guarding.

Team Position	Initial Order	After crossover counter with ➔ + P1	After crossover counter with ➔ + P2
Point Character	Member A	B	C
Partner 1	Member B	A	B
Partner 2	Member C	C	A

CROSSOVER COUNTERS AND TEAM HYPER COMBOS

UPON BLOCKING A LAGGY ATTACK, CROSSOVER COUNTER TO CHUN-LI—γ WITH ➔ + P1 or P2 CANCEL ⬇ ⬊ ➔ + ATK ATK, THC IRON MAN ➔ ⬇ ⬊ + ATK ATK

(447,100 damage, requires 3 hyper combo gauge bars) This combo, the opener of which is accomplished simply by guarding, shows a few important concepts:

- **Using a crossover counter aggressively, to strike an opponent during the recovery of a guarded move.**
- **Canceling a special move (in this case, the crossover counter) into a hyper combo.**
- **Performing a team hyper combo.**

1

Crossover counters can be performed when blocking on the ground with ⇨ + P1 or P2 .

2

The chosen partner, if available, becomes the point character and tags in with their crossover assist. One bar of hyper combo gauge is expended.

3

Not all crossover assists are created equal in this regard; some will be far more effective than others. A quick-hitting move like Chun-Li—γ Hyakuretsukyaku, or an invincible one, like Haggar—α Double Lariat, is ideal. Many, if not most, crossover assists are not suitable for use as crossover counters outside of a desperate situation.

4

Once the crossover counter is complete and the new point character is performing their crossover assist, control is already assumed. You can cancel the crossover assist with a hyper combo! By now, you've spent at least 2 bars of hyper combo gauge, but that's not bad considering you scored the opportunity simply by guarding.

5

As with crossover counters themselves, your mileage may vary regarding the effectiveness of following up with a hyper combo cancel, depending on the arsenal of your team.

6

Of course, performing a hyper combo means you can extend the punishment with a team hyper combo. Depending on who you tagged in originally for the crossover counter, this may even re-involve the character who blocked initially!

7

One of the most important things to consider when building your teams is team hyper combo potential. Team hyper combos allow you to easily extend combos, swap characters safely, and spend some of your hard-earned meter efficiently. Not just any character can be slapped with another and produce effective ***THC***s—you'll have to consider the angles, speeds, and effects of the hyper combos of each team member.

8

Just as with a hyper combo, the screen freezes briefly during a team hyper combo while the next character tags in and prepares their attack. This sometimes allows attacks to strike where they wouldn't otherwise. The pre-hyper cutscene frames of hyper combos are eliminated; slow hyper combos like Hail Storm really benefit.

9

Depending on your resources, positioning, and team, you may extend this even further with a THC to the remaining third character. Otherwise, it's often possible to use X-Factor to cancel the hyper combo into another.

THROWS

← OR → + (H) (ON GROUND OR IN AIR)

Active in 1 frame, throws are extremely quick.

The throw victim has 7 frames to input ← or → + (H) in order to ***break away*** from the throw. Characters are in an even frame situation afterward.

Most throws lead to an opportunity to OTG the throw victim, leading to even more damage.

As an **unblockable** close-range attack, throws are ideal for assaulting a **guarding** opponent. Throws cannot snag a character that is stuck in **guardstun**, actively guarding something, but they will grab passive foes that *expect* to guard (throws are also not possible for 4 frames after guardstun or hitstun ends). If you throw while an opponent's assist comes on screen, your point character will be invulnerable to whatever that assist does ,as long as the throw is actually being performed.

Throws are very important for breaking down the defense of passive, defensive opponents (who are sometimes called turtles—depending on who it's coming from, this title can be bestowed with either admiration or scorn!). The threat of throws (along with the threat of chip damage, and the threat of a time out loss) prevent guarding from being an impenetrable bulwark against damage.

BASIC ATTACK

(L) (M) (H)

Basic attacks are the building blocks of chain combos, and the foundation of any poking gameplan.

Basic attacks, or normal moves, are the basis of offense and defense. Basics attacks are performed by pressing (L), (M), or (H). The outcome will differ depending on whether your character is airborne, standing, or crouching. Basic attacks can be canceled into one another with **chain combos**, which are detailed in the **Combos** section of this chapter.

Basic attacks can all chain to command attacks and special attacks, and are all cancelable to special moves and hyper combos. Specific basic attacks can also be canceled with jumps or dashes.

BASIC ATTACK NOTATION

THROUGHOUT THIS GUIDE, BASIC ATTACKS AS DISCUSSED AS BEING PERFORMED CROUCHING, STANDING, OR AIRBORNE. CROUCHING AND STANDING ARE SOMETIMES ABBREVIATED AS CR. AND ST. FOR SPACE. IF A STATE IS NOT PROVIDED FOR A MOVE, ASSUME IT FOLLOWS THE SAME STATE AS THE PREVIOUS ONE, FOR EXAMPLE AIR (M), (M), (H), (S) REFERS TO A CHAIN OF BASIC ATTACKS IN THE AIR.

SPECIAL ATTACK

Special attack was referred to as "exchange" for much of MvC3's development. This button has two main purposes.

First, on the ground, (S) is a **launcher** attack that can be chained from most **basic attacks**, and which launches an opponent on hit. On a successful (S) hit, you can simply hold any upward direction to automatically **cancel** into a **super jump**, which will take you into position to **air combo** the opposing character.

Second, in the air, (S) is an aerial attack that has a unique property if used within an **air combo** that started from a grounded (S) **launcher**. Used at the end of a launcher combo, air (S) causes **flying screen**, an effect in which the air combo victim is tossed into an **unrecoverable knockdown** while the attacking character falls to pursue. This is an opportunity to pop the floored character up **o**ff **t**he **g**round with an **OTG-capable** attack. Many characters have attacks that OTG, and many crossover assists do as well—most assists labed as TILT DW type are intended as OTG tools.

(S) is also used as an input for several **special moves**, such as ↓↙← + (S) Flight for many chararacters, She-Hulk's ↓↓ + (S) charging stance, or variations of a direct body attack move with (S) + (ATK).

TEAM AERIAL COMBOS

Air ⇧ + Ⓢ during launcher combo: 48,500 damage, upward air tag

Air ⇨ or ⇦ + Ⓢ during launcher combo: 40,400 damage, half a hyper combo gauge bar, sideways air tag

Air ⇩ + Ⓢ during launcher combo: 40,400 damage, a full hyper combo gauge bar, ground bounce air tag

After the actual team aerial combo tag "flash," the victim has 15 frames to input the same command as the air tag used, in order to break out with a team aerial counter.

New to *MvC3* are team aerial combos, or **TAC**s. A team aerial combo starts by landing Ⓢ launcher, then super jumping with the victim and performing at least one air basic attack before chaining into direction + Ⓢ. (Diagonal directional inputs are interpreted as upward or downward) The direction you input dictates which kind of team aerial combo you'll initiate. Upward generally offers the best juggle positioning and a slight damage bonus, while sideways or downward offers great boosts to the hyper combo gauge—no small bonus whatsoever.

After the first tag hand-off in mid-air, the next character can perform an air chain as they normally can during a launcher combo. The new incoming character can also hand off to the second partner by using direction + Ⓢ again. No need to do at least one basic attack after the first tag, either; for the second tag, you can potentially just do air ⇧ or ⇨ or ⇩ + Ⓢ right away.

When direction + Ⓢ is input to spark a team aerial combo during an air combo, the victim has 15 frames following the brief freeze to input the break command. The correct break command is exactly the command used to start the air tag: ⇧ + Ⓢ if that's the air tag incoming, ⇩ + Ⓢ for the down air tag, and ⇨ or ⇦ + Ⓢ for the sideways air tag (either direction works). Only one Ⓢ input is accepted during this 15 frame window—a victim who can potentially input every possible escape perfectly during the 15 frame window is not guaranteed to break every team aerial combo; he'll only break them at random, if the first input he uses during the window happens to be right. Interestingly, a neutral Ⓢ input during the window will prevent a correct input right afterward from being used, even if accomplished during the break window.

A successful team aerial counter will toss the character who attempted to air tag off of the victim, while dealing 50,000 damage. The offender is invincible off of the wall bounce caused by a team aerial counter, so neither side is guaranteed anything—it's essentially a match reset.

The primary purpose of team aerial combos is to stave off hitstun deterioration and build tons of hyper combo gauge. Team aerial combos are weighted heavily in favor of the aggressor—you get far more out of successful team aerial combos than you do out of successful team aerial counters. A good team aerial combo can easily build three or more bars of hyper combo gauge, while easily dealing over 500,000 damage, which is nothing to sneeze at. And just like any other air combos, team aerial combos can lead to OTG opportunities right afterward, because flying screen is still possible.

Finally, it's worth noting that a victim stuck in an air combo, waiting to possibly get hit by a TAC starter, might just be mashing directions + Ⓢ. If you launch such a player, then leave a small gap in your air combo where you'd normally put direction + Ⓢ, the opponent will almost certainly begin to whiff air Ⓢ right in front of you. Depending on your character's air options, and who the opponent is, you may be able to make them pay quite hard for trying to guess their way out of a TAC!

TEAM AERIAL COMBOS

TEAM ORDER CHUN-LI, VIEWTIFUL JOE, IRON MAN: CHUN-LI BOX JUMP AIR Ⓜ, Ⓜ, LAND, CR. Ⓛ, CR. Ⓜ, ST. Ⓗ, CR. Ⓗ, Ⓢ CANCEL➡ SUPER JUMP, AIR Ⓜ, Ⓜ, Ⓗ CANCEL➡ DOUBLE JUMP, AIR Ⓜ, Ⓜ, Ⓗ CANCEL➡ TRIPLE JUMP, AIR Ⓜ, Ⓜ, Ⓗ, ⇧ + Ⓢ, VIEWTIFUL JOE AIR Ⓜ, Ⓜ, Ⓗ CANCEL➡ DOUBLE JUMP, AIR Ⓜ, Ⓜ, Ⓗ CANCEL➡ TRIPLE JUMP, AIR Ⓜ, Ⓗ, ⇧ + Ⓢ, IRON MAN AIR Ⓜ, Ⓗ CANCEL➡ DOUBLE JUMP, AIR Ⓜ, Ⓢ

(~460,300 damage, variable depending on actual chains used, before potential **OTG** at the end) This team aerial combo depicts the method and usefulness of TACs:

TACs are a mostly safe way to attempt to tag in your next partner; the worst thing that can happen is that they team aerial counter, which only deals 50,000 damage.

TACs allow for combos far longer than normal, since hitstun deterioration is scaled back for each new character who tags in. The amount that hitstun deterioration is scaled back varies from character to character. Characters with extended air chains, such as double and triple jump characters, or fliers, can use their normal air combos.

TACs build incredible meter, whether through sheer volume of hits, or by using sideways or downward air tags for big hyper combo gauge bonuses.

1 The team aerial combo starter must launch, then chain to air direction + Ⓢ. An opponent must not input the same command within 15 frames.

2 The first partner tags in, at the chosen angle.

3 After the first air tag, the new character can air chain to one more air tag.

4 Now the second partner tags in, again along the chosen angle.

5 At any point during a team aerial combo, neutral air Ⓢ can still be used to induce flying screen, which generates a possible OTG opportunity.

6 It's a long way down...

TEAM AERIAL COMBO ORDER QUIRK

NORMALLY, TEAM AERIAL COMBOS SIMPLY TAG TO THE NEXT CHARACTER IN LINE. ON A TEAM OF THREE HEROES, THE FIRST TAG SWAPS TEAMMATE A FOR TEAMMATE B, AND THE SECOND TAG THEN SWAPS TEAMMATE B FOR TEAMMATE C.

IF TEAMMATE B IS NOT AVAILABLE FOR SOME REASON WHEN A TEAM AERIAL COMBO IS ATTEMPTED, SOMETHING INTERESTING WILL HAPPEN. TEAMMATE A WILL AIR TAG TO TEAMMATE C INSTEAD. IF TEAMMATE C IS THEN MADE TO AIR TAG AGAIN, THE AIR SWITCH WILL BE *BACK* TO TEAMMATE A! TEAMMATE B NEVER COMES INTO PLAY, THE TEAM'S ORDER ULTIMATELY STAYS THE SAME, AND TEAMMATE A GETS TO DO TWO AIR COMBOS IN THE SAME COMBO!

THE EASIEST WAY TO SET THIS UP IS TO USE TEAMMATE B IN TEAMMATE A'S COMBO THAT LEADS UP TO Ⓢ LAUNCHER. THEN CHAIN TO AN AIR TAG BEFORE TEAMMATE B'S CROSSOVER ASSIST IS READY AGAIN.

COMMAND ATTACK

Command attacks extend chains, or possess special properties.

A command attack is a specialized **basic attack** that often has special properties, but special restrictions too. Some command attacks are **overheads**. Some command attacks cannot be **canceled**, or can only be chained into a particular way. Other command attacks basically function as another hit in ground chains before launching with Ⓢ. Some characters don't have command attacks at all. For specifics on command attacks for a particular character, visit that character's chapter in this book.

SPECIAL MOVE

Special moves have all sorts of uses.

Special moves are powerful attacks and abilities that are performed by inputting a directional sequence before pressing the appropriate button. There are motion special moves, charge special moves, and tap special moves.

After inputting the motion for a special move, you must press the button within 9 frames. This might not sound like a long time—it's less than 1/6th of a second—but this allows for some interesting execution tricks. As just one example, let's say you want to perform an air special move that has a command of ⇩ ⇘ ⇨ + ATK, but you want to do it as soon as possible after leaving the ground. To accomplish this, you can "tiger knee" a motion while standing on the ground, combining the move's directional sequence with an upward direction: ⇩ ⇘ ⇨ ⇗ . Now, jumps aren't airborne until the 4th frame after the upward input, so you must wait at least 4 frames before pressing ATK in this instance, but no longer than 9 frames total.

As another example, this 9 frame grace period can also be used for **option selects**, covering more than one option intentionally. Let's say Felicia is pressuring Ryu with ground attacks, with the intent of landing her special move throw (⇨ ⇘ ⇩ ⇙ ⇦ + ATK). A common method of attempting a throw is what is known as a tick throw. First, you "tick" the foe with a single light attack, which creates the expectation in them that a **chain combo** is coming. Then, while the opposing player continues to hold back, in anticipation of further attacks, you throw their character. This trick has been around since time immemorial (or, ok, since 1991, in *Street Fighter 2: The World Warrior*), and here, as in other Capcom fighting games, you can add a twist. Felicia's standing Ⓛ , when blocked, leaves her at a -2 frame disadvantage—in this case, Ryu can act 2 frames sooner than Felicia after guarding her attack. Furthermore, a character in guardstun cannot be thrown for 4 frames after guardstun ends. Further still, Ryu has perhaps the best attack in the game for negating this situation—his Shoryuken is invincible starting with the very first frame. If Felicia is made to go for her throw as soon as possible, Ryu will still be unthrowable because of guardstun. If she performs it as soon as possible, with a normal input method, Ryu might just Shoryuken her in the face. So, what does she do? If, instead of going for a throw right away, she **ticks** with standing Ⓛ , then immediately inputs ⇨ ⇘ ⇩ ⇙ ⇦ , but then *waits* as long as possible before pressing ATK to activate the throw, one of two things will happen. If Ryu comes out of guardstun with Shoryuken as fast as he can, Felicia will guard! After all, the motion ⇨ ⇘ ⇩ ⇙ ⇦ ends in a ⇦ input, which counts as blocking. But if Ryu *doesn't* Shoryuken, and instead just waits, Felicia's late ATK press will engage her throw and snag him.

HYPER COMBO

Like special moves, the uses and types of hyper combos are varied.

Hyper combos are powered-up versions of special moves, which require hyper combo gauge to use. Hyper combos have many uses. Most damaging combos feature hyper combos in some way. Many simply deal direct damage, whether through physical hits or an inescapable command throw. Some create high priority projectile threats, or high priority full screen beams. A few hyper combos serve to enhance your team with bonuses; Amaterasu and Viewtiful Joe have hyper combos that slow down an opponent's characters, while Arthur, Felicia, Hsien-Ko, Morrigan, Phoenix, Wolverine, and Zero have hyper combos that briefly enhance their abilities in some way. These enhancements are as varied as speed and ability boosts, shadow or kitty helpers, a healing aura, or permanent hyper armor.

HYPER COMBO CUTSCENES

EACH HYPER COMBO PROGRESSES IN A PARTICULAR MANNER: THE VERY FIRST FEW FRAMES OF THE HYPER COMBO WILL PLAY OUT, ACCOMPANIED BY THE DISTINCTIVE HYPER COMBO "FLASH." THEN, THE ACTION BRIEFLY FREEZES, WHILE A CUTSCENE OF THE CHARACTER GATHERING ENERGY FOR THE ATTACK PLAYS. THEN, ACTION STARTS BACK UP AGAIN AS THE CHARACTER ACTUALLY WINDS UP TO RELEASING THEIR HYPER COMBO.

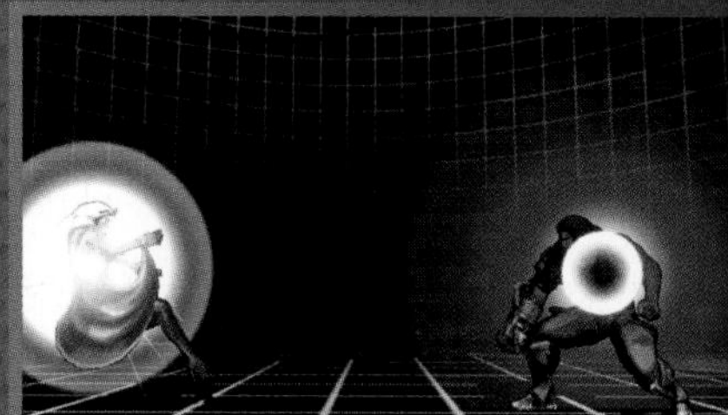

TEAM HYPER COMBO

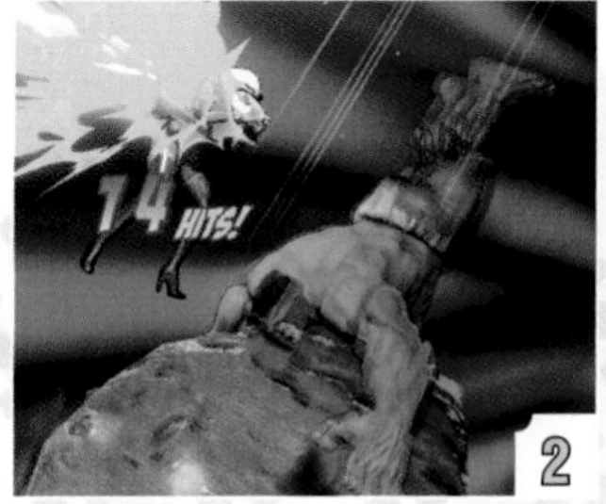

THCs greatly expand damage and combo potential, and are also the key to swapping in characters with less risk.

During level 1 hyper combos, you can team hyper combo to the next character simply by inputting a hyper combo command for the next hero in line, while the current hyper combo is in progress. You can THC at a single stretch up to twice, ultimately using one hyper combo from each partner. Level 3 hyper combos can finish, but not start, team hyper combos. When called into a THC, characters leap on the screen and perform their hyper combo as normal, going through hyper combo start and the hyper combo cutscene.

Team hyper combos are obviously useful for their damage and chip potential. For example, any combo ending in a beam hyper combo can easily be made much more powerful simply by team hyper combo canceling to another beam hyper combo. But team hyper combos are also important because of the safety you're potentially afforded. In most situations, tagging in a new point character with a crossover attack or crossover counter is risky. By burning a couple bars of hyper combo gauge, you can perform your current point character's safest hyper combo, then THC to the safest hyper combo for your next teammate.

Team Position	Initial Order	After 1 stage THC to partner 1	After 2 stage THC to partner 2
Point Character	Member A	B	C
Partner 1	Member B	A	A
Partner 2	Member C	C	B

SNAP BACK

↓↘→ + P1 or P2 (REQUIRES 1 BAR OF HYPER COMBO GAUGE), 50,000 DAMAGE

Snap backs are 1 frame attacks that require 1 bar of the hyper combo gauge to perform. Faster than any other physical attack, the purpose of snap backs is to rearrange an opponent's team order. Partner characters that are snapped in with red damage will have the red damage become permanent. Partner actions are not possible for 210 frames between teammates who've been swapped with a snap back.

If your opponent has a character with a lot of red damage, or a deadly THC order, or a weak character they're using just for the assist, snap backs can be your best friend.

↓↘→ + P1 will snap in their first partner, while ↓↘→ + P2 will snap in their second partner. If you happen to "double snap" the opposing team, hitting both their point character plus an assist at once, one of two things will happen:

If you double snap to their currently-unused character, that character will jump in even if the assist hasn't left play yet.

If you double snap to the partner that's currently on screen as an assist, you will be able to beat up the assist for a couple seconds, before jumping out of play as an assist, then right back into play as a point character (making all the red damage you just inflicted permanent!).

Team Position	Initial Order	After eating ↓↘→ + P1 snap back	After eating ↓↘→ + P2 snap back
Point Character	Member A	B	C
Partner 1	Member B	A	B
Partner 2	Member C	C	A

PROJECTILES & BEAMS

Projectiles and beams have their own hidden durability priorities and values that dictate what happens when different projectiles collide.

PROJECTILE PRIORITY

The first check is priority. There are three projectile priorities: low, medium, and high. Most standard projectiles and beams are low priority, which certain attacks, like Arthur's Golden Armor Lance, are medium priority. Projectile or beam hyper combos are high priority.

When projectiles of higher priority run into projectiles of lower priority, the higher priority projectile wins outright. It doesn't matter how many low priority projectiles a medium priority projectile plows through, for example; as long as it only encounters lower priority projectiles, it will always win.

DURABILITY POINTS

Durability points come into play when projectiles of the same priority collide. Projectiles pack their durability points into a single punch, while beams distribute their durability points across a certain number of frames. When projectiles collide, they mutually deplete durability according to their durability point ratings; projectiles as one blast of DP, beams as DP distributed evenly across their number of frames. When a projectile or beam is depleted of either clashing frames or durability points, it is destroyed.

COMBOS

Back in 1991, intended input leniency for special moves in *Street Fighter 2: The World Warrior* accidentally allowed basic attacks to strike before canceling into an unavoidable special. This afterthought became an official feature with the introduction of the combo meter in *Super Street Fighter 2*. In the mid-'90s, series like *Darkstalkers* and *Street Fighter Alpha*, along with the games *X:Men: Children of the Atom*, *Marvel Super Heroes*, and *X-Men vs. Street Fighter* and *Marvel Super Heroes vs. Street Fighter* (these the seeds of the *MvC* series) began to take combos to a whole different level. Outrageous, over-the-top, outstanding combos represent the number one source of serious damage in the *MvC* franchise and the *Vs.* games in general, as well as a good portion of their heart and soul.

The classics never die.

So, in fighting game terms, what is a combo? A combo is a sequence of hits that is guaranteed if the first attack is not blocked. Combos work because of **hitstun**, which is the period of time a character reels when struck by an attack. During hitstun, no actions are possible, blocking included. Hit the opponent, then during their hitstun cancel your current move into another, or link into another move after the initial one is fully recovered, and you'll create a combo. Combos are vital for the obvious purpose of dealing lots of damage, but more important in that good combos allow you, after two or three initial attacks, to **verify** whether your attacks are being guarded. Many combos and tactics are vulnerable to guaranteed retaliation if blocked—the S launcher possessed by every character is the best example—so confirming your hits before you reach the unsafe parts of a combo is a vital skill. Instead of finishing the combo, you can stop and switch to a back-up plan, or rethink your positioning if the blocking adversary pushes you away with advancing guard.

Number of Hits	Combo
3-4	YES!
5-6	COOL!
7-9	GOOD!
10-12	GREAT!
13-16	DUDE!
17-20	SWEET!
21-25	AWESOME!
26-30	WONDERFUL!
31-35	VIEWTIFUL!
36-42	EXCELLENT!

Number of Hits	Combo
43-49	STYLISH!
50-55	FANTASTIC!
56-64	AMAZING!
65-74	INCREDIBLE!
75-81	MIGHTY!
82-90	MARVELOUS!
91-100	UNCANNY!
101-110	CRAZY!
111-199	GALACTIC!
200+	UNSTOPPABLE!

COMBO LIMITATIONS

Great for style, and building hyper combo gauge? Yes. Good for damage or hitstun deterioration? No.

Plenty of combos are capable of knocking out any character outright. However, there are certain safeguards in place, to prevent some repetitious infinite combos from occurring, and to prevent combos with high numbers of hits from doing disproportionate damage compared to less sizable combos.

DAMAGE SCALING

As the first hit in a combo, all attacks deal their full damage. With each hit added to the combo, however, attacks deal a diminishing percentage of their full damage.

Damage scaling somewhat devalues certain attacks that do lots of hits quickly, like Sentinel's standing and crouching H mouth lasers, and Morrigan's standing H. These moves can still be excellent for other reasons, such as the extra time they grant you to hit-confirm a combo, but the damage of your follow-up suffers.

DAMAGE = (BASE_DAMAGE * MODIFIER ^ COMBO_COUNTER) / 100

BASE_DAMAGE is the listed base damage of an attack. COMBO_COUNTER is the current hit number in the combo. The "MODIFIER" value is as follows:

- **L basic attacks = 0.75**
- **M basic attacks = 0.8**
- **H basic attacks = 0.85**
- **S attacks, special moves, and hyper combos = 0.9**

Damage cannot be less than 10% of base damage. S attacks, special moves, and hyper combos reach the scaling cap on hit 23. The other attack strengths reach the scaling cap progressively earlier.

Because scaling is weighted by button and based on the current number of hits, light attacks don't adversely affect scaling for the entire combo; scaling for only the current move is affected. This is unlike many modern fighting games, where opening with a light attack is detrimental to scaling on down the line.

Throws immediately scale combo damage starting at 45%, which is noticeable if you throw an opponent, then start a combo off the throw. This is possible with most throws by landing an OTG-capable attack.

During X-Factor, the effects of damage scaling are greatly reduced. This is one of the reasons X-Factor is so powerful. Multi-hit moves in particular benefit greatly from lowered damage scaling during X-Factor.

HITSTUN DETERIORATION

As discussed before, **hitstun** is the period of time during which a struck character reels, unable to block. Hitstun lasts for a certain period of time, depending on the move used to inflict the blow. As a general rule, the heavier the attack, the longer the hitstun. However, as hits pile up within a combo, this hitstun period begins to shrink. Eventually, hitstun deteriorates so much that nothing is fast enough to continue the combo, and the victimized character is able to act again. This prevents most infinite combos and, in tandem with damage scaling, removes some of the luster from some multi-hit moves, which accelerate hitstun deterioration more quickly than single-hit attacks.

IHitstun deterioration is influenced differently by different attacks. Some attacks will make hitstun problematic sooner than others. The effects of hitstun deterioration are less noticeable at first while super jumping during air combos, simply because hitstun produced by super jumping basic attacks is higher than normal regardless.

Hitstun deterioration is scaled back considerably during **team aerial combos**, which allows incoming characters to score full air chains one after another. Hitstun deterioration is rapidly accelerated in combos that start after a throw.

X-FACTOR INFINITES

SOME SPECIAL KNOCKDOWN STATES, LIKE STAGGERS, IGNORE HITSTUN DETERIORATION. THESE EFFECTS WILL BE THE SAME NO MATTER HOW MANY TIMES THEY ARE APPLIED IN THE SAME COMBO. DURING CERTAIN LEVELS OF X-FACTOR, DUE TO SPEED BOOSTS, SOME CHARACTERS ARE ABLE TO LINK SPECIAL MOVES TOGETHER IN SUCH A WAY AS TO SKIRT AROUND THE ISSUE OF HITSTUN DETERIORATION ALTOGETHER.

ARTHUR, CAPTAIN AMERICA, DANTE, DEADPOOL, FELICIA, WOLVERINE, AND X-23 HAVE INFINITES THAT WORK ONLY BY LINKING CERTAIN SPECIAL MOVES TOGETHER INDEFINITELY DURING PARTICULAR LEVELS OF X-FACTOR. (CAPTAIN AMERICA AND WOLVERINE HAVE EXTRA SAFEGUARDS IN PLACE THAT PREVENT TRULY INFINITE X-FACTOR COMBOS BUT, BY THE TIME THOSE SAFEGUARDS HAVE KICKED IN, THEIR OPPONENT IS PROBABLY KNOCKED OUT REGARDLESS)

CHAIN COMBOS

Chain combos are sequences of basic attacks chained together by pressing attack buttons one after another. Most basic attacks chain upward in strength, from L light to M medium to H heavy, and most basic attacks can be chained into S special attack. S special attacks cannot be chained into anything else. Chains are possible crouching, standing, or airborne. Not every character can perform the same chain combos—there are a handful of chain combo archetypes, under which various characters fall.

MARVEL CHAIN ARCHETYPES

Character	Hunter Series	Marvel Series	2-hit Limited	3-hit Alternating	Full Normal Jump Chains	Rapid fire Light Attacks
Captain America	No	Yes	No	No	Yes	Standing Only
Deadpool	Yes	No	No	No	Yes	Yes
Doctor Doom	No	Yes	No	No	No	Crouching only
Dormammu	No	No	Yes	No	No	No
Hulk	No	No	Yes	No	No	No
Iron Man	Yes	No	No	No	Yes	Yes
Magneto	No	Yes	No	No	No	Yes
M.O.D.O.K	No	Yes	No	No	No	Yes
Phoenix	Yes	No	No	No	Yes	Yes
Sentinel	No	No	Yes	No	No	Crouching Only
She-Hulk	No	Yes	No	No	No	Crouching Only
Shuma-Gorath (DLC)	Yes	No	No	No	Yes	Yes
Spider-Man	No	Yes	No	No	Yes	Yes
Storm	Yes	No	No	No	Yes	Crouching only
Super-Skrull	Yes	No	No	No	Yes	Yes
Taskmaster	No	Yes	No	No	No	No
Thor	No	No	Yes	No	No	No
Wolverine	Yes	No	No	No	Yes	Crouching only
X-23	Yes	No	No	No	Yes	Yes

CAPCOM CHAIN ARCHETYPES

Character	Hunter Series	Marvel Series	2-hit Limited	3-hit Alternating	Full Normal Jump Chains	Rapid fire Light Attacks
Amaterasu	No	Yes	No	No	No	Yes
Akuma	No	Yes	No	No	No	Yes
Arthur	No	Yes	No	No	No	Yes
Chris	No	Yes	No	No	No	No
Chun-Li	No	Yes	No	No	Yes	Yes
C. Viper	No	Yes	No	No	Yes	Crouching Only
Dante	No	No	No	Yes	Yes	Crouching Only
Felicia	Yes	No	No	No	Yes	Yes
Haggar	No	Yes	No	No	No	No
Hsien-Ko	Yes	No	No	No	Yes	Yes
Jill (DLC)	Yes	No	No	No		Yes
Morrigan	Yes	No	No	No	Yes	Crouching only
Ryu	No	Yes	No	No	No	Yes
Spencer	No	Yes	No	No	No	Standing only
Trish	No	Yes	No	No	Yes	Yes
Tron	No	Yes	No	No	No	No
Viewtiful Joe	Yes	No	No	No	Yes	Yes
Wesker	No	Yes	No	No	No	No
Zero	No	Yes	No	No	Yes	No

GROUND CHAIN COMBO ARCHETYPES

MORRIGAN & CHAIN COMBOS

AIR Ⓜ, Ⓗ, LAND, ST. Ⓛ, CR. Ⓛ, ST. Ⓜ, CR. Ⓜ, ST. Ⓗ, CR. Ⓗ, → + Ⓗ CANCEL ⇨ NORMAL JUMP, AIR Ⓜ, Ⓜ, Ⓗ, Ⓢ, LAND, Ⓢ CANCEL ⇨ SUPER JUMP, AIR Ⓜ, Ⓜ, Ⓗ, Ⓢ, LAND

(381,700 damage with Astral Vision active, before potential **OTG** at the end) This Morrigan combo is a good demonstration of several points and concepts:

- **The usefulness of overhead attacks.**
- **The max potential of ground hunter chain combos.**
- **Transitioning from ground combos to normal jump air combos.**
- **Launching with Ⓢ, and causing flying screen with air Ⓢ after a launcher.**
- **Finishing with an unrecoverable knockdown, creating an opportunity for even more damage with an OTG.**

Characters with ***Flight*** or ***airdashes*** that lend themselves to being used as fast "triangle jump" ***overheads*** have an excellent opener to lean on when fishing for ***combos***. Here Morrigan is pictured airdashing at Iron Man with air Ⓜ.

Iron Man's Ⓢ is attempted as anti-air, but it's too late. Morrigan's Astral Vision is required for this combo mid screen, but not in the corner.

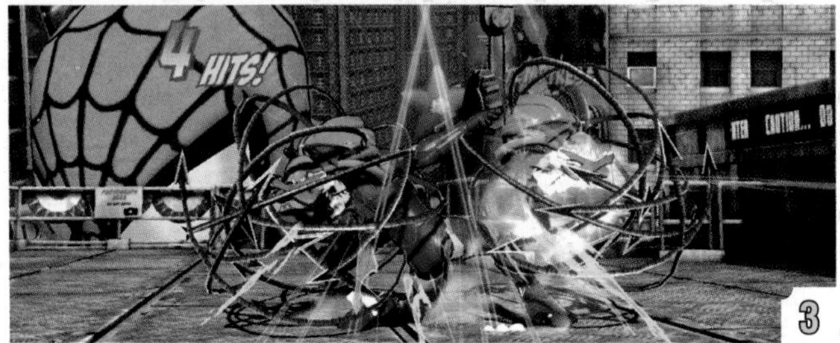

Air Ⓜ is chained to air Ⓗ. To chain basic attacks, simply press the next button in the sequence. Attacks within chains can often be delayed a great deal, but it's the rule rather than the exception that you generally want to speed through chains quickly. Exceptions apply of course, based on character and positioning.

After landing: standing Ⓛ

Crouching Ⓛ

Standing Ⓜ

Crouching Ⓜ...see a pattern forming?

Standing Ⓗ

Crouching Ⓗ

Morrigan's basic ***chain combo*** is done, but her ***command attack*** ⇨ + Ⓗ can be tacked onto the end.

This attack is ***normal jump cancelable***; simply holding ⇗ will interrupt the move with a forward leap, allowing the combo to continue in the air. As an alternative, ⇨ + Ⓗ can be chained into Ⓢ to ***launch*** into an ***air combo***.

Here, Morrigan links the normal jump cancel into air Ⓜ to start an air chain combo. Air chain rules differ from ground chain rules—during a super jump, any character can chain air Ⓛ, Ⓛ, Ⓜ, Ⓜ, Ⓗ, Ⓢ. During a normal jump that same chain is possible, but some characters are restricted to only three hits total. Morrigan is not one of those characters.

Air Ⓜ

Air Ⓗ

Air Ⓢ

Morrigan lands, and Ⓢ launcher can be linked on the ground.

Ⓢ for every character is ***super jump cancelable***. If Ⓢ hits, simply hold ⇧ or ⬀ to leap upward for an air combo.

Chain air Ⓜ, Ⓜ, Ⓗ, Ⓢ again.

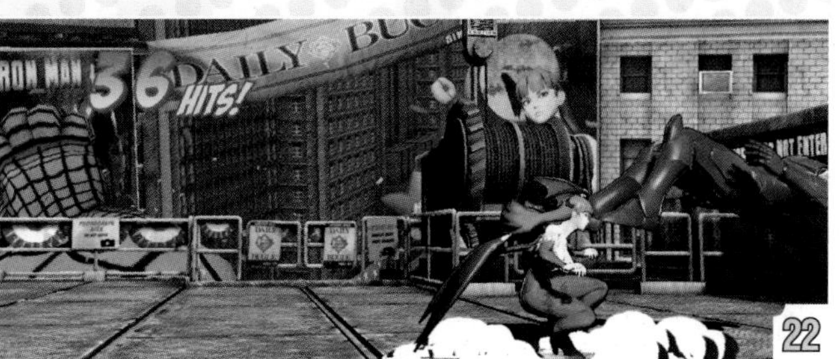

This time, since the air combo was started with grounded Ⓢ, air Ⓢ creates a ***flying screen unrecoverable knockdown***. Unrecoverable knockdowns grant an opportunity to ***OTG***—popping a foe up ***o***ff ***t***he ***g***round, for continued hits.

After flying screen, you can ***OTG*** with Morrigan's Shadow Servant hyper combo, or call a quick OTG-capable crossover assist, using that to link into her Darkness Illusion level 3 hyper combo.

HUNTER SERIES (FULL ALTERNATING)

A style of chaining that originated from the *Darkstalker* series; it is no surprise that Hsien-Ko, Felicia, and Morrigan all use this archetype. Characters with this type may chain one of each ground attack together from weakest to strongest. Attacks of the same strength can also be chained together only when alternating from the standing to crouching position (example, Super Skrull may chain standing Ⓛ, crouching Ⓛ, standing Ⓜ, crouching Ⓜ, standing Ⓗ, crouching Ⓗ).

MARVEL SERIES (STRAIGHT AHEAD)

This chain archetype only allows three attacks chained together from weakest to strongest. This chain set may NOT alternate from a standing to crouching attack of the same strength, unlike the Hunter series (with the exception of Chun-Li, who can chain standing Ⓗ into crouching Ⓗ).

2-HITS LIMITED

This chain set allows the player to only chain two attacks together. The sequence must start with a light attack (crouching or standing) before chaining into any medium or heavy attack.

3-HIT ALTERNATING

This chain type carries the chaining properties of the Hunter series—you can string together attacks from weakest to strongest while also alternate from standing to crouching attacks of the same strength, but you can only chain up to three attacks together within these limitations. Dante, for example, can normally chain crouching Ⓜ, standing Ⓗ then crouching Ⓗ. However, if the combo is started with an additional attack, like standing Ⓜ, crouching Ⓜ and then standing Ⓗ, you cannot follow-up with the final crouching Ⓗ.

AERIAL CHAIN ARCHETYPES

Only two types of air chains exist: a "Hunter Series" style of chaining where the player can chain two attacks each of light and medium before chaining to stronger attacks (air Ⓛ, Ⓛ, Ⓜ, Ⓜ, Ⓗ, Ⓢ), and a limited air chain where the player follows the same rules as the Hunter Series alternating chain method, but can only chain up to three attacks together. The full Hunter Series style of chaining is available to all characters during a super jump, and only to some characters during a normal jump. The three hit limited style of air chaining is seen only on some characters during their normal jump.

AIR-TO-AIR CHAINS WITH IRON MAN

SUPER JUMP AIR Ⓜ, ↓ + Ⓗ, Ⓢ CANCEL ↓ ↙ ← + Ⓢ, AIR Ⓜ, Ⓗ, ↓ + Ⓗ CANCEL ↓ ↙ ← + Ⓢ, AIR Ⓗ CANCEL DOUBLE JUMP, AIR Ⓗ, Ⓢ CANCEL ↓ ↘ → + Ⓛ

(427,500 damage) This combo demonstrates the differences between air combos that start air-to-air, versus those that begin with an Ⓢ launcher. It also helps illustrate how Flight and double jumps work in jumps and air combos:

Per each jump period, characters can either airdash, or double jump, but not both.

Exceptions are Chun-Li and Viewtiful Joe, who can triple jump, or double jump and airdash. Instead of double jumping, Chun-Li and Viewtiful Joe can also airdash twice.

Only three special moves are possible per jump period. Exception occurs if Flight is activated before three special moves are used—during Flight, there is no limit on the number of special moves that can be used.

Flight can only be activated once per jump period. Usage of Flight does not preclude double jumping after Flight expires or is canceled. Using an airdash at any time before or during Flight will prevent double jumping later, however.

The exception is M.O.D.O.K., who can initiate normal jump Flight by holding ↑ from the ground, and still activate ↓ ↙ ← + Ⓢ Flight later in the same airborne period.

Air attacks from a super jump or super jump Flight cause considerably more hitstun than air attacks from a normal jump or normal jump Flight. This means that some air combos are more difficult to perform during a normal jump, and some air combos only work during a super jump state.

Iron Man's air Ⓜ is an excellent air-to-air poke.

Air Ⓜ is chained into Iron Man's air ↓ + Ⓗ command attack.

Air ↓ + Ⓗ is chained into air Ⓢ. Air Ⓢ doesn't cause flying screen when used in an air combo that doesn't begin from a launcher. Instead, air Ⓢ behaves like a basic attack (although it cannot be canceled with a double jump).

Air Ⓢ is canceled into Flight by inputting ↓ ↙ ← + Ⓢ. The recovery of air Ⓢ is interrupted by the activation of Flight.

Air Ⓜ is linked after Flight activation. During Flight, characters can perform the same basic air attacks that they can while jumping.

Air Ⓜ is chained to air Ⓗ.

Air Ⓗ is chained to air ↓ + Ⓗ.

Flight cancelation can be used to cancel the recovery of basic attacks, just as Flight activation can. Input ↓ ↙ ← + Ⓢ to cancel Flight.

Immediately press Ⓗ to perform air Ⓗ as Iron Man begins to fall.

Tap ↗ to cancel air Ⓗ with a double jump. Only one double jump is possible per jumping period, and no double jump is possible if an airdash is used.

Double jump cancels are instant, and characters can accept input on the very next frame. Immediately press Ⓗ for another air Ⓗ.

Air Ⓗ chains to air Ⓢ. As before, since this air combo didn't start with a launcher, air Ⓢ does not cause flying screen.

This time, air Ⓢ is canceled into ↓ ↘ → + Ⓛ.

OTHER CHAIN TYPES

RAPID FIRE LIGHT ATTACKS

Some characters can chain light attacks into each other repeatedly. Whenever desired, you can transition from rapid fire light attacks to their regular chain combo.

TARGET COMBOS (CHARACTER SPECIFIC CHAIN COMBOS)

Some characters have unique chain combos. Though all characters initially fall into a chain archetype of some sort, these special combos, also known as target combos, bypass the normal rules of their chain structure.

Amaterasu: May chain (H) into crouching (H), but only within a 3-attack chain limit. May chain jumping (H) three times consecutively (this ability bypasses the 3-attack normal jump chain limit).

Chun-Li: standing (H), crouching (H).

Dante: crouching (L) into standing (L). Chain does not interfere with the 3-hit alternating hit rule.

Jill (DLC): crouching (L) into standing (L).

Captain America: standing (M), (M).

Sentinel: standing (H), crouching (H).

Shuma-Gorath (DLC): crouching (L) into standing (L).

Wolverine: standing (M), (L) (or air (M), (L).

COMMAND ATTACK CHAINS

Command attacks are much like basic attacks in many ways, but do not fit into chain combos in the same way. Command attacks play by their own rules, on a case by case basis; some command attacks can be chained into or out of, while some can't be used in chain combos at all.

LINKS

Akuma ⇨ + (M), linked into Goshoryuken, or Spencer ⇨ + (H), linked into Armor Piercer, are simple examples of link combos.

A link occurs when you wait until an attack has fully recovered before striking again. This is distinct from **chain combos**, in which (ATK) buttons are simply pressed in sequence, or **cancel** combos, in which recovery periods are interrupted with new actions. *MvC3* is not as link-intensive as some fighters, like *Super Street Fighter 4*, but links are still present. In absolute terms, links are present all over the place, just in a different form. When chaining into (S) to launch then performing an air combo, you are technically canceling (S) with a super jump, then linking into an aerial chain.

CANCELS CANCEL ➔

Smart Bomb L OTG CANCEL ➔ Proton Cannon
X-Factor Proton Cannon CANCEL ➔ Okami Shuffle

To cancel means to interrupt the recovery of one action with another action. Most (ATK) basic attacks are cancelable into command attacks, and command movements such as Flight or teleportation. Some basic attacks are jump, double/triple jump, or super jump cancelable—that is, the attack can be interrupted simply by holding an upward direction, or tapping down-up quickly. (S) special attacks are cancelable only on hit, and then only into super jump, while air (S) is not cancelable when used after a launch into an air combo (though air (S) is cancelable if used in an air combo that begins without a launch). Most (ATK) basic attacks and command attacks are cancelable into special moves and hyper combos, and all level 1 hyper combos can themselves be canceled into a team hyper combo (THC), in which the next partner tags in to continue the hyper combo punishment. Finally, X-Factor activation (X-Factor) can be used to cancel nearly any action on the ground.

CROSSOVER ASSISTS IN COMBOS

P1 or P2

Apart from their utility for zoning, protection, and distraction, crossover assists are invaluable combo tools. Each partner can be called once per combo. Partners cannot be called during hitstun, guardstun, special moves, super jumps, or super jump Flight. They can, be called during normal jumps, normal jump Flight, during or after ground and air recovery, and while on the ground performing (ATK) basic attacks or (S) special attacks. And basic attacks on the ground, or off of jump-ins (or advanced jump-ins like triangle jumps or box jumps), are where most combos begin.

The openings for using assists in combos are too numerous to bother listing many examples. The possibilities offered by *Vs.* games have driven hardcore experimenters and combo video producers for over a decade and a half.

You can't use the same crossover assist twice in one combo, but you *can* use each assist once. Assists can be used in combos to help with verification, to extend combos on the ground, and to OTG after a launcher combo that leads to flying screen. Combos can start off of errant or grazing hit from a crossover assist—an opponent may get clipped by, for example, the edge of Doctor Doom's Molecular Shield or Iron Man's Repulsor Blast, allowing you to start a combo if you juggle them in time. Sometimes this can be as simple as starting up a long-range hyper combo or linking (S) launcher, or it can be more complex.

This is one general possibility (of many) for the use of both assists in one combo: Catching a stray hit with a close range assist, then following up with a chain combo ending in (S) to launch them into an air combo, ending in (S) to create flying screen, where an OTG-capable partner can be called to continue further.

RYU + CROSSOVER ASSISTS

AIR ↓ ↙ ← + Ⓛ, LAND, CR. Ⓛ + P1 OR P2 MORRIGAN, CR. Ⓜ, CR. Ⓗ, → + Ⓗ CANCEL ← ↓ ↙ + Ⓛ WALL BOUNCE, ST. Ⓜ + P1 OR P2 CHRIS, ST. Ⓗ, → + Ⓗ CANCEL ← ↓ ↙ + Ⓛ, CHRIS'S MINE HITS, STANDING Ⓗ CANCEL ← ↓ ↙ + Ⓛ CANCEL → ↓ ↘ + ATK ATK, STANDING Ⓜ CANCEL → ↓ ↘ + Ⓗ CANCEL ↓ ↘ → + ATK ATK, HOLD ↑

(Requires corner, 4 bars, Morrigan—γ and Chris—γ, 1,088,700 damage) This powerful Ryu combo uses a wall bounce, two assists, two hyper combos, and three Jodan Sokuto Geri kicks. This combo highlights several advanced combo concepts:

- **Using assists to build hyper combo gauge.**
- **Using assists to prolong combos.**
- **Using multiple chains, assists, special moves, and hyper combos in the same combo.**
- **Using a wall bounce.**
- **Using the corner.**

Many characters have useful air attacks that can hit on either side of them. This makes these attacks useful for going for cross-ups on an opponent—or for faking a cross-up. Here, Ryu lands his air ↓ ↙ ← + Ⓛ Tatsumaki Senpukyaku L, which spins in a useful downward arc and hits regardless of the side that Ryu ends up on.

After landing: crouching Ⓛ + P1 OR P2 —depending on the slot Morrigan is in, this can be different. Buttons to call partners may be pressed while performing basic attacks on the ground or during a normal jump (and during Flight that begins from a normal jump, but that obviously doesn't apply to Ryu).

Crouching Ⓜ. Morrigan arrives.

Crouching Ⓗ. Morrigan's Dark Harmonizer grants Ryu roughly 30% of a hyper combo gauge bar.

Ryu's basic Marvel series chain combo is done, but you can tack on his → + Ⓗ command attack.

→ + Ⓗ is canceled into ← ↓ ↙ + Ⓛ, which causes a ***wall bounce***.

Standing Ⓜ + P1 OR P2 —depending on the slot Chris is in, this can be different. Standing Ⓜ juggles after the wall bounce.

Standing Ⓗ. Chris arrives.

→ + Ⓗ command attack is used again. Chris sets his mine up.

→ + Ⓗ is again canceled to ← ↓ ↙ + Ⓛ. Only one wall bounce is possible per combo, so this kick will not prolong the combo on its own...

...Chris's mine will, however.

Juggle after the mine explosion with standing Ⓗ.

Standing Ⓗ is canceled to yet another ← ↓ ↙ + Ⓛ.

With the wall bounce and both assists used up, it's time to go another route for prolonging the combo after a Jodan Sokuto Geri. Cancel ← ↓ ↙ + Ⓛ into → ↓ ↘ + ATK ATK, Ryu's Shin Shoryuken level 3 hyper combo.

Shin Shoryuken ends by hurling the foe high into the air. They must fall all the way back to earth before recovering, creating another juggle opportunity.

Standing Ⓜ.

Standing Ⓜ is canceled to → ↓ ↘ + Ⓗ, Shoryuken H. Ryu's standing Ⓜ, Ⓗ, → + Ⓗ chain is extremely reliable when juggling an opponent just off the ground, but it is not used here because this combo pushes the limits of ***hitstun deterioration*** as it is.

Shoryuken H is immediately canceled before Ryu leaves the ground into ↓ ↘ → + ATK ATK, Shinku Hadoken.

Holding ↑ directs the Shinku Hadoken almost straight up, where it catches the opponent who was launched up by the dragon punch.

Special Hit States in Combos

Using special states is a great way to perpetuate combos. This also enables you to think of combos in stages—before floor bounce, after floor bounce, after flying screen, and so on. Certain hit states can only show up once per combo—these are ground bounce, wall bounce, and crumple (multiple ground bounces are possible if you follow a ground bounce with a downward team aerial combo). There are technically no restrictions on the number of staggers, spinning knockdowns, unrecoverable knockdowns, incapacitations, and OTG hits, however. Those are limited in combos only by team makeup and hitstun deterioration.

The most universal special state is flying screen, caused by landing air Ⓢ in a launcher combo. After flying screen, the combo victim is left in an unrecoverable knockdown state, during which OTG-capable attacks will hit. OTGs are possible after flying screen, after most throws, and after certain special moves and hyper combos. While many characters can OTG without any help, some characters require a P1 or P2 partner to OTG.

OTG-Capable Crossover Assists
Akuma—γ
Arthur—γ (delayed)
Chris—γ (delayed)
C. Viper—β
Dante—β
Deadpool—β
Dormammu—β
Hulk—α
Iron Man—γ
Sentinel—β (delayed)
Sentinel—γ
She-Hulk—α
Shuma-Gorath—α (DLC)
Storm—β (delayed)
Viewtiful Joe—γ (delayed)
Wesker—β
X-23—β

Crossover Assists That Cause Ground Bounce
Akuma—γ (air hit only)
Deadpool—β
Felicia—γ (air hit only)
Haggar—γ
Jill—α (DLC)
Spider-Man—γ

Crossover Assists That Cause Wall Bounce
Jill—β (DLC)
Spencer—γ
Super-Skrull—α

Crossover Assists That Cause Spinning Knockdown
Chris—γ
Deadpool—α
Haggar—β
M.O.D.O.K.—β
Wesker—γ

Crossover Assists That Cause Crumple
She-Hulk—β

Crossover Assists That Cause Incapacitation
Magneto—β
Spider-Man—α
Trish—β

Alternatively, attack an opponent directly. Vary your opening attacks between low attacks that must be guarded crouching, quick airborne attacks (of which there are many, most of which must be blocked standing), and throws. All three can lead to combos, and each must be defended against differently.

When you start your **chain combo**, get to a point where you can cause a **wall bounce** or **ground bounce** with the fewest, hardest hits possible. Off the bounce, chain into Ⓢ launcher, then perform a brief **air combo** into Ⓢ to cause **flying screen**. Many attacks cause bounces, while flying screen is caused by air Ⓢ in a launcher combo. If you don't have attacks or assists available to create a wall or floor bounce, proceed directly to flying screen.

When performing air chain combos into air Ⓢ for flying screen, it's usually best to cause flying screen as low to the ground as possible. This is because the faster you land, the more likely it is you'll be able to OTG an opponent, which is what you want to do after flying screen. The best way to cause flying screen low enough to OTG afterward, before the opponent can get up, varies from character to character. For some, it's as simple as chaining very slowly, or using one air Ⓜ instead of two during air chains. For others, using Flight in an air combo helps. And naturally, because of the larger distance involved, following up with an OTG after flying screen is usually more difficult, or even impossible mid-screen (even though fast wavedashing can make what seems impossible work in many situations). Securing an OTG is much easier in a corner.

After the OTG, you're probably approaching 15 or 20 hits, the point at which **hitstun deterioration** starts to mean that combo extension is impossible soon. Get as close as you can to this limit as possible, then finish with something that either causes lots of damage, or sets you up to keep momentum. Ending with flying screen again is fine—at this point you might not be able to score another OTG into anything, but you'll be able to drop an assist right on top of an opponent when they recover, or perhaps score another combo. Otherwise, if you can, finish with a powerful **hyper combo**. From here, if necessary for the knockout, an **X-Factor cancel** into another hyper combo, and/or a **team hyper combo**, are strong options. Although damage scaling is at its heaviest by this point, many hyper combos add on enough total hits to add up damage quickly regardless. And while **THC**s from **level 3 hyper combos** aren't allowed, these costly maneuvers make great combo or THC enders, since level 3 hyper combos are unaffected by damage scaling!

The combo engine in *MvC3* manages to keep the outrageousness of the *Vs.* series combos alive, while eliminating one of the lingering problems with the openness of the *Vs.* series combo rules—the previous preponderance of infinite combos. The use of infinites in high level play for previous installments is the rule, rather than the exception. One of the best characters in *MvC1*, Red Venom, was essentially a hideously fast, walking infinite combo whose only deficiency was low stamina, and in *MvC2* Magneto continued that tradition. But that's only two examples. *MvC2* alone had Iron Man as a slower, more air-based version of Magneto. Between his Flight modes, normal jump infinite, and guard break potential he could turn one glancing aerial counterhit into three dusted characters. Here, there are still high-risk, high-reward offensive characters, and there are certainly incredible, high damage combos that annihilate any character's health bar (usually from X-Factor or using heavy resources). But between hitstun deterioration, the removal of guard breaks against normal jumps, and the ability to roll forward or backward with invulnerability from any wakeup, the frustration of eating a single random accident into a lost round is removed.

Disclaimer: This is not to say *MvC3* won't be full of huge swings and ridiculous damage; it wouldn't be *MvC* without it, would it? Getting your point and assist character both caught in a strong team hyper combo, crossover combination, or X-Factor combo is perhaps even worse then eating a double snap back into anti-assist infinite in *MvC2*—instead of losing one character to an accident, then perhaps being guard broken when your next character falls in, you just lose two characters simultaneously! At least your own X-Factor will be beefed up with only one character left, if you still have it... never give up!

Composing Strong Combos

A large part of being successful in fighting games is making the most of the opportunities that you have. Good opponents will give up little for free, so when a solid chance comes your way you need to make it count. The ways in which attacks **chain**, **cancel**, and **link** into one another, along with the limitations imposed by **damage scaling** and **hitstun deterioration**, suggest a certain approach to squeezing out the most damage when you score a hard-earned first hit.

Combos need to start somewhere. Call a **crossover assist** and wait to see if the attack is successful. If yes, start a combo. Bonus points here if you can put the assist in a place that makes it difficult to deal with—the best example is dropping an assist on one side of an opponent before **jumping**, **airdashing**, **flying**, or **teleporting** to the other side.

DANTE, X-FACTOR, AND JUMP CANCELING-EXPERT LEVEL COMBOS

ST. Ⓜ, CR. Ⓜ, ST. Ⓗ, → + Ⓗ [X-FACTOR] ST. Ⓜ, CR. Ⓜ, ST. Ⓗ, → + Ⓗ [CANCEL] Ⓢ + ATK [CANCEL] → ↓ ↘ + Ⓜ [CANCEL] ↓ ↙ ← ↖ + Ⓜ, LATE ST. Ⓗ, Ⓢ [CANCEL] SUPER JUMP, AIR Ⓜ, Ⓜ, Ⓗ [CANCEL] ↓ ↘ → + Ⓗ, LAND, ↓ ↙ ← + Ⓛ [CANCEL] ↓ ↘ → + ATK ATK

(2,717,000 damage if performed with X-Factor level 1 on opposing point plus partner; same combo is possible without X-Factor, minus the first chain) **X-Factor** activation instantly cancels any action on the ground, and boosts damage an astonishing amount. Meanwhile, partner characters performing crossover assists cannot block, and take 50% extra damage! Adding all that up, it's not hard to see that recognizing you've caught both the opposing point and assist before hit-confirming into a doubly-fatal X-Factor combo is one of the best tricks you can pull off in *MvC3*. This combo highlights several other things too:

The importance of hit-confirming, which goes hand-in-hand with picking solid places to use X-Factor; in this case, two full health characters are annihilated off a chance standing Ⓜ, which is an attack a Dante player should use constantly anyway.

Ground chain combos made necessary by the 3-hits alternating archetype.

Using a jump cancel, but then canceling the jump itself too! Canceling pre-jump frames with a special move, after command jump canceling another attack.

Canceling pre-jump frames with a special move, after normal jump canceling another attack.

Using a ground bounce.

Canceling a special move into a hyper combo.

1

Here, Dante dashes in to open with standing Ⓜ, his best basic poke. Doctor Doom is attempting to zone with projectiles and Dormammu assist.

2

Dante's standing Ⓜ counterhits Doctor Doom and Dormammu.

3

Standing Ⓜ chains to crouching Ⓜ. Dante's chain combo archetype is 3-hits alternating; he can chain standing to crouching attacks of the same strength like in a Hunter Series, but he cannot chain more than three basic attacks together in one grounded chain combo. This is just as well, since his crouching Ⓛ is irregular, his standing Ⓜ is fantastic, and he can continue his chains in innumerable ways anyway.

4

Crouching Ⓜ chains to standing Ⓗ. At this point, Dante's basic attack chain combo options are exhausted.

5

It's still possible to chain to his ⇨ + Ⓗ command attack, however. At this point, four attacks into the combo, it should be apparent that not only are you striking the opposing point character, but you've also caught the assist! There are several visual indicators that will all work together to help alert you that you've caught two-thirds of their team at once—the combo meter will be higher than expected, damage will appear on two opposing vitality gauges instead of one, the assist will be visible being hit, and the "Player 1" or "Player 2" markers will be above the assist's head. Focus on looking for these signs so you can make the most of unexpected hits against assists.

6

7

8

[X-FACTOR] X-Factor is activated by pressing Ⓛ + Ⓜ + Ⓗ + Ⓢ. X-Factor is available once per team per match. Only having one go at X-Factor per fight means you should spend it very carefully, but it's harder to suggest a more efficient place to use it than taking two characters out at once, which is what this combo does. This combo is possible the moment the match starts!

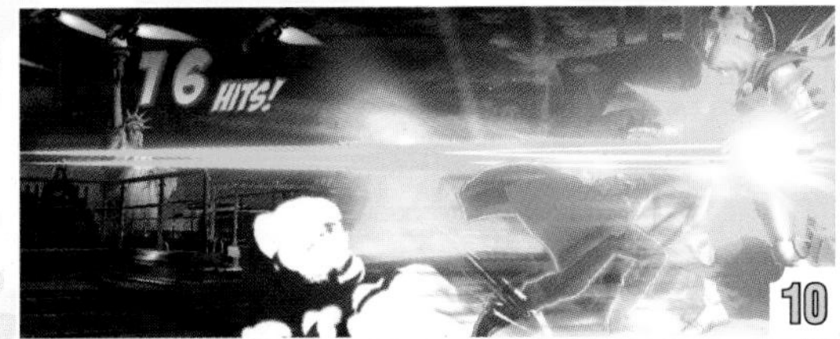

Like the activation of a hyper combo, X-Factor freezes action for just a moment. As soon as you can act again, repeat the initial chain of standing (M), crouching (M), standing (H), ⇨ + (H).

Dante's ⇨ + (H) is canceled with his (S) + (ATK) command jump. Shown here are the command jump's standing pre-jump frames. Here's where things get interesting, from an execution standpoint. Dante's ⇨ + (H) is NOT normally jump cancelable simply by hitting ⇗, but it IS cancelable into Dante's (S) + (ATK) command jump. This command jump operates the same as any other jump, meaning that it has 3 pre-jump frames where Dante is still considered standing. If the command for a special move or hyper combo is completed during this period, the special move will preempt the jump, and the jump will never occur.

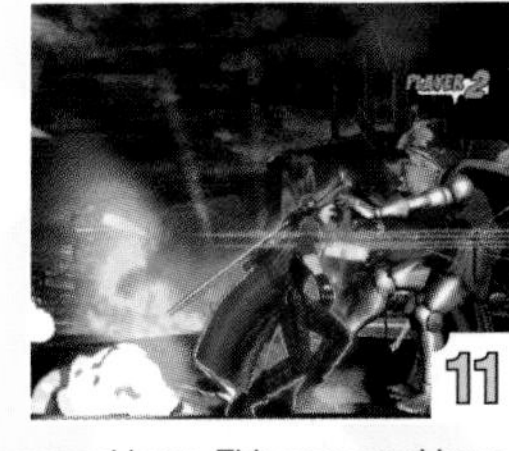

The ultimate effect of all this is that Dante can essentially cancel ⇨ + (H) into special moves, something he cannot normally do. Here, the command ⇨⇩⇘ + (M) is completed before (S) + (ATK) actually causes Dante to leave the ground.

⇨⇩⇘ + (M) hits. Here, execution gets interesting again. Unlike ⇨ + (H), ⇨⇩⇘ + (M) IS cancelable into a normal jump, simply by holding ⇗. Again, this normal jump has 3 pre-jump frames, during which special move and hyper combo inputs will be interpreted as ground moves, canceling jumps before they happen.

So, using these principles, by inputting ⇩⇙⇦⇖ + (M) when ⇨⇩⇘ + (M) hits, you can trigger Dante's grounded ⇩⇙⇦ + (M) special move. In the interests of leniency, inputs carry forward very slightly. Dante doesn't have a move with the actual command of ⇩⇙⇦⇖ + (M), so the game first registers the last directional input, ⇖, as an attempt to jump, then carries forward and cancels the pre-jump frames with ⇩⇙⇦ + (M).

⇩⇙⇦ + (M) causes a ground bounce. One ground bounce is possible per combo. The enemy bounces quite high here, so you'll want to wait a second and perhaps dash forward to reposition.

Catch the enemies low to the ground with standing (H).

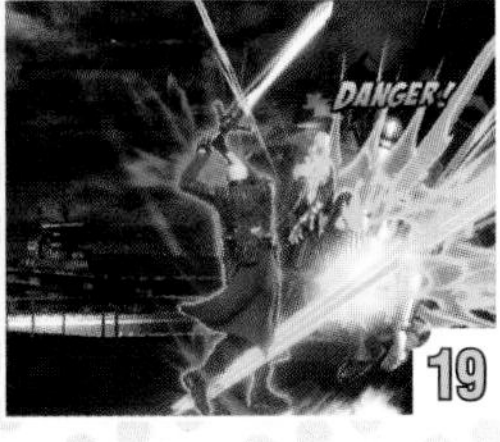

Standing (H) chains to (S), for a launch.

After the (S) launcher, super jump by holding ⇗.

After the (S) launcher, air (M), (M), (H) CANCEL ⇩⇘⇨ + (H) is performed.

While the results of ⇩⇘⇨ + (H) in an air combo can be irregular, usually you're left in position to land and connect ⇩⇙⇦ + (L).

⇩⇙⇦ + (L) is canceled into ⇩⇘⇨ + (ATK)(ATK), and two characters are guaranteed to bite the dust. And Dante is hardly the only character capable of insane nastiness with X-Factor and only one bar right at the start of the match...

TEAM BUILDING & SPACE CONTROL

Marvel vs. Capcom 3 requires you to think of your team as a whole entity, rather than simply a trio of different characters. The nature and character of a team doesn't just stem from what each character is capable of, but also what each enables for the others. When building a team, always consider:

Any character can (and absolutely should) team up with partners whose crossover assists (tap P1 or P2) help close gaps in offense or defense, or which emphasize strengths. For example, characters without options to OTG (off the ground) by themselves can team up with characters that have OTG-capable crossover assists. Characters that are good at zoning with long range projectiles can choose assist partners that further press this advantage. Rushdown-oriented characters can can be complimented by assists that make blocking problematic. Flying and airdashing characters can couple with low-hitting assists. Teleport-capable characters can drop pinning assists on one side then easily cross to the other, which makes blocking tricky, and safe retaliation almost impossible.

Some crossover assists also make great crossover counters (during guardstun, tap ⇨ + P1 or P2). A player could build an entire strategy around gaining meter and biding time to turn a match on its head with one solid crossover counter that hits both their point and their assist. Guard their pinning pressure tactics, then crossover counter, catch both characters, and cancel to hyper combo. Now, with either X-Factor cancel to another hyper combo, or a THC (team hyper combo) to your next partner, you've taken out two characters just from being patient and letting an opponent think they were getting what they wanted.

A solid team order should take into account team hyper combos. It is *much* more valuable to knock an opposing character out completely rather than just dealing heavy damage. If you don't maximize the opportunities that come your way, and try to put characters down when possible, you're leaving the door open for them to heal up in reserve and waste your efforts. Solid team hyper combos will often be the only way to continue a combo; the only way left to get that *last* little bit of damage to knock out a point or assist. It is *extremely* valuable to take opposing characters out completely when given the chance, no matter the cost.

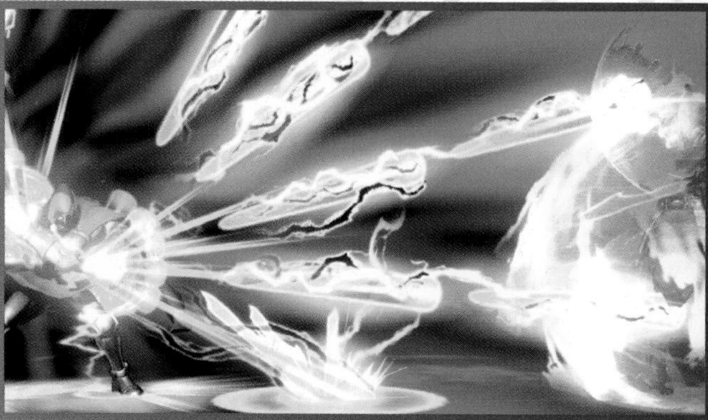

Of course, in addition to combo extension, team hyper combos also serve to rotate in a new point character. While there are several ways to switch characters, you will inevitably find yourself in a situation where most options are unavailable or unsafe. Crossover attacks can be read and punished; crossover counters aren't possible if an opponent doesn't give you anything to guard. Your opposition won't if they're on the lookout for some sort of switch in the first place. Team aerial combos require a clean hit, and what's more they require that an opponent doesn't properly team aerial counter. Often, the only remotely safe option to tag in a new character will be to activate the current character's fastest-activating hyper combo, then starting the next character's safest hyper combo. There are many hyper combos that are completely safe when guarded, which is the best quality for this purpose. The archetypal example here, of course, is Storm's Hail Storm.

Characters that lack great air combos on their own can score a launcher, then hand off the air combo to more combo-capable teammates with team aerial combos. Team aerial combos not only allow more flexibility in teammate switching and team construction, but also provide terrific damage and potentially insane hyper combo gauge rewards—how does maxed meter in one team air combo sound?

Of course, a lot of these techniques cost hyper combo gauge. So here there are more decisions. How will you build hyper combo gauge? Of the characters you favor, who is best suited to a "battery" role? Will you stockpile hyper combo gauge primarily for one purpose, such as a particular THC, a hyper combo that is safe to guess/chip with, or a crossover counter to hyper combo? Or you might save hyper combo gauge for a particular character. For example, so Phoenix can be ready to rise as Dark Phoenix, so Dormammu can unleash repeated Stalking Flares, or so characters like Ryu and Akuma can land their level 3 hyper combos. Perhaps you've picked a trio with a solid crossover combination; some pairings of characters and assist types create crossover combinations that knock many character out outright, or which deal incredible chip damage.

Regardless of your ultimate plans with team chemistry and construction, or with hyper combo gauge consumption, the point is mainly that you should have plans in the first place. Of course, things won't always go according to plan—inevitably, you will lose a partner to assist damage prematurely, or a character or two will disappear in seconds to a nasty X-Factor combo or THC, but you will control a lot more of your fate if you've at least thought about what you'll do ahead of time.

Team Hyper Combo and Crossover Combination Potential

A few characters can consistently K.O. foes on their own, but aside from using X-Factor, the best way to eek out severe damage usually involves swapping characters with team hyper combos, or bringing in everyone at once for a crossover combination. Team hyper combos are often also vital for relatively safe swap ins of partner 1 or 2.

Susceptibility to Mismatches

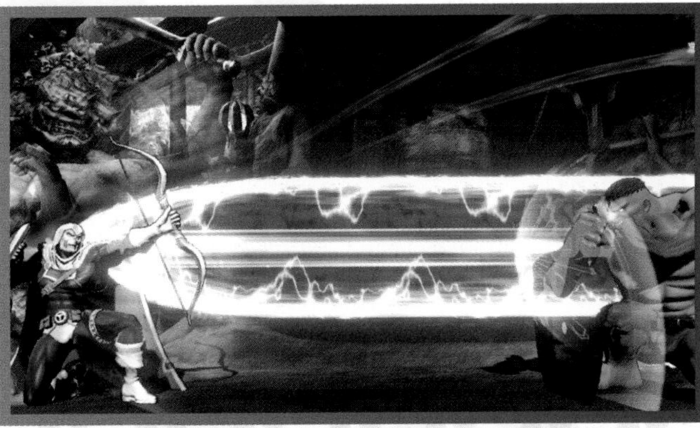

Certain types of characters just have problems with other types of characters. Low vitality, rushdown characters may have an uphill battle versus sturdy teams filled with high-health bruisers. Likewise, those same, sluggish bruisers are just never going to be at their best against characters that are good at zoning and keeping foes away. It's worth considering possible mismatches that stretch across your whole team.

Overall Vitality

Overall health is also a consideration. A team of Thor, Haggar, and Tron can simply handle a lot more punishment than Phoenix, Amaterasu, and Storm, for example.

Themed Teams

You may wish to build some teams around fun concepts or storyline partnerships. To name just a few, Felicia, Hsien-Ko, and Morrigan can make up Team Darkstalkers; X-23, Wolverine, and Deadpool can make up Team Weapon X, Thor, Iron Man, and Captain America can make up The Avengers, and so on. Playing around with such teams at least once is the basis for a few Trophies and Achievements, as well.

FRAME DATA

Going from a complete novice to an intermediate player requires grasping the fundamental concepts of the game—moving, guarding, attacking, and other concepts. Taking the extra step to becoming an expert player, to some degree, requires digging a little deeper and internalizing some rather esoteric concepts. The most prominent, measureable, and ultimately meaningful of these is the idea of frame advantage. Getting into this can be a little intimidating for a new player, so rest assured that Rome wasn't built in a day, and neither do you have to incorporate all this information and somehow translate it into improved gameplay all at once—as in any hobby or skill with depth, serious players measure the time they've put into fighting games in *years*, not days, weeks, or months. So don't fret if this seems overwhelming at first. A salad bar approach can work wonders here—take a little of what seems to help you at a time.

FRAMES

A frame is the game's unit of time measurement. Like most modern games, *MvC3* runs at 60 frames per second. Regarding the game using the actual frame data, when available, takes the discussion to a deeper and more useful place. The actual utility of a given move, for example, becomes much more apparent when looking at the frame data for that move. Visually, there is very little difference between an attack that hits in 4 frames versus a move that hits in 8 frames. To most human observers, there is not a difference at all—for this example, we're talking about the difference between "just under a tenth of a second" and "just over a tenth of a second." But in terms of the game, this miniscule, barely-perceptible difference can amount to a vast gulf.

STARTUP FRAMES

This is the number of frames it takes for an attack to become "active," or capable of hitting an opponent, after the command for the move is correctly input. The fastest moves in the game have 1 to 4 frames of startup, and are mostly throw attacks. For the purposes of this guide, startup frames naturally include the first frame of the active period. This is for ease of looking for links under frame advantage. If something in this guide is listed with an advantage of +6, then any attack with a startup of 6 frames of lower will work. This does mean, however, that if you add up the startup, active, and recovery frames, the sum is actually 1 frame longer than the real duration of the move.

ACTIVE FRAMES

This is the number of frames in which a move is actually capable of striking. For basic attacks, this number tends to be very small—usually no more than 3-5 frames. Exceptions apply, of course, and it's always worth noting when a move has an unusually high number of active frames.

RECOVERY FRAMES

This is the number of frames in which an attack is recovering, no longer active. Characters can't guard or perform other actions while recovering, so they are vulnerable to retaliation if the recovery period is lengthy. The recovery period is the portion that is circumvented when using any kind of cancel into other moves. For projectile attacks, recovery begins the moment the projectile is actually released.

ADVANTAGE ON HIT / ADVANTAGE IF GUARDED

When an attack strikes an opponent, two things happen: the attacking character's move goes through its recovery period, while the defending character either goes through their animation of guardstun or hitstun (depending, of course, on whether the attack was blocked). Different attacks have different recovery periods, and inflict different amounts of guardstun or hitstun. The attacking character will eventually fully recover from their attack and be ready to act again, just as the defending character will eventually leave the animation of guardstun or hitstun, ready to act again as well. The discrepancy between when the attacker and the defender can act is expressed exactly with the concept of frame advantage. A frame advantage of +10 means that the attacker can act a full ten frames before the defender—no small advantage at all. Many attacks are active in less than 10 frames, so in this hypothetical scenario the attacker can actually link any move faster than 10 frames, and there's nothing the defender can do about it. On the other hand, a frame advantage of +1 is not particularly noteworthy—yes, the attacker can act a whole single frame before the opponent, and the opportunity to act first is never a bad thing, but nothing is guaranteed.

So, how is this useful? In this guide, we've compiled almost complete frame data for every single character. The only data we did not manage to complete, due to time restrictions and logistic difficulties, was frame advantage on hit/guard for air attacks (these are variable both from normal to super jump, but also harder to determine because of the less exact nature of air-to-air combat, and the exigencies of air recovery).

What is here, however, should be a treasure trove to the novice gamer and the hardened tournament veteran alike.

CAPTAIN AMERICA

"A LOT OF PEOPLE LOOK UP TO ME. NOW I'M GONNA SHOW YOU WHY!"

BIO

REAL NAME

STEVEN "STEVE" ROGERS

OCCUPATION

SOLDIER, ADVENTURER

ABILITIES

EXTREMELY PROFICIENT IN BOXING, JUDO, AIKIDO, AND VARIOUS OTHER FIGHTING DISCIPLINES. HE ALSO UTILIZES WEAPONS-BASED FIGHTING STYLES USING HIS SHIELD.

WEAPONS

A SHIELD MADE FROM VIBRANIUM ALLOY. IT IS THE ONLY ONE IN EXISTENCE IN THE WORLD.

PROFILE

THE SOLE RECIPIENT OF THE SUPER-SOLDIER SERUM, CAP'S DEEP LOVE FOR HIS COUNTRY AND HIS UNPARALLELED SENSE OF JUSTICE MAKE HIM ONE OF THE MOST RESPECTED HEROES TODAY. HE HAS ALSO BEEN THE LONG-TIME LEADER OF THE AVENGERS, A GROUP DEDICATED TO KEEPING THE WORLD SAFE FROM HARM.

FIRST APPEARANCE

CAPTAIN AMERICA COMICS #1 (1941)

POWER GRID

3	INTELLIGENCE
3	STRENGTH
2	SPEED
3	STAMINA
1	ENERGY PROJECTION
6	FIGHTING ABILITY

*This is biographical, and does not represent an evaluation of the character's in-game combat potential.

ALTERNATE COSTUMES

PS3: ⓧ Xbox 360: Ⓐ

PS3: □ Xbox 360: Ⓧ

PS3: △ Xbox 360: Ⓨ

PS3: R1 Xbox 360: RB

ATTACK SET

STANDING BASIC ATTACKS

Screen	Command	Hits	Damage	Startup	Active	Recovery	Advantage on Hit	Advantage if Guarded	Notes
1	Standing Ⓛ	1	46,000	5	3	12	0	-2	—
2	Standing Ⓜ	1	68,000	10	2	20	-2	-4	—
3	Standing Ⓗ	1	80,000	16	4	24	-4	-6	⇩⬂⇨ + P1 or P2
4	Ⓢ	1	90,000	10	4	22	—	-4	Launcher attack, not special- or hyper combo-cancelable

1

2

3

4

CROUCHING BASIC ATTACKS

Screen	Command	Hits	Damage	Startup	Active	Recovery	Advantage on Hit	Advantage if Guarded	Notes
1	Crouching Ⓛ	1	30,000	4	3	15	-3	-5	Low attack
2	Crouching Ⓜ	1	48,000	9	4	19	-3	-5	—
3	Crouching Ⓗ	1	75,000	13	4	26	—	-8	Low attack, knocks down

1

2

3

AERIAL BASIC ATTACKS

Screen	Command	Hits	Damage	Startup	Active	Recovery	Notes
1	Air Ⓛ	1	50,000	5	3	14	Overhead attack
2	Air Ⓜ	1	65,000	9	4	20	Overhead attack
3	Air Ⓗ	1	70,000	12	10	16	Overhead attack
4	Air Ⓢ	1	85,000	15	5	21	Overhead attack, causes flying screen if used in launcher combo

1

2

3

4

COMMAND ATTACKS

Screen	Command	Hits	Damage	Startup	Active	Recovery	Advantage on Hit	Advantage if Guarded	Notes
1	(during st. M hit) M	1	48,000	9	4	19	-2	-5	—
2	Air ⇧ + H	1	73,000	10	3	23	—	—	Overhead attack
3	Air ⇩ + H	1	70,000	11	5	16	—	—	Overhead attack

1

2

3

AS A PARTNER-CROSSOVER ASSISTS

Screen	Type	P1+P2 Crossover Combination Hyper Combo	Description	Hits	Damage	Startup	Active	Recovery (this crossover assist)	Recovery (other partner)	Notes
1	α – Alpha	Hyper Charging Star	Shield Slash M	2	95,000	41	—	131	101	Shield is in play for 51 frames, each hit of Shield Slash has 5 low priority durability points
2	β – Beta	Hyper Stars & Stripes	Stars & Stripes H	3	108,300	29	12	145	115	Knocks down
3	γ – Gamma	Hyper Charging Star	Charging Star M	3	108,300	29	11	138	108	Knocks down

1

2

3

CAPTAIN AMERICA

SPECIAL MOVES

Screen	Name	Command	Hits	Damage	Startup	Active	Recovery	Advantage on Hit	Advantage if Guarded	Notes
1	Shield Slash L	↓↘→ + L	2	95,000	21	—	30	—	—	Each hit of Shield Slash has 5 low priority durability points, shield is in play for 52 frames if Captain America does not move
2	Shield Slash M	↓↘→ + M	2	95,000	17	—	34	—	—	Each hit of Shield Slash has 5 low priority durability points, shield is in play for 51 frames if Captain America does not move
3	Shield Slash H	↓↘→ + H	2	95,000	13	—	38	—	—	Each hit of Shield Slash has 5 low priority durability points, shield is in play for 50 frames if Captain America does not move
4,5,6	Air Shield Slash	(in air) ↓↘→ + ATK	2	95,000	15	—	Until grounded, 1 frame ground recovery	—	—	Each hit of Shield Slash has 5 low priority durability points, shield is in play for 51 frames if Captain America does not move
7	Stars & Stripes L	→↓↘ + L	1	80,000	5	5	44	-25	-27	Invincible from frames 1-4, knocks down
	Stars & Stripes M	→↓↘ + M	2	104,500	5	11	50	-32	-39	Invincible from frames 1-6, knocks down
	Stars & Stripes H	→↓↘ + H	3	135,400	5	12	57	-37	-47	Invincible from frames 1-9, knocks down
8	Charging Star L	↓↙← + L	1	100,000	5	9	30	—	-17	Nullifies all low and medium priority projectiles during frames 4-18, knocks down
	Charging Star M	↓↙← + M	2	133,000	5	11	35	-12	-22	Nullifies all low and medium priority projectiles during frames 4-18, knocks down
	Charging Star H	↓↙← + H	3	162,500	5	13	43	—	-17	Nullifies all low and medium priority projectiles during frames 4-18, knocks down
9	Backflip	S + ATK	—	—	—	34	—	—	—	Can pass through opponents

Shield Slash L: The Shield Slash attacks are unique projectiles that return back to Captain America after flying a set distance forward—the shield projectile hits both on the way forward and on the way back. The returning hit leaves you at a large frame advantage, allowing you to use Shield Slash to start combos if distances permit. Against airborne opponents the returning hit of Shield Slash knocks an opponent back toward Captain America, forming the basis of most of his combos.

If the shield projectile runs out of durability points by clashing with another projectile it instantly returns back to Captain America without an active hitbox; losing all durability points essentially destroys the shield projectile. If your opponent makes contact with you while your shield is in transit, the shield will no longer hit your foe on its return trip. The shield projectile essentially disappears if Captain America guards or gets hit. This is true for all versions of Shield Slash. Be sure not to cancel basic attacks into any versions of Shield Slash against a guarding opponent, as it is very unsafe. The initial hit of Shield Slash does not produce nearly enough guardstun to prevent your opponent from hitting you before you recover. This also prevents the shield from hitting on its way back!

Shield Slash L has the slowest startup speed and fastest recovery of all versions of the attack. Shield Slash L is the version that leaves Captain America with the highest possible frame advantage, allowing for more situations where it is possible to start a combo on a standing opponent. Shield Slash L is also the only version of the attack that reaches all the way across the screen. The optimal range to use Shield Slash L is at the distance from which both hits of the shield projectile register as a combo; about three-fourths of the screen away, or a single forward dash away from full-screen distance.

Shield Slash M: Shield Slash M has faster startup time and slower recovery time compared to Shield Slash L. The faster startup and higher-off-the-ground projectile make it easier to use, but the increased recovery also makes it more difficult to start combos.

Shield Slash H: Shield Slash H travels upwards at an angle, but the projectile initially appears much too low to reliably anti-air opponents. If your opponent jumps toward you from very far away Shield Slash H can anti-air well, and it will also lead to a full combo.

Air Shield Slash L: When performed as low as possible, Air Shield Slashes have significantly less recovery compared to their ground versions, making them much easier to start combos with or to set up Backflip cross-ups. Air Shield Slashes have a height restriction preventing you from performing them from too low, so fancy tricks like performing Air Shield Slash with ↓↘→↗ + ATK won't help you.

Air Shield Slash L is great for jumping forward over projectiles and counterattacking with one of your own. Captain America cannot keep up with the projectile durability point output that many other characters have, so tactics like this become necessary until you get into range for Charging Star H. In juggle combos, Air Shield Slash L is used when you need to lower the height of your opponent in order to continue the combo.

Air Shield Slash M: Air Shield Slash M is primarily used in combos, but can also be used to attack opponents relying mid-air zoning tactics.

Air Shield Slash H: Air Shield Slash H is rarely used, but can sometimes be effective to counter opponents relying on projectiles fired from super jump height.

Stars & Stripes: Stars & Stripes is a fast attack that is completely invincible, starting from the first frame. This is a great attack to use defensively. If your opponent has any small holes in their offense you can hit them using the invincibility of Stars & Stripes!

Stars & Stripes is very unsafe if guarded, however. If you aren't 100% sure that it will hit your opponent, try to cover yourself by calling a crossover assist, then immediately perform Stars & Stripes M. Stars & Stripes L runs out of invincible frames before it hits an opponent, and Stars & Stripes H has far too much recovery to easily cover up with a crossover assist. If your opponent is wary of running into Stars & Stripes and stops their offense short to guard, take advantage of the situation by attacking your opponent with basic attacks or throws instead of using Stars & Stripes!

Charging Star: Charging Star nullifies enemy projectiles during its active frames. This makes it great for blowing through tons of ranged attacks and hitting an opponent.

Charging Star L doesn't travel far, making it a safe way to advance forward against an opponent who is across the screen, firing projectiles. Instead of trying to jump over projectiles or guarding them from full-screen, use Charging Star L to safely move through them and gain a little ground.

Charging Star H is very fast and has the most range, but still only reaches about halfway across the screen. Still, against zoning characters, you'll want to safely work your way into range of Charging Star H to be able to counter their zoning tactics. If you hit your opponent you can perform a delayed hyper combo-cancel to Hyper Charging Star for a quick 420,400 damage. The timing on this is a little tricky, because it is easy to perform the cancel too early as well as too late. Practice this combo in training mode!

All Charging Star attacks are very unsafe if guarded. Calling a long ranged assist like Arthur—β immediately before using Charging Star will keep your opponent guarding during your recovery and allow you to keep attacking afterward.

Backflip: Backflip allows you to flip to the other side of an opponent, passing straight through them. This gives you the ability to set up cross-ups using crossover assists. Against a guarding opponent, call a crossover assist immediately before performing Backflip to force your opponent to guard in the opposite direction. If your opponent does not react in time to guard in the proper direction, you can begin a combo starting from the assist's hit!

Backflip is not invincible at all. If your opponent sticks out any attack your Backflip can be punished by a combo. It is also unsafe if canceled into from any basic attack; no basic attacks produce enough guardstun to prevent your opponent from punishing your Backflip. Always use a crossover assist in tandem with Backflip; not only to cross up opponents, but to make it a safe move to use.

HYPER COMBOS

Screen	Name	Command	Hits	Damage	Startup	Active	Recovery	Advantage on Hit	Advantage if Guarded	Notes
1	Hyper Stars & Stripes	⇨⇩⬂ + ATK ATK	5	290,800	12+0	11(7)12(7)13	38	-2	-25	Invincible from frames 1-24
2	Hyper Charging Star	⇩⬃⇦ + ATK ATK	10	274,100	5+2	11	45	—	-23	Destroys projectiles/ignores beams from frames 1-23, unrecoverable knockdown
3	Final Justice (Level 3 Hyper Combo)	⇩⬂⇨ + ATK ATK	8	440,000	22+2	16	18	—	-12	Invincible from frames 16-36, unrecoverable knockdown

Hyper Stars & Stripes: Hyper Stars & Stripes has a lot of invincible frames that you can use to blow through attacks. If you don't predict your opponent correctly, and your Hyper Stars & Stripes is guarded, you can team hyper combo to another character to keep Captain America safe.

Hyper Charging Star: Hyper Charging Star is a useful hyper combo that is invincible to all projectiles from the first frame. Unlike most projectile-invulnerable attacks, hyper charging star is also invincible to projectile-based hyper combos! Use Hyper Charging Star on reaction to the super freeze animation of an opponent's projectile hyper combo if you're within range—about two-thirds of the screen distance. If you hit with the very edge of Hyper Charging Star's range, you'll still get all ten hits for full damage.

Hyper Charging Star is Captain America's main combo ender. In almost all of your combos you'll want to juggle your opponent around ground level, so you can tack on a Hyper Charging Star for considerably more damage than no-meter combos can inflict. Each hit of Hyper Charging Star knocks your foe downward and very far away. This makes it very difficult to team hyper combo to another character afterwards, unless the partner character has an OTG-capable hyper combo.

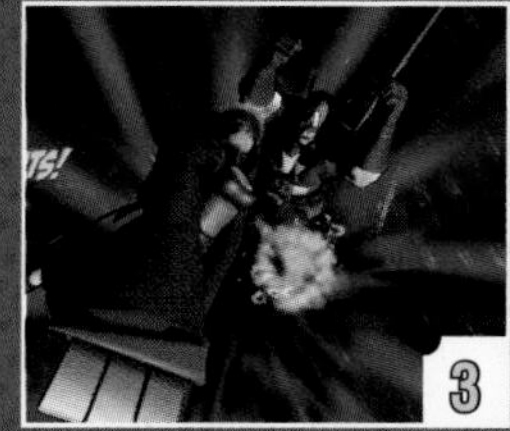

Final Justice: Level 3 hyper combos are not subject to damage scaling, so substituting Final Justice in for Hyper Charging Star at the end of a combo is a great way to add a lot of damage. Final Justice also has the dubious distinction of being one of the only level 3 hyper combos in the game that isn't invincible on the first frame. This limits its usage strictly to combos.

BATTLE PLAN

OVERVIEW

VITALITY: 1,050,000

CHAIN COMBO ARCHETYPE: MARVEL SERIES

X-Factor	Lv.1	Lv.2	Lv.3
Damage	130%	160%	190%
Speed	105%	110%	115%

Your goal with Captain America is to get within range to cross up your opponent with Backflip, while still having access to your primary crossover assist.

Why is this a good strategy?

Backflip can be used to flip to the other side of an opponent. Used in tandem with a crossover assist, this allows you to cross up your adversary with the assist attack and begin a combo.

Backflip cross-ups are the only reliable method for Captain America to attack an opponent and force damage; he has no overhead, you can't realistically base his gameplan around chip damage, and he has no great way to counter opponents that try to throw escape.

Captain America's zoning tools aren't strong enough to be solely relied upon, so attacking opponents is usually the more reliable option.

How does one get within Backflip range while still having access to a crossover assist?

Using Charging Star L to safely pass through projectiles from long range.

Jumping forward and using Air Shield Slash L to evade attacks and create some offensive momentum.

Using Charging Star H to punish mid range zoning attacks.

Forcing your opponent to guard or get hit by the returning hit of a Shield Slash.

Pushing your foe to the corner.

"I WILL ALWAYS FIGHT FOR WHAT'S RIGHT - NO MATTER WHAT!"

ON THE GROUND

Charging Star completely nullifies the projectiles of a zoning character. Get within range and counter any projectiles your opponent tries to throw out!

Use the invincibility of Stars & Stripes to get you out of sticky defensive situations. The threat of Stars & Stripes should cause opponents to stop their offense and guard, giving you the opportunity to strike!

Used from its optimal range, the two hits of Shield Slash produce a lot of guardstun on your opponent. Use a long ranged crossover assist to keep your offense moving and push your opponent to the corner!

Captain America best fills the role of either meter-builder or dedicated crossover assist character on a team. Captain America builds meter quickly with Shield Slash pressure and doesn't have many chances to use it effectively. As a dedicated assist character, Captain America supports teams with his Shield Slash—one of the more useful assists in the game.

The simplest way to get within cross-up Backflip range is to make contact with the return path of Shield Slash L or M. This gives you massive frame advantage on both hit or guard, plenty of time to dash forward and press a basic attack button simultaneously with P1orP2, then cancel the basic attack into Backflip to cross up your opponent. If you predict your foe will use advancing guard against the basic attack, skip the basic attack entirely and Backflip behind your adversary while they are expecting to guard something; your crossover assist will force them to guard in the opposite direction. If your opponent uses advancing guard against the second hit of Shield Slash you'll get pushed away and lose the mix-up situation—call your crossover assist while wavedashing forward and concentrate on pushing your opponent to the corner.

Captain America can give zoning characters a lot of trouble with his projectile-destroying Charging Star attack. From afar, use Charging Star L to go through projectiles safely while slowly gaining ground. When you work your way into range of Charging Star H it becomes much more risky for your opponent to continue to throw projectiles. Charging Star H can be performed on reaction to most non-beam projectiles to blow through and hit your challenger, before hyper combo-canceling into Hyper Charging Star or Final Justice for very good damage!

Beam projectiles are much more difficult to react to, so you'll have to make educated guesses on when to go in with Charging Star H. To mitigate the risk, call a long ranged crossover assist immediately before using Charging Star H to keep your opponent in guardstun for longer.

Unlike almost every other character in the game, Captain America's combos get substantially *weaker* against a cornered opponent! Shield Slash juggles do not knock an opponent backwards the requisite distance, and the shield's returning hit doesn't make contact until much later because it is off of the screen. Without any combo-friendly tools like wall bounces, ground bounces, or OTG-capable attacks to do respectable damage in the corner you'll need an OTG-capable crossover assist handy. As an alternative, you can begin a combo with a Backflip cross-up to bring your opponent out into mid-screen again!

On defense Captain America is better off than most characters, simply by virtue of having the invincible Stars & Stripes attack. However, due to the large risk in using the attack, you're generally better off simply using advancing guard and pushing your opponent away. If your foe manages to stick to you, despite your attempts to use advancing guard, then it is time to consider using Stars & Stripes to counter their attacks. Opponents trying to bait out a Stars & Stripes will often cut their offense short and guard—try to predict when this will happen and surprise your opponent with a Backflip cross-up! This is even more risky than using Stars & Stripes: if your opponent attacks they will likely hit both you and your crossover assist for a combo!

UP IN THE AIR

Air Shield Slash L performed as low as possible results in a huge amount of frame advantage.

If your opponent doesn't use advancing guard, you can land two air Ⓜ attacks within the same jump. This double-overhead attack is difficult to guard against!

Air Ⓗ, ⇧ + Ⓗ and ⇩ + Ⓗ are strong air-to-air attacks for all angles.

Captain America lacks any aerial movement options to give you an easier time in establishing Backflip range. The only way to alter Captain America's air trajectory is to use Air Shield Slash, which causes Captain America to slowly drop straight down from his current position.

Air Shield Slash L performed as low as possible is arguably Captain America's strongest asset outside of Backflip cross-ups. While jumping before using a Shield Slash makes its total startup time much slower than any of the ground versions, the recovery finishes as soon as Captain America touches the ground. This makes low Air Shield Slashes much safer to attack with, in addition to drastically increasing the frame advantage. When jockeying for position to establish cross-up Backflip range, use low Air Shield Slashes as often as you can get away with them.

If you predict your opponent will try to jump toward you to prevent you, use a low Air Shield Slash M instead. If it hits your opponent out of the air you can transition into a full combo!

Captain America has a strong set of basic air attacks for all purposes. Air Ⓢ covers a huge area of the screen, and is a good go-to attack whenever you're in the air. Air Ⓗ, ⇧ + Ⓗ, and ⇩ + Ⓗ are all great air-to-air attacks, provided you use the proper angle for the situation. Air Ⓜ is a strong attack to use when jumping toward a grounded opponent. If you attack the top of the opposing character's head and they do not use advancing guard, you have time to hit them with a second air Ⓜ before landing for a nasty surprise overhead attack!

COMBO USAGE

I. (MID-SCREEN REQUIRED) CR. Ⓛ, ST. Ⓜ, ST. Ⓗ, Ⓢ CANCEL ⇨ SUPER JUMP, AIR Ⓜ, ↓ + Ⓗ CANCEL ⇨ ↓ ↘ → + Ⓛ, LAND, JUMP FORWARD, AIR Ⓜ, Ⓗ CANCEL ⇨ ↓ ↘ → + Ⓜ, LAND, ST. Ⓗ, CANCEL ⇨ ↓ ↙ ← + Ⓛ CANCEL ⇨ ↓ ↙ ← + ATK ATK

(625,800 damage) Captain America can inflict very good damage against a mid-screen opponent with this cool-looking combo! After hitting the launcher, delay the initial air Ⓜ to get your opponent at the right height for the rest of the combo to work. Against very small characters you may want to use air Ⓗ instead of ↓ + Ⓗ if the combo doesn't seem to be working correctly. Finally, delay hyper combo-canceling the Charging Star L to get the Hyper Charging Star to juggle more consistently.

If your initial attacks are guarded, simply end with the standing Ⓗ attack to push yourself out to a safe distance. If your opponent isn't using advancing guard, use this as a chance to call a crossover assist and cancel into Backflip! Replacing Hyper Charging Star with Final Justice at the end of the combo inflicts 859,400 damage.

II. (MID-SCREEN REQUIRED, AIRBORNE OPPONENT) ↓ ↘ → + Ⓗ, JUMP FORWARD, AIR Ⓜ, Ⓗ CANCEL ⇨ ↓ ↘ → + Ⓜ, LAND, JUMP FORWARD, AIR Ⓜ, ↓ + Ⓗ CANCEL ⇨ ↓ ↘ → + Ⓛ, LAND, ST. Ⓗ CANCEL ⇨ ↓ ↙ ← + Ⓛ CANCEL ⇨ ↓ ↙ ← + ATK ATK

(584,200 damage) If you predict that a mid-screen opponent is going to jump toward you, Shield Slash H can be used to anti-air them and start a combo. However, Shield Slash H isn't a particularly reliable anti-air. It works much better if performed in anticipation and if an opponent comes in from farther away.

The exact same combo can be performed from a low Air Shield Slash M against an airborne opponent. Air Shield Slash L performed low to the ground is a staple of Captain America's offense, and can be mixed up with a low Air Shield Slash M if the opponent attempts to jump over it and attack.

III. CR. Ⓛ, ST. Ⓜ, ST. Ⓗ, Ⓢ CANCEL ⇨ SUPER JUMP, AIR Ⓜ, Ⓜ, Ⓗ, ↓ + Ⓗ, Ⓢ

(327,500 damage) Captain America's combos quickly become weaker against a cornered opponent. To perform better combos in this situation you'll need to either cross a cornered opponent up using Backflip, or have an OTG-capable assist available on your team. If neither of these conditions is met, you may want to use a team aerial combo starter for a chance for more substantial damage.

IV. P1 or P2, Ⓢ + ATK, ST. Ⓜ, ST. Ⓜ, ST. Ⓗ, Ⓢ CANCEL ⇨ SUPER JUMP, AIR Ⓜ, ↓ + Ⓗ CANCEL ⇨ ↓ ↘ → + Ⓛ, LAND, JUMP FORWARD, AIR Ⓜ, Ⓗ CANCEL ⇨ ↓ ↘ → + Ⓜ, LAND, ST. Ⓗ, CANCEL ⇨ ↓ ↙ ← + Ⓛ CANCEL ⇨ ↓ ↙ ← + ATK ATK

(601,400 damage, Arthur—β) This is a combo from a Backflip cross-up using a crossover assist. Backflip cross-ups comprise Captain America's main offensive threat, and are also a good way to get an opponent out of the corner so that you can do strong damage.

V. (MID-SCREEN REQUIRED) ↓ ↙ ← + Ⓗ CANCEL ⇨, JUMP, AIR Ⓜ, Ⓗ CANCEL ⇨ ↓ ↘ → + Ⓜ, LAND, JUMP, AIR Ⓜ, Ⓗ CANCEL ⇨ ↓ ↘ → + Ⓜ, LAND, ST. Ⓗ CANCEL ⇨ ↓ ↙ ← + Ⓛ CANCEL ⇨ ↓ ↙ ← + ATK ATK

(869,500 damage, level 1 X-Factor) Charging Star H is a huge threat to zoning opponents because of its ability to destroy projectiles, even if it typically doesn't lead to much more than 400,000 damage. Canceling it into X-Factor allows you to get much more damage, potentially enough to K.O. certain characters outright!

ASSISTS

Multi-hit projectile-using crossover assists like Arthur—β fill many roles in Captain America's gameplan.

OTG-capable assists substantially increase your combo damage against cornered opponents.

Captain America—α fires a multi-hit projectile attack which is a strong asset to any team.

Of Captain America's three assist types, choosing Shield Slash is essentially a no-brainer. Charging Star does not retain its projectile-destroying properties, and Stars & Stripes does not have invincibility at all as an assist. Next to these two disappointing assist types, Shield Slash is the most useful one by default! Luckily, Shield Slash is a great asset to any team, since multi-hit projectiles are always useful to every character. The unique juggle properties of Shield Slash M differentiate this assist from others like Arthur—β or powered-up Zero—β, adding a lot of potential damage to mid-screen combos.

Despite having a multi-hitting projectile, Captain America benefits most from having one as an assist. Arthur—β and powered-up Zero—β perform vital roles for Captain America, like allowing him to easily start combos using Backflip cross-ups, covering up the recovery of a guarded Charging Star H, and covering up holes between Shield Slash attacks.

Any OTG-capable crossover assist will allow you to nearly double the damage from your corner combos. OTG-capable assists with fast startup times like Deadpool—β and Wesker—β also allow you to start combos using a backwards air throw. The low-hitting Wesker attack will also allow you to potentially set up unguardable situations using air Ⓢ, greatly bolstering your offensive capabilities.

ADVANCED TACTICS

COUNTERING OPPONENT HYPER COMBOS

Between fully-invincible, close ranged Hyper Stars & Stripes and the projectile-invincible long ranged Hyper Charging Star, you have an answer to almost every situation where your opponent performs a hyper combo outside of a combo. For example, if a Ryu player tries to punish your attempt to Charging Star L through a Hadoken from afar with a Shinku Hadoken, you can hyper combo-cancel into Hyper Charging Star to blow through the Shinku Hadoken!

Almost all hyper combos that aren't considered projectiles will be within range of Hyper Stars & Stripes. For example, if a Chun-Li player attempts to use the invincibility of Hoyokusen to go through a Shield Slash, you can react to the super freeze cutscene and respond in turn with a hyper combo-cancel into Hyper Stars & Stripes to knock Chun-Li out of her attack!

Of course, using these hyper combos for their invincibility shouldn't be restricted to countering other hyper combos—these are just much easier to react to.

Many characters rely on hyper combos used outside of combos…

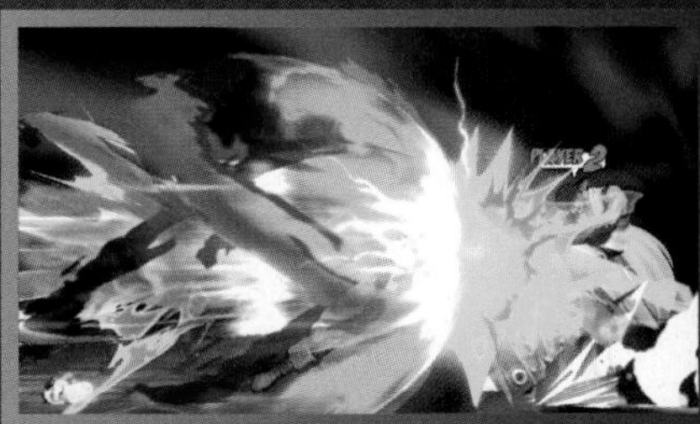

…but the invincibility of Captain America's hyper combos can nullify a lot of these tactics!

COMBO APPENDIX

GENERAL EXECUTION TIPS

After hitting a launcher attack, delay hitting the initial air Ⓜ to allow your opponent to reach the proper height.

After hitting a Charging Star, delay the hyper combo-cancel as much as possible without allowing the opponent to air recover.

Requirements (Position, meter, etc.)	Notes	Command Sequence	Damage
Wesker—β	Same combo works with both air throws	Backwards throw, P1 or P2, ⇩⇘⇨ + Ⓗ, jump forward, air Ⓜ, Ⓗ CANCEL ⇩⇘⇨ + Ⓜ, land, st. Ⓗ CANCEL ⇩⇙⇦ + Ⓛ CANCEL ⇩⇙⇦ + ATK ATK	504,100
Mid-screen only	Shield Slash must hit at opponent at a very specific range for this combo to work. Shield Slash L can also start the same combo	⇩⇘⇨ + Ⓜ, dash, st. Ⓛ, st. Ⓜ, st. Ⓗ, Ⓢ CANCEL super jump, air Ⓜ, ⇩ + Ⓗ CANCEL ⇩⇘⇨ + Ⓛ, land, jump forward, air Ⓜ, Ⓗ CANCEL ⇩⇘⇨ + Ⓜ, land, st. Ⓗ, CANCEL ⇩⇙⇦ + Ⓛ CANCEL ⇩⇙⇦ + ATK ATK	626,800
—	Combo from Charging Star H; very useful against zoning characters. Delay the hyper combo-cancel for as long as you can without allowing the opponent to air recover to successfully hit the Hyper Charging Star.	⇩⇙⇦ + Ⓗ CANCEL ⇩⇙⇦ + ATK ATK	420,400
Corner required, Deadpool—β	—	Cr. Ⓛ, st. Ⓜ, st. Ⓗ, Ⓢ CANCEL super jump, air Ⓜ, Ⓜ, Ⓗ, ⇩ + Ⓗ, Ⓢ, land, P1 or P2, st. Ⓗ CANCEL ⇩⇙⇦ + Ⓛ CANCEL ⇩⇙⇦ + ATK ATK	616,800
Mid-screen required, Deadpool—β	It is nearly impossible to start a combo from Captain America's forward air throw; use backwards air throw instead if you have a fast OTG-capable crossover assist	Backwards air throw, P1 or P2, land, ⇩⇘⇨ + Ⓗ, jump forward, air Ⓜ, Ⓗ CANCEL ⇩⇘⇨ + Ⓜ, land, st. Ⓗ CANCEL ⇩⇙⇦ + Ⓛ CANCEL ⇩⇙⇦ + ATK ATK	495,100

DEADPOOL

BIO

REAL NAME

WADE WILSON

OCCUPATION

MERCENARY

ABILITIES

A HEALING FACTOR COUPLED WITH ENHANCED PHYSICAL CONDITIONING. HE IS ALSO A SPECIALIST IN CLOSE-QUARTER COMBAT, AND HIS ASSASSINATION SKILLS ARE UNPARALLELED.

WEAPONS

USES VARIOUS WEAPONS INCLUDING HANDGUNS, MACHINE GUNS, GRENADES, SWORDS, NUNCHAKU, ETC. HE ALSO HAS A TELEPORTING DEVICE ON HIS BELT, BUT IT TENDS TO MALFUNCTION EASILY.

PROFILE

TO CURE HIS TERMINAL LUNG CANCER, WADE ATTEMPTED TO OBTAIN MUTANT POWERS ARTIFICIALLY. HOWEVER, THE SIDE EFFECTS OF THE PROCEDURE DISFIGURED HIM AND ALSO CAUSED PSYCHOLOGICAL DAMAGE. ALTHOUGH HE LOVES HAVING CHEERFUL CONVERSATIONS, BECAUSE OF HIS MADNESS NO ONE REALLY KNOWS WHAT HE'S SAYING.

FIRST APPEARANCE

THE NEW MUTANTS #98 (1990)

POWER GRID

2	INTELLIGENCE
3	STRENGTH
2	SPEED
4	STAMINA
1	ENERGY PROJECTION
6	FIGHTING ABILITY

*This is biographical, and does not represent an evaluation of the character's in-game combat potential.

ALTERNATE COSTUMES

PS3: ✕ Xbox 360: A	PS3: □ Xbox 360: X	PS3: △ Xbox 360: Y	PS3: R1 Xbox 360: RB

ATTACK SET

STANDING BASIC ATTACKS

Screen	Command	Hits	Damage	Startup	Active	Recovery	Advantage on Hit	Advantage if Guarded	Notes
1	Standing (L)	1	43,000	4	3	12	-2	-3	—
2	Standing (M)	2	63,000	8	6	17	-3	-4	—
3	Standing (H)	1	80,000	11	4	19	+3	-1	Knocks down, ⇩ ⇘ ⇨ + P1onP2 snap back
4	(S)	1	80,000	5	6	34	—	-18	Launcher, not special or hyper combo cancelable

CROUCHING BASIC ATTACKS

Screen	Command	Hits	Damage	Startup	Active	Recovery	Advantage on Hit	Advantage if Guarded	Notes
1	Crouching (L)	1	37,000	5	2	14	-3	-4	Low attack
2	Crouching (M)	1	60,000	7	3	19	-5	-5	Low attack, slightly launches opponent
3	Crouching (H)	1	70,000	12	13	19	—	-10	Low attack, knocks down

AERIAL BASIC ATTACKS

Screen	Command	Hits	Damage	Startup	Active	Recovery	Notes
1	Air (L)	1	44,000	5	3	15	Overhead attack
2	Air (M)	1	60,000	8	3	22	Overhead attack
3	Air (H)	1	75,000	12	8	11	Overhead attack
4	Air (S)	1	80,000	13	3	20	Overhead attack, unrecoverable knockdown when used in air combo after (S) launcher

COMMAND ATTACKS

Screen	Command	Hits	Damage	Startup	Active	Recovery	Advantage on Hit	Advantage if Guarded	Notes
1	⇨ + Ⓜ	2	63,000	25	7	14	—	+3	Overhead, unrecoverable knockdown, chains into Ⓢ
2	Select button	1	10,000	10	5	95	-74	-75	Cancelable into special moves, hyper combos, and Ⓢ
3	Jump backwards against wall, then press ⇗	—	—	8	—	—	—	—	Performs a wall jump, may initiate aerial attacks or movements after 8th frame

DEADPOOL

AS A PARTNER—CROSSOVER ASSISTS

Screen	Type	P1+P2 Crossover Combination Hyper Combo	Description	Hits	Damage	Startup	Active	Recovery (this crossover assist)	Recovery (other partner)	Notes
1	α – Alpha	Happy-Happy Trigger	Quick Work L	1	90,000	37	4	126	96	Ignores hitstun deterioration, spinning knockdown
2	β – Beta	Happy-Happy Trigger	Katana-Rama! H	1	70,000	37	3	122	92	OTG-capable, ground bounce
3	γ – Gamma	Happy-Happy Trigger	Trigger Happy H	10	97,300	39	21	112	82	Each projectile has 1 low priority durability point

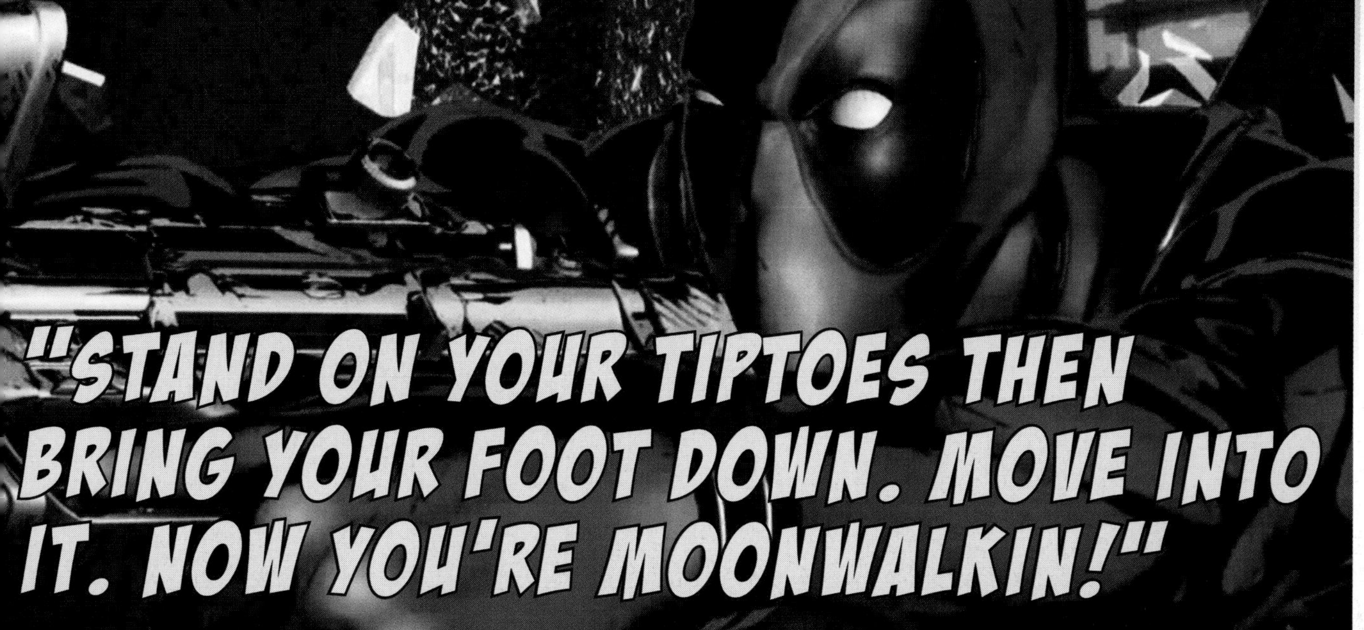

"STAND ON YOUR TIPTOES THEN BRING YOUR FOOT DOWN. MOVE INTO IT. NOW YOU'RE MOONWALKIN!"

SPECIAL MOVES

Screen	Name	Command	Hits	Damage	Startup	Active	Recovery	Advantage on Hit	Advantage if Guarded	Notes
1,2,3	Trigger Happy	⇩ ⇘ ⇨ + ATK	10	97,300	15	21	30	-8	-14	Each projectile has 0.8 low priority durability points
4	Air Trigger Happy L	(in air) ⇩ ⇘ ⇨ + Ⓛ	10	97,300	15	21	20	—	—	OTG-capable, each projectile has 1 low priority durability point
5	Air Trigger Happy M	(in air) ⇩ ⇘ ⇨ + Ⓜ	10	97,300	15	21	20	—	—	Each projectile has 0.8 low priority durability points
6	Air Trigger Happy H	(in air) ⇩ ⇘ ⇨ + Ⓗ	10	97,300	15	21	20	—	—	Each projectile has 0.8 low priority durability points
7	Ninja Gift L (in air OK)	(During Trigger Happy) Ⓛ	3	108,300	10	—	35	-5	-9	Can cancel Trigger Happy from frames 3-15, each projectile has 2 low priority durability points
8	Ninja Gift M (in air OK)	(During Trigger Happy) Ⓜ	1	80,000	10	—	35	—	+5	Can cancel Trigger Happy from frames 3-15, grenade detonates on contact or after 108 frames, projectile has 1 medium priority durability point
9	Ninja Gift H (in air OK)	(During Trigger Happy) Ⓗ	1	10,000	10	—	35	—	-6	Can cancel Trigger Happy from frames 3-15, projectile has 1 low priority durability point, places airborne opponent in special unrecoverable knockdown state during which all attacks are OTG-capable
10	Quick Work L	⇩ ⇙ ⇦ + Ⓛ	1	90,000	13	4	34	—	-16	Low attack, spinning knockdown, ignores hitstun deterioration
	Quick Work M	⇩ ⇙ ⇦ + Ⓜ	1	110,000	18	4	34	—	-16	Low attack, spinning knockdown, ignores hitstun deterioration
	Quick Work H	⇩ ⇙ ⇦ + Ⓗ	1	130,000	23	4	34	—	-16	Low attack, spinning knockdown, ignores hitstun deterioration
11	Katana-Rama! L	⇨ ⇩ ⇘ + Ⓛ	1	70,000	13	3	30	+8	-11	Knocks down
12	Katana-Rama! M	⇨ ⇩ ⇘ + Ⓜ	1	70,000	13	3	30	—	-11	Knocks down
13	Katana-Rama! H	⇨ ⇩ ⇘ + Ⓗ	1	70,000	13	3	30	—	-11	OTG-capable, ground bounce
14	Chimichangas!!	(During Katana-Rama!) Ⓗ	1	63,000	13	3	30	—	-11	Can cancel Katana-Rama! on hit/block during frames 15-20, wall bounce
15	TELEPORT	⇦ ⇩ ⇙ + ATK	—	—	18	—	12	—	—	Every third teleport Deadpool's teleporter will malfunction (see description)
16	TELEPORT Malfunction	—	1	100,000 (5,800 to Deadpool)	18	2	31	—	—	Unrecoverable knockdown on both characters, OTG-capable

Trigger Happy: Deadpool fires ten shots in variable directions: ⇩ ⇘ ⇨ + Ⓛ and Ⓜ fire horizontal shots low and high, while ⇩ ⇘ ⇨ + Ⓗ fires upward at an angle. Trigger Happy L and M act as long range attacks used preemptively to stop forward dashes, while also dealing chip damage. The stream of multiple hits makes it easy to verify whether the shots have hit or not; if they hit, cancel into Happy-Happy Trigger for an easy long range combo. Trigger Happy H acts as a hindrance to super jumps and flight, but only at long distances. Unfortunately, canceling into Happy-Happy Trigger does not work in this case. All versions of this attack are unsafe when guarded at close distances. Fire them only at long range. Each bullet also has an extremely low durability rating, so they can't always be relied upon in a firefight. If your opponent tries to counter your shots with a bigger projectile, cancel into Happy-Happy Trigger.

The aerial versions of Trigger Happy are even more effective than the ground versions. The go to attack for your aerial offense with Deadpool should be backward jumping air ⇩ ⇘ ⇨ + Ⓜ, which, when fired just as he falls from a jump, unleashes a sweep of bullets that cover both the ground and air. It also recovers faster than the ground versions of the attack, allowing you to jump and fire it again with little worry. Air ⇩ ⇘ ⇨ + Ⓛ should mainly be used during forward jumps to beat out anti-air attacks and to punish projectiles. A successful hit leads to ***Combo I***. Finally, air ⇩ ⇘ ⇨ + Ⓗ, like the ground version, is meant to be used to catch super jumping or flying enemies.

Ninja Gift: This is a supplement to Trigger Happy. ⇩ ⇘ ⇨ + Ⓛ CANCEL Ⓛ is a safe method of pushing away foes that move towards Deadpool. ⇩ ⇘ ⇨ + Ⓜ CANCEL Ⓜ, tosses a grenade that stays active for a long period of time, enabling you to control the ground while focusing on aerial fire. It also has a high enough durability rating to nullify most incoming projectiles. ⇩ ⇘ ⇨ + Ⓗ CANCEL Ⓗ is the most important of these tools — it throws a shot that incapacitates an opponent momentarily. It's used to preemptively stop anti-air attacks. Just jump forward and throw it when you believe an anti-air is coming. If the attack hits, follow-up with ⇩ ⇙ ⇦ + Ⓗ and transition into ***Combo VI***.

Quick Work: Deadpool slides forward with a katana cut. Use this strictly for combos involving heavy juggles. Hitstun deterioration has no effect on this attack, so it is suitable for a number of long and flashy combinations. In fact, its lack of hitstun loss enables you to juggle with Quick Work indefinitely when in X-Factor level 3, crushing the totality of a foe's vitality in seconds.

11

12

13

14

Katana-Rama!: Another attack used in heavy combos, Chimichangas!! the follow-up to Katana-Rama! causes a wall bounce. This can be used to create unusual combos that can be done from anywhere on the battlefield. The Ⓗ version of Katana-Rama is also OTG-capable and can be used to tack on damage after Deadpool's throws and other unrecoverable knockdowns.

15

16

TELEPORT: This unusual teleport quickly transports Deadpool to a position based on your button layout. If he's facing to the right, Ⓛ transports him to the left end of the screen, Ⓜ to the middle, and Ⓗ to the rightmost edge. These controls are reversed if Deadpool is facing left. TELEPORT is extremely fast and it can be difficult for an opponent to react to it, giving it numerous uses offensively while also offering an easy method of escaping corners. However, every third teleport malfunctions, causing an explosion that deals damage to Deadpool and any nearby foe. Adding further punishment to an already bad situation, Deadpool is knocked into an unrecoverable knockdown after the explosion, leaving him vulnerable to OTG-capable attacks (assuming that your opponent guards the explosion). This is troublesome indeed, because the TELEPORT is a necessary evil due to Deadpool's weak offense. There is one saving grace to the TELEPORT Malfunction, it's OTG-capable and hyper cancelable. If you're really itching to get more uses out of his TELEPORT, end any corner combo with an unrecoverable knockdown and OTG your foe with ⇦⇩⇙ + ATK CANCEL ⇩⇘⇨ + ATK ATK. You'll take a little damage from the explosion, but you'll have two TELEPORT moves to use again.

HYPER COMBOS

Screen	Name	Command	Hits	Damage	Startup	Active	Recovery	Advantage on Hit	Advantage if Guarded	Notes
1	Happy-Happy Trigger (in air OK)	⇩⇘⇨ + ATK ATK	40	238,400	13+1	114	41	-11	-20	Each projectile has 1 high priority durability point, air version is OTG-capable
	Air Happy-Happy Trigger	(in air) ⇩⇘⇨ + ATK ATK	40	238,400	13+1	97	24	-2	-5	Each projectile has 1 high priority durability point
2	Cuttin' Time	⇩⇙⇦ + ATK ATK	5	322,800	15+0	10	35	-17	-23	Frames 11-19 invincible, spinning knockdown
3	4th-Wall Crisis (Level 3 Hyper Combo)	⇨⇩⇘ + ATK ATK	3	400,000	5+1	80	24	—	—	5 frames invincibility, counters all attacks except beams/projectiles, unrecoverable knockdown

1

Happy-Happy Trigger: This is an all-purpose, long range attack. You can hyper combo cancel into it off of Trigger Happy from long distances, react to and counter incoming projectiles, or use it in long air combos. The aerial version is also OTG-capable, a useful property for dealing heavy damage off of Deadpool's throws and unrecoverable knockdowns.

2

Cuttin' Time: This hyper combo inflicts more damage than Happy-Happy Trigger initially but, after heavy damage reduction has occurred during a long combo, it ends up dealing less. Instead, use it to pass through projectiles from just outside of mid range. It has a short invulnerability window that lasts just long enough for this purpose, but this is difficult to time properly. Wait for the projectile to end up right in front of Deadpool, then input the command.

3

4th-Wall Crisis:. An invulnerable level 3 hyper combo that counters any physical attack that makes contact with it. Although this attack is expensive for a defensive hyper combo, it inflicts a ton of damage while leaving an opponent in an unrecoverable knockdown. This enables you to dash forward and OTG the opposing character with Katana-Rama! into an extended combo. Potentially, this can give you the lead if you are behind in the match.

BATTLE PLAN

OVERVIEW

VITALITY: 900,000

CHAIN COMBO ARCHETYPE: HUNTER SERIES

X-Factor	Lv.1	Lv.2	Lv.3
Damage	120%	150%	180%
Speed	110%	120%	130%

Deadpool is a hit & run character. Your goal while using him should be to annoy your foe from a distance to get them to recklessly move in on you then, when you see an opening to call an assist, charge in for a combo, a high attack, low attack, or a throw mix-up.

You should initially keep your distance with Deadpool because:

- **His mobility is poor, making it difficult to stay on top of a guarding opponent.**
- **His air ↓ ↘ → + Ⓜ, though weak against opposing projectile characters, covers a large portion of the screen and shuts down low altitude jumps.**
- **All of his Ninja Gift attacks move him backwards to avoid harm.**
- **The long range ↓ ↘ → + Ⓛ and Ⓜ both lead into ↓ ↘ → + ATK ATK on a successful hit.**
- **Calling assists in combination with a teleport that ends behind the opposing character is nearly impossible to guard.**

This goal is accomplished by:

- **Jumping backwards and firing air ↓ ↘ → + Ⓜ at the peak of Deadpool's jump. Jumping forward and firing air ↓ ↘ → + Ⓜ to punish opposing projectiles.**
- **Performing ↓ ↘ → + Ⓜ, Ⓜ to control the ground while moving backwards.**
- **Super jumping and throwing air ↓ ↘ → + Ⓛ CANCEL ▶ Ⓛ.**
- **Calling an assist when your opponent isn't readily looking for it, then dashing in and starting an attack.**

ON THE GROUND

Use ↓ ↙ → + Ⓗ CANCEL ▶ Ⓗ to escape bad situations. Of course, you shouldn't use it if you're cornered…

Attack with Ninja Gift M to fortify your ability to control space.

Keep your distance and watch your opponent's actions closely. If they try to approach via a forward dash, fire ↓ ↙ → + Ⓛ and check if it hits. If it does, cancel into ↓ ↙ → + ATK ATK for heavy damage. If they're prone to throwing projectiles, those with a low priority durability of 5 or less can be preemptively stopped by firing ↓ ↙ → + Ⓛ. Only three bullets will get through and hit your foe, but you can always hyper cancel into ↓ ↙ → + ATK ATK for additional damage. ↓ ↙ → + Ⓜ is harder to jump over but misses against most crouching characters, use it preemptively only when you think a low altitude jump is coming. Fire ↓ ↙ → + Ⓗ when your opponent super jumps away. If you're ever certain of an incoming jump, attack with **Combo IV** to punish it.

If the opposing player ever finds a gap in your offense and rushes their character in, use ↓ ↙ → + Ⓗ CANCEL ▶ Ⓗ. This moves Deadpool backwards very quickly, causing it to avoid most short range attacks (if done preemptively). A successful hit stuns your foe, leaving them open to a forward dashing **Combo I**. You may opt to use ↓ ↙ → + Ⓛ CANCEL ▶ Ⓛ instead, if your opponent uses an attack that is oddly low to the ground (which can sometimes slip under Ninja Gift H). Another alternative, ↓ ↙ → + Ⓜ CANCEL ▶ Ⓜ, lays a grenade that lingers for several seconds. Use this to keep your opponent's ground movement limited while you return to firing aerial Trigger Happy shots. You can also use the window that the grenade from Ninja Gift H creates as covering fire to move into close range.

At close distances, you will be reliant on assists with Deadpool (see Assists section), but when they aren't available you should focus on keeping your foe grounded with air throws (which lead to **Combo III**). This will condition your opponent into avoiding jumps and allow you to stage a worthwhile ground offense. From there, attack with a throw, **Combo I**, or the → + Ⓜ overhead attack (**Combo V**). → + Ⓜ can be chained into from any attack, including many of the opening attacks in **Combo I**, like crouching Ⓛ x 2. If this short sequence is guarded, halt the remainder of the combo and use → + Ⓜ instead. This may trick your opponent into taking a hit from the overhead, because of the previous low attacks. When the opposing player expects that pattern, go for a delayed **Combo I** again instead of the overhead, or walk up and throw your foe.

Advancing guard can throw many of the preceding patterns out the window, which is why assists are necessary. Without them you'll have to rely on canceling guarded attacks into ↓ ↙ → + Ⓜ CANCEL ▶ Ⓜ, which pushes you away from the opposition, but at least sets a grenade down to block your foe's path while you regain ground. Otherwise, you should retreat back to your long range offense to deal guard damage.

UP IN THE AIR

After sweeping airspace with air ↓↘→ + Ⓜ, use the fast landing period to throw ↓↘→ + Ⓜ CANCEL Ⓜ to cover the ground, fire ↓↘→ + Ⓜ to inflict chip damage, or jump and fire air ↓↘→ + Ⓜ again.

Forward jumping ↓↘→ + Ⓛ is not just a great way to punish projectiles; it also deals heavy guard damage while leaving you at a frame advantage on guard.

Your long range objective should be to shut down your opponent's ground and low altitude aerial movement. This can be done single handedly with air ↓↘→ + Ⓜ, which fires sweeping bullets across the playing field if this is performed just as Deadpool falls from the peak of his jump. Your opponent cannot choose to airdash or move forward with these shots on the screen. Their only recourse is to fire a projectile with a higher durability at you (which isn't difficult, Trigger Happy fires 10 bullets of 1 low priority durability), or super jump away to safety. Though Deadpool's forward jumping range is too short and slow to clear projectiles from a distance, jumping forward and firing a quick ↓↘→ + Ⓛ thrusts his momentum forward slightly while also hitting his foe really early, so early that you can merely react to their projectile and punish it. If the forward momentum puts you within range, you can land and link after the shots with **Combo I**. In rare cases where your foe recovers before the shots hit, the spray of bullets will cover your landing from anti-air attacks. If your opponent tries to super jump away in fear of your gun attacks, fire ↓↘→ + Ⓗ to force them back to the ground.

When you need to super jump away from an onslaught, you can fire the 3-way ↓↘→ + Ⓛ CANCEL Ⓛ shot to cover a retreat. Firing it early during a jump enables you to eventually double jump or act with basic attacks on the way down, making it the safest aerial special move that Deadpool has. His double jump and wall jump are also great for avoiding danger; they offer new avenues of attack. For example, if your opponent corners you, look for a moment to super jump away, then double jump out of the corner. If your foe is focused on stopping your air ↓↘→ + Ⓜ, which is generally done while jumping backwards, jump against a wall to bait out their projectile, then wall jump forward and spray them down with bullets from an air ↓↘→ + Ⓛ.

COMBO USAGE

I. CR. Ⓛ, CR. Ⓛ, CR. Ⓜ, ST. Ⓗ CANCEL ↓↙← + Ⓗ, FORWARD DASH, CR. Ⓜ, ST. Ⓗ CANCEL ↓↙← + Ⓜ, FORWARD DASH, Ⓢ CANCEL SUPER JUMP, EARLY AIR Ⓜ, Ⓗ, Ⓢ, LAND, →↓↘ + Ⓗ CANCEL Ⓗ, ↓↙← + Ⓗ CANCEL ↓↘→ + ATK ATK

(682,800 damage) This complex combo requires a lot of training mode time. Deadpool swaps sides with his foe when ↓↙← + Ⓗ hits, so play close attention and reverse the command for the next sequence. You also can't see Deadpool during Quick Work, making it difficult to time a dash attack to juggle your opponent again. Use your foe's height and fall speed to determine when it's best to dash in and attack again.

After →↓↘ + Ⓗ CANCEL Ⓗ causes a wall bounce, don't do ↓↙← + Ⓗ if your opposition is near a corner. Instead, do ↓↘→ + ATK ATK on its own to ensure everything hits properly.

II. FORWARD THROW, FORWARD DASH, →↓↘ + Ⓗ CANCEL Ⓗ, ST. Ⓗ CANCEL ↓↙← + Ⓗ, FORWARD DASH Ⓢ CANCEL SUPER JUMP, AIR Ⓜ, Ⓗ, Ⓢ, LAND, ↓↘→↗ + ATK ATK

(430,900 damage) A big throw combo. To quickly dash while performing Katana-Rama!, just input →→↓↘ + Ⓗ very quickly. The final attack, ↓↘→↗ + ATK ATK, performs the hyper right as you leave the ground for a jump.

III. FORWARD AIR THROW, LAND, →↓↘ + Ⓗ CANCEL Ⓗ, FORWARD DASH, LATE ST. Ⓗ CANCEL ↓↙← + Ⓜ, FORWARD DASH, Ⓢ CANCEL FORWARD SUPER JUMP, AIR Ⓗ, Ⓢ, LAND, ↓↘→↗ + ATK ATK

(449,400 Damage) Use this against opponents that try to jump away from your ground offense. The opening throw switches sides with your foe, which may be confusing initially. Wait for Deadpool to land fully before attacking with →↓↘ + Ⓗ.

IV. AGAINST AN AIRBORNE FOE, CR. Ⓜ, ST. Ⓗ CANCEL ↓↙← + Ⓜ, CR. Ⓜ, ST. Ⓗ CANCEL ↓↙← + Ⓜ, FORWARD DASH, Ⓢ CANCEL FORWARD SUPER JUMP, AIR [M,], Ⓗ, Ⓢ, LAND, →↓↘ + Ⓗ CANCEL Ⓗ, ↓↙← + Ⓗ CANCEL ↓↘→ + ATK ATK

(673,100 damage) A high damage, anti-air combo. This must done very late against an incoming jump attack or the first Quick Work slash will miss.

V. → + Ⓜ, →↓↘ + Ⓗ CANCEL Ⓗ, FORWARD DASH, LATE ST. Ⓗ CANCEL ↓↙← + Ⓜ, FORWARD DASH, Ⓢ CANCEL SUPER JUMP, EARLY AIR Ⓜ, Ⓗ, Ⓢ, LAND, ↓↘→↗ + ATK ATK

(557,200 damage) This combo starts off of Deadpool's overhead attack. You can verify if it hits or not before committing to the rest of the combo.

VI. ↓↘→ + Ⓗ CANCEL Ⓗ, ↓↙← + Ⓗ, FORWARD DASH, Ⓢ CANCEL SUPER JUMP, AIR Ⓜ, Ⓗ, Ⓢ, LAND, →↓↘ + Ⓗ CANCEL Ⓗ, ↓↙← + Ⓗ CANCEL ↓↘→ + ATK ATK

(614,200 damage) Attack with this combo while Ninja Gift H stuns a character. Like **Combo I**, if your foe is hit with →↓↘ + Ⓗ near a corner, omit the following ↓↙← + Ⓗ.

ASSISTS

Multi-hit projectile assists are of great use to you while you are playing Deadpool. On a basic level, calling a projectile assist and firing air ↓ ↘ → + (M) is very difficult for foes to get around. Projectile assists also open the window for Deadpool to finally move in for an attack. For instance, call Dante—γ, Arthur—β, or Taskmaster—α, then dash forward. If your opponent guards the shots, dash forward and attack with the overhead → + (M) (**Combo V**) or the low-hitting **Combo 1**. You can also use TELEPORT for cross-up assist trickery. For example, input standing (M) while calling Dante—α, then cancel into ← ↓ ↙ + (H) (assuming you're facing right). Deadpool will teleport to the other side of his foe just before Dante's assist hits, forcing your opponent to guard the opposite direction very quickly. You only get two TELEPORT moves per game until the device explodes, so save them for this tactic.

Katana-Rama! provides combo opportunities for character's that have poor combo options.

Save TELEPORT for assist cross-ups!

Deadpool's own assists are relatively varied, but his β assist still stands out as the strongest. It's OTG-capable and causes a ground bounce on hit, a great combination of properties that serves teammates with the inability to create those states themselves. His α assist deals heavy damage and causes a long aerial hitstun, making it useful for juggle combos. γ is an upward gunshot relegated to keeping the opposition from super jumping.

ADVANCED TACTICS

FUN WITH → + (M)

Blindside your adversary!

Deadpool's → + (M) overhead attack can hit the back of the opposing character's head, if done directly next to them, while they're crouching. This forces your opponent to guard the opposite direction. This is very easy to do if performed during a dash. It's also cancelable during either of its two hits—canceling the first hit into ↓ ↘ → + (H) CANCEL (H) causes the projectile to link, leaving your target vulnerable to a follow-up combo. Unfortunately, this only works against middle to large sized characters. Check out the Combo Appendix for an example combo.

COMBO APPENDIX

GENERAL EXECUTION TIPS

Quick Work combos require you to reverse your command when Deadpool slides to the other side of his foe, but you can't actually see his position because of camera movements. Don't let this dissuade you; Deadpool always slides to his foe's backside during Quick Work.

Extended combos that include Quick Work kill the length of your air chains, but in some instances you can land more hits than you normally can by attacking very early after an (S) launch.

Requirements (Position, meter, etc.)	Notes	Command Sequence	Damage
Requires 1 hyper combo gauge bar	Only works against medium sized crouching characters (i.e. no one smaller than Captain America), must cancel the first hit of → + (M) at a very close distance for projectile to combo, if → ↓ ↘ + (H) CANCEL (H) hits near a corner, omit the final ↓ ↙ ← + (H) and just perform ↓ ↘ → + (ATK)(ATK)	→ + (M) (1 hit) CANCEL ↓ ↘ → + (H) CANCEL (H), forward dash, cr. (M), st. (H) CANCEL ↓ ↙ ← + (H), forward dash, cr. (M), st. (H) CANCEL ↓ ↙ ← + (M), forward dash, (S) CANCEL super jump, early air (M), (H), (S), land, → ↓ ↘ + (H) CANCEL (H), ↓ ↙ ← + (H) CANCEL ↓ ↘ → + (ATK)(ATK)	633,200
Requires 4 hyper combo gauge bars	Your foe must attack Deadpool as the hyper combo is activated, once the hyper combo animation finished, input → → ↓ ↘ + (H) CANCEL (H), to immediately dash and OTG the opposition with Katana-Rama!	→ ↓ ↘ + (ATK)(ATK), counters enemy attack, forward dash, → ↓ ↘ + (H) CANCEL (H), forward dash, (S) CANCEL super jump, air (M), (H), (S), land, ↓ ↘ → ↗ + (ATK)(ATK)	800,300
Requires 1 hyper combo gauge bar, requires level 1 X-Factor	This combo takes heavy advantage of a long range hit, after canceling into X-Factor, perform ↓ ↙ ← + (H) as soon as the super freeze ends, if → ↓ ↘ + (H) CANCEL (H) hits your foe near a corner, bypass ↓ ↙ ← + (H) and do ↓ ↘ → + (ATK)(ATK) the opposite direction	↓ ↘ → + (L) (9 hits) from a distance X-FACTOR, ↓ ↙ ← + (H), forward dash, cr. (M), st. (H) CANCEL ↓ ↙ ← + (H), forward dash, st. (H) CANCEL ↓ ↙ ← + (M), forward dash, (S) CANCEL forward super jump, air (H), (S), land, → ↓ ↘ + (H) CANCEL (H), ↓ ↙ ← + (H) CANCEL ↓ ↘ → + (ATK)(ATK)	976,200
Requires 1 hyper combo gauge bar, requires level 1 X-Factor	—	Cr. (L), cr. (L), st. (M) (2 hits) X-FACTOR forward dash, cr. (M), st. (H) CANCEL ↓ ↙ ← + (H), forward dash, cr. (M), st. (H) CANCEL ↓ ↙ ← + (M), forward dash, (S) CANCEL forward super jump, air (H), (S), land, → ↓ ↘ + (H) CANCEL (H), ↓ ↘ → + (ATK)(ATK)	1,004,500
Requires 1 hyper combo gauge bar, requires level 2 X-Factor	The last sequence consists of back-to-back Quick Work, which swaps the side of the screen that Deadpool is on. Compensate by reversing the command as you pass under your foe	Cr. (L), cr. (L), st. (M) (2 hits) X-FACTOR forward dash, cr. (M), st. (H) CANCEL ↓ ↙ ← + (H), forward dash, cr. (M), st. (H) CANCEL ↓ ↙ ← + (M), forward dash, st. (H) CANCEL ↓ ↙ ← + (M), ↓ ↙ ← + (M), ↓ ↙ ← + (M), ↓ ↙ ← + (M) CANCEL ↓ ↘ → + (ATK)(ATK)	1,146,700
Requires level 3 X-Factor	Once the first ↓ ↙ ← + (H) hits, you can repeatedly do ↓ ↙ ← + (H) until your X-Factor bar has expired	X- Factor activated, cr. (L), cr. (M), st. (H) CANCEL ↓ ↙ ← + (H), ↓ ↙ ← + (H), ↓ ↙ ← + (H), ↓ ↙ ← + (H), ↓ ↙ ← + (H), ↓ ↙ ← + (H)...	100%

"EVEN GODS FALL BEFORE DOOM'S MIGHT."

DOCTOR DOOM

BIO

REAL NAME

VICTOR VON DOOM

OCCUPATION

MONARCH OF LATVERIA, WOULD-BE CONQUEROR

ABILITIES

DOOM IS A GENIUS IN PHYSICS, ROBOTICS, CYBERNETICS, GENETICS, WEAPONS TECHNOLOGY, BIO-CHEMISTRY, AND TIME TRAVEL. HE IS ALSO SELF-TAUGHT IN THE MYSTIC ARTS. DOOM IS A NATURAL LEADER, A BRILLIANT STRATEGIST, AND A SLY DECEIVER.

WEAPONS

HIS ARMOR IS LOADED WITH GIMMICKS, INCLUDING A HIGH-POWERED BLASTER ON HIS WAIST HOLSTER. HE HAS ALSO PERSONALLY INVENTED SOME NASTY SURPRISES.

PROFILE

THE MASKED GENIUS SCIENTIST WHO PLOTS FOR WORLD DOMINATION. HIS MASTERY OF THE MYSTIC ARTS AND TECHNOLOGICALLY ADVANCED WEAPONRY PERFECTLY COMPLEMENT HIS SINISTER PLANS, GIVING HIS SUPER HERO FOES PLENTY TO WORRY ABOUT.

FIRST APPEARANCE

FANTASTIC FOUR #5 (1962)

POWER GRID

6	INTELLIGENCE
4	STRENGTH
5	SPEED
6	STAMINA
6	ENERGY PROJECTION
4	FIGHTING ABILITY

*This is biographical, and does not represent an evaluation of the character's in-game combat potential.

ALTERNATE COSTUMES

PS3: ⊗ Xbox 360: Ⓐ	PS3: ▢ Xbox 360: Ⓧ	PS3: △ Xbox 360: Ⓨ	PS3: R1 Xbox 360: RB

ATTACK SET

STANDING BASIC ATTACKS

Screen	Command	Hits	Damage	Startup	Active	Recovery	Advantage on Hit	Advantage if Guarded	Notes
1	Standing L	1	55,000	5	3	12	+1	-1	Dash-cancelable
2	Standing M	2	72,000	10	4	17	+4	+2	OTG-capable, dash cancelable
3	Standing H	2	101,700	15	7	21	+2	0	OTG-capable, dash-cancelable
4	S	1	100,000	11	4	22	—	-2	Launcher attack, not special- or hyper combo-cancelable

CROUCHING BASIC ATTACKS

Screen	Command	Hits	Damage	Startup	Active	Recovery	Advantage on Hit	Advantage if Guarded	Notes
1	Crouching L	1	53,000	6	3	16	-3	-5	Low attack, dash-cancelable
2	Crouching M	1	70,000	9	4	21	-2	-4	Dash-cancelable
3	Crouching H	1	80,000	13	4	21	—	-1	Low attack, dash-cancelable, knocks down

AERIAL BASIC ATTACKS

Screen	Command	Hits	Damage	Startup	Active	Recovery	Notes
1	Air L	1	55,000	6	3	20	Overhead attack
2	Air M	2	81,000	10	7	19	Overhead attack
3	Air H	3	94,800	23	20	20	Inflicts chip damage, not special- or hyper combo-cancelable, beam durability: 1 frame x 1 durability points
4	Air S	1	90,000	11	Until grounded or contact	1 if whiffed, or until grounded	Causes flying screen if used in launcher combo, after hitting the opponent Doctor Doom bounces backwards in the air, not special-cancelable

COMMAND ATTACKS

Screen	Command	Hits	Damage	Startup	Active	Recovery	Advantage on Hit	Advantage if Guarded	Notes
1	⇨ + Ⓗ	1	90,000	8	4	24	—	-4	Launcher attack, dash-cancelable, ⇩ ⬃ ⇨ + P1 or P2 snap back
2	⇦ + Ⓗ	1~8	20,000~ 113,600	25	—	30	—	—	Can press Ⓗ rapidly for up to 7 extra missiles, OTG-capable, each missile has 1 low priority durability point
3	(in air) ⇨ + Ⓗ	1	90,000	12	Until grounded or contact	1	—	—	Can only be performed once per jump , after striking the opponent Doctor Doom bounces backwards in the air in neutral state

1

2

3

DOCTOR DOOM

AS A PARTNER-CROSSOVER ASSISTS

Screen	Type	P1+P2 Crossover Combination Hyper Combo	Description	Hits	Damage	Startup	Active	Recovery (this crossover assist)	Recovery (other partner)	Notes
1	α – Alpha	Photon Array	Plasma Beam M	8	113,600	46	20	109	79	Beam durability: 8 frame x 1 low priority durability points
2	β – Beta	Photon Array	Hidden Missile	6	93,500	49	37	149	119	OTG-capable, each missile has 1 low priority durability point
3	γ – Gamma	Sphere Flame	Molecular Shield M	9	111,800	34	25	126	96	Initial barrier lasts for 24 frames, inflicts 1 durability point of damage per frame, four rocks fired afterward, each rock has 1 durability point

1

2

3

SPECIAL MOVES

Screen	Name	Command	Hits	Damage	Startup	Active	Recovery	Advantage on Hit	Advantage if Guarded	Notes
1	Plasma Beam L	↓↘→ + L	5	81,700	22	15	14	—	+2	Knocks down, beam durability: 5 frame x 1 low priority durability points
1	Plasma Beam M	↓↘→ + M	8	113,600	22	20	17	—	+1	Knocks down, beam durability: 8 frame x 1 low priority durability points
1	Plasma Beam H	↓↘→ + H	12	143,000	22	25	19	—	+2	Knocks down, beam durability: 12 frame x 1 low priority durability points
2	Air Plasma Beam L	(in air) ↓↘→ + L	5	81,700	25	19	7	—	—	Knocks down, OTG-capable, beam durability: 5 frame x 1 low priority durability points
2	Air Plasma Beam M	(in air) ↓↘→ + M	8	113,600	25	20	16	—	—	Knocks down, OTG-capable, beam durability: 8 frame x 1 low priority durability points
2	Air Plasma Beam H	(in air) ↓↘→ + H	12	143,000	25	25	21	—	—	Knocks down, OTG-capable, beam durability: 12f x 1 low priority durability points
3	Photon Shot	↓↙← + ATK	5x2	122,600	27	—	33	-8	-10	Each projectile has 2 low priority durability points
4	Air Photon Shot	(in air) ↓↙← + ATK	5	122,600	27	—	33	-8	-10	Each projectile has 2 low priority durability points
5	Molecular Shield L	→↓↘ + L	7	103,100	7	15	39	-11	-12	Initial barrier lasts for 14 frames, inflicts 1 durability point of damage per frame, four rocks fired afterward, each rock has 1 durability point
5	Molecular Shield M	→↓↘ + M	9	111,800	10	25	34	-7	-8	Initial barrier lasts for 24 frames, inflicts 1 durability point of damage per frame, four rocks fired afterward, each rock has 1 durability point
5	Molecular Shield H	→↓↘ + H	11	118,900	13	35	28	-1	-2	Initial barrier lasts for 34 frames, inflicts 1 durability point of damage per frame, four rocks fired afterward, each rock has 1 durability point
6	Flight (in air OK)	↓↙← + S	—	—	15	—	—	—	—	Activates Flight mode, lasts for 100 frames

Plasma Beam: Plasma Beam is a very useful long ranged attack. Doctor Doom can fight his way through most firefights with Plasma Beam alone—its monstrous 12 durability points easily surpasses what most characters can output. When trying to keep offensive characters away, all versions of Plasma Beam inflict substantial chip damage: Plasma Beam L inflicts 30,000 damage, Plasma Beam M does 48,000 damage, and Plasma Beam H results in a whopping 72,000 points of chip damage!

Plasma Beam L finishes 15 frames faster than Plasma Beam H, making it less of a commitment to fire off. However, if you're going to use Plasma Beam at all you should at least be confident that it's going to make contact with your opponent; there isn't much value in using any versions of the attack other than Plasma Beam H. Amaterasu and Morrigan can crouch under Plasma Beam completely; if you are fighting against these characters from long range use Molecular Shield or Air Photon Shot.

Air Plasma Beam: Air Plasma Beam fires at too steep of an angle to effectively use often; the best time to use this version of the Plasma Beam is after super jumping toward a full-screen opponent. For what it's worth, Air Plasma Beam is the only long-ranged attack Doctor Doom can perform more than once in the air.

Photon Shot: Photon Shot is a great way to control almost the entire screen—its large spread attacks opponents both on the ground and at super jump height. While you can use Photon Shot on reaction to an opponent super jumping toward you, note that this only works well at long ranges. There is a large "dead zone" in the Photon Shot's coverage area directly above Doctor Doom's head, and opponents that aren't full-screen away will reach that spot much more easily.

If your opponent's character is trying to close the distance, repeated use of Photon Shot L is almost certain to slow them down and inflict a small amount of chip damage. This works best when used in conjunction with a long-ranged crossover assist. Again, you'll have to stop firing Photon Shots when your challenger gets halfway across the screen; from there they can easily reach the dead zone above Doctor Doom's head. If you predict that your opponent is going to try to reach that area, use the air H horizontal beam attack to cut them off.

Photon Shots aren't particularly useful in a long ranged firefight; each shot has a small number of durability points and is easily nullified. The chip damage from Photon Shots is negligible as well; they're mainly used to control the movements of an opponent.

Air Photon Shot: The air version of Photon Shot covers a huge area that can only be avoided by super jumping above it or by wavedashing under it. While this is an extremely useful attack, it has a special limitation: Air Photon Shot can only be performed once per jump, even if you activate Flight afterward (which normally allows a character to continue using special moves even beyond the usual three-specials-per-airborne-period limit). As such, this attack can't be relied upon to consistently keep firing on an opponent from afar. Instead, its best usage is covering fire: super jump toward your opponent and fire Air Photon Shot L, then airdash diagonally down-forward towards your foe behind the projectiles. From there you can safely start Doctor Doom's offense.

Molecular Shield: Molecular Shield creates a momentary barrier around Doctor Doom that protects him from the neck down, also nullifying projectiles. After the barrier disappears, four rock projectiles are fired forward.

While this attack inflicts a substantial amount of chip damage on a guarding opponent when it is performed up close, Doctor Doom has much stronger in-close options to use that will lead to much more damage. Instead, this attack is best used in long ranged firefights: if a projectile is incoming that you don't have enough time to power through with Plasma Beam, use the faster startup time on Molecular Shield to destroy the opposing projectile. After the projectile has been destroyed, Molecular Shield will fire four more rocks at your foe to help you get farther ahead in the firefight.

Flight: Flight Mode is relatively useful for Doctor Doom: canceling attacks like air → + H, air S and air M into Flight can lead to some cool tricks, especially if your airdash has already been used up. Flight mode only lasts for 100 frames however, so it's difficult to base any lasting strategy around its usage.

HYPER COMBOS

Screen	Name	Command	Hits	Damage	Startup	Active	Recovery	Advantage on Hit	Advantage if Guarded	Notes
1	Photon Array	↓↙← + ATK ATK	25x2	287,900	10+1	40	34	+4	+2	Each projectile has 1 high priority durability point
2	Air Photon Array	(in air) ↓↙← + ATK ATK	25	287,900	10+1	40	59	—	—	OTG-capable, Each projectile has 1 high priority durability point
3	Sphere Flame	→↓↘ + ATK ATK	57	340,000	8+1	66	47	—	—	Each projectile has 1 high priority durability point
4	Doom's Time (level 3 hyper combo)	↓↘→ + ATK ATK	13	440,000	4+0	1	49	—	-27	Frames 1-9 invincible, unrecoverable knockdown

Photon Array: The ground version of Photon Array quickly covers up practically the entire screen, but isn't particularly useful due to the laughable damage it inflicts at long ranges. Up close to an opponent Photon Array does respectable damage, but still generally isn't worth using because Doctor Doom's other options are better overall.

Air Photon Array: Air Photon Array is Doctor Doom's primary combo ender. To get the maximum damage from the hyper combo the target must be positioned perfectly in front of Doom's fingers, allowing all of the projectiles to hit.

Ending combos with Air Photon Array will usually leave the opponent's character in hitstun all the way until landing on the ground. Using a team hyper combo to nearly any other character can be done very easily.

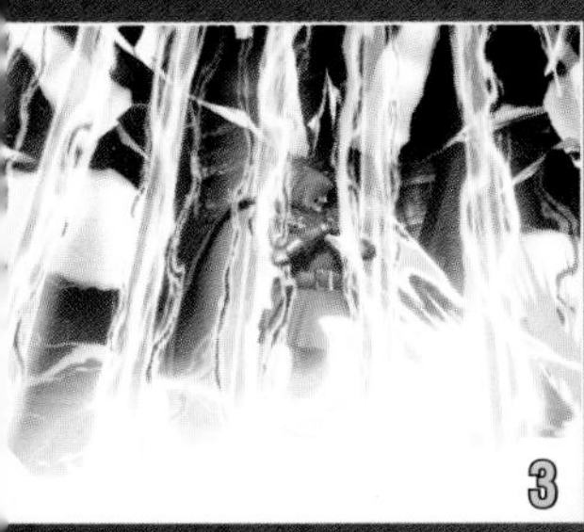

Sphere Flame: The damaging Sphere Flame is used in combos or situations whenever you need to attack directly above Doctor Doom's head. This hyper combo inflicts more damage the lower the challenger is, but the vast majority of the damage is still dealt with the final explosion at the top of the screen.

If Sphere Flame misses completely, the upward projectile will still explode and create a full-screen rain of projectiles afterward. Doctor Doom has recovered fully at this point and can use the projectiles to safely move around or to tag another character in.

Doom's Time: As a level 3 hyper combo, Doom's time is invincible and isn't subject to damage scaling. It's also very fast, making it ideal for ending long corner combos when hitstun has been severely deteriorated.

The fast speed and invincibility of Doom's Time make it relatively easy to use in defensive situations: any attack your opponent does that has a frame disadvantage of -4 or more will be punished after guarding. That's a large percentage of attacks in the game! Doom's Time is also the only invincible attack that you have at your disposal; if your opponent is smothering you with attacks and they are not attacking from very high off the ground, you may want to take a gamble and try to blow through their offense with this hyper combo.

BATTLE PLAN

OVERVIEW

VITALITY: 1,000,000

CHAIN COMBO ARCHETYPE: MARVEL SERIES

X-Factor	Lv.1	Lv.2	Lv.3
Damage	130%	160%	190%
Speed	110%	120%	130%

Your goal with Doctor Doom is to corner your opponent.

Given Doctor Doom's arsenal of special moves, one would think that he should be played as a zoning character. Why would you concentrate on cornering your opponent?

Doctor Doom's corner combos are much, much stronger than their mid-screen equivalents.

In the corner it is much more difficult to defend against Doctor Doom's airdash mix-ups.

In the corner Doom's ground forward throw and air forward throw both lead to strong combos.

How does one push an opponent to the corner using Doctor Doom?

Using dash-canceled attacks to combat advancing guard.

Attacking safely behind the cover of Air Photon Shot L.

Jumping toward your opponent and harassing them with air Ⓗ.

Attacking safely behind the cover of Hidden Missiles.

ON THE GROUND

Doctor Doom is a versatile character than can fill any role on a team well. As a meter-builder he has both strong zoning abilities and safe offensive options to build bar quickly, and he doesn't necessarily need to expend any meter to be effective. As a meter-user he gains the ability to end every combo with Air Photon Array, which is also a great way to set up damaging team hyper combos. The Sphere Flame and Doom's Time hyper combos also have a lot of utility in general match situations. Doctor Doom is great even as a dedicated crossover assist character because Plasma Beam is one of the best all-around support attacks in the game.

Doctor Doom is one of the few characters in the game that cannot cancel his dash—during a dash you cannot stop and guard or do basic attacks. This also prevents you from wavedashing. These dashes are jump-cancelable, so you can cancel the startup frames of the jump into a grounded special move. Jump-canceled dashes into grounded special moves don't come in handy very often with Doctor Doom, besides the occasional Molecular Shield to destroy an incoming projectile. As you may expect, not having a conventional dash severely limits Doctor Doom's mobility on the ground. As such, you'll have to rely mostly on airdashes to get around. However, by jump-canceling a dash early and airdashing diagonally down-forward back down the ground, you can simulate an approximation of a wavedash that is still much faster than an un-canceled dash.

He has these restrictive dashes for a reason. Doctor Doom has the unique ability to cancel most of his basic attacks into a forward or backward dash! While canceling attacks into an un-cancelable dash doesn't immediately seem amazing, the potential starts to shine through when you begin to jump-cancel the dashes. Airdashing forward immediately after the jump allows you to keep attacking your opponent even after they use advancing guard! See the Advanced Tactics section for more details.

Pushing a zoning character back to the corner is an arduous task, since you usually cannot just airdash toward them without running into an errant projectile or two. Against these characters your focus switches a bit to out-gunning them while looking for opportunities to safely move forward. Your biggest asset in a firefight is Plasma Beam H. With its combined 12 points of durability you can simply out-muscle most other characters from long range. Characters that can't keep up with Plasma Beam H will likely have to resort to firing projectiles at you from super jump height, or they'll have to switch gears and come to you.

In either case, this is your cue to maneuver in and begin pushing your opponent back to the corner.

The characters with higher durability outputs, like Arthur and Iron Man, will quickly outpace you if they employ a long ranged crossover assist. If you don't have one of your own, you'll have to go out of your way to counter this tactic. Since all of your opponent's efforts are concentrated on the ground to deal with your Plasma Beam H, this should make it safe for you to super jump over the projectiles, toward your opponent, and fire a Photon Shot L. Once the projectiles are in play, airdash down toward your opponent and begin your offense. Since your opponent had just used their crossover assist, you will have a brief window in which you can attack without having any extra worries.

As an alternate solution, you can use Molecular Shield H to absorb all of the projectiles coming your way if they are relatively condensed together. If you successfully destroy the incoming projectiles with the shield, you'll fire a group of rocks back toward your challenger and get back ahead in the firefight.

The ← + Ⓗ Hidden Missile attack can be useful in almost every match-up if you can find time to safely do it. A single missile will usually suffice; it recovers much faster than multiple missiles, and will still do a decent job at disrupting your opponent's actions a few seconds down the line. More is better, to be sure, but finding time to fire all seven missiles can be difficult against a live opponent.

Doctor Doom has no invincible moves or tools to quickly get away from an opponent. If your foe gets close to you to and is maintaining offensive pressure, you'll have to resort to universal defensive options to get breathing room—using advancing guard every chance you get and finding opportunities to air throw your challenger. On the plus side, a successful backwards air throw always leads into a full combo! See the Combo Usage section for details.

To prevent your foe from smothering you in the first place, you'll need to reliably anti-air your opponent. While air throws are reliable and lead to a decent combo, they can be throw escaped and require your opponent to be very close. ← + Ⓗ can be very effective against opponents coming in from farther away and goes straight into a launcher combo if hit. Pressing Ⓢ works great against opponents coming in from directly above or even behind, and also goes straight into launcher combos.

Doctor Doom has the unique ability to cancel almost all of his basic attacks into dashes. Use this to maintain offense against opponents that use advancing guard!

Photon Beam H can blast through 12 projectile durability points—more than enough to get you through most long ranged firefights.

Hidden Missiles is a great attack, whenever you have time to perform it. The missiles can be used as covering fire to get near your opponent, and they can also be used to momentarily prevent your opponent from attacking you.

COMBO USAGE

I. CR. Ⓛ, CR. Ⓜ, CR. Ⓗ, Ⓢ (CANCEL) ⇒ SUPER JUMP, AIR Ⓜ (2 HITS), → + Ⓗ (CANCEL) ⇒ ↘ + ATK ATK, AIR Ⓜ (2 HITS), LAND, CR. Ⓜ, CR. Ⓗ, Ⓢ (CANCEL) ⇒ SUPER JUMP, AIR Ⓜ, (2 HITS), → + Ⓗ (CANCEL) ⇒ ↘ + ATK ATK, AIR Ⓜ (2 HITS), LAND, CR. Ⓜ, CR. Ⓗ, Ⓢ (CANCEL) ⇒ SUPER JUMP, AIR Ⓜ (2 HITS), Ⓜ (2 HITS), → + Ⓗ (CANCEL) ⇒ ATK ATK, AIR Ⓜ (2 HITS), Ⓢ

(580,300 damage) With a bit of practice, you can do some huge meterless damage with Doctor Doom mid-screen! After airdash-canceling the first two air → + Ⓗ attacks, wait as long as possible before hitting the opponent with air Ⓜ. This keeps the opponent low enough to juggle with crouching Ⓜ. If you attack with air Ⓜ too early, often it is possible to still salvage the combo by immediately relaunching with → + Ⓗ.

Omitting the third launcher and hyper combo canceling the crouching Ⓗ into Sphere Flame inflicts 665,700 damage. Replacing the final air Ⓢ with Air Photon Array inflicts about 657,300 damage and allows for THC opportunities.

II. (CORNER REQUIRED) CR. Ⓛ, CR. Ⓜ, CR. Ⓗ, Ⓢ (CANCEL) ⇒ SUPER JUMP, → + Ⓗ, Ⓢ, LAND, ST. Ⓗ (2 HITS) OTG, Ⓢ (CANCEL) ⇒ SUPER JUMP, AIR Ⓜ (2 HITS), Ⓜ (2 HITS), → + Ⓗ, (CANCEL) ⇒ ATK ATK, AIR Ⓜ (2 HITS), Ⓢ, Ⓢ, LAND, ST. Ⓗ (2 HITS) OTG, Ⓢ (CANCEL) ⇒ SUPER JUMP, AIR Ⓜ (2 HITS), Ⓜ (2 HITS), → + Ⓗ (CANCEL) ⇒ ATK ATK, AIR Ⓜ (2 HITS), Ⓢ, LAND, ST. Ⓗ (2 HITS) OTG

(651,700 damage) Due to his unique OTG-capable basic attacks, Doctor Doom's corner combos are a whole lot more damaging than his mid-screen combos. If your opponent isn't completely flush with the corner when the combo begins, simply omit the first super jump repetition; go right into the airdash-canceled → + Ⓗ attacks.

Dash-canceling the final standing Ⓗ attack gives you a great chance to continue with your offense, especially when combined with a crossover assist. Dash forward and threaten your air-recovering opponent with an air throw!

UP IN THE AIR

Doctor Doom has a number of strong air mobility options, chief of which is his eight-way airdash. While Doctor Doom's airdash is mostly standard fare, it has a much lower height restriction than others; you can normal jump and input the airdash command almost immediately and it will still execute.

Air Ⓢ isn't an overhead, but it causes Doctor Doom to change his air trajectory to a steep downward angle while attacking. Performed from high enough above your opponent, this attack can be difficult to stop without an invincible attack. Air Ⓢ isn't special-cancelable, and has the strange effect of making the height restriction for an airdash much higher. It is hyper combo-cancelable however, so if you hit your foe with it at a low height you can add on an Air Photon Array for some quick damage. Against a standing opponent the Air Photon Array is unsafe even if hit however, so be sure you have enough bar to team hyper combo to another character. If the air Ⓢ does hit from within the height restriction of an airdash, canceling the air Ⓢ into a down-forward airdash will allow you to land and link a crouching Ⓛ afterwards for a combo. You can also cancel it into a forward airdash and attack with air Ⓜ, which also happens to combo if the air Ⓢ hits. If guarded, air Ⓢ will bounce Doctor Doom away in a very vulnerable state where he can do nothing but hyper combo-cancel, airdash cancel (if within the height restriction), or call a crossover assist. Calling a crossover assist simultaneously with the air Ⓢ hit is often the best choice, and will usually let you dash forward again to continue attacking.

Air ⇨ + Ⓗ is similar, but it cause Doctor Doom to soar almost completely horizontally forward. This is great for covering a lot of distance at normal jump height while attacking, which also allows you to call a crossover assist while Doom is flying forward. Air ⇨ + Ⓗ doesn't have all of the restrictions that air Ⓢ has; it is special-cancelable and retains Doctor Doom's extremely low height restriction for airdashes. Attacking the opponent from across the screen with air ⇨ + Ⓗ and canceling it into an airdash is a very strong tactic! Even if you don't cancel the attack, after bouncing back Doctor Doom is still in a neutral state free to do anything, including guard. Falling down from the bounce with an air Ⓗ laser beam allows you to keep attacking your opponent from this position. Air ⇨ + Ⓗ has some additional quirks: it can only be performed once per jump, and against a cornered foe an air ⇨ + Ⓗ that hits the wall behind the opposing character will actually switch sides and cause Doctor Doom to land into the corner. Use this to your advantage and surprise your opponent with a sneaky cross-up using a crossover assist!

A large portion of Doctor Doom's ability to push an opponent to the corner stems from aerial maneuvers. In addition to airdash-canceling air ⇨ + Ⓗ, another strong tactic is to super jump toward the opposing character and fire Air Photon Shot L. If your opponent doesn't react fast enough to super jump over it or wavedash under it, immediately follow the projectiles with a down-forward airdash to begin attacking your foe almost completely safely.

Doctor Doom doesn't have a lot of basic air attacks to choose from. Thankfully, air Ⓜ is pretty good when used from an airdash!

Air ⇨ + Ⓗ is a great way to attack opponents from afar. Once you make contact, cancel into a forward airdash and begin your attack!

Super jumping toward your foe and firing Air Photon Shot L, then airdashing behind it is a great way to start your offense safely.

At mid range, simply jumping toward your opponent repeatedly while firing air Ⓗ laser beams can be difficult to deal with, provided the opposing character does not have a projectile-based attack. The laser beam is easily nullified by any projectile that has even a small amount of durability points, however. The laser beam of air Ⓗ travels too slowly to be effectively used for zoning purposes; at best it will travel about two-thirds of the screen distance when fired from a normal jump.

When you're close enough to your opponent, begin attacking by jumping and airdashing straight forward, then immediately attacking with air Ⓜ. The two hits of this attack are both overheads and allow you to land and combo afterwards. While this by itself isn't particularly difficult to guard, there are several ways you can build upon this foundation to mix up your opponent. Instead of airdashing forward, airdashing down-forward will cause you to land almost instantly. From here you can surprise your foe with a crouching Ⓛ low attack and start a combo, or do a backwards throw if you're mid-screen; after a backwards throw Doctor Doom can land a full combo without help from a crossover assist starting with a standing Ⓗ OTG hit. If your adversary is in the corner, a forward throw goes into a much more damaging combo; see the Combo Usage section for details on both of these throw combos.

To add more layers to the mix-up, you can cancel the first hit of air Ⓜ to another air Ⓜ attack. The startup on air Ⓜ is too slow for it to hit before Doctor Doom lands, allowing you to do single-hit overhead Ⓜ into a low-hitting crouching Ⓛ))!

If your opponent uses advancing guard against your air Ⓜ attack, cancel it into air ⇨ + Ⓗ to fly back toward your foe and keep pushing the opposing character back toward the corner. If the air ⇨ + Ⓗ makes contact with your opponent after an advancing guard, immediately cancel it into Air Photon Shot L. This will cause you to instantly land without firing the shots, and prevent yourself from bouncing backwards after the air ⇨ + Ⓗ. From here dash forward and keep your offense going!

Doctor Doom's airdash-based offense really begins to shine when you start to add crossover assists into the equation. Long ranged assists are great for pinning an opponent down whenever you are flying back in with air ⇨ + Ⓗ, and low-hitting assists can easily make all your airdash Ⓜ attacks unguardable!

DOCTOR DOOM

III. BACKWARDS THROW, ST. Ⓗ (2 HITS) OTG, Ⓢ CANCEL ⇨ SUPER JUMP, AIR Ⓜ (2 HITS), → + Ⓗ CANCEL ⇨ ↘ + ATK ATK, AIR Ⓜ (2 HITS), LAND, CR. Ⓜ, CR. Ⓗ, Ⓢ CANCEL ⇨ SUPER JUMP, AIR Ⓜ (2 HITS), → + Ⓗ CANCEL ⇨ ↘ + ATK ATK, AIR Ⓜ (2 HITS), LAND, → + Ⓗ CANCEL ⇨ SUPER JUMP, AIR Ⓜ (2 HITS), Ⓜ (2 HITS), → + Ⓗ CANCEL ⇨ ATK ATK, AIR Ⓜ (2 HITS), Ⓢ

(425,700 damage) Doctor Doom has the very convenient ability to combo after a backwards ground throw with no crossover assist required. Use backwards throws with caution. Missing your throw attempt will result in an accidental Hidden Missile activation!

If you want to save the meter, ending the combo with air Ⓢ results in 249,700 damage. Due to the large amount of hitstun deterioration caused by the throw, the combo cannot be ended with Plasma Beam H in the same way that Doctor Doom's normal mid-screen combo can. The exact same combo can be performed from a backwards air throw. However, in this case the combo does 514,300 due to a strange lack of additional damage scaling after the air throw.

IV. (CORNER REQUIRED) FORWARD THROW, CR. Ⓜ, CR. Ⓗ, Ⓢ CANCEL ⇨ SUPER JUMP, AIR Ⓜ (2 HITS), → + Ⓗ, Ⓢ, LAND, ST. Ⓗ (2 HITS) OTG, Ⓢ CANCEL ⇨ SUPER JUMP, AIR Ⓜ (2 HITS), Ⓜ (2 HITS), → + Ⓗ, CANCEL ⇨ ATK ATK, AIR Ⓜ (2 HITS), Ⓢ, LAND, ST. Ⓗ (2 HITS) CANCEL ⇨ → ↓ ↘ + ATK ATK

(572,300 damage) Against cornered opponents, Doctor Doom's offense becomes much scarier due to his damaging combos that start with a forward throw. Throws introduce a large amount of hitstun deterioration into combos, so you won't be able to get as many re-launches as you would normally.

V. (CORNER REQUIRED) FORWARD AIR THROW, AIR Ⓜ (2 HITS), LAND, CR. Ⓜ, CR. Ⓗ, Ⓢ CANCEL ⇨ SUPER JUMP, → + Ⓗ, Ⓢ, LAND, ST. Ⓗ (2 HITS) OTG, Ⓢ CANCEL ⇨ SUPER JUMP, AIR Ⓜ (2 HITS), Ⓜ (2 HITS), → + Ⓗ, Ⓢ, LAND, ST. Ⓗ (2 HITS) OTG CANCEL ⇨ → ↓ ↘ + ATK ATK

(546,000 damage) Doctor Doom also gains the ability to start a combo from a forward air throw against a cornered opponent. This comes in handy more than you would think; many of Doctor Doom's corner combos end with an opportunity to reset an opponent with an air throw.

ASSISTS

Low-hitting crossover assists make Doctor Doom's offense of constant air Ⓜ attacks completely unguardable!

Chun-Li—γ lets you perform a much more damaging corner combo, and is also great for pinning down your opponent when used in tandem with dash-canceled attacks.

Projectile-based crossover assists are a great help all-around, but are especially handy for keeping opponents on defense so that they can be pushed to the corner.

All of Doctor Doom's assist types are much better than average: Hidden Missile is a great all-around support attack that can be used to insure that your opponent will momentarily be forced to guard in a few moments. Frequent use of this assist can be very frustrating to deal with, and will often lead to combo openings due to the opponent getting hit by a string of missiles. Molecular Shield is one of the best crossover assists for keeping your opponent pinned down; it's like a Chun-Li Hyakuretsu assist that fires a group of projectiles afterward! Doctor Doom's Plasma Beam assist type stands above the others in terms of all-around usefulness. Having a beam-based crossover assist is of great use to literally every character in the game!

Doctor Doom's offense is mostly predicated on the two-hit air Ⓜ, performed from a forward airdash. Both hits of the air Ⓜ are overheads, so it's a no-brainer that adding a quick low-hitting assist to the mix like Wesker—β will result in lots of unguardable attacks! To create the proper timing for the set-up, simply press P1 or P2 immediately before jumping, then airdash and press Ⓜ as normal. Chun-Li—γ lets you pin your enemy in guardstun for a long period of time whenever you get near them. Used in combination with dash-cancelable attacks, this allows you to stay near the opponent and perform an airdash mix-up. The Hyakuretsu assist also lets you perform an even more damaging corner combo, and by a large margin! See the Combo Appendix section for details.

ADVANCED TACTICS

DASH-CANCELING VERSUS ADVANCING GUARD

If you dash-cancel at around the same time that your opponent inputs the advancing guard command, the dash completely cancels out the advancing guard attempt; it's like it never even happened! The fastest-possible dash cancel nullifies a fast advancing guard. Your opponent will likely react a little later, so dash-canceling just a touch later will cancel out the most common timings for your opponent to input the advancing guard command. If your opponent uses advancing guard especially late, this is easily countered by doing the fastest-possible dash cancel, then using the forward airdash to cancel out the advancing guard!

As such, the same idea can be applied to air attacks canceled into airdashes: forcing your opponent to guard Doctor Doom's air ➡ + Ⓗ isn't particularly difficult. If your foe doesn't use advancing guard, you can cancel the attack into a forward airdash and initiate some offense. If your adversary begins to use advancing guard, try to cancel the attack into the airdash at the same time as your opponent's advancing guard input to cancel it out.

The best attacks to use for dash-canceling are crouching Ⓗ and ➡ + Ⓗ. Both attacks produce the most guardstun out of Doctor Doom's basic attacks and give you the most time to attack afterward. The fastest-possible dash cancel from these two moves will leave you at -1 in front of your opponent if guarded. Jump-canceling early on allows you to move before the opponent; attack with a forward airdash Ⓜ!

If you can predict when your opponents will input the advancing guard command, you can negate it completely by canceling into a forward dash!

COMBO APPENDIX

GENERAL EXECUTION TIPS

When dash-canceling attacks, use ATK ATK rather than ⇨⇨; it's much more efficient and frees up your left hand to jump-cancel the dash more easily.

Requirements (Position, meter, etc.)	Notes	Command Sequence	Damage
—	A lot of attack sequences that begin with your opponent dashing toward you can be countered by quickly jumping up and hitting them with Ⓢ. If you're not above the height restriction for an airdash, this combo is the most you can get out of the situation. This combo isn't safe even if it hits your opponent; you'll have to team hyper combo to a different character to keep Doctor Doom safe. On a more positive note, Air Photon Array leaves your foe standing, allowing you to easily combo into almost any other hyper combo!	Air Ⓢ CANCEL➡ ⇩⬃⇦ + ATK ATK	363,400
—	—	Air ⇨ + Ⓗ CANCEL➡ ATK ATK, Ⓜ (2 hits), land, cr. Ⓜ, cr. Ⓗ, Ⓢ CANCEL➡ super jump, air Ⓜ (2 hits), Ⓜ (2 hits), ⇨ + Ⓗ CANCEL➡ ATK ATK, Ⓜ (2 hits) CANCEL➡ ⇩⬃⇦ + ATK ATK	525,900
Corner required	—	Cr. Ⓛ, cr. Ⓜ, cr. Ⓗ, Ⓢ CANCEL➡ super jump, ⇨ + Ⓗ, Ⓢ, land, st. Ⓗ (2 hits) OTG, Ⓢ CANCEL➡ super jump, air Ⓜ (2 hits), Ⓜ (2 hits), ⇨ + Ⓗ CANCEL➡ ATK ATK, Ⓜ (2 hits), Ⓢ, land, st. Ⓗ (2 hits) OTG, Ⓢ CANCEL➡ super jump, air Ⓜ (2 hits), Ⓜ (2 hits), ⇨ + Ⓗ CANCEL➡ ATK ATK, Ⓜ (2 hits), Ⓢ, land, st. Ⓗ (2 hits) OTG CANCEL➡ ⇩⬂⇨ + ATK ATK	1,091,700
Corner required, Chun-Li—γ	While your opponent is getting juggled by Chun-Li's Hyakuretsu, letting them fall slightly before hitting them with Photon Beam H results in the most damage	Cr. Ⓛ, cr. Ⓜ, cr. Ⓗ, Ⓢ CANCEL➡ super jump, ⇨ + Ⓗ, Ⓢ, land, st. Ⓗ (2 hits) OTG, Ⓢ CANCEL➡ super jump, air Ⓜ (2 hits), Ⓜ (2 hits), ⇨ + Ⓗ, CANCEL➡ ATK ATK, Ⓜ (2 hits), Ⓢ, Ⓢ, land, st. Ⓗ (2 hits) OTG, Ⓢ CANCEL➡ super jump, air Ⓜ (2 hits), Ⓜ (2 hits), ⇨ + Ⓗ, CANCEL➡ ATK ATK, Ⓜ (2 hits), Ⓢ Ⓢ, land, P1 or P2 + st. Ⓗ (2 hits) OTG CANCEL➡ dash, st. Ⓛ, CANCEL➡ ⇩⬂⇨ + Ⓗ CANCEL➡ ⇨⇩⬂ + ATK ATK	917,700
Mid-screen only, Wesker—β	Combo starting from unguardable set-up	P1 or P2, jump, ATK ATK, air Ⓜ (2 hits), land, cr. Ⓜ, cr. Ⓗ, Ⓢ CANCEL➡ super jump, air Ⓜ (2 hits), Ⓜ (2 hits), ⇨ + Ⓗ CANCEL➡ ATK ATK, Ⓜ (2 hits) CANCEL➡ ⇩⬂⇨ + Ⓗ	406,900

DORMAMMU

"WHAT HOPE DO YOU HAVE AGAINST ONE WHO WIELDS THE DARK MAGICKS?"

BIO

REAL NAME

DORMAMMU

OCCUPATION

DESPOT, CONQUEROR

ABILITIES

AMONG HIS MANY ABILITIES ARE MATTER TRANSMUTATION, INTERDIMENSIONAL TELEPORTATION, SIZE AND SHAPE ALTERATION, ELEMENT CONTROL, TELEPATHY, CREATION OF ARTIFICIAL BEINGS, AND EMPOWERMENT OF OTHERS.

WEAPONS

NONE

PROFILE

MASTER OF THE DARK DIMENSION, THE DREAD DORMAMMU HAS CROSSED OVER TO THE REAL WORLD IN THE HOPES OF CONQUERING IT.

FIRST APPEARANCE

STRANGE TALES #126 (1964)

POWER GRID

6	INTELLIGENCE
7	STRENGTH
7	SPEED
7	STAMINA
7	ENERGY PROJECTION
4	FIGHTING ABILITY

*This is biographical, and does not represent an evaluation of the character's in-game combat potential.

ALTERNATE COSTUMES

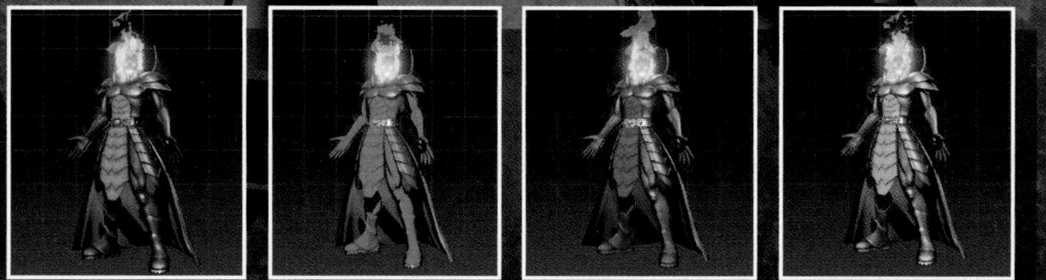

PS3: ⨂ Xbox 360: Ⓐ

PS3: ▢ Xbox 360: Ⓧ

PS3: △ Xbox 360: Ⓨ

PS3: R1 Xbox 360: RB

ATTACK SET

STANDING BASIC ATTACKS

Screen	Command	Hits	Damage	Startup Frames	Active Frames	Recovery Frames	Frame Advantage on Hit	Frame Advantage if Guarded	Notes
1	Standing L	1	48,000	6	2	12	0	-1	—
2	Standing M	1	70,000	8	10	16	-7	-8	Nullifies low and medium priority projectiles
3	Standing H	1	90,000	13	5	21	-2	-3	Nullifies low and medium priority projectiles, knocks opponent upward ↓↘→ + P1 or P2
4	S	1	95,000	9	20	12	—	-9	Nullifies low and medium priority projectiles, launcher, not special or hyper combo-cancelable

1

2

3

4

CROUCHING BASIC ATTACKS

Screen	Command	Hits	Damage	Startup Frames	Active Frames	Recovery Frames	Frame Advantage on Hit	Frame Advantage if Guarded	Notes
1	Crouching L	1	45,000	7	2	13	-1	-2	Low attack
2	Crouching M	1	70,000	9	8	17	+6	-7	Nullifies low and medium priority projectiles, launches opponent slightly
3	Crouching H	1	90,000	13	4	24	—	-5	Nullifies low and medium priority projectiles, low attack, knocks down opponent

1

2

3

AERIAL BASIC ATTACKS

Screen	Command	Hits	Damage	Startup Frames	Active Frames	Recovery Frames	Notes
1	Air L	1	50,000	7	3	16	Overhead attack
2	Air M	1	50,000	10	11	15	Nullifies projectiles low and medium priority, overhead attack
3	Air H	1	85,000	10	5	29	Nullifies projectiles low and medium priority, overhead attack
4	Air S	1	90,000	14	5	27	Nullifies projectiles low and medium priority, overhead attack

1

2

3

4

COMMAND ATTACKS

Screen	Command	Hits	Damage	Startup Frames	Active Frames	Recovery Frames	Frame Advantage on Hit	Frame Advantage if Guarded	Notes
1	→ + H	1	80,000	20	—	26	—	-3	Wall bounces opponent, inflicts chip damage, not special- or hyper combo-cancelable, projectile has 1 low priority durability point
2	↘ + H	5	81,700	15	—	31	+5	+4	Creates pool of fire on the ground that lasts 180 frames, only one pool of fire per player can be in play at a time, OTG-capable, inflicts chip damage, not special- or hyper combo-cancelable, beam durability: 5 frames x 1 low priority durability point

1

2

DORMAMMU

AS A PARTNER-CROSSOVER ASSISTS

Screen	Type	P1+P2 Crossover Combination Hyper Combo	Description	Hits	Damage	Startup Frames	Active Frames	Recovery Frames (this crossover assist)	Recovery Frames (other partner)	Notes
1	α – Alpha	Chaotic Flame	Dark Hole M	9	122,200	50	34	103	68	Knocks down opponent beam durability: 10 frames x 3 low priority durability points
2	β – Beta	Chaotic Flame	Purification L	4	120,300	56	23	103	73	Spinning knockdown beam durability: 5 frames x 3 low priority durability points
3	γ – Gamma	Stalking Flare	Liberation	Variable	Variable	Variable	Variable	Variable	Variable	Attack performed depends on how many Destruction or Creation points stored

1

2

3

SPECIAL MOVES

Screen	Name	Command	Hits	Damage	Startup Frames	Active Frames	Recovery Frames	Frame Advantage on Hit	Frame Advantage if Guarded	Notes
1	Dark Spell: Destruction	↓↙← + L	—	—	15	—	20	—	—	Stores 1 Destruction point, if 3 Dark Spell points already stored then performs Liberation instead
2	Dark Spell: Creation	↓↙← + M	—	—	15	—	20	—	—	Stores 1 Creation point, if 3 Dark Spell points already stored then performs Liberation instead
3	Liberation (empty)	↓↙← + H	1	80,000	15	5	21	+5	-3	Performed with 0 stored points, knocks down opponent, attack nullifies projectiles, projectile has 5 low priority durability points
4	Liberation (Destruction 1)	↓↙← + H	3	94,800	15	10	16	—	+1	Requires 1 Destruction point, uses all stored Dark Spell points, knocks down opponent, nullifies projectiles, projectile has 5 low priority durability points
5	Liberation (Destruction 2)	↓↙← + H	6	163,800	15	10	16	—	+1	Requires 2 Destruction points, uses all stored Dark Spell points, knocks down opponent, nullifies projectiles, beam durability: 6 frames x 1 low priority durability point
6	Liberation (Destruction 3)	↓↙← + H	10	195,000	15	15	21	—	-5	Requires 3 Destruction points, uses all stored Dark Spell points, knocks down opponent, nullifies projectiles, beam durability: 10 frames x 1 low priority durability point
7	Liberation (Creation 1)	↓↙← + H	3	108,300	12	10	24	—	-10	Requires 1 Creation point, uses all stored Dark Spell points, knocks down opponent, nullifies projectiles, projectile has 5 low priority durability points
8	Liberation (Creation 2)	↓↙← + H	9	183,400	12	10 (9) 10 (10) 10	35	—	-10	Requires 2 Creation points, uses all stored Dark Spell points, knocks down opponent, nullifies projectiles, projectile has 5 low priority durability points
9	Liberation (Creation 3)	↓↙← + H	1	0	15	—	36	-21	-23	Requires 3 Creation points, uses all stored Dark Spell points, on hit opponent cannot jump for 300 frames
10	Liberation (Mixed)	↓↙← + H	~19	~174,200	15	54	36	—	—	Requires 1 Destruction and 1 Creation point, meteors inflict unrecoverable knockdown on airborne opponents , OTG-capable, nullifies projectiles, beam durability: each meteor has 3 frames x 3 low priority durability points
11	Liberation (Destruction Mix)	↓↙← + H	variable	80,000 (flame pillar) 15,000 (per meteor)	20	20	21	—	—	Requires 2 Destruction points and 1 Creation point, meteors inflict unrecoverable knockdown on airborne opponents , all attacks are OTG-capable, flame pillar attack knocks down opponent, all attacks nullify projectiles, ground spike has 100 durability points, beam durability: each meteor has 1 frame x 1 low priority durability point
12	Liberation (Creation Mix)	↓↙← + H	~22	~222,2000	27	79	14	—	—	Requires 2 Creation points and 1 Destruciton point, meteors inflict unrecoverable knockdown on airborne opponents, OTG-capable, nullifies projectiles, beam durability: each meteor has 3 frames x 3 low priority durability points
13	Dark Hole	↓↘→ + ATK (in air OK)	9	122,200	26	34	6	—	+7	Knocks down opponent, Dark Hole disappears if Dormammu receives damage, air version does not recover until landing (unless in Flight mode), beam durability: 10 frames x 3 low priority durability points
14	Purification	→↓↘ + ATK	4	120,300	32	23	11	+11	+2	OTG-capable, spinning knockdown, beam durability: 5 frames x 3 low priority durability points
15	Mass Change	←↓↙ + ATK (in air OK)	—	—	13	—	17	—	—	—
16	Flight	↓↙← + S (in air OK)	—	—	21	—	—	—	—	Activates Flight mode, Flight mode lasts for 120 frames, activating Flight while already in Flight mode cancels Flight mode, has 0 recovery

Dark Spell: Destruction: Stores 1 Destruction point. Store Destruction or Creation points whenever you get the chance, preferably when your opponent is guarding a crossover assist or is high up in the air after being hit by a Purification.

Dark Spell: Creation: Stores 1 Creation point. Usage is the same as Dark Spell: Destruction.

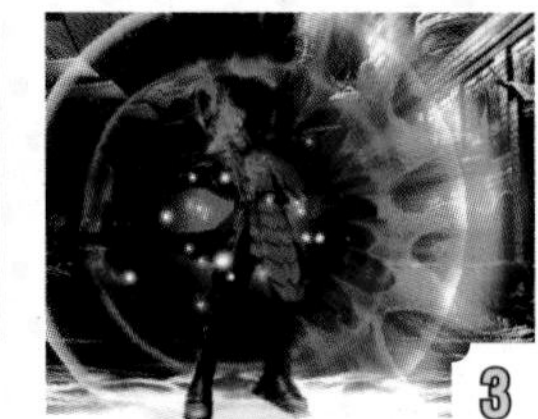

Liberation (empty): Liberation (empty) is the only move Dormammu has that hits directly above his head, other than any of the meteor-using Liberation moves. This makes it occasionally useful as an anti-air against super jumping opponents. Its relatively slow startup makes it difficult to use in other situations.

Liberation (Destruction 1): Not particularly useful for much outside of corner combos; it's generally better to save your Destruction point and build up to something better.

Liberation (Destruction 2): Substantially more useful than Liberation (Destruction 1), this version creates a huge explosion in front of Dormammu, great for countering any movement your opponent does in that range, especially in the air. Liberation (Destruction 2) can be hit-confirmed into Chaotic Flame very easily, though it is generally more prudent to use that time to store a Dark Spell.

ASSISTS

Beam-based crossover assists like Iron Man's UniBeam perform many roles in Dormammu's game, like cross ups!

Long-ranged low assists allow Dormammu make attacks from Mass Change H incredibly difficult to guard, if not impossible!

Doctor Doom's unique crossover assist essentially gives you more meteors to throw around!

Dormammu's three crossover assist types are all extremely specialized: Dark Hole M never seems to cover the area of the screen that you need it to, but it is the assist type with the most range and pins down opponents for the longest period of time. Purification L is OTG-capable, but is typically too slow to make use of easily in combos. It also knocks the opponent too high into the air to follow up with anything particularly threatening. Purification L is generally best used as an anti-air against super jumping foes. Liberation has enormous potential as a crossover assist, but isn't very realistic to use in a real match since it requires you to store Dark Spells as Dormammu then tag him out. As such, Dark Hole M is the easiest assist to recommend.

Beam-based assists like Iron Man—α and Doctor Doom —α are a huge boon to Dormammu, and could even be considered a necessity. Against offensive characters, beam assists push opponents backwards while simultaneously buying you time to lay down more defenses or store Dark Spells. Against other zoning characters, beam-based assists help immensely in letting you keep up with your opponent in the projectile war. Against all characters, beam assists allow you to attack from anywhere on the screen with a cross up Mass Change M; simply call the crossover assist about a half-second before teleporting. This is very scary to deal with, since it is nearly impossible to guard on reaction. This will often force your opponent to jump around, giving you an even greater advantage on the ground.

On a similar note, long-ranged, low-hitting crossover assists like She-Hulk —α and Felicia —α can be used similarly, except now the result is essentially unblockable! Since both of these assists only hit once, the resulting combo does much more damage than a beam assist cross up combo due to less damage scaling. She-Hulk —α also has the additional benefit of being OTG-capable.

Dormammu is great at doing ridiculous damage to your opponent's crossover assists. Simply hitting an assist with Dark Hole into Chaotic Flame can do anywhere between 50% to 90% damage, depending on whether the assist being juggled stays onscreen or not, and whether the opponent's point character is guarding your assist combo.

If your opponent's back is against the corner, hitting an assist with Liberation (Destruction 3), juggling Dark Hole, then hyper combo-canceling into Chaotic Flame will do 100% damage to most any crossover assist if the opponent's point character is guarding; the point character guarding at any point in the combo resets damage scaling on the assist combo! If the point character gets hit as well, the assist takes about 70% damage, but the point character also takes 45%.

ADVANCED TACTICS

USING NORMAL ATTACKS TO NULLIFY PROJECTILES

Dormammu's match-ups against other zoning characters are very specialized; you need to employ a variety of tactics to keep up with the sheer output of projectiles other characters can create. Most important of these tactics is his unique ability to nullify projectiles with his Ⓜ, Ⓗ and Ⓢ normal attacks.

Dormammu's standing M is the best overall move to nullify projectiles with. Cancel it into a Dark Spell or Purification.

If a character like Zero puts a stream of L Hadangekis on the screen, Dormammu won't have time to call a crossover assist or Dark Hole between projectiles. Attempting to Mass Change H over Zero's head is risky as well, since the Zero player can read that and counter with a variety of moves.

To keep up with Zero, Dormammu can nullify projectiles with standing Ⓜ. After nullifying a projectile, you can cancel the standing Ⓜ into any special move while simultaneously calling a crossover assist. For example, nullify a projectile with standing Ⓜ while calling Ryu's Hadoken assist, then cancel the attack into Dark Spell: Destruction. Ryu's Hadoken cancels out the next projectile, and you've now come out ahead in the exchange by having a Destruction point stored.

You can also cancel standing Ⓜ into a Purification, which will likely hit the opponent if they continue to toss projectiles. This also buys you time to store a Dark Spell.

LIBERATION COMBOS USING SUPER JUMP CANCEL

Storing the necessary points for the two mixed Liberation moves can be beneficial for a variety of tactical reasons, and it can also lead to improved combos should the situation arise.

Comboing into Liberation (Destruction Mix) or Liberation (Creation Mix) requires a super jump cancel, but the rewards are great.

Both moves do a large amount of damage if the opponent gets caught in them at about a single-screen height. The problem is, how does one get the opponent that high in a combo-able state? The Ⓢ special attack launcher isn't special-cancelable.

Launchers are super jump-cancelable on hit, however. In addition, the initial frames of a jump can be canceled into any special move or super. This allows you to launch the opponent high into the air, cancel the launcher into a jump, then cancel the jump into your Liberation move. This is performed with ↓↙←↖ + Ⓗ.

When an opponent is juggled by these Liberation moves in this way, they are launched into a large group of meteors, which pull the opponent back down towards you to continue a juggle combo into another launcher. As an added bonus, the multitude of hits from the Liberation moves grant you an entire hyper combo gauge bar on their own!

The damage from these moves is especially exaggerated after X-Factor activation. Juggling Liberation (Destruction) after X-Factor-canceling a Chaotic Flame adds a whopping 6,000,000 damage! And it still allows another combo into launcher!

COMBO APPENDIX

GENERAL EXECUTION TIPS

When hitting opponents with Purification OTG into Chaotic Flame, try to super-cancel the Purification after only one or two hits. Practice the timing for this in Training Mode until it becomes second nature.

Requirements (Position, meter, etc.)	Notes	Command Sequence	Damage
—	Hyper combo cancel the Purification as early as possible	Forward/back air throw, ⇨⇩⇘ + (M) OTG CANCEL ⇩⇘⇨ + ATK ATK	369,700
Corner required	—	Forward/back air throw, land, cr. (M), ⇨ + (H), cr. (H), (S) CANCEL super jump, air (M), (M), (H), (S), land, ⇨⇩⇘ + (M) OTG CANCEL ⇩⇘⇨ + ATK ATK	494,100
—	—	⇩⇘⇨ + ATK CANCEL ⇩⇘⇨ + ATK ATK	332,700
Against airborne opponent	—	Air (H), (S), land, cr. (M), (S) CANCEL super jump, air (M), (M), (H), (S), land, ⇨⇩⇘ + (M) OTG CANCEL ⇩⇘⇨ + ATK ATK	642,400
2 Creation points, 1 Destruction point required	Due to the random nature of the meteors, this combo is very inconsistent	Cr. (L), cr. (M), (S) CANCEL super jump cancel CANCEL ⇩⇙⇦ + (H), dash, walk forward, cr. (L), cr. (M), (S) CANCEL super jump, air (M), (M), (H), (S), land, ⇨⇩⇘ + (M) OTG CANCEL ⇩⇘⇨ + ATK ATK	683,600
Corner required, 2 Destruction points, 1 Creation point stored	After hitting the launcher, cancel the pre-jump frames into Liberation (Destruction Mix) by doing ⇩⇙⇦⇖ + (H)	Cr. (L), cr. (M), ⇨ + (H), cr. (H), (S) CANCEL super jump cancel CANCEL ⇩⇙⇦ + (H), st. (H), (S) CANCEL super jump, air (M), (M), (H), (S), land, ⇨⇩⇘ + (L) OTG CANCEL ⇩⇘⇨ + ATK ATK, st. (M)	~796,900
Corner required, 2 Destruction points, 1 Creation point stored, X-Factor Level 1	Completely pointless max damage combo to mess around with in training mode. Liberation (Destruction Mix) does insane damage after X-Factor! Ending the combo with just a Purification L OTG after the Liberation does 1,230,700 damage; something much more realistic to use in a match	Air (H), land, cr. (M), ⇨ + (H), cr. (H), (S) CANCEL super jump, air (M), (M), (H), (S), land, ⇨⇩⇘ + (L) OTG CANCEL ⇩⇘⇨ + ATK ATK CANCEL X-Factor, ⇩⇙⇦ + (H), ⇨⇩⇘ + ATK ATK OTG, ⇨⇩⇘ + (L) OTG CANCEL ⇩⇘⇨ + ATK ATK	2,041,500
—	If opponent jumps into ⇘ + (H)	⇘ + (H), st. (H), (S) CANCEL super jump, air (M), (M), (H), (S), land, ⇨⇩⇘ + (M) OTG CANCEL ⇩⇘⇨ + ATK ATK	470,400
Iron Man —α crossover assist	Combo from cross up beam assist	P1 or P2, ⇦⇩⇙ + (M), air (H), land, cr. (M), (S) CANCEL super jump, air (M), (M), (H), (S), land, ⇨⇩⇘ + (M) OTG CANCEL ⇩⇘⇨ + ATK ATK	463,700
She-Hulk —α crossover assist	Combo from virtually unblockable set up with She-Hulk's Torpedo	P1 or P2, ⇦⇩⇙ + (H), air (H), land, cr. (H), (S) CANCEL super jump, air (M), (M), (H), (S), land, ⇨⇩⇘ + (M) OTG CANCEL ⇩⇘⇨ + ATK ATK	646,400
She-Hulk —α crossover assist	Delay the initial air M to allow more time for She-Hulk's Torpedo to hit OTG	Cr. (L), cr. (M), ⇨ + (H), cr. (H), (S) CANCEL super jump, air (M), (M), (H), (S), land, P1 or P2, dash, (S) CANCEL super jump, air (M), (M), (H), (S), land, ⇨⇩⇘ + (M) OTG CANCEL ⇩⇘⇨ + ATK ATK	676,200

"THIS PLANET IS MINE! AND NOW, YOU DIE!"

HULK
"YOU MAKE HULK ANGRY! YOU NOT LIKE HULK ANGRY!"
BIO
REAL NAME
ROBERT BRUCE BANNER
OCCUPATION
FORMER NUCLEAR PHYSICIST
ABILITIES
AS BANNER HE HAS A GENIUS-LEVEL INTELLECT. AS THE HULK, HE IS ONE OF THE MOST POWERFUL BEINGS ON THE PLANET. HIS BODY IS ABLE TO WITHSTAND EVEN THE MOST EXTREME CONDITIONS.
WEAPONS
NONE
PROFILE
A GENIUS SCIENTIST, BRUCE ACCIDENTALLY ABSORBED HUGE AMOUNTS OF GAMMA RADIATION DURING A BOMB TEST. AS A RESULT, WHEN HIS ANGER OR NEGATIVE EMOTIONS REACH A BOILING POINT, HE TRANSFORMS INTO THE GREEN-SKINNED HULK, COMPLETE WITH INCREDIBLE POWER THAT SETS THE STANDARD FOR STRENGTH.
FIRST APPEARANCE
THE INCREDIBLE HULK #1 (1962)
POWER GRID
6 INTELLIGENCE
7 STRENGTH
3 SPEED
7 STAMINA
1 ENERGY PROJECTION
4 FIGHTING ABILITY
*This is biographical, and does not represent an evaluation of the character's in-game combat potential.
ALTERNATE COSTUMES
PS3: Xbox 360:
PS3: Xbox 360:
PS3: Xbox 360:
PS3: R1 Xbox 360: RB

ATTACK SET

STANDING BASIC ATTACKS

Screen	Command	Hits	Damage	Startup	Active	Recovery	Advantage on Hit	Advantage if Guarded	Notes
1	Standing L	1	85,000	9	3	27	-11	-14	—
2	Standing M	1	90,000	13	3	33	-10	-10	1 hit of Super Armor during frames 3-15, knocks down opponent, P1 on P2 snapback
3	Standing H	1	120,000	15	4	37	—	-15	1 hit of Super Armor during frames 6-18, ground bounces opponent, unrecoverable knockdown
4	S	2	121,000	10	2(2)3	36	—	-13	Launcher attack, not special or hyper combo-cancelable

1

2

3

4

CROUCHING BASIC ATTACKS

Screen	Command	Hits	Damage	Startup	Active	Recovery	Advantage on Hit	Advantage if Guarded	Notes
1	Crouching L	1	58,000	9	3	19	-3	-6	Low attack
2	Crouching M	1	85,000	14	3	26	-5	-9	—
3	Crouching H	1	100,000	12	4	34	—	-12	Knocks down

1

2

3

AERIAL BASIC ATTACKS

Screen	Command	Hits	Damage	Startup	Active	Recovery	Notes
1	Air L	1	60,000	7	3	18	Overhead attack
2	Air M	1	90,000	13	3	19	Overhead attack
3	Air H	1	110,000	16	5	18	Overhead attack, staggers grounded opponents for 49 frames
4	Air S	1	130,000	17	3	36	Overhead attack, causes flying screen if used in launcher combo, otherwise ground bounces opponent

1

2

3

4

AS A PARTNER-CROSSOVER ASSISTS

Screen	Type	P1+P2 Crossover Combination Hyper Combo	Description	Hits	Damage	Startup	Active	Recovery (this crossover assist)	Recovery (other partner)	Notes
1	α – Alpha	Gamma Tsunami	Gamma Wave M	3	108,300	47	28	123	93	OTG-capable, knocks down, each projectile has 5 low priority durability points
2	β – Beta	Gamma Quake	Gamma Charge M (Anti-Air)	4	137,400	29	19	130	100	1 hit of super armor during frames 23-32
3	γ – Gamma	Gamma Crush	Gamma Charge M	4	137,400	33	8	131	101	1 hit of super armor during frames 27-36

1

2

3

HULK

SPECIAL MOVES

Screen	Name	Command	Hits	Damage	Startup	Active	Recovery	Advantage on Hit	Advantage if Guarded	Notes
1	Gamma Wave L	← (charge), → + L	2	76,000	19	—	34	—	-1	OTG-capable, knocks down, projectiles are in play a total of 23 frames, each projectile has 5 low priority durability points
	Gamma Wave M	← (charge), → + M	3	108,300	23	—	36	—	-5	OTG-capable, knocks down, projectiles are in play a total of 28 frames, each projectile has 5 low priority durability points
	Gamma Wave H	← (charge), → + H	4	137,400	27	—	36	—	-6	OTG-capable, knocks down, projectiles are in play a total of 32 frames, each projectile has 5 low priority durability points
2	Gamma Charge L	↓ ↘ → + L	3	135,400	9	6	36	-12	-12	Knocks down
	Gamma Charge M	↓ ↘ → + M	4	171,800	9	8	39	-15	-15	Knocks down
	Gamma Charge H	↓ ↘ → + H	5	204,600	9	10	42	-18	-18	Knocks down
3	Gamma Charge 2nd L	(During Gamma Charge) L	1	70,000	9	10	27	—	-11	1 hit of super armor during frames 3-15, must input command during frames 9-25 of Gamma Charge, knocks down
4	Gamma Charge 2nd M	(During Gamma Charge) M	1	70,000	7	19	35	-28	-28	1 hit of super armor during frames 3-15, must input command during frames 9-25 of Gamma Charge, knocks down
5	Gamma Charge 2nd H	(During Gamma Charge) H	1	70,000	9	10	32	—	-16	1 hit of super armor during frames 3-15, must input command during frames 9-25 of Gamma Charge, knocks down
6	Gamma Charge L (Anti-Air)	→ ↓ ↘ + L	3	135,400	5	6	44	-20	-22	1 hit of super armor during frames 6-11, knocks down
	Gamma Charge M (Anti-Air)	→ ↓ ↘ + M	4	171,800	5	19	38	-25	-29	1 hit of super armor during frames 6-11, knocks down
	Gamma Charge H (Anti-Air)	→ ↓ ↘ + H	5	204,600	5	25	48	-39	-43	1 hit of super armor during frames 6-11, knocks down
7	Gamma Charge 2nd L (Anti-Air)	(During Gamma Charge (Anti-Air)) L	1	70,000	10	6	Until grounded, 10 frames of ground recovery	—	—	Must input command during frames 5-25 of Gamma Charge (Anti- Air), knocks down
8	Gamma Charge 2nd M (Anti-Air)	(During Gamma Charge (Anti-Air)) M	1	70,000	10	6	Until grounded, 10 frames of ground recovery	—	—	Must input command during frames 5-25 of Gamma Charge (Anti- Air), knocks down
9	Gamma Charge 2nd H (Anti-Air)	(During Gamma Charge (Anti-Air)) H	1	70,000	10	6	Until grounded, 15 frames of ground recovery	—	+5	Ground bounces opponent, must input command during frames 5-25 of Gamma Charge (Anti- Air), knocks down
10	Gamma Tornado L	→ ↘ ↓ ↙ ← + L	2	60,000	11	2	28	—	—	Throw attack, unrecoverable knockdown
	Gamma Tornado M	→ ↘ ↓ ↙ ← + M	2	60,000	16	2	23	—	—	Throw attack, unrecoverable knockdown
11	Gamma Tornado H	→ ↘ ↓ ↙ ← + H	2	60,000	18	2	21	—	—	Air throw attack, unrecoverable knockdown

1

Gamma Wave: Gamma Wave is one of the most important attacks at Hulk's disposal, since it gives him a strong full-screen presence. Gamma Wave alone prevents Hulk from being dominated from across the screen by zoning characters—each hit of Gamma Wave has 5 low priority durability points, more than enough to keep up with and even overpower most other characters! Against many characters, you can actually use Gamma Wave repeatedly from across the screen and force them to come to you—right into the range of Gamma Tornado and your super armor attacks. Gamma Wave is OTG-capable, and is great for ending combos in situations where the corner is too close to get much damage from Gamma Tsunami, and too far away to use Gamma Quake.

Gamma Charge: Gamma Charge is mainly used as way to make Hulk's attacks a little safer. Every single one of Hulk's basic attacks are very unsafe if guarded. Verifying that an attack is guarded, canceling into Gamma Charge H, then retreating with Gamma Charge 2nd can make it much more difficult for an opponent to punish it. Attacking with Gamma Charge in this way can also be a relatively safe way to inflict chip damage on opponents.

2

3

Gamma Charge 2nd L: When you hit your opponent with Gamma Charge, you can visually confirm the hits and cancel into Gamma Charge 2nd L for additional damage and a knockdown. If you are mid-screen you can add a Gamma Tsunami for a small amount of additional damage, or Gamma Crush in the corner for a whole lot of damage! Gamma Charge 2nd L also has a single hit of super armor very early on. This is difficult to utilize effectively, since you must whiff an entire Gamma Charge first to be able to go through something with Gamma Charge 2nd L—if Gamma Charge is guarded, Gamma Charge 2nd L does not leave any time at all for your opponent to stick anything out, making the super armor a non-factor.

4

Gamma Charge 2nd M: Gamma Charge 2nd M causes Hulk to attack straight up. Even though this attack has super armor, it is difficult to Gamma Charge 2nd M effectively in actual matches. Theoretically, you could use Gamma Charge 2nd M to attack an opponent jumping over a Gamma Charge, but this is easily guarded and punished.

Gamma Charge 2nd H: Gamma Charge 2nd H is a retreating attack that can be used in attempt to make Gamma Charge safer if it is guarded. Gamma Charge 2nd H can still be punished with fast, long ranged hyper combos like Wesker's Phantom Dance or Dormammu's Chaotic Flame. If your opponent's character can punish Gamma Charge 2nd H, you may want to use Gamma Charge 2nd L instead and hyper combo-cancel into Gamma Quake.

5

6

Gamma Charge (Anti-Air): Gamma Charge (Anti-Air) has super armor frames, but they don't kick in until after the active frames have already started. This makes it fairly rare that the super armor comes into play. Gamma Charge (Anti-Air) is still a strong anti-air, and when it is canceled into Gamma Charge 2nd H (Anti-Air) it leads into a damaging combo. If performed when the opposing character isn't too low, canceling into Gamma Charge 2nd H (Anti-Air) keeps you safe if the attacks are guarded.

7

Gamma Charge 2nd L (Anti-Air): If Gamma Charge (Anti-Air) hits and your opponent is too high above you to hit Gamma Charge 2nd H (Anti-Air), use the L version instead to a quick free extra hit.

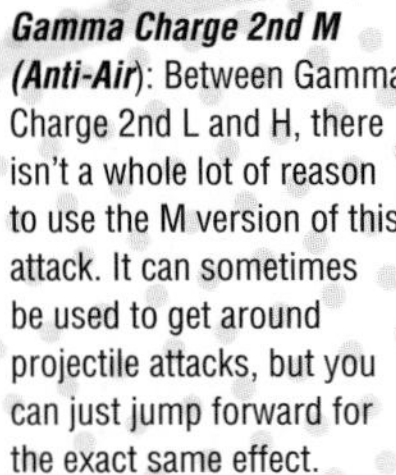

Gamma Charge 2nd M (Anti-Air): Between Gamma Charge 2nd L and H, there isn't a whole lot of reason to use the M version of this attack. It can sometimes be used to get around projectile attacks, but you can just jump forward for the exact same effect.

8

9

Gamma Charge 2nd H (Anti-Air): Gamma Charge 2nd H (Anti-Air) ground bounces an opponent, allowing for huge combos. This is an important facet of Hulk's combos, and makes Gamma Charge (Anti-Air) a hugely threatening attack. If your foe starts to jump and guard for fear of getting hit by a combo stemming from this attack, that's your cue to jump and air throw your opponent, or grab them with Gamma Tornado H! Gamma Charge 2nd H (Anti-Air) is safe if a standing opponent guards it, so you can sometimes use it as an alternative means of closing the distance on your opposition.

Gamma Tornado L and M: Gamma Tornado L and M are throw attacks with huge range that leave an opponent in an unrecoverable knockdown state, allowing you to add on one of Hulk's OTG-capable hyper combos. If you have an OTG-capable crossover assist, the Gamma Tornado attacks can lead into huge combos—see the Combo Appendix section for details. Gamma Tornado M recovers much faster after the throw animation completes, and is much easier to start a combo from than Gamma Tornado L.

10

One of the more common ways to set up Gamma Tornado is after you perform a crouching (L) to crouching (M) chain: if it hits, chain into a launcher and combo. If it is guarded and your opponent doesn't have a fast attack that will reach you, perform a late cancel into Gamma Tornado M to grab your adversary.

If your opponent is guarding near you, expecting you to use super armor attacks like standing (M) or standing (H), that's another great opportunity to grab your opponent with Gamma Tornado L or M. Finally, any time your opponent is relying on advancing guard to push you away, dash forward and jump cancel your dash into Gamma Tornado M by inputting ⇨⇘⇩⇙⇦⇖ + (M).

11

Gamma Tornado H: Gamma Tornado H is slow, but can grab airborne opponents for a combo. Unlike air throws, your opponent cannot use throw escapes to get away from Gamma Tornado H. The most common times to use this are against opponents jumping away from you after guarding a crouching (L) chain. Perform a late cancel into Gamma Tornado H to grab your opponent immediately out of their jump! Gamma Tornado H can also be used in situations when your opponent used air recovery near you, such as in the corner or after being hit by a crossover assist. It also works fairly well as anti-air against opponents super jumping towards you.

HYPER COMBOS

Screen	Name	Command	Hits	Damage	Startup	Active	Recovery	Advantage on Hit	Advantage if Guarded	Notes
1	Gamma Tsunami	⇩⇘⇨ + ATK ATK	5	327,400	6+15	24	39	—	-11	OTG-capable, knocks down, each projectile has 3 high priority durability points
2	Gamma Crush	⇩⇙⇦ + ATK ATK	8	403,700	5+10	56	48	—	-25	Invincible from frames 1-73, unrecoverable knockdown
3	Gamma Quake	⇨⇩⇘ + ATK ATK	11	301,400	6+9	81	89	—	+13	OTG-capable, knocks down, rocks will begin hitting a standing opponent 34 frames after quake is initiated, each projectile has 3 high priority durability points

Gamma Tsunami: Gamma Tsunami is a projectile hyper combo that quickly covers the screen, making it fairly easy to hit a character in many situations. It deals much more damage the closer you are to your foe, and will miss several hits if your opponent reaches the corner while Gamma Tsunami is hitting. This attack is also OTG-capable, making it the preferred ender for mid-screen combos. If your opponent is relatively close to the corner, the increased damage becomes fairly marginal. You may want to opt to save your meter and just OTG your opponent with Gamma Wave H instead.

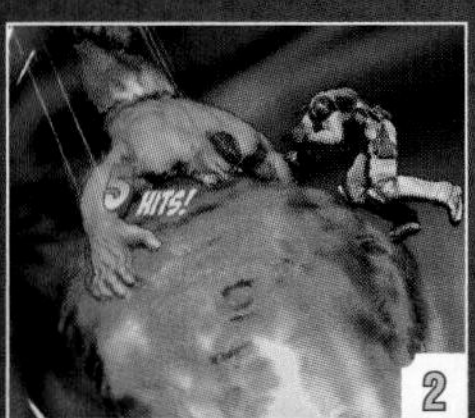

Gamma Crush: Gamma Crush has a lot invincibility to work with. That makes this a great, high-reward hyper combo to use defensively against opponents that are above you. Gamma Crush inflicts an insane 400,000 damage against opponents if it successfully hits! This also makes Gamma Crush a great move to use in team hyper combos. Any hyper combo that ends with your opponent high in the air is an opportunity to add on Gamma Crush! Gamma Crush is very unsafe if guarded, so make sure you have enough meter to team hyper combo to something safer if you plan to use Gamma Crush defensively.

Gamma Quake: The OTG-capable Gamma Quake is most often used as a combo ender in the corner, where Gamma Tsunami will miss most of its hits. Outside of combos Gamma Quake is used to hyper combo-cancel Gamma Charge attacks that are guarded, making them much safer and giving you frame advantage to continue your offense.

There is a large gap between the point where Hulk pounds the ground and when the rocks actually start hitting an opponent. This gives certain characters time to dash forward slightly and grab Hulk with a special throw attack—during throw animations the other character is invincible, allowing them to cleanly punish Gamma Quake without receiving damage. Level 3 hyper combos will also punish Gamma Quake cleanly; during the "cutscene" that happens the attacker is completely invincible as well. If you're within range of your opponent's launcher attack, they can hit you with the launcher and jump cancel, then guard the falling rocks in the air. Characters with a teleport can also get right behind Hulk and punish with a combo. Outside of these situations, if an opponent attempts to hit Hulk out of Gamma Quake they will most likely get hit by the rock avalanche for a lot of damage.

"HULK SMASH! HULK WIN! HULK IS STRONGEST!"

BATTLE PLAN

OVERVIEW

VITALITY: 1,200,000

CHAIN COMBO ARCHETYPE: 2-HIT LIMITED

X-Factor	Lv.1	Lv.2	Lv.3
Damage	130%	180%	230%
Speed	100%	100%	100%

Your goal with Hulk is to get within range to threaten your opponent with Gamma Tornado.

What makes this an effective strategy?

Gamma Tornado is a throw attack with huge range, and with an OTG-capable crossover assist it leads to major damage.

Gamma Tornado can be mixed with Gamma Tornado H or air throws, grabbing opponents that try to jump away.

Opponents trying to stay out of range of Gamma Tornado will eventually corner themselves!

How do you get within range of Gamma Tornado?

Using Gamma Wave H from across the screen, forcing your opponent to come to you!

Advancing forward behind the covering fire of a crossover assist.

Cornering your opponent.

Attacking your opponent with Gamma Charge, then hyper combo-canceling into Gamma Quake to maintain offense and push your opponent farther towards the corner.

ON THE GROUND

Using Gamma Wave H, you can actually dominate long ranged firefights against most characters!

Hulk's standing (M) and (H) have super armor and can absorb attacks. Take advantage of these to counterattack opponents and transition into damaging combos.

Gamma Tornado M has enormous range! Use it to grab opponents while you keep Hulk out of range of your opponent's attacks!

Hulk best performs the role of meter-user on a team—his combos deal extremely high damage when ended with a hyper combo, and he is also one of the few characters in *Marvel vs. Capcom 3* that doesn't build at least one bar during the course of his combos. He also becomes much stronger in matches where an opponent can't reliably punish Gamma Quake.

Hulk's dashes travel a long distance, but cannot be canceled into basic attacks or guard. This can often be a liability, since dashing forward will often run you right smack into a projectile. You also cannot quickly dash forward and attack your opponent with basic attacks. You can cancel Hulk's dashes into jumps, which allow you to instantly guard. You can also cancel the initial startup frames of a jump into a special move like Gamma Charge by inputting ↓ ↖ → ↗ + (ATK), which is useful to quickly cover ground with an attack. Dashing forward and jump-canceling to Gamma Tornado is also effective. Canceling the initial frames of a dash into a jump causes the momentum of the dash to carry over into the jump as well, resulting in some distance and speed on the jump. The difference isn't huge, but the normally-immobile Hulk can use all the help he can get!

Gamma Wave is one of the most important tools at Hulk's disposal. Each rock on the screen has 5 low priority durability points, allowing you to actually out-gun most zoning characters with Gamma Wave M or H! The startup on Gamma Wave is slow, so you'll often have to jump backwards over a projectile first to be able to respond with a Gamma Wave. If you're still finding it difficult to find time to use Gamma Wave, try using a crossover assist to take the hits from your opponent's projectiles. Once you get going with repeated Gamma Wave H projectiles, you usually can perform them indefinitely and completely shut down any ground-based projectile attacks that your opponent may have. In response your opponent will have to either come to you, or fire projectiles from the air (if they are able to). If they come to you, great! They just accomplished your goal for you!

If your opposition can fire projectiles from the air that can reach you from full-screen, things get a little trickier. Most of these projectiles can be dodged by simply jumping backwards from across the screen. Wait until your adversary has to land, then force them to guard a Gamma Wave H! While this is a very slow way to press your advantage, if you have the lead you can keep this up until you win by a timeout. In this situation, your opponent will likely give in and come to you.

When your foe gets within striking range you'll want to put them in a simple mix-up—beat their attacks with standing (M) or (H), or grab their attempts to guard with Gamma Tornado M! Standing (M) and (H) have super armor: a special property of the attack that allows Hulk to absorb one hit without going into hitstun. This allows you to take an attack from your opponent and hit them in return with your own attack, either of which leads into a damaging combo. Standing (M) and (H) work especially well as anti-air!

Both standing (M) and (H) can chain into a launcher, but all three of these attacks are very unsafe if guarded. When using these super armor attacks, press the (P1 or P2) button simultaneously with your (S) launcher—if the attacks are guarded your crossover assist will keep your opponent in guardstun for longer and keep Hulk safe. If the attacks hit, super jump-canceling the launcher will allow you to perform a combo without interference from your crossover assist in most cases. If your crossover assist is especially fast, like Chun-Li—γ, then you can simply press the (P1 or P2) button later.

There are some key differences between standing (M) and standing (H). The super armor of standing (M) kicks in much faster, at only 3 frames of startup. This allows you to use standing (M) in situations where you barely even have time to move! On the flip side, standing (M) will not combo into a launcher at farther ranges. It can also be cleanly crouched under by many characters:

Amaterasu	**Deadpool**	**Hsien-Ko**	**Phoenix**	**Super-Skrull**	**Wolverine**
Arthur	**Dormammu**	**Magneto**	**Spider-Man**	**Trish**	**X-23**
Dante	**Felicia**	**Morrigan**	**Storm**	**Viewtiful Joe**	**Zero**

The super armor of standing (H) kicks in at the sixth frame; noticeably slower than standing (M). On the plus side it ground bounces an opponent, leading into combos much more consistently at all ranges. It also has a much larger area-of-effect around Hulk. To avoid getting hit by super armor attacks, your opponent may try to simply guard when they get within range. If you can predict this, surprise your opponent by grabbing them with Gamma Tornado M! A successful grab leads into a combo opportunity. You can either dash forward, then jump-cancel and land before performing Gamma Tsunami, or go straight into Gamma Quake if your foe ends up in the corner. If you have an OTG-capable assist you can deal much more damage from a Gamma Tornado—see the Combo Usage section for details.

Smarter opponents will try to counter your super armor attacks by avoiding them completely, using movement options like double jumps or airdashes. In these cases you can't rely on a crossover assist to cover you; Hulk and the crossover character will probably be hit by a combo. Instead, try canceling your whiffed super armor attack into Gamma Charge or Gamma Charge (Anti-Air). Both of these attacks can be followed with their (H) enders, making them much more safe. Barring that, hyper combo-cancel into Gamma Quake!

If you must be proactive and come to your opponent, due to timer concerns, it's almost mandatory that you have a long ranged crossover assist to use for covering fire—call your assist, then dash forward and jump while guarding. As an alternative, you can also gain ground after calling assists using Gamma Charge H, then Gamma Charge 2nd L. You may want to counter all projectile attacks entirely with Gamma Tsunami. It will only inflict 216,700 damage from all the way across the screen, but it knocks your opponent down and buys you time to call a long ranged crossover assist, then dash forward and jump.

Without a long ranged assist for covering fire, gaining ground on your opponent is an uphill battle while you are using Hulk. Your only real options to advance are to dash and jump forward, super jump, and Gamma Charge H. From Gamma Charge H you can attempt to use the super armor of Gamma Charge 2nd L to blow through an attack from your opponent, but timing this correctly is rare. If your opponent guards Gamma Charge 2nd L, hyper combo-cancel into Gamma Quake if your opponent's character cannot reliably punish it. From there you can use the frame advantage to continue attacking, pushing your opponent back to the corner.

Whenever you get into striking range with Hulk you have a chance to mix your opponent up. If your opponent guards crouching (L) to crouching (M), you can perform a late cancel into Gamma Tornado M to grab them. Most characters cannot easily interrupt the Gamma Tornado because it is out of range of their fast attacks. If your opponent tries to jump away, simply perform a late cancel into Gamma Tornado H instead. If your challenger uses advancing guard you cannot perform this mix-up. However, if your opponent is waiting to use advancing guard, simply grab them right away with Gamma Tornado! It's useful to be able to dash forward and cancel the dash into Gamma Tornado in situations like these: input → →, then ↖ ↓ ↙ ← ↖ + (ATK)

UP IN THE AIR

You do not have any special aerial movement options or special moves to work while you are playing Hulk. The only way you can change Hulk's air trajectory is by using air Ⓗ, which stops all of his vertical momentum briefly before dropping him back down. This can be used on the way up from a super jump to result in a jump arc that's somewhere halfway between a normal jump and a super jump—you jump high enough to avoid most ground projectiles, but don't stay in the air quite long enough for your opponent to easily wavedash under you. When using this "clap jump", attack with air Ⓢ on the way down if your adversary is below you. It covers a large area below Hulk and results in a ground bounce if it hits.

Air Ⓢ can cross up opponents, leading into a combo!

If your opponent guards air Ⓛ, you can surprise them with a second overhead attack before landing…

…and if your opponent uses advancing guard on the air Ⓛ, immediately dash forward to keep attacking!

When you get into range to attack, jumping at your opponent and attacking with air Ⓛ is a strong option. Once it makes contact you can chain into air Ⓜ, resulting in a sneaky, double-overhead attack that is extremely difficult to guard. If your opponent begins guarding the air Ⓜ, you can simply omit it and go straight into crouching Ⓛ, or land and grab your foe with Gamma Tornado L. Unfortunately, unless your challenger is in the corner, this mix-up can be nullified if advancing guard is used against the air Ⓛ.

However, by inputting ⇨⇨ while pressing Ⓜ, a nice option select is created. If your opponent does not use advancing guard your air Ⓜ makes contact. If they do use advancing guard, the air Ⓜ completely whiffs, and in the absence of guardstun you immediately dash forward upon landing! From there you can jump-cancel the dash into Gamma Tornado L, or jump forward and air throw a jumping opponent!

As an alternative to Gamma Tornado mix-ups, you can also try to dash forward and jump over an opponent, then hit them with a surprise cross-up air Ⓢ! Air Ⓢ ground bounces an opponent, so no matter how high in your jump you hit your foe, you'll still be able to land and transition into a full combo.

COMBO USAGE

I. (MID-SCREEN REQUIRED) CR. Ⓛ, CR. Ⓜ, Ⓢ CANCEL➡ SUPER JUMP, AIR Ⓜ, Ⓜ, Ⓗ, Ⓢ, LAND, DASH CANCEL➡ JUMP CANCEL CANCEL➡ ⬇⬊➡ + ATK ATK

(573,100 damage) Hulk's combo from a crouching Ⓛ is all very simple and basic until you must perform the final hyper combo—Gamma Tsunami does more damage the closer you are to an opponent, making it worthwhile to dash forward after flying screen. However, Hulk's dash isn't normally cancelable into anything besides jumps. You can cancel the initial frames of a jump into the Gamma Tsunami by inputting ⬇⬊➡⬈ + ATK ATK.

If the initial attacks are guarded you have a few options: perform a late cancel into Gamma Tornado M to grab a guarding opponent, or a late cancel into Gamma Tornado H against jumping opponents. For a safer option, cancel the crouching Ⓜ into Gamma Charge H, then retreat with Gamma Charge 2nd H. Be wary of opponents that can still punish Gamma Charge 2nd H! In that situation you may want to use Gamma Charge 2nd L instead, then hyper combo-cancel into Gamma Quake.

II. (MID-SCREEN REQUIRED) CR. Ⓛ, CR. Ⓗ CANCEL➡ ➡⬇⬊ + Ⓗ (1 HIT) CANCEL➡ (DURING GAMMA CHARGE (ANTI-AIR) Ⓗ, WALK FORWARD, ST. Ⓛ, CR. Ⓗ, Ⓢ CANCEL➡ SUPER JUMP, AIR Ⓜ, Ⓜ, Ⓗ, Ⓢ, LAND, DASH CANCEL➡ JUMP CANCEL CANCEL➡ ⬇⬊➡ + ATK ATK

(695,700 damage) By chaining into crouching Ⓗ instead of crouching Ⓜ you can perform a combo that inflicts much more damage. This combo requires you to be very close to an opponent; if you're even a little bit too far, the Gamma Charge (Anti-Air) or crouching Ⓗ are very likely to whiff.

III. (MID-SCREEN REQUIRED) ST. Ⓗ, Ⓢ CANCEL➡ SUPER JUMP, AIR Ⓜ, Ⓜ, Ⓗ, Ⓢ, LAND, DASH CANCEL➡ JUMP CANCEL CANCEL➡ ⬇⬊➡ + ATK ATK

(609,400 damage) Hulk's super armor attacks are among the scariest tools he has at his disposal, punishing your opponent for attacking with major damage. Other than the jump-canceled dash at the end, this combo is among the easiest in the game. Pressing P1 or P2 simultaneously with Ⓢ makes this a safe combo to go for, provided your crossover assist isn't very slow.

IV. (MID-SCREEN REQUIRED) ➡⬊⬇⬋⬅ + ATK, DASH CANCEL➡ JUMP FORWARD, P1 or P2, LAND, JUMP FORWARD, AIR Ⓗ, Ⓢ, LAND, CR. Ⓗ, Ⓢ CANCEL➡ SUPER JUMP, AIR Ⓜ, Ⓜ, Ⓗ, Ⓢ, LAND, DASH CANCEL➡ JUMP CANCEL CANCEL➡ ⬇⬊➡ + ATK ATK

(581,300 damage, Wesker—β) Gamma Tornado leaves your opponent in an unrecoverable knockdown state for an extended period of time, allowing you to use even very slow OTG-capable assists like Super-Skrull—α. Wesker—β is one of the best all-around crossover assists in *Marvel vs. Capcom 3*, so it is used in this example combo. Note that Gamma Tornado L has significantly more recovery than the other versions of the attack; this actually requires you to use one of the fast OTG-capable crossover assists midscreen.

Ending the combo with Gamma Quake in the corner results in 625,000 damage. Ending the combo with Gamma Wave H results in 445,300 damage.

V. (MID-SCREEN REQUIRED) AIR THROW, P1 or P2, LAND, ➡⬇⬊ + Ⓗ CANCEL➡ (DURING GAMMA CHARGE (ANTI-AIR) Ⓗ, CR. Ⓗ, Ⓢ CANCEL➡ SUPER JUMP, AIR Ⓜ, Ⓜ, Ⓗ, Ⓢ, LAND, DASH CANCEL➡ JUMP CANCEL CANCEL➡ ⬇⬊➡ + ATK ATK

(628,300 damage, Wesker—β) You get a lot of opportunities to land air throws as Hulk; opponents will typically jump backwards in desperation whenever you get close. As such, being able to convert these air throws into major damage is very important. Unlike Gamma Tornado combos, Hulk requires one of the faster OTG-capable assists to combo from an air throw, like Wesker—β or Deadpool—β.

ASSISTS

Hulk's crossover assist types are something of a mixed bag. Gamma Wave is OTG-capable and is handy for nullifying other projectiles, but it is also very slow and doesn't reach all the way across the screen. It also doesn't have the slow-traveling threat of a projectile assist, nor does it have the quick, full-screen utility of a beam assist. Gamma Charge and Gamma Charge (Anti-Air) can be very useful because of their super armor properties, but still have a vulnerable frame before the super armor kicks in. Gamma Charge (Anti-Air) is faster and easier to time, but also doesn't have the horizontal range. Both of the Gamma Charge assists are difficult to protect; careless use can quickly result in a lost character. For most teams, Gamma Wave is the recommended crossover assist type to use, simply because it is a long ranged assist.

Wesker—β greatly increases your damage potential as Hulk!

Projectile-based crossover assists are practically a necessity to close the distance on opponents safely.

Hulk isn't nearly as fearsome without the ability to convert Gamma Tornado and air throws into huge damage. While most OTG-capable crossover assists in the game will allow you to combo from Gamma Tornado, only the fastest ones will allow you to combo from Hulk's air throw. Deadpool—β is the fastest OTG-capable crossover assist in the game, but Katanarama! causes a ground bounce; this reduces Hulk's overall damage potential. Wesker—β emerges as the clear choice—not only is he a fast, OTG-capable assist that doesn't ground bounce, he also hits low for additional offensive potential!

You won't always be able to Gamma Wave your opponents into submission and force them to approach you. In particular, if you're lower on health and the clock is ticking, you'll have to make a move and approach your challenger. Hulk is very immobile and has difficulty getting around zoning defenses, he essentially requires you to have a long ranged assist for covering fire. Long ranged assists perform a variety of other roles—making Gamma Charges safe, making super armor attacks safe, helping you find time to Gamma Wave H in a long ranged firefight, and even for dash cross-ups! See the Advanced Tactics section for details.

ADVANCED TACTICS

DASH CROSS-UP VERSUS CROUCHING CHARACTERS

Hulk's unique dash allows you to dash straight over many characters if they are crouching. Cross up your opponent using crossover assists!

While Hulk's dash is mostly a liability, it also offers a distinct benefit—you can dash straight over more than half of the characters in the game if they are crouching! This allows you to perform tricky cross-ups using crossover assists, which can lead into combos.

The following characters can be dashed over if they are crouching:

Amaterasu	Dormammu	Morrigan	Super-Skrull	Wolverine
Arthur	Felicia	Phoenix	Taskmaster	X-23
Dante	Hsien-Ko	Spider-Man	Trish	Zero
Deadpool	Magneto	Storm	Viewtiful Joe	

Some characters are easier to dash over than others; Amaterasu can be crossed up from almost any point in your dash. Taskmaster on the other hand can barely be cleared if you begin the dash at a very close distance.

COMBO APPENDIX

GENERAL EXECUTION TIPS

When ending combos with dash into Gamma Tsunami, jump-cancel the dash, then cancel the jump into the hyper combo. This is performed by inputting ⇩⇘⇨⇗ + ATK ATK.

To avoid getting an accidental Gamma Quake using the above method, dash forward by pressing ATK ATK instead of using ⇨⇨.

Requirements (Position, meter, etc.)	Notes	Command Sequence	Damage
Corner required	—	Cr. Ⓛ, cr. Ⓜ CANCEL ▶ ⇨⇩⇘ + Ⓗ (5 hits) CANCEL ▶ (during Gamma Charge (Anti-Air) Ⓗ, st. Ⓛ, cr. Ⓗ, Ⓢ CANCEL ▶ super jump, air Ⓜ, Ⓜ, Ⓗ, Ⓢ, land, ⇨⇩⇘ + ATK ATK OTG	741,100
Mid-screen required	Combo starting from standing Ⓜ, which has super armor from the third frame. Cancel into Gamma Charge to make it safer. Omitting the Gamma Tsunami results in 311,300 damage. In the corner, ending the combo with Gamma Crush results in 594,000 damage	St. Ⓜ CANCEL ▶ ⇩⇘⇨ + Ⓗ CANCEL ▶ (during Gamma Charge] Ⓛ CANCEL ▶ ⇩⇘⇨ + ATK ATK	511,300
Mid-screen required	Combo from standing Ⓜ at close range	St. Ⓜ, Ⓢ CANCEL ▶ super jump, air Ⓜ, Ⓜ, Ⓗ, Ⓢ, land, dash CANCEL ▶ jump cancel CANCEL ▶ ⇩⇘⇨ + ATK ATK	592,100
Mid-screen required	This combo works after air throws in both directions	Air throw, land, ⇩⇘⇨ + ATK ATK	394,600
Mid-screen required	—	⇨⇘⇩⇙⇦ + Ⓜ, dash CANCEL ▶ forward jump, land, ⇩⇘⇨ + ATK ATK OTG	325,100
Mid-screen required	Combo from cross-up air Ⓢ	Air Ⓢ, land, walk forward, st. Ⓛ, cr. Ⓗ, Ⓢ CANCEL ▶ super jump, air Ⓜ, Ⓜ, Ⓗ, Ⓢ, land, dash CANCEL ▶ jump cancel CANCEL ▶ ⇩⇘⇨ + ATK ATK	684,600
Corner required	Ending the combo with Gamma Tsunami mid-screen results in 656,400 damage	⇨⇩⇘ + Ⓗ (5 hits) CANCEL ▶ (during Gamma Charge (Anti-Air) Ⓗ, walk forward, st. Ⓛ, cr. Ⓗ, Ⓢ CANCEL ▶ super jump, air Ⓜ, Ⓜ, Ⓗ, Ⓢ, land, ⇨⇩⇘ + ATK ATK OTG	681,400
Corner required, level 1 X-Factor	Cancel the Gamma Quake into X-Factor as soon as Hulk's fist hits the ground, then quickly perform Gamma Charge H to hit while the rocks are still hitting an opponent	Cr. Ⓛ, cr. Ⓜ CANCEL ▶ ⇨⇩⇘ + Ⓗ (5 hits) CANCEL ▶ (during Gamma Charge (Anti-Air) Ⓗ, st. Ⓛ, cr. Ⓗ, Ⓢ CANCEL ▶ super jump, air Ⓜ, Ⓜ, Ⓗ, Ⓢ, land, ⇨⇩⇘ + ATK ATK OTG CANCEL ▶ X-Factor, ⇩⇘⇨ + Ⓗ CANCEL ▶ ⇩⇙⇦ + ATK ATK	1,250,100

IRON MAN

"GOT TO CALL PEPPER. LOOKS LIKE I'M GOING TO BE FASHIONABLY LATE TO YET ANOTHER PARTY."

BIO

REAL NAME

ANTHONY "TONY" EDWARD STARK

OCCUPATION

ADVENTURER, PRESIDENT EMERITUS OF STARK INDUSTRIES

ABILITIES

TONY'S SHARP MIND AND TECHNOLOGICAL KNOW-HOW ALLOW HIM TO DEVELOP AND MAINTAIN HIS OWN BATTLE SUIT. AS IRON MAN, HIS ARMOR IS EQUIPPED WITH VARIOUS WEAPONS, AS WELL AS THE ABILITY TO FLY.

WEAPONS

HE HAS VARIOUS WEAPONS, INCLUDING THE REPULSOR RAY HE CAN FIRE FROM BOTH HANDS, ANTI-TANK MISSILES, AND THE UNIBEAM HE FIRES FROM HIS CHEST. HE HAS SEVERAL ARMORS WITH DIFFERENT FUNCTIONALITY.

PROFILE

CAPTURED BY A TERRORIST GROUP IN A WAR-TORN REGION, TONY CREATED A BATTLE SUIT TO HELP HIM ESCAPE. AFTERWARDS, HE IMPROVED THE BATTLE SUIT TO BECOME IRON MAN, AND HAS DEDICATED HIMSELF TO PROTECTING THE PEACE SINCE.

FIRST APPEARANCE

TALES OF SUSPENSE #39 (1963)

POWER GRID

6	INTELLIGENCE
6	STRENGTH
5	SPEED
6	STAMINA
6	ENERGY PROJECTION
3	FIGHTING ABILITY

*This is biographical, and does not represent an evaluation of the character's in-game combat potential.

ALTERNATE COSTUMES

PS3: ⓧ Xbox 360: Ⓐ	PS3: ▢ Xbox 360: Ⓧ	PS3: △ Xbox 360: Ⓨ	PS3: R1 Xbox 360: RB

ATTACK SET

STANDING BASIC ATTACKS

Screen	Command	Hits	Damage	Startup	Active	Recovery	Advantage on Hit	Advantage if Guarded	Notes
1	Standing L	1	47,000	5	3	8	+2	+1	Rapid fire
2	Standing M	1	70,000	8	4	12	+1	0	↓ ↘ → + P1 or P2 snap back
3	Standing H	1	90,000	13	5	32	-14	-16	—
4	S	1	80,000	13	3	31	—	-13	Launcher, not special or hyper combo cancelable

CROUCHING BASIC ATTACKS

Screen	Command	Hits	Damage	Startup	Active	Recovery	Advantage on Hit	Advantage if Guarded	Notes
1	Crouching L	1	45,000	5	3	11	-1	-2	Low attack, rapid fire
2	Crouching M	1	68,000	7	4	20	—	-3	Low attack, knocks down opponent
3	Crouching H	1	80,000	20	—	17	+9	+4	Not special- or hyper combo-cancelable, knocks down, projectile has 5 low priority durability points

AERIAL BASIC ATTACKS

Screen	Command	Hits	Damage	Startup	Active	Recovery	Notes
1	Air L	1	50,000	4	3	17	Overhead attack, double jump-cancelable
2	Air M	1	70,000	8	8	17	Overhead attack, double jump-cancelable
3	Air H	1	80,000	11	6	29	Overhead attack, double jump-cancelable
4	Air S	1	90,000	13	6	29	Overhead attack, causes flying screen when used in launcher combo

COMMAND ATTACKS

Screen	Command	Hits	Damage	Startup	Active	Recovery	Notes
1	Air ⇧ + Ⓗ	1	80,000	11	6	29	Overhead attack, double jump-cancelable
2	Air ⇩ + Ⓗ	1	80,000	11	6	29	Overhead attack, double jump-cancelable

AS A PARTNER-CROSSOVER ASSISTS

Screen	Type	P1+P2 Crossover Combination Hyper Combo	Description	Hits	Damage	Startup	Active	Recovery (this crossover assist)	Recovery (other partner)	Notes
1	α – Alpha	Proton Cannon	Unibeam M	8	113,600	47	25	108	78	Beam is full-screen in 56 frames, beam durability: 8 frames x 1 low priority durability points
2	β – Beta	Angled Proton Cannon	Repulsor Blast M	5	122,600	40	55	103	73	Knocks down opponent, beam durability: 5 frames x 3 low priority durability points
3	γ – Gamma	Proton Cannon	Smart Bomb H	10	129,900	44	—	133	103	OTG-capable, , two beam-like projectiles with 5 frames x 3 low priority durability points each

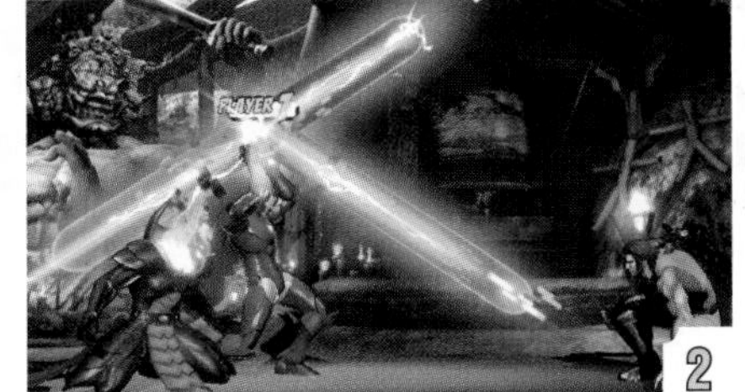

SPECIAL MOVES

Screen	Name	Command	Hits	Damage	Startup	Active	Recovery	Advantage on Hit	Advantage if Guarded	Notes
1	Unibeam L	↓↘→ + L	5	81,700	18	20	15	0	-15	Beam is full-screen in 26 frames, beam durability: 5 frames x 1 low priority durability points
	Unibeam M	↓↘→ + M	8	113,600	23	25	15	+4	-11	Beam is full-screen in 31 frames, beam durability: 8 frames x 1 low priority durability points
	Unibeam H	↓↘→ + H	10	129,900	28	30	15	+5	-10	Beam is full-screen in 36 frames, beam durability: 11 frames x 1 low priority durability points
2	Repulsor Blast L	↓↙← + L	5	81,700	11	50	10	—	-8	Knocks down opponent, beam durability: 5 frames x 3 low priority durability points
3	Repulsor Blast M	↓↙← + M	5	102,300	16	55	10	—	-13	Knocks down opponent, beam durability: 5 frames x 3 low priority durability points
4	Repulsor Blast H	↓↙← + H	5	122,600	21	60	10	—	-18	Knocks down opponent, beam durability: 5 frames x 3 low priority durability points
5	Repulsor Spread	↓↙← + H during Repulsor Blast	1	80,000	1	6	24	—	-9	Spinning knockdown, explosion has 8 low priority durability points
6	Smart Bomb L	→↓↘ + L	2	57,000	20	—	24	-1	-3	OTG-capable, two projectiles with 1 low priority durability point each
	Smart Bomb M	→↓↘ + M	6	84,200	20	—	36	-8	-10	OTG-capable, two beam-like projectiles with 3 frames x 1 low priority durability points each
	Smart Bomb H	→↓↘ + H	10	103,700	20	—	41	-10	-12	OTG-capable, two beam-like projectiles with 5 frames x 1 low priority durability points each
	Air Smart Bomb L	→↓↘ + L	2	57,000	20	—	18	—	—	OTG-capable, two projectiles with 1 low priority durability point each
	Smart Bomb M (in air OK)	→↓↘ + M	6	84,200	20	—	23	—	—	OTG-capable, two beam-like projectiles with 3 frames x 1 low priority durability points each
	Smart Bomb H (in air OK)	→↓↘ + H	10	103,700	20	—	29	—	—	OTG-capable, two beam-like projectiles with 5 frames x 1 low priority durability points each
7	Flight	↓↙← + S	—	—	14	—	—	—	—	Enters Flight mode, flight lasts 106 frames

Unibeam: Iron Man's direct beam attack. Number of hits, overall damage, durability points, and startup time are increased in higher strength versions. Iron Man's beam is a little bit slower and less durable than Doctor Doom's equivalent attack, and Iron Man will also lose beam firefights with Arthur, Magneto, Storm, or a resourceful Dormammu or Taskmaster. Against characters with standard projectiles, or no projectiles at all, Unibeam H gives Iron Man a solid solution for winning zoning wars. Err toward using the H version; while weaker versions are faster, they also lose much of the potency that allows Unibeam H to plow through most other projectiles.

Unibeam can be performed in the air, which can prove useful for cutting off two horizontal planes of the screen at once, by calling a ground beam assist before leaping to perform air Unibeam. Conversely, you could use Unibeam to cut off horizontal space while Dante—α or Dormammu—β cut off vertical space.

Repulsor Blast L

Repulsor Blast M

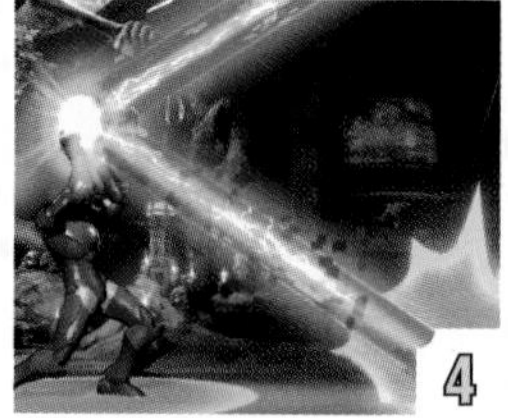

Repulsor Blast H

Repulsor Blast: Iron Man creates a linear, warping cross of laser energy that pulsates around his raised hands. It is important to note that Repulsor Blast H is faster than both Unibeam M and H at mid range, for the purposes of poking opponents with a projectile! It can also be hit-confirmed into either Proton Cannon, or Repulsor Spread (then, if you feel like it and you have three bars, Iron Avenger!).

Repulsor Blast is technically a beam, just like Unibeam, that will exchange durability points with other low priority projectiles. This means, with a little finesse, you can use Repulsor Blast canceled into Repulsor Spread to eat up a lot of your foe's projectiles. It's the slowest version, but try to use Repulsor Blast H for this purpose—this version easily eats up the most screen space, giving you the most potential to score stray hits and absorb incoming projectiles.

Repulsor Blast (then Repulsor Spread) also works as a great preemptive defense against aggressive teleport or triangle jump oriented characters (they'll just run into the energy, and you can then blast them away with Repulsor Spread or Proton Cannon). It can also be used to provide a shield for incoming assists. Calling a zoning oriented assist like Doctor Doom—β or Taskmaster—γ, then performing Repulsor Blast H into Repulsor Spread to essentially guarantee the assist call, this can buy you time and also force your foe to block a Unibeam or two as the assist eventually pins them. Then you can call the assist and Repulsor Blast H again!

Repulsor Spread: This interesting follow-up special can only be activated during a Repulsor Blast. Iron Man dissipates all the energy from his palms at once, creating a large, instant explosion. Repulsor Spread is technically tied for the fastest attack in the game, along with some command throws, since it hits on the first frame. In practice, it's not that sneaky—it's only possible after 23+ frames of a Repulsor Blast. Still, this is an excellent attack. Repulsor Spread allows Iron Man to use Repulsor Blasts as long, invincible mid range pokes without actually taking much risk—whenever an opponent guards or evades a Repulsor Blast, just use Repulsor Spread to cancel the Repulsor Blast recovery. You can actually wait a bit, and cancel Repulsor Blast into Repulsor Spread quite late. This can hit foes who attempt to rush in at the end of Repulsor Blast, expecting to punish Iron Man's recovery.

On hit Repulsor Spread produces a spinning knockdown. Anytime you successfully land Repulsor Spread, you can hyper combo cancel into Iron Avenger. You don't have to hyper combo cancel right away—in fact, if you do, the hyper combo might whiff by sliding under the spinning foe too early.

Smart Bomb: Smart Bombs are the foundation of Iron Man's offense. Smart Bombs are not quite beams, not quite projectiles—while the Ⓛ version just fires two projectiles, the Ⓜ and Ⓗ versions behave more like two separate beams, dealing durability damage to other projectiles over time. Unlike beams (and more like projectiles), Smart Bombs do not disappear if Iron Man takes a hit after releasing them.

Smart Bombs can be performed on the ground or in the air. On the ground, Smart Bombs are most useful for their OTG capability—Smart Bomb L makes the best OTG attack, as it has the lowest number of hits (heavier Smart Bombs actually weaken the combo overall because of rapidly accelerated damage scaling). From the air, Smart Bombs temporarily assure control of a downward sloping corridor that extends a little less than half the playing field away. Smart Bomb H is the best while airborne. From the air you'll want the highest durability and number of hits to hold an opponent. In much the same way as Akuma with his aerial projectile, Iron Man can set up safe aggressive paths to to his target by getting above them and raining down Smart Bombs. Smart Bombs done low enough to the ground allow you to airdash in with ↓ + Ⓗ afterward, or fall with air Ⓗ to score extra hits. Depending on position, you may get a full combo.

Flight: Iron Man has the best Flight mode in the game, in terms of speed. He's free to move 14 frames after activation, or immediately after cancelation. Coupled with his 4 frame air Ⓛ and his excellent array of air Ⓗ attacks, Iron Man has flexibility in attacks and chains during Flight that no one else has.

IRON MAN

HYPER COMBOS

Screen	Name	Command	Hits	Damage	Startup	Active	Recovery	Advantage on Hit	Advantage if Guarded	Notes
1	Proton Cannon	↓↘→ + ATK ATK	36	276,800	3*22+1	6*111	47	—	-47	Knocks down opponent, beam durability: 35 frames x 1 high priority durability points
1	Angled Proton Cannon	→↓↘ + ATK ATK	36	276,800	3*22+1	6*111	47	—	-47	Knocks down opponent, beam durability: 35 frames x 1 high priority durability points
3	Iron Avenger	↓↙← + ATK ATK	68	430,000	10+3	11	41	—	-31	Level 3 hyper combo, unrecoverable knockdown, unaffected by damage scaling, frames 1-21 invincible

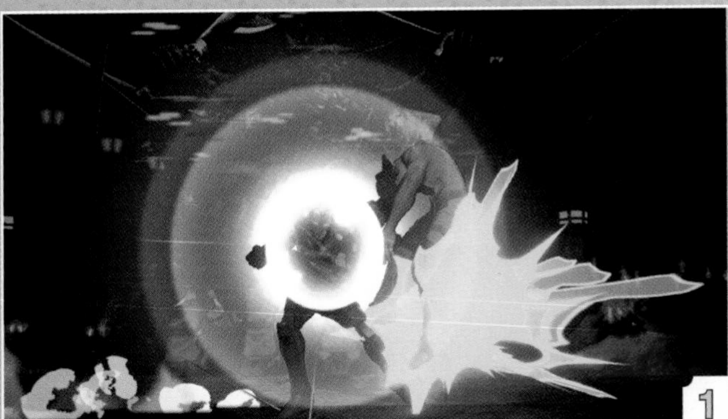

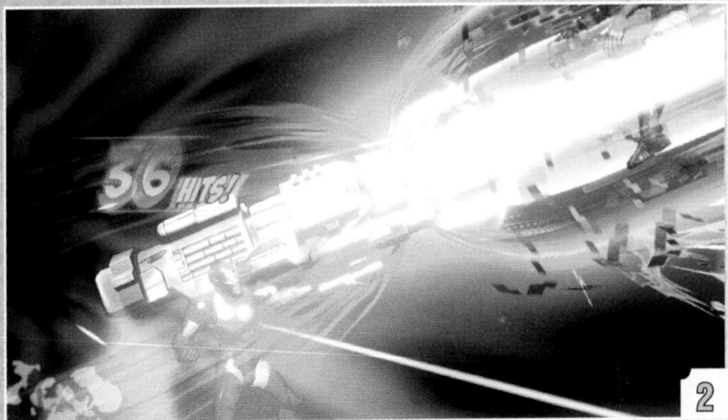

Proton Cannon & Angled Proton Cannon: While Proton Cannon couldn't quite be called sluggish, it is relatively slow full screen compared to beam hyper combos like Akuma's Messatsu-Gohado Ungyo or Dormammu's Chaotic Flame. Because of its nature (causing a screen freeze a few frames more quickly than other hyper combos) an opponent is given slightly more time to react to your hyper combo activation if they're not yet committed to an action. In other words, it's very guardable on reaction if the opposing player didn't already hit a button. It can still be used to punish some things from full screen on reaction, especially opposing crossover assists or recovering attacks, but it can't punish quite so many things.

Interestingly, it's one of the fastest close range attacks in the game—the motion Iron Man makes to summon the Proton Cannon hits up close on the third frame! This is extremely fast for a physical hit. This means that, although Proton Cannon has no invulnerability, it's still fast enough to punish or interrupt many close range tactics. It can almost be thought of as a 3 frame, close range tick that happens to deal almost 300,000 damage! If guarded or avoided Proton Cannon is unsafe, but you can use the opportunity to team hyper combo in your next character, preferably with a hyper combo that is safe and deals decent chip damage, or with an enhancing hyper combo ability. Even planning to THC isn't totally safe, however; if an attentive opponent blocks the third frame hit and ***doesn't*** use advancing guard, they have plenty of time to start up a full ground chain on Iron Man in between the third frame hit and before Proton Cannon actually fires. However, there's another layer here, because you can wait for the opposing player to start an attack, then THC out of Proton Cannon to a close range hyper combo before Iron Man is interrupted. Tricking a challenger with this even once should make them hesitant to punish blocked, close range Proton Cannons in the future. In general, the less frequently and predictably you use Proton Cannon as a close range desperation move, the more often it will actually hit.

Proton Cannon's quick first hit has a hitbox in a big circle around Iron Man. This makes it easy to stick a Proton Cannon onto the end of any combo or juggle that leaves Iron Man on the ground and an opponent within one character width away.

Iron Avenger: Iron Man's extremely damaging level 3 hyper combo. Like all level 3 hyper combos, Iron Avenger is not affected by damage scaling. Iron Man's combos deal solid damage already, so tacking on an Iron Avenger (if you have the hyper combo gauge available to do it, and especially if you'll knock out a character), is usually worth it.

Iron Avenger is invulnerable from activation until the 22nd frame, and by then it's crossed the entire screen. Iron Avenger can thus be used on reaction to all kinds of full screen actions. Something as simple as throwing a single projectile takes on heavy consequences against an Iron Man player looking to use Iron Avenger. Happily, if a crossover assist is between Iron Man and the opposing point character as he pushes forward during Iron Avenger, he'll simply brush the assist aside and continue toward the point character for the remainder of active frames.

Needless to say, Iron Avenger as a counter move becomes much more potent with X-Factor burning. Iron Avenger deals 752,500 damage by itself during level 3 X-Factor!

BATTLE PLAN

OVERVIEW

VITALITY: 950,000

CHAIN COMBO ARCHETYPE: HUNTER SERIES

X-Factor	Lv.1	Lv.2	Lv.3
Damage	130%	180%	230%
Speed	107%	114%	121%

Your goal with Iron Man is to keep your foe at mid range. Imagine an oval five character widths wide and two character heights high around Iron Man, on the ground at the center. This is Iron Man's bubble. Keep your opposition out of it. In this way you can also think of Iron Man as a vehicle for deploying and defending assists. Once your opponent either is forced into passivity by your mid range zoning, is pushed back into the corner, or accidentally runs into something, you should go on the offensive.

Why is Iron Man effective from mid range? Because his entire arsenal is basically designed for this purpose, and it's a fine arsenal indeed:

Air Ⓗ and its command attack variants (⇧ + Ⓗ and ⇩ + Ⓗ) are some of the best air attacks in the game; they have enormous range, lots of active frames, can be canceled into Flight or double jumps, and Iron Man does not project a vulnerable hitbox beyond his hands.

Unibeam H overpowers most low priority projectiles while dealing good chip damage and building significant meter, even when guarded.

Repulsor Blast H can be used as a "guess" poke against a huge portion of the playing field from mid range, and can be made essentially safe by canceling into Repulsor Spread.

Smart Bombs dropped directly onto (or right in front of) an opposing character are very hard for an opponent to deal with; and from this range even if they get around Smart Bombs, either dashing underneath or jumping above, they'll still have to deal with the invincible tip of air Ⓗ!

Iron Man has some excellent offensive capabilities to utilize when an opponent is passive:

Air Ⓛ is a 4 frame basic attack, making for fast close range triangle jumps.

Any of air Ⓜ, Ⓗ, and ⇩ + Ⓗ makes a great overhead from longer range, or out of a box jump.

In much the same way that Akuma and Doctor Doom can use an air projectiles to provide cover to rush in, Iron Man can drop Smart Bombs and airdash behind them (or fall with Ⓗ, or more Smart Bombs).

Iron Man has the fastest Flight mode in the game. He can fly to enhance combos, to escape dangerous situations, and to drop crossover assists in confusing ways.

Iron Avenger has the speed and invulnerability to punish many full screen actions for heavy damage.

COMBO USAGE

I. CROUCHING Ⓛ, CROUCHING Ⓜ, STANDING Ⓗ, Ⓢ CANCEL⇨ SUPER JUMP, AIR Ⓜ, Ⓜ, Ⓗ, ⬇ + Ⓗ, Ⓢ, LAND, DASH, ➡⬇↘ + Ⓛ OTG CANCEL⇨ ⬇↘➡ + ATK ATK

(600,000 damage, 844,700 damage during level 1 X-Factor) For the heavy damage it causes, and the perfect THC position Proton Cannon places an opponent in, this combo is extraordinarily easy. The only trouble spots: rush through the ground chain as fast as possible, hit as soon as possible with the first air Ⓜ, and rush the air chain, but be careful not to get direction + Ⓢ instead of neutral Ⓢ at the end (unless you'd like to use this as a team aerial combo starter). This combo actually does more damage using the Ⓛ version of Smart Bomb to OTG—heavier versions have many more hits, which adversely affects damage scaling.

When at least 3 bars are ready, end the combo with Iron Man's level 3 hyper combo, Iron Avenger, instead of Proton Cannon. This deals 800,100 damage (1,059,800 during level 1 X-Factor) an enormous amount for a relatively simple combo.

You may sometimes land the initial low chain outside of the range to launch with Ⓢ. Hitting from outside of point blank range, you'll have to cancel after standing Ⓗ into Repulsor Blast L, then hyper combo cancel into Proton Cannon. Still a respectable 459,900 damage and great THC position, but not quite as rewarding as the air combo version.

This combo can be beefed up in damage, bar building, and difficulty by chaining to Ⓢ launcher, pausing slightly before super jumping, then performing: air Ⓜ, Ⓜ, Ⓗ, ⬇ + Ⓗ CANCEL⇨ double jump, air Ⓜ, ⬇ + Ⓗ, Ⓢ, land, dash (or wavedash), ➡⬇↘ + Ⓛ CANCEL⇨ ⬇↘➡ + ATK ATK. Perform the air chain prior to the double jump slowly, so Iron Man drifts down from the apex of his jump slightly. This allows the attacks after the double jump to connect, rather than just whiff above a foe. After double jumping, link air Ⓜ, ⬇ + Ⓗ immediately, but pause briefly before chaining to air Ⓢ for flying screen. The longer you can manage to wait, the easier it will be to dash forward and OTG with Smart Bomb L.

II. CROUCHING Ⓛ, CROUCHING Ⓜ, STANDING Ⓗ CANCEL⇨ ⬇↙⬅ + Ⓛ CANCEL⇨ ⬇↙⬅ + Ⓗ CANCEL⇨ ⬇↙⬅ + ATK ATK

(799,100 damage, requires 3 levels of hyper combo gauge) This is how you can land Iron Avenger in a combo outside the range of Ⓢ, without using an assist. This makes this combo much more valuable in during X-Factor level 2 or 3, when you have less partners left and the combo becomes a knockout on most characters (1,014,400–1,197,400 damage!). This combo means that you can afford to be more aggressive, faster and requiring less precision, the stickier the situation gets!

If you feel like getting fancy, insert a Flight cancel. Perform crouching Ⓛ, crouching Ⓜ, standing Ⓗ CANCEL⇨ ⬇↙⬅ + Ⓢ, air Ⓛ, Ⓜ, Ⓗ, Ⓢ, land, standing Ⓜ, standing Ⓗ CANCEL⇨ ⬇↙⬅ + Ⓛ CANCEL⇨ ⬇↙⬅ + Ⓗ CANCEL⇨ ⬇↙⬅ + ATK ATK. Because of damage scaling, this actually does slightly less than the listed version—7,000 less—but it builds more hyper combo gauge, and there's no accounting for style points. Go through everything as quickly as possible, but pause briefly before canceling Repulsor Spread into Iron Avenger. While this combo is slightly weaker normally, it deals about 100,000 more during X-Factor.

ON THE GROUND

Repulsor Blast H has surprising reach, and it can easily clip opposing point characters and assists.

Ⓢ launcher isn't as good when it is used as an anti-air, as it was in MvC2. By the time the flash extends from Iron Man's heel, the active period of the attack is already over—if you're going to use this as anti-air do it late, not early.

While Iron Man has great combos, and access to high/low mix-ups with a fantastic triangle jump and Flight mode, your focus should be mid range dominance while you use him. Iron Man can be used to do many things from mid range that an opponent really can't do much about. At worst, Iron Man's attacks are guarded, but you can keep him in the best position—with his enemy literally at arm's length. The edge of most of Iron Man's basic attacks is invulnerable, with no hittable portion of Iron Man exposed.

Your basic objective should be to constantly put the tips of invulnerable, mid range moves in your opponent's way from about half a screen away. This goal remains the same whether Iron Man is grounded or airborne, whether he is standing, jumping, or flying. From the ground, this means poking with the edges of the flash from crouching Ⓜ, standing Ⓜ, and standing Ⓗ, looking for places to make your opponent block Unibeam H, or for times when you have clearance to safely perform Repulsor Blast H from about half the screen away. From here, the tip of the Repulsor Blast will catch and drag in point characters or assists. Repulsor Blast might seem like a laggy attack to throw out at random, but it can be made much safer by canceling into Repulsor Spread, and the payoff and deterrence of the move are great. If you happen to catch your opponent's assist, cancel into Proton Cannon and THC into another hyper combo to assure a knockout.

If you have suitable crossover assists available, you should call them just before zoning with Iron Man's special moves. Upward arcing and vertical assists can bisect screen space when you use Unibeam; long range beam assists are both covered by and provide extra cover to Repulsor Blast; assists are also useful before dropping Smart Bombs during a normal jump, or when using the tip of air Ⓗ when normal jumping or flying.

Iron Man can't cancel his dash or backdash with guarding or basic attacks until 11 frames of the dash have elapsed. This is one of the reasons why your focus shouldn't be based as much on all-out rushdown, despite the fact that Iron Man has a very solid set of rushdown attacks. Dashing forward with crouching Ⓛ or Ⓜ isn't nearly as fast as it is with characters who can dash forward and dash cancel into a fast low attack right away. The one thing that Iron Man can cancel the first 11 frames of a dash into is a jump, so you can feint a dash and take to the skies. Otherwise, you'll need empty triangle jumps, or a low hitting assist, to truly threaten low with some speed.

III. TRIANGLE JUMP Ⓜ, LAND, CROUCHING Ⓛ, CROUCHING Ⓜ, STANDING Ⓗ, Ⓢ [CANCEL] SUPER JUMP, AIR Ⓜ, Ⓗ [CANCEL] ↓ ↙ ← + Ⓢ, AIR Ⓜ, Ⓗ [CANCEL] ↓ ↙ ← + Ⓢ, DOUBLE JUMP IMMEDIATELY, AIR Ⓜ, Ⓗ [CANCEL] → ↓ ↘ + Ⓗ, ↓ ↘ → + Ⓗ

(420,400 + ~36,600 damage) This is a combo to use when you'd like to build bar rather than burn it. After canceling Flight, double jump immediately and press Ⓜ, Ⓗ [CANCEL] → ↓ ↘ + Ⓗ as fast as possible. The final command is for an air Unibeam H that your opponent is virtually guaranteed to be forced to block in mid air, after air recovering from Smart Bomb H. This is a good team aerial combo start sequence, too; if you'd like to go for a TAC, end the air combo with (direction + Ⓢ) rather than Smart Bomb H.

IV. AIR-TO-AIR: AIR Ⓜ, Ⓗ, [CANCEL] DOUBLE JUMP UP-FORWARD, AIR Ⓜ, Ⓗ [CANCEL] ↓ ↙ ← + Ⓢ, AIR Ⓜ, Ⓗ [CANCEL] → ↓ ↘ + Ⓗ, ↓ ↘ → + Ⓗ

(350,700 + ~36,000 damage) A consistent combo for super jumping to go air to air with airborne foes. Depending on positioning, you can embellish upon this quite a bit, but consistently maximizing damage depending on actual angles will take great reactions and a lot of practice. For example, if the opposing character is at Iron Man's head level or lower, air Ⓜ, Ⓗ, ↓ + Ⓗ can open the air combo; ↑ + Ⓗ can often be added at the end (but this may cause Smart Bomb H to miss). The Unibeam H on the end is for forced block damage after your foe recovers in mid air.

V. FORWARD THROW + [P1⇒P2] AKUMA—γ, Ⓢ [CANCEL] SUPER JUMP, AIR Ⓜ, Ⓜ, Ⓗ, ↓ + Ⓗ, Ⓢ, LAND, DASH, → ↓ ↘ + Ⓛ OTG [CANCEL] ↓ ↘ → + ATK ATK [CANCEL] ↓ ↘ → + ATK ATK (HOLD Ⓗ)

(602,800+ damage, requires 2 bars of hyper combo gauge, Akuma—γ) Akuma—γ is a great assist for enhancing Iron Man's offensive potential. Akuma—γ is both an overhead attack, and an attack that allows Iron Man to combo after his throw. Call Akuma just before performing the forward throw, then launch immediately upon regaining control of Iron Man. Go through the air chain as quickly as possible.

Akuma—γ isn't just for combos, however. It's an overhead attack, causes a ground bounce, and is OTG-capable. Akuma and Iron Man make natural THC partners, and their assists are complimentary. Just watch the red damage carefully on partner Akuma; he's one of the least-sturdy characters, especially as an assist.

UP IN THE AIR

Air Ⓗ (and its command attack variants) is one of the best air basic attacks in the game.

If your opposition doesn't use advancing guard to push you away after a single box jump air Ⓜ, a second Ⓜ can be performed unbelievably low to the ground. Go low immediately upon landing. If your opponent blocks this, they basically just got lucky.

Iron Man's set of air basic attacks is the envy of the entire cast of *MvC3*. Air Ⓛ is active in 4 frames and makes for an excellent triangle jump (but it is the only one of Iron Man's attacks with a hitbox that leaves something to be desired—the attacking area is actually quite small). All other basic attacks have a lot of active frames, are fast for their purposes, and have *huge* hitboxes that extend very far away from Iron Man. Air Ⓗ in particular, and its command attack variants, hits characters at a huge distance away. Try to position yourself to strike continually with the tips of air Ⓗ variants, aimed appropriately depending on the opposing character's position.

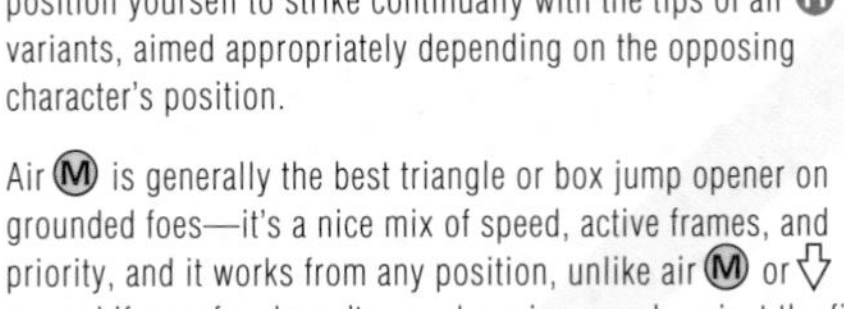

Air Ⓜ is generally the best triangle or box jump opener on grounded foes—it's a nice mix of speed, active frames, and priority, and it works from any position, unlike air Ⓜ or ⇩ + Ⓗ. After box jumping in from long range with the tip of air Ⓜ, you can perform a follow-up air Ⓜ extremely low to the ground if your foe doesn't use advancing guard against the first hit. This is essentially impossible to guard consistently. Box jump air Ⓜ, ⇩ + Ⓗ also makes an excellent jump-in chain that works from very far away. From Flight, you can airdash in on your opponent and perform air Ⓜ, ⇩ + Ⓗ, Ⓢ for a chain that automatically returns Iron Man to the ground, where the combo can continue.

Apart from looking for opportunities to go for overheads with airdashes and Flight, your job in the air matches your job on the ground—keep the opposition at the tip of Iron Man's effective range. In the air, this is the range of air Ⓗ. Properly spaced, air Ⓗ will beat almost anything most characters can do in mid air. Depending on positioning, you can score hefty combos off of counterhit air Ⓗ. There are tons of variables going air to air and some improvisation is required, but flying air Ⓗ, Flight canceled to immediate falling air Ⓗ, double jump canceled to air Ⓗ, Ⓢ, canceled into Smart Bombs H or Unibeam L generally works, if performed very quickly. The first two hits—flying air Ⓗ Flight canceled to immediate falling air Ⓗ—are extremely effective to do frequently just to keep hitboxes on an opponent; call assists that help close up gaps while you put air Ⓗ on your target as frequently as possible.

Finally, it's hard to go wrong dumping Smart Bomb H on your foe whenever you have an altitude and distance advantage. Launch Smart Bombs from diagonally up and above your opponent, rather than from very far away, or directly above them. After dropping Smart Bomb, you can follow up, depending on what you expect from your opponent. Unibeam here can keep your foe from jumping out from behind Smart Bomb, while falling ⇩ + Ⓗ, Ⓢ is an effective chain to fall on top of any character that dashed under Smart Bomb. Or, you can just drop Smart Bomb H again, or use active Flight and reposition.

ASSISTS

Assists that cut off more angles of the screen are great for Iron Man. For example, call Doctor Doom—β, perform Repulsor Blast into Repulsor Spread to insure he launches Hidden Missiles, then perform Unibeam H while your opponent is forced to guard the missiles as they come back down.

Between Repulsor Blast and Smart Bomb, Iron Man can cover his assist very well.

Iron Man doesn't have a bad crossover assist. You might find use for all three of them on various teams. Iron Man—α is Unibeam M, while Iron Man—β is Repulsor Blast M. Both have applications in combos, and can be used to get ahead in firefights between low priority projectiles; Unibeam by blasting across the screen directly, Repulsor Blast by destroying projectiles that approach while shielding the current point character. Iron Man—γ is a little different. At first glance, it just seems to be Smart Bomb H—ten hits, good damage but heavy damage scaling, OTG-capable. That's all true, but as an unexpected bonus, Smart Bomb H as an assist packs *twice* the durability point punch as it does from Iron Man on point! This also holds true for Iron Man—γ used as a crossover counter.

While all of Iron Man's assists can easily be used in combos, they're not that great for this purpose—all assists have a high number of hits, which means they ramp up damage scaling and hitstun deterioration excessively. Iron Man's assists are more about the physical space that they help you control: α full screen, β in a warping cross around the point character, and γ at a sharp downward angle out to about the length of a dash.

Unsurprisingly, like other strong projectile-oriented characters, Iron Man's zoning is aided strongly by pairing him with a good beam or projectile assist. Dante—α and Dormammu—β create vertical walls to the ceiling at the edge of the range Iron Man likes to defend. Doctor Doom—β and Taskmaster—γ create projectile rain from above, a perfect supplement to crouching Ⓗ, air Ⓗ, Unibeams, and Repulsor Blasts.

With the right tactics and assist, Iron Man becomes a safe battery even without landing clean hits. When you are within mid range and you are confident that your opponent isn't about to start up something fast, call Amaterasu—γ or Morrigan—γ, then immediately perform Repulsor Blast H. Whether it hits or it is blocked, cancel it into Repulsor Spread. If a grazing hit from Repulsor Blast catches your foe, the whole sequence generates slightly more than half a bar. Even if they guard, Iron Man builds about 35~40% of a bar! Similarly, "tiger knee" Smart Bomb H (⇨ ⬀ ⇩ ⬂ + Ⓗ) done just after calling a bar building assist generates 40~50% of a bar whether on hit or guard! The same holds true for calling an assist before Unibeam H.

As is the case with many characters, Wesker—β works well. He strengthens Iron Man's low threat considerably. Call Wesker—β, then immediately either perform Smart Bomb H just off the ground aimed on top of your opponent, or triangle jump in with air Ⓜ or air ⇩ + Ⓗ just as Wesker's gunshot hits. Dropping Smart Bomb doesn't create an unguardable situation, but if your foe attempts to guard Smart Bomb while standing (as they will if they attempt to jump, but don't quite leave the ground before being forced into guardstun), Wesker shoots them low. This option is much safer to attempt; you can essentially call Wesker and drop Smart Bombs with impunity, if you perform Smart Bomb H in the right place (just at the top of normal jump height, out of the grounded horizontal plane). If you happen to have both an overhead and a low assist, you can alternate between them while dropping Smart Bomb repeatedly.

ADVANCED TACTICS

MID AIR HIT-CONFIRMATION

Perform quick actions like flying air Ⓗ, Flight cancel, falling air Ⓗ, aiming the tips of the heavy attacks over where you anticipate your foe will be, then watch for the result.

Just like on the ground, there are certain chains in mid air that you should learn to start doing whether or not they hit, before hit-confirming to see what else to perform. On the ground, this amounts to hit-checking your opponent with chains like crouching Ⓛ, crouching Ⓜ. In mid air, this becomes jumping air Ⓜ, Ⓗ, or flying air Ⓗ, Flight canceled to falling air Ⓗ. The idea is that you perform these first two hits from either aerial state, whether or not your foe gets hit or blocks; you're using the time to establish what to do next. If you realize your opponent is eating the air attacks, you can visually confirm and cancel the second attack into a double jump, allowing the air combo to continue.

TIGER KNEE SMART BOMB

The angles on Iron Man's attacks, coupled with the openness of the playing field and the variety of assists, allow you to control certain angles at will.

Smart Bomb can be performed very close to the ground, at an angle that is very hard for your opponent to either punish, dash under, or jump around. "Tiger knee" Smart Bomb H is performed with → ↗ ↓ ↘ or ↗ → ↓ ↘ + Ⓗ. Call a horizontal crossover assist beforehand and you can virtually assure your safety. Your opponent won't be able to hit either Iron Man or his assist without getting tagged by the other character.

COMBO APPENDIX

GENERAL EXECUTION TIPS

Perform ground chains as quickly as possible.

Pause slightly before super jumping after landing Ⓢ launcher. If opening with air Ⓜ, Ⓜ, Ⓗ, ⇩ + Ⓗ, perform chain as slowly as possible.

Always perform attacks after either activating or deactivating Flight, or after double jumping, as quickly as possible.

Where neutral air Ⓗ is required, be careful not to get ⇧ or ⇩ + Ⓗ; when chaining into Ⓢ after air ⇧ or ⇩ + Ⓗ, be careful not to start a team aerial combo with ⇧ + ⇩ + Ⓢ accidentally.

Don't cancel Repulsor Spread into Iron Avenger too early—you can wait a beat.

Requirements (Position, meter, etc.)	Notes	Command Sequence	Damage
Requires 1 bar of hyper combo gauge	Pause slightly before super jumping after Ⓢ, perform air chain before double jump slowly, hit double jump air Ⓜ as fast as possible, leave a long gap between ⇩ + Ⓢ and Ⓢ to make OTG follow-up easier.	Triangle jump air Ⓜ, land, cr. Ⓜ, st. Ⓗ, Ⓢ CANCEL ➡ super jump, air Ⓜ, Ⓜ, Ⓗ, ⇩ + Ⓗ CANCEL ➡ double jump, air Ⓜ, ⇩ + Ⓗ, Ⓢ, land, dash (or wavedash), ⇨⇩⬂ + Ⓛ OTG CANCEL ➡ ⇩⬂⇨ + ATK ATK	634,700
Requires 1 bar of hyper combo gauge	—	Triangle jump air Ⓜ, land, cr. Ⓛ, cr. Ⓜ, st. Ⓗ CANCEL ➡ ⇩⬃⇦ + Ⓛ CANCEL ➡ ⇩⬂⇨ + ATK ATK	487,700
Requires 1 bar of hyper combo gauge, Akuma—γ	—	Triangle jump air Ⓜ, land, cr. Ⓛ, cr. Ⓜ, st. Ⓗ + P1 or P2 Akuma CANCEL ➡ ⇩⬃⇦ + Ⓛ, Ⓢ CANCEL ➡ super jump, air Ⓜ, Ⓗ, Ⓢ, land, dash, ⇨⇩⬂ + Ⓗ	598,000
Requires 1 bar of hyper combo gauge, Akuma—γ	Max range combo	Box jump air Ⓜ, Ⓜ, land, cr. Ⓜ, st. Ⓗ + P1 or P2 Akuma CANCEL ➡ ⇩⬂⇨ + Ⓛ CANCEL ➡ ⇩⬂⇨ + ATK ATK	519,800 (676,100+ with THC to Akuma)
Fly-in opening, requires corner	Team aerial combo starter, or flying screen (OTG possible afterward with Smart Bomb or assist)	Flight, airdash down-forward air Ⓜ, Ⓜ, ⇩ + Ⓗ, Ⓢ, land, cr. Ⓜ, st. Ⓗ, Ⓢ CANCEL ➡ super jump, air Ⓜ, Ⓗ CANCEL ➡ ⇩⬃⇦ + Ⓢ, air Ⓜ, Ⓗ CANCEL ➡ ⇩⬃⇦ + Ⓢ, air Ⓗ CANCEL ➡ double jump, air Ⓗ, (direction + Ⓢ or Ⓢ)	469,900+
From team aerial combo starter aerial combo. (up to twice in one combo)	Team aerial combo follow-up, causes another upward team aerial combo tag-in. Press neutral Ⓢ early at any time for flying screen and an OTG opportunity.	Air Ⓗ CANCEL ➡ double jump up, air Ⓜ, Ⓗ CANCEL ➡ ⇩⬃⇦ + Ⓢ, air Ⓜ, Ⓗ, ⇧ + Ⓗ, ⇧ + Ⓢ	433,800+

"YOU PUT UP A GOOD FIGHT, BUT I HAD THE SUPERIOR TECH, SKILLS, AND EXPERIENCE."

M.O.D.O.K.

BIO

REAL NAME

GEORGE TARLETON

OCCUPATION

LEADER OF A.I.M., WOULD-BE CONQUEROR, TERRORIST

ABILITIES

HE IS CAPABLE OF VARIOUS TYPES OF ATTACKS USING HIS PSIONIC ABILITIES, AND ALSO HAS SUPERHUMAN CALCULATING ABILITY.

WEAPONS

VARIOUS WEAPONS DESIGNED FOR KILLING OUTFITTED INTO HIS HOVER-CHAIR.

PROFILE

FORMERLY JUST A REGULAR HUMAN, GEORGE WAS FORCED TO BECOME A LIVING HUMAN EXPERIMENT AND WAS SUBSEQUENTLY TURNED INTO M.O.D.O.K. (MENTAL ORGANISM DESIGNED ONLY FOR KILLING). CALLING HIMSELF THE SCIENTIST SUPREME AND USING HIS VAST INTELLECT AND PSIONIC POWERS, HE ANNIHILATED ALL THOSE WHO WERE INVOLVED IN HIS EXPERIMENT.

FIRST APPEARANCE

TALES OF SUSPENSE #93 (1967)

"ALL IN THIS WORLD ARE BENEATH ME AND MUST PERISH BECAUSE OF IT."

POWER GRID

6 INTELLIGENCE

1 STRENGTH

1 SPEED

1 STAMINA

6 ENERGY PROJECTION

1 FIGHTING ABILITY

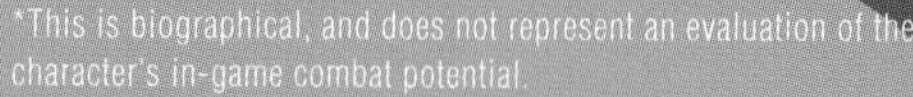

*This is biographical, and does not represent an evaluation of the character's in-game combat potential.

ALTERNATE COSTUMES

PS3: ⊗ Xbox 360: Ⓐ

PS3: ▢ Xbox 360: Ⓧ

PS3: △ Xbox 360: Ⓨ

PS3: R1 Xbox 360: RB

ATTACK SET

STANDING BASIC ATTACKS

Screen	Command	Hits	Damage	Startup	Active	Recovery	Advantage on Hit	Advantage if Guarded	Notes
1	Standing Ⓛ	1	45,000	7	12	11	-1	-1	—
2	Standing Ⓜ	5	67,000	10	9	17	+3	+3	Fires 5 projectiles of 3 low priority durability points
3	Standing Ⓗ	1	80,000	16	10	20	+1	-4	Knocks down, jump cancelable
4	Ⓢ	1	80,000	10	12	22	—	-8	Launcher, not special or hyper combo cancelable

CROUCHING BASIC ATTACKS

Screen	Command	Hits	Damage	Startup	Active	Recovery	Advantage on Hit	Advantage if Guarded	Notes
1	Crouching Ⓛ	1	45,000	5	6	10	0	0	—
2	Crouching Ⓜ	1	60,000	10	—	25	0	0	Projectile has 3 low priority durability points, the puddle created upon landing hits low, projectile is active for 60 frames
3	Crouching Ⓗ	1	80,000	15	10	21	+3	-5	Low attack, ↓↘→ + P1 or P2 snap back, jump cancelable

AERIAL BASIC ATTACKS

Screen	Command	Hits	Damage	Startup	Active	Recovery	Notes
1	Air Ⓛ	2~14	18,700-177,000	6	Until grounded	1	Overhead attack
2	Air Ⓜ	1	70,000	10	10	16	Overhead attack
3	Air Ⓗ	1	80,000	13	10	23	Overhead attack
4	Air Ⓢ	1	90,000	13	8	20	Overhead attack, unrecoverable knockdown when used in air combo after Ⓢ launcher, causes ground bounce when done at a low height

COMMAND ATTACKS

Screen	Command	Hits	Damage	Startup	Active	Recovery	Advantage on Hit	Advantage if Guarded	Notes
1	→ + H	1	80,000	18	10	13	—	+3	Wall bounce, jump cancelable
2	← + H	—	—	30	—	15	—	—	Creates a shield that negates most attacks that are not hyper combos, projectile stays active for 122 frames
3	(With Psionic power charged) ← + S	—	—	30	—	15	—	—	Creates a shield that negates most attacks that are not hyper combos, projectile stays active for 184 frames
4	↙ + H	1	80,000	18	10	13	+18	+3	Jump cancelable

1

2

3

4

AS A PARTNER-CROSSOVER ASSISTS

Screen	Type	P1+P2 Crossover Combination Hyper Combo	Description	Hits	Damage	Startup	Active	Recovery (this crossover assist)	Recovery (other partner)	Notes
1	α – Alpha	Hyper Psionic Blaster	← + H	—	—	54	—	107	77	Creates a shield that negates most attacks that are not hyper combos, shield lasts 122 frames
2	β – Beta	Hyper Psionic Blaster	Balloon Bomb M	1	80,000	64	—	117	87	Projectile lasts 182 frames, does not interact with other projectiles, causes spinning knockdown
3	γ – Gamma	Hyper Psionic Blaster	Psionic Blast M	4	103,000	44	20	108	78	Knocks down, Beam durability: 4 frames x 3 low priority durability points

1

2

3

SPECIAL MOVES

Screen	Name	Command	Hits	Damage	Startup	Active	Recovery	Advantage on Hit	Advantage if Guarded	Notes
1	Battering Ram	S + ATK	1	90,000	13	10	23	-7	-7	Can be performed in any direction
2	Psionic Blast L (in air OK)	↓↘→ + L	3	81,200	12	20	14	—	-4	Knocks down, beam durability: 3 frames x 3 of low priority durability points
	Psionic Blast M (in air OK)	↓↘→ + M	4	103,000	20	20	16	—	-4	Knocks down, beam durability: 4 frames x 3 low priority durability points
	Psionic Blast H (in air OK)	↓↘→ + H	5	122,600	28	20	18	—	-4	Knocks down, beam durability: 5 frames x 3 low priority durability points
3	Psionic High Blast	(With Psionic power charged) ↓↘→ + S	5	163,600	28	20	18	+17	-9	Beam durability: 5 frames x 5 low priority durability points, staggers
4	Analysis Cube L (in air OK)	↓↙← + ATK	1	50,000	10	—	30	-5	-5	Charges Psionic power on hit, projectile has 1 low priority durability point, projectile stays active for 60 frames
	Analysis Cube M (in air OK)	↓↙← + ATK	1	50,000	10	—	30	-5	-5	Charges Psionic power on hit, projectile has 1 low priority durability point, projectile stays active for 60 frames
	Analysis Cube H (in air OK)	↓↙← + ATK	1	50,000	15	—	30	-5	-5	Charges Psionic power on hit, projectile has 1 low priority durability point, projectile stays active for 60 frames
5	Balloon Bomb L	→↓↘ + L	1	80,000	30	—	25	—	+1	Spinning knockdown, projectile has 1 medium priority durability point, projectile stays active for 182 frames
	Balloon Bomb M	→↓↘ + M	1	80,000	40	—	25	—	+1	Spinning knockdown, projectile has 1 medium priority durability point, projectile stays active for 182 frames
	Balloon Bomb H	→↓↘ + H	1	80,000	50	—	25	—	+1	Spinning knockdown, projectile has 1 medium priority durability point, projectile stays active for 182 frames
	Air Balloon Bomb L	(in air) →↓↘ + L	1	80,000	30	—	25	—	—	Spinning knockdow , projectile has 1 medium priority durability point, projectile stays active for 181 frames
	Air Balloon Bomb M	(in air) →↓↘ + M	1	80,000	40	—	25	—	—	Spinning knockdown, projectile medium priority has 1 medium priority durability point, projectile stays active for 181 frames
	Air Balloon Bomb H	(in air) →↓↘ + H	1	80,000	50	—	25	—	—	Spinning knockdown, projectile has 1 medium priority durability point, projectile stays active for 181 frames
6	Jamming Bomb	(With Psionic power charged) →↓↘ + S	1		50	—	25	—	+1	Spinning knockdown, reverses opponent's controls, for 300 frames homes in on opponent, projectile has 1 medium priority durability point, projectile stays active for 302 frames
7	Flight	↓↙← + S	—	—	10	—	—	—	—	Lasts 300 frames

1

2

3

Battering Ram: M.O.D.O.K. charges forward with a head attack. You can determine the way it flies by holding the corresponding direction. Outside of its use in combos involving Hyper Battering Ram, its variable directions of attack make it useful for moving around the screen in a quick manner. Up to three of them can done at a time during a jump or Flight to stay airborne.

Psionic Blast & Psionic High Blast: Fire this beam to control ground movement and to counter an opponent's low priority projectiles. The L version counters the vast majority of other low priority shots, which, like Ryu's Hadoken and Morrigan's Soul Fist, often have a low priority durability of 5 (Psionic Blast L hits three times, each hit has a low priority durability of 3). More threatening shots with higher durability, like Arthur's Axe Toss, can be destroyed with Psionic Blast M. All versions if this beam can be hyper canceled into Hyper Psionic Blast for additional damage, but you cannot verify if the beam hits or not before doing so.

Psionic High Blast is possible when you've hit a foe with an Analysis Cube. Its frame data is similar to Psionic Blast H, but it inflicts additional damage and staggers an opponent. The stagger enables you to follow-up with ↓↘→ + L CANCEL ↓↘→ + ATK ATK from as far as the opposite end of the screen.

Analysis Cube: M.O.D.O.K. summons a small projectile that hovers in place momentarily. The area it appears in is dependant on the strength of the button used; ↓↙← + Ⓛ plants it right by his feet, ↓↙← + Ⓜ a character length away in the air, and ↓↙← + Ⓗ summons it out at a distance. Since these attacks have a sizable amount of screen activity (60 frames), the base use of the Analysis Cube attacks is to control space. A successful hit drains information from the opponent and stores away 1 psionic power charge (up to 9 total can be stored). This power-up is used to initiate the Psionic High Blast, Jamming Bomb, and ← + Ⓢ, which uses up one charge when initiated. Each charge stored also powers up the Hyper Psionic Blast hyper combo, which inflicts massive 441,100 damage at 9 charges and also leaves a foe in an unrecoverable knockdown that's vulnerable to OTG attacks. This carries enough comeback potential to warrant saving Analysis Cube charges for it, along with orienting your game play and combos around obtaining charges.

Balloon Bomb & Jamming Bomb: This attack fires a slow moving bomb that stays active for a great deal of time. The bomb has a medium priority durability of 1, meaning it cannot be nullified easily by a majority of opposing projectiles. This can act as a shield against an opponent's approaches and their projectiles. Unfortunately, the wind-up period for this attack is too slow for you to throw it out recklessly. Summon a Analysis Cube first, or perform crouching Ⓜ CANCEL ▶ →↓↘ + ATK to cover its release. Note that only one Balloon Bomb can be on the screen at a time, firing a second with another already around causes the first to explode.

Jamming Bomb requires a psionic charge to be used. Once fired, it homes in on an opponent's location and actively chases them for roughly 5 seconds, or until it makes contact. A successful hit puts the opposing character into a special state that reverses their control scheme. This is very difficult to compensate for 100% of the time, making it a valuable method of crippling an opponent's defense. It's too risky to use at random because of its heavy starting period, so find ways to combo into it; assists like Dante—α are absolutely necessary to do this.

Flight: Inputting ↓↙← + Ⓢ initiates Flight mode, which is exactly like the Flight mode done when inputting ↖, ↑, or ↗. The major difference is that you can cancel basic attacks into Flight or you can initiate it after a super jump. Unlike Flight with other characters, performing an airdash cancels Flight mode altogether (as does the Battering Ram). You can still perform an unlimited number of aerial special moves, though, and this enables you to stay in the air while tossing repeated Analysis Cube attacks for as long as you like.

HYPER COMBOS

Screen	Name	Command	Hits	Damage	Startup	Active	Recovery	Advantage on Hit	Advantage if Guarded	Notes
1	Hyper Psionic Blast (in air OK)	↓↘→ + ATK ATK	22~100	129,100 ~ 441,100	10+1	120	36	—	30	Each charge of Psionic power up to 9 increases the number of hits and amount of damage Hyper Psionic Blaster does, uses all existing charges of Psionic Power, beam durability: 22 frames x 5 high priority durability points, unrecoverable knockdown
2	Hyper Battering Ram (in air OK)	↓↙← + ATK ATK	3~15	72,700 ~ 305,00	4+4	11	24	—	-5	Pressing ATK repeatedly allows more hits and control of flight path, knocks down
3	Killer Illumination	→↓↘ + ATK ATK	30	300,000	18+0	10	40	—	—	Frames 1-24 invincible, throw, unrecoverable knockdown

Hyper Psionic Blast: This is a standard beam hyper combo until it has been powered up with the Analysis Cube. Use it in ranged combos, or fire it against projectiles that you anticipate from your opponent to punish them. When powered up, Hyper Psionic Blast gains a significant damage boost. Levels 7 through 9 are the only versions worth using in terms of damage output, otherwise the Hyper Battering Ram inflicts more damage. Acquire psionic charges via Analysis Cube combos, then fire the level 9 Hyper Psionic Blast to obliterate your opponent's vitality.

Hyper Battering Ram: M.O.D.O.K.'s second hyper combo can be used in combos when Hyper Psionic Blast is less damaging. After activation, input ATK and a directional command to move M.O.D.O.K. in that direction. This can be done up to 5 times if different directions and buttons presses are inputted as quickly as possible.

Killer Illumination: A throw hyper combo with a horrendous starting period, this is difficult to use for aggressive throw setups because an opposing character can always jump away from it after activation. Instead, use its long window of invulnerability to counter close range ground attacks. You can OTG your opponent after it recovers to add additional damage to a successful counter.

BATTLE PLAN

OVERVIEW

VITALITY: 950,000

CHAIN COMBO ARCHETYPE: MARVEL SERIES

X-Factor	Lv.1	Lv.2	Lv.3
Damage	130%	160%	190%
Speed	105%	110%	115%

Your objective with M.O.D.O.K. should be to push your opponent towards a corner. He has numerous methods for zoning an opponent and making their life miserable, but he truly shines when he has an opposing character cornered, where his ← + Ⓗ shield, Analysis Cube, airdash pressure, and combos are especially threatening.

This strategy is effective because:

M.O.D.O.K.'s massive list of projectiles allows him to quickly shutdown an opponent's avenues of movement.

His unmatched aerial mobility can be used to both avoid attacks and to easily pressure guarding foes.

Many of M.O.D.O.K.'s best combos carry an opposing character to the far end of the screen, pushing them ever closer to the corner.

His zoning options and corner combos are vastly improved, so much that he can inflict up to 1,000,000 in a single combo at the cost of only two hyper combo bars.

This goal is accomplished by:

Setting up Analysis Cubes, Balloon Bombs, and the ← + Ⓗ shield to fortify his position, then firing Psionic Blasts to push a challenger backwards.

Firing crouching Ⓜ and canceling it into Flight, then airdashing forward to shield an aggressive move into close range.

Catching an opponent with → + Ⓗ and following up with a combo that pushes them into the corner.

ON THE GROUND

Almost always place crouching Ⓜ when firing the Analysis Cube or Balloon Bomb.

Analysis Cube M can always be placed near a foe to stop their airdash attempts for a short window of time.

Control the battlefield with your various projectiles. Much if this strategy starts with crouching Ⓜ, which fires a green slime that lingers for a while after it hits the ground. Cancel this attack as it fires into Analysis Cube Ⓜ, which appears in the sky. Placing both projectiles on the screen at the same time cuts off your opponent's ability to dash or airdash towards you. For the moment that they are both on the screen, you can safely fire ↓ ↘ → + ATK, Analysis Cube H, Ballon Boom M, or summon the ← + Ⓗ shield. Balloon Bomb M travels forward slowly, opening a window for you to follow behind and position yourself closer to your opponent. The shield nullifies any projectile or physical attack that is not a hyper combo, fully protecting you from almost any frontal threat. If your foe ever tries to stop these "wall" techniques by throwing a projectile with high durability, cancel any recovery period into ↓ ↘ → + ATK ATK. This stops anything that isn't a hyper combo.

When your foe stays on the ground, use your projectile cover to move forward and pressure them with → + Ⓗ (**Combo V**) or standing Ⓜ (which can be chained into **Combo II** if it hits). → + Ⓗ should be used to preemptively stop jumps and slow ground attacks, causing a wall bounce when it hits. Standing Ⓜ is faster than → + Ⓗ and is better for stopping an opponent's forward movement. It leaves you at a slight frame advantage when guarded, and creates an opportunity to follow-up with a dashing throw or a delayed **Combo II**. If your opponent uses advancing guard, cancel into ↓ ↙ ← + Ⓢ and airdash forward to stay on top your opposition. Landing **Combo II** carries your challenger across most of the screen, bringing them closer to the corner.

While you are using M.O.D.O.K. a cornered adversary should equal a dead adversary. Your first goal is to make your opposition afraid to jump. This can be done in numerous ways via Analysis Cube M, which hovers directly above the opposing character's head when done at mid range. One way is to purposefully fire crouching Ⓜ so that the puddle lands right in front of your opponent (without hitting, leaving the puddle on the ground), and then cancel into Anaylsis Cube M. Your foe cannot dash forward with the puddle in front them, nor can they jump with the cube hovering over their head. This can be done repeatedly until your opponent's counter measure is anticipated, which is completely dependent upon the character match up. For example, if positioned perfectly, Ryu can't escape this tactic without taking a hit. This is due to his oddly shaped hit box, which gets wider as he stands; even though it will continue to miss as he stays crouching, standing up causes him to run into the slime on the floor, which can't be guarded because it hits low. He can't jump away for the same reason, nor can he throw a projectile—this also causes him to run into the slime. Some other characters have no such issue. Instead, these characters can escape by jumping and airguarding the Analysis Cube and using advancing gaurd against it to push M.O.D.O.K. out. This is countered on your end by canceling crouching Ⓜ into ↓ ↙ ← + Ⓢ, then airdashing forward and air throwing your opponent. In the rare instance that your foe can fire a projectile to nullify your shot, hyper cancel at any point into ↓ ↘ → + ATK ATK.

You can also easily transition into an aerial offense off of crouching Ⓜ. Like the previous air throw example, cancel crouching Ⓜ as the shot comes out into ↓ ↙ ← + Ⓢ, then airdash forward. Since crouching Ⓜ hits low as it turns into a puddle, a quick airdashing Ⓛ following it is extremely difficult for an opponent to guard consistently.

UP IN THE AIR

In addition to his airdash, M.O.D.O.K.'s normal jump is an automatic Flight activation. He has the fastest Flight starting period of any other character, along with the longest Flight time. When combined with his Battering Ram and Analysis Cube, you can keep him in the air for long stretches of time. For example, super jump and use the Battering Ram twice to fly in whatever direction you desire, airdash one time, then start Flight as you recover. Activating Flight allows you to indefinitely perform aerial special moves until Flight ends. From there you can start repeating Analysis Cubes to continue floating for several more seconds. Flight patterns like this help you play "keep away", or create a defensive style of play designed to force your opponent to come to you. This is a great option when the round timer is about to expire, so it is worth considering.

If you need to stay out of trouble, activate Flight mode and keep creating Analysis Cubes.

Condition your opponent with M.O.D.O.K.'s massive of list of fast overhead air attacks, then attack low with crouching (H).

Knowing this, keep your distance and fire at your opponent from the air. You can fight off nearby foes with air (M), (H), (S) if your opposition tries to start air-to-air battles. If you anticipate a super jump during your ground offense, super jump with your foe and blast them with air ↓ ↙ → + (L). When your opposition chooses to stay on the ground, fire downwards at them with air ↓ ↙ → + (H). If the threat of a super jump followed by a frontal attack is a possibility, summon Analysis Cube M in front of M.O.D.O.K. before firing. Remember, even if your opponent manages to get relatively close, you can always use the Battering Ram to quickly move away to safety.

When transitioning to a close range offense, rely heavily on M.O.D.O.K.'s jump cancelable ground attacks and airdashes. Forcing your opponent to guard crouching (H) or → + (H), for example, leads to a varied aerial offense. Cancel either of these attacks into Flight by holding ↗, then immediately do a forward airdash. Attack with an early air (L) for the fastest air attack (which hits twice), or air (S) which hits later during the jump. An alternate way to do this is to airdash forward and miss on purpose with air (H), then land and either throw (**Combo III**) your opponent or attack with the low-hitting **Combo II**. You don't need to airdash if you need a fast overhead while you are directly next to your foe, simply press up and hit (L) or (S) to perform either attack right off the ground very quickly. When your opponent is wary of your fast high attacks, jump forward and immediately input ↖ + ATK ATK to airdash back to the ground. This effectively baits your opponent into thinking an air attack is coming. When you land, attempt a throw or go for **Combo II**.

COMBO USAGE

I. AIR (S), LAND, ↓ ↙ ← + (L), → + (H) CANCEL ↓ ↙ ← + (H), FORWARD DASH TWICE (WAVEDASH), (S) CANCEL FORWARD SUPER JUMP, AIR (M), (H), (S), LAND, CR. (M) CANCEL ATK + (S) CANCEL ↓ ↙ ← + ATK ATK, AFTER INITIAL 3 HITS, → + ATK, ↓ + ATK, ↑ + ATK

(597,700 damage) A big combo starting off an overhead attack. Perform ↓ ↙ ← + (L) right as you land from air (S) to ensure that your opponent bounces off of it late enough for the remainder of the combo to work. Near corners, → + (H) CANCEL ↓ ↙ ← + (H) misses, so instead do → + (H) CANCEL ↓ ↙ ← + (L).

II. CR. (H) CANCEL FORWARD JUMP, FORWARD AIRDASH, AIR (M), LAND, FORWARD DASH, CR. (M), CR. (H) CANCEL FORWARD JUMP, FORWARD AIR DASH, AIR (S) LAND, ↓ ↙ ← + (L), (S) CANCEL FORWARD SUPER JUMP, AIR (M), (M), (H), (S), LAND, ↓ + (M) CANCEL ↓ ↘ → + (L) CANCEL ↓ ↘ → + ATK ATK

(592,800 damage) This difficult, low-hitting combo requires that you cancel crouching (H) into a forward airdash, then dash again. Be sure to cancel into forward jump, which will leave you closer to your opponent during the remainder of the sequence.

III. BACK THROW OR AIR BACK THROW, FORWARD DASH, ↓ + (M) CANCEL ↓ ↙ ← + (S), FORWARD AIRDASH, AIR (M), LAND, (S) CANCEL FORWARD SUPER JUMP, AIR (M), (M), (H), (S)

(330,100 damage) The opening segment to this throw combo requires you to OTG a fallen foe, then airdash and juggle them before they hit the ground. You must cancel crouching (M) into ↓ ↙ ← + (S) before the slime even makes contact, or else there's not enough time for you to fly over and hit your foe while they are in the air.

IV. WITH PSIONIC POWER CHARGED, HIT ENEMY WITH ↓ ↘ → + (S), ↓ ↘ → + (L) CANCEL ↓ ↘ → + ATK ATK

(303,400 damage) This simple combo is possible at great distances. Go for it when you're certain your opponent wants to fire a low priority projectile at you.

V. → + (H) CANCEL ↓ ↙ ← + (H), FORWARD DASH TWICE (WAVEDASH), (S) CANCEL FORWARD SUPER JUMP, AIR (M), (H), (S), LAND, CR. (M) CANCEL ATK + (S) CANCEL ↓ ↙ ← + ATK ATK, AFTER INITIAL 3 HITS, → + ATK, ↓ + ATK, ↑ + ATK

(565,200 damage) As with the similar **Combo I**, do → + (H) CANCEL ↓ ↙ ← + (L) instead when you are near a corner.

VI. → ↓ ↘ + ATK ATK, CR. (M) CANCEL ↓ ↙ ← + (S), FORWARD AIRDASH, AIR (M), LAND, (S), FORWARD SUPER JUMP, AIR (M), (H), (S), LAND, FORWARD DASH, CR. (M) CANCEL ATK + (S) CANCEL ↓ ↙ ← + ATK ATK, AFTER INITIAL 3 HITS, → + ATK, ↓ + ATK, ↑ + ATK

(570,000 damage) This giant combo starts of the invulnerable Killer Illumination hyper combo. You don't have to move any closer after this attack to OTG with crouching (M), you're well within range as it ends.

ASSISTS

Use assists with low attacks along with M.O.D.O.K.'s Flight mode to create nearly unblockable situations.

M.O.D.O.K.'s shield can prevent opponents from advancing on the ground and force them into the air.

M.O.D.O.K. lacks fast low attacks, so the best assist choice is clear, load up with X-23—β, She-Hulk—α, or Wesker—β low-hitting assists. You can call these assists while M.O.D.O.K. is in Flight mode (only when activated from the ground), enabling for unblockable situations. For example, fly over an opponent's head with M.O.D.O.K., call X-23—β, then press air (L) to drop down with a flurry of kicks. If timed so that both attacks make contact together, your opponent will be not able to guard it.

M.O.D.O.K.'s own α assist creates a shield that nullifies all attacks that make contact with it, including physical attacks. This is probably the most useful option, since as you can hide behind it in any bad situation to avoid harm. β summons the slow-moving Balloon Bomb, which can be used to shield an approach toward a foe. His γ assist is just his generic Psionic Blast attack, which does have some use in combos.

ADVANCED TACTICS

COMPENSATING FOR CROUCHING (H)

Crouching (H) doesn't have to be a complete hindrance to your close range offense.

Unlike the majority of the cast, M.O.D.O.K.'s attacks should be used to condition an opponent to guard high with constant overhead attacks, and then attack with his slow, low-hitting crouching (H) when your opposition isn't looking for it. Unfortunately, even veteran players can sometimes react to the low attack and guard it. You can avoid this problem by utilizing a feint of sorts—perform crouching (H), then *before* it hits, kara-cancel it into ↓ ↙ ← + (S), then come down out of the air with air (S) or (L). This effectively tricks your opponent into thinking you have chosen a low attack, but then you quickly cancel Flight into a dropping overhead attack. Use this against veteran players who are used to the normal attack options.

COMBO APPENDIX

GENERAL EXECUTION TIPS

After a normal (S) launch, wait until M.O.D.O.K. reaches the same height as his foe before doing an air chain.

Requirements (Position, meter, etc.)	Notes	Command Sequence	Damage
Requires corner, 2 hyper combo gauge bars	—	Cr. (H) CANCEL ↓ ↙ ← + (L), cr. (H) CANCEL ↓ ↙ ← + (L), Cr. (H) CANCEL ↓ ↙ ← + (L), cr. (H), → + (H) CANCEL ↓ ↙ ← + (L), st. (H), → + (H), ↓ ↙ ← + (S), forward airdash, air (S), land, → + (H) CANCEL ↓ ↙ ← + (L), → + (H) CANCEL ↓ ↙ ← + (L) CANCEL ↓ ↘ → + ATK ATK, cr. (M) CANCEL ↓ ↙ ← + ATK ATK, direct it forward, then upward, then downward	1,027,600
Requires corner, 1 hyper combo gauge bar	—	Air (S), land, ↓ ↙ ← + (L), cr. (H) CANCEL ↓ ↙ ← + (L), cr. (H) CANCEL ↓ ↙ ← + (L), cr. (H), → + (H) CANCEL ↓ ↙ ← + (L), st. (H), → + (H), ↓ ↙ ← + (H) CANCEL ↓ ↘ → + ATK ATK	647,800

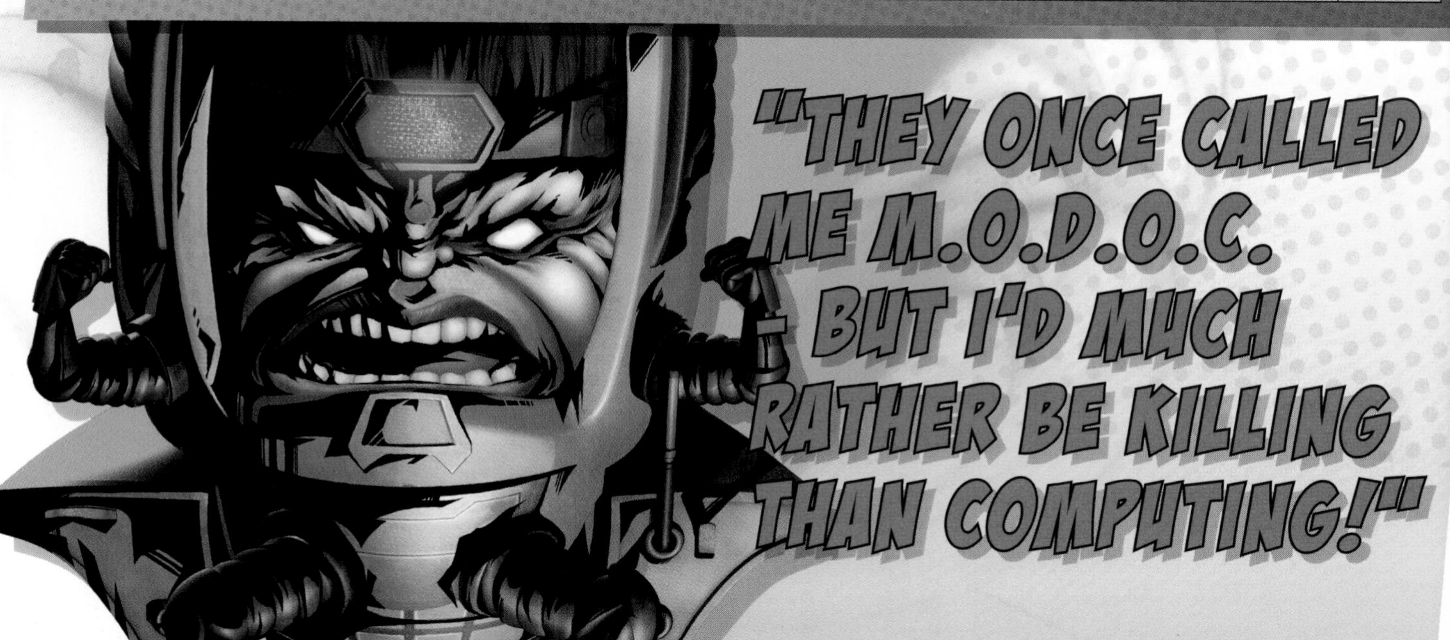

"THEY ONCE CALLED ME M.O.D.O.C. - BUT I'D MUCH RATHER BE KILLING THAN COMPUTING!"

PHOENIX

BIO

REAL NAME

JEAN GREY-SUMMERS

OCCUPATION

ADVENTURER

ABILITIES

TELEKINETIC POWERS, AS WELL AS TELEPATHY SO STRONG SHE CAN CONTROL OTHERS' THOUGHTS OR FORCE THEM INTO UNCONSCIOUSNESS. ALSO SERVES AS AN AVATAR FOR THE COSMIC PHOENIX FORCE.

WEAPONS

NONE

PROFILE

WHILE RETURNING FROM SPACE, JEAN WAS EXPOSED TO LETHAL LEVELS OF SOLAR RADIATION. HER LIFE WAS SAVED BY THE COSMIC ENTITY KNOWN AS THE PHOENIX FORCE., THOUGH ITS POWER HAS AT TIMES CONSUMED HER TO THE POINT OF EVIL AS DARK PHOENIX.

FIRST APPEARANCE

THE X-MEN #1 (1963)

"LEAVE WHILE YOU CAN... BEFORE SHE COMES."

POWER GRID

3 INTELLIGENCE
2 STRENGTH
7 SPEED
7 STAMINA
7 ENERGY PROJECTION
4 FIGHTING ABILITY

*This is biographical, and does not represent an evaluation of the character's in-game combat potential.

ALTERNATE COSTUMES

PS3: ⊗ Xbox 360: Ⓐ

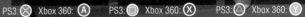

PS3: □ Xbox 360: Ⓧ

PS3: △ Xbox 360: Ⓨ

PS3: R1 Xbox 360: 

ATTACK SET

STANDING BASIC ATTACKS

Screen	Command	Hits	Damage	Startup	Active	Recovery	Advantage on Hit	Advantage if Guarded	Notes
1, 2	Standing Ⓛ	1/2	30,000/+24,000	5/4	3/4	11	0/+4	-1/+1	Dark Phoenix fires 1 feather straight forward
3, 4	Standing Ⓜ	1/4	46,000/+24,000 x 3	8	3	16	0/-1	-1/-3	Dark Phoenix fires 3 feathers in a 90 degree arc
5, 6	Standing Ⓗ	1/6	67,000/+24,000 x 5	11/10	10	10	+4/+8	+3/+5	⇩ ⇙ ⇨ + P1 or P2 snap back, Dark Phoenix fires 5 feathers in a 180 degree arc
7	Ⓢ	1	80,000	10	5	21	—	-3/0	Launcher attack, not special- or hyper combo-cancelable

CROUCHING BASIC ATTACKS

Screen	Command	Hits	Damage	Startup	Active	Recovery	Advantage on Hit	Advantage if Guarded	Notes
1, 2	Crouching Ⓛ	1/2	33,000/ +24,000	4/3	3	11	0/+4	-1/+1	Low attack/*Dark Phoenix fires 1 feather straight forward*
3, 4	Crouching Ⓜ	1/4	50,000/ +24,000x3	9	8	19	-8/-9	-9/-11	Low attack/*Dark Phoenix fires 3 feathers in a 90 degree arc, at a 45 degree angle*
5, 6	Crouching Ⓗ	1/6	60,000/ +24,000x5	12	4	23	—	-4/-11	Low attack, knocks down opponent/*Dark Phoenix fires 5 feathers in a 90 degree arc, at a 45 degree angle*

AERIAL BASIC ATTACKS

Screen	Command	Hits	Damage	Startup	Active	Recovery	Notes
1, 2	Air Ⓛ	1/2	33,000/+24,000	5	3	18	Overhead attack/*Dark Phoenix fires 1 feather straight forward*
3, 4	Air Ⓜ	1/4	47,000/+24,000 x 3	9/8	3	20	Overhead attack/*Dark Phoenix fires 3 feathers in a 90 degree arc*
5, 6	Air Ⓗ	1/4	70,000/+24,000 x 3	8	11	17	Overhead attack/*Dark Phoenix fires 5 feathers in a 180 degree arc, at a 90 degree angle*
7, 8	Air Ⓢ	1/6	70,000/+24,000 x 5	10	12	24	Overhead attack, causes flying screen if used in launcher combo/*Dark Phoenix fires 5 feathers in a 90 degree arc, at a -45 degree angle*

ADVANCED TACTICS

DARK PHOENIX FEATHER CROSS-UPS

While in Dark Phoenix mode, all basic and command attacks fire feather projectiles. Normal attacks can be canceled at any point into a special move, including Teleportation M. Add these two points together, and you can create several feather cross-ups that will keep opponents guessing!

The simplest feather cross-up to set up probably uses crouching Ⓜ. Perform crouching Ⓜ at a little farther than backdash distance, then quickly cancel the attack into Teleportation M as soon as the feathers are created. This set-up looks exceptionally sneaky! A simple way to set this up is to let the opponent advancing guard you from point-blank range, preferably after rushing them with an air Ⓛ triangle jump attack or crouching Ⓛ. After being pushed away, immediately slide back at your opponent using crouching Ⓜ, then use Teleportation M at the last second to complete the cross-up.

Dropping on top of an opponent's head with air ↓ + Ⓗ, then canceling the attack into Teleportation after they guard it is another great way to set up a cross-up. Your vertical height here is key: attacking from too low will cause the feathers to be guarded instantly, and attacking from too high will be too far away from the feathers to even reach your opponent. An easy way to set up the proper height is to super jump above the opposing character's head, airdash down, then perform air ↓ + Ⓗ. Be sure to perform the input motion for Teleportation in the proper direction; unintentional side-switches can be very common in this situation.

A situation that comes up much more frequently in matches is when your opponent is about to descend from a jump onto your stream of standing Ⓛ feathers. When you recognize this is about to happen, cancel your current standing Ⓛ into Teleportation M! From there if you had enough projectiles out you can continue juggling your target with standing Ⓗ into → + Ⓗ, canceled into TK Trap L.

Using air Ⓜ while jumping forward is another great way to advance forward behind a wall of feather projectiles. If you notice that your foe is pinned down by an incoming downward feather, time a Teleportation M to cross up at the last moment!

Normal attacks can be canceled at any time into Teleportation M...

...this allows you to set-up some very unpredictable cross-ups with the feather projectiles!

III. (CORNER REQUIRED) CR. Ⓛ, CR. Ⓜ, CR. Ⓗ, → + Ⓗ, Ⓢ CANCEL SUPER JUMP, AIR Ⓜ, Ⓜ, Ⓗ, AIR → + Ⓗ, AIR ↓ + Ⓗ, LAND, ↓ ↙ ← + Ⓛ, → + Ⓗ, Ⓢ CANCEL SUPER JUMP STRAIGHT UP, AIR Ⓜ, Ⓜ, Ⓗ, Ⓢ, LAND, AIR ↓ ↘ → + Ⓛ (OTG), → ↓ ↘ + Ⓗ

(425,800 damage) Phoenix's combo in the corner. Vary your opening between crouching Ⓛ or → + Ⓜ to crack your opponent's defense. Phoenix's corner combo potential becomes vastly stronger once she transforms into Dark Phoenix.

IV. (AS DARK PHOENIX) CR. Ⓛ, CR. Ⓜ, CR. Ⓗ, → + Ⓗ CANCEL → ↓ ↘ + Ⓛ, CR. Ⓛ, ST. Ⓗ, → + Ⓗ, CANCEL ↓ ↙ ← + Ⓛ, → + Ⓗ CANCEL ↓ ↙ ← + Ⓛ, → + Ⓗ, Ⓢ CANCEL SUPER JUMP STRAIGHT UP, AIR Ⓜ, Ⓜ, Ⓗ CANCEL ↓ ↘ → + ATK ATK

(~1,056,500 damage) Dark Phoenix gains access to easy combos that will do 100% damage to most characters. This combo alone builds about 2.9 bars of hyper combo gauge, so always ending the combo with a Phoenix Rage is a good idea. Since the combo will likely K.O. your opponent, you can then immediately activate Healing Field afterward and still have a net gain!

Some characters bounce higher after juggle hits than others. These characters won't get hit enough times by the initial TK Overdrive L to able to continue the combo. Against these characters you can juggle TK Trap L instead, gaining one more repetition of → + Ⓗ into TK Trap L. The resulting combo is slightly weaker, but is still higher than 900,000 damage.

V. (AS DARK PHOENIX, CORNER ONLY) CR. Ⓛ, CR. Ⓜ, CR. Ⓗ, → + Ⓗ CANCEL → ↓ ↘ + Ⓛ, CR. Ⓛ, ST. Ⓗ, → + Ⓗ CANCEL ↓ ↙ ← + Ⓛ, ST. Ⓗ, → + Ⓗ CANCEL ↓ ↙ ← + Ⓜ, ↓ ↙ ← + Ⓛ, ST. Ⓗ, → + Ⓗ CANCEL ↓ ↘ → + Ⓛ CANCEL ↓ ↘ → + ATK ATK

(~1,134,100 damage, more or less depending on opposing character) As Dark Phoenix you can perform a modified combo in the corner to get a little more damage. Larger characters receive much more damage, due to getting hit by more feather projectiles.

COMBO APPENDIX

GENERAL EXECUTION TIPS

For OTG combos, do air TK Shot L and M low to the ground by performing ↓ ↘ → ↗ + (ATK).

If you're still having trouble doing low air TK Shots, try doing the input motion slowly, and pressing the attack button slightly late.

Ground bounces are almost always followed by TK Trap L, then a standing (H) attack. Press (H) slightly late to get the opponent lower to the ground; this allows you to super jump forward without going under the opponent.

Requirements (Position, meter, etc.)	Notes	Command Sequence	Damage
Corner required	—	Cr. (L), cr. (M), cr. (H), (S) CANCEL super jump, air (M), (M), (H), air ↓ + (H), ↓↙← + (L), (S) CANCEL super jump straight up, air (M), (M), (H), (S), land, air ↓↘→ + (L) OTG, dash, (S) CANCEL super jump, air (H) CANCEL ↓↘→ + (L) CANCEL ↓↘→ + (ATK)(ATK)	553,700
—	Meter-less combo mid-screen. Delaying the aerial chain combo after the second launcher gives you more time to hit the TK Shot M OTG. Hyper combo-canceling the air TK Shot M into Phoenix Rage results in 530,200 damage	Cr. (L), cr. (M), cr. (H), (S) CANCEL super jump, air (M), (M), (H), air ↓ + (H), land, ↓↙← + (L), st. (H), (S) CANCEL super jump, air (M), (M), (H), (S), land, air ↓↘→ + (M) OTG	387,100
—	Combo from → + (M) overhead attack. A standing (H) can be added for extra damage, but most characters can crouch under it	→ + (M), cr. (H), (S) CANCEL super jump, air (M), (M), (H), air ↓ + (H), land, st. (H), (S) CANCEL super jump, air (M), (M), (H), (S), land, air ↓↘→ + (M) OTG	411,100
—	Combo from Teleportation mix-up using TK Shot H	↓↘→ + (H), ←↓↙ + (ATK), cr. (L), cr. (M), cr. (H), (S) CANCEL super jump, air (M), (M), (H), air ↓ + (H), land, ↓↙← + (L), (S) CANCEL super jump straight up, air (M), (M), (H), (S)	294,500
Dark Phoenix mode required	Combo from Teleportation mix-up using TK Shot H while in Dark Phoenix mode	↓↘→ + (H), ←↓↙ + (ATK), cr. (L), cr. (M), cr. (H), → + (H) CANCEL →↓↘ + (L), cr. (L), st. (H), → + (H) CANCEL ↓↙← + (L), → + (H) CANCEL ↓↙← + (L), → + (H) CANCEL →↓↘ + (M) CANCEL ↓↘→ + (ATK)(ATK)	~1,011,500
Corner required	Hitting the air (H) after the air throw requires very tight timing	Forward air throw, air (H), (S), land, st. (H), (S) CANCEL super jump straight up, air (M), (M), air ↓ + (H), land, ↓↙← + (L), st. (H), (S) CANCEL super jump straight up, air (M), (M), (H), (S), land, air ↓↘→ + (L) OTG	279,100
Corner, Dark Phoenix mode required	—	Forward air throw, air (H), (S), land, st. (H), → + (H) CANCEL ↓↙← + (L), st. (H), → + (H) CANCEL ↓↙← + (L), st. (H), → + (H) CANCEL →↓↘ + (M) CANCEL ↓↘→ + (ATK)(ATK)	852,200
Airborne opponent, Dark Phoenix mode required	Combo from anti-air standing (L) in Dark Phoenix mode	St. (L), st. (L), st. (H) CANCEL ↓↙← + (L), → + (H) CANCEL ↓↙← + (L), → + (H) CANCEL ↓↙← + (L), → + (H), (S) CANCEL super jump, air (M), (M), (H) CANCEL ↓↘→ + (ATK)(ATK)	896,500
Dark Phoenix mode required	Combo if opponent gets hit by TK Trap L	↓↙← + (L), → + (H) CANCEL ↓↙← + (L), → + (H) CANCEL ↓↙← + (L), → + (H) CANCEL ↓↙← + (L), → + (H) (S) CANCEL super jump straight up, air (M), (M), (H) CANCEL ↓↘→ + (ATK)(ATK)	~995,700
Dark Phoenix mode required	Combo if opponent gets hit by TK Trap M	↓↙← + (M), ←↓↙ + (L), cr. (M), st. (H), → + (H) CANCEL ↓↙← + (L), → + (H) CANCEL ↓↙← + (L), → + (H), (S) CANCEL super jump straight up, air (M), (H) CANCEL ↓↘→ + (ATK)(ATK)	~902,800
Corner, Dark Phoenix mode required	—	Forward throw, air ↓↘→ + (L) OTG, st. (M), st. (H), → + (H), (S) CANCEL super jump, air (M), (M), (H) CANCEL ↓↘→ + (L) CANCEL ↓↘→ + (ATK)(ATK)	~687,300
Corner, Dark Phoenix mode required, Phoenix tagged in via ↓ + (S) team aerial combo starter	—	Air (M), (H), (S) land, air ↓↘→ + (L) OTG, (S) CANCEL super jump, air (M), (M), (H), (S), land, air ↓↘→ + (L) OTG, →↓↘ + (L) CANCEL ↓↘→ + (ATK)(ATK)	Damage variable depending on scaling
Corner, Dark Phoenix mode required, Phoenix tagged in via ↑ + (S) team aerial combo starter	—	Air (M), (H), (S), land, air ↓↘→ + (L) OTG, (S) CANCEL super jump, air (M), (M), (H) CANCEL ↓↘→ + (ATK)(ATK)	Damage variable depending on scaling

"I'VE DESTROYED WHOLE PLANETS, SO WHAT CHANCE DID YOU HAVE REALLY?"

SHE-HULK

BIO

REAL NAME
JENNIFER "JEN" WALTERS

OCCUPATION
LAWYER, ADVENTURER

ABILITIES
LIKE HER COUSIN, JENNIFER POSSESSES GREAT STRENGTH, DURABILITY, ENDURANCE, AND A HEALING FACTOR. UNLIKE HER COUSIN, SHE ALMOST ALWAYS RETAINS HER FULL INTELLIGENCE AND PERSONALITY AS SHE-HULK.

WEAPONS
NONE

PROFILE
ROBERT BRUCE BANNER'S (HULK) COUSIN. AFTER BEING GRAVELY INJURED, SHE RECEIVED A BLOOD TRANSFUSION FROM BANNER WHICH ALLOWED HER TO TRANSFORM INTO SHE-HULK. HER TRANSFORMATION EXTENDS AS FAR AS HER PERSONALITY, GOING FROM MEEK AND MOUSY TO STRONG-WILLED AND CONFIDENT.

FIRST APPEARANCE
THE SAVAGE SHE-HULK #1 (1980)

"I DON'T WANT YOU TO THINK I WENT EASY ON YOU; I WANT YOU TO KNOW I WENT EASY ON YOU."

POWER GRID

3	INTELLIGENCE
7	STRENGTH
3	SPEED
6	STAMINA
1	ENERGY PROJECTION
4	FIGHTING ABILITY

*This is biographical, and does not represent an evaluation of the character's in-game combat potential.

ALTERNATE COSTUMES

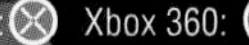

PS3: ⨂ Xbox 360: Ⓐ | PS3: ▢ Xbox 360: Ⓧ | PS3: △ Xbox 360: Ⓨ | PS3: R1 Xbox 360: RB

ATTACK SET

STANDING BASIC ATTACKS

Screen	Command	Hits	Damage	Startup	Active	Recovery	Advantage on Hit	Advantage if Guarded	Notes
1	Standing L	1	55,000	7	4	11	+1	-2	—
2	Standing M	1	70,000	8	4	15	+2	-2	—
3	Standing H	1	90,000	10	4	17	+5	+1	⇩ ⬃ ⇨ + P1 or P2 snap back
4	S	1	90,000	10	3	26	—	-7	Launcher, not special or hyper combo cancelable

1

2

3

4

CROUCHING BASIC ATTACKS

Screen	Command	Hits	Damage	Startup	Active	Recovery	Advantage on Hit	Advantage if Guarded	Notes
1	Crouching L	1	48,000	7	3	11	+2	-1	Low attack, chains into standing L
2	Crouching M	1	67,000	9	4	19	-2	-6	Low attack
3	Crouching H	1	80,000	13	10	23	—	-11	Low attack, knocks down, press ⇨ between frames 21-30 to cancel into Chariot, press ⇦ between frames 21-30 to cancel into Catapult

1

2

3

AERIAL BASIC ATTACKS

Screen	Command	Hits	Damage	Startup	Active	Recovery	Notes
1	Air L	1	55,000	6	8	17	Overhead attack
2	Air M	1	70,000	7	4	26	Overhead attack
3	Air H	1	85,000	9	4	26	Overhead attack
4	Air S	1	90,000	10	4	27	Overhead attack, unrecoverable knockdown when used in air combo after S launcher

1

2

3

4

COMMAND ATTACKS

Screen	Command	Hits	Damage	Startup	Active	Recovery	Advantage on Hit	Advantage if Guarded	Notes
1	⇨ + Ⓗ	1	90,000	25	3	15	+8	+4	Overhead attack, press ⇨ between frames 21-32 to cancel into Chariot, press ⇦ between frames 21-32 to cancel into Catapult
2	(in air) ⇩ + Ⓗ	1	100,000	20	Until grounded	19	—	—	Overhead attack, OTG-capable, cancelable into TAC attack, 1 hit of Super Armor during frames 14-26, knocks down
3	Jump backwards against wall, then press ⬀	—	—	8	—	—	—	—	Performs a wall jump, may initiate aerial attacks or movements after 8th frame

1

2

3

AS A PARTNER-CROSSOVER ASSISTS

Screen	Type	P1+P2 Crossover Combination Hyper Combo	Description	Hits	Damage	Startup	Active	Recovery (this crossover assist)	Recovery (other partner)	Notes
1	α – Alpha	Emerald Cannon	Torpedo	1	75,000	47	8	117	87	Low attack, OTG-capable
2	β – Beta	Emerald Cannon	Clothesline	1	90,000	53	4	140	110	1 hit of Super Armor during frames 45-56, crumples for 124 frames on hit
3	γ – Gamma	Emerald Cannon	Somersault Kick M	2	114,000	30	11	132	102	—

1

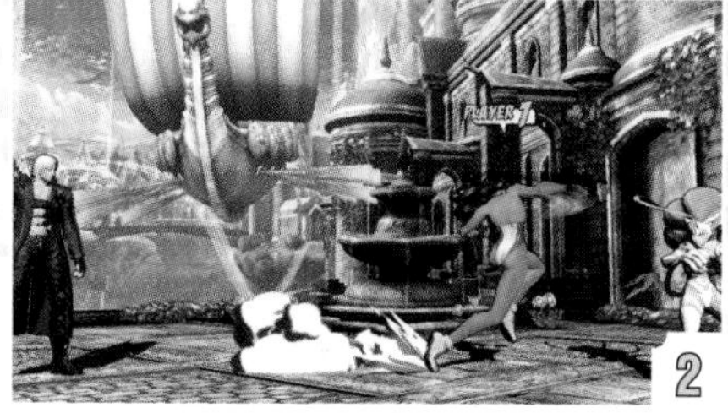
2

3

SPECIAL MOVES

Screen	Name	Command	Hits	Damage	Startup	Active	Recovery	Advantage on Hit	Advantage if Guarded	Notes
1	Heavy Strike L	⇩ ⇘ ⇨ + (L)	1	56,000	10	1	25	—	—	Throw, stuns opponent for 120 frames
2	Heavy Strike M	⇩ ⇘ ⇨ + (M)	1	56,000	9	4	23	—	—	Throw, only hits airborne opponents, stuns opponent for 120 frames
3	Heavy Strike H	⇩ ⇘ ⇨ + (H)	2	106,400	20	6	20	—	—	Throw, stuns opponent for 120 frames
	Somersault Kick L	⇨ ⇩ ⇘ + (L)	1	100,000	8	10	21	-6	-9	Press ⇨ between frames 34-38 to cancel into Chariot, press ⇦ between frames 34-38 to cancel into Catapult
4	Somersault Kick M	⇨ ⇩ ⇘ + (M)	2	133,000	6	11	39	-12	-26	Press ⇨ between frames 51-55 to cancel into Chariot, press ⇦ between frames 51-55 to cancel into Catapult
	Somersault Kick H	⇨ ⇩ ⇘ + (H)	3	162,500	4	13	59	-29	-49	Press ⇨ between frames 66-75 to cancel into Chariot, press ⇦ between frames 66-75 to cancel into Catapult
5	Runner's Start	⇩ ⇩ + (S)	—	—	9	—	—	—	—	Pressing (S) any time from frame 10 and onward causes She-Hulk to go into a 5 frame recovery period
6	Chariot	(During Runner's Start) ⇨	—	—	1	36	—	—	—	—
7	Torpedo	(During Chariot) (L)	1	80,000	9	8	24	+4	-10	Low attack, OTG-capable, spinning knockdown, cancels into Runner's start
8	Clothesline	(During Chariot) (M)	1	110,000	15	4	37	—	-19	1 hit of Super Armor during frames 7-18, crumples for 124 frames on hit, cancels into Runner's start
9	Somersault Kick+	(During Chariot) (H)	2	133,000	6	10	40	-7	-21	Press ⇨ between frames 46-50 to cancel into Chariot, press ⇦ between frames 46-50 to cancel into Catapult
10	Emergency Stop	(During Chariot) (S)	—	—	5	—	5	—	—	Returns She-Hulk to neutral state
11	Catapult	(During Runner's Start) ⇦	—	—	26	—	—	—	—	She-Hulk jumps back and then jumps forward off the wall, stays airborne for frames 27-65, may initiate any Catapult maneuver during that time, cannot air guard during jumps entire duration
12	Shooting Star	(During Catapult) (L)	1	90,000	6	Until grounded	8	—	—	Ground bounce
13	Flying Drop Kick	(During Catapult) (M)	1	110,000	10	Until grounded	15	—	—	Wall Bounce
14	Diving Senton	(During Catapult) (H)	1	110,000	12	Until grounded	19	—	—	1 hit of Super Armor during frames 14-26, Ground bounce, OTG-capable
15	Emergency Landing	(During Catapult) (S)	—	—	—	—	Until grounded	—	—	She-Hulk's forward momentum stops and she falls straight down

Heavy Strike: This varied command throw comes in three flavors: ⇩ ⇘ ⇨ + (L) performs a forward grab, ⇩ ⇘ ⇨ + (H) grabs a foe out of the air, and ⇩ ⇘ ⇨ + (H) does a lunging throw with a slow starting period. All versions of the throw stun an opponent and leave them open to a combo. Use Heavy Strike L at close proximities to grab guarding characters, or cancel into Heavy Strike H from basic attacks to grab an opponent from afar. Heavy Strike M is strictly for stopping attempts to jump away from the previous variations.

Somersault Kick: Perform this early against aerial attacks. The (H) version is the most consistent counter because of its fast starting speed, but its recovery period is massive. Somersault Kick (L) has the least amount of recovery so it's difficult to punish, but its slow wind-up forces you to do it very early against air attacks. All versions of the Somersault Kick can be shifted into Catapult or Chariot by holding ⇦ or ⇨ respectively. Even though it is generally not recommended that you do this if its guarded, shifting into Catapult and coming down with one of its attacks is useful for evading a move and transitioning into an offense.

Runner's Start: This special stance shifts into the Catapult and Chariot movement options by inputting ⇦ or ⇨. This charging period cannot be exited without canceling into either variance, so use it only when you're ready to commit to them.

Chariot: An aggressive forward run that occurs when inputting ⇨ during Runner's start, crouching (H), ⇨ + (H), or Somersault Kick. Its purpose is to move you back into a dangerous position against an opponent whenever you're pushed away. The most prominent option is the Emergency Stop ((S) during Chariot), a quick slide that cancels the Chariot run in 5 frames. The base use for this is to stop the run after you've moved into throw range, an option that works when your foe is wary of the Clothesline and Torpedo options. You can also use it to lower the recovery period on basic attacks. For example, canceling standing (H) into Runner's Start CANCEL Chariot CANCEL Emergency stop as fast as possible nets a +9 frame advantage on hit, a slight improvement over its normal +5 value. The next option, Torpedo, is a sliding low attack that is OTG-capable. Use it in combos starting off of an (S) launcher to land the Emerald Cannon hyper combo. Clothesline ((M) during Chariot), has super armor during the swing, enabling it to stop any attack option that isn't a throw. Use it when you're using Chariot in disadvantageous situations when you can't use Emergency Stop, and a quick light attack to stop a counter offensive. Oddly, you can cancel both Clothesline and Torpedo's recovery periods into ⇩ ⇩ + (S), allowing you to safely keep your offense going when they're guarded. Finally, you can perform the Somersault Kick by hitting (H) during Chariot. This is the fastest option in this arsenal and it is perfect for preemptively countering fast attacks. Don't let its backward movement fool you, it is very vulnerable to dashing attacks when guarded.

Catapult: She-Hulk jumps to the wall behind her and leaps off of it with one of three attacks. You can direct where she flies by holding ← or → when airborne—this movement is cancelable at any time during its flight by pressing Ⓢ. All of the jump techniques have very similar trajectories, Ⓛ is the fastest and safest of the bunch, while Ⓗ has protective super armor, but is punishable when it lands. Version Ⓜ is a drop kick that seems to offer nothing interesting outside of the wall bounce that it causes.

The Catapult is used to move in on a foe from afar and to lure out anti-air attacks. Leaping off of the wall and pressing Ⓢ to cancel the jump just before you reach your target can bait your opponent into doing an anti-air. Though risky, the Ⓗ attack's super armor can blow through anti-air attempts for a ground bounce. Use these abilities in combination with the Chariot to create a varied and confusing offense.

SHE-HULK

HYPER COMBOS

Screen	Name	Command	Hits	Damage	Startup	Active	Recovery	Advantage on Hit	Advantage if Guarded	Notes
1	Emerald Cannon	↓↘→ + ATK ATK	1	120,000	10+4	8	62	—	-48	Wall bounce, unrecoverable knockdown
2	Emerald Impulse	(During Emerald Cannon) ↓↘→ + Ⓢ	1	120,000	26	31	41	—	—	Unrecoverable knockdown
3	Emerald Disaster	(During Emerald Impulse) ↓↘→ + Ⓢ	1	120,000	46	22	21	—	—	Unrecoverable knockdown
4	Taking out the Trash	→↓↘ + ATK ATK	10	260,000	4+3	88-92	93-154	—	—	Frames 1-8 invincible, air throw, wall bounce
5	Road Rage (Level 3 Hyper Combo)	↓↙← + ATK ATK	3	180,000 ~ 400,000	18+0	1	3	—	—	Frames 1-19 invincible, throw, projectile has 4 high priority durability points

Emerald Cannon: This hyper combo is used strictly for combos, more often than not after an OTG Torpedo. Its two extensions serve as a method of taking advantage of varied combos depending on the amount of meter available. With only 1 meter it is best to go for both extensions. When 2 meters are available you can opt to stop the command at Emerald Impulse, then OTG with Torpedo CANCEL ↓↘→ + ATK ATK to score a small amount of extra damage.

Taking out the Trash: A dominant anti-air, hyper combo with few weaknesses. This unblockable throw has just enough invulnerability to blow through any aerial attack, assuming that it is performed as late as possible. A successful hit leads to an air combo. Additionally, the invulnerability and inability to guard it makes it perfect for "resets", or tactics used to hit a foe flipping out of an aerial hit. For example, perform a combo that causes an unrecoverable knockdown, then OTG your foe with ↓↓ + Ⓢ CANCEL → CANCEL Ⓛ. When they flip out, wait a moment to see what direction they move towards, then do →↓↘ + ATK ATK. Your opponent cannot attack to escape this option, which is only escapable if they have a double jump or invincible air special move.

Road Rage: An unusual level 3 throw hyper combo that summons a car projectile if the throw misses. Road Rage is extremely slow and cannot be linked into via a combo, relegating its use to a reversal. Even then, the cost is rather high for something with no guarantee of success.

BATTLE PLAN

OVERVIEW

VITALITY: 1,150,000

CHAIN COMBO ARCHETYPE: MARVEL SERIES

X-Factor	Lv.1	Lv.2	Lv.3
Damage	130%	160%	190%
Speed	110%	120%	130%

She-Hulk is a close range character that is designed to easily compensate for advancing guard use. Her flexibility at close distances is unmatched, and she can easily deal with players that attempt to jump away from this offense. With that said, the objective with She-Hulk should be to move into close range with a secondary goal of cornering the opposition.

Moving into close range is effective because:

Runner's Start followed by Chariot moves She-Hulk right back into a threatening position whenever an attack is guarded.

She-Hulk's → + Ⓗ overhead is fast and leaves her at a frame advantage, this is a good compliment to her powerful, low-hitting combos.

The three command throws at her disposal all lead to extended combos, adding further "oomph" to her close range options.

Taking out the Trash is an invulnerable air throw that deters a foe's constant use of air dash attacks and attempts to escape She-Hulk's close range setups.

This goal is accomplished by:

Using projectile assists to shield an approach.

Baiting an opponent into making poorly calculated anti-air attacks with the Catapult extensions.

Jumping at an opponent and beating their anti-air attack with ↓ + Ⓗ.

Using Clothesline's super armor to blast through an incoming projectile.

ON THE GROUND

Your goal while playing She-Hulk is to move into close range, but this is no easy task. At long range you have little to work with in regards to countering projectiles, so relying on projectile assists is a must. You also have access to the Catapult options (↓ ↓ + Ⓢ CANCEL ←), which are designed to lure out and counter anti-air attempts, while avoiding projectiles. Use Catapult to leap off of a wall, then attack with Shooting Star (↓ ↓ + Ⓢ CANCEL ← CANCEL Ⓛ) to move into close range. When your foe is aware of your intentions and readies an anti-air, leap off of the wall and perform Emergency Landing (↓ ↓ + Ⓢ CANCEL ← CANCEL Ⓢ) to kill your jump momentum and drop to the ground. This effectively tricks the opposing player into using an anti-air attack that misses. In addition to these options, Diving Senton (↓ ↓ + Ⓢ CANCEL ← CANCEL Ⓗ) has a short window of super armor that can plow through anti-air attacks. It's not safe when guarded, so use it sparingly.

Some projectiles can be preemptively stopped with the Clothesline (↓ ↓ + Ⓢ CANCEL → CANCEL Ⓜ) which has super armor. This must be done very early in anticipation of the shot. When this is too risky, rely instead on crouching Ⓗ which can be used as a general poke for preemptively stopping projectiles and other ground attacks. Its range is massive, enabling you to perform this attack when She-Hulk is just within long range. It is safe when guarded from a distance, so have little fear when using it unless your opponent is reliant on airdashes. You can also verify if it hits or not—if it hits, chain into a late Ⓢ to shift into an air combo; if it doesn't, cancel into ↓ ↘ → + Ⓗ to grab a guarding foe, or ↓ ↓ + Ⓢ to shift into the Runner's Start then tap → to dash towards your adversary.

Enemy jump attacks become an issue when using crouching Ⓗ. Luckily, She-Hulk has one anti-air option that trumps all others, → ↓ ↘ + ATK ATK. This hyper combo air throw is unblockable and invulnerable, making a perfect anti-air. It also leads to **Combo V** on a successful hit. The threat of this alone should dissuade an aggressive opponent from using airdash tactics to attack. When meter isn't available, use → ↓ ↘ + Ⓛ instead. This attack does not have invulnerability, but is still fast enough to stop most air attacks. It also shifts into the Catapult movement (→ ↓ ↘ + Ⓗ CANCEL ←), which makes it difficult to punish when guarded against most characters. When your foe starts to air guard, you can air throw them to the ground and transition into **Combo VI**.

Catapult (and its many variations) is useful for confusing your opponent's defense, but be wary of beam hyper combos, which can preemptively punish it.

Chariot moves you back into close range after failed attacks, but don't rely on the Clothesline to counter reversals. Input Ⓢ to cancel the dash and guard instead.

Your close range offense should consist of varying between the Heavy Strike (↓ ↘ → + ATK) throw, low-hitting **Combo I**, and **Combo IV** (which starts off of an overhead). **Combos I** and **IV** have flexible attack openings that can be canceled into Chariot to compensate for failed attacks. Both crouching Ⓗ and → + Ⓗ can do this automatically when you hold → after they hit, or input ↓ ↓ + Ⓢ CANCEL → to do it manually. The manual input shifts into the Chariot much faster than the auto version, a necessary attribute for consistently countering an opponent's attempts to stop the dash. When your challenger doesn't use advancing guard to push you away, cancel crouching Ⓗ into ↓ ↓ + Ⓢ CANCEL → CANCEL Ⓢ to stop the run, then perform **Combo I** without a gap in guard stun. Use this same tactic when you attempt Heavy Strike L (transition into **Combo II**). You can also cancel crouching Ⓗ into the → + Ⓗ overhead to keep your opponent on their toes. When the opposing player uses advancing guard against these common openings, cancel into the Chariot to move back into a threatening position. Although it is risky because of its heavy recovery, an early Clothesline can be used to crash through your opponent's attempts to attack you during Chariot. If your foe tries to jump away from a Chariot offense, cancel the run with Emergency Stop, then grab your target out of the air with Heavy Strike M or → ↓ ↘ + ATK ATK.

She-Hulk's offense is far more difficult to push away with advancing guard near corners. There are smaller gaps between attacks canceled into Chariot CANCEL Emergency Stop, and you're always in range for Heavy Strike H when it is canceled into from a basic attack. If your foe jumps vertically over Heavy Strike H to avoid it, catch them as they fall with → ↓ ↘ + ATK ATK to land a giant combo.

UP IN THE AIR

↓ + Ⓗ crushes anti-air attacks, but the risk in using it far out ways its benefits, unless an assist is used to cover it.

She-Hulk's aerial options are limited. In most cases, you will be reliant on using basic jump attacks to punish projectiles and to stage an offense. Air Ⓗ is the best attack to use during a forward jump, which allows for a basic mix-up whenever it is blocked—perform air Ⓗ then land and go for **Combo I**, or chain air Ⓗ into air Ⓢ to hit your foe when they are expecting the previous variation. When your opposition is looking to anti-air your jumps, you can use the super armor property of air ↓ + Ⓗ to plow through it. This is risky, because ↓ + Ⓗ is punishable by throws when it is blocked.

She-Hulk also has access to wall jumps. This is a possible option for escaping corners, even though the jump itself has little range. This has the effect of putting you into cross-up range when your foe is one character length away, which occasionally makes up for its poor range. Perform the swinging air Ⓗ when going for cross-ups in this situation.

COMBO USAGE

I. CR. Ⓛ, CR. Ⓜ, CR. Ⓗ, Ⓢ CANCEL SUPER JUMP, AIR Ⓜ, Ⓜ, Ⓗ, Ⓢ, LAND, ↓↓ + Ⓢ CANCEL → CANCEL Ⓛ CANCEL ↓↘→ + ATK ATK CANCEL ↓↘→ + Ⓢ CANCEL ↓↘→ + Ⓢ

(587,300 damage) She-Hulk's basic, low-hitting combo. After the initial Ⓢ launch, delay each input for the air chain to ensure air Ⓢ hits as low as possible in the air. This makes it easier to OTG your foe with ↓↓ + Ⓢ CANCEL → CANCEL Ⓛ. Omit the crouching Ⓜ from this combo if your opponent is prone to using advancing guard. Doing so keeps you near your opposition, regardless of its use.

II. ↓↘→ + Ⓛ OR Ⓜ OR Ⓗ, ↓↓ + Ⓢ CANCEL → CANCEL Ⓜ, ↓↓ + Ⓢ CANCEL ← CANCEL Ⓗ, LAND, Ⓢ CANCEL SUPER JUMP FORWARD, AIR Ⓜ, Ⓜ, Ⓗ, Ⓢ, LAND, ↓↓ + Ⓢ CANCEL → CANCEL Ⓛ CANCEL ↓↘→ + ATK ATK CANCEL ↓↘→ + Ⓢ CANCEL ↓↘→ + Ⓢ

(551,700 or 557,400 damage) This combo works after any of She-Hulk's command grabs. Don't rush the clothesline after she recovers from the command throw, there's plenty of time. After inputting ↓↓ + Ⓢ CANCEL ← CANCEL Ⓗ, there's no need to input directions for it to hit an opponent, it will track their location on its own.

III. ↓↓ + Ⓢ CANCEL → CANCEL Ⓜ, ↓↓ + Ⓢ CANCEL ← CANCEL Ⓗ, LAND, Ⓢ CANCEL SUPER JUMP FORWARD, AIR Ⓜ, Ⓜ, Ⓗ, Ⓢ, LAND, ↓↓ + Ⓢ CANCEL → CANCEL Ⓛ CANCEL ↓↘→ + ATK ATK CANCEL ↓↘→ + Ⓢ CANCEL ↓↘→ + Ⓢ

(683,000 damage) A high damage combo done when Clothesline plows through an attack. Take caution, it's completely unsafe when guarded.

IV. → + Ⓗ, CR. Ⓛ, CR. Ⓜ, CR. Ⓗ, Ⓢ, CANCEL SUPER JUMP, AIR Ⓜ, Ⓜ, Ⓗ, Ⓢ, LAND, ↓↓ + Ⓢ CANCEL → CANCEL Ⓛ CANCEL ↓↘→ + ATK ATK CANCEL ↓↘→ + Ⓢ CANCEL ↓↘→ + Ⓢ

(605,500 damage) → + Ⓗ CANCEL → shifts into the Chariot, which keeps you near your challenger if they use advancing guard against the opening attack. This is far better than doing → + Ⓗ on its own, since advancing guard will eliminate any momentum that you have gained. You can still link into the same combo by performing Emergency Stop after the Chariot (→ + Ⓗ CANCEL → CANCEL Ⓢ) to leave you at a frame advantage. It is harder to link into crouching Ⓛ in that situation, but the added flexibility helps when an attack fails.

V. AGAINST AN AIRBORNE FOE, →↓↘ + ATK ATK, WAIT A MOMENT, CR. Ⓗ, Ⓢ CANCEL SUPER JUMP FORWARD, AIR Ⓜ, Ⓜ, Ⓗ, Ⓢ, ↓↓ + Ⓢ

(350,400 damage) This invincible air throw is used against high priority jump attacks. Mid-screen you must dash forward after the initial throw before you perform crouching Ⓗ. Near corners you should just wait a moment before doing it.

VI. AIR THROW, ↓↓ + Ⓢ CANCEL → CANCEL Ⓛ CANCEL ↓↘→ + ATK ATK CANCEL ↓↘→ + Ⓢ CANCEL ↓↘→ + Ⓢ

(424,800 damage) When hyper combo meter isn't available for **Combo V**, and your opponent is prone to guarding normal anti-air attacks, use this option. Nothing difficult here, just land from the throw and perform the remainder of the commands.

SHE-HULK

ASSISTS

Projectile assists are the only way to move in without taking unfavorable risks.

She-Hulk's—α assist has unmatched attacked range for an OTG-capable attack.

She-Hulk has no means of approaching enemies with projectiles. To deal with this issue, you should pick projectile assists that hit multiple times, like Dante—γ, Arthur—α, or Taskmaster—α. With a projectile on screen, wavedash forward and attack with **Combo I** or **Combo IV** to mount a basic high/low attack.

There's a clear winner in regards to She-Hulk's own assists, and that's the low-hitting α assist. Outside of its long attacking range, its OTG capabilities allow it to extend combos for numerous characters that require improved damage output. Its low-hitting property allows it to also be used for a number of attack setups that are completely un-guardable. She-Hulk's β assist is the Clothesline, which has a short window of super armor that's good for countering projectiles. Her third γ assist is a basic anti-air attack with a fast wind-up. γ is the best option for crossover counters, even if it doesn't lead to additional damage on a successful hit.

ADVANCED TACTICS

↓ + H CANCEL → TAC WHIFF

AIR COMBO!
8 HITS!

8 HITS!

9 HITS!

No other character can take advantage of such an odd technique.

A She-Hulk player will have a hard time dealing heavy damage without meter, but there's a way to compensate by using a special technique. Air ↓ + H is OTG-capable and TAC cancelable. Normally, canceling into a TAC attack tags into another character. However, if you make the TAC attack whiff, She-Hulk stays on screen. Perform a S launcher and follow your foe up with an immediate air M, H, S. Perform the air chain as soon as you take to the air. After S knocks the opposing character to the floor, perform air ↓ + H as She-Hulk is falling to OTG the character. Just as the attack hits, cancel into ↓ + S, which will miss entirely, allowing She-Hulk to recover from ↓ + H earlier than she normally does. Immediately attack with crouching M, crouching H, then S to hit and re-launch your foe. Move along to the Combo Appendix to see examples for using this damaging technique.

COMBO APPENDIX

GENERAL EXECUTION TIPS

After launching your opponent with S, start a chain late in the air and slightly delay each attack. This gives you additional time to OTG the opposing character with ↓ ↓ + S CANCEL → → CANCEL → L.

Requirements (Position, meter, etc.)	Notes	Command Sequence	Damage
Requires 1 hyper combo gauge bars	—	Cr. L . cr, M, cr. H, S CANCEL → forward super jump, air M, M, H, S, land, ↓ ↓ + S CANCEL → →, L CANCEL → ↓ ↓ + S, → CANCEL → S (cancel), S CANCEL → forward super jump, early air H, S, ↓ + H CANCEL → ↓ + S (TAC tag hit whiffs), land, cr. H, S CANCEL → forward super jump, air M, M, H, S, land, ↓ ↓ + S CANCEL → →, L CANCEL → ↓ ↘ → + ATK ATK CANCEL → ↓ ↘ → + S, ↓ ↘ → + S, ↓ ↓ + S CANCEL → →, L	712,800
Requires 1 hyper combo gauge bar, requires level 1 X-Factor	—	Cr. L, cr. M, st. H X-Factor forward dash, cr. M, cr. H, S CANCEL → super jump, early air M, H, S, wait a moment, ↓ + H CANCEL → ↓ + S (TAC tag hit whiffs), land, cr. M, S CANCEL → super jump forward, air M, M, H, S, land, ↓ ↓ + S CANCEL → → CANCEL → L CANCEL → ↓ ↘ → + ATK ATK CANCEL → ↓ ↘ → + S CANCEL → ↓ ↘ → + S	1,172,000
Requires 1 hyper combo gauge bar, requires level 1 X-Factor	—	↓ ↘ → + L, cr. M, st. H X-Factor forward dash, cr. M, cr. H, S CANCEL → super jump, early air M, H, S, wait a moment, ↓ + H CANCEL → ↓ + S (TAC tag hit whiffs), land, cr. M, cr. H, S CANCEL → super jump forward, air M, M, H, S, land, ↓ ↓ + S CANCEL → → CANCEL → L CANCEL → ↓ ↘ → + ATK ATK CANCEL → ↓ ↘ → + S CANCEL → ↓ ↘ → + S	1,192,800

"YOU JUST
GOT PULVERIZED
BY 700 POUNDS
OF LEAN GREEN
MUSCLE, SWEETIE."

SPIDER-MAN

BIO

REAL NAME

PETER BENJAMIN PARKER

OCCUPATION

FREELANCE PHOTOGRAPHER

ABILITIES

IN ADDITION TO STICKING TO WALLS AND CEILINGS, HE CAN ALSO SHOOT WEBS FROM THE WEB-SHOOTERS ON HIS WRISTS, USEFUL FOR CATCHING BAD GUYS OR TRAVELING BY WEB-SWINGING. HIS "SPIDER-SENSE" ALLOWS HIM TO SENSE WHEN DANGER IS PRESENT.

WEAPONS

NONE

PROFILE

WHILE ATTENDING A PUBLIC SCIENCE EXHIBIT, YOUNG PETER WAS BITTEN BY A RADIOACTIVE SPIDER; THIS GRANTED HIM SPECIAL ABILITIES, AND HE BECAME THE HERO SPIDER-MAN. WHEN HIS BELOVED UNCLE WAS KILLED BY A CRIMINAL PETER COULD HAVE APPREHENDED BUT CHOSE NOT TO, HE SWORE TO LIVE BY THE CREED OF "WITH GREAT POWER THERE MUST ALSO COME GREAT RESPONSIBILITY."

FIRST APPEARANCE

AMAZING FANTASY #15 (1962)

POWER GRID

4	INTELLIGENCE
4	STRENGTH
3	SPEED
3	STAMINA
1	ENERGY PROJECTION
4	FIGHTING ABILITY

*This is biographical, and does not represent an evaluation of the character's in-game combat potential.

ALTERNATE COSTUMES

PS3: ⓧ Xbox 360: Ⓐ

PS3: ▢ Xbox 360: Ⓧ

PS3: △ Xbox 360: Ⓨ

PS3: R1 Xbox 360: RB

ATTACK SET

STANDING BASIC ATTACKS

Screen	Command	Hits	Damage	Startup	Active	Recovery	Advantage on Hit	Advantage if Guarded	Notes
1	Standing L	1	43,000	4	3	9	+2	+1	—
2	Standing M	1	60,000	8	3	15	+1	-1	—
3	Standing H	1	70,000	10	6	24	-6	-8	↓↙← + P1 or P2 snap back
4	S	1	80,000	9	4	26	—	-8	Launcher, not special or hyper combo cancelable

CROUCHING BASIC ATTACKS

Screen	Command	Hits	Damage	Startup	Active	Recovery	Advantage on Hit	Advantage if Guarded	Notes
1	Crouching L	1	40,000	6	2	11	+1	0	Low attack, chains into standing L
2	Crouching M	1	57,000	5	6	18	-5	-7	—
3	Crouching H	1	67,000	10	7	37	—	-22	Low attack, knocks down

AERIAL BASIC ATTACKS

Screen	Command	Hits	Damage	Startup	Active	Recovery	Notes
1	Air L	1	44,000	5	3	22	Overhead attack
2	Air M	1	60,000	7	4	17	Overhead attack
3	Air H	1	70,000	10	8	16	Overhead attack
4	Air S	1	78,000	9	8	11	Overhead attack, unrecoverable knockdown when used in air combo after S launcher

COMMAND ATTACKS

Screen	Command	Hits	Damage	Startup	Active	Recovery	Advantage on Hit	Advantage if Guarded	Notes
1	Jump backwards against wall, then press ↗	—	—	8	—	—	—	—	Performs a wall jump, may initiate aerial attacks or movements after 8th frame

AS A PARTNER-CROSSOVER ASSISTS

Screen	Type	P1+P2 Crossover Combination Hyper Combo	Description	Hits	Damage	Startup	Active	Recovery (this crossover assist)	Recovery (other partner)	Notes
1	α – Alpha	Crawler Assault	Web Ball L	1	10,000	40	—	124	91	Stuns for 30 frames on hit, projectile has 5 low priority durability points
2	β – Beta	Crawler Assault	Web Swing H	1	90,000	44	20	114	84	—
3	γ – Gamma	Crawler Assault	Spider Sting M	1	80,000	35	21	137	107	—

SPECIAL MOVES

Screen	Name	Command	Hits	Damage	Startup	Active	Recovery	Advantage on Hit	Advantage if Guarded	Notes
1	Web Ball L (in air OK)	↓↘→ + L	1	10,000	16	—	29	+5	-13	Incapacitates opponent for 34 frames on hit, projectile has 5 low priority durability points
	Web Ball M	↓↘→ + M	1	10,000	22	—	33	+10	-17	Incapacitates opponent for 43 frames on hit, projectile has 5 low priority durability points
	Web Ball H	↓↘→ + H	1	10,000	28	—	38	+15	-22	Incapacitates opponent for 53 frames on hit, projectile has 5 low priority durability points
	Air Web Ball L	(in air) ↓↘→ + L	1	10,000	18	—	29	—	—	Incapacitates opponent for 34 frames on hit, projectile has 5 low priority durability points
	Air Web Ball M	(in air) ↓↘→ + M	1	10,000	22	—	35	—	—	Incapacitates opponent for 43 frames on hit, projectile has 5 low priority durability points
	Air Web Ball H	(in air) ↓↘→ + H	1	10,000	26	—	41	—	—	Incapacitates opponent for 53 frames on hit, projectile has 5 low priority durability points
2	Spider Sting L	→↓↘ + L	1	70,000	7	21	20	-10	-19	Knocks down
	Spider Sting M	→↓↘ + M	1	80,000	9	21	26	-16	-25	Knocks down
	Spider Sting H	→↓↘ + H	1	90,000	11	21	44	-34	-43	Knocks down
3	Spider Bite	(During Spider Sting) H	1	45,000	3	3-8	Until grounded, 1 frame ground recovery	—	—	Ground bounce
4	Web Swing L (in air OK)	←↓↙ + L	1	70,000	12	10	6	+15	+6	Air version is an overhead attack, knocks down
	Web Swing M (in air OK)	←↓↙ + M	1	80,000	16	16	6	+9	0	Air version is an overhead attack, knocks down
	Web Swing H (in air OK)	←↓↙ + H	1	90,000	20	20	2	—	0	Air version is an overhead attack, knocks down
5	Web Throw L	→↘↓↙← + L	3	150,000	20	—	28	—	-15	Unrecoverable knockdown, projectile has 3 low priority durability points
	Web Throw M	→↘↓↙← + M	3	150,000	16	—	27	—	-10	Unrecoverable knockdown, projectile has 3 low priority durability points
	Web Throw H	→↘↓↙← + H	3	150,000	14	—	26	—	-4	Unrecoverable knockdown, projectile has 3 low priority durability points
6	Web Glide (can be directed, in air OK)	S + ATK	1	20,000	16 (upward), 18 (downward)	Until contact	—	+19	+17	Holding ↗, ↘, ↙, or ↖ fires the shot at an angle in the corresponding direction, Spider-Man instantly recovers in air upon contact, projectile has 1 low priority durability point

1

Web Ball: Spider-Man's projectile wraps the opposition in webbing, leaving them stunned and vulnerable momentarily. The length of the stun is determined by the strength of the attack; L creates only a short 34 frame stun, while H causes a heavy 53 frame stun. The button also determines how slow its starting period is. Web Ball L is the best version to use because of its faster release and slower traveling speed. The H version is very slow to start but travels faster after it is finally shot. Fire Web Ball L to control your foe's ground movements and to shield an approach—when you are wary of brashly charging into the fray, shoot Web Ball L and either wavedash or air dash behind it. If Web Ball ever hits, dash forward and hit the stunned foe with a combo. Aerial Web Balls have similar frame data. The major difference is their angled line of attack. You can fire up to two air Web Ball Ls during a super jump before landing. Doing this controls a lot of space and forces an opponent to take awkward measures to make an approach. If needed, you can also fire a single air Web Ball before doing an airdash or Web Glide to protect your move.

2

3

Spider Sting: This flying uppercut is used only in combos, despite its anti-air influenced appearance. Its biggest asset is its Spider Bite extension, which causes a ground bounce on hit. Take advantage of the opening by attacking with an immediate air combo afterwards. There's no reason to use any version other than the damaging Spider Sting H. Since you'll only be doing it in combos, there's no need to worry about its extended recovery period.

4

Web Swing: A leaping kick used for combos and offensive patterns. Web Swing creates a hefty hitstun on contact while leaving Spider-Man in the air. This allows for follow-up air combos that are long and damaging. Additionally, Web Swing L grants frame advantage on guard, as does the M and H versions, as long as they hit on later active frames. This makes Web Swing a powerful tool near corners to combat advancing guard. For instance, cancel attacks that your foe uses advancing guard against into Web Swing H, which swings you back into close range. Once the kick is guarded, drop down with the air attack of your choice to keep your foe pinned before you land.

The aerial version of the Web Swing is an overhead attack. Although it is normally difficult to use because of its high altitude, doing ←↓↙↖ + L command performs the Web Swing just as you leave the ground for a super jump. After inputting ↖, you must allow at least 4 frames to pass before hitting L, or else one of the 3 pre-jump grounded frames will cancel into the ground version of the Web Swing, which is not an overhead. You'll know you're getting the air version if you see a cone of dust fly upwards (a dust effect that plays during a super jump). Take note that this does not work against smaller crouching characters, like Dante, Deadpool, Felicia, Hsien-ko, Morrigan, Viewtiful Joe, Wolverine, X-23, and Spider-Man himself.

5

Web Throw: Spider-Man fires a long web that grabs an opponent and tosses them. This is strictly a long range tool for preemptively countering attempts to act after your opponent has guarded Web Ball L. A common reaction is to assume another Web Ball is coming after the first, causing your foe to jump or try to match your shot with their own projectile. Firing →↘↓↙← + M in this situation will catch a jump, while →↘↓↙← + L will hit a projectile's start-up frames, assuming your initial Web Ball is guarded at a distance (causing Spider-Man to recover before the Web Ball even makes contact, thus giving the Web Throw plenty of time to fire). Web Throw also uniquely leads to high damage combos if you are able to toss your foe into a nearby corner. This only occurs if Spider-Man's back is facing a wall. Take a look at the Combo Appendix for an example of this powerful, but rare, scenario.

6

Web Glide: Spider-Man's trademark web swinging is finally possible in a fighting game. Web Glide is an all-purpose mobility option that is great for defensive and aggressive play. When on the ground, inputting ATK + S on its own fires a web upwards at an angle. You can direct the web to fire directly upwards by holding ↑, or backwards by holding ← or ↖. In the air the default direction is angled downward, while hitting ↑ or ← shoots in those corresponding directions. Once the web attaches to a wall or player, Spider-Man zooms toward his target at a blinding speed. Outside of using this to move around the screen, you're left in an aerial state that allows for air attacks, granting the opportunity to combo after the web grab. This is good for punishing an opponent's projectiles when you're jumping vertically, or for simply moving into close range against a guarding foe.

HYPER COMBOS

Screen	Name	Command	Hits	Damage	Startup	Active	Recovery	Advantage on Hit	Advantage if Guarded	Notes
1	Maximum Spider (in air OK)	↓↘→ + ATK ATK	15	271,600	7~23+4	8~11	68	—	-54	Invincible until Spider-Man reaches the wall, unrecoverable knockdown
2	Crawler Assault	→↓↘ + ATK ATK	8	292,100	20+4	3 (5) 3 (5) 3 (5) 3 (5) 3 (5) 3 (5) 3 (10) 5	52	—	-36	Frames 1-26 invincible, last hit wall bounces
3	Ultimate Web Throw	→↘↓↙← + ATK ATK	1	300,000	29+3	15	76	—	—	Frames 1-20 invincible, air throw, unrecoverable knockdown

Maximum Spider: Spider-Man leaps off of a wall before pummeling his opponent with multiple kicks. Maximum Spider has some use in air combos when canceled into off of air Web Swing. Unfortunately, this occasionally misses. Maximum Spider must touch a nearby wall before traveling, so it sometimes takes too long to reach the final destination if the wall is at a distance. An alternative to dealing with this problem is to use OTG-capable assists to improve the number of ways that you can link into this hyper combo.

Crawler Assault: This multi-hit hyper combo has few uses outside of its invulnerability window, which can counter close range attacks. It is unsafe when guarded, and this limits its uses to performing it as an invincible method of escaping the battlefield with a team hyper combo.

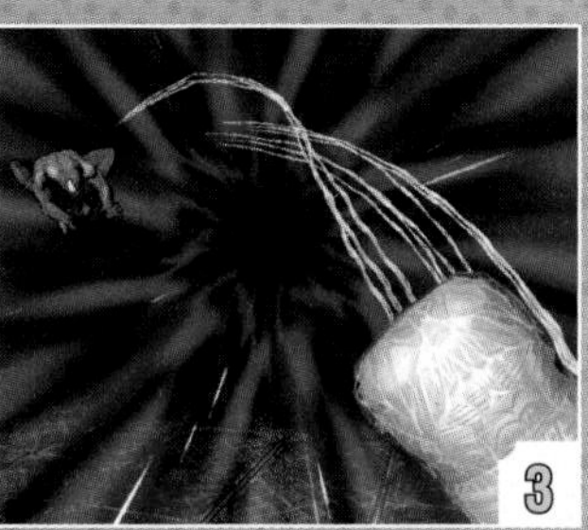

Ultimate Web Throw: This is an aerial throw used to stop jumps from long range. Its invulnerability runs out before the attack initiates, making it difficult to use it as an anti-air at close distances. Save it only for an opponent's jumps done from afar. It has some uses in a few aerial throw tricks—do a combo that allows you to land and juggle an airborne foe with standing L, then cancel into Ultimate Web Throw. Your opponent recovers directly into the web, which can't be guarded. Sadly, even this can be countered, if the enemy performs a forward air recovery followed by an air attack. Needless to say, you may want to avoid using this hyper combo in favor of the other options.

BATTLE PLAN

OVERVIEW

VITALITY: 900,000

CHAIN COMBO ARCHETYPE: MARVEL SERIES

X-Factor	Lv.1	Lv.2	Lv.3
Damage	125%	150%	175%
Speed	113%	123%	139%

Your friendly neighborhood Spider-Man patrols the battleground looking for a way to get close and personal. He has a few projectile attacks that help round him out in matches where he can't just rush in, but don't let that dissuade you from utilizing his strongest position in a fight; glide past your opponent's defenses and move into close range.

This strategy is effective because:

Spider-Man's Web Glide and airdash both allow you to easily punish projectiles and ground attacks, along with enabling you to perform fast aerial attacks that are very close to the ground as quick overheads.

The air version of Web Swing L can be done very close to the ground as a very fast overhead that leads to air combos, which compliments Spider-Man's powerful, low-hitting combos.

Spider-Man's Web Ball L travels slowly across the field, allowing him to dash behind it to safely approach an opponent.

Accomplish this strategy by:

Countering a ground attack or projectile with an airdash or Web Glide.

Throwing Web Ball L and wavedashing behind it.

Super jumping and throwing air Web Ball L before airdashing behind it.

ASSISTS

OTG-capable assists make is easier to combo into Maximum Spider.

Stick with Spider-Man's—α assist, additional space control is never a bad thing

Spider-Man has relatively strong combos, but very few of them efficiently take advantage of hyper combos. Use OTG-capable assists to compensate for this problem, which allow you to easily tack on Maximum Spider after unrecoverable knockdowns once the assist hits. For example, perform **Combo I** near a corner with the variation that ends with a air Ⓢ. While your challenger is floored, call Wesker—β then immediately perform ↓ ↘ → + ATK ATK. If done quickly, Wesker will shoot the floored opponent and bump them into the air just as Maximum Spider activates. Dante—β, X-23—β, and She-Hulk—α are also options for doing this. See the Combo Appendix for an example.

As a partner, Spider-Man's assists are lackluster. Web Ball is the best option because it is usable for general space control and combos (it wraps foes in webbing momentarily, allowing for easy follow-up combos). However, its damage is very low, and it creates damage reduction for little reward. Web Swing covers a lot of area and deals the most damage out of the rest of his assists, offering some use in air combos. Spider Sting is a basic anti-air assist that's faster than the other options. Its fast speed makes it a strong option for crossover counters. When it hits, hyper cancel into Maximum Spider for additional damage.

ADVANCED TACTICS

UNBLOCKABLE ASSIST SETUPS

You can use She-Hulk from as far out as long range to go for a completely unguardable attack!

She-Hulk—α already improves Spider-Man's combo capabilities. It also provides a powerful mix-up option that's impossible to guard due to the assist's low-hitting property. For example, call She-Hulk—α and airdash towards your foe, then attack with air Ⓢ. If both attacks are timed to hit at the same time, your opponent cannot guard. When it hits, jump forward and perform air Ⓜ, Ⓜ, Ⓗ CANCEL ← ↓ ↙ + Ⓜ, Ⓜ, Ⓢ to combo off of it.

COMBO APPENDIX

GENERAL EXECUTION TIPS

After canceling into a super jump from an (S) launcher, follow your foe into the sky and perform your chosen air chain late in the air.

When canceling into (ATK) + (S) to link into air moves, start attacking as soon as possible after you're lifted in the air. The best string to link into is air (M), (M), (S), which will push your foe away when done at mid-screen. Dash forward after landing to move back into range for more hits.

Requirements (Position, meter, etc.)	Notes	Command Sequence	Damage
Requires corner, requires 1 hyper combo gauge bar, She-Hulk—α	During the final air chain sequence, delay each input to drop Spider-Man's height slightly, this ensures he lands soon enough after air (S) to OTG with She-Hulk—α	Cr. (L), st. (L), cr. (M), cr. (H) CANCEL→ →↓↘ + (H) CANCEL→ (H), st. (H) CANCEL→ ←↓↙ + (M), air (M), (M), (S), land, st. (M), (S) CANCEL→ super jump, air (M), (M), (H), (S), land, P1 or P2, ↓↘→ + (ATK)(ATK)	619,800
Enemy must be standing	Position yourself directly next to your opponent for Web Glide to hit, Web Glide cannot hit smaller characters at all, like Amaterasu, Arthur, and Zero.	Cr. (L), st. (M), st. (H) CANCEL→ (ATK) + (S), air (M), (M), (S), land, forward dash, cr. (M), cr. (H) CANCEL→ ←↓↙ + (L), air (M), (M), (S), land, st. (M), st. (H), (S) CANCEL→ super jump, air (M), (M), (H), (S)	459,800
Requires Spider-Man to be cornered, requires 1 hyper combo gauge bar, Wesker—β	The →↘↓↙←↖ + (H) command cancels a super jump's pre-jump frames into the Web Throw, after slapping your foe to the ground with air (S), call Wesker—β then immediately perform ↓↘→ + (ATK)(ATK) without a delay	Cr. (L), cr. (M), cr. (H), (S) CANCEL→ →↓↘ + (H) CANCEL→ (H), st. (H), (S) CANCEL→ →↘↓↙←↖ + (H), forward dash, cr. (M), cr. (H) CANCEL→ ←↓↙ + (L), air (M), (M), (S), land, st. (H), (S) CANCEL→ super jump, air (M), (M), (H), (S), land, P1 or P2, ↓↘→ + (ATK)(ATK)	791,900
Requires level 1 X-Factor	—	Cr. (L), cr. (M), st. (H) (X-Factor) forward dash, cr. (M), cr. (H) CANCEL→ →↓↘ + (H), st. (H) CANCEL→ ←↓↙ + (M), air (M), (M), (S), land, st. (M), st. (H), (S) CANCEL→ super jump, air (M), (M), (H), (S)	828,600

"SOMETHING TELLS ME PETER PARKER GOT SOME NICE SHOTS OF YOUR HUMILIATING DEFEAT FOR TOMORROW'S DAILY BUGLE."

STORM

"I MAY TREASURE PEACE, BUT I AM VERY GOOD AT MAKING WAR."

BIO

REAL NAME

ORORO MUNROE

OCCUPATION

QUEEN OF WAKANDA

ABILITIES

STORM COMMANDS THE WEATHER—SHE CAN FREELY MANIPULATE ATMOSPHERIC TEMPERATURE, PRESSURE, HUMIDITY, ETC. SHE CAN ALSO CONTROL THE SURROUNDING ATMOSPHERE, CREATING HURRICANES OR EVEN SHOOT LIGHTNING.

WEAPONS

NONE

PROFILE

THOUGH SHE SURVIVED THE ORDEAL, ORORO'S PARENTS DIED WHEN A PLANE CRASHED INTO THEIR HOME. BEING BURIED UNDER RUBBLE PROVED A TRAUMATIC EXPERIENCE THAT WOULD LEAVE HER WITH SEVERE CLAUSTROPHOBIA. ORPHANED, SHE BECAME A STREET THIEF IN ORDER TO GET BY. SHE WAS LATER RECRUITED BY CHARLES XAVIER, AND DECIDED TO PUT HER POWERS TO USE FOR GOOD AS A MEMBER OF THE X-MEN.

FIRST APPEARANCE

GIANT-SIZED X-MEN #1 (1975)

POWER GRID

2	INTELLIGENCE
2	STRENGTH
3	SPEED
2	STAMINA
5	ENERGY PROJECTION
4	FIGHTING ABILITY

*This is biographical, and does not represent an evaluation of the

ALTERNATE COSTUMES

ATTACK SET

STANDING BASIC ATTACKS

Screen	Command	Hits	Damage	Startup	Active	Recovery	Advantage on Hit	Advantage if Guarded	Notes
1	Standing L	1	33,000	5	3	9	+3	+2	—
2	Standing M	1	55,000	9	11	10	-2	-4	Normal jump cancelable
3	Standing H	1	70,000	15	12	5	+7	+5	—
4	S	1	80,000	13	12	11	—	-1	Launcher, not special or hyper combo cancelable

1

2

3

4

CROUCHING BASIC ATTACKS

Screen	Command	Hits	Damage	Startup	Active	Recovery	Advantage on Hit	Advantage if Guarded	Notes
1	Crouching L	1	30,000	5	3	8	+3	+2	Low attack
2	Crouching M	1	53,000	9	10	12	-3	-5	—
3	Crouching H	1	67,000	13	11	14	—	-3	Low attack, knocks down opponent, normal jump cancelable

1

2

3

AERIAL BASIC ATTACKS

Screen	Command	Hits	Damage	Startup	Active	Recovery	Notes
1	Air L	1	35,000	4	3	18	Overhead attack
2	Air M	1	53,000	11	6	19	Overhead attack
3	Air H	1	68,000	12	7	19	Overhead attack
4	Air S	1	75,000	13	15	11	Overhead attack

1

2

3

4

AS A PARTNER—CROSSOVER ASSISTS

Screen	Type	P1+P2 Crossover Combination Hyper Combo	Description	Hits	Damage	Startup	Active	Recovery (this crossover assist)	Recovery (other partner)	Notes
1	α – Alpha	Hail Storm	Whirlwind M	5	102,300	44	—	130	100	Whirlwind active for 30 frames, 5 projectiles with 3 low priority durability points each
2	β – Beta	Hail Storm	Double Typhoon M	6	140,300	87	—	108	78	Typhoon active for 30 frames, beam durability: 6 frames x 5 low priority durability points
3	γ – Gamma	Lightning Storm	Lightning Attack ↗	1	60,000	37	13	122	92	—

1

2

3

SPECIAL MOVES

Screen	Name	Command	Hits	Damage	Startup	Active	Recovery	Advantage on Hit	Advantage if Guarded	Notes
1	Whirlwind L	↓↘→ + L (in air ok)	3	67,000	15	—	30 (air: 35)	-4 (air: -9)	-6 (air: -11)	Whirlwind active for 22 frames, 3 projectiles with 3 low priority durability points each
2	Whirlwind M	↓↘→ + M (in air ok)	5	102,300	20	—	37	-11	-13	Whirlwind active for 30 frames, 5 projectiles with 3 low priority durability points each
3	Whirlwind H	↓↘→ + H (in air ok)	7	130,200	25	—	40	-14	-16	Whirlwind active for 38 frames, 7 projectiles with 3 low priority durability points each
4, 5, 6	Double Typhoon	↓↙← + ATK (in air ok)	6	140,300	63	—	15	+42	+31	Whirlwind active for 30 frames, knocks down, air versions do not recover until Storm lands, beam durability: 6 frames x 5 low priority durability points
7	Lightning Attack 1~3x	S + ATK up to 3 times (can be directed, in air OK)	1~3	80,000 ~ 216,700	13	13	26	—	-16	Can be repeated three times in a row, subsequent Lightning Attacks have 15 frames startup, knocks down
8, 9, 10	Lightning Sphere	(in air) →↓↘ + ATK	5	110,100	20	—	41	0	-3	—
11	Flight	↓↙← + S	—	—	22	—	—	—	—	Flight lasts for 99 frames

1

Whirlwind L

2

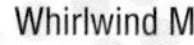
Whirlwind M

3

Whirlwind H

Whirlwind: Whirlwind acts a little differently than any other projectile. It crosses the screen like a beam, but it is actually a group of static projectiles firing down a line in a timed sequence, one after the other. This means that Whirlwind interrupts essentially anything along its path, once released; projectiles that destroy early stages of Whirlwind have no effect on later stages. Whirlwind will even pierce M.O.D.O.K.'s Barrier! Like a beam, though, the entire attack disappears if Storm takes a hit.

The L version creates three tornados that reach to mid range. The M version creates five tornados that read almost to full screen. The H version creates seven tornados that stretch across the entire playing field. The lighter the version, the shorter the startup and recovery period.

Relative to some primary projectiles, Whirlwind requires a big time investment, but it has great payoffs for successful use. Each individual tornado within Whirlwind pushes the opponent back whether on hit or guard, and in turn the next tornado pushes them farther down the line—Whirlwind H pushes the opponent all the way across the screen!

Whirlwind's odd nature makes it extremely powerful in zoning wars—Storm can keep up with Doctor Doom backed with Iron Man—α (or vice versa) all by herself. Her Whirlwind H will cut through both of their beams and strike the two of them. However, due to the odd, timed nature of Whirlwind, occasional beam or projectile hits may squeeze through and hit Storm as well. Opponents looking to out-shoot Storm in a projectile war must either hit her with quick projectiles before she even releases Whirlwind, or simply give up and look for ways around Whirlwind. But there is no beating Whirlwind head-on once Storm has unleashed it.

Whirlwind can be used in combos, most notably to use Whirlwind H to combo into Hail Storm from a ground chain at mid screen. Unless you want to push the opponent all the way across the screen, there are better things to do in ground combos, though. And for zoning wars, Whirlwind L and M don't provide sufficient deterring power. For both combos and zoning, stick to Whirlwind H.

Double Typhoon: Double Typhoon takes over a second to summon, but once released creates a huge vertical cyclone that extends to just under super jump height. Double Typhoon is OTG-capable, though lengthy startup prevents this from having much use outside of air throw follow ups or specialized assist combos. Double Typhoon also boasts tremendous low priority projectile durability. Its behavior is similar to Dormammu's Purification pillars. Double Typhoon is really just an extremely sturdy vertical beam—though it does not extend to the ceiling as Purification does. Double Typhoon won't hit opponents at high altitude.

Double Typhoon L

Double Typhoon M

Double Typhoon H

Used while jumping, Double Typhoon causes Storm to fall like a stone after release. You have two choices to avoid this. Either activate Flight before performing air Double Typhoon, or cancel the very end of the recovery of air Double Typhoon into Lightning Attack. You have to cancel right away—if you actually wait for Storm to start falling after Double Typhoon, it's too late for her Lightning Attack to break her fall. This is similar to Spencer canceling the recovery of Air Wire Grapple into Swing Wire, if he wants to avoid falling like a brick. Of course, note that if you don't precede Double Typhoon by activating Flight, she'll still drop like a rock after the Lighting Attacks too, so either use the Lighting Attacks to link Lighting Storm after a successful Double Typhoon hit, or to return to the ground.

You can stall decently by super jumping, activating Flight, then tossing Double Typhoon L. The enemy may possibly run into the vortex as they try to chase you. If the enemy runs into Double Typhoon, you can usually follow-up with Lightning Attack x1, hyper combo canceled into Lightning Storm. Excellent damage for baiting the opponent into running into a giant vertical projectile!

Lightning Attack: A combination movement technique and direct body attack employed by Storm. Lightning Attack can be aimed in any direction, and can be canceled into itself twice. Subsequent Lightning Attacks do not have to be aimed in the same direction as the first. After a Lighting Attack that leaves Storm airborne, she falls to the ground unable to act or block, just like after Double Typhoon—again, unless you activate Flight first.

The primary purpose of Lightning Attack is to add heavy damage to combos. Simply performing Lightning Attack x3, hyper combo canceled into Lightning Storm, deals 464,300 damage! Performing Lightning Attack x3 requires solid precision, but it's worth learning. The three Lightning Attack hits add serious damage to any combo they're in, and the damage boost over just using one or two Lightning Attacks isn't paltry. It's worth learning to combo all three consistently.

Lightning Attack is not safe if guarded, so don't use it as a poke on its own unless you call a crossover assist first to provide cover, or you plan on canceling to a Lightning Attack that is directed back away from the enemy.

Lightning Sphere: Lightning Sphere is a projectile Storm can only throw while airborne. It can be directed up-forward, straight forward, or down-forward. Once Lightning Sphere actually hits an opponent, whether on hit or guard, it expands into a larger ball for a second while dealing damage. This projectile deals decent damage, but doesn't have noteworthy projectile durability. Its biggest bonus is the slow speed of the projectile, which allows you to use Lightning Sphere to cover certain angles. For example, you can super jump backward, activate Flight, perform Double Typhoon L or M, then follow up with Lightning Sphere L. This pattern makes it very hard for the enemy to get at you for a few seconds, unless they're right on top of you from the start.

Lightning Sphere L

Lightning Sphere M

Lightning Sphere H

Flight: Since Storm falls without being able to block or act after performing air Double Typhoon or air Lightning Attack, Flight is crucial for her to use these moves in the air freely, without handing a free opportunity over to a watchful foe. If Storm performs these moves while flying, she won't be so helpless when falling to the ground afterward, and can guard or attack as normal.

Storm's Flight has a relatively long startup time compared to some Flight modes, so apart from increasing her mobility and making her aerial zoning offense safer, it's not as important for specialized use, such as combo extension.

HYPER COMBOS

Screen	Name	Command	Hits	Damage	Startup	Active	Recovery	Advantage on Hit	Advantage if Guarded	Notes
1	Hail Storm	↓↙← + ATK ATK	35	282,900	40+1	81	1	—	+7	Knocks down, OTG-capable
2	Lightning Storm	↓↘→ + ATK ATK	15	289,000	18+1	51	53	—	-42	Knocks down
3	Elemental Rage	→↓↘ + ATK ATK	15	266,900	8+3	30	32	—	-29	Knocks down, OTG-capable, causes wall bounce

Hail Storm: Hail Storm is one of the more versatile hyper combos in the game. While it has a slow startup before the hyper combo cutscene compared to most hyper combos, it has ample advantages to make up for this. For one, it's more or less instant after the cutscene. It also hits the entire screen, and is OTG-capable—the easiest way to tack on solid damage after a flying screen air combo is to simply perform Hail Storm upon landing! Hail Storm is also safe if guarded, making it a great hyper combo to occasionally throw out seemingly at random, whether to chip the enemy or potentially deal heavy damage to their errant assist calls. Finally, since the pre-cutscene hyper combo startup is circumvented in team hyper combos, Hail Storm is one of the best hyper combos in the game to team hyper combo into from another character—if not THE best. For its full-screen hit area, damage, and safety, it's also excellent in crossover combinations, whether guarded or on hit.

Lightning Storm: Lightning Storm is Storm's standard combo-ending hyper combo. Anytime you combo into Lightning Attack (preferably three of them), you can hyper combo cancel into Lightning Storm for extra damage. Lightning Storm is extremely unsafe if guarded, so save it for combos exclusively.

Elemental Rage: Like Hail Storm, Elemental Rage is OTG-capable. Unlike Hail Storm, Elemental Rage is much faster to start. Elemental Rage is actually fast enough to OTG with after using Storm's normal ground throws! Ultimately, that's the purpose of Elemental Rage—to score an OTG hit in situations where Hail Storm is too slow. Elemental Rage causes a wall bounce, which isn't useful for Storm herself—she's still recovering from the hyper combo—but this does make normal throw into Elemental Rage an excellent team hyper combo starter for many horizontal hyper combos.

BATTLE PLAN

OVERVIEW

VITALITY: 850,000

CHAIN COMBO ARCHETYPE: HUNTER SERIES

X-Factor	Lv.1	Lv.2	Lv.3
Damage	125%	%150	175%
Speed	115%	130%	145%

Storm is a versatile character, who can be played any way you like. That said, she has great strengths at both rushdown, and keepaway, and one of her advantages is how easy it is for her to transition between them.

Why is Storm a good aggressive character?

Her array of basic attacks allows for varied high and low mix-ups that the opponent won't be able to guard against consistently.

Her jump cancelable basic attacks and generally safe moveset allow her to attack freely and keep up momentum when pushed away with proper guarding and advancing guard.

She has some of the best mobility in the cast. She has a lightning quick dash, an even quicker wavedash, a fast 8-way airdash that allows for box jumps and triangle jumps, Flight, and a float maneuver that allows for extra mid-air positioning, and extremely fast overheads.

While her combos don't inflict quite the damage of some characters, they still do more than enough. 500,000 or more damage is still more than half life on most characters.

Why is Storm also a good keepaway character?

Her Whirlwind projectile finds a way to overpower most other projectiles, one way or another, and pushes characters it hits very far away, whether on hit or guard.

Her mobility advantage also applies to the sky far away, where she can fly and rain down Double Typhoons and Lightning Spheres.

Safety and momentum are never farther than a "random" Hail Storm away.

Finally, Storm makes both a great teammate, and an ideal character for holding a lead. This is because you can use another character to build hyper combo gauge and get a clean hit on the opponent, then cancel to their hyper combo and THC to Hail Storm. This works with virtually every hyper combo in the game: Hail Storm hits the whole screen on the first frame after the hyper combo cutscene. Your THC to Hail Storm deals massive damage, hopefully knocking out a character (or two, if you caught an assist also!). This provides tons of momentum for Storm to simply play it safe for a while, letting the enemy throw themselves carelessly into Hail Storms and pokes as they try to regain their footing.

STORM

ON THE GROUND

If you wanted to stay back as a general mandate, Storm can perform as well as any hero. Whirlwind H gives her a constant, reliable option against all but the fastest projectiles, the edges of her basic attacks do not have vulnerable hitboxes, and she has the speed and air mobility to stay away. While sizing up the enemy, you may just hang back and see how they act, while peppering them with Whirlwind H when possible. Cover yourself with assists preemptively to insure an airdash or teleport character doesn't get the jump on you. You might occasionally deploy Double Typhoon over wherever you expect your opponent to be, but you really need to cover yourself with an assist first (or be fighting a very passive foe) in order to actually release a ground Double Typhoon without getting punished for it. Double Typhoon is one of the slowest-starting moves in the game.

Storm's basic attacks generate small whirlwinds with hitboxes past her vulnerable limbs. Strike with the tips of these attacks for essentially invulnerable pokes!

Opponents who guard crouching Ⓗ but don't use advancing guard have a terrible time guarding instant float follow ups consistently.

Anytime you successfully release Whirlwind H (or Double Typhoon), you have an opportunity to hyper combo cancel into Hail Storm, hitting the entire screen. While Hail Storm has lengthy startup, Whirlwind H (and perhaps whichever assist you called, or Double Typhoon if you did manage to position it over the enemy) will protect from most frontal threats. Once the Hail Storm cutscene ends, Hail Storm strikes the entire screen immediately, and combos for heavy damage against point characters and assists who ate the preceding Whirlwind, assist, or Typhoon! Even if your challenger guards, they'll incur a fair bit of chip damage.

Zoning them for a bit may frustrate the opponent and cause them to employ increasingly desperate things to get at Storm. You'll be building hyper combo gauge bars all the while, too (assuming you are at least forcing the enemy to block some assists and Whirlwinds). Hail Storm alone means that Storm likes to use meter, and some players will certainly find themselves spending hyper combo gauge bars with Storm as soon as she earns them. Aside from keeping the opponent away with Whirlwind H and Hail Storm, she has effective tactics zoning from the air, as well, covered in Up in the Air.

You don't have to think of Whirlwind H as solely a vehicle for Hail Storm, though. This projectile is great on its own. It deals excellent damage, while pushing the opponent extremely far away. Note however that Whirlwind is one of the few moves (like Captain America's Shield Toss) that is actually *worse* against a cornered enemy. Most of the tornadoes are simply generated offscreen past the corner, behind the enemy's back! Against a cornered foe it's time to abandon zoning and rush them down anyway, though.

Whenever you feel the time is right, transition from running to rushing. Storm has great options attacking low, high, or with throws. If poking at grounded opponents at mid range, use standing Ⓜ. Standing Ⓜ is Storm's longest-range basic attack, and has 8 active frames on the hitting whirlwind area that are not a part of Storm herself. Closer up, use crouching Ⓛ. With 5 frames of startup, her crouching Ⓛ is one of the fastest low attacks in the game. At point blank range you can mix in the threat of throws, and a normal throw in either direction can lead to an Elemental Rage hyper combo OTG hit. As a mix-up against these, she can attack with amazingly fast overheads from the air, in a variety of ways.

When on the defensive, grounded Ⓢ launcher should work for all anti-air needs that don't come down directly on top of Storm. The hitbox hits the same exact width and range as crouching Ⓗ, but reaches much, much higher—almost to the top of the screen! Of course, from a successful anti-air Ⓢ, you get a launcher combo. Instant float ⇨ + Ⓗ also makes an excellent anti-air option select, even against threats directly above Storm. Air ⇨ + Ⓗ just off the ground may either air throw an incoming foe, break *their* air throw, or produce air Ⓗ, which is an excellent air-to-air jousting attack.

In advantaged situations, like against rising opponents or during chains the opponent is blocking, but hasn't pushed away with advancing guard, standing Ⓗ and crouching Ⓗ both have use. On hit, standing Ⓗ grants enough advantage to combo light attacks; on counterhit, medium attacks will work. Of course, you can also just chain to crouching Ⓗ, as Storm's chain combo archetype is hunter. Her reach is just so narrow that it's hard to do *Darkstalkers*-style chains consistently. Perform standing Ⓗ with ⇨ + Ⓗ, so you also give yourself the option of scoring a throw (or accidentally breaking one) instead. Unfortunately though, standing Ⓗ whiffs cleanly over many crouching characters. Instead, you may choose to use meaty crouching Ⓗ when you have frame advantage, like against an opponent rising from ground recovery. This attack has tons of active frames, hits low, and can lead into either Ⓢ launcher, or any normal jump or instant float follow ups you might prefer. Mix up between instant float overheads and crouching Ⓗ into instant float overheads against defensive opponents. If they're extremely passive, simply normal throw them and OTG immediately with Elemental Rage, or call a crossover assist like Amaterasu—β just before going for the throw.

UP IN THE AIR

Storm has a lot of latitude in the sky. She can activate Flight first in order to safely shell the ground with Double Typhoon. She can vary this aerial attack by mixing in Lightning Sphere L to stop enemies who try to rise quickly past anticipated Double Typhoons. Depending on positioning, you can usually follow up connected air Double Typhoons with Lightning Attack x1, hyper combo canceled into Lightning Storm. Doing more than one Lightning Attack is inconsistent because you have to cancel into Lightning Storm during the frames in which Storm is still considered flying; if Flight has technically expired, the amount of special moves she's done becomes relevant again, (it's irrelevant during Flight) and the hyper combo won't activate.

With Flight, Double Typhoon, and Lightning Sphere, Storm can stall from mid air with the best of them.

Any mid air hit, whether from an air chain or a Double Typhoon, can usually lead into Lightning Attack, hyper combo canceled into Lightning Storm.

Whirlwind is also decent in mid air, but best close to the ground—only do it at great height if you're certain the enemy will be parallel to you. Also, air Whirlwind doesn't cause Storm to fall straight down, so use it before Flight, not after, if you're planning to fly during that jump.

Whether going air-to-air or air-to-ground, air ⇨ + (H) tends to be your best bet. It's the ultimate mix of the speeds and hitboxes of air (M) and air (S) and, by performing it as ⇨ + (H), you add the potential of an air throw. Storm gets a nice hyper combo setup after air throws at any height; see Combo Usage for details. Air-to-air (M) is good when coming up under targets, while air (S) is great for aiming down-away, especially against ground targets. Its reach is surprising!

There are several ways to approach the enemy from the air. From far away, you can use Storm's airdash to box jump in behind the cover of an assist, falling with air (S) or air ⇨ + (H). These moves have terrific reach and hitboxes that extends far from Storm's vulnerable hands. From mid range, triangle jumping with air (L) works well. And up close, of course, instant float overheads are usually the way to go, preferably mixed up with or without crouching (H) right before them.

COMBO USAGE

I. CR. (L), ST. (M), CR. (H), (S) CANCEL⇨ SUPER JUMP, AIR (H) CANCEL⇨ AIRDASH FORWARD, AIR (H) CANCEL⇨ ↗ + (S) + (ATK) X3 CANCEL⇨ ↓↘⇨ + (ATK)(ATK)

(548,300 damage) Storm has quite a bit of variation on what she can do with her "bread and butter" combo. This is merely the simplest and most consistent version. Crouching (L) is a natural opener because it must be guarded crouching. Crouching (M) isn't actually a low attack, and standing (M) is normal jump cancelable, so standing (M) is the best place to go from crouching (L). Following up with crouching (H) is natural—it must be guarded crouching, it's *also* normal jump cancelable, and it chains to (S) for a launcher. Standing (H) in the same chain often pushes the opponent too far away for (S) to connect.

If the opponent successfully guards crouching (L), and then uses advancing guard to push you away during standing (M) or crouching (H), then these normal jump cancelable basic attacks come in very handy. You can jump cancel standing (M) or crouching (H) and airdash right back in with another attack, negating the space the enemy created with advancing guard.

As an easy alternative, you can just chain to air (S) for flying screen, then land and perform Hail Storm to OTG.

Using either normal jump cancels, and/or instant float can make this combo considerably more complicated. Crouching (H) is a sweep that knocks the enemy down, and is jump cancelable. After a successful sweep you can hold up-forward for the jump cancel, then immediately hit air (M), (M), (S), land, and ground chain into launcher. The damage increase over the standard combo isn't huge, but you will build more hyper combo gauge. Alternatively, after crouching (H), tap up for the jump cancel, *immediately* tap up again for instant float, then hit air (S) before landing again. It's possible to perform a few loops of crouching (H) CANCEL⇨ instant float air (S), land, standing (M), crouching (H) CANCEL⇨ instant float air (S), land, and so on using this technique! Mid screen Storm will usually be pushed too far to use instant float more than once in a combo, but on a cornered foe you can be much more creative.

II. INSTANT FLOAT AIR → + (H), DASH, CR. (L), ST. (M), CR. (H) CANCEL⇨ JUMP FORWARD, AIR (M), (M), (S), LAND, ST. (H), CR. (H), (S) CANCEL⇨ SUPER JUMP, AIR (M), (M), (H) CANCEL⇨ ↗ + (S) + (ATK) X2 CANCEL⇨ ↓↘→ + (ATK)(ATK)

(502,600 damage, requires 1 bar of hyper combo gauge) This is an example of a more complicated storm combo. The damage can actually be less, but the meter gained during basic attacks is much higher. You want to do two Lightning Attacks in the air combo here instead of three because of hitstun deterioration.

III. NORMAL JUMP HEIGHT AIR THROW, LAND, ↓↙← + (L), DASH, JUMP FORWARD AIR (H) CANCEL⇨ ↗ + (S) + (ATK) X3 CANCEL⇨ ↓↘→ + (ATK)(ATK)

(307,400 damage, requires 1 bar of hyper combo gauge) Storm's normal jump height throw air combo. You can wait until landing to perform Double Whirlwind L. The dash before jumping air (H) isn't always necessary, but it doesn't hurt.

IV. SUPER JUMP HEIGHT AIR THROW, ↓↙← + (L) OTG, ↘ + (S) + (ATK) X2 CANCEL⇨ ↓↘→ + (ATK)(ATK)

(299,700 damage, requires 1 hyper combo gauge bar) Storm's air combo from a super jump height air throw. You must cancel the very end of Double Typhoon L recovery into down-forward Lightning Attack; if you wait too long, Double Typhoon L's recovery simply causes Storm to fall to the ground, unable to act.

V. FRONT OR BACK THROW, →↓↘ + (ATK)(ATK)

(307,300 damage, requires 1 bar of hyper combo gauge) Storm's combo off a normal ground throw requires the use of Elemental Rage. Because Elemental Rage ends in a wall bounce, this is an excellent starter for team hyper combos.

ASSISTS

Storm's best assist is Storm—α, Whirlwind M. It doesn't quite reach full screen, but it almost does, and it shares the same advantage of point Whirlwind: decent damage, great at overpowering other projectiles, pushes the enemy very far away. Storm—β, Double Typhoon M, could also see some use on specialized zoning teams, or for combos that require a delayed OTG assist. Storm—γ is lacking compared to these options. It doesn't have much utility as an assist, and it as a crossover counter the Lightning Attack cannot be directed or canceled into itself (though it can be canceled into Lightning Storm).

Storm on point can work well with a wide variety of assists. Projectile or beam assists only enhance her ranged advantage, and allow her to use Double Typhoon a little more freely. Ideal partners for this purpose include Amaterasu—β, Iron Man—α, and Sentinel—α.

For the most part, except against extremely fast projectiles, Storm can handle the lateral angle on her own with Whirlwind. A vertical assist like Dormammu—β or Dante—α helps her bisect the screen.

Assists that take up a lot of space or create artificial barriers enhance Storm's attack against rising opponents.

These same kind of partners, including M.O.D.O.K.—α, an irregular barrier that basically creates an artificial corner, are also great for Storm when you create an unrecoverable knockdown, or an aerial recovery. Storm can dash with ease under or over floored or flipping foes, crossing back and forth with rapid dashes several times before dropping an assist on one side, then dashing one final time to the other side. With a properly timed rhythm of dashes, you can simply use the ATK ATK command dash and not worry about direction; Storm always dashes toward the enemy, even just after they begin to rise or roll past her. Once you have an assist going on one side and you're safe on the other, make them choose between guarding a quick overhead, or meaty crouching Ⓗ into its possible follow up options.

ADVANCED TACTICS

INSTANT FLOAT

Tap up just after jumping to float immediately...

...then attack for a lightning quick overhead!

By holding any upward direction while jumping, you'll cause Storm to float, drifting back to the ground more slowly. This has the obvious use of fine positioning in mid air, but the less obvious use of leading to extremely fast high attacks! You see, float can be inputted on the very first frame Storm is airborne—as early as the 4th frame after inputting the upward direction for the jump! So if you jump, then tap up very briefly after at least 4 frames have elapsed and Storm is actually airborne, her upward momentum will be cut off and she'll float right off the ground. Air attacks used from this position are *extremely* fast overheads.

Work on precision for this technique. You want to tap up cleanly and quickly after just one upward tap to initially register the jump. With imprecise inputs, you may end up jumping then immediately airdashing upward, or sideways.

Once you're comfortable getting air attacks just off the ground using instant float, you can begin incorporating this trick into your mix-ups and combos. Standing Ⓜ and crouching Ⓗ are both normal jump cancelable, which means they can both combo into instant float attacks! This is especially useful from crouching Ⓗ, which is a low attack.

FLOATING STANCE QUIRKS

Storm doesn't actually stand flush with the ground while standing, as almost everyone else does (except Magneto). This means, among other things, that it's less obvious to the opposition when she jumps since no dust cloud is produced! Storm's slim personal profile and floating stance also make some throw situations more difficult. Storm actually *can't* throw crouching Sentinel unless she pushes deep into Sentinel's animation with an empty triangle jump first. Just walking forward, she literally can't throw Sentinel.

Storm's floating properties also extend to the invisible hitboxes that determine when she'll "push" against other characters. For Storm, these boxes don't actually touch the floor, so she can pass cleanly over many characters who are on their feet! This is distinct from the ability many characters have (including Storm) to dash over characters while they're knocked down.

Storm can simply pass through some opponents, depending on who it is and whether they're standing or crouching. For others, she has to knock them into hitstun first before dashing through.

By passing totally through an opponent, you can go for cross-ups or drop an assist before switching sides, without needing to jump! In practice you can use this very much like a situational teleport.

With many characters, usually the small ones, Storm can simply dash through their bodies! With other characters, Storm can only dash through immediately after hitting the enemy with a particular airborne attack. The enemy's reeling posture during hitstun is lowered enough to allow Storm to dash through them.

In high-level *MvC2*, it was often a better idea for strong rushdown characters like Storm to intentionally pass up hyper combo opportunities or full combos, in favor of smaller combos and resets broken up together. This worked because Storm was able to mix-up so quickly after intentionally dropping combos early in certain positions. It's far too early for us to make a judgment of the ultimate usefulness of being able to pass through characters in these situations, but if fighting game history is our guide, the ability to reset hits and create cross-ups in awkward ways is never a bad thing to have in your wheelhouse.

Storm can "walk" through:
Viewtiful Joe (crouching)

Storm can dash through:
Arthur (crouching, point blank, use dash Ⓛ or Ⓜ)
Felicia (crouching, use dashing Ⓛ or Ⓜ)
Hsien-Ko (standing)
Morrigan (crouching)
Spider-Man (crouching)
Viewtiful Joe (standing, use dash Ⓜ)
Viewtiful Joe (crouching)
X-23 (crouching)

Storm can dash through after air Ⓜ/Ⓗ/Ⓢ:
Akuma (crouching)
Arthur (crouching)
Chun-Li (crouching)
Deadpool (crouching)
Wesker (crouching)
Zero (crouching)

Storm can dash through after air Ⓗ/Ⓢ:
Arthur (standing)
Captain America (crouching)
Chris (crouching)
Iron Man (crouching)
Taskmaster (crouching)
Thor (crouching)
Tron (crouching)

COMBO APPENDIX

GENERAL EXECUTION TIPS

Storm has a very slim profile, but also pushes opponents back far on hits. Dash whenever possible during ground combos to maintain proximity and assure consistency.

Perform inputs for consecutive Lightning Attacks deliberately and precisely. There must be slight pauses between each Lightning Attack input.

Requirements (Position, meter, etc.)	Notes	Command Sequence	Damage
—	—	Instant float air H, land, dash, cr. L, st. M, cr. H CANCEL normal jump forward, air M, M, S, land, st. H, cr. H, S CANCEL super jump, air M, M, H CANCEL airdash up-forward, air S	335,000
Mid screen only, requires 1 bar of hyper combo gauge	Don't hyper combo cancel into Hail Storm until Storm releases Whirlwind H	Cr. L, st. M, cr. H CANCEL ↓↘→ + H CANCEL ↓↙← + ATK ATK	430,900
Corner only	—	Air S, land, st. M, cr. H CANCEL jump, instant float air S, land, st. M, cr. H CANCEL jump, instant float air S, land, st. M, st. H CANCEL S + ATK CANCEL ↗ + S + ATK x2 CANCEL ↓↘→ + ATK ATK	577,300
Requires 1 bar of hyper combo gauge	Basic combo, but starting with an air S overhead	Air S, land, cr. L, st. M, cr. H, S CANCEL super jump, air H CANCEL airdash forward, air H CANCEL ↗ + S + ATK x3 CANCEL ↓↘→ + ATK ATK	565,600
Requires 1 bar of hyper combo gauge	—	Instant float air → + H, land, st. M, cr. H CANCEL instant float air S, land, st. M S CANCEL super jump, air M, M, H CANCEL airdash forward, air H CANCEL direction + S + ATK x3 CANCEL ↓↘→ + ATK ATK	575,500
Requires 1 bar of hyper combo gauge, Spencer—γ, mid screen only	—	Cr. L + P1 or P2 Spencer, st. M, cr. H CANCEL ↓↙← + H CANCEL ↓↙← + ATK ATK	527,600
Requires 1 bar of hyper combo gauge, X-Factor level 1	—	Cr. L, st. M, cr. H X-FACTOR st. M, st. H, S CANCEL super jump, air M, M, H CANCEL airdash forward, air H CANCEL ↗ + S + ATK x3 CANCEL ↓↘→ + ATK ATK	815, 900
Requires 1 bar of hyper combo gauge	Juggle the first standing M as low as you can to keep the opponent lower to the ground, allowing you to juggle after the second Lightning Attack	Cr. L, st. M, cr. H CANCEL normal jump forward, ↘ + S ATK, land, st. M, cr. H CANCEL normal jump forward, ↘ + S + ATK, land, st. M, S CANCEL super jump, air H CANCEL airdash forward, air H CANCEL ↗ + S + ATK x3 CANCEL ↓↘→ + ATK ATK	579,300

"AS LONG AS NATURE IS MY ALLY, I WILL NEVER LOSE."

SUPER-SKRULL

"THERE'S FAR TOO MUCH TRASH IN THE UNIVERSE."

BIO

REAL NAME

KL'RT

OCCUPATION

SOLDIER OF THE SKRULL EMPIRE

ABILITIES

TOGETHER WITH THE SKRULL ABILITY OF SHAPESHIFTING, KL'RT IS ALSO CAPABLE OF HYPNOTISM. HE HAS ALL THE POWERS OF THE FANTASTIC FOUR, AND CAN UTILIZE THEM AT THE SAME TIME.

WEAPONS

NONE

PROFILE

A GENETICALLY-ENGINEERED SUPER SOLDIER CREATED BY THE SKRULLS TO DEFEAT THE FANTASTIC FOUR, WHO STOPPED THEIR INVASION OF EARTH. HIS PRIDE AND TENDENCY TO LOOK DOWN ON OTHERS IS NOT UNIQUE TO HIM, BUT A CHARACTERISTIC OF THE SKRULL RACE IN GENERAL.

FIRST APPEARANCE

FANTASTIC FOUR #18 (1963)

POWER GRID

2	INTELLIGENCE
6	STRENGTH
5	SPEED
6	STAMINA
6	ENERGY PROJECTION
4	FIGHTING ABILITY

*This is biographical, and does not represent an evaluation of the character's in-game combat potential.

ALTERNATE COSTUMES

PS3: ⓧ Xbox 360: Ⓐ

PS3: □ Xbox 360: Ⓧ

PS3: △ Xbox 360: Ⓨ

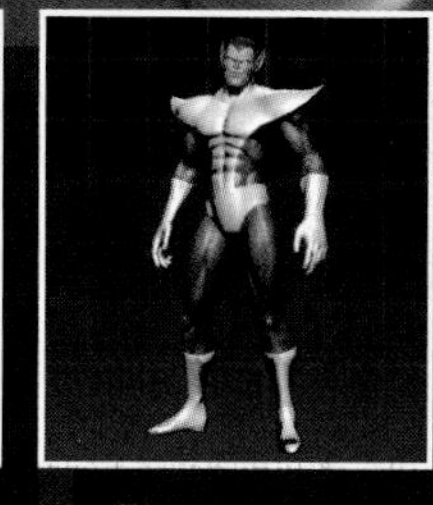

PS3: R1 Xbox 360: RB

ATTACK SET

STANDING BASIC ATTACKS

Screen	Command	Hits	Damage	Startup	Active	Recovery	Advantage on Hit	Advantage if Guarded	Notes
1	Standing L	1	50,000	6	3	11	0	-1	Low attack
2	Standing M	2	72,000	9	4	21	-4	-5	—
3	Standing H	1	90,000	13	4	17	-	+2	Ground bounces opponent, ⇩⇙⇨+ P1orP2 snap back
4	S	1	100,000	11	4	24	-	-5	Launcher, not special- or hyper combo-cancelable

CROUCHING BASIC ATTACKS

Screen	Command	Hits	Damage	Startup	Active	Recovery	Advantage on Hit	Advantage if Guarded	Notes
1	Crouching L	1	45,000	6	3	12	-1	-2	—
2	Crouching M	1	75,000	8	3	18	+8	-3	Slightly launches opponent
3	Crouching H	1	80,000	11	4	24	-	-5	Low attack, knocks down opponent
4	⇙ + H	1	90,000	15	4	22	-2	-3	—

AERIAL BASIC ATTACKS

Screen	Command	Hits	Damage	Startup	Active	Recovery	Notes
1	Air L	1	55,000	6	3	15	Overhead attack
2	Air M	1	75,000	9	3	20	Overhead attack
3	Air H	1	85,000	11	7	19	Overhead attack
4	Air S	1	90,000	15	4	15	Overhead attack

SUPER-SKRULL

COMMAND ATTACKS

Screen	Command	Hits	Damage	Startup	Active	Recovery	Advantage on Hit	Advantage if Guarded	Notes
1	⇨ + Ⓗ	1	90,000	15	4	22	-2	-3	—
2	Standing Ⓗ (hold)	1	120,000	52	6	22	—	-5	OTG-capable, wall bounces opponent, jump-cancelable, not special- or hyper combo-cancelable, inflicts chip damage
3	⇨⇨⇨ + Ⓗ	1	130,000	26	3	24	—	-4	Unrecoverable knockdown, inflicts chip damage
4	⇩⇩ + Ⓗ	3	84,000	1	2	29	—	—	Only hits grounded opponents, not special- or hyper combo-cancelable, opponent remains grounded
5	Crouching Ⓗ (hold)	1	110,000	48	4	34	—	-15	Spinning knockdown, jump cancelable, not special- or hyper combo-cancelable, inflicts chip damage
6	Air ⇩ + Ⓗ	2	115,000	15	Until landing*6	16	—	-9	Overhead attack, OTG-capable, floor bounces, knocks down, not special- or hyper combo-cancelable, inflicts chip damage
7	Air Ⓢ (hold)	1	120,000	37	6	—	—	—	Overhead attack, ground bounces opponent, not special- or hyper combo-cancelable, inflicts chip damage

AS A PARTNER-CROSSOVER ASSISTS

Screen	Type	P1+P2 Crossover Combination Hyper Combo	Description	Hits	Damage	Startup	Active	Recovery (this partner)	Recovery (other partner)	Notes
1	α – Alpha	Inferno	Stone Smite	1	120,000	58	6	113	83	OTG-capable, wall bounces opponent
2	β – Beta	Inferno	Orbital Grudge M	6	158,600	39	19	114	84	Knocks down opponent
3	γ – Gamma	Skrull Torch	Tenderizer H	10	121,600	42	3(4)3(4)3(4)3(4)3 (4)3(5)3(4)3(4) 3(9)3	118	88	Knocks down opponent

SPECIAL MOVES

Screen	Name	Command	Hits	Damage	Startup	Active	Recovery	Advantage on Hit	Advantage if Guarded	Notes
1	Orbital Grudge L	⇩⇘⇨ + Ⓛ	4	94,800	10	11	30	—	-10	Knocks down opponent, 1 hit of super armor during frames 10-20
	Orbital Grudge M	⇩⇘⇨ + Ⓜ	6	140,300	15	19	22	—	-4	Knocks down opponent, 1 hit of auper armor during frames 15-28
	Orbital Grudge H	⇩⇘⇨ + Ⓗ	9	171,100	20	20	21	—	-8	Knocks down opponent, 1 hit of super armor during frames 20-34
2	Fatal Buster	(During Orbital Grudge) ⇩⇙⇦ + Ⓗ	1	70,000	15	4	37	—	-18	Wall bounces opponent, unrecoverable knockdown
3,4,5	Tenderizer (in air OK)	ATK	10	121,600	18	3 (4) 3 (4) 3 (4) 3 (4) 3 (4) 3 (5) 3 (4) 3 (4) 3 (9) 3	25	—	-5	Knocks down opponent, Ⓛ version is OTG-capable, final hit of Ⓛ version ground bounces
6,7,8	Elastic Slam	⇩⇙⇦ + ATK	5	180,000	21	1	44	—	—	Throw attack, unrecoverable knockdown
9	Meteor Smash	⇨⇩⇘ + ATK	2	125,000	22	26*4	32	—	-21	Frames 6-19 invincible, OTG-capable, hits overhead, knocks down opponent

Orbital Grudge: The primary use of Orbital Grudge is to extend combos after hitstun deterioration has reached a point where normal launcher combos become impossible. Combos involving X-Factor or crossover assists often necessitate the use of Orbital Grudge into Fatal Buster.

All of the versions of the Orbital Grudge moves have a single hit of super armor during their active frames, but the prohibitively long startup times for these attacks make it difficult to take advantage of this property. Orbital Grudge attacks can also be used to inflict the last big hit of chip damage that may be needed to K.O. a cornered opponent.

The Ⓜ version of Orbital Grudge is mostly safe when it is guarded, but you should be wary of opposing characters with fast command throws that can reach you after the attack completes.

Fatal Buster: Accessible only from the Orbital Grudge special move, Fatal Buster strikes a large portion of the screen and wall bounces an opponent. Unfortunately, the lengthy recovery from this attack doesn't leave you enough time to land a standard combo. The wall bounce leaves the opposing character in an unrecoverable knockdown state and it allows you to land a Meteor Smash OTG hit. Fatal Buster is very unsafe if it is guarded, which limits its use outside of combos.

Tenderizer L

Tenderizer M

Tenderizer H

Tenderizer: The Ⓛ version of Tenderizer is the fastest way to inflict OTG hits at medium range. This comes in handy most at the end of extended flying screen combos that don't leave you enough time to land a Meteor Smash. The final hit of Tenderizer L ground bounces an opponent, allowing you to combo this move into a Skrull Torch hyper combo. Typically, you'll want to use Meteor Smash in OTG combos instead because it results in much more damage.

Using Tenderizer outside of combos isn't recommended. Your challenger only needs to use advancing guard against the initial hits, and suddenly Super-Skrull becomes very vulnerable as he whiffs punches.

Elastic Slam: The Elastic Slam is the most important move in Super-Skrull's arsenal. The Ⓛ and Ⓜ versions of this attack function as command throws with insane range. The Ⓛ version has a range of about three character widths, while the Ⓜ version has a range of about five character widths. However, this move has a dead zone at close range. Any version of the Elastic Slam can lead to an easy combo—Meteor Smash into Inferno for 478,500 damage, essentially forcing your opponent to stay off the ground at all times.

The Ⓜ version of Elastic Slam can sometimes be used on reaction, if your opponent throws a mid-range projectile at Super-Skrull. While using this attack, Super-Skrull's extended arm does not have a vulnerable hitbox and it can cleanly grab your foe through the projectile.

Elastic Slam L

Elastic Slam M

Elastic Slam H

The Ⓗ version of the Elastic Slam not only functions as a simple mix-up to the other two versions, it's also a great way to reset opponents as they air recover.

All versions of the Elastic Slam have very lengthy recovery times if they don't connect with your challenger, so try not to get overzealous with your grab attempts.

Meteor Smash: The Meteor Smash allows Super-Skrull to land OTG hits from anywhere on the screen. Used in almost all of Super-Skrull's combos to lead into Inferno, the Meteor Smash is the main reason Super-Skrull's damage output is high.

Outside of combos, the delayed invulnerability of Meteor Smash can be used to escape the corner against characters who are too slow to punish it—like Haggar. This move can also be used occasionally as a risky countermeasure against zoning projectile attacks, as a surprise anti-air against super jumping opponents, as well as a surprise cross-up attack. However, you should use the Meteor Smash very sparingly outside of combos, since it is incredibly unsafe on block.

The button used to determine the final destination of the Meteor Smash is screen-relative; the Ⓛ version will always end up on the left side of the screen, Ⓜ in the middle, and Ⓗ on the right. This takes some getting used to when you are performing Super-Skull's combos on both sides, but it quickly becomes second nature.

HYPER COMBOS

Screen	Name	Command	Hits	Damage	Startup	Active	Recovery	Advantage on Hit	Advantage if Guarded	Notes
1	Skrull Torch	↓↘→ + ATK ATK (in air OK)	30	293,200	10+1	43	51	—	—	Frames 4-19 (4-11 in air) invincible, knocks down opponent, Super-Skrull can be directed up or down using the controller
2	Inferno	↓↙← + ATK ATK (in air OK)	50	284,100	10+2	57	14	+5	-22	Beam durability: 50 frames x3 durability points, all hits except for final hit cannot be advancing guarded
3	Death Penalty	→↓↘ + ATK ATK	13	450,000	20+6	8	45	—	-19	24 frames invincibility, OTG-capable, hits overhead, button combination determines location of attack

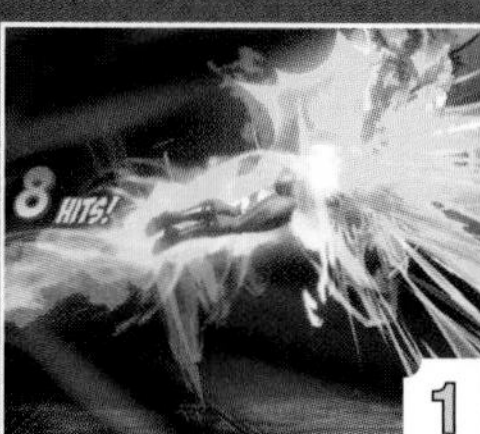

Skrull Torch: While this hyper combo may be viewed as a combo finisher after Tenderizer, its true strength lies in its versatility. Skrull Torch can be activated on the ground or in the air, it has a fast traveling speed, it can be aimed to reach nearly anywhere in front of Super-Skrull, and it has a lot of invincibility frames. This combination of attributes makes for a hyper combo you can use very often if you're looking for opportunities and you are willing to spend the hyper combo gauge.

More specifically, the Skrull Torch is the only defensive deterrent that Super-Skrull has when offensive characters get too close for comfort. Blow through the opposing character's offense with a Skrull Torch—just make sure you have two hyper combo gauge bars to use a team hyper combo if your opponent blocks!

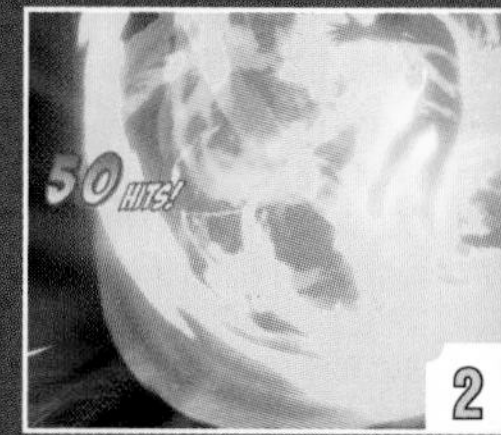

Inferno: This hyper combo has a huge area of effect, but it is also slow and it does not have invincibility. This makes Inferno difficult to use outside of combos, which is just as well; almost every single combo Super-Skrull has ends with an Inferno!

***Death Penalty*:** The Death Penalty is essentially a level 3 hyper combo version of the Meteor Smash—they're both used to land OTG hits from anywhere on the screen. Death Penalty is among the more damaging level 3 hyper combos, however, so ending extended combos with Death Penalty can often be a good idea if it will K.O. the opposing character.

Like the Meteor Smash, the buttons used to activate the Death Penalty determines where Super-Skrull performs the attack: Ⓛ + Ⓜ hits the left side of the screen, Ⓜ + Ⓗ hits the right, while Ⓛ + Ⓗ hits the middle.

BATTLE PLAN

OVERVIEW

VITALITY: 1,000,000

CHAIN COMBO ARCHETYPE: HUNTER SERIES

X-Factor	Lv.1	Lv.2	Lv.3
Damage	120%	150%	180%
Speed	110%	120%	130%

Your goal with Super-Skrull should be to get into position and threaten your opponent using Elastic Slam, with the secondary objective of cornering your opposition.

Super-Skrull's Elastic Slam is the cornerstone of his gameplan for several reasons:

- **It is an unblockable throw attack that can reach incredible ranges, and it creates a constant threat for opponents who want to keep the fight on the ground.**
- **It leads to about 50% damage on hit, with anywhere between 85% and 117% damage if X-Factor is used.**
- **The lack of vulnerable hitboxes on Super-Skrull's arm allows you to actually shut down a lot of your opponent's ground-based tactics.**

When you corner your opponent, their options for avoiding the Elastic Slam become extremely limited; normal moves from up close can be canceled directly into Elastic Slam—even if your challenger uses an advancing guard!

Here are the ways to get Super-Skrull into position to use an Elastic Slam attack. In order of effectiveness:

- **Advancing forward behind the cover of a crossover assist.**
- **Patiently wavedashing forward and blocking, mixed with jumping forward and blocking—this depends on your opponent's actions.**
- **Airdashing over the opposing character's head and coming down with air ↓ + Ⓗ.**
- **Advancing forward using → → → + Ⓗ.**

ON THE GROUND

Advancing behind the cover of an assist is the easiest way for Super-Skrull to close the distance.

⇘ + (H) has a very small hitbox; you must be very precise when using it.

Elastic Slam M is a terrifying move; use it to preemptively counter certain ground tactics!

Super-Skrull should be the main meter-user on your team. One of his primary strengths is the ability to tack on a Meteor Smash OTG onto almost anything, which then cancels into Inferno for major damage.

On offense, the points listed above in the overview are the main tools that Super-Skrull has to close distance. Super-Skrull doesn't have any great character-specific options for dealing with projectiles, so you must do things the old-fashioned way and push towards the opposing character with patience. Fortunately, he has one of the fastest wave-dashes in the game, and this helps to close distance much more quickly. Simply jumping forward and blocking is also a necessary tactic. You should attempt an airdash when it is safe to do so; however, you cannot block during the initial portion of an airdash. You should avoid getting impatient and super jumping at your opponent because smart players will simply wave-dash under this and negate all the forward progress you've made. Don't be afraid to block projectiles and take chip damage. As long as you don't get hit by any zoning moves and make slow, constant progress it should all pay off in the end.

Fortunately, Super-Skrull doesn't have to advance very far before he gets within range of Elastic Slam M. However, there are often situations where the opposing character may have a frame advantage at that range, preventing you from executing Elastic Slam M in time. If you're constantly being shut down at mid-range, try normal jumping and airdashing above your opponent, then call your crossover assist before dropping down with air ⇩ + (H). Depending on the assist, you should generally have enough time to wavedash back in close at an advantage, even after your opponent uses an advancing guard.

When Super-Skrull is in close with frame advantage, you should simply mix up Elastic Slam L with standing (L). Standing (L) hits low, essentially covering all of your opponent's options besides guarding and invincible moves—Elastic Slam grabs guarding opponents. If your crossover assist is still available, calling it during a chain combo usually allows you to continue your offense if your opponent chooses to use an advancing guard. If your opponent doesn't use an advancing guard, standing (H) gives a +2 frame advantage, allowing you to counter hit anything your foe does with standing (L) afterwards. If your opponent continues to block, cancel the standing (H) into Elastic Slam L!

Super-Skrull's anti-air options are a bit limited, especially against characters with airdashes. Against characters with more predictable jump arcs, ⇘ + (H) and even Elastic Slam H work great, provided that you can react to this movement quickly enough. Note that both of those moves only have attacking hitboxes near the tip of Skrull's arms. If the opposing character is too close, these moves will whiff completely.

A more reliable move is Super-Skrull's crouching (M). If it is used early enough and within range, it can be employed as an anti-air against most attacks, including those done from an airdash. If this attack hits, you can chain into standing (H) and continue into a full combo. If crouching (M) is beaten by your opponent's air attacks, you'll have to make do with the universal anti-air attacks—air throws and advancing guard.

When you must play defensively, Super-Skrull tends to struggle a little. As mentioned, using anti-air attacks effectively against an aerial assault presents a bit of a problem, making it fairly difficult to keep the opposing character out of range. Super-Skrull also has slower-than-average (L) moves, at 6 frames, and no moves that are instantly invincible except the Skrull Torch hyper combo. When faced with an offense that has few holes, try to use an advancing guard to work your way out of a bad situation while you look for opportunities to land an air throw against your opponent.

A number of new options open up to you once your opponent's character is cornered. Most prominently, close attacks that your opponent uses an advancing guard against still leave you in range to immediately cancel into an Elastic Slam M! This isn't guaranteed by any means, but is still very likely to connect. If your challenger begins holding up or up/forward after the advancing guard, you can be aggressive and counter this movement with a late-cancel into Elastic Slam H instead. If you decide to be a little safer, doing a ⇘ + (H) in this same situation also works. In the corner, a ⇘ + (H) that hits leads to a reset opportunity with Elastic Slam H that is difficult for your opponent to escape! Lastly, advancing in behind the Super Armor property of Orbital Grudge M becomes fairly viable, especially when coupled with a crossover assist.

You can make great use of Super-Skrull's X-Factor—any Meteor Smash OTG hit can be canceled into X-Factor to add huge damage to a combo. Even with X-Factor at Level 1, a single Elastic Slam can lead to an X-Factor combo that will do 860,900 damage. This is enough to K.O. several characters outright!

COMBO USAGE

I. ST. (L), CR. (M), ST. (H), CR. (H), (S) CANCEL⇒ SUPER JUMP, AIR (M), (M), (H), (S), LAND, → ↓ ↘ + (H) OTG CANCEL⇒ ↓ ↙ ← + (ATK)(ATK)

(662,900 damage) Super-Skrull can deal some hefty damage off of a clean standing (L) hit! To perform this combo consistently, wait until Super-Skrull is just before the peak of the super jump before you perform the air combo. If the combo is blocked, end the chain combo at standing (H), then continue to attack behind the + 4 frame advantage!

** The combos listed in this section all assume that Super-Skrull is on the 1p side of the screen; if not, Meteor Slams must be performed with the (L) button instead.*

Substituting the Inferno with the level 3 hyper combo Death Penalty does 883,800 damage. Canceling the Meteor Slam with X-Factor and performing another launcher combo into Inferno does 1,053,300 damage at Level 1 X-Factor.

II. ↓ ↙ ← + (ATK), → ↓ ↘ + (L) OTG CANCEL⇒ ↓ ↙ ← + (ATK)(ATK)

(478,500 damage) Skrull's standard combo from an Elastic Slam. Be sure to perform the Meteor Smash as early as possible, and try to hit-confirm the two hits of the Meteor Smash before canceling into Inferno.

III. ST. (L), CR. (M), CR. (H), (S) CANCEL⇒ SUPER JUMP, AIR (M), (M), (H), (S), LAND, P1 or P2, → ↓ ↘ + (H) OTG, (S) CANCEL⇒ SUPER JUMP, AIR (M), (M), (H), (S), → ↓ ↘ + (L) OTG

(543,900 damage, Phoenix—γ) With certain assists, Super-Skrull can do over 50% damage to most characters without even expending hyper combo gauge. Other crossover assists that work are M.O.D.O.K—β and Chris—γ. These combos also can end in a reset set-up: see the Advanced Section for details.

UP IN THE AIR

Super-Skrull's aerial movement options are average. He does not have a double jump or any air special moves that travel across the screen. He does have an airdash, albeit a fairly offbeat one. Super-Skrull's airdash only travels diagonally up-forward. This is a mixed blessing. The direction of the airdash prevents Super-Skrull from attacking directly with airdash attacks, but it's great for maneuvering into position to drop down with air ⇩ + Ⓗ. It also allows Super-Skrull to travel even higher to avoid zoning projectiles than a normal jump, allowing access to crossover assists.

Air ⇩ + Ⓗ is an incredible move. This move is deceptively safe, hits overhead, knocks down, inflicts chip damage, and leads to a full combo on hit! This attack is a great way to get your offense started when it is coupled with a crossover assist. To combo after air ⇩ + Ⓗ at midscreen, you should quickly dash and juggle your opponent's character with standing Ⓛ, while using Ⓜ + Ⓗ to dash. Attacking with air ⇩ + Ⓗ without a crossover assist to support it becomes creates a risky situation. Even if your opponent can't normally punish this attack on block, they can employ a wavedash to move their character under Super-Skrull before the elbow drop, causing this move to whiff while Super-Skrull hops backwards into a waiting opponent.

Super-Skrull has a unique airdash, one that is exceptionally good for setting up air ⇩ + Ⓗ.

Air ⇩ + Ⓗ is an incredibly useful move, especially in tandem with crossover assists!

Air Ⓢ (hold) may seem like a great way to control space, but the attacking hitbox is much smaller than you think it is.

Super-Skrull's aerial options other than air ⇩ + Ⓗ are a little subpar. Tenderizer is very risky to throw out, since it doesn't recover until he reaches the ground. Air Ⓛ and Ⓗ have decent enough speed and hitboxes to use them as air-to-ground attacks, but a direct approach via normal or super jumps is remarkably slow and unlikely to work. Air Ⓜ is good for intercepting super jumping characters, and air Ⓢ can cross-up a foe if the situation arises. Air Ⓢ (hold) looks great. This move covers a huge chunk of the screen, does chip damage, and wall bounces on hit. Unfortunately, the actual attacking hitbox of this move isn't much larger than a normal air Ⓢ.

In short, Super-Skrull should only be used in the air for three reasons: to air throw, to avoid attacks and advance, or to use an air ⇩ + Ⓗ.

ASSISTS

Super-Skrull's special moves outside of Elastic Slam aren't particularly great, so it should come as no surprise that his crossover assist attacks are equally lackluster. Stone Smite and Tenderizer H are far too slow for normal use, and are only useful in very specialized combo situations. However, Stone Smite does hit OTG and wall bounce, which are two useful attributes.

In the end, Orbital Grudge M is probably Super-Skrull's most useful crossover assist—it has a hit of super armor during the active frames, it moves forward, and it can cause interference for your opponent. On hit, it leaves the opposing character with enough hitstun for you to dash forward and juggle fairly easily.

Sentinel—α uses the Sentinel Force special move, directing three drones to slowly traverse the screen. This creates an ideal cover for Super-Skrull to wave-dash in to close range. Sentinel Force sends the drones diagonally upward, which means that distant foes can crouch under them to avoid this attack. This is fine, since they are in a prime position to be grabbed with Elastic Slam M!

This crossover assist is relatively slow. However, it has two major effects on gameplay. First, when using air ⇩ + Ⓗ against an opponent, Sentinel—α must be called before jumping. Second, it's slow enough to be called after a flying screen knockdown, and can still hit opponents who have been hit by a Meteor Smash OTG! While this creates a situation that is slightly awkward to combo from at midscreen, it's great for hitting opponents with an Elastic Slam H reset after they air recover. If the reset connects, the total damage of the combo becomes 954,700!

When Chris—γ is called, Chris performs Grenade Toss L, laying a land mine at Super-Skrull's feet. This works well with Super-Skrull for a number of reasons. Most importantly, it improves his subpar defensive capabilities—guarding an attack from an opponent while calling Chris—γ all but prevents your opponent from moving back in to close range for the next few seconds. If your opponent decides not to respect the land mine and attacks anyway, you get a free launcher after the opposing character is hit. Secondly, this crossover assist allows you to extend your midscreen combos to do substantially more damage, without using hyper combo gauge—see above Combo Usage section for details. Unfortunately, Chris—γ doesn't really help Super-Skrull close the distance against zoning opponents, so a Super-Skrull oriented team needs another supporting assist.

Wesker—β, Samurai Edge (lower), is a low-hitting attack. This creates an area of opportunity for Super-Skrull: virtually unblockable air ⇩ + Ⓗ attacks! Unblockable elbow drops still go into full combos! To properly do this joint attack, time the crossover assist button simultaneously with your jump, then perform an airdash and ⇩ + Ⓗ as normal. Wesker's gun shot is also OTG-capable, allowing you to easily extend combos by substituting the crossover assist for a Meteor Smash.

Not only does Sentinel—α give you great covering fire to advance behind, he also creates opportunities for reset Elastic Slams!

Zoning-type players typically employ a crossover assist to aid them while they attempt to fill up portions of the screen with projectiles. They'll also typically fall into patterns when calling these assists, confident that their own projectiles are sufficient to protect them. If you have two bars of hyper combo gauge, Super-Skrull has a great answer for these predictable patterns—Meteor Smash the assist and cancel into Inferno, then team hyper combo into nearly any other hyper combo to K.O. the assist!

Assists take 50% more damage than normal, so just the Meteor Smash to Inferno alone does 597,200 damage. Following-up with a team hyper combo that will fully hit the assist should easily do more than 1,000,000 damage.

Of course, it's preferable if the hyper combo that you team hyper combo into is safe if it is guarded, since your opponent will probably be blocking with their point character while they helplessly watching their assist character get knocked out. If not, it's up to you to make the judgment call on whether taking out the assist character is worth the retaliation that you're about to receive.

IV. (CORNER ONLY) ST. Ⓛ, CR. Ⓜ, ST. Ⓗ, CR. Ⓗ, Ⓢ CANCEL SUPER JUMP, AIR Ⓜ, Ⓜ, Ⓗ, Ⓢ, LAND, ST. Ⓗ (HOLD) OTG, Ⓢ CANCEL SUPER JUMP, AIR Ⓜ, Ⓜ, Ⓗ, Ⓢ, LAND, → ↓ ↘ + Ⓛ CANCEL ↓ ↙ ← + ATK ATK

(714,800 damage) Super-Skrull can squeeze in some additional damage in the corner, albeit with a more difficult combo. The timing of the first attack in the air combo is key—wait just long enough, so the opposing character is above Super-Skrull by the time the air Ⓢ hits. Otherwise, you won't have enough time to land the Stone Smite OTG. Substituting the final Inferno for Death Penalty does 932,400 damage.

V. AIR ↓ + Ⓗ, DASH, ST. Ⓛ, CR. Ⓜ, CR. Ⓗ, Ⓢ CANCEL SUPER JUMP, AIR Ⓜ, Ⓜ, Ⓗ, Ⓢ, LAND, → ↓ ↘ + Ⓗ OTG CANCEL ↓ ↙ ← + ATK ATK

(629,800 damage) After hitting an air ↓ + Ⓗ midscreen, you'll have to quickly dash in before juggling with standing Ⓛ. To perform this more easily, press Ⓜ + Ⓗ to dash, then quickly press Ⓛ. Note that the standing Ⓗ is omitted from this combo. The air ↓ + Ⓗ ground bounces your foe, and you only get one ground bounce per combo.

SUPER-SKRULL

ADVANCED TACTICS

ELASTIC SLAM RESET SET UP

After any combo involving two full launcher juggles, hitstun degrades to the point where a Meteor Smash OTG hit will cause an opponent to air recover instead of being knocked down. You can use this to your advantage by immediately hitting the character out of the air recovery with Elastic Slam H!

Of course, the Elastic Slam H isn't guaranteed; characters with fast aerial movement options like 8-way airdashes can avoid the Elastic Slam. However, most members of the cast will have a very difficult time avoiding the Elastic Slam if they air recover backwards (the natural reaction to the situation), or don't air recover at all.

An air recover forward will escape the Elastic Slam with any character, and will even allow the opposing player to score a combo on Super-Skrull while he is still recovering from the whiffed grab.

Once the combo meter gets high enough, you have a great opportunity to reset an opposing character after a Meteor Slam OTG.

COUNTERS TO FORWARD AIR RECOVERY

Once your opponent begins an air recover forward out of your reset attempts, you can put them in yet another mix-up! You have several options here—dash under your opponent and perform crouching Ⓜ into a combo is the safest option. This attack will anti-air most cross-up attacks that your opponent may try. To mix it up, you can immediately wave-dash twice to make Super-Skrull dash back in front of his foe! This is very tricky, but be careful when the opposing player immediately presses buttons out of their air recovery, since Super-Skrull can be hit by a combo if you try to employ a double-cross up. Alternatively, you can backdash immediately and make your opponent land into an Elastic Slam M, or you can choose to jump up and perform an air throw.

An Air recover forward may get your foe out of the reset, but it still puts them in a very dangerous position!

"YOUR DEFEAT IS JUST A PRELUDE TO WHAT AWAITS THE ENTIRE UNIVERSE!"

COMBO APPENDIX

GENERAL EXECUTION TIPS

Always wait a bit before doing the first hit in an air combo. You'll want the opposing character higher than yours before you put them in a flying screen state; it gives you much more time to hit your foe with an OTG attack.

You don't have to cancel Meteor Smash into Inferno quickly at all. You can verify the successful OTG hits before inputting the cancel.

Try not to accidentally hold any buttons down. Super-Skrull has several moves that can be held, making them much slower.

Requirements (Position, meter, etc.)	Notes	Command Sequence	Damage
—	Damage on standard combo without canceling to Inferno	st. Ⓛ, cr. Ⓜ, st. Ⓗ, cr. Ⓗ, Ⓢ CANCEL ➡ super jump, air Ⓜ, Ⓜ, Ⓗ, Ⓢ, land, ⇨⇩⇘ + Ⓗ OTG	433,800
—	Easier than Meteor Smash OTG	⇩⇙⇦ + ATK, Ⓛ))) CANCEL ➡ ⇩⇘⇨ + ATK ATK	393,700
—	—	Any ground throw or air throw, ⇨⇩⇘ + ATK OTG CANCEL ➡ ⇩⇙⇦ + ATK ATK	403,400
X-Factor Level 1	Will outright K.O. several characters off of one Elastic Slam	⇩⇙⇦ + ATK, ⇨⇩⇘ + Ⓛ OTG CANCEL ➡ X-FACTOR, Ⓢ CANCEL ➡ super jump, air Ⓜ, Ⓜ, Ⓗ, Ⓢ, land, ⇨⇩⇘ + Ⓗ CANCEL ➡ ⇩⇙⇦ + ATK ATK	860,900
—	Can hit-confirm before performing Meteor Smash	⇨⇨⇨ + Ⓗ CANCEL ➡ ⇨⇩⇘ + Ⓗ OTG CANCEL ➡ ⇩⇙⇦ + ATK ATK	509,600
Wesker—β	511,200 damage without using Inferno	st. Ⓛ, cr. Ⓜ, st. Ⓗ, cr. Ⓗ, Ⓢ CANCEL ➡ super jump, air Ⓜ, Ⓜ, Ⓗ, Ⓢ, land, dash, P1 or P2, Ⓢ CANCEL ➡ super jump, air Ⓜ, Ⓜ, Ⓗ, Ⓢ, land, ⇨⇩⇘ + Ⓛ OTG CANCEL ➡ ⇩⇙⇦ + ATK ATK	718,000
Sentinel—α	509,700 damage without using Inferno, backdash not necessary midscreen	st. Ⓛ, cr. Ⓜ, st. Ⓗ, cr. Ⓗ, Ⓢ CANCEL ➡ super jump, air Ⓜ, Ⓜ, Ⓗ, Ⓢ, land, P1 or P2, ⇨⇩⇘ + Ⓗ OTG, backdash, ⇩⇘⇨ + Ⓛ (whiff) CANCEL ➡ ⇩⇙⇦ + Ⓗ, ⇨⇩⇘ + Ⓗ OTG CANCEL ➡ ⇩⇙⇦ + ATK ATK	719,900

THOR

BIO

REAL NAME

THOR ODINSON

OCCUPATION

WARRIOR, ADVENTURER

ABILITIES

TRAINED AS A WARRIOR, THOR EXCELS AT HAND-TO-HAND COMBAT, SWORD FIGHTING, AND THROW TECHNIQUES. WITH HIS OTHER-WORLDLY STAMINA AND SUPERHUMAN STRENGTH, ORDINARY ATTACKS HAVE NO EFFECT ON HIM.

WEAPONS

THOR WIELDS MJOLNIR, A HAMMER FORGED FROM URU METAL. MJOLNIR IS VIRTUALLY UNBREAKABLE, AND ALLOWS THOR TO COMMAND THE POWERS OF THE STORM: RAIN, THUNDER AND LIGHTNING.

PROFILE

THOR IS THE SON OF ODIN, RULER OF ASGARD, THE HOME OF THE GODS. KNOWN AS THE STRONGEST WARRIOR IN ASGARD, HIS PRIDEFUL WAYS WERE REFORMED AFTER SPENDING TIME LIVING AS A HUMAN. CURRENTLY, HE IS A MEMBER OF THE EARTH'S MIGHTIEST HEROES, THE AVENGERS.

FIRST APPEARANCE

JOURNEY INTO MYSTERY #83 (1962)

"THOSE FOOLISH ENOUGH TO CHALLENGE THOR SHALL LEARN TO REGRET THEIR DECISION."

POWER GRID

2	INTELLIGENCE
7	STRENGTH
7	SPEED
6	STAMINA
6	ENERGY PROJECTION
4	FIGHTING ABILITY

*This is biographical, and does not represent an evaluation of the character's in-game combat potential.

ALTERNATE COSTUMES

PS3: ⊗ Xbox 360: Ⓐ

PS3: ▢ Xbox 360: Ⓧ

PS3: △ Xbox 360: Ⓨ

PS3: R1 Xbox 360: RB

ATTACK SET

STANDING BASIC ATTACKS

Screen	Command	Hits	Damage	Startup	Active	Recovery	Advantage on Hit	Advantage if Guarded	Notes
1	Standing Ⓛ	1	65,000	8	3	23	-8	-10	—
2	Standing Ⓜ	1	90,000	13	3	30	-10	-13	—
3	Standing Ⓗ	1	110,000	18	2	36	-7	-12	Knocks down
4	Ⓢ	1	110,000	11	4	28	—	-6	Launcher, not special or hyper combo cancelable

1

2

3

4

CROUCHING BASIC ATTACKS

Screen	Command	Hits	Damage	Startup	Active	Recovery	Advantage on Hit	Advantage if Guarded	Notes
1	Crouching Ⓛ	1	63,000	7	3	24	-9	-11	Low attack
2	Crouching Ⓜ	3	97,600	13	12	19	-2	-5	Low attack
3	Crouching Ⓗ	1	105,000	16	4	36	—	-14	Low attack, knocks down

1

2

3

AERIAL BASIC ATTACKS

Screen	Command	Hits	Damage	Startup	Active	Recovery	Notes
1	Air Ⓛ	1	68,000	6	8	17	Overhead attack
2	Air Ⓜ	1	85,000	13	4	27	Overhead attack
3	Air Ⓗ	1	100,000	16	Until grounded or contact	1	Overhead attack
4	Air Ⓢ	1	110,000	14	5	37	Unrecoverable knockdown when used in air combo after Ⓢ launcher

1

2

3

4

AS A PARTNER—CROSSOVER ASSISTS

Screen	Type	P1+P2 Crossover Combination Hyper Combo	Description	Hits	Damage	Startup	Active	Recovery (this crossover assist)	Recovery (other partner)	Notes
1	α – Alpha	Mighty Thunder	Mighty Spark M	7	114,100	47	22~27	124	94	Initial spark has 1 low priority durability point, beam durability: 3 frames x 5 low priority durability points
2	β – Beta	Mighty Tornado	Mighty Smash	2	95,000	37	5(16)10	114	84	Causes ground bounce
3	γ – Gamma	Mighty Tornado	Mighty Strike M	2	133,000	44	11	126	96	20 nullifies projectiles during active frames, knocks down

1

2

3

SPECIAL MOVES

Screen	Name	Command	Hits	Damage	Startup	Active	Recovery	Advantage on Hit	Advantage if Guarded	Notes
1	Might Spark L	↓↘→ + L	3	90,700	15	19	12	+8	+5	Initial spark has 1 low priority durability point, beam durability: 1 frame x 5 low priority durability points
	Might Spark M	↓↘→ + M	7	123,000	23	32	3	+16	+12	Initial spark has 1 low priority durability point, beam durability: 3 frame x 5 low priority durability points
	Might Spark H	↓↘→ + H	11	154,000	30	45	0	+18	+14	Initial spark has 1 low priority durability point, beam durability: 5 frame x 5 low priority durability points
2	Mighty Smash L	→↓↘ + L	2	133,000	12	6 (17) 3	28	—	-4	Unrecoverable knockdown
	Mighty Smash M	→↓↘ + M	2	160,000	12	6 (17) 3	33	—	-9	Causes ground bounce
	Mighty Smash H (Can be charged)	→↓↘ + H	5~7	203,700~226,100	13~38	6 (19) 3 (6) 8~12	13~9	+9	+9~8	OTG-capable, causes spinning knockdown, fully-charged version adds more hitsun and hitstun
3	Mighty Strike L (Can be charged)	←↓↙ + L	2~3	133,000~175,900	20~41	11~11 (1) 11	35~22	-10	-18~-7	Knocks down, fully-charged version adds more hits and hitstun, nullifies projectiles during active frames
4	Mighty Strike M (Can be charged)	←↓↙ + M	2~3	133,000~175,900	20~41	11~11 (1) 11	23~10	+2	-6~+5	Knocks down, fully-charged version adds more hits and hitstun, nullifies projectiles during active frames
5	Mighty Strike H (Can be charged)	←↓↙ + H	2~3	133,000~175,900	20~41	11~11 (1) 11	23~10	+2	-8~-7	Knocks down, fully-charged version adds more hits and hitstun, nullifies projectiles during active frames
3	Air Mighty Strike L (Can be charged)	(in air) ←↓↙ + L	2~3	133,000~175,900	20~41	11~11 (1) 11	15~1	—	-5~+12	Knocks down, fully-charged version adds more hits and hitstun, nullifies projectiles during active frames
6	Air Mighty Strike M (Can be charged)	(in air) ←↓↙ + M	2~3	133,000~175,900	20~41	11~11 (1) 11	15~1	—	+13~+13	Knocks down, fully-charged version adds more hits and hitstun, nullifies projectiles during active frames, 11 frames ground recovery
7	Air Mighty Strike H (Can be charged)	(in air) ←↓↙ + H	2~3	133,000~175,900	20~41	11~11 (1) 11	15~1	—	+13~+13	Knocks down, fully-charged version adds more hits and hitstun, nullifies projectiles during active frames, 11 frames ground recovery
8	Mighty Hurricane L (in air OK)	→↘↓↙← + L	1	130,000	5	1	40	—	—	Throw
	Mighty Hurricane M (in air OK)	→↘↓↙← + M	1	150,000	3	1	42	—	—	Throw
	Mighty Hurricane H (in air OK)	→↘↓↙← + H	1	180,000	1	2	43	—	—	Throw
9	Flight (in air OK)	↓↙← + S	—	—	30	—	—	—	—	—
10	Mighty Speech	↓↓ + H (hold down)	—	—	18	—	22	—	—	Charges hyper combo gauge

Mighty Spark: Use this to combat enemy projectiles and to halt horizontal movement. The L version has the fastest startup period, while the stronger versions are too slow for firefights. All strengths leave you at a frame advantage when guarded, allowing you to link after them at close distances. This is another property that works well with the combo-friendly Mighty Spark L, which is the only strength that combos after a canceled light attack.

Mighty Smash: The Mighty Smash is used in combos and to punish projectiles. Mighty Smash M causes a ground bounce on hit, while Mighty Smash H is OTG-capable. Mighty Smash H also has the most attack range and leaves you at a frame advantage when blocked, making it ideal for punishing projectiles. It can be charged, which increases the damage and guardstun it causes.

Mighty Strike: This lunging hammer strike nullifies projectiles during active frames. All strengths can be charged to increase their damage and hitstun durations. The ground versions have heavy recovery periods, while the aerial variations recover almost instantly after their active hit periods expire. You can perform an "instant" version of the aerial Mighty Strike L (←↓↙↖ + L), doing it right as you leave the ground for a jump to mimic the ground version of the same move while eliminating its poor recovery.

Mighty Hurricane: Thor's powerful command throw. The L version inflicts little damage but has a large attack range. Mighty Hurricane H deals the most damage but requires you to be directly next to an opposing character to grab them; it's also 1 frame, making it usable as reversal. This applies to both the ground and air versions of the move. Use the Mighty Hurricane to grab foes who rely on guarding too often. If your opponent ever attempts to jump away from your throw, use the aerial version of the same move to grab them out of the sky!

Flight: Inputting ↓↙← + S activates Thor's Flight mode, which lasts roughly two seconds. It's used only to keep Thor out of trouble when vitality is low, or when your challenger has too many resources at their disposal (causing you to opt for a defensive position).

Mighty Speech: Thor's speech charges the hyper combo gauge as long as the button is held. Its starting and recovery periods are horrendous, making it far too risky to commit to. Use it only when there's an assist shielding you.

HYPER COMBOS

Screen	Name	Command	Hits	Damage	Startup	Active	Recovery	Advantage on Hit	Advantage if Guarded	Notes
1	Mighty Tornado (in air OK)	↓↘→ + ATK ATK	15	321,600	20+2	85	58	—	-35	Final hit knocks down, beam durability: 15 frames x 1 high priority durability points
2	Mighty Thunder	→↓↘ + ATK ATK	4	383,700	24+14	40	63	—	-72	OTG-capable, unrecoverable knockdown, each projectile has 1 high priority durability point
3	Mighty Punish	→↘↓↙← + ATK ATK	2	310,000	4+0	1	23	—	—	Frames 3-6 invincible, throw, unrecoverable knockdown

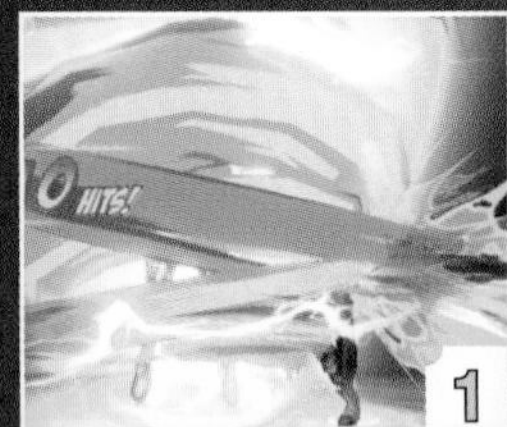

Mighty Tornado: This damage-heavy hyper combo is used predominantly in air combos. The ground version causes a long juggle state that the opposition doesn't recover from until they hit the ground, which is useful for team hyper combos. The aerial version causes the defender to flip out earlier than normal, but recovers faster than its ground counterpart.

Mighty Thunder: Mighty Thunder is used strictly for OTG combos. Prime times to use it are after → ↓ ↘ + (L) hits or after you nail your target with air (S) during a launcher combo. Since it covers a large portion of screen very quickly, it's also good for safely getting Thor off of the screen via a THC.

Mighty Punish: A throw hyper combo with some invulnerability, Mighty Punish is used in place of the Mighty Hurricane when your opponent uses slow normal attacks or throws to stop it. This is also a good method of countering your foe's attempts to punish the heavy recovery periods on Thor's moves.

BATTLE PLAN

OVERVIEW

VITALITY: 1,250,000

CHAIN COMBO ARCHETYPE: 2-HIT LIMITED

X-Factor	Lv.1	Lv.2	Lv.3
Damage	160%	190%	220%
Speed	100%	105%	110%

Thor is an oddly flexible "grappler" character, or a character whose sole focus is to establish close range and force an opponent to guess between a throw and a combo. His access to a projectile and strong aerial mobility is a first for this archetype, giving him valuable ways of handling a wide spectrum of matches. The cost for these gifts is severe, since he has terribly unsafe recovery periods on almost all of his main combo openings; and in spite of his air mobility, has difficulty keeping offensive momentum against advancing guard use. Your objective doesn't change despite these problems, but you'll have to be heavily reliant on assists to accomplish it—move into short range to stage an attack, and try to corner your opponent when possible. Use assists to fortify both strategies and to compensate for Thor's risky move set.

Establishing close range is effective because:

Thor's Mighty Hurricane is usable on either the ground or in the air, allowing him to rely on it for both aerial and ground-based attacks.

Thor inflicts absolutely massive damage off of a successful throw or combo mix-up.

His flexible set of special attacks and mobility gives him clear-cut answers against an opponent's ranged offense—rare options for a grappler, which makes it easier to secure a close position.

Accomplish this objective by:

Using airdashes to fly over ground attacks and projectiles.

Calling an assist to cover an approach.

Attacking with Mighty Spark L (↓ ↘ → + (L)) to bait and punish jumps.

Using the "instant, tiger knee" version of the aerial Mighty Strike L (← ↓ ↙ ↖ + (L)) to plow through projectiles.

ON THE GROUND

Fire the Mighty Spark down your opponent's avenues of attack!

Always threaten with the Mighty Throw!

There are numerous ways of establishing close range, all of which depend on the opposition and the range that you're fighting at. Your main long range goal is to use ↓↘→ + L to control your challenger's movements, lure out mistakes, and to thwart projectile attacks. Your secondary goal is to look for a projectile to punish with →↓↘ + H or the "instant" version of air Mighty Strike (input ←↓↙↖ + L). Attack with Mighty Spark L when you anticipate a forward ground dash, or jump and use it just as you leave the ground to stop low-altitude jumps and airdashes. You can fire it off somewhat late to nullify projectiles containing 5 or fewer durability points, but if you're 100% certain a projectile is coming, you should punish it instead with Mighty Smash H or "instant" air Mighty Strike L. Both attacks leave you with frame advantage when guarded, so press your advantage if your opponent doesn't counter you outright.

Your options at mid range are extremely limited, but necessary nonetheless. Counter jump attempts with **Combo VI** or crouching M CANCEL→ →↓↘ + H. Attack with standing M to thwart forward movement of any sort. The recovery period is horrendous, so cancel standing M into Mighty Spark L if it whiffs against a grounded opponent, or into Mighty Smash H to catch an airborne foe trying to punish it with a jump.

Thor's close range options are heavily reliant on his triangle jump air L (covered in Up in the Air), which is his only 100% safe attack opening. Apart from going for triangle jump air L, you can also attack with Mighty Hurricane when your opponent guards, or **Combos I**, **II**, or **IV** when they try to stop the throw. **Combo IV** is used for basic Mighty Hurricane counterhit setups. For example, a common method of landing the Mighty Hurricane is to force your opponent to guard crouching L, then immediately perform →↘↓↙← + ATK right as you recover. When you're certain that your challenger will counter the throw, chain crouching L into standing H, which leaves just enough of a gap between hits to allow your opponent to stick out an attack. Standing H counterhits if they do, allowing for the above combo. Note that your foe can always do a throw to stop this set up; if you expect this, chain to crouching M instead of standing H. Revert back to using standing H when your opposition tries to react to a visible gap in your sequence.

UP IN THE AIR

If you're wary of running into an anti-air during a forward jump, drop to the floor with ↓↓ or ↓ + ATK + ATK.

Thor's triangle jump air L is the foundation for your close range offense.

Thor's 8-way airdash (hold any direction and press ATK ATK) and Flight (↓↙← + S) helps both your defensive and offensive purposes. When keeping your distance, watch what your opponent does and use various combinations of super jumps, air Mighty Sparks, airdashes, and Flight to avoid their actions. ↓ + ATK ATK or air Mighty Strike H should be used to quickly drop under horizontal projectiles fired from the air. Use forwards and backwards airdashes to soar over and punish upward projectiles, or to pass over the opposing character's head when they try to move under you. Flight should be used to stay in the air longer than your super jump and airdash times allow. Try to only use Flight at the peak of a super jump—any closer to the ground and you put yourself at risk.

Aggressive movements are done with air → + ATK ATK, ↘ + ATK ATK, or ←↓↙ + M. Come out of horizontal airdashes with air H, which stays out for the entire duration of a jump. Attack with air L, Thor's fastest air attack, after diagonal "triangle jump" airdashes. The angled air Mighty Strike M has a giant area of effect in front of it that nullifies projectiles and stops most anti-air attacks (leading to **Combo V** on hit). It even beats pillar-esque projectiles, like Dante's Jam Session!

Forcing your opponent to guard a single air attack or Mighty Strike leads to a potent mix-up opportunity when you land: land and attempt →↘↓↙← + M (**Combo III**), **Combo I or II**, jump vertically then immediately drop to the ground with ↓ + ATK ATK then do →↘↓↙← + ATK, or jump vertically and input air ↘ + ATK ATK to air dash over the opposing character's head, then hit air L on the way down to cross them up. You can also do air ↘ + ATK ATK then a quick air H, which whiffs, then land and transition into **Combo I**. This tricks your challenger into believing that you'll attack high, when instead you actually perform a low-hitting attack. Using triangle jump tricks in this manner is the foundation of Thor's close range offense.

COMBO USAGE

I. CR. Ⓛ CANCEL ↓↘→ + Ⓛ, CR. Ⓛ, CR. Ⓗ CANCEL →↓↘ + Ⓜ, Ⓢ CANCEL SUPER JUMP, AIR Ⓜ, Ⓜ, Ⓗ CANCEL ←↓↙ + Ⓛ CANCEL ↓↘→ + ATK ATK

(592,600 damage) This is Thor's only safe combo that doesn't require an assist to shield its recovery. This is due to ↓↘→ + Ⓛ, which leaves you at a frame advantage on guard. Unfortunately, Mighty Spark does not hit properly against Arthur and numerous crouching characters: C. Viper, Dante, Felicia, Hsien-ko, Morrigan, Phoenix, Spiderman, Storm, Super-Skrull, Trish, Wesker, Wolverine, X-23, and Zero. Additionally, the full combo does not work if started with an air attack, in which case you must change the opening portion to crouching Ⓛ CANCEL ↓↘→ + Ⓛ, crouching Ⓛ, Ⓢ.

So why spend time learning a combo with so many issues? Thor has very few safe ways to attack, especially those that leave him at a frame advantage. Study the match-ups where this combo is effective and use it when possible.

II. CR. Ⓛ, CR. Ⓜ CANCEL →↓↘ + Ⓜ, Ⓢ CANCEL SUPER JUMP, AIR Ⓜ, Ⓜ, Ⓗ CANCEL ←↓↙ + Ⓛ CANCEL ↓↘→ + ATK ATK

(588,300 damage) This is the alternative to the above combo that works against all characters. All elements of this combo are at least throw-punishable when blocked, including crouching Ⓜ. You can cancel into a delayed →↓↘ + Ⓜ to counterhit some incoming attempts to punish your recovery, →↘↓↙← + ATK to grab foes who expect the previous option, or ↓↙← + Ⓢ to activate Flight. Since all of these options are risky, you should probably use assists to shield yourself from counter attacks after crouching Ⓜ has been blocked.

III. (THROW OR →↘↓↙← + Ⓗ OR AIR →↘↓↙← + Ⓗ), →↓↘ + Ⓜ, Ⓢ CANCEL SUPER JUMP, AIR Ⓜ, Ⓜ, Ⓗ CANCEL ←↓↙ + Ⓛ CANCEL ↓↘→ + ATK ATK

(448,600 or 656,300 damage) A high damage throw combo. After recovering from any of the mentioned throws, perform →↓↘ + Ⓜ as soon as possible for it to properly juggle. Note that it's much easier to juggle after the aerial version of →↘↓↙← + ATK because of its extended air time.

ASSISTS

Call assists to fend of enemy counter attacks.

Thor is in desperate need of assists to help protect his recovery-heavy ground chains. The typical batch of multi-hit assists like Dante—α, Arthur—β, Ryu—γ, and Captain America—α all work well for this, but almost any fast projectile assist will do.

As an assist, Thor—α is a beam that has 3 frames with 5 durability points each, a high number for an assist. Thor—β causes a ground bounce on hit, which is useful when paired with characters who can't cause this state on their own, like Trish. Its fast starting speed and the ability to juggle after it also makes it a great crossover counter, when you need to tag Thor in defensively. Finally, Thor—γ is a little slow as anti-air, but you can use it to counter projectiles fired from the air at a downward angle.

Thor—β, Mighty Smash, is a powerful crossover counter.

IV. COUNTERHIT ST. Ⓗ CANCEL➡ DELAYED → ↓ ↘ + Ⓜ, Ⓢ CANCEL➡ SUPER JUMP, AIR Ⓜ, Ⓜ, Ⓗ CANCEL➡ ← ↓ ↙ + Ⓛ CANCEL➡ ↓ ↘ → + ATK ATK

(702,700 damage) This is used in counterhit setups to score heavy damage. You can verify whether standing Ⓗ hits or not before canceling into → ↓ ↘ + Ⓜ.

V. AIR ← ↓ ↙ + Ⓛ OR Ⓜ, LAND, Ⓢ CANCEL➡ SUPER JUMP, AIR Ⓜ, Ⓜ, Ⓗ CANCEL➡ ← ↓ ↙ + Ⓛ CANCEL➡ ↓ ↘ → + ATK ATK

(629,500 damage) A basic combo done after the air Mighty Strike counterhits an anti-air attempt. Depending on the height at which the first attack hits, you may have to wait a moment before juggling with Ⓢ to ensure that your foe doesn't get knocked too high in the air.

VI. MEET AN AIRBORNE ENEMY WITH FORWARD JUMPING AIR Ⓛ, Ⓜ, DELAYED Ⓢ, LAND, JUMP FORWARD, AIR Ⓛ, Ⓜ, DELAYED Ⓗ, LAND, ST. Ⓜ, Ⓢ CANCEL➡ SUPER JUMP, AIR Ⓜ, Ⓜ, Ⓗ CANCEL➡ ← ↓ ↙ + Ⓛ CANCEL➡ ↓ ↘ → + ATK ATK

(662,900 damage) This is designed to preemptively stop jumps at close distances. If air Ⓛ whiffs entirely, come back down from the jump with air Ⓛ to attack, or airdash backwards to retreat. Any input prefaced with "delayed" should be press slightly later than normal. This ensures the attack is done closer to the ground, giving you more time to re-jump and continue the combo.

THOR

ADVANCED TACTICS

KARA CANCEL MIGHTY HURRICANE

Kara-canceling can hide your intentions.

Performing crouching Ⓛ, then doing the Mighty Hurricane is a common "tick," or command throw setup. Chaining crouching Ⓛ into standing Ⓗ is the secondary option for counterhitting enemies expecting the throw. The only major problem with this setup, outside of its weakness to throws, is that crouching Ⓛ has a very obvious and long recovery period, making it easy to tell when the Mighty Hurricane is coming. There's a way to prevent this problem via kara-canceling (or canceling a basic attack into a special move before it hits). Chain crouching Ⓛ into standing Ⓗ, then just before standing Ⓗ hits, cancel it into → ↘ ↓ ↙ ← + Ⓜ. If done properly, standing Ⓗ will visibly come out just before canceling into the throw, which may coerce your opponent to continue blocking in fear of the hit.

MIGHTY STRIKE SETUP

Never let them escape!

In those rare instances where you don't have hyper combo gauge to spare, end air combos with Mighty Strike L like you normally would, then airdash ↗ towards your opponent. Regardless of whether they air recover forwards or backwards, you can attack with air Ⓛ, Ⓢ CANCEL➡ ↓ ↘ → + Ⓜ when you think they'll try to attack, or → ↘ ↓ ↙ ← + ATK (Combo III) when they guard. A similar mix-up opportunity occurs after hitting a foe with → ↓ ↘ + Ⓗ. Jump forward and airdash towards them to move in for the kill!

COMBO APPENDIX

GENERAL EXECUTION TIPS

After a standard (S) launcher, start your air chain early during the super jump.

Linking after ↓ ↘ → + (ATK) takes slightly stricter timing than chain combos. If you're having trouble executing the combo, try brushing your fingers across the follow-up attack button twice rapidly. This compensates for execution errors involving inputting the button too early.

Requirements (Position, meter, etc.)	Notes	Command Sequence	Damage
Requires corner, requires one hyper combo gauge bar	—	→ ↘ ↓ ↙ ← + (H), st. (M) CANCEL→ → ↓ ↘ + (M), cr. (H), (S) CANCEL→ super jump, air (M), (M), (H) CANCEL→ ← ↓ ↙ + (L) CANCEL→ ↓ ↘ → + (ATK)(ATK)	676,600
Requires corner, requires one hyper combo gauge bar	—	Air → ↘ ↓ ↙ ← + (H), st. (H) CANCEL→ → ↓ ↘ + (M), cr. (H), (S) CANCEL→ super jump, air (M), (M), (H) CANCEL→ ← ↓ ↙ + (L) CANCEL→ ↓ ↘ → + (ATK)(ATK)	691,600
Requires level 1 X-Factor, requires one hyper combo gauge bar	—	Cr. (L), cr. (M) X-FACTOR cr. (L), cr. (H) CANCEL→ → ↓ ↘ + (M), (S) CANCEL→ super jump, air (M), (M), (H) CANCEL→ ← ↓ ↙ + (L) (1 hit) CANCEL→ ↓ ↘ → + (ATK)(ATK)	1,190,900
Requires level 1 X-Factor, requires one hyper combo gauge bar	—	→ ↘ ↓ ↙ ← + (H) or air → ↘ ↓ ↙ ← + (H), → ↓ ↘ + (M), X-FACTOR, (S) CANCEL→ super jump, air (M), (M), (H) CANCEL→ ← ↓ ↙ + (L) CANCEL→ ↓ ↘ → + (ATK)(ATK)	1,075,300
Requires corner, requires 2 hyper combo gauge bars	It's possible to juggle after the aerial version of ↓ ↘ → + (ATK)(ATK), but it must hit your opponent while they are low to the ground	Air (H) CANCEL→ air ↓ ↘ → + (ATK)(ATK), land, → ↓ ↘ + (M), cr. (H), (S) CANCEL→ super jump, air (M), (M), (H) CANCEL→ ← ↓ ↙ + (L) (1 hit) CANCEL→ ↓ ↘ → + (ATK)(ATK)	624,200

"ASGARDIANS AND
MIDGARDIANS ALIKE
CAN REST EASY
KNOWING THOR
IS THEIR ETERNAL
GUARDIAN!"

WOLVERINE

BIO

REAL NAME

JAMES HOWLETT

OCCUPATION

ADVENTURER

ABILITIES

WITH HIS MUTANT HEALING FACTOR AND ADAMANTIUM CLAWS, WOLVERINE IS THE BEST THERE IS AT WHAT HE DOES...BUT WHAT HE DOES BEST ISN'T VERY NICE.

WEAPONS

CLAWS COATED IN VIRTUALLY INDESTRUCTIBLE ADAMANTIUM, WHICH HE CAN FREELY RELEASE FROM BOTH HANDS. THE CLAWS ARE PART OF HIS SKELETON, WHICH IS ALSO COATED IN ADAMANTIUM.

PROFILE

BENEATH HIS GRUFF AND CRUDE EXTERIOR LIES A NOBLE SPIRIT WHO GENUINELY TREASURES HIS COMRADES. HOWEVER, IN THE FACE OF HIS ENEMIES HE IS MERCILESS, OFTEN EMPLOYING EXTREME MEASURES IN HIS METHODS.

FIRST APPEARANCE

THE INCREDIBLE HULK #180 (1974)

POWER GRID

2	INTELLIGENCE
4	STRENGTH
2	SPEED
4	STAMINA
1	ENERGY PROJECTION
7	FIGHTING ABILITY

*This is biographical, and does not represent an evaluation of the character's in-game combat potential.

ALTERNATE COSTUMES

PS3: ⨂ Xbox 360: A

PS3: ▢ Xbox 360: X

PS3: △ Xbox 360: Y

PS3: R1 Xbox 360: RB

ATTACK SET

STANDING BASIC ATTACKS

The second frame data value is for Wolverine with Berserker Charge active.

Screen	Command	Hits	Damage	Startup Frames	Active Frames	Recovery Frames	Frame Advantage on Hit	Frame Advantage if Guarded	Notes
1	Standing Ⓛ	1	53,000	4/4	3/3	11/8	0/+3	-1/+2	—
2	Standing Ⓜ	—	67,000	6/5	3/3	22/17	-6/-1	-8/-3	—
3	Standing Ⓗ	1	95,000	11/9	4/4	24/18	-2/+4	-6/0	Knocks down opponent, ⇩ ⇘ ⇨ + P1⇔P2 snap back
4	Ⓢ	1	80,000	9/7	4/4	27/21	—	-9/-3	Launcher attack, not special- or hyper combo-cancelable

1

2

3

4

CROUCHING BASIC ATTACKS

The second frame data value is for Wolverine with Berserker Charge active.

Screen	Command	Hits	Damage	Startup Frames	Active Frames	Recovery Frames	Frame Advantage on Hit	Frame Advantage if Guarded	Notes
1	Crouching Ⓛ	1	48,000	6/5	3/3	12/9	-1/+2	-2/+1	Low attack
2	Crouching Ⓜ	1	70,000	7/6	3/3	19/14	-5/0	-5/-3	Knocks opponent into the air
3	Crouching Ⓗ	1	78,000	12/10	4/4	20/15	—	-2/+3	Low attack, knocks down

1

2

3

AERIAL BASIC ATTACKS

The second frame data value is for Wolverine with Berserker Charge active.

Screen	Command	Hits	Damage	Startup Frames	Active Frames	Recovery Frames	Frame Advantage on Hit	Frame Advantage if Guarded	Notes
1	Air Ⓛ	1	50,000	4/4	7/6	12/9	—	—	Overhead attack
2	Air Ⓜ	1	70,000	6/5	3/3	24/18	—	—	Overhead attack
3	Air Ⓗ	1	80,000	8/7	2/2	26/20	—	—	Overhead attack
4	Air Ⓢ	1	90,000	11/9	4/4	21/16	—	—	Overhead attack, causes flying screen state if comboed after a launcher attack

1

2

3

4

AMATERASU

"WOW, WE DIDN'T EVEN NEED THE CELESTIAL BRUSH FOR THAT FIGHT."

BIO

REAL NAME

AMATERASU OKAMI

OCCUPATION

SUN GOD

ABILITIES

ABLE TO PERFORM 13 TYPES OF MIRACLES WITH THE CELESTIAL BRUSH; ALSO WIELDS THREE DIVINE WEAPONS.

WEAPONS

THE THREE DIVINE WEAPONS; THE THUNDER EDGE, THE DEVOUT BEADS, AND THE SOLAR FLARE. EACH WEAPON POSSESSES UNIQUE ATTRIBUTES, GIVING AMATERASU A VARIETY OF OPTIONS IN BATTLE.

PROFILE

100 YEARS AGO, AMATERASU SEALED AWAY TRUE OROCHI, BUT LOST HER PHYSICAL FORM DUE TO INJURIES SUSTAINED IN BATTLE. HER SPIRIT WAS CONTAINED WITHIN A STATUE, AND SHE WAS LATER RESURRECTED, ALTHOUGH WITHOUT HER CELESTIAL BRUSH POWERS. SHE BEGAN A JOURNEY TO RESTORE BEAUTY TO THE NIPPON WHILE REGAINING HER POWERS. SHE LOOKS LIKE AN ORDINARY WOLF TO THE AVERAGE PERSON.

FIRST APPEARANCE

OKAMI (2006)

POWER GRID

5	INTELLIGENCE
3	STRENGTH
7	SPEED
4	STAMINA
6	ENERGY PROJECTION
6	FIGHTING ABILITY

*This is biographical, and does not represent an evaluation of the character's in-game combat potential.

ALTERNATE COSTUMES

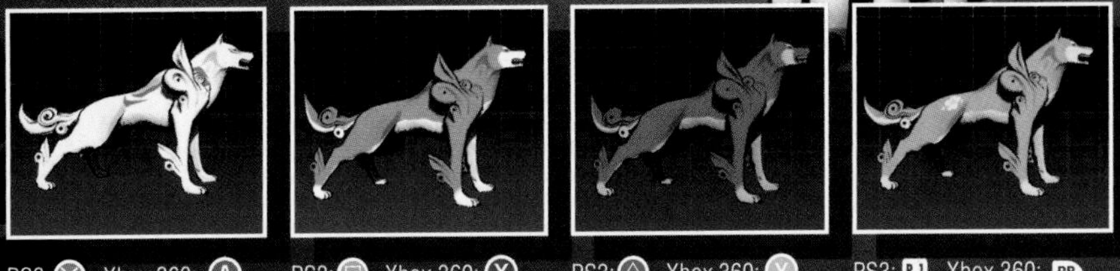

PS3: ⓧ Xbox 360: Ⓐ

PS3: ▢ Xbox 360: Ⓧ

PS3: △ Xbox 360: Ⓨ

PS3: R1 Xbox 360: RB

ATTACK SET

STANDING BASIC ATTACKS

Screen	Command	Hits	Damage	Startup	Active	Recovery	Advantage on Hit	Advantage if Guarded	Notes
1	Standing Ⓛ	1	30,000	3	2	11	+1	0	—
2	Standing Ⓜ	1	50,000	6	6	12	+1	-1	↓ ↘ → + P1 or P2 snapback
3	(With Solar Flare) Standing Ⓗ	1	60,000	8	4	16	+4	+2	Jump cancelable, chains into crouching Ⓗ
4	(With Thunder Edge) Standing Ⓗ	1	80,000	13	4	17	+3	+1	Chains into crouching Ⓗ
5	(With Devout Beads) Standing Ⓗ	4	79,500	15	4	30	-7	-9	Chains into crouching Ⓗ
6	Ⓢ	1	70,000	7	6	18	—	-2	Launcher, not special or hyper combo cancelable

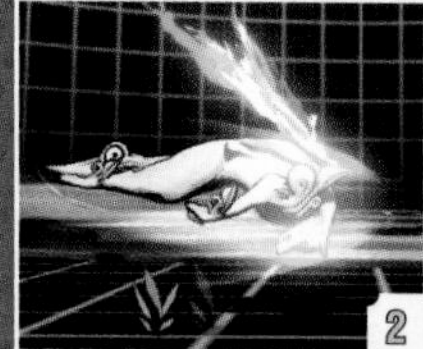

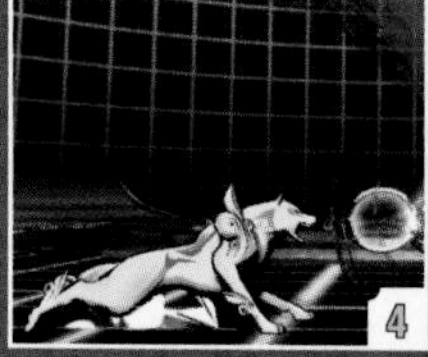

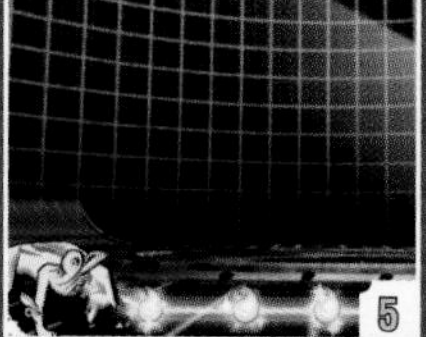

CROUCHING BASIC ATTACKS

Screen	Command	Hits	Damage	Startup	Active	Recovery	Advantage on Hit	Advantage if Guarded	Notes
1	Crouching Ⓛ	1	28,000	4	2	12	0	-1	Low attack, rapid fire, chains into standing Ⓛ
2	Crouching Ⓜ	1	50,000	7	3	15	+1	-1	Low attack
3	(With Solar Flare) Crouching Ⓗ	1	60,000	9	4	16	—	+2	Low attack, jump cancelable
4	(With Thunder Edge) Crouching Ⓗ	1	80,000	13	4	19	—	-1	Low attack
5	(With Devout Beads) Crouching Ⓗ	4	79,500	13	4	26	—	-5	Low attack

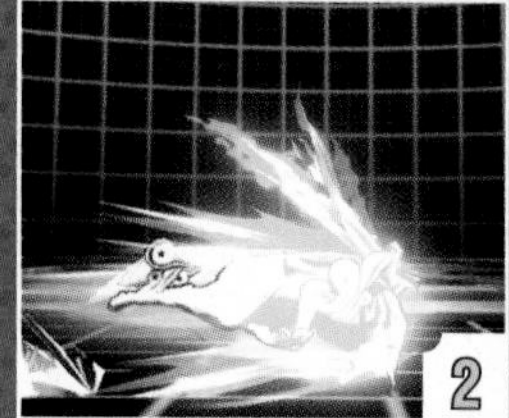

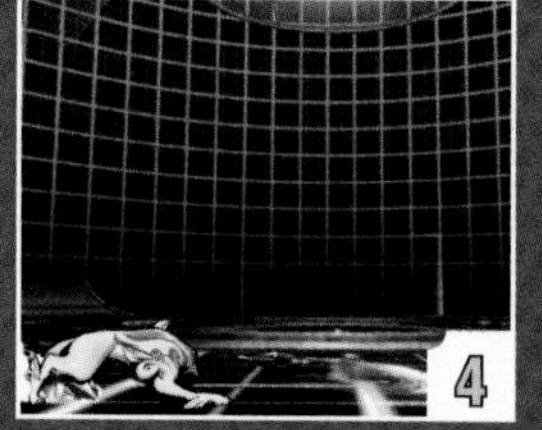

AERIAL BASIC ATTACKS

Screen	Command	Hits	Damage	Startup	Active	Recovery	Advantage on Hit	Advantage if Guarded	Notes
1	Air Ⓛ	1	35,000	4	4	14	—	—	Overhead attack
2	Air Ⓜ	1	48,000	7	3	20	—	—	Overhead attack
3	(With Solar Flare) Air Ⓗ	1	60,000	9	5	20	—	—	Overhead attack, chains into itself up to 3 times
4	(With Thunder Edge) Air Ⓗ	1	90,000	17	4	17	—	—	Overhead attack
5	(With Thunder Edge) hold air Ⓗ	1	110,000	36	4	17	—	—	Overhead attack, causes ground bounce on hit, does not use up ground bounce state if comboed into another hold air Ⓗ, unaffected by hitstun deterioration
6	(With Devout Beads) Air Ⓗ	4	79,500	18	5	18	—	—	Overhead attack
7	Air Ⓢ	1	70,000	11	3	22	—	—	Overhead attack, unrecoverable knockdown when used in air combo after Ⓢ launcher

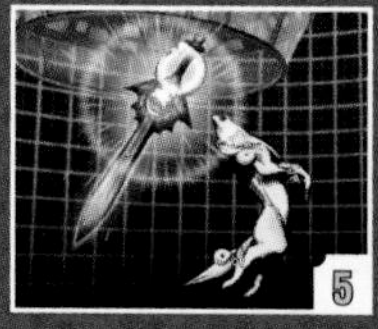

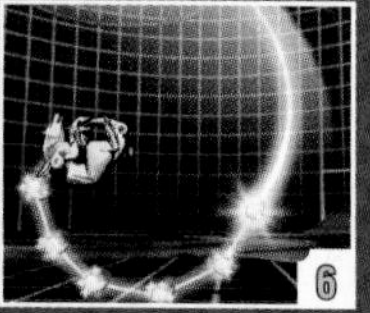

COMMAND ATTACKS

Screen	Command	Hits	Damage	Startup	Active	Recovery	Advantage on Hit	Advantage if Guarded	Notes
1	(With Solar Flare) ⇨ + Ⓗ Ⓗ Ⓗ Ⓗ Ⓗ	5	222,400	12	4 (11) 4 (11) 4 (11) 4 (11) 4	21	-1	-3	Chains into Ⓢ, unaffected by hitstun deterioration
2	(With Thunder Edge) ⇨ + Ⓗ Ⓗ Ⓗ Ⓗ	4	254,900	14	5 (14) 5 (14) 5 (14) 5	18	—	-1	Unaffected by hitstun deterioration
3	(With Thunder Edge) ⇨ + hold Ⓗ, hold Ⓗ, hold Ⓗ, hold Ⓗ	4	318,600	47	5 (46) 5 (46) 5 (46) 5	18	—	-1	All 4 hits cause stagger
4	(With Devout Beads) ⇨ + Ⓗ Ⓗ Ⓗ Ⓗ Ⓗ	20	163,900	17	5 (16) 5 (16) 5 (16) 5 (16) 5	23	—	-7	Knocks down
5	(With Thunder Edge, in air) ⇘ + Ⓗ	1	90,000	11	Until hit or grounded	43	—	—	OTG-capable, causes ground bounce on aerial or OTG hit, chains into TAC attack
6	(With Thunder Edge, in air) hold ⇘ + Ⓗ	1	120,000	43	Until hit or grounded	43	—	—	OTG-capable, causes ground bounce on aerial or OTG hit, chains into TAC attack

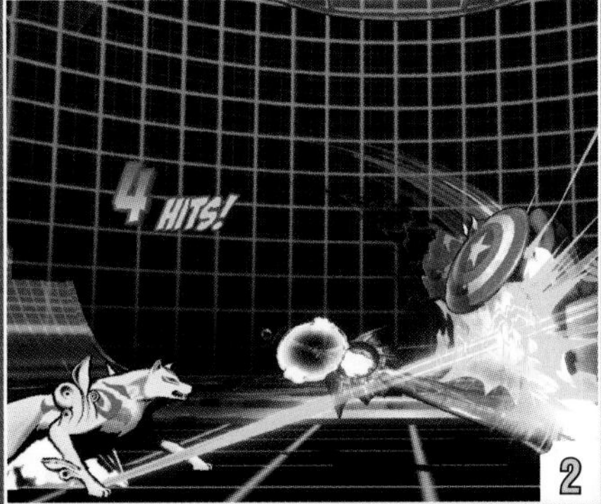

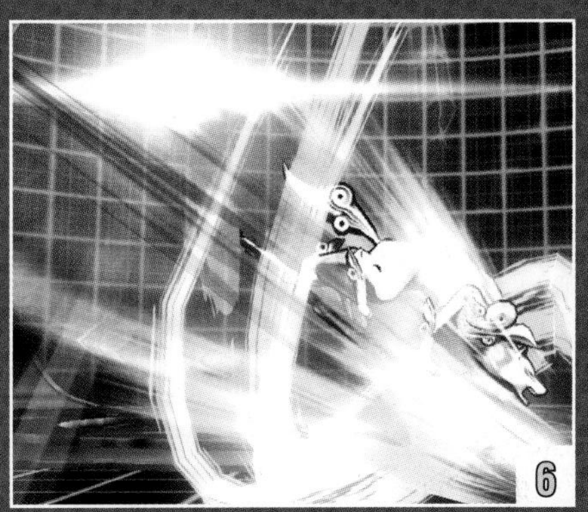

AMATERASU

AS A PARTNER-CROSSOVER ASSISTS

Screen	Type	P1+P2 Crossover Combination Hyper Combo	Description	Hits	Damage	Startup	Active	Recovery (this crossover assist)	Recovery (other partner)	Notes
1	α – Alpha	Okami Shuffle	Solar Flare	—	—	30	25	98	68	Nullifies certain beam attacks, reflects projectiles
2	β – Beta	Okami Shuffle	Cold Star	8	113,600	42	68	126	96	Each projectile has 1 durability point
3	γ – Gamma	Okami Shuffle	Bloom	—	—	25	—	181	151	Fills hyper combo gauge by 30%

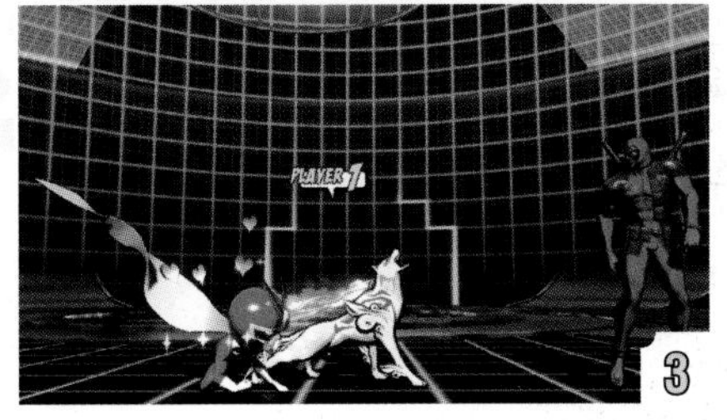

SPECIAL MOVES

Screen	Name	Command	Hits	Damage	Startup	Active	Recovery	Advantage on Hit	Advantage if Guarded	Notes
1	Head Charge L	(in air) ↓ ↘ → + (L)	1	70,000	13	15	13	—	—	—
2	Head Charge M	(in air) ↓ ↘ → + (M)	1	70,000	13	15	13	—	—	—
3	Head Charge H	(in air) ↓ ↘ → + (H)	1	70,000	18	Until hit or grounded	50	—	—	Causes ground bounce, causes Amaterasu to bounce upwards into the air in neutral state
4, 5, 6	Power Slash	↓ ↙ ← + ATK	1	80,000	10	—	26	+8	+6	Power Slash stun is not affected by hitstun deterioration, projectile has 1 low priority durability point
7	Weapon Change	↓ ↓ + ATK	—	—	10	—	—	—	—	The strength used determines what weapon you change to: (L) for Solar Flare, (M) for Thunder Edge, and (H) for Devout Beads
8	Fireworks	(With Solar Flare) → ↓ ↘ + (L) or (M)	—	150,000	6	15	7	—	—	The (L) version shifts into a counter throw if a mid or high attack makes contact with the shield, the (M) version counters low and mid attacks, holding the button increases its counter duration
9	Solar Flare	(With Solar Flare) → ↓ ↘ + (H)	1	—	3	21	4	—	—	Reflects projectiles, holding the button increases its duration
10, 11, 12	Thunder Edge (Can be charged)	(With Thunder Edge) ↓ ↘ → + ATK	1	100,000~ 150,000	12 (33 fully charged)	6	20	+1/—	-1/+1	Charging the attack improves damage and hitstun length, staggers opponent, causes spinning knockdown when fully charged
13	Glaive Chop	(In air, with Thunder Edge) ↓ ↘ → + (S)	8	88,600	21	Until hit or grounded*8	31	—	—	Resets the 1 ground bounce per combo rule, final hit causes spinning knockdown, projectile has 1 low priority durability point
14	Cold Star L	(With Devout Beads) ↓ ↘ → + (L)	1~8	20,000~ 113,600	13	—	23(33)	+1(-9)	-1(-11)	Each projectile has 1 low priority durability point
15	Cold Star M	(With Devout Beads) ↓ ↘ → + (M)	1~8	20,000~ 113,600	13	—	24(36)	+1(-9)	-1(-11)	Each projectile has 1 low priority durability point
16	Cold Star H	(With Devout Beads) ↓ ↘ → + (H)	1~8	20,000~ 113,600	18	—	33(31)	-10(-5)	-12(-9)	Each projectile has 1 low priority durability point

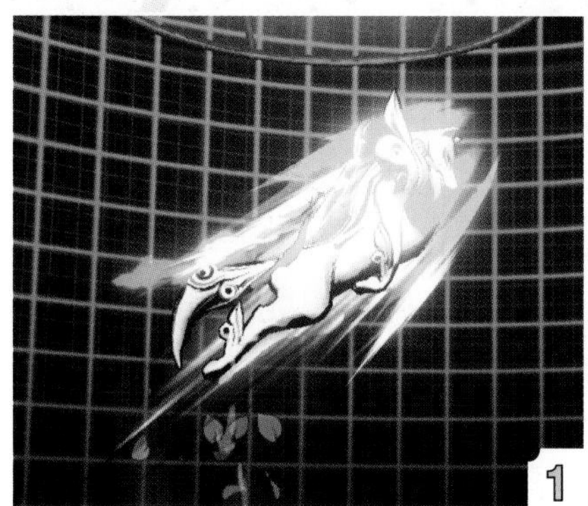
Head Charge L

Head Charge M

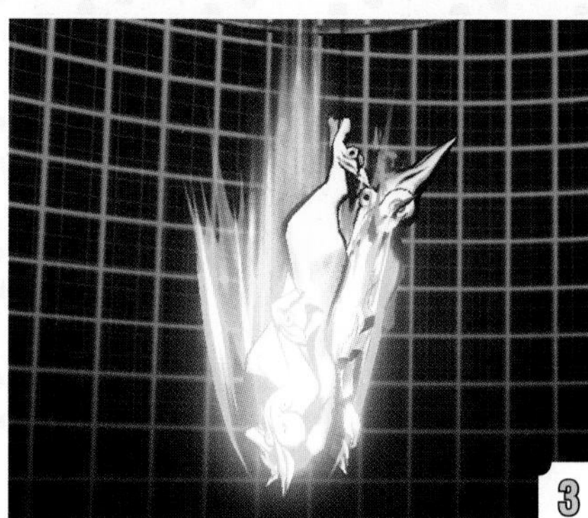
Head Charge H

Head Charge: This attack thrusts Amaterasu in various directions (depending on the strength of button used). It should be used to aggressively approach an opponent; Amaterasu's head has a giant hit box that's difficult to stop. The later it hits, the more frame advantage you have to work with. When it hits as late as possible, come out of the attack with air (L) to link into a combo.

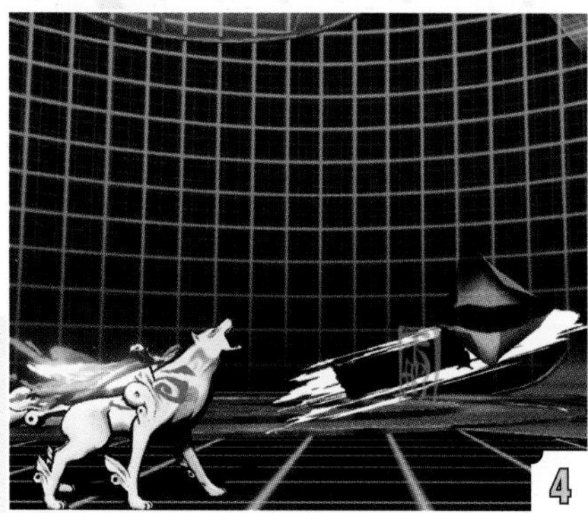
Power Slash L

Power Slash M

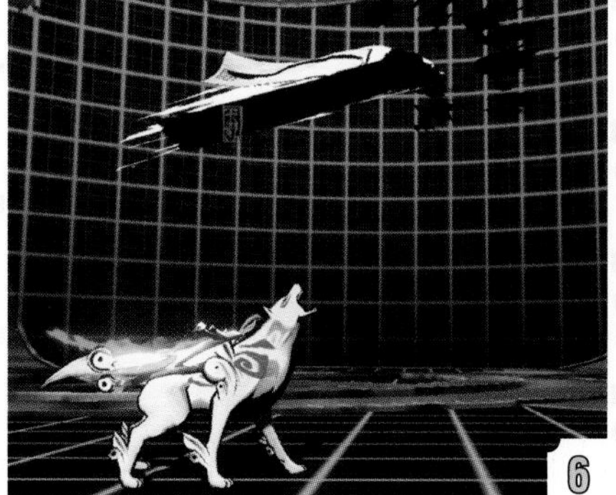
Power Slash H

Power Slash: Amaterasu swipes in front of her to summon a floating projectile. The button strength used determines where it appears. The (L) version is used for massive combos and as a frontal poking attack, while the (M) and (H) versions shield you against aerial attacks. Protecting yourself from aerial assaults is especially important when in Devout Beads mode, which relies on a long range offense that lacks anti-air. The projectile disappears if Amaterasu is hit, however, so it must make contact with the enemy. Finally, the Power Slash always leaves you at a frame advantage when blocked, so use it liberally at close distances.

Weapon Change: Inputting ↓ ↓ + (ATK) changes Amaterasu's weapon or "mode." The strength of button determines the mode: (L) for Solar Flare, (M) for Thunder Edge, and (H) for Devout Beads. The change duration is extremely fast—so quick that you can cancel into it from (M) or (H) basic attacks and then link afterwards. This is your primary method of changing modes at close distances. From afar, do ↓ ↙ ← + (H) to cover yourself, then change modes.

Fireworks: This shield counters attacks that make contact with it. The (L) version counters only high attacks, while the (M) version stops low-hitting moves. Upon activation it inflicts 150,000 damage and leaves the opposing character open for a combo. Even though the (M) version is not very useful, the (L) version is a very effective anti-air attack. Use it often if your opponent is reliant on airdashes to attack (like Morrigan, C. Viper, and Iron Man).

Solar Flare: A green version of Fireworks, this reflects projectiles. Beams and a few other unique projectiles do not reflect back, but are nullified entirely. This does not work against hyper combos of any sort.

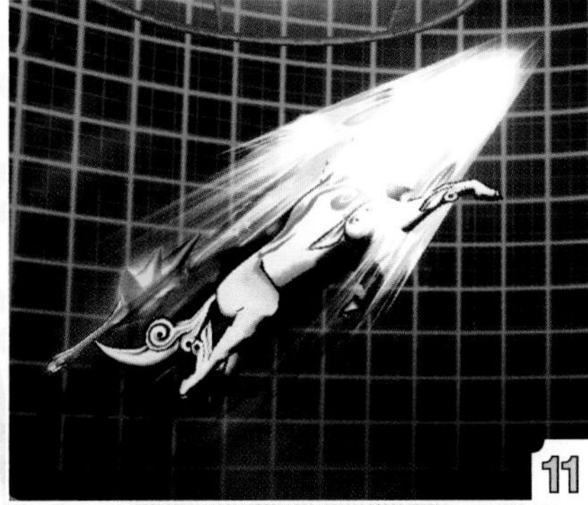

Thunder Edge L

Thunder Edge M

Thunder Edge H

Thunder Edge: Amaterasu charges forward with a sword swing. Thunder Edge L is used in both high damage combos and offensive patterns. Although it's -1 on guard normally, using it from a distance causes it to hit later than normal, leaving you at a 0~+4 advantage (the further away it hits, the more frame advantage you'll have). This is great for moving back into a threatening position after failed attacks. Thunder Edge M soars upwards at an angle, covering the sky from aerial attack. You can come out of it with air attacks shortly after the slash—a useful way of performing combos after countering a jump. Thunder Edge H shoots directly upwards, an odd option that's only useful against characters falling from super jump height on top of you.

All versions of the Thunder Edge can be charged by holding the attack button down after the command. This improves the damage and lengthens the hitstun it causes. The charging animations between each of the strengths looks identical. This is useful for hiding the version that you choose to use. If your opponent believes the charged (L) version is coming, charge Thunder Edge M instead, and release it if your foe tries to jump away.

Glaive Chop: This is primarily used in combos that involve air ↘ + (H), an OTG-capable dive attack that's cancelable into the Glaive Chop. It also resets the 1 ground bounce per combo rule on hit, allowing you to perform multiple bounces in a single combo. This is quite powerful when canceled into from air (L), an attack used right after leaving the ground as a quick overhead.

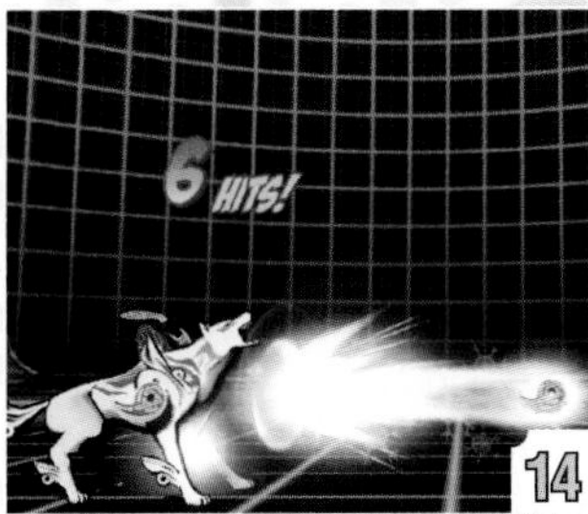

Cold Star L

Cold Star M

Cold Star H

Cold Star: Devout Beads Cold Star fires shots in various directions; ↓ ↘ → + (L) fires shots horizontally, ↓ ↘ → + (M) fires upward at an angle, and ↓ ↘ → + (H) causes Amaterasu to leap in the air before firing shots downward at a 45 degree angle. The (L) version is used to cover the ground, while (M) thwarts aerial attacks. The (H) variation stops ground-based projectiles by leaping over them before firing. This is a necessary tool, since the Cold Star has a low number of projectile points. This means that it can be easily nullified by many opposing projectiles if it is fired straight-on. All versions can fire up to 8 shots when the corresponding button is pressed repeatedly. The ability's recovery period increases drastically when firing more than one shot, so you should fire single shots unless you're certain it'll hit. On the rare occurrence that a full stream hits, cancel into the Okami Shuffle (↓ ↘ → + (ATK)(ATK)) for additional damage.

HYPER COMBOS

Screen	Name	Command	Hits	Damage	Startup	Active	Recovery	Advantage on Hit	Advantage if Guarded	Notes
1	Okami Shuffle (in air OK)	↓↘→ + ATK ATK	35	311,600	18+4	25 (20) 30 (22) 88	5	—	+1	Knocks down, projectile 1 (fire) has 10 high priority durability points, Each projectile 2 (ice) has 3 high priority durability points, each projectile 3 (lightning) has 5 high priority durability points
2	Vale of Mist (in air OK)	↓↙← + ATK ATK	—	—	20+3	—	28	—	—	Slows enemy movement speed by 25%, effect lasts for 300 frames
3	Divine Instruments (level 3 hyper combo)	→↓↘ + ATK ATK	25	400,000	8+2	15	35	—	-28	19 frames invincibility, unaffected by damage scaling, knocks down opponent

Okami Shuffle: Even though it is mostly used for combos, the Okami Shuffle covers the entire screen, making it useful for quickly inflicting damage to assists on reaction to their appearance. This attack is also completely safe if guarded, removing any worry of randomly using it.

Vale of Mist: Upon activation, the Vale of Mist slows the opposing character's actions, crushing their ability to fend off your attacks. This also allows for extended combos because of their slowed hitstun recovery. Take caution, Vale of Mist has a heavy starting period. You should shield its activation by using an assist or super canceling into it from a Ⓜ or Ⓗ Power Slash.

Divine Instruments: As a level 3 hyper combo that inflicts heavy damage, Divine Instruments is good for last ditch comebacks. It also has a heavy window of invulnerability, making it viable for countering jump-in attacks.

BATTLE PLAN

OVERVIEW

VITALITY: 800,000

CHAIN COMBO ARCHETYPE: MARVEL SERIES

X-Factor	Lv.1	Lv.2	Lv.3
Damage	120%	140%	150%
Speed	100%	100%	100%

Amaterasu is a well-rounded character that can fight from any position in any manner; short range bombardment, long range run away—you want it, she's got it. There's a clear standout strength amongst these capabilities, however; her short range, anti-advancing guard pressure. Because of this, your goal with Amaterasu is to push the opposing character to the corner. A cornered opponent has less means to escape her frame advantage-heavy offense.

This strategy is effective because:

- Many of Amaterasu's key attacks either leave her at a frame advantage or allow for jump canceling. Both are used to stay on top of a foe even when they use advancing guard.
- Her forward airdash has a *massive* travel distance, giving her a quick way of moving in when she's pushed away.
- All of her most flexible attack options lead to far more damage when near a corner.

This goal is accomplished by:

- Repeatedly attacking with the forward-moving standing Ⓜ.
- Cutting off enemy mobility with assists and Devout Beads ranged attacks.
- Airdashing over an opponent's ground attacks.
- Using Head Charge M or Thunder Edge L to move in.

ON THE GROUND

Standing Ⓜ is absurdly powerful. Abuse it!

Power Slash M or H should always be set whenever there's a lull in the action.

Amaterasu has three weapons to change between. Your ground game strategy relies on switching between these weapons based on your position. Solar Flare is your base weapon—a simplified collection of close range options that are effective against advancing guard usage. The cornerstone of your offense is standing Ⓜ, a lunging head charge that leaves you with frame advantage whenever it's guarded from a distance. This attack is barely pushed away when advancing guard is used, especially near corners where it can be done repeatedly without the fear of losing momentum. It's possible to link into **Combo I** if it hits from a distance, increasing its value even further. When your opponent doesn't attempt to push you away, use the advantage to attack with **Combo I** or **Combo IV**. A jump is the only thing that can safely deal with this tactic, so ready an air throw when you read their intentions. Standing Ⓗ should also be used to supplement standing Ⓜ. In rare cases where standing Ⓜ hits too closely (leaving you at a -1 frame disadvantage), chain into standing Ⓗ to thwart an incoming attack. If it hits, link afterwards with **Combo I.** When guarded, use the frame advantage to attack again, or cancel into a jump and airdash forward to deal with advancing guard attempts.

Solar Flare is the only weapon mode with consistent defensive options. Fireworks raises a shield that deflects incoming physical attacks; the Ⓛ version counters high attacks, while the Ⓜ version stops low strikes. The Ⓜ variation works great as an anti-air, leading to heavy damage on a successful deflection (**Combo V**). The heavy use of Power Slash (↓↙← + ATK) is also needed to shield Amaterasu from harm. The initial slash animation is fast, allowing you to easily vary between the Ⓜ and Ⓗ versions to stop an air assault even from close distances. Use the Ⓛ version to stop frontal movement, and the Ⓜ and Ⓗ versions to shield against air attacks.

The Thunder Edge mode is often used at mid range. Its jump-crushing standing Ⓗ and the ranged Thunder Edge special attack (↓↘→ + ATK) are both useful from this position. When done from a distance, ↓↘→ + Ⓛ leaves you at a frame advantage. This is the backbone of your Thunder Edge offense. Whenever a failed attack is blocked, cancel into ↓↘→ + Ⓛ to move right back into close range again. If your opponent doesn't push you away with advancing guard, Thunder Edge's oddly powerful short range mix-up comes into play: attack with the low-hitting **Combo II**, throw (**Combo IV**), or perform an immediate air Ⓛ just as you leave the ground with a jump, and transition into **Combo VI**.

The Devout Beads weapon is predominantly used from long distances. Controlling your opponent's position is the key to using it properly, but it's difficult to protect yourself from aerial attacks. Fortify your strategy by using ↓↙← + Ⓜ or Ⓗ to shield your head. Once the projectile is floating above you, mount your attack by eliminating your foe's paths of travel. Devout Beads standing Ⓗ is used to stop forward ground movement. If it hits your challenger, chain into crouching Ⓗ. Against enemies who try to move backwards to avoid standing Ⓗ, dash forward and attack with crouching Ⓗ to catch them standing. If your foe ever accidentally misses a big attack from a distance, punish them with → + ⒽⒽⒽⒽⒽ. Mix in upward Cold Star shots (↓↘→ + Ⓜ) to combat distant jumps; use a single shot if you're uncertain of your opponent's intentions (it has a faster recovery period), or multiple shots when you're certain your foe will attack from the air. Fire the horizontal Cold Star when you're certain your opponent will stay grounded or attack with something slow. This pushes your foe towards the corner while inflicting heavy damage. If it happens to hit, cancel into ↓↘→ + ATK ATK to tack on even more!

If your challenger ever hesitates to attack when you're using Devout Beads, dash in and strike with standing Ⓜ. Cancel it into ↓↓ + Ⓛ or Ⓗ to transition into one of your short range weapons. You're left at a frame advantage in either case, so mount an attack if guarded, or shift into **Combo I or II** when it connects. Methodically switching between modes like this must be learned in order to attack effectively.

UP IN THE AIR

Amaterasu's airdash travels great lengths. Use it when covered by an assist to attack from long distances.

The Head Charge keeps you mobile when in the air.

Amaterasu's forward airdash command (→→ or ATK ATK) can be held to travel across the majority of the playing field. This works wonders with your anti-advancing guard strategy, since you can always catch up to your foe regardless of how far away they are. This is also useful for escaping corners. Whenever there's a gap in your adversary's offense, super jump and airdash to the other end of the screen. When offensively airdashing forward against advancing guard attempts, stop the dash before passing over your challenger to attack from the front, or fly over the opposing character's head and attack their back. Solar Flare's air Ⓗ is great for this tactic because it crosses up! Thunder Edge's air Ⓗ has a giant attack arc that also acts as a cross-up, but its lengthy wind-up time forces you to use it very early during a jump.

When you are on defense, use the Devout Beads to control airspace while staying mobile. Air Ⓗ is a cancelable attack with a giant area of effect. You can cancel it into ↓↘→ + Ⓛ or Ⓗ to cut its recovery animation into a forward or upward air movement, which can then be followed by another air Ⓗ or Head Charge. Head Charges are great for avoiding enemy attacks, or to strike at jumps performed from a distance.

The ↘ + ATK ATK version of the air dash is mostly a short range tool. Performing this move just as you leave the ground allows for quick overhead attacks that are difficult to defend against. Once airborne, attack with air Ⓛ, Ⓛ, Ⓜ, or perform a late whiffed air Ⓢ and throw as you land. Air Ⓛ x2 hits enemies who guard low after the first air Ⓛ in anticipation of a low combo.

COMBO USAGE

I. SOLAR FLARE CR. Ⓛ, ST. Ⓜ, ST. Ⓗ CANCEL ⇒ → + ⒽⒽⒽⒽⒽ CANCEL ⇒ Ⓢ CANCEL ⇒ SUPER JUMP, AIR Ⓜ, Ⓜ, Ⓗ, Ⓗ, Ⓗ CANCEL ⇒ ↓ ↘ → + Ⓗ, LAND, Ⓢ CANCEL ⇒ SUPER JUMP, Ⓜ, Ⓗ, Ⓗ, Ⓗ, Ⓢ

(370,000 damage) This is Solar Flare's main mid-screen combo. After the first launch, perform the air Ⓜ, Ⓜ chain slightly late during the jump to avoid passing over the enemy. Against middle sized characters like Captain America, Doctor Doom, Chris, Wesker, Ryu, etc., you can tack on additional damage by canceling the final hit of → + ⒽⒽⒽⒽⒽ into ↓ ↙ ← + Ⓛ. After the projectile hits, link into standing Ⓜ, Ⓢ to continue the combo. Near corners this combo's size increases immensely (see Combo Appendix).

When the first two hits of this chain are guarded, throw when you recover, or chain into a delayed standing Ⓗ to counterhit enemy attempts to stick out an attack (if it hits, link into **Combo I**). If standing Ⓗ is guarded, use the frame advantage (+2) to attack with **Combo I** again, or cancel it into a forward jump and perform an immediate ↘ + ATK ATK airdash and attack with air Ⓛ.

Countering advancing guard is dependant on what attack your challenger uses it against. If they push crouching Ⓛ away (a rare occurrence), cancel the whiffed standing Ⓜ into → ↓ ↘ + Ⓛ or Ⓜ to stop incoming low or mid attacks. When your opponent uses advancing guard against standing Ⓜ, dash forward and attack with standing Ⓜ again (near corners you don't even need to dash!). If your foe pushes away standing Ⓗ, jump cancel the move and immediately airdash forward to stay on top of them if they push you away. This type of lateral airdashing just off the ground is often called box jumping, or square jumping.

II. THUNDER EDGE CR. Ⓛ, CR. Ⓜ, CR. Ⓗ CANCEL ⇒ ↓ ↘ → + Ⓛ, ST. Ⓛ, ST. Ⓜ, ST. Ⓗ CANCEL ⇒ ↓ ↘ → + Ⓛ, ST. Ⓜ CANCEL ⇒ Ⓢ CANCEL ⇒ SUPER JUMP, AIR Ⓜ, Ⓜ, Ⓢ, ↘ + Ⓗ CANCEL ⇒ ↓ ↘ → + Ⓢ (2 HITS) CANCEL ⇒ ↓ ↘ → + ATK ATK

(570,900 damage) The juggle after the first ↓ ↘ → + Ⓛ is relatively difficult; do standing Ⓛ just before your foe hits the ground. After air Ⓢ knocks your opponent down during the launcher segment, the next ↘ + Ⓗ isn't canceled into from Ⓢ; simply do it when you recover. Additional damage can be added to this combo near corners (see Combo Appendix).

III. DEVOUT BEADS CR. Ⓛ, CR. Ⓛ, ST. Ⓜ CANCEL ⇒ ↓ ↓ + Ⓜ, THUNDER EDGE CR. Ⓛ, CR. Ⓜ, CR. Ⓗ CANCEL ⇒ ↓ ↘ → + Ⓛ, ST. Ⓛ, ST. Ⓜ, ST. Ⓗ CANCEL ⇒ ↓ ↘ → + Ⓛ, ST. Ⓜ CANCEL ⇒ Ⓢ CANCEL ⇒ SUPER JUMP, AIR Ⓜ, Ⓜ, Ⓢ, ↘ + Ⓗ CANCEL ⇒ ↓ ↘ → + Ⓢ (2 HITS) CANCEL ⇒ ↓ ↘ → + ATK ATK

(496,600 damage) After the weapon change to Thunder Edge, do the follow-up crouching Ⓛ as fast as possible to keep the combo going. If the opening three attacks are guarded, cancel into Cold Star L to push your challenger away, or cancel into Thunder Edge and strike with either **Combo II**, **Combo V**, or **Combo VIII**.

IV. SOLAR FLARE CR. Ⓜ, ST. Ⓗ, CR. Ⓗ CANCEL ⇒ ↓ ↓ + Ⓜ, THUNDER EDGE ST. Ⓜ, ST. Ⓗ CANCEL ⇒ ↓ ↘ → + Ⓛ, ST. Ⓜ, ST. Ⓗ CANCEL ⇒ ↓ ↘ → + Ⓛ, ST. Ⓜ, Ⓢ CANCEL ⇒ SUPER JUMP, AIR Ⓜ, Ⓜ, Ⓢ, ↘ + Ⓗ CANCEL ⇒ ↓ ↘ → + Ⓢ

(430,400 damage) Use this combo to transition from Solar Flare into Thunder Edge's heavier damage output. After the weapon change, perform Thunder Edge's standing Ⓜ as soon as possible to continue the combo. When blocked, cancel Solar Flare's standing or crouching Ⓗ into a box jump.

V. FORWARD THROW, (SOLAR FLARE DASH FORWARD Ⓜ, Ⓢ CANCEL ⇒ SUPER JUMP, AIR Ⓜ, Ⓜ, Ⓗ, Ⓗ, Ⓗ CANCEL ⇒ ↓ ↘ → + Ⓗ, LAND, Ⓢ CANCEL ⇒ SUPER JUMP, AIR Ⓜ ,Ⓗ, Ⓗ, Ⓗ, Ⓢ) *OR* (THUNDER EDGE DASH FORWARD Ⓜ, Ⓢ CANCEL ⇒ SUPER JUMP, AIR Ⓜ, Ⓜ, Ⓢ, ↘ + Ⓗ CANCEL ⇒ ↓ ↘ → + Ⓢ CANCEL ⇒ ↓ ↘ → + ATK ATK)

(224,100 or 399,600 damage) This combo only works if you perform a forward throw (→ + Ⓗ). Throwing your opponent the opposite direction tosses them too far away to juggle with the dashing Ⓜ. If you use a back throw instead, do ↓ ↘ → + ATK ATK when Amaterasu recovers for easy damage.

VI. FORWARD AIR THROW, ↓ ↘ → + ATK ATK

(306,400 damage) Though simplistic, this is an easy way to add damage to a successful air throw. It's possible to do the longer combos shown in **Combo V** instead, but the throw must be done at a low altitude or near a corner.

VII. SOLAR FLARE → ↓ ↘ + Ⓛ VS. A JUMPING ATTACK (OR → ↓ ↘ + Ⓜ VS. A LOW ATTACK), ↓ ↘ → + ATK ATK

(395,000 damage) Perform this combo when you manage to land the Fireworks counter. There's not much to it, when Amaterasu recovers after bouncing your foe off of the ground, input ↓ ↘ → + ATK ATK.

VIII. THUNDER EDGE INSTANT AIR Ⓛ CANCEL ⇒ ↘ + Ⓗ CANCEL ⇒ ↓ ↘ → + Ⓢ, ST. Ⓜ, ST. Ⓗ CANCEL ⇒ ↓ ↘ → + Ⓛ, Ⓜ, Ⓢ CANCEL ⇒ SUPER JUMP, AIR Ⓜ, Ⓜ, Ⓢ, ↘ + Ⓗ CANCEL ⇒ ↓ ↘ → + Ⓢ CANCEL ⇒ ↓ ↘ → + ATK ATK

(488,200 damage) The opening jumping Ⓛ is supposed to be done the absolute second you leave the ground for a jump, making it useful as a very fast overhead as close range. ↘ + Ⓗ must be canceled into ↓ ↘ → + Ⓢ as fast as possible for the combo to work. If your opponent pushes air Ⓛ or ↘ + Ⓗ away with advancing guard, cancel the missed ↘ + Ⓗ into air ↓ ↘ → + Ⓜ. This moves you back into short range behind frame advantage (attack with air Ⓛ or land and throw as you recover from the charge).

ASSISTS

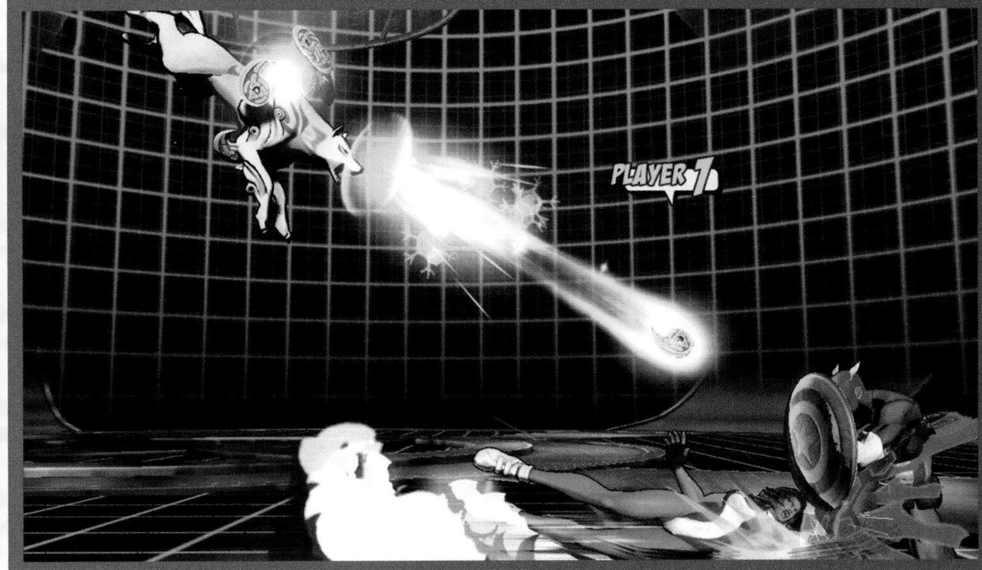

Keep the enemy pinned with an assist!

Amaterasu needs multi-hit assists to cover approaches and to help push a challenger to a corner. Dante—γ Weasel Shot, Arthur—β Dagger Toss, and Sentinel—α Sentinel Force are all good for this. Weasel Shot and Dagger Toss are especially effective when used with Divine Beads, which allow you to combo after its standing H and ⇨ + H H H H H attacks. Call the assist just before doing standing H, or call it during the last hit of ⇨ + H H H H H to enable you to dash forward and link into M, S.

Both β Cold Star and γ Bloom have uses when Amaterasu is used as an assist. Cold Star is considered ideal for aggressive characters that need an assist to keep an enemy pinned (Dante, C. Viper, Iron Man, Wesker, X-23 and Morrigan make great use of it). Bloom fills your hyper combo gauge by about 30%, which is useful for characters that are reliant on meter usage (like Trish, Storm and Sentinel). Amaterasu's α Solar Flare reflects non-hyper combo projectiles, a trait that's rarely useful in most circumstances.

ADVANCED TACTICS

HYPER COMBO USAGE

Blast assists with Okami Shuffle!

Both of Amaterasu's level 1 hyper combos are fantastic. The Okami Shuffle, outside of its uses in combos, fills the screen with a completely safe barrage of projectiles. This is extremely useful for reacting to assist calls and damaging them from any position!

The Vale of Mist crushes your opponent's game plan by slowing their actions down by 25%. This makes it difficult for them to stop your offense while also lengthening the types of combos you can do. This is especially powerful with a last ditch X-Factor activation, which improves your chances of scoring a hit. Finally, you can cancel team hyper combos into the Vale of Mist to perform extended combos. For example, perform Trish's Round Harvest, then team hyper combo into the Vale of Mist. From there, dash forward and start hitting your foe. It works the other way around too—activate Vale of Mist, then cancel into Felicia's Kitty's Helper hyper combo. Not only will your foe have a world of difficulty stopping Felicia's leaping cat offense, but she can do combos she couldn't do before (for example, she can link up to seven of her → ↓ ↘ + L attacks in a row)!

COMBO APPENDIX

GENERAL EXECUTION TIPS

After launching the enemy with (S), start your air combo early during the jump if the enemy is cornered. When in the middle of the screen, wait until you've glided up to the enemy to ensure hits don't miss.

Requirements (Position, meter, etc.)	Notes	Command Sequence	Damage
Starts in Solar Flare mode. Requires corner	Does not work against X-23	St. (M), st. (H) CANCEL ⇩⇙⇦ + (L), St. (M), st. (H) CANCEL ⇩⇙⇦ + (L), St. (M), st. (H), ⇨ + (H)(H)(H)(H)(H) CANCEL ⇩⇙⇦ + (L), (S) CANCEL super jump, air (M), (M), (H), (H), (H) CANCEL ⇩⇘⇨ + (H), land, (S) CANCEL super jump, air (M), (M), (H), (H), (H), (S)	482,600
Starts in Thunder Edge mode. Requires corner. Requires 2 hyper combo gauge bars	In air ⇩⇘⇨ + (S) must hit 3 times after ⇘ + (H). This causes a spinning stun state to occur, resetting the 1 OTG rule for the follow-up ground hit. It's possible to do up to three Okami Shuffles in one combo with this method, but it's very difficult!	Cr. (L), cr. (M), cr. (H) CANCEL ⇩⇘⇨ + (L), st. (L), st. (M), st. (H) CANCEL ⇩⇘⇨ + (L), st. (M) CANCEL (S) CANCEL super jump, air (M), (M), (S), ⇘ + (H) CANCEL ⇩⇘⇨ + (S) (2 hits) CANCEL ⇩⇘⇨ + ATK ATK, air ⇘ + (H) CANCEL ⇩⇘⇨ + (S) (1 hit) CANCEL ⇩⇘⇨ + ATK ATK	706,500
Starts in Thunder Edge mode. Requires corner. Requires 2 hyper combo gauge bars	After the ground throw, perform the first ⇩⇘⇨ + (L) slightly late. If you instead start with an air throw, perform ⇩⇘⇨ + (L) as fast as possible	Throw or air throw, Thunder Edge ⇩⇘⇨ + (L), st. (M) CANCEL ⇩⇘⇨ + (L), (M) CANCEL ⇩⇘⇨ + (L), (M), (S) CANCEL super jump, air (M), (M), (S), ⇘ + (H) CANCEL ⇩⇘⇨ + (S) CANCEL ⇩⇘⇨ + ATK ATK, air ⇘ + (H) CANCEL ⇩⇘⇨ + (S) CANCEL ⇩⇘⇨ + ATK ATK	588,900
Starts in Solar Flare mode. Requires corner. Requires 2 hyper combo bars	Combo must be started early after Vale of Mist activation	Activate Vale of Mist, cr. (M), st. (H) CANCEL ⇩⇙⇦ + (L), dash forward, st. (M), st. (H) CANCEL ⇩⇙⇦ + (L), dash forward, st. (M), st. (H) CANCEL ⇩⇙⇦ + (L), dash forward, st. (M), st. (H) CANCEL ⇩⇙⇦ + (L), dash forward, st. (M), st. (H) CANCEL ⇨ + (H)(H)(H)(H)(H), (S) CANCEL super jump, air (M), (M), (H), (H), (H), (S), land, ⇩⇩ + (M), Thunder Edge air ⇘ + (H) CANCEL (S) CANCEL ⇩⇘⇨ + ATK ATK	661,300
Starts in Solar Flare mode. Requires corner. Requires 2 hyper combo gauge bars	After causing the flying screen with Solar Flare's air (S), land, quickly switch to Thunder Edge, then jump and perform ⇘ + (H) as close the ground as possible.	St. (M), st. (H) CANCEL ⇩⇙⇦ + (L), St. (M), st. (H) CANCEL ⇩⇙⇦ + (L), St. (M), st. (H), ⇨ + (H)(H)(H)(H)(H) CANCEL ⇩⇙⇦ + (L), (S) CANCEL super jump, air (M), (M), (H), (H), (H), (S), land, ⇩⇩ + (M), Thunder Edge air ⇘ + (H) CANCEL ⇩⇘⇨ + (S) (3 hits) CANCEL ⇩⇘⇨ + ATK ATK, air ⇘ + (H) CANCEL ⇩⇘⇨ + (S) (1 hit) CANCEL ⇩⇘⇨ + ATK ATK	740,200
Starts in Thunder Edge mode. Requires corner, level 1 X-factor, and 1 hyper combo gauge bar	—	Cr. (L), st. (M), st. (H) CANCEL ⇩⇘⇨ + (L) X-FACTOR cr. (M), cr. (H) CANCEL ⇩⇘⇨ + (L), st. (L), st. (M), st. (H) CANCEL ⇩⇘⇨ + (L), st. (M) CANCEL (S) CANCEL super jump, air (M), (M), (S), ⇘ + (H) CANCEL ⇩⇘⇨ + (S) (2 hits) CANCEL ⇩⇘⇨ + ATK ATK, air ⇘ + (H) CANCEL ⇩⇘⇨ + (S)	1,119,300
Starts in Solar Flare mode, requires corner, requires 1 hyper combo gauge bar	After the first launch with (S), allow air (S) to fully recover, then OTG with air ⇘ + (H), ⇘ + (H) must be canceled into ⇩ + (S) just before the blade hits the ground, this causes the inital TAC attack to whiff, and then the TAC explosion hits soon after, after landing fromm the missed TAC, you must then juggle with another (S) launcher before the explosion knocks the opponent to the ground to create the ground bounce state, this ensures that you can continue to hit with multiple TACs	St. (M), st. (H) CANCEL ⇩⇙⇦ + (L), st. (M), st. (H) CANCEL ⇩⇙⇦ + (L), st. (M), st. (H), ⇨ + (H)(H)(H)(H)(H) CANCEL ⇩⇩ + (M), (Thunder Edge (S) CANCEL forward super jump, early air (S), ⇘ + (H) (allow blade to almost hit ground) CANCEL ⇩ + (S) TAC whiff, flames hit) x 3 additional times, ⇩⇙⇦ + ATK ATK, vertical jump, early air (H) (hold), land, vertical jump, early air (H) (hold), land, vertical jump, early air (H) (hold), land, vertical jump, early air (H) (hold), land, ⇩⇘⇨ + ATK ATK	726,100

"AMMY! CHILL OUT! DON'T YOU KNOW IT'S BAD TO BITE PEOPLE WHO ARE DOWN ON THEIR LUCK?"

SIR ARTHUR...
IS READY TO DO BATTLE!

ARTHUR

BIO

REAL NAME

ARTHUR

OCCUPATION

KNIGHT

ABILITIES

CAN RAPIDLY HURL SPEARS, SWORDS, ETC. TOWARD HIS ENEMIES. WHEN WEARING GOLD ARMOR, HE GAINS THE ABILITY TO USE MAGIC.

WEAPONS

HIS INVENTORY INCLUDES LARGE LANCES, SWORDS, FIRE BOTTLES, BOMBS, BOOMERANG SCYTHES, THE SWALLOW BLADE, VINE WHIPS, ETC.

PROFILE

THE LEGENDARY KNIGHT WHO JUMPED INTO THE DEMON WORLD ALL BY HIMSELF TO SAVE THE PRINCESS WHO HAD BEEN KIDNAPPED BY SATAN. WHILE BEST KNOWN FOR HIS DAUNTLESS COURAGE IN THE FACE OF TERRIFYING MONSTERS AND LIFE-THREATENING TRAPS, HE ALSO ENJOYS WEARING STRAWBERRY-PRINT BOXER SHORTS. THOUGH HE LOOKS LIKE AN OLD MAN, HE'S REALLY ONLY 28 YEARS OLD.

FIRST APPEARANCE

GHOSTS 'N GOBLINS (1985)

POWER GRID

4	INTELLIGENCE
5	STRENGTH
3	SPEED
2	STAMINA
5	ENERGY PROJECTION
6	FIGHTING ABILITY

*This is biographical, and does not represent an evaluation of the character's in-game combat potential.

ALTERNATE COSTUMES

PS3: ⓧ Xbox 360: Ⓐ

PS3: ▢ Xbox 360: Ⓧ

PS3: △ Xbox 360: Ⓨ

PS3: R1 Xbox 360: RB

ATTACK SET

STANDING BASIC ATTACKS

Screen	Command	Hits	Damage	Startup	Active	Recovery	Advantage on Hit	Advantage if Guarded	Notes
1	Standing Ⓛ	1	30,000	6	3	11	0	-1	—
2	Standing Ⓜ	1	48,000	12	3	23	-5	-7	Has autoguard property versus mid/high attacks throughout active frames
3	Standing Ⓗ	1	65,000	14	5	22	-3	-5	⇩ ⬂ ⇨ + P1 or P2 snap back
4	Ⓢ	1	70,000	9	4	31	—	-13	Launcher attack, not special- or hyper combo-cancelable

1

2

3

4

CROUCHING BASIC ATTACKS

Screen	Command	Hits	Damage	Startup	Active	Recovery	Advantage on Hit	Advantage if Guarded	Notes
1	Crouching Ⓛ	1	28,000	7	2	12	0	-1	Low attack
2	Crouching Ⓜ	1	45,000	10	3	22	-4	-6	Low attack
3	Crouching Ⓗ	1	63,000	15	4	24	—	-6	Low attack, knocks down

1

2

3

AERIAL BASIC ATTACKS

Screen	Command	Hits	Damage	Startup	Active	Recovery	Notes
1	Air Ⓛ	1	30,000	7	9	10	Overhead attack
2	Air Ⓜ	1	47,000	9	3	22	Overhead attack
3	Air Ⓗ	1	63,000	11	5	20	Overhead attack
4	Air Ⓢ	1	65,000	12	Until grounded	5	Overhead attack, causes flying screen if used in launcher combo

1

2

3

4

UP IN THE AIR

Arthur's aerial movement options leave much to be desired. His jump is very slow and floaty, making each jump something of a commitment. The only way to alter Arthur's jump trajectory is by using a double jump, which puts you in another floaty jump.

Besides the "wall" tactics explained in the On the Ground section, Arthur doesn't have very many reasons to be in the air. In dire situations that require you to attack your opponent, jumping or super jumping toward them with Air Fire Bottle Toss can be a safe and effective way to get some offensive momentum going. If guarded, this can be followed with the ground version of Fire Bottle Toss, then Lance Toss to do a large amount of chip damage while pushing your opponent back towards the corner.

If you're in a tough situation and need to start attacking your opponent, super jumping forward and using Air Fire Bottle Toss is a good way to get your offense started.

While in Golden Armor state, Air Scatter Crossbow can be used to safely attack an opponent from super jump height.

While in Golden Armor state, Air Scatter Crossbow is a great way to attack your opponent while jumping forwards or backwards. Super jumping towards your opponent with Air Scatter Crossbow is much more difficult to avoid than Air Fire Bottle Toss, but the frame advantage afterwards is much lower. Air Ⓢ is one of the more interesting options available to you should you need to attack—it attacks very far below Arthur and is difficult to anti-air. Depending on the timing and distance, it can also cross up opponents if it is set up correctly!

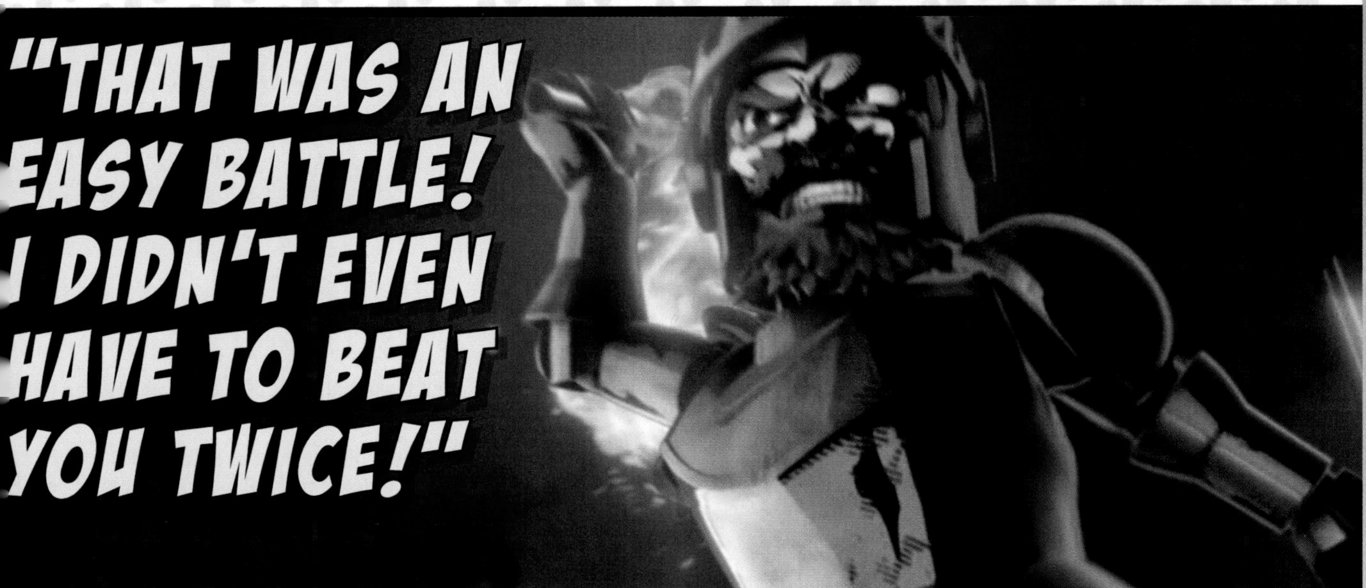

"THAT WAS AN EASY BATTLE! I DIDN'T EVEN HAVE TO BEAT YOU TWICE!"

ARTHUR

ASSISTS

Any long ranged crossover assist is a huge boon for Arthur's zoning game.

Air throws are a critical part of defense, and Deadpool—β is the only OTG-capable crossover assist fast enough to consistently combo after Arthur's air throws.

Haggar—α is completely invincible and can interrupt offensive opponents for a free combo.

Arthur has two crossover assist types that are exceptional: Fire Bottle Toss is OTG-capable, but is typically too slow to be used after most flying screen combos. However, the flames are great for pinning opponents down in a huge amount of guardstun, allowing for very easy offense. This assist gets considerably stronger if Arthur is in Golden Armor state; hitstun and guardstun become much longer, and the flames are still created even if the bottle hits an opponent directly.

Dagger Toss is easily the recommended crossover assist type to use—it is one of the best all-around assist types in the game, a long-ranged crossover assist that inflicts a lot of hitstun and guardstun to opponents, and doesn't cause major damage scaling in combos. Arthur—β can be used as a dedicated assist character on many teams.

As for assists that compliment Arthur's game, any long ranged crossover assist will fill that role nicely. Of course, the better long ranged assists like Doctor Doom—α and powered-up Zero—β are preferable, but anything at all that puts more projectiles on the screen is a huge boon.

Combining long ranged crossover assists with "wall" tactics can be incredibly difficult for an opponent to penetrate without first taking massive amounts of chip damage!

Air throws are critical for any defensive character, so assists that allow you to combo from air throws make a huge difference. The only OTG-capable assist fast enough to consistently hit after Arthur's air throws is Deadpool—β. Even though Deadpool's role is extremely specialized, he greatly increases Arthur's damage output and gives you one more strong way to push your way out of the corner!

Since Arthur is at his weakest when enemies are up close and applying pressure, the invincible Double Lariat of Haggar—α can be a huge deterrent for opponents attacking at close range. If the Double Lariat hits, you can easily start a combo afterwards starting from a Fire Bottle Toss OTG hit.

ADVANCED TACTICS

EXPLOITING SHIELD DEFLECT HITBOXES

Shield Deflect has absolutely no vulnerable hitboxes behind Arthur. Use it to nullify cross-up mix-ups!

Shield Deflect has one strange property—Arthur has no vulnerable hitboxes behind him all the way until he recovers! This can be used against characters with side-switching mix-ups like Wolverine. If Wolverine crosses Arthur up with Berserker Slash while Shield Deflect is active, the attack will whiff completely! While Shield Deflect has too much recovery time to punish Wolverine afterward, you can effectively nullify the mix-up if you know it is coming. If Wolverine stays in front of you with Berserker Slash, your opponent will trigger the counter and allow for a combo!

INSTANT OVERHEAD AIR (S)

If you absolutely have to make some offense happen, instant overhead air (S) is about the only scary thing Arthur has.

Making comebacks with Arthur can be very difficult, especially if the time on the clock is getting low. Even if you do manage to get near your opponent, Arthur's offensive potential isn't exactly the best thing in the world. For the most part, your opponent can just avoid getting hit by an air throw and you have no other way to inflict major damage on them.

However, you do have one option at your disposal, air (S) can be used as an instant overhead against every character in the game! If you call a crossover assist immediately before hitting with the overhead, you'll be able to land a full combo afterwards! See the Combo Appendix section for a sample combo from instant overhead air (S).

There are two main ways to set up this instant overhead air (S). The first is by simply cornering your opponent using Air Fire Bottle Toss and Air Scatter Crossbow while in Golden Armor state. From there you can get close enough to your opponent to mix them up with instant overhead air (S) or crouching (L).

The other way to set up instant overhead air (S) is against opposing players who use forward ground recovery with their characters as a method to get near Arthur. Opponents getting hit out o the air by Axe Toss or a crossover assist will often get knocked down, allowing your opponent to use an invincible ground recovery roll to cover much of the screen safely. Counter this by calling your crossover assist ahead of time and surprising them with an instant overhead air (S)!

COMBO APPENDIX

GENERAL EXECUTION TIPS

To consistently link more than one Goddess' Bracelet, pay attention to the combo gauge—you'll want to input the next hyper combo when the combo gauge is about 18 hits higher than what it currently is.

To properly perform "wall" tactics with Air Dagger Toss or Air Lance Toss, you'll have to delay the final dagger or lance cancel. When practicing in Training Mode, press the buttons harder than you normally would—this allows you to learn the proper timing by hearing the rhythm of the button presses.

Requirements (Position, meter, etc.)	Notes	Command Sequence	Damage
Mid-screen required, during Golden Armor state	Combo from anti-air standing (M) during Golden Armor state	St. (M), st. (H) CANCEL ➡ ⇨⇩⇘ + (H), st. (H), (S) CANCEL ➡ super jump, air (M), (M), (H), (S), land, ⇩⇙⇦ + (L) OTG, ⇩⇘⇨ + (M) CANCEL ➡ ⇩⇘⇨ + (ATK)(ATK), ⇗ as needed	599,700
Corner required	Corner combo deals less damage due to not being able to use extended Fire Bottle Toss OTG hits	cr. (L), cr. (M), cr. (H) CANCEL ➡ ⇨⇩⇘ + (H), (S) CANCEL ➡ super jump straight up, air (M) CANCEL ➡ jump forward, air (M), (M), (H), (S), land, ⇩⇙⇦ + (L) OTG CANCEL ➡ ⇩⇘⇨ + (ATK)(ATK), ⇗ as necessary	509,800
Mid-screen required, Deadpool—β	Works from both forwards and backwards air throw	Air throw, P1 OR P2, land, cr. (H), (S) CANCEL ➡ super jump, air (M), (M), (H), (S), land, ⇩⇙⇦ + (L) OTG, ⇩⇙⇦ + (H) CANCEL ➡ ⇩⇘⇨ + (ATK)(ATK), ⇗ as necessary	478,900
Doctor Doom—α	Combo from an instant overhead air (S)	P1 OR P2, jump forward, air (S) CANCEL ➡ ⇩⇘⇨ + (L) CANCEL ➡ (during Air Dagger Toss) (L) CANCEL ➡ (during Air Dagger Toss) (L), land, cr. (M), cr. (H), (S) CANCEL ➡ super jump, air (M), (M), (H), (S), land, ⇩⇙⇦ + (L) OTG CANCEL ➡ ⇩⇘⇨ + (ATK)(ATK), ⇗ as necessary	451,600
Corner required, level 2 X-Factor	The increased speed resulting from X-Factor level 2 and 3 allow you to link Fire Bottle Toss in the corner indefinitely until the X-Factor timer runs out. Hyper combo-canceling into Goddess' Bracelet inflicts more damage while X-Factor is still active, so perform the hyper combo cancel when the combo gauge is at 22 hits. To link the second Goddess' Bracelet, try to time it exactly when the combo gauge is going to reach 42 hits.	Cr. (L), st. (M), st. (H), ⇨ + (H) CANCEL ➡ ⇩⇙⇦ + (L) CANCEL ➡ [X-Factor], ⇩⇙⇦ + (L) x17 CANCEL ➡ ⇩⇘⇨ + (ATK)(ATK), ⇩⇘⇨ + (ATK)(ATK)	1,205,600

CHRIS REDFIELD

"NO ONE'S DYING ON MY WATCH."

BIO

REAL NAME

CHRIS REDFIELD

OCCUPATION

BSAA OPERATIVE

ABILITIES

HAS PLENTY OF EXPERIENCE WITH ALL TYPES OF WEAPONS. ALSO SKILLED IN HAND-TO-HAND COMBAT AS WELL AS WITH A KNIFE. HAS GOOD OBSERVATIONAL AND PERCEPTION SKILLS, IMPORTANT FOR SURVIVAL.

WEAPONS

VARIOUS FIREARMS SUCH AS HANDGUNS, SUB-MACHINE GUNS, SHOTGUNS, ETC. ALSO ARMED WITH A MILITARY-ISSUE KNIFE AND MACHETE.

PROFILE

EVER SINCE THE RACCOON CITY INCIDENT, HE HAS BEEN FIGHTING CONTINUOUSLY AGAINST THE SPREAD OF BIOTERRORISM DESPITE THE DISSOLUTION OF UMBRELLA. HE IS ALSO SEARCHING FOR HIS FORMER PARTNER JILL, WHOSE WHEREABOUTS ARE UNKNOWN.

FIRST APPEARANCE

RESIDENT EVIL (1996)

POWER GRID

5	INTELLIGENCE
5	STRENGTH
4	SPEED
5	STAMINA
1	ENERGY PROJECTION
5	FIGHTING ABILITY

*This is biographical, and does not represent an evaluation of the character's in-game combat potential.

ALTERNATE COSTUMES

PS3: ⨂ Xbox 360: A

PS3: ▢ Xbox 360: X

PS3: △ Xbox 360: Y

PS3: R1 Xbox 360: RB

ATTACK SET

STANDING BASIC ATTACKS

Screen	Command	Hits	Damage	Startup	Active	Recovery	Advantage on Hit	Advantage if Guarded	Notes
1	Standing L	1	48,000	6	3	11	-1	-2	—
2	Standing M	1	65,000	8	3	18	-3	-4	—
3	Standing H	1	80,000	10	3	21	-1	-2	⇩⇙⇨ + P1⇔P2 snapback
4	S	1	80,000	9	4	27	—	-9	Launcher, not special- or hyper combo-cancelable

1

2

3

4

CROUCHING BASIC ATTACKS

Screen	Command	Hits	Damage	Startup	Active	Recovery	Advantage on Hit	Advantage if Guarded	Notes
1	Crouching L	1	45,000	6	3	13	-3	-4	Low attack
2	Crouching M	1	80,000	8	3	18	-3	-4	Low attack
3	Crouching H	1	90,000	17	2	19	+2	+1	Low attack, OTG-capable, inflicts chip damage, not special- or hyper combo-cancelable, projectile has 3 low priority durability points

1

2

3

AERIAL BASIC ATTACKS

Screen	Command	Hits	Damage	Startup	Active	Recovery	Notes
1	Air L	1	50,000	5	5	19	Overhead attack
2	Air M	1	70,000	8	3	27	Overhead attack
3	Air H	1	90,000	10	3	26	Overhead attack
4	Air S	1	85,000	11	3	32	Overhead attack, causes flying screen during launcher combo

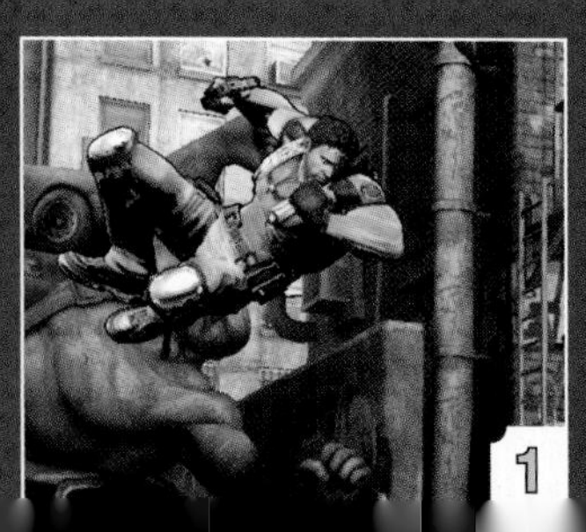
1

2

3

4

COMMAND ATTACKS

Screen	Command	Hits	Damage	Startup	Active	Recovery	Advantage on Hit	Advantage if Guarded	Notes
1	→ + M	1	90,000	15	4	22	-3	-4	OTG-capable, inflicts chip damage, not special- or hyper combo-cancelable, projectile has 3 low priority durability points
2	→ + H	1	90,000	15	3	25	-5	-6	Inflicts chip damage
3	← + H	9 - 25	110,000 – 166,800	20	17	22	0	-1	Inflicts chip damage, button can be held for extra hits, not special-cancelable, beam durability: 60 frames x 1 low priority durability points
4	Air ↓ + H	1	90,000	15	—	Until landing	—	—	Inflicts chip damage, not special- or hyper combo-cancelable, projectile has 3 low priority durability points

AS A PARTNER—CROSSOVER ASSISTS

Screen	Type	P1+P2 Crossover Combination Hyper Combo	Description	Hits	Damage	Startup	Active	Recovery (this crossover assist)	Recovery (other partner)	Notes
1	α – Alpha	Sweep Combo	Combination Punch H	2	112,000	34	2(16)2	134	104	Unrecoverable knockdown
2	β – Beta	Grenade Launcher	Gun Fire M	8	125,00	49	—	114	84	Each projectile has 1 low priority durability point
3	γ – Gamma	Grenade Launcher	Grenade Toss L	1	117,000	41	—	116	86	Spinning knockdown, projectile has 1 low priority durability point

Special Moves

Screen	Name	Command	Hits	Damage	Startup	Active	Recovery	Advantage on Hit	Advantage if Guarded	Notes
1	Combination Punch L	↓↙← + Ⓛ	2	104,000	10	2(15)3	21	-1	-2	—
2	Body Blow	(During Combination Punch L) Ⓛ	1	50,000	12	3	26	-3	-4	—
3	Heavy Blow	(During Body Blow) Ⓜ	1	60,000	13	3	30	-5	-6	—
4	Payoff	(During Heavy Blow) Ⓗ	3		15	3 (18) 3 (17) 4	21	—	-3	2nd hit knocks down opponent, 3rd hit wall bounces
5	Combination Punch M	↓↙← + Ⓜ	2	122,000	10	2(24)3	22	—	-3	First hit staggers opponent, 2nd hit knocks down
6	Magnum Combo	(During Combination Punch M) Ⓗ	1	150,000	22	—	34	—	-12	Wall bounces opponent, unrecoverable knockdown, projectile has 10 low priority durability points
7	Combination Punch H	↓↙← + Ⓗ	2	131,000	10	2 (16) 2	41	—	-20	Unrecoverable knockdown
8	Grenade Toss L	→↓↘ + Ⓛ	1	130,000	17	—	28	—	-7	Spinning knockdown, land mine is created on 15th frame, land mine explodes on contact, or persists for 90 frames before detonating, land mine can be detonated by projectiles from either player, and also detonates whenever Chris receives damage, explosion has 1 medium priority durability point
9	Grenade Toss M	→↓↘ + Ⓜ	1	150,000	20	—	25	—	—	Grenade detonates after 90 frames, can bounce off of walls, can be detonated by projectiles, and also detonates whenever Chris receives damage, causes spinning knockdown, explosion has 5 low priority durability points
10	Grenade Toss H	→↓↘ + Ⓗ	1+5	130,000 + 61,300	25	—	26	—	—	Grenade detonates after 120 frames, can bounce off of walls, can be detonated by projectiles, and also detonates whenever Chris receives damage, explosion causes spinning knockdown, creates flame pool upon detonation, flame pool lasts for 120 frames, explosion has 1 medium priority durability point, fire pool has 5 flames with 1 low priority durability point
11	Gun Fire L	↓↘→ + Ⓛ (in air OK)	10	133,400	25	—	30	+7	+6	On counterhit will stagger the opponent if the first hit is a headshot, each projectile has 1 low priority durability point
12	Gun Fire M	↓↘→ + Ⓜ (in air OK)	8	120,900	25	13	22	+1	0	Fires 8 shots, each projectile has 1 low priority durability point
13	Gun Fire H	↓↘→ + Ⓗ (in air OK)	1	150,000	22	—	34	—	-12	Ground version wall bounces opponent and causes unrecoverable knockdown, air version bounces opponent, projectile has 10 low priority durability points
14	Prone Position	↓↓ + Ⓗ	—	—	27	—	—	—	—	Can move left or right while in Prone Position, exit Prone Position by tapping up on the controller
15	Prone Shot	(During Prone Position) Ⓗ	1	90,000	—	—	—	—	—	Not hyper combo-cancelable, projectile has 3 low priority durability points

1

Combination Punch L: While fancy, the Combination Punch L series only has one very specialized use—it's the best way to combo into Grenade Launcher by hyper combo-canceling Heavy Blow. For all other combo enders you will generally get more damage doing other moves, like Combination Punch M.

The timing to get the follow-up attacks to Combination Punch L can be a little tricky. See the caption for each follow-up attack for details.

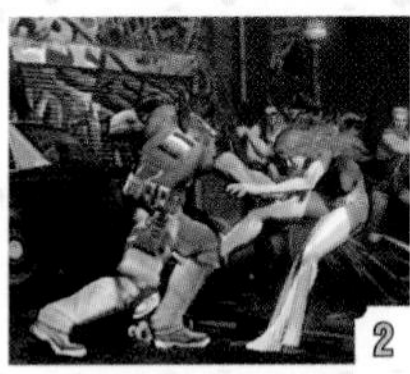

2

3

4

Body Blow: To activate Body Blow, simply press Ⓛ immediately after the second punch from Combination Punch L hits the opponent. The timing window is very lenient at 10 frames.

Heavy Blow: To activate Heavy Blow, press Ⓜ immediately after Body Blow hits. The timing window here is still very lenient, at 9 frames. If you intend to combo into Grenade Launcher, this is the point from which you'll want to hyper combo cancel. Cancel as early as possible!

Payoff: Activating Payoff takes a bit of practice to master. The timing window on it is considerably tighter: 4 frames immediately after Heavy Blow hits an opponent. If you're having trouble getting Payoff to activate, you're likely pressing Ⓗ too late.

5

Combination Punch M: Combination Punch M goes into Magnum Combo for a wall bounce, and is used in Chris's corner combos for maximum damage. Although the second punch pushes Chris away to a safe distance if guarded, there is a four frame gap in-between the first and second punch that allows an opponent to get a guaranteed throw on you.

6

Magnum Combo: The timing to activate Magnum Combo is a little awkward, and takes a bit of practice to master. The window is 4 frames long, timed 7 frames after the second punch of Combination Punch M makes contact. Pressing Ⓗ on the final frame of your 4 frame window will still cause the shot to miss many characters, making the window effectively smaller.

7

Combination Punch H: Combination Punch H creates an unrecoverable knockdown on hit, making it the preferred way to combo into Satellite Laser in the corner. Combination Punch H is also typically the best way to end combos when hitstun deterioration starts to get heavy—both punches will usually combo no matter how bad hitstun has deteriorated, and the unrecoverable knockdown leads to OTG opportunities.

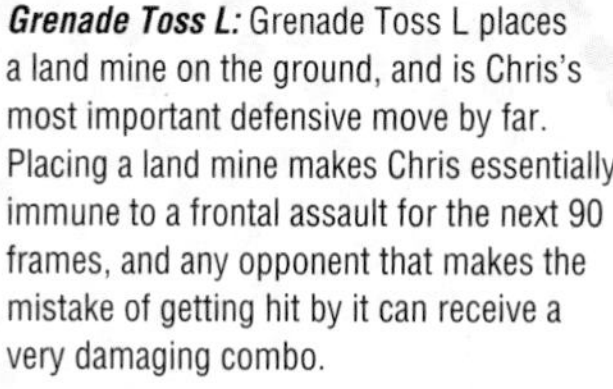
8

Grenade Toss L: Grenade Toss L places a land mine on the ground, and is Chris's most important defensive move by far. Placing a land mine makes Chris essentially immune to a frontal assault for the next 90 frames, and any opponent that makes the mistake of getting hit by it can receive a very damaging combo.

Oddly enough, Grenade Toss L is probably Chris's best anti-air. If you successfully get the land mine out in time, your opponent will hit you with their air attack, then proceed to get blown up by the land mine—if Chris receives damage it causes the land mine to immediately detonate! From there you can still convert the hit into a full combo by using ⇨ + Ⓗ into a launcher.

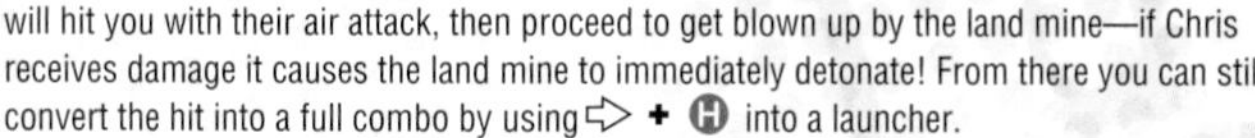

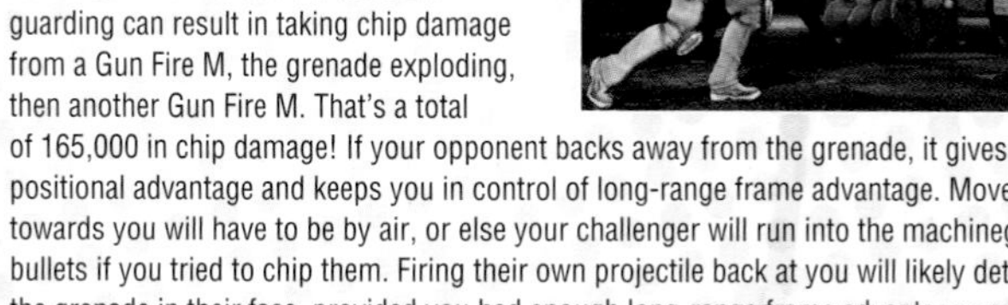
9

Grenade Toss M: Grenade Toss M throws a slow-detonating grenade at your opponent, reaching three-quarters of the screen in length. It is best used at that range, particularly when you have long-range frame advantage on your opponent.

Throwing a grenade at your opponent's feet forces them to make a decision: guarding can result in taking chip damage from a Gun Fire M, the grenade exploding, then another Gun Fire M. That's a total of 165,000 in chip damage! If your opponent backs away from the grenade, it gives you positional advantage and keeps you in control of long-range frame advantage. Movement towards you will have to be by air, or else your challenger will run into the machinegun bullets if you tried to chip them. Firing their own projectile back at you will likely detonate the grenade in their face, provided you had enough long-range frame advantage on your opponent. That said, calling a crossover assist is a great way to buy yourself time to toss grenades.

Your own projectiles can detonate grenades as well, resulting in big damage if your opponent decides to move forward. Grenades are detonated most easily by Gun Fire M and air ⇩ + Ⓗ.

10

Grenade Toss H: The uses for Grenade Toss H are similar to Grenade Toss M, but with one major difference: Grenade Toss H leaves a lingering pool of fire on the ground after detonation, preventing a ground-based approach from the opponent for short period of time.

The downside of this is that Grenade Toss H takes longer to both throw and recover, and the detonation of the grenade does less damage than Grenade Toss M.

The lingering pool of fire also detonates additional grenades you throw at it. This allows you to create a persistent pool of fire by performing Grenade Toss H a bunch of times!

11

Gun Fire L: The ground version of Gun Fire L isn't particularly useful, but it does give substantial frame advantage on hit or block. However at close ranges most characters can crouch under it entirely, making it a moot point.

The air version of Gun Fire L is an incredible move, and is the cornerstone of Chris's offense. Chris can jump at his opponents from a considerable distance away and attack with the shotgun—it will beat nearly any anti-air due to it being a projectile, and produces a huge amount of hitstun if it hits his opponent. On a successful hit, you have enough time to easily dash forward and do a crouching Ⓜ into a full combo. If guarded, air Gun Fire L has the potential to do 75,000 points of chip damage if all ten shots connect. Even better, it can produce an incredible +35 frame advantage if guarded!

Gun Fire L has a peculiar special property—it staggers opponents that are hit by a counterhit headshot. This is essentially a random occurrence in a real match situation, but happens much more frequently when attacking with air Gun Fire L at close range. If you successfully get a counterhit headshot, the next jumping shotgun you do will combo from the first, allowing you to easily hit-confirm and convert to a full combo.

12

Gun Fire M: Chris's machinegun is his standard tool to attack opponents from across the screen. Gun Fire M is one of the most damaging projectiles in the game in terms of chip damage, at 60,000 damage total on a guarding opponent.

The machinegun can be used in a manner similar to beam projectiles, but with one major difference—Chris's bullets are much worse at nullifying other projectiles. In a firefight across the screen with another zoning character Chris will generally have to rely on either Gun Fire H to pierce through their projectiles, or Prone Position to avoid them entirely.

The air version of Gun Fire M can sometimes be useful against a full-screen opponent if done early in a super jump. Chris can fire shots at another zoning foe without having to be in their line of fire.

13

Gun Fire H: Gun Fire H has a very specific use—it powers through nearly every other projectile in the game, beams included, and continues to travel until it blasts an opponent in the face. The magnum shot wall bounces a foe, but it's generally impossible to get any extra damage off of it without the help of a crossover assist. You can quickly hyper combo cancel into Grenade Launcher and get a single hit, or get a full juggle combo at close range in the corner, but neither of these things are very useful to apply in a real, competitive match.

Trying to attack with Gun Fire H doesn't work very well, since most characters can crouch under the magnum bullet completely. Stick to using Gun Fire M and air Gun Fire L for attacking purposes.

The air version of the magnum shot (Gun Fire H) floor bounces an opponent, but is generally only used to extend combos. In general battle situations, air Gun Fire L or M are probably better options.

14

Prone Position: Prone Position gives Chris an edge against many other characters in a long-ranged fight, as he can simply go prone under their attacks while firing back with Prone Shot. This tactic will often force the opponent to move toward Chris and attack him head on, something that zoning characters generally aren't good at. When using Prone Position beware of characters with beam-based hyper combos, as Chris cannot prone under those. Also, Chris can still call crossover assists while in Prone Position.

15

Prone Shot: Prone Shot allows Chris to fire back at opponents who likely won't be able to retaliate. You'll generally only want to fire the Prone Shot if your opponent won't have time to avoid it; the recovery time on Prone Shot is lengthy and leaves Chris in the still-vulnerable Prone Position. This can be mitigated if you have a defensive crossover assist handy, however.

HYPER COMBOS

Screen	Name	Command	Hits	Damage	Startup	Active	Recovery	Advantage on Hit	Advantage if Guarded	Notes
1	Grenade Launcher	↓↘→ + ATK ATK	4	343,700	15+4	111	36	—	—	First hit incapacitates opponent for 113 frames, does not incapacitate airborne opponents, 2nd hit causes spinning knockdown, 3rd hit cause knockdown, 4th hit causes spinning knockdown, and has homing capability, each projectile has 1 high priority durability point
2	Sweep Combo	→↓↘ + ATK ATK	22	290,400	10+2	4 (10) 3 (27) 8 (27) 17 (20) 7 (43) 20	53	—	-31	2nd hit floor bounces opponent, 21st and 22nd hits cause spinning knockdown
3	Satellite Laser (Level 3 Hyper Combo)	↓↙← + ATK ATK	27	445,500	35+1 (Lock On 14)	37	43	—	—	Invulnerable for (35+7) frames, creates a cursor to aim Satellite Laser, pressing any button fires, allows three shots within time limit, each shot is OTG-capable, time limit is 260 frames, each shot has 20 frames of start up, each projectile has 1 high priority durability point

1

Grenade Launcher: Grenade Launcher is one of the most damaging hyper combos in the game, but unfortunately does not fully juggle against airborne opponents. This severely limits its usefulness in combos, since you can almost always get more damage with Chris's juggle options. It does allow for extended combos in the corner however, if you wish to spend more than one bar in a combo.

In battle situations, the Grenade Launcher can be used as an anti-projectile tool like Gun Fire H. While the Grenade Launcher fires more quickly than the magnum, allowing you to nullify projectiles faster, the grenade round travels across the screen considerably slower than the magnum shot. This requires quicker reactions to use effectively than the magnum.

If the Grenade Launcher is guarded or avoided, the skyward shot that Chris fires effectively protects him from getting hit by a combo; even if your opponent starts hitting you the skyward grenade will come down and disrupt the combo. In some situations, you can actually convert that hit into a full combo with → + H!

Grenade Launcher has great team hyper combo potential when hit from far away—immediately after the fourth round is fired, team hyper combo into a fast-recovering hyper combo like Wolverine's Berserker Charge or Phoenix's Healing Wave, then wavedash in and get a full juggle combo!

2

Sweep Combo: Sweep Combo is Chris's only hyper combo that can reliably be used to juggle opponents. Unfortunately, it also has a ground bounce in its second hit. This means that if Chris has already juggled his opponent with air Gun Fire H ground bounce, Sweep Combo will not connect fully. This makes the additional damage from juggling into Sweep Combo too marginal to use outside of corner combos involving Combination Punch M.

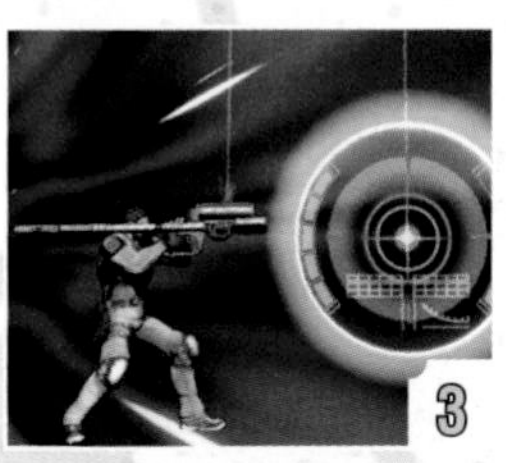
3

Satellite Laser: Satellite Laser is a strange level 3 hyper combo that allows you to manually aim a targeting reticle on the screen and fire three OTG-capable beams. Like all level 3 hyper combos, Satellite Laser is not subject to damage scaling and can add a substantial amount of damage to a combo.

However, the excruciatingly slow start up and cursor speed movement of Satellite Laser make it nearly impossible to combo into except against cornered opponents. The massive start up time on Satellite Laser is completely invulnerable however; this allows for some specialized situations in which you can pass through and punish entire hyper combos from your opponent.

BATTLE PLAN

OVERVIEW

VITALITY: 1,100,000

CHAIN COMBO ARCHETYPE: MARVEL SERIES

X-Factor	Lv.1	Lv.2	Lv.3
Damage	135%	175%	210%
Speed	105%	110%	115%

Your goal with Chris is simple: inflict chip damage on your opponent while staying out of trouble. Why would you be happy with just chip damage?

Chris has two of the most damaging special moves in the game in terms of chip damage: Gun Fire M and air Gun Fire L.

Air Gun Fire L is a great all-around attacking tool, and leads to a full combo if it hits an opponent.

Chris lacks offensive capability otherwise; he doesn't have many good ways to set up and earn clean hits on his opponent. As such, the majority of his damage must come from pelting his opponent with projectiles.

How does Chris inflict chip damage while staying out of trouble?

Use air Gun Fire L liberally when in range.

Use Gun Fire M when given the opportunity from across the screen.

Employ Grenade Toss L and H to prevent frontal assaults temporarily.

Air ↓ + H and Prone Position allow Chris to attack and chip opponents from afar while dodging incoming attacks.

ON THE GROUND

From across the screen your main focus is to make contact with Gun Fire M while avoiding damage.

Magnum shots pierce through most other projectiles in the game; use them if you think you have a good read on your opponent's projectile patterns.

Chris best fills the role of meter-builder on a team—you won't use his hyper combos often and he builds a ton of bar while pelting his opponent with shotguns and machineguns. In addition, Chris's lack of practical combos that lead into hyper combos gives him a small dependency on characters that he can team aerial combo with.

Against attacking opponents you'll want to keep them across the screen for as long as possible using Gun Fire M, Grenade Toss H, and any projectile-throwing crossover assists you may have. From across the screen you can put encroaching opponents in a simple mix-up—attack with Gun Fire M if they're going to approach by ground, or wait for them to jump forward. If they jump, make them land into a Gun Fire M! Each Gun Fire M that hits or is guarded is a small victory; they do substantial chip damage and push your opponent farther back across the screen. If you have a projectile-throwing crossover assist, use that to buy time to use Grenade Toss H. The pool of fire completely removes the option of approaching via the ground for a short period of time; expect your opponent to jump over it and make them land into a Gun Fire M!

When your opponent eventually gets into mid-range, things start to get a little dangerous. At this range your opponent is now within striking range of air attacks or dash attacks, so you'll want to lay down a Grenade Toss L land mine to keep them off of you. Laying down the land mine takes 15 frames, so you'll have to evaluate whether you have time to pull it off or not. (To give you an idea, 15 frames is exactly how long you must hold P1=P2 to tag in another character with a crossover attack.) However, don't worry about getting hit after those 15 frames have elapsed; if your opponent hits you during that time the land mine will automatically detonate and allow you to retaliate with a full combo.

If you successfully lay down a land mine without getting hit, things can get a little silly, depending on the character match-up. Laying down a land mine makes it almost completely safe to do a Gun Fire M and push your opponent out. If they jump over it and hit you, they are launched by the land mine into a full combo. The land mine explodes on its own immediately after Gun Fire M finishes, allowing you to drop another land mine. This is extremely hard for an opponent to deal with without projectiles, or a way to reliably get behind Chris—the most consistent method is to guard the Gun Fire M, immediately wavedash towards Chris, then guard the next Grenade Toss L. This puts the challenger at a +7 frame advantage, able to punish Chris if they're in range. If your opponent's character has a fast enough dash, they can dash in and hit Chris out of the very small window between the Gun Fire M and the next land mine that is dropped. If you have a crossover assist that pushes your opponent backwards a large distance on block, calling that assist between the Grenade Toss L and Gun Fire M will nullify these counters. If you don't have a crossover assist of that sort handy, counter their attempts to dash in after the Gun Fire M by simply jumping back and doing air Gun Fire L.

If your opponent gets on top of you and prevents you from finding time to drop a land mine, you'll have to rely on universal defensive options—advancing guard, air throws, and super jump. Chris has no fast or invincible moves that can be pulled off in a pinch; you need to be patient and find a hole in your opponent's offense to use an advancing guard and drop a land mine.

By the same token, Chris doesn't have any great reliable anti-airs except for Grenade Toss L. Keep your opponent away and try to ensure that you always have time to drop the land mine, or you may find it near-impossible to get your opponent off of you. If your challenger super jumps at you, either drop a land mine on reaction or use the opportunity to wavedash under your opponent to get more distance between your character and the corner.

Against another zoning character the dynamic of the match completely changes. Against these characters you'll generally want to take the stance of reacting to and countering your opponent's actions, rather than trying to overpower them in a firefight.

Grenade Toss L is far and away your most important defensive move; be sure to have one out if your opponent gets within mid-range.

Each bullet in Gun Fire M only has one durability point; this means that it takes five bullets to nullify most single-hit projectiles in the game, and that all eight bullets are typically nullified by any beam attack or multi-hit projectile. When confronted with a situation in which your firepower is less than your opponent's, you have the following options:

Evade your opponent's projectile by going under it with Prone Position, then attacking back with Prone Shot.

Evade your challenger's projectile by going over it, jumping straight up with air ↓ + H at two-thirds screen distance, or jumping towards the opponent at the same distance with air Gun Fire L.

Blowing through your foe's projectiles entirely with Gun Fire H or Grenade Launcher.

Using a projectile-throwing crossover assist.

Only use Gun Fire M when you're sure your opponent is in a defensive position, such as after blocking an assist. Your aim here is to frustrate your opponent from across the screen and make them feel as if fighting from long range is futile. If they come towards you, they are putting themselves in position to be rushed down with air Gun Fire L.

In a long-ranged firefight, Chris seemingly has a weakness against characters that can attack from super jump height. However, in almost all instances these characters can only attack from full-screen at the peak of their super jump height, which means that they can only fire off one attack that you'll have to deal with. Simply jump over that attack and make your opponent land on a Gun Fire M. If the ranged attack cannot easily be jumped over, like Doctor Doom's Photon Shots (of which he can only perform one in a single jump), you can counter that by super jumping towards the opponent and attacking with air Gun Fire H.

If you're not near full-screen distance from an opponent that can attack from super jump height, you'll want to either wavedash under your foe and place a land mine under them, or wavedash backwards to create the necessary room. If you're in the corner you may have to guard a few projectiles and use an advancing guard against your opponent to create room, depending on how difficult it is to approach.

UP IN THE AIR

Air Gun Fire L is ridiculously good. Abuse it!

Air ⇩ + Ⓗ is a great tool for attacking from long range while still remaining mobile.

Super jumping and attacking with Gun Fire M at full-screen is a good way to attack while avoiding both the point and assist character's projectiles.

Chris has none of the aerial movement options that other characters have—he has no airdashes, no aerial special moves that alter his trajectory, and no Flight special move. This isn't as much of a problem for Chris as it would be for other characters, since you are not typically trying to get Chris near his opponents. It does limit his escape options, however, and places even more emphasis on having a land mine out whenever you may be in trouble.

When Chris is in the air, the vast majority of the time he's only doing one of three things:

Air Gun Fire L to attack opponents.

Air ⇩ + Ⓗ to chip opponents from across the screen.

Air throws for defense.

Air Gun Fire L is an amazing move, and should be considered whenever your opponent is anywhere within two-thirds screen distance from you. Attacking with jumping shotguns can be very difficult for an opponent to deal with; the projectiles will beat most any anti-air your opponent can muster, allowing you to dash in and get a full combo. If guarded, the massive amount of guardstun from the shotgun allows you to jump and fire again with near-impunity. The jumping shotgun can have a frame advantage of up to +35 if guarded! Your opponent must use advancing guard against the shotgun blast to push you away. If you expect this you can land and immediately fire a Gun Fire M which your opponent must block. Just one air Gun Fire L and ground Gun Fire M adds up to 135,000 chip damage!

To counter air Gun Fire L, your opponent must meet you in the air and counter with faster jump attacks. To prevent your challenger from directly countering you, only attack with air Gun Fire L from further distances, or attack behind the massive frame advantage of a previous jump-in. Almost any counter that the opposition may have for air Gun Fire L that does not involve a projectile will also typically get hit by a Grenade Toss L.

To make jumping shotguns even more difficult to deal with, call a crossover assist after landing from your jump! Depending on your assist, this will often keep your opponent in guardstun long enough for you to wavedash back in close and resume the jumping shotgun offense. Attacking with jumping shotguns also has the additional benefit of pushing your opponent back towards the corner.

It gets better against a cornered opponent, since you can repeatedly do jumping shotguns until your opposition uses an advancing guard against you several times, or until your opponent attempts to escape by using advancing guard and jumps after it. If you read this, you can do a Grenade Toss L land mine upon landing; if your opponent had jumped towards you and attacked they'll get hit by the land mine, leading to a full corner combo. If they jump backwards, they become pinned even more by the land mine!

If one jumping shotgun blast hits your opponent, the massive hitstun allows you to dash in and land a full combo. Even better, if you hit your opponent with a counterhit headshot your challenger becomes staggered, allowing a second jumping shotgun to combo! When this happens it becomes very easy to hit-confirm the shotgun blast and dash in. While all these hits from the shotgun pellets scale the combo damage severely, it still grants you some free damage and hyper combo bar, as well as the ability to push your opponent all the way to the corner with a standard combo.

From farther away, air ⇩ + Ⓗ is a strong option. It allows you remain mobile while still attacking from a long distance, and is useful in both long-ranged firefights and against enemies attempting to close the distance on you.

COMBO USAGE

I. CR. Ⓛ, CR. Ⓜ, ST. Ⓗ, → + Ⓗ, Ⓢ CANCEL⇨ SUPER JUMP, AIR Ⓜ, Ⓜ, Ⓗ CANCEL⇨ AIR ↓ ↘ → + Ⓗ, LAND, → + Ⓗ, Ⓢ CANCEL⇨ SUPER JUMP, AIR Ⓜ, Ⓜ, Ⓗ, Ⓢ, LAND, CR. Ⓗ OTG

(482,600 damage) Chris's standard combo does considerable damage, bearing in mind that it uses no hyper combo bar or assists. It's also very easy for a *Marvel vs. Capcom 3* combo, with very straight-forward execution. Since Chris can't easily combo into a hyper combo it may be worth handing off the air combo at the end to a partner with a team aerial combo, since other characters have stronger finishing options in the air or after flying screen than Chris.

Beginning the combo with an air Gun Fire L instead of crouching Ⓛ inflicts anywhere between 257,200 and 417,300 damage, depending on how few shotgun pellets hit the opponent.

This combo nearly takes the opposing character from one corner all the way to the other, putting your opponent in prime position to be rushed down with jumping shotguns. The crouching Ⓗ OTG forces your foe to recover in the air, which is an opportunity to either reset with an air throw or place Grenade Toss L directly under them.

II. (CORNER REQUIRED) CR. Ⓛ, CR. Ⓜ, ST. Ⓗ, → + Ⓗ CANCEL⇨ ↓ ↙ ← + Ⓜ CANCEL⇨ (DURING COMBINATION PUNCH M) Ⓗ, CR. Ⓜ, ST. Ⓗ, → + Ⓗ CANCEL⇨ ↓ ↙ ← + Ⓗ CANCEL⇨ → ↓ ↘ + ATK ATK

(671,900) Chris can do substantially more damage in the corner against a grounded opponent. The corner combo is trickier to execute than Chris's basic combo, but is still easy enough with some practice. Juggling Magnum Combo off of Combination Punch M has a 3 frame window; see the Special Moves section for details on when exactly that window is. The timing for juggling the Sweep Combo off of the Combination Punch H is a little unintuitive; canceling the second punch right away will cause Sweep Combo to miss completely. Canceling too late is very possible as well, so spend some time practicing before you try this combo in a real match.

Starting this combo with air Gun Fire L instead of crouching Ⓛ does anywhere between 437,400 damage and 572,100 damage.

ASSISTS

The Whirlwind attack of Storm—α pushes opponents backwards a huge distance, allowing you to keep attackers at bay more easily.

Beam-based crossover assists are great for Chris in general, useful for both keeping opponents across the screen and for winning long-ranged firefights.

The slow speed of Thor's Mighty Spark actually helps Chris juggle from his Gun Fire H, increasing Chris's damage output significantly in firefights.

All three of Chris's crossover assist types can be very useful. Gun Fire M is an all-around useful assist, with applications very similar to a beam projectile. It also does more chip damage and pushes opponents back further than most beam attacks. Grenade Toss L is useful for any character defensively, and is an easy way to add a sizeable chunk of damage to many combos. Combination Punch H is the most specialized of Chris's assist types, being mainly used to extend combos. Causing a high knockback and unrecoverable knockdown state makes it very useful in corner combos.

Chris benefits most from having a good beam-based crossover assist handy, like Doctor Doom—α or Iron Man—α. These assists help keep offensive characters far across the screen, add a lot of necessary firepower in a long-ranged fight, and also greatly increase Chris's ability to punish crossover assists. Without a beam assist, Chris's only ways to damage assists behind an opponent are Gun Fire H and pre-emptive Grenade Toss M or H.

Storm's Whirlwind attack is a unique projectile in that it pushes opponents back almost all the way to the opposite end of the screen. This is great for keeping attacking characters at bay, especially when used in tandem with Grenade Toss L. On the flip side, Storm's Whirlwind does not reach full-screen distance—it only goes about 90% of the way across. Also, unlike most projectile assists, Storm appears in front of Chris when performing her Whirlwind attack; this makes it much more difficult to ensure that Storm has a chance to perform her Whirlwind uninterrupted.

Thor's Mighty Spark attack has a very specialized use for Chris—it allows him to land a small combo off of a full-screen Gun Fire H. While this significantly increases his damage output in long-ranged match-ups, it's very difficult to make use of otherwise; Mighty Spark is very slow and can be crouched under by most characters, and also appears in front of Chris instead of behind him. To create the correct timing to juggle Mighty Spark off of Gun Fire H, simply press the crossover assist button immediately before performing the move. Beware of pressing P1⇔P2 *during* the ⇩ ⬂ ⇨ motion, however, as this may actually prevent the assist from appearing—if Chris actually starts his special move animation before the assist has begun to jump onscreen, they won't come out!

Single-hit projectile assists like Ryu—β or Zero—β can be used to juggle after Gun Fire H as well, but the crossover assist button must be pressed earlier. This makes it more difficult to land the combo in an actual match situation. The timing for when to press the crossover assist button also varies depending on the distance between you and your opponent, making things even trickier. These assists are generally more useful all-around however than Thor—α, and can also be used to combo off of Chris's air throw.

"PHEW... WHAT'S THE POINT OF ALL THIS FIGHTING?"

III. → ↓ ↘ + (L), → + (H), (S) CANCEL⇨ SUPER JUMP, AIR (M), (M), (H) CANCEL⇨ ↓ ↘ → + (H), LAND, → + (H), (S) CANCEL⇨ SUPER JUMP, AIR (M), (M), (H), (S), LAND, CR. (H) OTG

(561,800 damage) Your foe must walk or jump into an already-placed land mine for this combo to work. This combo is one of the main reasons Chris can give offensive characters fits; land mines are already difficult to deal with. Land mines leading to over 50% damage without using hyper combo are almost ridiculous!

IV. (CORNER REQUIRED) FORWARD THROW, CR. (H) OTG, ST. (L), CR. (M), (S) CANCEL⇨ SUPER JUMP, AIR (M), (M), (H) CANCEL⇨ AIR ↓ ↘ → + (H), LAND, → + (H), (S) CANCEL⇨ SUPER JUMP, AIR (M), (M), (H), (S), LAND, CR. (H) OTG

(286,100 damage) Against a cornered opponent Chris can link after his crouching (H) OTG if hitstun hasn't deteriorated much. This allows Chris to get a lot of free damage and hyper combo bar off of a throw against a cornered opponent. The damage following a throw is scaled considerably, but this can be avoided if desired by activating X-Factor after the throw but before the initial OTG.

V. (CORNER REQUIRED) CR. (L), CR. (M), ST. (H), → + (H) CANCEL⇨ ↓ ↙ ← + (L) CANCEL⇨ (DURING COMBINATION PUNCH L) (L) CANCEL⇨ (DURING BODY BLOW) (M) CANCEL⇨ ↓ ↘ → + (ATK)(ATK), → + (H) CANCEL⇨ ↓ ↙ ← + (H) CANCEL⇨ ↓ ↙ ← + (ATK)(ATK), (ATK) OTG, (ATK) OTG, (ATK) OTG, CR. (H) OTG

(1,004,100 damage) Chris can create a ton of damage off of a clean hit if you're willing to spend the bar on Satellite Laser. Hyper combo canceling Heavy Blow into Grenade Launcher successfully takes a bit of practice; make sure you're canceling Heavy Blow as early as possible.

ADVANCED TACTICS

CORNER BEAM ASSIST SET-UP

Call your beam assist at the same time as your crouching Ⓗ OTG...

...then mix your opponent up as they land!

Chris can take the opponent fully into the corner with almost any of his combos. His combos almost all end with a crouching Ⓗ OTG shot, which causes an opponent to recover in the air. If you call a beam crossover assist simultaneously while pressing crouching Ⓗ, the beam will be on top of your opponent as they recover in the air, preventing them from doing anything but guarding on the way down.

If the beam hits, you can hit-confirm and juggle your challenger for another full combo. If the beam is guarded, you can wait for your foe to land and perform a three-way mix-up of throw, jump back and air Gun Fire L, or crouching Ⓛ. Doing a throw will grab a guarding or attacking character. Chris gets a full combo off of a throw in the corner—see the Combo Appendix section for details. Jumping back and firing the shotgun will counter an opponent attempting to tech the throw; they will unintentionally perform a standing Ⓗ attack instead of a throw, which gets shot by the shotgun. You can then dash back in and get another combo. If the opposition tries to avoid the mix-up by jumping, crouching Ⓛ will hit them out of their pre-jump startup frames.

You can also add another dimension to this mix-up by jumping up and air throwing your foe before they land on top of the beam projectile. However, since you had just used a crossover assist, you only get to combo with a crouching Ⓗ OTG shot unless you want to activate X-Factor.

Your opponent can avoid this mix-up by air recovering forward, unless you had dashed backwards first before pressing crouching Ⓗ. Doing so makes the opposing character land on top of a beam no matter which way they air recover. Doctor Doom—α stands farther back behind Chris, so there's no need for the backwards dash if you're using that particular assist.

This set-up works best with Iron Man—α and Doctor Doom—α. Other beam assists are either too slow or do not have enough active frames.

Characters can use aerial movement options to escape the mix-up, and your counters to those are situation-specific and beyond the scope of this guide.

COMBO APPENDIX

GENERAL EXECUTION TIPS

Practice the timing to juggle Magnum Combo from Combination Punch M, it's slightly after the point of impact of the second punch.

When attempting to convert stray juggle hits into a combo, try to hit → + Ⓗ as late as possible; you'll want the opponent lower to the ground in your aerial combo to hit your challenger with the air Gun Fire H.

Requirements (Position, meter, etc.)	Notes	Command Sequence	Damage
Corner required	Heavy Blow must be canceled into Grenade Launcher as soon as possible	Cr. Ⓛ, cr. Ⓜ, st. Ⓗ, → + Ⓗ CANCEL ▶ ↓↙← + Ⓛ CANCEL ▶ (During Combination Punch L) Ⓛ CANCEL ▶ (During Body Blow) Ⓜ CANCEL ▶ ↓↘→ + ATK ATK, → + Ⓗ CANCEL ▶ ↓↙← + Ⓗ CANCEL ▶ →↓↘ + ATK ATK	748,200
Level 1 X-Factor	Allows Chris to combo into Satellite Laser even when started in the opposite corner	Cr. Ⓛ, cr. Ⓜ, st. Ⓗ, → + Ⓗ, Ⓢ CANCEL ▶ super jump, air Ⓜ, Ⓜ, Ⓗ CANCEL ▶ air ↓↘→ + Ⓗ, land, → + Ⓗ, Ⓢ CANCEL ▶ super jump, air Ⓜ, Ⓜ, Ⓗ, Ⓢ, land, cr. Ⓗ OTG CANCEL ▶ X-FACTOR, ↓↙← + Ⓗ CANCEL ▶ ↓↙← + ATK ATK, ATK OTG, ATK OTG, ATK OTG, cr. Ⓗ OTG	1,237,300
Corner required	—	Cr. Ⓛ, cr. Ⓜ, st. Ⓗ, → + Ⓗ CANCEL ▶ ↓↙← + Ⓜ CANCEL ▶ (During Combination Punch M) Ⓗ, cr. Ⓜ, st. Ⓗ, → + Ⓗ CANCEL ▶ ↓↙← + Ⓗ CANCEL ▶ ↓↙← + ATK ATK, ATK OTG, ATK OTG, ATK OTG, cr. Ⓗ OTG	917,800
Doctor Doom—α	Delay the crouching Ⓗ hit for as long as possible to give the crossover assist more time to hit. The same combo with Storm—α does 521,100 damage	Cr. Ⓛ, cr. Ⓜ, st. Ⓗ, → + Ⓗ, Ⓢ CANCEL ▶ super jump, air Ⓜ, Ⓜ, Ⓗ CANCEL ▶ air ↓↘→ + Ⓗ, land, → + Ⓗ, Ⓢ CANCEL ▶ super jump, air Ⓜ, Ⓜ, Ⓗ, Ⓢ, land, P1 or P2, cr. Ⓗ OTG, ↓↙← + Ⓗ, cr. Ⓗ OTG	537,600
Thor—α	Combo from fullscreen Gun Fire H	P1 or P2, ↓↘→ + Ⓗ, ↓↘→ + Ⓗ	313,600

CHUN-LI

"THERE'S MORE TO FIGHTING THAN JUST STRENGTH!"

BIO

REAL NAME
CHUN-LI

OCCUPATION
INTERPOL OFFICER

ABILITIES
EXTREMELY PROFICIENT IN KUNG-FU, SHE IS WELL-KNOWN FOR HER VARIED AND BEAUTIFUL KICKS MORE THAN HER PUNCHES. LIKE RYU, SHE IS ALSO ABLE TO UTILIZE HER SPIRITUAL ENERGY IN BATTLE.

WEAPONS
NONE

PROFILE
SHE TIRELESSLY CONTINUES HER INVESTIGATION TO TAKE DOWN THE CRIMINAL ORGANIZATION SHADALOO. WHILE HER STRONG SENSE OF DUTY AND OBLIGATION ARE READILY APPARENT, SHE ALSO LONGS TO LIVE THE LIFESTYLE OF AN ORDINARY GIRL.

FIRST APPEARANCE
STREET FIGHTER II (1991)

POWER GRID

5 INTELLIGENCE

3 STRENGTH

7 SPEED

4 STAMINA

5 ENERGY PROJECTION

6 FIGHTING ABILITY

*This is biographical, and does not represent an evaluation of the character's in-game combat potential.

ALTERNATE COSTUMES

PS3: ⓧ Xbox 360: Ⓐ

PS3: ◻ Xbox 360: Ⓧ

PS3: △ Xbox 360: Ⓨ

PS3: R1 Xbox 360: 

ATTACK SET

STANDING BASIC ATTACKS

Screen	Command	Hits	Damage	Startup	Active	Recovery	Advantage on Hit	Advantage if Guarded	Notes
1	Standing L	1	35,000	4	2	12	-1	-2	—
2	Standing M	1	50,000	6	3	16	-1	-2	—
3	Standing H	1	70,000	10	3	18	+2	+1	Jump cancelable, ⇩ ⇙ ⇨ + P1 or P2 snap back
4	S	1	70,000	8	5	27	—	-10	Launcher attack, not special- or hyper combo-cancelable

CROUCHING BASIC ATTACKS

Screen	Command	Hits	Damage	Startup	Active	Recovery	Advantage on Hit	Advantage if Guarded	Notes
1	Crouching L	1	33,000	4	2	11	0	-1	—
2	Crouching M	1	48,000	6	3	14	+1	0	Low attack
3	Crouching H	1	60,000	8	5	23	—	-6	Low attack, knocks down, jump-cancelable

AERIAL BASIC ATTACKS

Screen	Command	Hits	Damage	Startup	Active	Recovery	Advantage on Hit	Advantage if Guarded	Notes
1	Air L	1	40,000	4	3	16	—	—	Overhead attack
2	Air M	1	55,000	6	6	18	—	—	Overhead attack
3	Air H	1	70,000	8	4	18	—	—	Overhead attack
4	Air S	1	70,000	8	4	18	—	—	Overhead attack , causes flying screen if hit during a launcher combo

CHUN-LI

COMMAND ATTACKS

Screen	Command	Hits	Damage	Startup	Active	Recovery	Advantage on Hit	Advantage if Guarded	Notes
1	⇨ + Ⓗ	1	80,000	29	3	8	+12	+11	Airborne from frame 6, overhead attack, jump-cancelable, not special-cancelable
2	(In air) ⇩ + Ⓜ	1	65,000	4	11	6	—	—	Overhead attack, attack cancels into a diagonally up-forward bounce if hit, Chun-Li is in neutral state during bounce
—	Jump backward against the wall, then press ⇗	1	—	8	—	—	—	—	Performs a wall jump, may initiate aerial attacks or movement after 8th frame

1

2

AS A PARTNER-CROSSOVER ASSISTS

Screen	Type	P1+P2 Crossover Combination Hyper Combo	Description	Hits	Damage	Startup	Active	Recovery (this crossover assist)	Recovery (other partner)	Notes
1	α – Alpha	Kikosho	Kikoken L	1	50,000	43	—	126	96	Projectile lasts 88 frames, projectile has 5 low priority durability points
2	β – Beta	Kikosho	Tenshokyaku M	5	81,700	27	1 (1) 2 (3) 1 (5) 1 (8) 1	126	96	Knocks down opponent
3	γ – Gamma	Hoyokusen	Hyakuretsukyaku H	10	71,300	31	61	93	63	Knocks down opponent

1

2

3

SPECIAL MOVES

Screen	Name	Command	Hits	Damage	Startup	Active	Recovery	Advantage on Hit	Advantage if Guarded	Notes
1	Kikoken L	⇦⇙⇩⇘⇨ + L	1	50,000	19	—	26	-2	-3	Projectile lasts 88 frames, projectile has 5 low priority durability points
	Kikoken M	⇦⇙⇩⇘⇨ + M	1	70,000	19	—	26	0	-1	Projectile lasts 32 frames, projectile has 5 low priority durability points
	Kikoken H	⇦⇙⇩⇘⇨ + H	1	90,000	19	—	26	+2	+1	Projectile lasts 8 frames, projectile has 5 low priority durability points
2	Kikoanken	(During Kikoken H) H	1	100,000	11	5	18	—	+4	Causes crumple stun
3	Spinning Bird Kick L (in air OK)	⇩ (charge), ⇧ + L	2	76,000	9	20	27 (in air, until grounded)	-6	-15	Knocks down opponent, air version has an additional 2 frames of grounded recovery
	Spinning Bird Kick M (in air OK)	⇩ (charge), ⇧ + M	3	94,800	9	30	21 (in air, until grounded)	+3	-12	Knocks down opponent, air version has an additional 2 frames of grounded recovery
	Spinning Bird Kick H (in air OK)	⇩ (charge), ⇧ + H	4	113,400	9	40	21 (in air, until grounded)	+5	-8	Knocks down opponent. air version has an additional 2 frames of grounded recovery
4	Hyakuretsukyaku L (in air OK)	L)))	4-9	51,500 – 91,500	7	22	1	+24	+15	Knocks down opponent, can be mashed for additional hits
	Hyakuretsukyaku M (in air OK)	M)))	5-11	61,300 - 102,500	7	22	1	+24	+14	Knocks down opponent, can be mashed for additional hits
	Hyakuretsukyaku H (in air OK)	H)))	8-15	85,100 – 118,600	7	22	1	+24	+12	Knocks down opponent, can be mashed for additional hits
5	Tenshokyaku L	⇨⇩⇘ + L	3	78,400	3	1 (1) 2 (4) 3	19	-1	0	Airborne from frame 1, knocks down opponent
	Air Tenshokyaku L	(in air) ⇨⇩⇘ + L	3	78,400	3	3 (6) 3	Until grounded, 1 frame ground recovery	—	—	Knocks down opponent
	Tenshokyaku M	⇨⇩⇘ + M	5	101,400	3	1 (1) 2 (3) 1 (5) 1 (8) 1	23	-3	-17	Airborne from frame 1, knocks down opponent
	Air Tenshokyaku M	(in air) ⇨⇩⇘ + M	5	101,400	3	3 (5) 2 (4) 2 (7) 3	Until grounded, 1 frame ground recovery	—	—	Knocks down opponent
	Tenshokyaku H	⇨⇩⇘ + H	7	120,000	3	1 (1) 1 (5) 1 (5) 1 (8) 1 (5) 1 (8) 3	13	+8	-23	Airborne from frame 1, knocks down opponent
	Air Tenshokyaku H	(in air) ⇨⇩⇘ + H	7	120,000	3	3 (5) 2 (4) 2 (7) 2 (4) 2 (7) 3	Until grounded, 1 frame ground recovery	—	—	Knocks down opponent

1

Kikoken: Kikoken L recovers quickly and fires a slow-traveling projectile, making it useful as both a zoning tool to keep out attacking characters, and as covering fire to advance behind. Kikoken L travels about 80% of the screen's length before dissipating, substantially farther than the other two versions of the attack.

Kikoken M and H deal progressively more damage to an opponent, but also dissipate much more quickly. This makes these versions of the attack difficult to use effectively.

2

Kikoanken: Kikoanken is performed by pressing H during the startup animation of Kikoken H. It is mainly used in combos, dealing a large amount of damage in a single hit and causing a crumple stun state.

Kikoanken has a frame advantage of +4 if guarded, but you'll usually want to cancel attacks into Hyakuretsukyaku instead for much more frame advantage.

3

Spinning Bird Kick: Spinning Bird Kick can be used in tandem with a long-ranged crossover assist to quickly cover a lot of distance while attacking. The air version of Spinning Bird Kick recovers much more quickly if done low to the ground, allowing combos afterwards if it hits successfully. Most characters can crouch completely under a Spinning Bird Kick done in the air, however.

The air version of Spinning Bird Kick only has 2 frames of grounded recovery. This can make it very difficult for any opposition to catch Chun-Li if you are employing Spinning Bird Kick to run away.

4

Hyakuretsukyaku: Tapping the same button three times in quick succession will activate Hyakuretsukyaku. This attack is Chun-Li's all-around, most useful move—a quick attack that allows for combos if it hits and massive frame advantage if it is guarded. Hyakuretsukyaku can also be performed in the air making it useful in several combos, in addition to a method of turning Chun-Li around to attack an opponent that she has airdashed over.

The main weakness of Hyakuretsukyaku is that its many hits severely scale damage in combos when used early on. While Hyakuretsukyaku allows many attacks to be combo-starters that wouldn't be otherwise, these combos will generally only inflict around 300,000 damage.

5

Tenshokyaku: Tenshokyaku isn't invincible at all, but still manages to be a strong anti-air attack due to its quick 3 frame startup speed. If you perform your anti-air Tenshokyaku too late and get hit out of the startup, you'll get knocked out of the air, because the attack is considered airborne from the first frame. This makes it more difficult for an opponent to hit you with a combo in this situation, but not impossible.

Tenshokyaku L is safe if guarded—Chun-Li recovers in a neutral airborne state afterwards. If your opponent guards the attack, you can often beat retaliatory attempts with air L afterward. Depending on the height at which Tenshokyaku was blocked, you may be at a frame disadvantage afterward. In these situations you're probably better off double jumping backwards and guarding.

HYPER COMBOS

Screen	Name	Command	Hits	Damage	Startup	Active	Recovery	Advantage on Hit	Advantage if Guarded	Notes
1	Kikosho	↓↘→ + ATK ATK	14	286,300	8+1	88	38	—	-32	Knocks down opponent, beam durability: 14 frames x 3 high priority durability points
2	Hoyokusen	↓↙← + ATK ATK	14	230,000	10+3	38 (7) 34 (7) 6	42	—	-26	Invincible from frames 1-16, final hit is a launcher attack
3	Shichisei Ranka (level 3 hyper combo)	→↓↘ + ATK ATK	14	410,000	10+3	2 (2) 2 (2) 2 (2) 2 (20) 3	27	—	-8	Invincible from frames 1-21, unrecoverable knockdown

1

Kikosho: The Kikosho hyper combo creates a huge projectile sphere around Chun-Li after its startup frames have completed, essentially making Chun-Li invulnerable during the duration of the active frames. Combined with its relatively fast startup speed, this makes Kikosho a good defensive hyper combo in a variety of situations such as anti-air and anti-teleport. Its strong damage also makes this the preferred combo-ender if you have an OTG-capable crossover assist available. Kikosho is very unsafe if guarded. Unless you are able to team hyper combo to a safe hyper combo, try to only use it in guaranteed situations. Kikosho is very easy to use within THC combos—the huge projectile sphere easily connects after nearly any hyper combo.

2

Hoyokusen: Hoyokusen ends with a launcher attack, allowing for full combos afterward. However it also causes a large amount of hitstun deterioration, which can make the following aerial combo substantially weaker if used late in a combo. As such, combos that use Hoyokusen usually have only a marginal damage increase over meter-less versions of the same combo.

Hoyokusen has a very large amount of invincibility, and can be used to blow through close-ranged attacks to result in a full combo. However, it also unsafe if guarded, so be sure you can team hyper combo to a safer hyper combo if you're not guaranteed to hit your opponent.

Another character on your team using a THC combo into Hoyokusen makes for some interesting possibilities, but generally in these situations hitstun has been deteriorated to the point where post-launcher aerial combos don't amount to much. However, you can use a team aerial combo attack to reset hitstun deterioration, as well as create flashy combos with over three character changes!

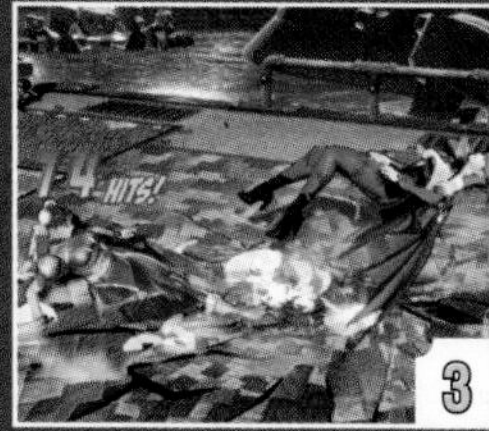

3

Shichisei Ranka: Like all level 3 hyper combos, Shichisei Ranka is not subject to damage scaling, making it ideal to end extended combos with. Like Kikosho, you'll need access to an OTG-capable crossover assist to be able to combo into Shichisei Ranka after an aerial combo. Shichisei Ranka also has a very large amount of invincibility, making it useful for blowing through attacks at higher angles.

BATTLE PLAN

OVERVIEW

VITALITY: 850,000

CHAIN COMBO ARCHETYPE: MARVEL SERIES

X-Factor	Lv.1	Lv.2	Lv.3
Damage	110%	130%	150%
Speed	115%	135%	150%

Your goal with Chun-Li is to establish close range with frame advantage, with the secondary goal of pushing your opponent to the corner.

Why is establishing close range beneficial with Chun-Li?

- **Chun-Li has many offensive tools that allow her to keep offensive momentum on a guarding opponent, such as jump-cancelable normal attacks, a fast airdash, and Hyakuretsukyaku with massive frame advantage if guarded.**
- **At close range she can set up cross ups which are difficult to guard, like airdash into cross up air Ⓛ, airdash into cross up Hyakuretsukyaku, or even ➔ ✚ Ⓗ.**
- **She can hit opponents with instant overhead ↓ ✚ Ⓜ or air Ⓛ, both of which can lead into full combos.**
- **With a low-hitting crossover assist, she can easily set up many unblockable overhead attacks.**

Why would you want to push your opponent to the corner with Chun-Li?

- **In the corner it is much easier to maintain offensive momentum after your challenger uses advancing guard.**
- **Chun-Li gains the ability to combo airdash Ⓗ after hitting with an instant overhead air ↓ ✚ Ⓜ, making her offense incredibly difficult to guard against.**
- **Chun-Li can easily maintain offensive momentum after a corner combo ending with flying screen.**

How do you establish close range at frame advantage with Chun-Li?

- **Using Chun-Li's excellent aerial mobility options to maneuver around zoning defenses.**
- **Wavedashing towards an opponent whenever they attempt to preemptively stop you from jumping.**
- **Wavedashing forward behind the cover of Kikoken L or a crossover assist.**
- **Reading when your opponent will attempt to advancing guard and countering with more forward movement.**

How does Chun-Li push the opponent to the corner?

- **Hitting your challenger with a combo.**
- **Not allowing your opponent to ground recover forward past Chun-Li by backdashing and staying in front of the opponent.**
- **Maintaining close-range momentum, forcing your challenger to use an advancing guard and push themselves back toward the corner.**
- **Maintaining momentum after your opponent uses advancing guard with a combination of instant airdash attacks, long-ranged crossover assists and Kikoken L.**

ON THE GROUND

Standing and crouching Ⓗ are both jump-cancelable. Immediately airdash after jump-canceling to maintain offensive momentum!

Hyakuretsukyaku inflicts chip damage while leaving you at a massive frame advantage if guarded. Repeated use of this attack forces your opponent to use advancing guard to push you away.

Kikoken L can provide you a safe way to approach your challenger.

Chun-Li is an execution-heavy, offensive character. Be prepared to spend a considerable amount of time in Training Mode perfecting her combos and set-ups! Chun-Li best fills the role of meter-builder on a team. Her standard combo is so long, it builds 1.8 bars of hyper combo gauge by itself! She also typically doesn't use any meter on her own when played, due to the fact that she requires a fast OTG-capable assist to be able to end combos with Kikosho or Shichisei Ranka.

To accomplish your goal of establishing close range with your opponent, you'll normally want to take to the air and take advantage of Chun-Li's air mobility. However, that discussion is covered in the Up in the Air section. To advance forward on the ground, your most common option is to simply wavedash forward when your challenger is expecting you to jump. Against characters that don't have a projectile, or don't have many projectile points on their projectile attacks, using Kikoken L and wavedashing behind the projectile can be a safe and effective way to advance forward. If you have a projectile-using crossover assist like Ryu—β or Arthur—β, you can call that assist immediately before using Spinning Bird Kick H to safely cover a large distance in a flash.

When you successfully get into close range with frame advantage, attacking with Hyakuretsukyaku H or Kikoanken both produce enough frame advantage for you to be able to attack continuously. There isn't much your opponent can do about this besides advancing guard. Knowing this, opponents may use advancing guard every chance they get—being able to maintain offense after an opponent uses advancing guard is the key to playing Chun-Li effectively.

If you anticipate that the opposition is going to use advancing guard against your next attack, use standing or crouching Ⓗ. These attacks are jump-cancelable, allowing you to immediately jump and airdash forward and attack with air Ⓜ to maintain offense. Your opponent will likely use advancing guard against your air Ⓜ as well, which will push you too far out of range to use another airdash to air Ⓜ. However, this sequence pushes your challenger backwards a considerable distance towards the corner, working toward your secondary goal. If you have a projectile-using crossover assist you can call that assist simultaneously with your air Ⓜ attack, then wavedash forward and establish close range again.

If your opponent manages to get away from you and creates a neutral situation across the screen, you'll have to work your way in again. Be sure to prevent your opponent from neutralizing your forward progress by getting behind you—constantly moving forward will give teleportation characters an opportunity to teleport behind you, counter this by not moving forward and punishing their teleportation attempt. Don't get impatient and super jump, since this will allow your opponent to wavedash under you. Details on what to do when you eventually corner your opponent are covered in the Up in the Air section.

Chun-Li's crouching Ⓛ does not hit low, making her only low attacks crouching Ⓜ and crouching Ⓗ. Crouching Ⓜ is as fast as many characters' crouching Ⓛ, so using it as a low attack isn't much of a compromise. Crouching Ⓜ also has a lot of range, allowing you to dash forward and attack with it from a considerable distance. If you hit with it at the very tip, chain to standing Ⓗ then hyper combo-cancel into Hoyokusen; nothing else will reach your opponent at that range.

Chun-Li's standing and crouching Ⓛ are very fast, having a startup speed of only 4 frames. This makes Chun-Li strong in situations with very slight frame advantage or disadvantage; Chun-Li's faster attacks will often beat out an opponent's. If you find yourself still getting hit in these situations, simply guarding is your best bet.

You'll initially want to keep some characters away, waiting for a safe opportunity to start your offense. In these situations throwing out a constant stream of Kikoken L can be very effective, essentially forcing your challenger to jump towards you unless they have an anti-projectile move. If your foe jumps toward you, they will inevitably land into a Kikoken. Stop throwing Kikokens when your opponent jumps and instead use the frame advantage from the situation to mount your offense. Even if your opposition has strong anti-projectile measures, getting a single Kikoken L onto the screen and countering the opposing player's attempts to get around it can be a strong tactic.

Chun-Li's main anti-air is Tenshokyaku L. It recovers in a neutral airborne state and is safe if guarded, and its fast 3 frame startup speed make it a very viable anti-air despite its lack of invincibility. If the attack hits, your opponent will likely air recover backwards. Take advantage of the situation by immediately airdashing forward, then dashing forward upon landing. This allows you to cross-under your challenger while off-screen and surprise them with a crouching Ⓛ! If Tenshokyaku L is guarded you should either attack on the way down with air Ⓛ, or double jump backwards and guard if you're at a significant frame disadvantage.

Once your opponent attempts to jump towards you and guard your Tenshokyaku L, that's your cue to anti-air with air throws. If you have a fast OTG-capable crossover assist like Wesker—β or Deadpool—β, you can land a full combo after a backwards air throw—see the Combo Appendix section for details.

UP IN THE AIR

Chun-Li has a unique airdash that travels at a slight downward angle very quickly.

Air Ⓜ from an airdash is very difficult to anti-air, and is huge component of Chun-Li's offense.

Air⇩ + Ⓜ can be used as an instant overhead on every character in the game.

Chun-Li has excellent aerial mobility options, making her a character that is often more at home in the air than she is on the ground. Chun-Li is one of only two characters in the game that can triple jump, giving her great options for continually changing her jump arc in unpredictable ways. This gives you the ability to maneuver around zoning projectiles at little to no risk, holding back on the controller after double or triple jumping makes it very unlikely to get hit. Using a triple jump from a normal jump lets you reach a great height while still having access to crossover assists. Using this tactic essentially forces your opponent to meet you in the air to counter you.

She has one of the best airdashes in the game—a unique forward airdash with a slight downward angle and incredible speed. This airdash is the cornerstone of Chun-Li's offense, but each airdash counts towards your double jump total. For example, you can super jump and then airdash twice, but you won't be able to double jump after the second airdash. This restriction also prevents you from jumping, airdashing, double jumping, and then airdashing again. Use Chun-Li's airdash when you need quick, abrupt forward movement while in the air. Airdashes are almost always followed by an air Ⓜ attack—Chun-Li's air attack with the farthest range.

Chun-Li also has the ability to wall jump; another rarity in *Marvel vs. Capcom 3*. The main purpose of a wall jump is simply to get even higher in the air. Note that wall jumps cannot be used directly from a super jump—you must use a double jump first to be able to wall jump. Wall jumps have two strong potential uses: if you normal jump backwards toward a wall, you can do a repeated sequence of wall jump to double jump backwards until you've used all your jumps. This allows you to reach super jump height while still in normal jump state, giving you access to crossover assists! Wall jumps are also a strong component of Chun-Li's stalling game. Super jump backwards towards a wall, double jump backwards, then wall jump forward. If the HUD marker denoting the location of your opponent is near you, then airdash and perform a Spinning Bird Kick H. You'll fly clear over your opponent away to safety, able to repeat the sequence in the other corner. If your opponent's HUD marker is on the other end of the screen, drop down instead of trying to fly over your foe. If your opponent's HUD quickly moves toward you during your decent, use your last remaining jump to triple jump toward the wall, then wall jump and Spinning Bird Kick over your opponent!

Air Ⓜ is Chun-Li's main air attack, having long range and great speed. If used from an airdash against an opponent that doesn't use advancing guard, you have enough time to attack with a very deep second air Ⓜ, which will likely hit as a surprise overhead attack.

If your opponent does use advancing guard against your air Ⓜ, simply jump, airdash and use air Ⓜ again if you're in range. This maintains offensive momentum and pushes your challenger back toward the corner, especially when combined with a long-ranged crossover assist.

Air Ⓛ is Chun-Li's fastest air attack, at 4 frames. It is most often used as an air-to-air attack against jumping opponents, leading to a full combo if you hit with it at normal jump height. Air Ⓛ is also Chun-Li's most reliable cross-up air normal attack, even though it still doesn't fill this role very well due to its very short hitbox extending backwards. Even so, a properly set up cross up airdash air Ⓛ can be incredibly effective.

Hyakuretsukyaku in the air isn't just combo filler—it can also be used to turn Chun-Li around in the air when jumping or airdashing past an opponent. This makes Hyakuretsukyaku a very effective cross-up, but it is difficult to execute due to its input command. Hyakuretsukyaku almost always allows you to combo your foe if it hits. The most effective way to set up a cross-up Hyakuretsukyaku is to airdash behind your challenger at close range, then immediately cancel the airdash into Hyakuretsukyaku. This requires a lot of practice!

Air⇩ + Ⓜ performed immediately after jumping is an instant overhead that works against every character in the game. Against all but extremely small characters you can hit a combo after air⇩ + Ⓜ by immediately airdashing and performing Hyakuretsukyaku M—see the Combo Appendix for details. Getting the Hyakuretsukyaku to combo after the instant overhead is very difficult to do consistently, so other options should be considered. On larger characters, air Ⓛ can be used as an instant overhead. This can then be canceled into Hyakuretsukyaku L, leading into a full combo. See the Combo Usage section for details on the combo and characters it works against. Lastly, you can call a crossover assist before you hit your opponent with an instant overhead air⇩ + Ⓜ. This causes the crossover assist to combo after the instant overhead, giving you enough time to airdash, land and continue into a full combo. Instant overheads should be considered whenever you are able to get within point-blank of the opponent. Once the opponent starts to guard your overheads, start mixing in crouching Ⓜ.

Once you have your opposition in the corner it becomes much easier to maintain your offense even after they use advancing guard, and you also gain access to an easy combo after an instant overhead: air⇩ + Ⓜ used as an instant overhead can easily combo into an airdash air Ⓗ in the corner. Once this attack hits you can transition into your best combo! In the corner it becomes much easier to establish point-blank range and set-up this instant overhead, especially if you use a long-ranged crossover assist to pin your challenger down. If Wesker is on your team, you also gain access to an incredibly powerful unblockable set-up against a cornered opponent. See the Advanced Tactics section for details.

Once you have your enemy in the corner, it becomes even more important to keep your offensive momentum after your opponent uses advancing guard. Stick to using jump-cancelable normal attacks and airdash Ⓜ for as long as possible. Save your long-ranged crossover assist for situations where you've been pushed too far away to keep up your offense otherwise, then wavedash towards your opponent and perform another mix-up of instant overhead air⇩ + Ⓜ or crouching Ⓜ. In the event that you're pushed away and do not have access to a long-ranged crossover assist, be ready to prevent whatever action your opponent does to escape the corner. In most cases the opposition will attempt to super jump; be ready to super jump with your foe and air throw them back down to the ground. If you accidentally get air Ⓗ instead of an air throw, rapidly press Ⓗ to cancel it into air Hyakuretsukyaku H. If your opponent uses advancing guard, double jump and airdash towards them again to keep pushing them back.

Chun-Li can inflict a lot of damage during her aerial combos, but it is often difficult to end her combos with a hyper combo. This makes her a great candidate for using team aerial combo starters! After all of your double jumps have been used in a combo, and hitstun has been deteriorated to the point where further combos become nearly impossible, sneaking in a team aerial combo starter can result in a drastic increase in combo damage. Ideally, you'll want to use team aerial combos to switch to a character that can easily end with a hyper combo; this will let you team hyper combo back to Chun-Li against an opponent that is most likely in the corner!

On a similar note, in a long combo using two team aerial combo starters, Chun-Li's huge meter-less aerial combo makes her the ideal second character in the combo. See the Combo Appendix sections for details on what combos to do with Chun-Li depending on which team aerial combo starter was used to tag her in.

COMBO USAGE

I. CR. Ⓛ, CR. Ⓜ, ST. Ⓗ CANCEL ← ↙ ↓ ↘ → + Ⓗ CANCEL (DURING KIKOKEN H) Ⓗ, ST. Ⓗ, CR. Ⓗ CANCEL JUMP, AIR Ⓛ, Ⓜ, Ⓜ, Ⓗ, Ⓢ, LAND, ST. Ⓛ, ST. Ⓜ, ST. Ⓗ, CR. Ⓗ, Ⓢ CANCEL SUPER JUMP STRAIGHT UP, AIR ↓ + Ⓜ, AIR ↓ + Ⓜ, AIR Ⓗ CANCEL Ⓗ)), DOUBLE JUMP, AIR Ⓜ, Ⓜ, Ⓗ CANCEL Ⓗ)), TRIPLE JUMP, AIR Ⓜ, Ⓜ, Ⓗ, Ⓢ

(463,900 damage) Chun-Li can dish out surprisingly respectable damage without using hyper combo gauge bars, but doing so requires you to perform one of the most challenging basic combos in the game. During the normal jump portion, be sure to delay the air Ⓢ as long as possible to be able to continue the combo afterwards. When super jump-canceling the launcher, be sure to super jump straight up; the air ↓ + Ⓜ will not connect with your opponent otherwise. After the two headstomps, make sure not to tap Ⓗ)) too quickly or the air Ⓗ will be canceled before the startup of the attack has time to finish. Juggling the air Hyakuretsukyakus takes a bit of practice. The most important point to remember is to not spaz out mashing Ⓗ; press Ⓗ three times in a controlled rhythm and the combo becomes much easier.

This combo not only does good damage, it also builds 1.8 bars of hyper combo gauge. In addition, it carries your opponent 75% of the way across the stage towards the corner.

Since Chun-Li has difficulty ending combos with a hyper combo without help from an OTG-capable crossover assist, attempting a team aerial combo during the triple jump can be a good idea to increase combo damage significantly.

II. (AGAINST JUMPING OPPONENT) AIR Ⓛ, Ⓜ, Ⓗ, Ⓢ, LAND, STANDING Ⓛ, STANDING Ⓜ, STANDING Ⓗ, CROUCHING Ⓗ, Ⓢ CANCEL SUPER JUMP, AIR ↓ + Ⓜ, AIR ↓ + Ⓜ, AIR Ⓗ CANCEL Ⓗ)), DOUBLE JUMP, AIR Ⓜ, Ⓜ, Ⓗ CANCEL Ⓗ)), TRIPLE JUMP, AIR Ⓜ, Ⓜ, Ⓗ, Ⓢ

(401,100 damage) Chun-Li's air Ⓛ is very fast, making it a great anti-air move if you're prepared to react. The main trick to landing this combo is delaying the air Ⓢ just the right amount of time. It will often take a bit of improvisation due to the opponent's height in the air, but it's a very learnable skill.

III. (CORNER REQUIRED) AIR ↓ + Ⓜ, AIR DASH, AIR Ⓗ, LAND, CR. Ⓜ, ST. Ⓗ CANCEL ← ↙ ↓ ↘ → + Ⓗ CANCEL (DURING KIKOKEN H) Ⓗ, ST. Ⓗ, CR. Ⓗ CANCEL ↓ ↙ ← + ATK ATK CANCEL SUPER JUMP, AIR ↓ + Ⓜ, AIR ↓ + Ⓜ, AIR Ⓗ CANCEL Ⓗ)), AIR ↓ + Ⓜ, AIR ↓ + Ⓜ, AIR Ⓜ, Ⓗ CANCEL Ⓗ)), AIR ↓ + Ⓜ, AIR Ⓗ CANCEL Ⓗ)), AIR Ⓢ, LAND, P1 OR P2, → ↓ ↘ + ATK ATK

(1,043,600 damage, Wesker—β) Insane damage off of an instant overhead air ↓ + Ⓜ! Ending the combo with a Kikosho instead of a Shichisei Ranka will inflict 810,000 damage, allowing you to team hyper combo to another character for potentially more efficient meter usage.

IV. AIR Ⓛ CANCEL Ⓛ)), AIR Ⓜ, LAND, ST. Ⓜ, ST. Ⓗ, CR. Ⓗ, Ⓢ CANCEL SUPER JUMP STRAIGHT UP, AIR ↓ + Ⓜ, AIR Ⓗ CANCEL Ⓗ)), DOUBLE JUMP, AIR Ⓜ, AIR Ⓗ CANCEL Ⓗ)), TRIPLE JUMP, AIR Ⓜ, AIR Ⓗ CANCEL Ⓗ))

(295,200 damage) Chun-Li's air Ⓛ can be performed immediately after jumping, making it an instant overhead attack on the larger crouching characters.

Vulnerable to instant overhead air Ⓛ:

- Captain America
- Hulk
- Iron Man
- M.O.D.O.K.
- Sentinel
- Taskmaster
- Thor
- Tron
- Wesker (extremely difficult)

Performing instant overhead air ↓ + Ⓜ after a dash, then quickly airdashing and doing Hyakuretsukyaku M works on most characters, but is much more difficult to do consistently. See the Combo Appendix section for details.

V. (CORNER REQUIRED) CR. Ⓛ, CR. Ⓜ, ST. Ⓗ CANCEL ← ↙ ↓ ↘ → + Ⓗ CANCEL (DURING KIKOKEN H) Ⓗ, ST. Ⓗ, CR. Ⓗ CANCEL JUMP, AIR Ⓛ, Ⓜ, Ⓜ, Ⓗ, Ⓢ, LAND, ST. Ⓛ, ST. Ⓜ, ST. Ⓗ, CR. Ⓗ, Ⓢ CANCEL SUPER JUMP STRAIGHT UP, AIR ↓ + Ⓜ, AIR ↓ + Ⓜ, AIR Ⓗ CANCEL Ⓗ)), DOUBLE JUMP, AIR Ⓜ, Ⓜ, Ⓗ CANCEL Ⓗ)), TRIPLE JUMP, AIR Ⓜ, Ⓜ, Ⓗ, Ⓢ, LAND, P1 OR P2, ↓ ↘ → + ATK ATK

(648,300 damage, Wesker—β) Having a fast OTG-capable crossover assist substantially increases Chun-Li's damage potential. Putting a Hoyokusen into Chun-Li's standard combo increases damage and doesn't require help from a crossover assist, but it also doesn't increase the damage by much. Hoyokusen introduces so much hitstun deterioration to the combo that the subsequent launcher combo does not result in much damage. See the Combo Appendix section for details.

This combo only requires that the combo eventually ends up in the corner, so that you don't have to dash forward to be in range for the Wesker—β OTG hit. This combo will work mid-screen with a faster OTG-capable crossover assist, like Deadpool—β. Substituting Shichisei Ranka for Kikosho at the end of the combo results in 881,900 damage.

ASSISTS

Wesker—β performs many roles for Chun-Li: OTG-capable attack to extend combos, low attack for unguardable set-ups, and is fast enough to combo after instant overheads!

Multi-hit projectile assists create the ideal cover for Chun-Li to advance forward with.

Beam-based crossover assists are useful all-around, and also are a vital component in maintaining offense against cornered opponents.

Chun-Li has two strong assist types, depending on what your needs are. Hyakuretsukyaku is great for extending combos and pinning down your opponent with guardstun, but will harshly scale the damage of a combo if used early on. Kikoken is good for covering fire, since it places a slow-moving projectile on the screen that remains an active threat for a long period of time.

Chun-Li as a character becomes much stronger when paired with Wesker—β. Wesker performs several vital roles for Chun-Li: as a fast OTG-capable assist, Wesker—β allows you get much more damage after her standard combos in addition to her forward ground throw and backwards air throw. Since Wesker—β is also a low-hitting attack, it allows you to create several practical set-ups which are unguardable for an opponent; see the Advanced Tactics section for details. The low-hitting gunshot is also useful in various other situations—you can triple jump at your foe while calling Wesker—β, surprising the opponent with a low-hitting attack while Chun-Li is still very high in the air. Calling Wesker during airdash Ⓜ attack patterns is also incredibly difficult to defend against.

There are other assists that are OTG-capable or low-hitting, but none of them are as fast and easy to use as Wesker—β. Even if you have another OTG-capable assist that's easier to use, like Deadpool—β or C. Viper—β, you won't find a low-hitting crossover assist that's faster than Wesker.

With the OTG-capable and low-hitting responsibilities taken care of, Chun-Li also benefits greatly from having a crossover assist that keeps opposing characters in guardstun from long ranges. Both beam-based and projectile-based assists work well in this regard, with multi-hit projectiles performing this role best. As such, Arthur—β and powered-up Zero—β are great crossover assists for Chun-Li. Both of these assists remain an active threat on the screen for a long time and induce very long guardstun and hitstun on challengers, making it much easier for you to wavedash close after they use advancing guard. These assists will also allow you to set up instant overhead mix-ups much more easily, as well as let you attack safely with Spinning Bird Kick H from across the screen.

Finally, beam-based crossover assists like Iron Man—α and Doctor Doom—α are useful all-around for keeping your opponent in guardstun. They also play a vital role in keeping momentum on a cornered opponent after a flying screen combo. See the Advanced Tactics section for details.

ADVANCED TACTICS

UNGUARDABLE SET-UPS USING WESKER—β

The easiest and most common way to set up an unguardable air Ⓜ attack is to press the P1 or P2 button simultaneously with a jump cancelable attack, usually standing Ⓗ. From there if you jump cancel and immediately attack with airdash Ⓜ you'll create the perfect timing to hit simultaneously with Wesker's low-hitting gunshot. A mid-screen opponent can use advancing guard against the standing Ⓗ and escape the set-up. However, it becomes very difficult for an opponent to escape this set-up in the corner.

Wesker—β is a low-hitting attack, and can easily be used in tandem with Chun-Li's air attacks to create unguardable set-ups.

Another strong set-up for an unguardable air Ⓜ is to normal jump towards the opponent, then double jump at the apex of your jump. At the double jump's apex, triple jump and press P1 or P2 slightly after jumping. This creates the timing for Wesker to hit your opponent simultaneously with Chun-Li coming down and attacking with air Ⓜ. Even better, Wesker doesn't even show up on the screen until after he's fired his shot! It a strong play to call Wesker slightly earlier, hitting your opponent with a surprise low attack that your air Ⓜ will combo after.

At close ranges, pressing P1 or P2 immediately before doing ➔ + Ⓗ creates an interesting situation: if your opponent stays on the ground guarding, Chun-Li's ➔ + Ⓗ overhead attack will hit simultaneously with Wesker's gunshot, allowing you to continue with a combo after the unguardable hits. If doing ➔ + Ⓗ happens to throw your foe, Wesker's gunshot will still OTG after the throw, allowing you to continue with a full combo regardless!

SET-UP AFTER FLYING SCREEN IN THE CORNER

After knocking down your opponent in the corner with a combo ending with flying screen, it's especially important for a Chun-Li player to maintain offensive momentum regardless of the direction that your opponent ground recovers in. If you have a beam-based crossover assist, you can distill the guessing game down to whether or not the opponent performed a ground recover at all.

Beam-based crossover assists allow you to continue attacking the opponent in the corner no matter what direction they ground recover in.

After finishing your combo with flying screen, immediately dash backwards and call your beam assist. If you see the opponent ground recover towards you, simply stand still: your challenger will ground recover right next to you while guarding the beam. This is a perfect opportunity to mix up your opponent with an instant overhead or crouching Ⓜ! If the opposing player chooses to ground recover backwards into the corner, you'll have plenty of time to see that happening, dash forward, and perform the same mix-up while your challenger is guarding the beam attack.

If your opponent chooses not to ground recover, call your assist immediately upon landing from the aerial combo, then dash backwards anyway. This way your opponent will have no visual stimuli to react to in deciding whether or not they should ground recover. If your opponent indeed does not ground recover, immediately dash forward again and mix them up after the guardstun from the beam assist.

COMBO APPENDIX

GENERAL EXECUTION TIPS

Simply tapping H three times quickly will result in air H cancelled into Hyakuretsukyaku H. Don't mash!

When using jump-canceled crouching H in combos, perform the air L, M, M, H chain as fast as possible, then delay the air S for as long as possible.

Chun-Li combos are more difficult than most combos in the game. Keep practicing!

Requirements (Position, meter, etc.)	Notes	Command Sequence	Damage
—	Chun Li's air version of her Spinning Bird Kick covers the screen incredibly quickly, is safe if guarded, and leads to combos if hit. To do the air version of the Spinning Bird Kick right off the ground, simply charge ↓, press ↑, then wait a fraction of a section before pressing H. Most characters can crouch under the air Spinning Bird Kick, however, so use with caution.	Air (charge) ↓, ↑ + H, st. M, st. H, cr. H, S CANCEL→ super jump, air ↓ + M, air ↓ + M, air H CANCEL→ H)), double jump, air M, M, H CANCEL→ H)), triple jump, air M, M, H CANCEL→ H))	349,200
—	Mash the Hyakuretsukyaku for extra hits before hyper combo-canceling into Shichisei Ranka	Cr. L, cr. M, st. H CANCEL→ ←↙↓↘→ + H CANCEL→ (during Kikoken H) H, st. H, cr. H CANCEL→ jump, air L, M, M, H, S, land, st. L, st. M, st. H, cr. H CANCEL→ H)) CANCEL→ →↓↘ + ATK ATK	772,500
—	This combo results in a damage increase of only about 80,000 more than the standard meter-less combo. Substituting Hyakuretsukyaku H for air S results in 552,800 damage	Cr. L, cr. M, st. H CANCEL→ ←↙↓↘→ + H CANCEL→ (during Kikoken H) H, st. H, cr. H CANCEL→ ↓↙← + ATK ATK CANCEL→ super jump, air ↓ + M, air ↓ + M, air H CANCEL→ H)), double jump, air M, M, H CANCEL→ H)), triple jump, air M, M, H, S	544,800
—	Full combo starting from instant overhead air ↓ + M midscreen, works against most characters in the game.	Air ↓ + M, airdash, M)), air M, land, st. M, st. H, cr. H, S CANCEL→ super jump, air ↓ + M, air ↓ + M, air H CANCEL→ H)), double jump, air M, M, H CANCEL→ H)), triple jump, air M, M, H, S	306,500
Wesker—β	Combo from unguardable set-up	P1 or P2, jump, airdash, air M, land, cr. M, st. H CANCEL→ ←↙↓↘→ + H CANCEL→ (during Kikoken H) H, st. H, cr. H CANCEL→ jump, air L, M, M, H, S, land, st. L, st. M, st. H, st. H, S CANCEL→ super jump straight up, air ↓ + M, air ↓ + M, air H CANCEL→ H)), double jump, air M, M, H CANCEL→ H)), triple jump, air M, M, H, S	512,500
Wesker—β, opponent must be no higher than normal jump height	—	Back air throw, P1 or P2, land, dash, st. M, st. H, cr. H, S CANCEL→ super jump, straight up, air ↓ + M, air ↓ + M, air H CANCEL→ H)), double jump, air M, M, H CANCEL→ H)), triple jump, air M, M, H, S	341,400
Wesker—β	Press the P1 or P2 button immediately before throwing the opponent. If you unintentionally get a throw instead of an unguardable → + H set-up, you can still get a full combo on the opponent.	P1 or P2, forward throw, jump, air L, M, M, H, S, land, st. L, st. M, st. H, cr. H, S CANCEL→ super jump, super jump straight up, air ↓ + M, air ↓ + M, air H CANCEL→ H)), double jump, air M, M, H CANCEL→ H)), triple jump, air M, M, H, S	361,600
Corner required	Chun-Li can do marginally more damage against a cornered opponent. Hitstun deterioration gets very pronounced by the end of the combo, which prevents you from easily integrating Chun-Li's remaining two jumps in the combo. The final air S can be substituted for a team aerial combo starter.	cr. L, cr. M, st. H CANCEL→ ←↙↓↘→ + H CANCEL→ (during Kikoken H) H, st. H, cr. H CANCEL→ jump, air L, M, M, H, S, land, st. L, st. M, st. H, cr. H, S CANCEL→ super jump straight up, air ↓ + M, air ↓ + M, air H CANCEL→ H)), air ↓ + M, air ↓ + M, air M, H CANCEL→ H)), double jump, air M, H CANCEL→ H)), S	489,900
Corner required, Chun-Li tagged in via ↓ + S team aerial combo starter	If tagged in via ↑ + S team aerial combo starter, omit the first air ↓ + M. Final air S can be exchanged with another team aerial combo starter.	Air ↓ + M, air H CANCEL→ H)), air ↓ + M, air ↓ + M, air M, M, H CANCEL→ H)), air ↓ + M, air ↓ + M, air M, M, H CANCEL→ H)), double jump, air M, M, H CANCEL→ triple jump, air M, M, H, S	Damage variable depending on damage scaling
Chun-Li tagged in via → + S team aerial combo starter	—	Air M, H CANCEL→ H)), double jump, air M, M, H CANCEL→ H)), triple jump, air M, M, H, S	Damage variable depending on damage scaling

"I'LL ROOT OUT EVIL
WHEREVER I FIND IT!
COUNT ON IT!"

"I DON'T HAVE TIME FOR THIS NOW, BE A DEAR AND GIVE UP ALREADY. OK?"

C. VIPER

BIO

REAL NAME

UNKNOWN

OCCUPATION

CIA AGENT

ABILITIES

HAS HIGH PHYSICAL ABILITIES, COMPLEMENTED BY HER SPECIAL BATTLE SUIT EQUIPPED HEAD TO TOE WITH WEAPONRY. SHE USES A FIGHTING STYLE CALLED "COVERT FIGHTING TOOLS", WHICH SHE CREATED.

WEAPONS

HER BATTLE SUIT, WHICH HAS VARIOUS WEAPONS INTEGRATED INTO IT.

PROFILE

WHEN IT COMES TO WORK, SHE LEAVES HONOR AND EMOTIONS BEHIND AND KEEPS IT ABOUT BUSINESS. HER DILIGENCE AND EFFICIENCY EARNED HER THE NICKNAME "MISS PERFECT". HOWEVER, IN FRONT OF HER DAUGHTER SHE BECOMES A GENTLE, LOVING MOTHER.

FIRST APPEARANCE

STREET FIGHTER IV (2008)

POWER GRID

5	INTELLIGENCE
4	STRENGTH
5	SPEED
4	STAMINA
4	ENERGY PROJECTION
5	FIGHTING ABILITY

*This is biographical, and does not represent an evaluation of the character's in-game combat potential.

ALTERNATE COSTUMES

PS3: ⨂ Xbox 360: Ⓐ

PS3: ▢ Xbox 360: Ⓧ

PS3: △ Xbox 360: Ⓨ

PS3: R1 Xbox 360: RB

ATTACK SET

STANDING BASIC ATTACKS

Screen	Command	Hits	Damage	Startup	Active	Recovery	Advantage on Hit	Advantage if Guarded	Notes
1	Standing L	1	40,000	5	3	10	0	-1	Low attack
2	Standing M	1	63,000	7	3	19	-4	-5	—
3	Standing H	1	75,000	9	3	22	-2	-3	—
4	S	2	75,000	8	5 (3) 6	24	—	-8	Launcher, second hit not special- or hyper combo-cancelable

1

2

3

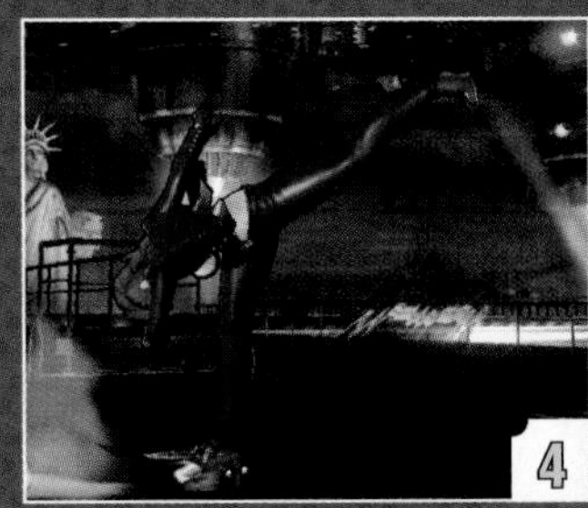
4

CROUCHING BASIC ATTACKS

Screen	Command	Hits	Damage	Startup	Active	Recovery	Advantage on Hit	Advantage if Guarded	Notes
1	Crouching L	1	38,000	4	2	11	0	-1	Rapid fire, chains into standing L
2	Crouching M	1	60,000	7	3	20	-5	-6	Low attack
3	Crouching H	1	72,000	9	4	19	0	-1	—

1

2

3

AERIAL BASIC ATTACKS

Screen	Command	Hits	Damage	Startup	Active	Recovery	Advantage on Hit	Advantage if Guarded	Notes
1	Air L	1	43,000	6	3	15	—	—	Overhead attack
2	Air M	1	60,000	8	3	19	—	—	Overhead attack
3	Air H	1	73,000	7	3	24	—	—	Overhead attack
4	Air S	1	75,000	9	4	23	—	—	Overhead attack, unrecoverable knockdown when used in air combo after S launcher

1

2

3

4

COMMAND ATTACKS

Screen	Command	Hits	Damage	Startup	Active	Recovery	Advantage on Hit	Advantage if Guarded	Notes
1	⇨ + Ⓜ	2	65,000	22	4	13	+1	0	Overhead attack, chains into Ⓢ attacks, may be canceled into a special move while in the air or during landing recovery
2	Ⓢ + ATK (can be charged)	2	70,000, 80,000 or 90,000	25~77 (on release 12)	3	23	-3	-4	Attack charges minimum 14 frames, after the 6th frame up to the 4th frame of recovery Viper will absorb all incoming attacks, taking damage without entering hitstun, Viper returns to her normal state once the attack's active frames have expired, charging improves damage in three stages: release the command during frames 1~32 for a level 1 attack, after 33 frames for a level 2 attack, and after 66 frames for a level 3 attack, both the level 2 and level 3 attack cause a crumple stun, the level 3 version is unguardable

1

2

AS A PARTNER-CROSSOVER ASSISTS

Screen	Type	P1+P2 Crossover Combination Hyper Combo	Description	Hits	Damage	Startup	Active	Recovery (this crossover assist)	Recovery (other partner)	Notes
1	α – Alpha	Emergency Combination	Thunder Knuckle H	1	80,000	29	7	131	101	Can be canceled with Ⓢ when used as a crossover counter, nullifies projectiles during active frames, knocks down opponent
2	β – Beta	Burst Time	Seismic Hammer	1	80,000	40	8	110	80	OTG-capable, can be canceled with Ⓢ when used as a crossover counter, knocks down opponent
3	γ – Gamma	Burst Time	Burning Kick	1	90,000	49	5	112	82	Overhead attack, can be canceled with Ⓢ when used as a crossover counter, knocks down opponent

1

2

3

C. VIPER

SPECIAL MOVES

Screen	Name	Command	Hits	Damage	Startup	Active	Recovery	Advantage on Hit	Advantage if Guarded	Notes
1	Thunder Knuckle L	↓↘→ + L	1	90,000	15	7	14	+2/+11	+1/+10	To cancel before hit, input S between 7th and 16th frame, input S on frames 15-16 to hit before recovering, second number in each frame field shows data when canceled, projectile has 10 medium priority durability points
2	Thunder Knuckle M	↓↘→ + M	1	90,000	13	7	16	0/+11	-1/+10	To cancel before hit, input S between 4th and 14th frame, input S on exactly the 14th frame to hit before recovering, second number in each frame field shows data when canceled, nullifies projectiles during active frames
3	Thunder Knuckle H	↓↘→ + H	1	100,000	5	7	44	—	-29/+10	To cancel before hit, input S between 2nd and 7th frame, input S between frames 15-16 to hit before recovering, second number in each frame field shows data when canceled, projectile has 10 medium priority durability points, knocks down opponent
4	Burning Kick L	↓↙← + L	1	90,000	23	10	26	—	-14	Overhead attack, projectile has 5 low priority durability points, to cancel before hit input S between frames 7 through 15
	Burning Kick M	↓↙← + M	1	90,000	25	10	18	—	-6	Overhead attack, projectile has 5 low priority durability points, to cancel before hit, input S between frames 10 through 17
	Burning Kick H	↓↙← + H	1	90,000	27	10	13	—	-1	Overhead attack, projectile has 5 low priority durability points, to cancel before hit input S between frames 11 through 18
	Burning Kick L	(in air) ↓↙← + L	1	90,000	21	10	Until grounded, 17 frames ground recovery	—	-6	Overhead attack, projectile has 5 low priority durability points, to cancel before hit input S between frames 7 through 15
	Burning Kick M	(in air) ↓↙← + M	1	90,000	19	10	Until grounded, 19 frames ground recovery	—	-10	Overhead attack, projectile has 5 low priority durability points, to cancel before hit input S between frames 10 through 17
	Burning Kick H	(in air) ↓↙← + H	1	90,000	17	10	Until grounded, 21 frames ground recovery	—	-11	Overhead attack, projectile has 5 low priority durability points, to cancel before hit input S between frames 11 through 18
5	Seismic Hammer	→↓↘ + ATK	1	80,000	16	8	35	—	-21	Jump cancelable, projectile has 5 low priority durability point, to cancel before hit input S between frames 7 through 12

Thunder Knuckle L: Use this lunging punch to safely attack from mid range. It cannot be punished when guarded, since you're left at a +1 frame advantage. On counterhit, it's possible to link afterward with crouching L. This may be useful in those rare instances when you duck under a high attack with Thunder Knuckle L. Look out for the red counterhit spark to take advantage of this. Lastly, you can cancel this attack, or 'fake' it, by inputting S just before it hits. Chaining into this off of a blocked basic attack thrusts you next to your foe with frame advantage—the perfect means of salvaging failed attacks.

Thunder Knuckle M: The second version of Thunder Knuckle has a much larger attack range, but it leaves you at a slight disadvantage when blocked. Use it as a general, long distance poke to preemptively stop ground movement. If your opponent ever defends in fear of this attack, input ↓↘→ + M and press S just before it hits to cancel it out, then throw the opposing character.

Thunder Knuckle H: C. Viper flies into the air with an electric uppercut. Use this as an anti-air against enemy jump attacks. Even though this is normally risky because of air blocking, you can stop the attack from soaring into the air by inputting S just before it leaves the ground. If done properly, you'll eliminate the risk involved with using the move, while opening up combo opportunities on a successful hit (see ***Combo III***). It's also possible to cancel it before it even hits, which is great for extending ground combos (see the Combo Appendix).

Burning Kick L, M, and H: Burning Kick is an overhead attack used for mounting confusing, short range assaults. The L and M versions are faster than the H version, but are extremely vulnerable when blocked. Save these attacks for air combos. Burning Kick H crosses an opponent up at close distances, forcing them to block the opposite direction. This is a valuable tool when you are on offense; it's exceedingly difficult for your opponent to guard against it when they expect frontal hits. Adding further confusion to the mix, you can also feint Burning Kick by inputting S just before it hits, causing C. Viper to stay in front of the challenger in an aerial state. From there you can perform air attacks to hit the front of the opposing character. Mixing between both variations makes it impossible to guard with consistency. Burning Kick H is also safer than the other versions—it's only vulnerable to throws on guard.

Seismic Hammer:
C. Viper punches the ground, summoning a geyser of fire. The strength of the button used determines where the flames appear. This allows you to instantly attack specific positions of the field. Preemptively stopping projectiles, ground movement, and low altitude jumps are its main purposes. It's also good for catching landing periods. For example, a super jump's screen movement makes it difficult for a player to see below them. Slipping in a Seismic Hammer to meet a foe as they land (preferably from afar) often hits because of its unexpected nature. This is also used to punish the recovery periods of aerial special attacks done from a distance. Finally, the Seismic Hammer is cancelable into a jump or super jump as soon as it's released. This is great for combos, and has numerous tactical uses (see **On the Ground** in the System and Gameplay chapter).

C. VIPER

HYPER COMBOS

Screen	Name	Command	Hits	Damage	Startup	Active	Recovery	Advantage on Hit	Advantage if Guarded	Notes
1	EX Thunder Knuckle	↓↘→ + S (burns 1 bar of hyper combo gauge)	1	150,000	10	38	28	—	-44	Frames 1-10 invincible, can cancel between frames 7-10 with S, can be canceled into other EX attacks or hyper combos, crumple stuns opponent, crumple stuns opponent
2	EX Burning Kick (in air OK)	↓↙← + S (burns 1 bar of hyper combo gauge)	4	119,700	9	10(5)5	20/ /until grounded, 15 frames ground recovery	—	-3/-4	Projectile has 5 low priority durability points, can be canceled by inputting S between frames 11 through 15, can be canceled into other EX attacks or hyper combos, final hit is an overhead attack
3	EX Seismic Hammer	→↓↘ + S (burns 1 bar of hyper combo gauge)	3	135,400	6	10(5)5	19	—	-6	Frames 1-15 invincible, 3 pillars with 5 durability points each, can be canceled by inputting S between frames 6 through 12, can be jump canceled any time after hit, can be canceled into other EX attacks or hyper combos, knocks down opponent
4	Emergency Combination	↓↘→ + ATK ATK	4	274,400	14	8	19	—	-5	36 frames invincibility, third and fourth hits knock down opponent
5	Burst Time	↓↙← + ATK ATK	5	273,300	10+4	5 (17) 6 (13) 6 (17) 6	72	—	-79	Frames 6-13 are invincible, OTG-capable, knocks down opponent
6	Viper Full Throttle	→↓↘ + ATK ATK (level 3 hyper combo)	22	430,000	9+1	4 (26) 64	57	—	-98	Frames 1-14 invincible, unrecoverable knockdown

EX Thunder Knuckle: The electric sphere at the end of C. Viper's fist has a large projectile durability value (10 medium priority durability points), allowing it plow through projectiles and most beams. A successful hit leaves the opposing character vulnerable to additional hits. This is also makes it great for combos. Take a look at the Combo Appendix for high-damage examples.

EX Burning Kick: The powered-up Burning Kick is only useful for combos. The final kick causes a massive hitstun when it connects in the air, making it valuable for extending combos where hitstun deterioration has taken effect. You can also cancel it by inputting S anytime during the first three hits (the spinning segment). Despite the ability to link after it when canceled, the first few hits inflict terrible damage while raising hitstun deterioration and damage scaling significantly. If you're going to do it, use it near the end of a combo.

EX Seismic Hammer: Boasting a giant window of invulnerability, the EX Seismic Hammer can be used to safely reverse both mid and close range attacks. A successful hit leads to a combo (see Combo Appendix); when guarded, cancel into a jump and airdash to safety. Also, fire it off when you anticipate a low-altitude jump because it's even harder to avoid than the normal Seismic Hammer!

Emergency Combination: Outside of its use in basic combos, Emergency Combination has a massive window of invulnerability that protects its journey across the screen. Use it to punish projectiles at mid range.

Burst Time: This hyper combo can OTG fallen enemies for heavy damage, making it the perfect combo ender near corners. Unfortunately, it has no other uses outside of OTG and juggle combos.

Viper Full Throttle: C. Viper dashes forward and pummels her challenger for heavy damage. Full Throttle is easily linked into after basic Thunder Knuckle M combos, and even some juggle combos. It has no other uses outside of this; save it only for combos when you need a substantial lead.

BATTLE PLAN

OVERVIEW

VITALITY: 900,000

CHAIN COMBO ARCHETYPE: MARVEL SERIES

X-Factor	Lv.1	Lv.2	Lv.3
Damage	125%	150%	175%
Speed	110%	120%	130%

C. Viper's game plan is to establish short range via all-out aggression, with the secondary objective of cornering the enemy. A cornered opponent has less methods of escaping C. Viper's offense, including a less effective advancing guard.

This strategy is effective because:

- **Viper's versatile mobility allows her stay close to the foe despite their use of advancing guard.**
- **Her move set consists of fast overheads, powerful low-hitting combos, and numerous moves that cross-up, making her offense nearly impossible to guard against consistently.**
- **All of her attack options lead to long, high damage combos.**

C. Viper achieves this goal in these ways, in order of effectiveness:

- **By using her air mobility to evade ground attacks.**
- **Attacking with Seismic Hammer (→ ↓ ↘ + ATK) to limit ground movement and stop normal jumps; on hit or guard this leads to a combo or the opportunity to move in with an airdash.**
- **Countering a projectile with her EX Thunder Knuckle (↓ ↘ → + S).**
- **Attacking a grounded foe with Thunder Knuckle M and performing her 1 frame cancel to eliminate its recovery period (↓ ↘ → + M, then input S just as the punch hits). Its instant recovery allows for follow-up dashes into short range.**

ON THE GROUND

Halt the enemy's advance with the Seismic Hammer.

Super jump canceling allows you to chain multiple Seismic Hammers together, a powerful way of pushing the enemy to a corner.

Condition your opponent into playing passively so it's easier to move in, or push them into the corner with brute force. The foundation of this strategy involves using long distance Seismic Hammers to control low altitude jumps, ground movement, and projectiles. Be wary of your challenger's movement patterns and attack with it accordingly. Seismic Hammer's pillar-like area-of-effect, and the ability to cancel it into a jump (press ↖, ↑, or ↗, even when it whiffs), makes it virtually impossible to punish with anything that isn't a beam. When your foe manages to airdash or super jump over Seismic Hammer, cancel its recovery into a jump and air guard their attack. Characters with beam attacks or quick invincible moves can punish Seismic Hammer, but you can lure them out by faking it—input → ↓ ↘ + ATK CANCEL S to cancel it just as C. Viper lifts her arm up. The flash on her arm telegraphs the use of the attack, baiting some players into taking action. It also lures out super jumps, which are countered with air throws (transition into **Combo V** if you grab them) or Thunder Knuckle H (leads to **Combo III**). Standing H is also an effective anti-air against frontal jumps, which shields the top of C. Viper's head against an incoming onslaught. Cancel it into Seismic Hammer L and then follow-up with a jump to score an air combo.

An advanced use of canceling makes this Seismic Hammer strategy exceedingly powerful (but difficult to perform). The very early starting frames of a jump are cancelable into special moves. Since the Seismic Hammer is cancelable into a jump, you can endlessly chain into back-to-back Seismic Hammers! When done quickly, it's possible to rapidly blast numerous positions on field to severely limit enemy mobility. This is your best method of pushing your opponent into a corner. To do this technique, input → ↓ ↘ → + ATK to do the first Seismic Hammer, then as it hits, perform ↓ ↘ → ↗ + ATK. The → input added to the first command covers (or buffers) the → input of the second Seismic Hammer. Rolling the stick to the ↗ position activates a jump just before the second Seismic Hammer command is finished, which is then canceled into the special move with the final button press. If done too slowly, you'll cancel the Seismic Hammer into just a jump. Once the second Seismic Hammer is released, continue to input ↓ ↘ → ↗ + ATK to repeatedly launch additional blasts.

Also use this tactic to cancel into other ground attacks. If your foe tries to punish a missed Seismic Hammer with a beam or projectile, input ↓ ↘ → ↗ + S to cancel its recovery into the projectile-crushing EX Thunder Knuckle (transition into **Combo VI** if it hits). Super jump cancel into Thunder Knuckle H (↓ ↘ → ↗ + H after a Seismic Hammer is released) to anti-air foes who manage to jump over your offense.

When your ranged offense has limited your opponent's use of projectiles and airdashes, move in. A raw forward dash works if your opponent is too scared to stick out attacks. Strike with **Combo I, Combo II,** or a throw (**Combo V**) when you move into range. There's also tricky way to transition into an aggressive movement using the aforementioned jump cancellation trick—force your opponent to block a Seismic Hammer, then input ↑ + S + ATK to super jump cancel into Viper's Focus Attack, then quickly perform → → or ATK + ATK to initiate a forward dash. Canceling the Seismic Hammer into a dash leaves you at a heavy frame advantage when guarded, so attack with **Combo I, Combo II,** or a throw when you get close. In cases where your challenger uses advancing guard against your Seismic Hammer to push you away, the forward dash keeps you close enough to fire-off another Seismic Hammer.

At close range, your options consist of the aforementioned **Combos I**, **II**, **V**, and Burning Kick H. **Combos I** and **II** are extremely flexible and allow for a follow-up offense when guarded. At point blank range Burning Kick hits your challenger's back side, forcing them to guard the opposite direction (a successful hit leads to **Combo IV**). It's also possible to cancel the Burning Kick (↓ ↙ ← + H CANCEL S); canceling the kick does not cause you to pass behind your foe, it instead leaves you in front of them while airborne. This is a powerful 50/50 mix-up situation. Not only does the opposing player have to guess between blocking in opposite directions, but the canceled version of the Burning Kick, followed by air L, H, acts as an extremely fast overhead. Options like these make C. Viper an aggressive beast.

C. VIPER

UP IN THE AIR

Strike when your opponent is less willing to use anti-air.

When your foe's defenses are down, or when they use a recovery heavy ground attack, start an offense by jumping towards your challenger. Viper's versatile air mobility stems from her 8-way airdash, which is done by holding a direction and pressing ATK ATK together while in the air. Upwards and backwards airdashes (which can also be accomplished with ⇧ ⇧ and ⇦ ⇦) are good for quick retreats. A downwards airdash is often used to lure out anti-air attempts—jump towards your foe to coerce them into readying their air throw or attack, then just before you enter their attack range, input ⇩ + ATK ATK to drop to the floor. This causes their attack to whiff, giving you just enough time to punish it with a combo. A forward airdash should be used to punish projectiles and the like (air ⇨ + ATK ATK, or ⇨ ⇨).

C. Viper's strongest movement asset is her 45 degree downward airdash (air ↘ + ATK ATK), which is used in combination with air Ⓛ or Ⓗ to apply constant pressure. Using diagonal down-forward airdashes offensively is often called triangle jumping. The goal is to continually attack with triangle jumps to lure out reversals and other defensive measures. Triangle jump Ⓗ is the better option of the two, as it causes more guardstun and also covers jumps—C. Viper's aerial Ⓗ hits both below and above her body while sharing the same input as her air throw (⇨ + Ⓗ), which automatically comes out if your opponent tries to jump away (shift into **Combo V** when you grab them). When you expect a reversal attempt (which generally occurs after they block a previous jump attack), either block or jump upwards before dropping to the floor with ⇩ + ATK ATK or ⇩ ⇩ .

When your opponent is less willing to anti-air your attacks, start going for a more varied offense (assuming they didn't use an advancing guard against the initial jump attack). A single blocked jumping Ⓗ opens the window for basic ground mix-ups. Going for **Combo I**, **Combo II**, or a throw are the obvious choices. You can also jump straight up and triangle jump with air Ⓗ, which can cross your challenger up. Keep this option diverse by super jumping straight up, air dashing straight down to quickly land, then attacking with a throw or **Combo I**. Also occasionally use triangle jump Ⓛ as the opening attack, which is faster than air Ⓗ. It's also easier to cancel into—if you want to get really crazy, cancel it into air ⇩ ↙ ⇦ + Ⓗ to unexpectedly hit your foe's backside. Alternatively, hit Ⓢ to cancel the Burning Kick to stay in front of the opposing character.

In cases when your opponent uses an advancing guard against your air attack to push you out, you can almost always land and dash forward to stay near your opposition. Mid-screen you must jump and airdash again after the forward dash to stay close, near corners you don't. You can also air dash at them without doing a jump attack and immediately throw as you land, circumventing problems with your foe pushing blocked attacks away. Occasionally replace the throw with the low-hitting **Combo I**, which may hit your foe if they expect a jump attack.

Outside of your offensive capabilities, keep your challenger out of the air with air throws (**Combo V**) or combos starting with jumping Ⓜ (**Combo VII**). Jumping Ⓜ recovers before you land, so if your attack whiffs, strike again as you fall or airdash backwards to safety. To avoid other bad defensive situations, like getting cornered, super jump over your foe, then use three canceled back-to back Burning Kicks (⇩ ↙ ⇦ + Ⓛ CANCEL➡ Ⓢ) to float to the opposite end of the screen. You can airdash after the third flip to create even more room between you and your adversary.

C. Viper's offense is second to none.

COMBO USAGE

I. ST. (L), ST. (M), ST. (H) ⇒CANCEL⇒ → ↓ ↘ + (L) ⇒CANCEL⇒ FORWARD JUMP, IMMEDIATE FORWARD AIRDASH, (M), (S), LAND, (M), (S) (1 HIT) ⇒CANCEL⇒ → ↓ ↘ + (L) ⇒CANCEL⇒ FORWARD JUMP, IMMEDIATE FORWARD AIRDASH, (M), (S), LAND, (M), (H), (S) (2 HITS) ⇒CANCEL⇒ SUPER JUMP, AIR (M), (M), (H) ⇒CANCEL⇒ DOUBLE JUMP, (M), (H), (S)

(479,500 damage) Additional damage can be added to the beginning of this combo by including a Thunder Knuckle H cancel (st. (L), st. (M), st. (H) ⇒CANCEL⇒ ↓ ↘ → + (H) ⇒CANCEL⇒ (S), cr. (M), st. (H) ⇒CANCEL⇒ → ↓ ↘ + (L), etc). The difficulty level to do this is high, so focus on nailing the original sequence first. The forward airdash proceeding → ↓ ↘ + (L) must be done as fast as possible, or else there isn't enough time to juggle with (M). Upon landing from that air chain, juggle with the (M) just before the enemy hits the ground (too early and your foe will be too high for future aerial hits). During the final air chain segment (air (M), (M), (H) ⇒CANCEL⇒ (M), (H), (S)) omit one (M) from the first 3 hits if your challenger is knocked too high above you. Finally, if this combo knocks your opponent into a corner, you can OTG your enemy with → ↓ ↘ + (L) ⇒CANCEL⇒ ↓ ↙ ← + (ATK)(ATK) for additional damage.

When the first 2–3 hits of this combo is guarded, stage a follow-up attack by canceling into ↓ ↘ → + (M) ⇒CANCEL⇒ (S). This moves you back into close range with frame advantage, or if your opponent uses advancing guard moves you closer than you would be normally. Alternatively, cancel into ↓ ↙ ← + (L) ⇒CANCEL⇒ (S) then air (L) ⇒CANCEL⇒ (H) to go for a quick overhead attack.

II. → + (M), (S) ⇒CANCEL⇒ → ↓ ↘ + (L) ⇒CANCEL⇒ FORWARD JUMP, IMMEDIATE FORWARD AIRDASH, (M), (S), LAND, (M), (S) (1 HIT) ⇒CANCEL⇒ → ↓ ↘ + (L) ⇒CANCEL⇒ FORWARD JUMP, IMMEDIATE FORWARD AIRDASH, (M), (S), LAND, (M), (H), (S) (2 HITS) ⇒CANCEL⇒ SUPER JUMP, AIR (M), (M), (H) ⇒CANCEL⇒ DOUBLE JUMP, (M), (H), (S)

(459,400 damage) → + (M) is an overhead attack. Its recovery period is cancelable into special moves or (S) launcher. This cancel is much easier to do if your foe is crouching, which is the only time it would hit anyways.

III. ↓ ↘ → + (H) ⇒CANCEL⇒ (S) (CANCEL IT AFTER THE HIT), → ↓ ↘ + (L) ⇒CANCEL⇒ SUPER JUMP, (M), (M), (H) ⇒CANCEL⇒ DOUBLE JUMP, (M), (H), (S) ⇒CANCEL⇒ ↓ ↙ ← + (L)

(384,700 damage) Use this anti-air combo against jumps. It must be done very late, i.e. when your challenger is as close to the ground as possible, or else you won't be able to cancel ↓ ↘ → + (H) (it must hit as it is still on the ground). This also stops you from soaring into the air when it's blocked, keeping you safe from harm.

IV. ↓ ↙ ← + (H) (CROSS UP), (L), (M), (H), (S) (1 HIT) ⇒CANCEL⇒ → ↓ ↘ + (L) ⇒CANCEL⇒ FORWARD JUMP, IMMEDIATE FORWARD AIRDASH, (M), (S), LAND, (M), (H), (S) (2 HITS) ⇒CANCEL⇒ SUPER JUMP, AIR (M), (M), (H) ⇒CANCEL⇒ DOUBLE JUMP, (M), (H), (S)

(448,900 damage) The opening attack is extremely unsafe when blocked, so use it sparingly. The juggle after the kick hits is difficult to do, so be sure to attack as fast as possible after you land.

V. THROW OR AIR THROW, LAND, → ↓ ↘ + (L) ⇒CANCEL⇒ FORWARD JUMP, IMMEDIATE FORWARD AIRDASH, (M), (S), LAND, (M), (S) (1 HIT) ⇒CANCEL⇒ → ↓ ↘ + (L) ⇒CANCEL⇒ FORWARD JUMP, IMMEDIATE FORWARD AIRDASH, (M), (S), LAND, (M), (H), (S) (2 HITS) ⇒CANCEL⇒ SUPER JUMP, AIR (M), (M), (H) ⇒CANCEL⇒ DOUBLE JUMP, (M), (H), (S)

(324,400 damage) You absolutely must perform a forward jump after → ↓ ↘ + (L) hits to ensure you'll be in range for the air chain follow-up. Tack on → ↓ ↘ + (L) ⇒CANCEL⇒ ↓ ↙ ← + (ATK)(ATK) near corners for additional damage.

VI. ↓ ↘ → + (S), → ↓ ↘ + (L) ⇒CANCEL⇒ FORWARD JUMP, IMMEDIATE FORWARD AIRDASH, (M), (S), LAND, (M), (S) (1 HIT) ⇒CANCEL⇒ → ↓ ↘ + (L) ⇒CANCEL⇒ FORWARD JUMP, IMMEDIATE FORWARD AIRDASH, (M), (S), LAND, (M), (H), (S) (2 HITS) ⇒CANCEL⇒ SUPER JUMP, AIR (M), (M), (H) ⇒CANCEL⇒ DOUBLE JUMP, (M), (H), (S)

(556,600 damage) This combo counters projectile attacks. The opening move is very vulnerable to punishment when blocked. If this combo knocks the opponent into a corner, add → ↓ ↘ + (L) ⇒CANCEL⇒ ↓ ↙ ← + (ATK)(ATK) for additional damage.

VII. AGAINST AN AIRBORNE OPPONENT, AIR (M), (M), (H) ⇒CANCEL⇒ JUMP, (M), (M), (H) ⇒CANCEL⇒ ↓ ↙ ← + (S), LAND, PERFORM A LATE ST. (H), (S) ⇒CANCEL⇒ AIR (M), (H) ⇒CANCEL⇒ JUMP, (M), (H), (S)

(414,500 damage) This is a basic anti-air combo that's safer than **Combo III**. If the opening strike (air (M), (M)) is blocked, chain into a delayed air (H) to safely land, while locking your opponent down.

ADVANCED TACTICS

Ⓢ + (ATK) COMMAND JUMP OFFENSIVE

The Ⓢ + (ATK) command jump allows for a continued offense when your standard attacks are blocked, but your opponent can stop it with an anti-air if you're not careful. To reduce risk when using it, cancel into it off of standing Ⓗ or → + Ⓗ, which causes more guardstun than other attacks. This gives you more time to attack before your opponent is able to act. Depending on whether or not your foe uses advancing guard against the opening attack, you have several offensive options once airborne:

Jump-canceling guarded moves, whether using Ⓢ + (ATK) Bold Move to interrupt basic attacks, or simply normal jump canceling a special move like Volcano, is a great way to vary your offense when an initial assault is blocked.

If your opponent uses advancing guard:

- Airdash forward with air Ⓗ. If your opponent blocks it, dash forward as you land and go for a throw or Combo I.
- Fire Air Play (↓ ↘ → + Ⓗ) at your opponent. This stops long range anti-air attempts. If the shot hits the enemy near corners, airdash forward with jumping Ⓜ and transition into Combo II.

If your challenger doesn't use advancing guard:

- Perform ↓ ↘ → + Ⓛ ↓ ↘ → + Ⓛ when you anticipate an anti-air attack. This attack is invulnerable, enabling it to blow through any type of anti-air, including invincible techniques like Ryu's Shoryuken.
- Airdash towards your opponent as soon as possible, then attack with jumping Ⓢ. This hits your foe with a frontal jump attack.
- Perform a forward airdash at the peak of Dante's jump. This causes the movement to pass over your foe's head. Attack with jumping Ⓜ to hit the enemy's back.

Ⓢ + (ATK) JUMP CANCELLATION

It will take some practice, but learning to cancel the three pre-jump frames of a jump or Bold Move will pay great dividends, allowing for otherwise-impossible techniques. Here, Dante's → + Ⓗ is canceled into Bold Move, and then Volcano is performed before Dante actually becomes airborne! Volcano itself can then be jump-canceled into Revolver with ↓ ↙ ← ↖ + Ⓜ, again taking advantage of pre-jump frames!

Dante's Ⓢ + (ATK) command jump has a secondary use. Just like with other jumps, the 3 pre-jump frames before the jump is actually airborne are cancelable into ground-based special moves. This technique has a very powerful use—Dante's → + Ⓗ is normally not cancelable on hit, but by canceling into Ⓢ + (ATK) just before inputting a special move, you'll cancel the → + Ⓗ into a command jump, and then into a special move, without becoming airborne! This has two applications. You can increase the damage of Dante's combos by canceling → + Ⓗ at opportune times (see the Combo Appendix for advanced uses of this), or use the technique to cancel → + Ⓗ into ↓ ↓ + Ⓢ. → + Ⓗ causes more guardstun than any of Dante's other basic attacks, making it harder for your opponent to counter your teleport behind them. This is mainly powerful when combined with assists. For example, with Amaterasu's Cold Star assist, input → + Ⓗ while calling the assist at the same time, then Ⓢ + (ATK) jump cancel into ↓ ↓ + Ⓢ. If using Arthur's Dagger Toss assist instead, the daggers will actually *combo* after → + Ⓗ from long distances, allowing you to come out of Air Trick and link into Combo II.

HAMMER TIME

No other character has this kind of "hammer" in their proverbial toolkit…pound foes into submission.

The Hammer delivers a downward jumping attack that's completely invulnerable until Dante lands. It's an overhead, causes an unrecoverable knockdown on hit, and leaves you with an absolutely massive frame advantage when guarded. These attributes lend itself towards a powerful tactic—when The Hammer is performed very close to the ground, just low enough so it still hits (too low and it'll whiff entirely), you'll recover almost instantly. To do this, input ↓ ↘ → ↗, hold ↗ for half a second, then input Ⓛ ↓ ↘ → + Ⓛ. Using it in this manner nets you +20 frame advantage if your adversary blocks it. Also, if your foe tries to use advancing guard to push you away, the massive frame advantage allows an immediate forward dash to bypass the pushback. This enables you to stay on top of your foe regardless of their defensive posture. To make the most of this tactic, *always* dash forward after The Hammer connects, hit or guard. If it hits, perform Volcano (→ ↓ ↘ + Ⓗ) to hit your grounded foe and transition into an air combo. When blocked, strike with Combo I if you believe they'll counter attack, go for a throw when you expect the opposing player to guard, or immediately jump and airdash forward with air Ⓜ to go for a cross up.

Adding further mayhem to this potent strategy, you can dash forward after a blocked Hammer and simply do it again. If performed as fast as possible, characters without fast reversals *cannot stop the second Hammer with an attack.* The only method of escape is to jump away, which still leaves Dante safe from harm. Anticipate these jumps and punish them with an air throw to reset the situation.

Finally, use The Hammer's invulnerability to stop reversals as your foe stands up from a knockdown. The opposing character passes through you if your opposition performs a reversal with invincibility, giving you ample time to punish the recovery with a combo. You can also perform The Hammer even closer to the ground than normal to make it purposely whiff (input ↓ ↘ → ↗ + Ⓛ). Since it's normally an overhead, whiffing it directly in front of your opponent gets them blocking high, giving you an opportunity to land a low-hitting combo.

COMBO APPENDIX

GENERAL EXECUTION TIPS

After launching your opponent with (S), always perform the follow-up air chain ((M), (M), (H), etc.) as early as possible during the jump.

When performing → + (H) CANCEL (S) + (ATK) and then canceling the 3 pre-jump frames into → ↓ ↘ + (M), you can 'buffer' the (S) + (ATK) input by hitting it well before → + (H) actually lands (the jump still comes out despite the early input). This gives you more time to perform → ↓ ↘ + (M) just as → + (H) hits.

Requirements (Position, meter, etc.)	Notes	Command Sequence	Damage
Requires 1 hyper combo gauge bar	The third attack in the (S) CANCEL (H) CANCEL (S) chain must be done late to fully connect. The ↓ ↘ → + (L) ↓ ↘ → ↗ + (L) command jump cancels into a grounded Acid Rain. The bolts must hit as high in the air as possible for the remaining juggles to work. The two ↓ ↘ → + (M) ↓ ↘ → + (M) attacks must be done as early as possible to leave time for ↓ ↙ ← + (L)	Cr. (L), st. (L), st. (M), st. (H), → + (H) CANCEL (S) + (ATK) CANCEL → ↓ ↘ + (M) CANCEL forward jump, air (M), (M) CANCEL double jump, (M), (H) CANCEL ↓ ↘ → + (L), land, (S) CANCEL (H) CANCEL delayed (S) CANCEL and, late (S) CANCEL (H) CANCEL delayed (S), ↓ ↘ → + (L) ↓ ↘ → ↗ + (L), ↓ ↘ → + (M) ↓ ↘ → + (M), ↓ ↘ → + (M) ↓ ↘ → + (M), ↓ ↙ ← + (L) CANCEL (H) (CANCEL ↓ ↘ → + (ATK)(ATK))	489,700 (or 657, 700)
Requires corner, requires 1~3 hyper combo gauge bars	—	St. (M), cr. (M), st. (H), → + (H) CANCEL (S) + (ATK) CANCEL → ↓ ↘ + (M) CANCEL forward jump, air (M) CANCEL double jump, (M), (H) CANCEL ↓ ↘ → + (L), land, late (S) CANCEL (H) CANCEL delayed (S), ↓ ↘ → + (L) ↓ ↘ → ↗ + (L), ↓ ↘ → + (L) ↓ ↘ → + (L), air (S), land, ↘ + (H)(H)(H) CANCEL → + (H) CANCEL (S) + (ATK) CANCEL ↓ ↘ → + (M) ↓ ↘ → ↗ + (M), → + (H) CANCEL (S) + (ATK) CANCEL → ↓ ↘ + (M) → ↓ ↘ + (M) CANCEL ↓ ↘ → + (ATK)(ATK) (or → ↓ ↘ + (ATK)(ATK))	764,600~ 1,022,600
Requires level 1 X-factor, requires 1 hyper combo gauge bar	—	St. (M), cr. (M), st. (H) (XF) st. (M), st. (H), → + (H) CANCEL (S) + (ATK) CANCEL → ↓ ↘ + (M) CANCEL forward jump, air (M), (M) CANCEL double jump, (M), (H) CANCEL ↓ ↘ → + (L), land, (S) CANCEL super jump air (M), (M), (H) CANCEL ↓ ↘ → + (H) CANCEL ↓ ↘ → + (ATK)(ATK)	1,058,100
Requires 1 hyper combo gauge bar	—	St. (M), cr. (M), st. (H) (XF) st. (M), st. (H), → + (H) CANCEL (S) + (ATK) CANCEL → ↓ ↘ + (M) CANCEL forward jump, air (M), (M) CANCEL double jump, (M), (H) CANCEL ↓ ↘ → + (L), land, (S) CANCEL (H) CANCEL delayed (S) CANCEL and, late (S) CANCEL (H) CANCEL delayed (S), ↓ ↘ → + (L) ↓ ↘ → ↗ + (L), ↓ ↘ → + (M) ↓ ↘ → + (M), ↓ ↘ → + (M) ↓ ↘ → + (M), ↓ ↙ ← + (L) CANCEL (H) (CANCEL ↓ ↘ → + (ATK)(ATK))	1,196,000
Requires corner, requires 1 hyper combo gauge bar	—	St. (M), cr. (M), st. (H), → + (H) CANCEL (S) + (ATK) CANCEL → ↓ ↘ + (M) CANCEL forward jump, air (M), (M) CANCEL double jump, (M), (H) CANCEL ↓ ↘ → + (L), land, st. (H), (S) CANCEL super jump, air (M), (M), (H) CANCEL ↓ ↘ → + (H), land, ↓ ↙ ← + (L) CANCEL (H) CANCEL ↓ ↘ → + (ATK)(ATK)	642,600
Requires corner	—	St. (M), cr. (M), st. (H), (S) CANCEL super jump, air (M), (M), (H) CANCEL ↓ ↘ → + (M), (H), (S), land, ↘ + (H)(H)(H) CANCEL → + (H) CANCEL (S) + (ATK) CANCEL ↓ ↘ → + (M) ↓ ↘ → + (M), → + (H) CANCEL (S) + (ATK) CANCEL → ↓ ↘ + (M) → ↓ ↘ + (M), → + (H) CANCEL (S) + (ATK) CANCEL → ↓ ↘ + (M) → ↓ ↘ + (M)	518, 900
Requires corner	—	Counterhit (H) CANCEL ← + (H), (M), (H), → + (H) CANCEL (S) + (ATK) CANCEL → ↓ ↘ CANCEL jump cancel, air (M), (M) CANCEL double jump, (M), (H) CANCEL ↓ ↘ → + (L), land, st. (H), (S) CANCEL super jump, air (M), (M), (H) CANCEL ↓ ↘ → + (H), land, ↓ ↙ ← + (L) CANCEL (H)	440,400
—	—	cr. (M), st. (H), → + (H) CANCEL (ATK) + (S) CANCEL ↓ ↙ ← + (ATK)(ATK), link Devil Trigger form st. (M), st. (H), → + (H) CANCEL (S) + (ATK) CANCEL → ↓ ↘ + (M) CANCEL jump, air (M), (M) CANCEL double jump, (M), (H) CANCEL ↓ ↘ → + (L), st. (H), (S) CANCEL super jump, air (M), (M), (H) CANCEL → ↓ ↘ + (S), air (S), ↘ + (H)(H)(H) CANCEL → + (H) CANCEL (S) + (ATK) CANCEL ↓ ↘ → + (M) ↓ ↘ → + (M), → + (H) CANCEL (S) + (ATK) CANCEL → ↓ ↘ + (M) → ↓ ↘ + (M) CANCEL ↓ ↘ → + (ATK)(ATK)	806,300
Requires corner, requires 4 hyper combo gauge bars	—	cr. (M), st. (H), → + (H) CANCEL (ATK) + (S) CANCEL ↓ ↙ ← + (ATK)(ATK), link Devil Trigger form st. (M), st. (H), → + (H) CANCEL (S) + (ATK) CANCEL → ↓ ↘ + (M) CANCEL jump, air (M), (M) CANCEL double jump, (M), (H) CANCEL ↓ ↘ → + (L), land, (S) CANCEL super jump, air (M), (M), (H) CANCEL ↓ ↘ → + (H) CANCEL → ↓ ↘ + (ATK)(ATK)	1,000,000

"OH MAN, I'M STARVING, WHERE'S MY PIZZA?"

FELICIA

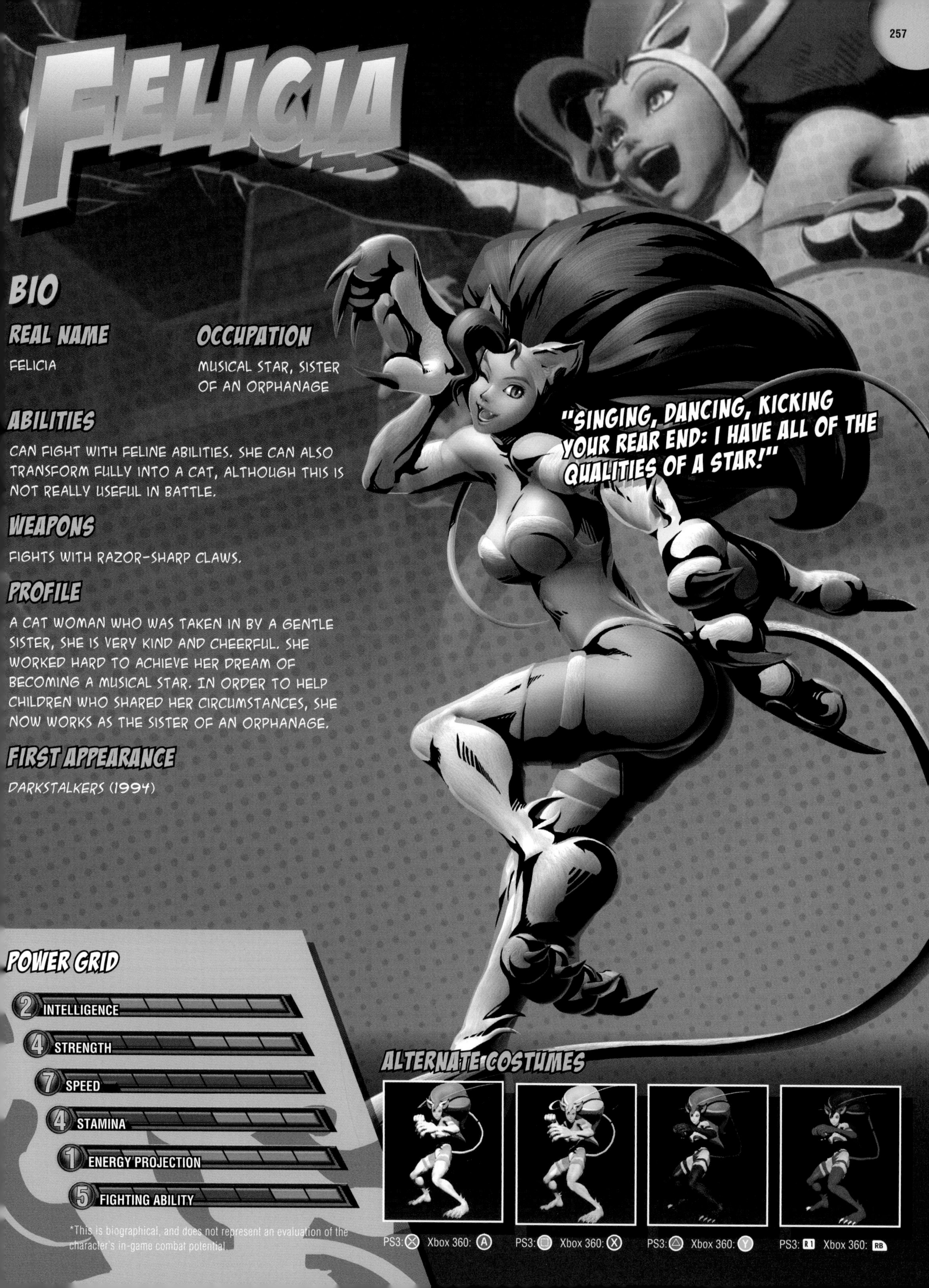

"SINGING, DANCING, KICKING YOUR REAR END: I HAVE ALL OF THE QUALITIES OF A STAR!"

BIO

REAL NAME

FELICIA

OCCUPATION

MUSICAL STAR, SISTER OF AN ORPHANAGE

ABILITIES

CAN FIGHT WITH FELINE ABILITIES. SHE CAN ALSO TRANSFORM FULLY INTO A CAT, ALTHOUGH THIS IS NOT REALLY USEFUL IN BATTLE.

WEAPONS

FIGHTS WITH RAZOR-SHARP CLAWS.

PROFILE

A CAT WOMAN WHO WAS TAKEN IN BY A GENTLE SISTER, SHE IS VERY KIND AND CHEERFUL. SHE WORKED HARD TO ACHIEVE HER DREAM OF BECOMING A MUSICAL STAR. IN ORDER TO HELP CHILDREN WHO SHARED HER CIRCUMSTANCES, SHE NOW WORKS AS THE SISTER OF AN ORPHANAGE.

FIRST APPEARANCE

DARKSTALKERS (1994)

POWER GRID

2	INTELLIGENCE
4	STRENGTH
7	SPEED
4	STAMINA
1	ENERGY PROJECTION
5	FIGHTING ABILITY

*This is biographical, and does not represent an evaluation of the character's in-game combat potential.

ALTERNATE COSTUMES

PS3: ✕ Xbox 360: A

PS3: □ Xbox 360: X

PS3: △ Xbox 360: Y

PS3: R1 Xbox 360: RB

ATTACK SET

STANDING BASIC ATTACKS

Screen	Command	Hits	Damage	Startup	Active	Recovery	Advantage on Hit	Advantage if Guarded	Notes
1	Standing Ⓛ	1	35,000	4	3	10	0	-2	Rapid fire
2	Standing Ⓜ	1	55,000	7	3	16	-3	-3	—
3	Standing Ⓗ	3	77,100	10	12	17	0	-2	↓↘→ + P1 or P2 snap back
4	Ⓢ	1	70,000	8	5	23	—	-7	Launcher, not special or hyper combo cancelable

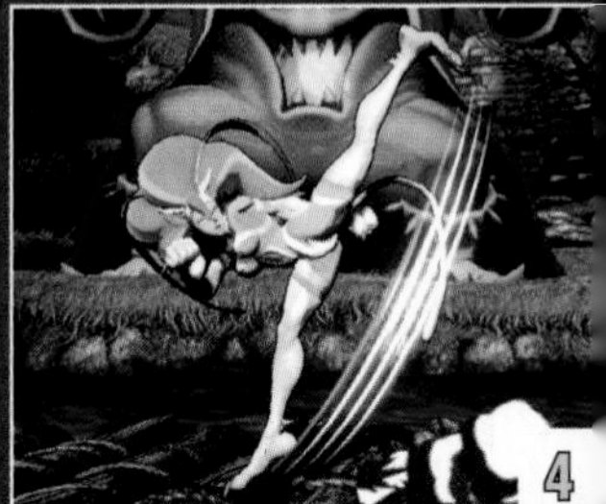

CROUCHING BASIC ATTACKS

Screen	Command	Hits	Damage	Startup	Active	Recovery	Advantage on Hit	Advantage if Guarded	Notes
1	Crouching Ⓛ	1	44,000	5	2	11	0	-2	Low attack, rapid fire
2	Crouching Ⓜ	1	53,000	7	3	18	-5	-5	—
3	Crouching Ⓗ	1	65,000	10	4	26	—	-9	Low attack, knocks down

AERIAL BASIC ATTACKS

Screen	Command	Hits	Damage	Startup	Active	Recovery	Notes
1	Air Ⓛ	1	45,000	5	3	19	Overhead attack
2	Air Ⓜ	1	55,000	8	4	29	Overhead attack
3	Air Ⓗ	1	70,000	8	5	23	Overhead attack
4	Air Ⓢ	1	70,000	9	4	33	Unrecoverable knockdown when used in air combo after Ⓢ launcher

UP IN THE AIR

Outside of projectiles, Felicia's other major weakness is her lack of flexible aerial options. She has no double jump, no airdash, and no aerial special moves at all. Her only unique ability is her Wall Cling (when back is to a wall, jump towards it and hold ⇦), which cannot be done during a super jump and leaves her very vulnerable. This causes her to have tremendous difficulty against highly mobile, aerial opponents. A minimalist's approach to this problem is the only way to go—load up on strong anti-air assists (see Assists section), super jump often, and rely on **Combos III** and **VI** to keep your foe out of the sky. If you manage to nail your opponent to the floor, keep your ground offense going and never let them escape.

Anti-air assists are an absolute necessity.

The Wall Cling seems like fun, but you're better off avoiding it.

In the rare occurrence that you jump towards a grounded foe instead of using a Cat Spike, air Ⓜ and Ⓢ are your best attacks. Ⓜ is designed to stop frontal anti-air attacks, while air Ⓢ has a hit box that swings below Felicia. Air Ⓢ also crosses-up, but the only decent time to land it is after a wall jump—this is risky. If you ever force your opponent to block air Ⓜ, land and attack with **Combo I,** or chain into air Ⓢ to catch someone crouching in anticipation of a low attack.

COMBO USAGE

I. CR. Ⓛ, CR. Ⓛ, CR. Ⓜ, ← + Ⓗ (2 HITS) CANCEL⇨ ↓ ↘ → + Ⓜ CANCEL⇨ Ⓜ, ST. Ⓛ, ST. Ⓜ, ↘ + Ⓜ CANCEL⇨ FORWARD JUMP, AIR Ⓜ, Ⓜ, Ⓗ, Ⓢ, LAND, Ⓢ CANCEL⇨ SUPER JUMP, AIR Ⓜ, Ⓜ, Ⓗ, Ⓢ

(377,400 damage) This is your most flexible attack opening. After ↓ ↘ → + Ⓜ CANCEL⇨ Ⓜ hits, the standing Ⓛ juggle must be done very quickly for the remainder of the combo to work. If your foe ever uses advancing guard to make any of the first four attacks whiff, cancel into → ↓ ↘ + Ⓜ or ← ↓ ↙ + Ⓜ to lung your way into short range again.

II. → ↓ ↘ + Ⓜ, ST. Ⓜ → ↓ ↘ + Ⓛ, ST. Ⓛ, ST. Ⓜ CANCEL⇨ ↓ ↘ → + Ⓜ CANCEL⇨ Ⓜ, ST. Ⓛ, ST. Ⓜ, ↘ + Ⓜ CANCEL⇨ FORWARD JUMP, AIR Ⓜ, Ⓜ, Ⓗ, Ⓢ, LAND, Ⓢ CANCEL⇨ SUPER JUMP, Ⓜ, Ⓜ, Ⓗ, Ⓢ

(447,100 damage) This difficult combo deals heavy damage off of Cat Spike M. This works whether the opening attack hits the front or back of your adversary. The ↓ ↘ → + Ⓜ CANCEL⇨ Ⓜ may miss if you do not input the second Ⓜ command fast enough. Press it at the exact time ↓ ↘ → + Ⓜ makes contact with your opponent.

III. AIR THROW OR → ↘ ↓ ↙ ← + Ⓗ, DASH FORWARD, ↘ + Ⓜ CANCEL⇨ FORWARD JUMP, AIR Ⓜ, Ⓜ, Ⓗ, Ⓢ, LAND ST. Ⓜ, CR. Ⓜ, ← + Ⓗ (1HIT), Ⓢ CANCEL⇨ SUPER JUMP, AIR Ⓜ, Ⓜ, Ⓗ, Ⓢ

(258,900 or 309,600) After ↘ + Ⓜ hits, cancel into a forward jump and immediately start the air Ⓜ, Ⓜ, Ⓗ, Ⓢ chain. When you land, wait a moment before doing Ⓜ, Ⓢ to ensure that your opponent isn't knocked too high.

IV. COUNTERHIT → ↓ ↘ + Ⓛ, ← + Ⓗ (2 HITS) CANCEL⇨ → ↓ ↘ + Ⓜ, ST. Ⓜ, ← + Ⓗ CANCEL⇨ ↓ ↘ → + Ⓜ CANCEL⇨ Ⓜ, ST. Ⓛ, ST. Ⓜ, ↘ + Ⓜ CANCEL⇨ FORWARD JUMP, AIR Ⓜ, Ⓜ, Ⓗ, Ⓢ, LAND, Ⓢ CANCEL⇨ SUPER JUMP, AIR Ⓜ, Ⓗ, Ⓢ

(449,100 damage) Use this combo to counterhit your opposition's attempts to stop your throws. When → ↓ ↘ + Ⓛ is guarded, follow-up with → ↘ ↓ ↙ ← + ATK or **Combo I.** If your opponent uses advancing guard to push you away, move back in with a dash or → ↓ ↘ + Ⓜ.

V. ← ↓ ↙ + Ⓗ (1 HIT), ST. Ⓛ, ST. Ⓜ, ← + Ⓗ (2 HITS) CANCEL⇨ ↓ ↘ → + Ⓜ CANCEL⇨ Ⓜ, ST. Ⓛ, ST. Ⓜ, ↘ + Ⓜ CANCEL⇨ FORWARD JUMP, AIR Ⓜ, Ⓜ, Ⓗ, Ⓢ, LAND, ST. Ⓜ, Ⓢ CANCEL⇨ SUPER JUMP, Ⓜ, Ⓜ, Ⓗ, Ⓢ

(352,300 damage) This is a basic combo for punishing projectiles at long range. Have no fear if it's blocked, you're left with just enough frame advantage to stage a secondary offense. Attack with **Combo I**, → ↘ ↓ ↙ ← + ATK, or cross-up → ↓ ↘ + Ⓜ when you recover.

VI. AGAINST A JUMPING FOE, AIR Ⓛ, Ⓜ, Ⓜ, Ⓢ, LAND Ⓜ, Ⓢ CANCEL⇨ SUPER JUMP, AIR Ⓜ, Ⓜ, Ⓗ, Ⓢ

(281,700 damage) Verify whether the first three hits connect or not. If your opponent air guards the attack, delay the final air Ⓢ to meet your challenger just as they land. If the air Ⓛ misses completely, guard or attack with a falling air Ⓢ.

ASSISTS

Equip yourself with Dante—α, the Jam Session assist, to keep your adversary on the ground.

Slip behind your foe with (S) + (ATK) while calling an assist, they'll never see it coming.

Felicia has a lot of weaknesses to cover with assists, so many that it's difficult to focus on just one. Your two biggest concerns are to find ways to combat projectile usage and to counter super jumps and Flight. Any sort of beam attack is useful in a firefight, along with assists like Arthur—β Dagger Toss and Amaterasu—α Solar Flare. Many of the same projectile assists also help you shield you an approach. Against aerial enemies, use Dante—α, Dormammu—β, or Doctor Doom—β.

Multi-hit assists that compliment Felicia's Foreground Dash are powerful options to choose. Dante—α, Doctor Doom—γ, and Chun-Li—γ are good candidates. If the assist is called just as Felicia dashes behind it, your opponent must guard in the opposite direction. This is very difficult to react to. Combo into a launcher after the assist hits for additional damage. This is a great surprise attack when you're pummeling your target with Felicia's corner traps.

Felicia's own assists are lackluster. α Rolling Buckler ends with a low attack that's useful for characters with fast overhead techniques. It's also a great crossover counter as you can transition into an air combo after it hits (see Rolling Buckler elements from **Combo I**). γ Cat Spike M causes a ground bounce against aerial foes, which is good for characters who can't cause that state on their own. β Sand Splash does very little for your team, so go with your other assist options instead.

ADVANCED TACTICS

↘ + (M) JUMP CANCELLATION

↘ + (M) leads to heavy damage regardless of the combo size.

↘ + (M) is cancelable into a jump, a helpful property for hitting a floored character and transitioning into an air combo. Unfortunately, hitstun deterioration often makes it impossible to juggle after ↘ + (M) with much (assuming the combo before the final hit is really long). For example, if you perform Combo I near a corner and OTG with ↘ + (M) after the final hit, you can't do much more than a single air (M). To make use of the attack despite hitstun deterioration, you can jump cancel ↘ + (M) into ground special moves and hyper combos to still earn respectable damage. When no meter is available, for example, quickly perform ↘ + (M) [CANCEL] ↓↘→↗ + (H) [CANCEL] (H) to juggle with the Rolling Uppercut. If you have one bar of your hyper combo gauge full, instead do ↘ + (M) [CANCEL] ↓↘→↗ + (ATK)(ATK). Both instances knock your opposition into an aerial state where they quickly recover, so you may opt to not do the OTG combo so it's easier to hold onto momentum. But, if the damage is needed, or if you can team hyper combo into a strong hyper combo, take advantage of this technique.

X-FACTOR LEVEL 2~3

No one crushes entire teams like X-Factor Felicia can.

The level 2 and 3 versions of X-Factor improve the overall speed of Felicia's attacks. This improvement allows for combos and pressure patterns that aren't normally possible. For example, Cat Spike L does not normally link into itself. With X-Factor 2~3 activated, it's possible to link into back-to-back Cat Spikes L attacks for as long as your gauge remains! This outright kills *any* character it touches, no exceptions! On top of this, the drastically increased speed and guard damage on Felicia's Cat Spike M and Delta Kick H make for a few incredibly powerful traps. For instance, X-Factor's Delta Kick H is so fast that it can be repeated over and over again, without the defender ever leaving guardstun! This pattern's only weakness is that small characters can crouch under Delta Kick's third hit, and other mid-sized characters can crouch and use advancing guard on the last hit to gain some breathing room (although this is a *very* small amount). However, large characters like Haggar, Hulk, and Sentinel cannot use either option, and instead must rely on a perfectly timed crossover counter to escape. If no meter or teammate is available for a crossover counter, then they have no choice but to take the heavy guard damage dealt from the repeated kicks. Up to 60~70% chip damage is inflicted with this pattern (which is reduced down to 40~50% damage if they sporadically use advancing guard)! Against mid-sized characters that can lightly push you away with advancing guard, activate Kitty's Helper to cover these minor gaps, then mix in the occasional low attack as the overhead cat splash is about to hit. If your attack connects, link into the Cat Spike L loop to instantly K.O. the opposing player's character.

COMBO APPENDIX

GENERAL EXECUTION TIPS

After hitting a standard (S) launcher, super jump and wait a moment before starting an air chain.

Performing combos after →↓↘ + (L) technically requires you to do a difficult link combo (into standing (L)). Buffering makes this easier than it seems, though. If you need even more help, try brushing your fingers across the (L) button twice rapidly. This compensates for execution errors involving inputting the button too early.

Requirements (Position, meter, etc.)	Notes	Command Sequence	Damage
Requires corner, requires 1 hyper combo gauge bar	After landing from air (M), (M), (H), (S), perform st. (M), cr. (M) a little late so that the opponent is low enough for Rolling Buckler to hit	→↘↓↙← + (H), dash forward, ↘ + (M) [CANCEL] forward jump, air (M), (M), (H), (S), land st. (M), cr. (M) [CANCEL] ↓↘→ + (L) [CANCEL] (L) [CANCEL] ↓↘→ + (ATK)(ATK)	420,600
Requires 1 hyper combo gauge bar	The ↘ + (M) [CANCEL] ↓↘→↗ + (H) [CANCEL] (H) cancels the OTG into a jump, then cancels the jump's 3 frame start-up into Rolling Buckler; there's no need to rush the command, input it precisely and it'll work	Cr. (M), ← + (H) [CANCEL] →↓→ + (L), st. (L), st. (M) [CANCEL] ↓↘→ + (M) [CANCEL] (M), st. (L), st. (M), ↘ + (M) [CANCEL] forward jump, air (M), (M), (H), (S), (S) [CANCEL] super jump, air (M), (M), (H), (S), land, ↘ + (M) [CANCEL] ↓↘→↗ + (H) [CANCEL] (H) (or ↓↘→↗ + (ATK)(ATK))	454,000 or 581,000
Requires 1 hyper combo gauge bar	—	→↓↘ + (M), st. (M) [CANCEL] →↓↘ + (L), st. (L), st. (M) [CANCEL] ↓↘→ + (M) [CANCEL] (M), st. (L), st. (M), ↘ + (M) [CANCEL] forward jump, air (M), (M), (H), (S), (S) [CANCEL] super jump, air (M), (M), (H), (S), land, ↘ + (M) [CANCEL] ↓↘→↗ + (ATK)(ATK)	622,100
Requires 3 hyper combo gauge bars	—	Cr. (M), ← + (H) [CANCEL] →↓↘ + (L), st. (L), st. (M) [CANCEL] ↓↘→ + (M) [CANCEL] (M) [CANCEL] ↓↙← + (ATK)(ATK)	663,800
Requires level 2~3 X-factor	You can indefinitely perform →↓↘ + (L) after the first as long as you're in X-factor; each must be performed as fast as possible	Cr. (L), st. (M), ← + (H) [CANCEL] →↓↘ + (L) [CANCEL] [X-FACTOR] →↓↘ + (L) [CANCEL] →↓↘ + (L) [CANCEL] →↓↘ + (L) [CANCEL] →↓↘ + (L)...	100%

HAGGAR

BIO

REAL NAME

MIKE HAGGAR

OCCUPATION

MAYOR OF METRO CITY

ABILITIES

MOVES RETAINED FROM HIS TIME AS A PRO-WRESTLER, AS WELL AS HIS EXPLOSIVE POWER COMBINE FOR DANGEROUS ATTACKS.

WEAPONS

BE IT A STEEL PIPE, A 2X4, OR A HAMMER, WITH HIS FULL FORCE BEHIND IT ANY WEAPON HE SWINGS BECOMES EXTREMELY EFFECTIVE.

PROFILE

FORMER PROFESSIONAL WRESTLER WHO BECAME THE MAYOR OF METRO CITY. TAKING ON THE NAME "FIGHTING MAYOR," HE TEAMED UP WITH HIS FRIENDS AND TOOK ON THE MAD GEAR CRIME SYNDICATE, GIVING BACK THE DESTRUCTION THEY HAD REAPED IN SPADES.

FIRST APPEARANCE

FINAL FIGHT (1989)

POWER GRID

4	INTELLIGENCE
7	STRENGTH
2	SPEED
7	STAMINA
1	ENERGY PROJECTION
5	FIGHTING ABILITY

*This is biographical, and does not represent an evaluation of the character's in-game combat potential.

ALTERNATE COSTUMES

PS3: ✕ Xbox 360: A

PS3: □ Xbox 360: X

PS3: △ Xbox 360: Y

PS3: R1 Xbox 360: RB

ATTACK SET

STANDING BASIC ATTACKS

Screen	Command	Hits	Damage	Startup	Active	Recovery	Advantage on Hit	Advantage if Guarded	Notes
1	Standing L	1	65,000	7	3	16	-2	-3	—
2	Standing M	1	83,000	11	3	20	-1	-2	—
3	Standing H	1	100,000	14	4	21	—	+1	Ground bounces opponent, ↓↘→ + P1 or P2 snap back
4	S	1	100,000	11	3	23	—	0	Launcher attack, not special or hyper combo cancelable

1

2

3

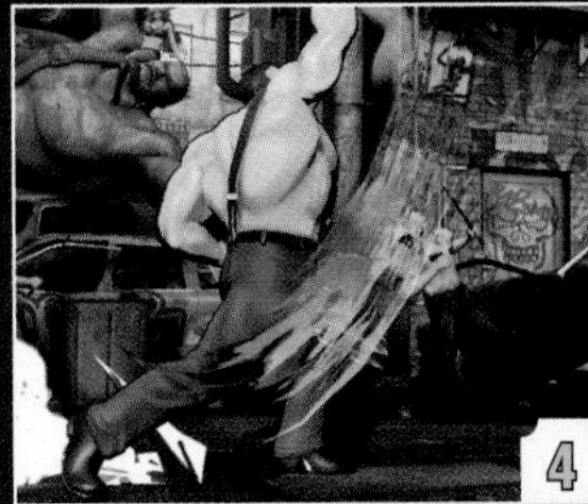
4

CROUCHING BASIC ATTACKS

Screen	Command	Hits	Damage	Startup	Active	Recovery	Advantage on Hit	Advantage if Guarded	Notes
1	Crouching L	1	62,000	8	3	14	0	-1	Low attack
2	Crouching M	1	80,000	12	3	21	-2	-3	Low attack
3	Crouching H	1	97,000	16	6	49	—	-29	Low attack, puts Haggar in unrecoverable knockdown state, invincible after frame 50, knocks down opponent

1

2

3

AERIAL BASIC ATTACKS

Screen	Command	Hits	Damage	Startup	Active	Recovery	Notes
1	Air L	1	58,000	7	Until grounded	1	Overhead attack
2	Air M	1	75,000	13	Until grounded	1	Overhead attack
3	Air H	1	100,000	16	Until grounded	2	Overhead attack
4	Air S	1	110,000	14	4	23	Overhead attack, causes flying screen if used in launcher combo

1

2

3

4

COMMAND ATTACKS

Screen	Command	Hits	Damage	Startup	Active	Recovery	Advantage on Hit	Advantage if Guarded	Notes
1	⇨ + Ⓗ	1	110,000	19	3	24	+10	+9	Ground bounces airborne opponents, unrecoverable knockdown versus airborne opponents
2	(in air) ⇧ + Ⓗ	1	100,000	8	4	19	—	—	Overhead attack, if attack counterhits a standing opponent causes dizzy state, if counterhits airborne opponent causes special knockdown state; unrecoverable knockdown, everything is OTG-capable
3	(in air) ⇩ + Ⓗ	1	120,000	14	3	29	—	—	Overhead attack, ground bounces opponent, unrecoverable knockdown

1

2

3

HAGGAR

AS A PARTNER-CROSSOVER ASSISTS

Screen	Type	P1+P2 Crossover Combination Hyper Combo	Description	Hits	Damage	Startup	Active	Recovery (this crossover assist)	Recovery (other partner)	Notes
1	α – Alpha	Giant Haggar Press	Double Lariat	3	108,300	32	45	121	91	Frames 1-67 invincible, converts 10,000 of Haggar's vitality into red vitality, unrecoverable knockdown
2	β – Beta	Giant Haggar Press	Violent Axe M	2	122,000	42	5(12)4	110	80	Causes spinning knockdown
3	γ – Gamma	Giant Haggar Press	⇨ + Ⓗ	1	110,000	43	3	117	87	Ground bounces opponent, unrecoverable knockdown

1

2

3

SPECIAL MOVES

Screen	Name	Command	Hits	Damage	Startup	Active	Recovery	Advantage on Hit	Advantage if Guarded	Notes
1	Violent Axe L	↓↘→ + L	1	110,000	15	4	22	+10	0	Spinning knockdown
2	Violent Axe M	↓↘→ + M	2	122,000	18	5(12)4	17	+16	+5	First hit staggers opponent, second hit causes spinning knockdown
3	Violent Axe H	↓↘→ + H	3	160,600	20	5(11)4(14)3	19	—	+5	First hit staggers opponent, third hit ground bounces
4	Hoodlum Launcher L	→↓↘ + L	2	140,000	14	6	16	—	+4	Launcher attack
4	Hoodlum Launcher M	→↓↘ + M	2	140,000	26	8	32	—	—	Launcher attack, throw attack
5	Hoodlum Launcher H	→↓↘ + H	2	140,000	30	14	43	—	—	Launcher attack, air throw attack
6	Flying Piledriver L	→↘↓↙← + L	1	160,000	5	1	30	—	—	Throw attack, unrecoverable knockdown
6	Flying Piledriver M	→↘↓↙← + M	1	190,000	3	1	32	—	—	Throw attack, unrecoverable knockdown
6	Flying Piledriver H	→↘↓↙← + H	1	220,000	1	2	33	—	—	Throw attack, unrecoverable knockdown
7	Skyhigh Back Drop L	(in air)→↘↓↙← + L	1	160,000	5	1	35	—	—	Air throw attack, unrecoverable knockdown
7	Skyhigh Back Drop M	(in air)→↘↓↙← + M	1	190,000	3	1	37	—	—	Air throw attack, unrecoverable knockdown
7	Skyhigh Back Drop H	(in air)→↘↓↙← + H	1	220,000	1	2	38	—	—	Air throw attack, unrecoverable knockdown
8	Double Lariat	S + ATK	3	108,300	8	45	28	—	-31	40 frames invincibility, converts 10,000 of Haggar's vitality into red vitality, unrecoverable knockdown
9	Wild Swing	(in air)↓↘→ + S	12	221,500	17	3	21	—	—	Does more damage and more hits the higher Haggar is, unrecoverable knockdown

1

Violent Axe L: Violent Axe L is used in most of Haggar's basic combos. It does a large amount of damage in a single hit and allows for a standing L juggle afterward. Outside of combos Violent Axe L is more difficult to use. While it has surprisingly long range and a large hitbox, it's also very slow on startup. While it is safe against grounded opponents, players that choose to guard it in the air can often land and punish you.

2

Violent Axe M: Violent Axe M is generally only used in Haggar's corner combos. It allows for a standing M juggle afterward, which can then juggle a Violent Axe L—see the Combo Usage section for details. Violent Axe M can also be used to combo from → + H at a great range. While the potential here is large, it's also very risky; if your opponent uses advancing guard after the → + H the Violent Axe M will whiff completely.

3

Violent Axe H: Violent Axe H doesn't have much of a role in Haggar's general gameplan. While it leads into easy combos, it also uses up a ground bounce that you would have normally caused with air ↓ + H. The result is that combo damage becomes much lower when Violent Axe H is used.

4

Hoodlum Launcher L and M: The Hoodlum Launcher attacks are the centerpiece of Haggar's offense. Hoodlum Launcher L is classified as an attack—it can hit opponents during combos and can be guarded. If guarded, Haggar is left at a +4 frame advantage. From here, standing L will beat almost any non-invincible attacks your opponent can stick out. Now, perform a chain combo of standing L to standing M and cancel into another Hoodlum Launcher L. The entire sequence is a combo if it hits and leads into perpetual frame advantage if guarded. Your opponent must use advancing guard to push you away.

Hoodlum Launch M looks similar to the L version, but is classified as a throw instead of an attack! From within range this creates a simple mix-up—attack with Hoodlum Launch L to create frame advantage, or use Hoodlum Launch M against opponents waiting to use advancing guard. This mix-up is nullified by an opponent jumping backwards, however; the hitbox on Hoodlum Launcher L is fairly low, and Hoodlum Launcher M cannot grab airborne characters at all. Against foes that jump back, simply advance forward and gain more positional advantage as your opponent willingly backs away toward the corner.

If either Hoodlum Launcher hits, Haggar will automatically launch his opponent for an aerial combo. This results in every successful Hoodlum Launcher leading to over 500,000 damage! See the Combo Usage section for details.

5

Hoodlum Launcher H: At first glance, Hoodlum Launcher H seems like it should be used as a mix-up to prevent opponents from jumping away from the other two versions of the attack. Unfortunately, its exceedingly slow startup and travel speed make it terrible for that use. Hoodlum Launcher H also does not recover until Haggar reaches the ground, making it very unsafe to use as a pure guess.

In spite of all this, Hoodlum Launcher H has one very key use: resetting opponents after they air recover! When set up correctly, a well-placed Hoodlum Launcher H can grab the opposing character immediately after their invincibility from air recovering wears out, allowing for another full combo that will probably lead to a K.O.

Hoodlum Launcher H is the only attack in the game that is classified as a mid-air, launcher attack. This means you can super jump cancel after the attack hits, even though you are already in the air!

6

Flying Piledriver: While Haggar's Flying Piledriver does a large amount of damage on its own, it is virtually impossible to land a combo afterwards in a real match situation. This makes its damage low in relation to other special throws in the game.

Each strength of Flying Piledriver does progressively more damage with faster startup, but has progressively less range. Flying Piledriver H has only 1 frame of startup, making it very useful defensively for grabbing opponents that have tiny gaps in their offense. The range on Flying Piledriver H is slightly shorter than even a normal throw, however. Flying Piledriver L has more range than the other two versions, but still only reaches marginally further than a regular throw. This makes Flying Piledriver H generally the most useful version of the attack.

COMMAND ATTACKS

Screen	Command	Hits	Damage	Startup	Active	Recovery	Advantage on Hit	Advantage if Guarded	Notes
1	⇨ + Ⓜ	1	70,000	12	6	22	+5	+3	Staggers opponent on counterhit, ⇩ ⬃ ⇨ + P1 or P2 snap back
2	⇨ + Ⓗ	1	70,000	11	5	29	-13	-13	Jump-cancelable, knocks down

1

2

MORRIGAN

AS A PARTNER-CROSSOVER ASSISTS

Screen	Type	P1+P2 Crossover Combination Hyper Combo	Description	Hits	Damage	Startup	Active	Recovery (this crossover assist)	Recovery (other partner)	Notes
1	α – Alpha	Shadow Servant	Shadow Blade H	5	102,300	27	15	132	102	Knocks down
2	β – Beta	Finishing Shower	Soul Fist L	1	70,000	39	—	128	98	Projectile has 5 low priority durability points
3	γ – Gamma	Finishing Shower	Dark Harmonizer	—	—	25	—	110	80	Fills hyper combo gauge by 30%

1

2

3

"I COULD USE A NICE PLAYTHING LIKE YOU."

SPECIAL MOVES

Screen	Name	Command	Hits	Damage	Startup	Active	Recovery	Advantage on Hit	Advantage if Guarded	Notes
1	Flight	↓↙← + S	—	—	15	—	1	—	—	Activates Flight mode for 106 frames, may cancel any special move into Flight
2,3	Soul Fist	↓↘→ + ATK	1	70,000	15	—	36	-14	-16	Projectile has 5 low priority durability points
4	Air Soul Fist L	(in air) ↓↘→ + L	1	70,000	10	—	42	—	—	Projectile has 5 low priority durability points
4	Air Soul Fist M	(in air) ↓↘→ + M	1	70,000	10	—	45	—	—	Projectile has 5 low priority durability points
5	Air Soul Fist H	(in air) ↓↘→ + H	1	70,000	10	—	48	—	—	Projectile has 5 low priority durability points
6	Shadow Blade L (in air OK)	→↓↘ + L	1	80,000	3	8	32/Until grounded, 11 frames ground recovery	-4	-19	Knocks down
6	Shadow Blade M (in air OK)	→↓↘ + M	3	94,800	3	7	48/Until grounded, 11 frames ground recovery	-15	-30	Knocks down
6	Shadow Blade H (in air OK)	→↓↘ + H	5	114,500	3	15	50/Until grounded, 11 frames ground recovery	-21	-36	Knocks down
7	Vector Drain L	→↘↓↙← + L	1	120,000	5	2	20	—	—	Throw, unrecoverable knockdown
7	Vector Drain M	→↘↓↙← + M	1	150,000	3	2	22	—	—	Throw, unrecoverable knockdown
7	Vector Drain H	→↘↓↙← + H	1	170,000	1	2	24	—	—	Throw, unrecoverable knockdown

1

Flight: Morrigan's Flight has one unique quirk, something that sets her apart from the rest of the cast and defines her as a character—all of her special moves can be canceled into Flight mode! This drastically cuts down on the recovery time of her special moves. Soul Fist and Shadow Blade all have at least 32 frames of recovery, which can be cut down to 15 by using Flight-cancels! Even better, if these special moves are performed while Morrigan is already in Flight mode, you can cancel them into "unfly", resulting in a single frame of recovery!

Flight can only be activated once per jump. This essentially gives you access to one Flight-cancel and one unfly-cancel before Morrigan touches the ground. Morrigan's Flight mode has 15 frames of startup, which is marginally faster than other characters. Combined with her 4 frame air L, you can use Flight mode cancels in combos with a larger degree of hitstun deterioration than normal. Activating Flight mode lasts for 106 frames, during which you can freely control Morrigan in the air using the controller.

Other than canceling recovery frames of attacks, Flight mode has a few strong benefits—during Flight mode there are no restrictions on how many special moves or airdashes you can use in a single jump. This allows you to perform four Air Soul Fist projectiles within a single super jump—fire two projectiles, activate Flight mode, then fire two more, then cancel the fourth projectile into unfly! It's important to note that Flight counts as one special move towards the three-special-moves-per-jump limitation that is universal to all characters; you cannot fire three air Soul Fist projectiles and Flight-cancel the third one.

During Flight mode you can cancel airdashes into other airdashes, giving Morrigan some "interesting" movement abilities. Forwards and backwards airdashes cannot be canceled into each other very quickly, however. Morrigan's funky, parabolic upwards and downwards airdashes behave differently during Flight mode: Morrigan moves a small distance down (or up) before simply moving straight forward. It's important to note that you have access to crossover assists during Flight mode, as long as Flight mode wasn't activated during a super jump. However, Morrigan can get hit out of a super jump, air recover, then activate Flight to be considered in normal jump state—this allows you activate Flight mode and call crossover assists even at the top of the screen!

2

3

***Soul Fist*:** Soul Fist is a fairly average projectile attack, but it is still an important part of Morrigan's toolset. Against characters that do not have a projectile of their own, you can mount a respectable zoning defense with Morrigan by using Soul Fist L, the upward-angled Soul Fist H, and air Soul Fist H. Repeated use of Soul Fist L forces your opponent to take their character to the air to get around it, while Soul Fist H and Air Soul Fist H both cut off air routes. Soul Fist projectiles should be Flight-canceled whenever possible to significantly cut down on recovery time. However, if you plan on simply doing two or more Soul Fist L projectiles in a row, you can save yourself the effort of doing repeated Flight-cancels into immediate unfly-cancels; the benefit of doing such is negligible in this case.

Soul Fist L is a strong way to begin a full-screen approach to your foe: toss the projectile, then jump and airdash forward all the way across the screen behind the cover of the Soul Fist! While in transit, you can also call a crossover assist to prolong your offensive momentum. As an alternative, you can cancel Soul Fist L into Flight, then manually fly Morrigan across the screen behind the projectile. You cannot airdash from Flight due to the height restriction required to airdash.
Soul Fist M travels faster across the screen compared to the L version of the attack, which generally isn't as useful. Soul Fist H is aimed diagonally upward, making it a strong choice against opponents that are jumping at mid range. It is also great for fighting against characters that are trying to attack with projectiles from the air.

4

5

***Air Soul Fist*:** Air Soul Fist L and M allow you to attack opponents from all the way across the screen at super jump height. This gives Morrigan something of an edge against other projectile-using characters, even if she can't match most of them in sheer output of durability points. Evade your opponent's attacks by super jumping forward, then rain down up to three Air Soul Fist projectiles! Air Soul Fist L is also a great way to set up an aerial approach—simply fire Air Soul Fist L, then airdash forward behind the projectile. Air Soul Fist L and M become much stronger when it is Flight-canceled: fire Air Soul Fist L, Flight-cancel, immediately perform Air Soul Fist M and unfly-cancel. From there you can airdash toward your opponent with the perfect covering fire!

Air Soul Fist H fires straight forward, which is useful for preemptively countering your opponent's attempts to fire their own aerial projectiles at you. You can perform Air Soul Fist H very low to the ground by inputting ↓↘→↗ + H. This fires a projectile that controls the screen at normal jump height. Use this as a fairly safe method to stop jumps from opposing characters. When performed low to the ground, Air Soul Fist H recovers considerably faster than the ground version of Soul Fist.

6

Shadow Blade: Shadow Blade may look like a Shoryuken-style attack, but unfortunately it lacks invincibility frames to be used as such. While it does function reasonably well as an anti-air because its speed and hitboxes, it is extremely unsafe if guarded. This can be easily remedied by Flight-canceling Shadow Blade! If your opponent guards a Flight-canceled Shadow Blade, drop down on them with air (S) and mount an offense! It's important to note that Shadow Blade cannot be canceled with unfly—using Shadow Blade while already in Flight mode is extremely unsafe!

Shadow Blade is mainly used in combos. This attack creates a large amount of hitstun that allows it to be hyper combo-canceled into Finishing Shower or Darkness Illusion, even when hitstun has been severely deteriorated. The large amount of hitstun also allows you to Flight-cancel it and link air basic attacks afterward.

7

Vector Drain: Vector Drain is a command throw that leaves your opponent in an unrecoverable knockdown state. Unfortunately, it is generally impossible to combo from Vector Drain unless Morrigan ends up in the corner, in which case you can add on the OTG-capable Shadow Servant for good damage.

Increased strengths of Vector Drain deal more damage and are progressively faster, with Vector Drain H having only 1 frame of startup. This allows you to use Vector Drain H defensively, whenever your opponent is near you and on the ground. If your opponent is in range, Vector Drain H will grab them out of anything that isn't airborne or invincible. The increased strengths of Vector Drain also require progressively less range, but Vector Drain H still outranges a normal ground throw.

The whiff animation of Vector Drain can be Flight-canceled at any time. This leads to a strong option select—input the command for Vector Drain H, then immediately press (S) afterwards. If your opponent was on the ground and able to be thrown, Vector Drain H grabs them. Otherwise (immediately after the grab fails to register), you'll Flight-cancel instead and bypass almost the entire whiff animation!

HYPER COMBOS

Screen	Name	Command	Hits	Damage	Startup	Active	Recovery	Advantage on Hit	Advantage if Guarded	Notes
1	Finishing Shower (in air OK)	⇩⇘⇨ + ATK ATK	35	251,900	18+2	69	21	+13	+14	Missiles can be aimed up or down using the controller, each projectile has 1 high priority durability point
2	Astral Vision	⇩⇩ + ATK ATK	—	—	10+6	—	13	—	—	Creates an Astral Vision that lasts for 590 frames, using a hyper combo ends Astral Vision
3	Shadow Servant	⇨⇩⇘ + ATK ATK	5	271,300	10+10	44	21	—	-45	Invincible from frames 1-29, OTG-capable, knocks down
4	Darkness Illusion (Level 3 Hyper Combo, in air OK)	⇩⇙⇦ + ATK ATK	33~35	405,000	16+0	79	Until grounded	—	-21	Invincible from frames 1-27, unrecoverable knockdown

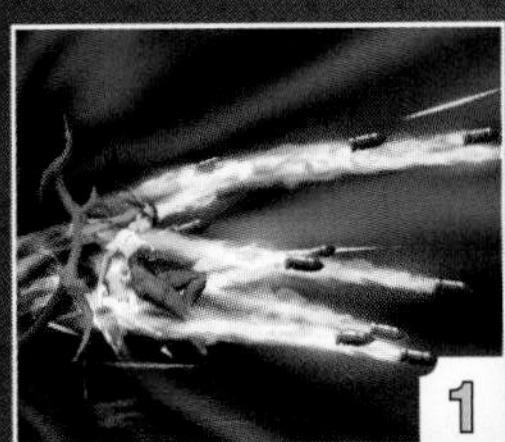

1

Finishing Shower: Finishing Shower fires a volley of 35 missiles across the screen. These missiles can be aimed up or down with the controller. While Finishing Shower is too slow to be used as a conventional projectile hyper combo, it is almost impossible to avoid entirely when it is employed from across the screen—unless your opponent has a teleport. If guarded, Finishing Shower leaves you at a large frame advantage, giving you time to airdash forward and gain substantial ground on your opponent.

Finishing Shower is most often used in combos, since it deals more damage than Shadow Servant. In corner combos, Finishing Shower leaves an opponent in enough hitstun to continue with further damage. If you have meter to spare you can use Finishing Shower several times within the same combo!

2

Astral Vision: Activating Astral Vision creates a mirror image of Morrigan that appears on the other side of an opponent, equidistant with the real version of Morrigan. The Astral Vision effectively doubles the hits in your combos, substantially increasing damage. If your opponent does not use advancing guard, being sandwiched between Morrigan and the Astral Vision almost completely negates the pushback of attacks, allowing you to stay much closer to your opponent during combos and attack patterns.

Since many characters have asymmetrical hitboxes, it is possible for the Astral Vision to hit an opponent while the "true" Morrigan's attacks whiff. In these situations, you will not get pushed away if your opponent uses advancing guard!

Astral Vision can be used as a safe way to tag in Morrigan when used in team hyper combos. It can also be used to further extend combos from another character, but hitstun deterioration will often prevent you from adding a significant amount of damage.

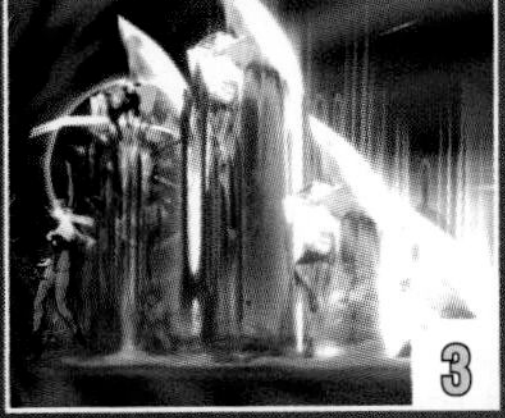

3

Shadow Servant: Shadow Servant is OTG-capable, making it an easy and consistent way to end combos. However, the damage from Shadow Servant is generally less than what you would get by using Finishing Shower, and it also misses several hits against an opponent that is near the corner. Shadow Servant has a large amount of invincibility frames, making it useful defensively or to counter several tactics on reaction. It is very unsafe if guarded, so be wary of using it recklessly unless you can team hyper combo to something safer.

3

Darkness Illusion: Darkness Illusion is a level 3 hyper combo, ignoring all damage scaling even at the end of long combos. It is also easily added into any combo Morrigan has, making it a great way to finish off an opponent. Darkness Illusion leaves your foe in an unrecoverable knockdown state, allowing you to combo into Shadow Servant afterwards! While this is an incredibly expensive and inefficient use of meter, it can be very useful for ending matches. The meter cost of Morrigan's combos can also be offset somewhat by using her Dark Harmonizer crossover assist!

BATTLE PLAN

OVERVIEW

VITALITY: 950,000

CHAIN COMBO ARCHETYPE: HUNTER SERIES

X-Factor	Lv.1	Lv.2	Lv.3
Damage	120%	140%	160%
Speed	115%	130%	145%

Your goal using Morrigan is to get into position to attack using her aerial basic attacks; with the secondary objective of cornering your opponent.

Morrigan's air-based offense is strong for several reasons:

- **You can attack with airdash Ⓛ and Ⓜ overheads, and can perform double overhead attacks against opponents that don't use advancing guard.**
- **The frontal overheads can be mixed up with cross-up airdash Ⓜ or Ⓗ.**
- **Against opponents attempting to guard the mix-up, you can airdash downwards and whiff air Ⓢ, then immediately land and grab an opponent with Vector Drain.**
- **Morrigan's overhead-heavy offense can be combined with a low-hitting crossover assist to create situations that are nearly impossible to guard.**

How do you get into position to attack from the air? In order of effectiveness:

- **Beat your opponent from long range with Soul Fist-based zoning, forcing your opponent to come to you.**
- **Fire Soul Fist L and follow it with a forward airdash.**
- **Super jump and fire an unfly-canceled Air Soul Fist, followed by a forward or downward airdash—depending on range.**
- **Use Finishing Shower from across the screen, then airdash forward as your opponent is guarding the missiles.**

Why is cornering an opponent beneficial to a Morrigan player?

- **Morrigan can deal significantly more damage to cornered opponents with combos that involve multiple Finishing Shower hyper combos.**
- **Opponents that jump backwards defensively are much easier to counter.**
- **Grabbing a cornered opponent with Vector Drain allows you to continue your offense.**

How does one corner an opponent using Morrigan?

- **Hitting the opposing character with combos.**
- **Using crossover assists in conjunction with Morrigan's airdash offense to keep foes in guardstun for extended periods of time.**
- **Using Finishing Shower from across the screen to push your opponent backwards a great distance while allowing you to mount an offense.**

ON THE GROUND

Morrigan can fill the role of meter-user on a team relatively well; in fact, there are too many ways to spend the entire meter. Her corner combos can use up to five bars to deal over 1,000,000 damage—not the most efficient use of meter, but still more than sufficient to knock out a good majority of the cast. Astral Vision is always nice to activate, since it increases overall damage, makes Morrigan's offense more confusing to guard against, and can enable offense that is immune to advancing guard. Having meter to burn on Finishing Shower is also handy, because it can ensure your ability to control the pace of the match for the next few moments.

Morrigan's meter-building, Dark Harmonizer crossover assist also makes her an ideal dedicated assist character on some specialized, meter-hungry teams. Team her up with a strong defensive character and you will be amazed at your rate of meter gain! Of course, all of the meter gained from Dark Harmonizer can also be used to finance Morrigan's incredibly expensive combos!

Try to beat your foes from across the screen with Soul Fist projectiles and force them to come to you!

Even though it isn't invincible, Shadow Blade still works great as an anti-air. If it is guarded, hyper combo-cancel into Finishing Shower to remain safe and attack your opponent behind the cover of the missiles!

Morrigan doesn't have a standard dash—her dash causes her to go into a sort of upward-angled airdash from the ground. Holding forward on the controller (or back if you're doing a backdash) causes Morrigan to continue flying in that direction up to a set distance. Attacks cannot be performed out of the forward dash until 15 frames have passed, preventing you from performing insanely low overhead attacks. Strangely, the backwards dash doesn't allow you to attack for 25 frames! Practice the timing for attacking out of the dash as soon possible. Dashing forward and attacking with air Ⓢ isn't blindingly fast, but at a combined 20 frames of startup it's still perfectly capable of catching an opponent off guard. If air Ⓢ hits, transition into a full combo.

The preferred strategy with Morrigan is to force your challenger to come to you, employing a strong long ranged game that employs various Soul Fist projectiles. Fire off Soul Fist L repeatedly from all the way across the screen and force your opponent to deal with it. If your opponent responds by jumping towards you, begin mixing in low Air Soul Fist H—performed by inputting ⇩ ⇘ ⇨ ⇗ + Ⓗ. Between uses of Soul Fist you should bolster your long ranged game as much as possible by using any projectile-based crossover assists that you may have.

If you develop fast hands and reflexes, you can Flight-cancel your Soul Fist projectiles by repeating the following sequence—Soul Fist L, Flight-cancel, Air Soul Fist H, unfly-cancel. Performed correctly, this sequence sends repeated walls of two Soul Fist projectiles stacked on top of each other. If your opponent does not have a character-specific way to get through these projectiles, they will essentially have no choice but to super jump forward. They can also opt to dash forward and guard a projectile with each repetition, and eventually close the distance that way, but they'll sustain a large chunk of chip damage during that time.

When your opponent eventually works their way into range to threaten you with air basic attacks, you can use ⇨ + Ⓜ to anti-air almost all jumps from a relatively low angle. ⇨ + Ⓜ can even be chained into a launcher for a combo! If your foe is approaching at a very high angle, ⇨ + Ⓗ will generally work if performed early enough. ⇨ + Ⓗ is jump-cancelable, also leading into combos. Against aerial moves that are difficult to anti-air with the previous two attacks, Shadow Blade will typically work reliably. However, you won't get a full combo from an anti-air Shadow Blade like you would with the other attacks. The best you can normally do is Shadow Blade H, Flight-cancel, then perform another Shadow Blade H.

As opposed to straight-forward anti-air tactics, typically the best air defense is to evade the attack and begin your own offense by jumping backwards, then airdashing forward with air Ⓜ! Call a crossover assist as you're attacking with air Ⓜ to keep your opponent in guardstun as long as possible, increasing your chances of scoring a clean hit.

Against a zoning character, you typically won't be able to keep up with their projectile output with just Soul Fist projectiles—even if you Flight-cancel them. Instead, evade their projectiles by super jumping forward, then immediately fire a couple of Flight-canceled, Air Soul Fist projectiles from above. Follow the projectiles with an airdash and you can begin your offense.

UP IN THE AIR

Morrigan has a great set of aerial mobility options that is very distinct from the rest of the cast. She can airdash in four different directions, two of which eventually end in crazy parabolic arcs. However, Morrigan's height restriction for airdash is higher than average—super jumping before airdashing allows you to reach the minimum height requirement more quickly and makes your airdash offense that much more deadly.

Morrigan has forward and backward airdashes that allow her to travel the length of the entire screen; all you have to do is continue holding the controller in the direction of the airdash. This allows you to cross the entire screen quickly and easily while staying above threats like ground-level projectiles—following a Soul Fist L projectile with a horizontal airdash is a great way to approach an opponent. In addition, if you perform a horizontal airdash from a normal jump you can soar across the screen while still having access to crossover assists!

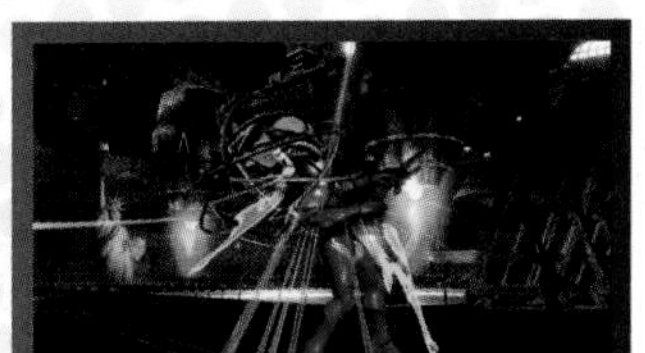

Airdashing forward behind the cover of Soul Fist L is a great way to approach an opponent. You can also call a crossover assist during your airdash!

Air (H) can hit opponents at a relatively far distance behind Morrigan, making it great for use in cross-ups using forward or upward airdashes.

When you're within melee range of your opponent, jumping up and performing a forward airdash can result in a nice, self-contained mix-up: attacking with air (M) will stay in front of your opponent unless you are very close, and attacking with air (H) will cross your opponent up and hit from behind! Airdashing forward with air (H) also has a secondary use—opponents attempting to jump away from Morrigan's offense will often jump right into an unintentional air throw! When attacking from the front with air (M), you have time to chain into air (M) or (H) for some double-overhead action!

Forward airdashes are especially strong when performed in conjunction with a low-hitting crossover assist like Wesker—β. While the initial overhead attack from a forward airdash isn't difficult to guard on reaction, adding low-hitting assists into the mix makes it suddenly very difficult, if not impossible to guard!

Pressing ⇩ + ATK ATK during a jump will cause Morrigan to airdash down and towards her foe, allowing you to attack with quick (L) or (M) overheads. Airdashing downwards and attacking with air (L) will usually give you enough time to attack with a second air (L) overhead, which can be mixed up by simply performing a single air (L) and transitioning into standing (L) for a low attack. You can also airdash downwards and whiff air (S) to land instantly, then use Vector Drain H or standing (L) for an extra dose of trickiness!

Airdashing downward and not canceling with an attack at all results in a strange movement—Morrigan's diagonally downward airdash bends upward and eventually rockets her up into the air! Ironically enough, Morrigan's downward airdash leaves her at the greatest height, when compared to the other directions. This parabolic airdash has a few uses: calling a crossover assist immediately before airdashing downward at close range will cause Morrigan to airdash into her opponent menacingly—your opponent will likely guard high expecting an overhead attack. However, she'll then bend upwards and fly behind the opposing character, creating a sneaky cross-up using the crossover assist if timed correctly! Another use of the downward airdash is to quickly get high above the head of a cornered opponent. Jump, airdash down, and soar above the opposing character's head, where you can proceed to perform Flight-canceled Air Soul Fist attacks! Note that since you had already used your one airdash per jump already, the only way you can airdash after a Soul Fist is to perform the airdash while within Flight mode. This opens up some interesting possibilities with unfly-canceled attacks during your airdash!

Pressing ⇧ + ATK ATK causes Morrigan to airdash diagonally up and forward and short distance before traveling downward in another parabolic arc. This can be thought of as a faster double jump. This movement is useful for evading attacks by traveling over them, while remaining in normal jump state with access to crossover assists. Spaced correctly, upwards airdashes can set up cross-up air (H) attack very well, and is especially difficult to guard when combined with a crossover assist.

While you'll be spending a lot of time in Flight mode from Flight-canceled attacks, generally you won't be spending any of that time actually flying around using the controller. Take advantage of your unlimited amount of airdashes and zoom across the screen with alternating down and forward airdashes! From this point you can attack your challenger with an unfly-canceled Soul Fist L and drop with air (S), or airdash straight into your foe and attack with a full air chain.

In summary, Morrigan's aerial options give you many ways to get into range to attack with airdashes. Chief among these methods is firing an unfly-canceled Air Soul Fist L or M and following it with an airdash. This is very difficult for an opponent to counter directly, and often guarantees some offensive momentum. Once you get near your foe, attack using airdash overheads, cross-ups using forward airdash (H), low attacks, and throws using downward airdash (S) to whiff and land quickly. Mixing low-hitting assists into all of this can make Morrigan's offense absolutely lethal!

COMBO USAGE

I. ST. (L), ST. (M), CR. (M), CR. (H), → + (H) [CANCEL] FORWARD JUMP, AIR (M), (M), (H), (S) (1~2 HITS), LAND, ST. (M), → + (M), (S) [CANCEL] FORWARD SUPER JUMP, AIR (M), (M), (H) [CANCEL] ↓ ↙ ← + (S), (L), (M), (H) [CANCEL] → ↓ ↘ + (M) [CANCEL] ↓ ↘ → + ATK ATK

(470,900 damage) Morrigan's standard, low-hitting combo. The first (M), (M), (H), (S) sequence must be performed as fast as possible for air (S) to hit. When you land from the chain, wait a moment, then juggle with standing (M), → + (M), (S). If you perform the chain any earlier, your target will be knocked too high in the air for a full air chain after.

II. BACK THROW, → ↓ ↘ + ATK ATK

(337,700 damage) This is a simple throw combo that unfortunately doesn't work with her nearly identical forward throw. It also inflicts less damage if you throw your foe into the corner. Save it for instances when you have meter to THC into a partner's hyper combo.

III. AGAINST AIRBORNE FOE, AIR (L), (M), (H), (S), LAND, ST. (M), → + (H) [CANCEL] FORWARD JUMP, AIR (M), (H), (H), (S), LAND, ST. (M), (S) [CANCEL] FORWARD SUPER JUMP, AIR (M), (M), (H) [CANCEL] → ↓ ↘ + (M) [CANCEL] ↓ ↘ → + ATK ATK

(452,900 damage) A preemptive air-to-air combo with a flexible opening. If air (L) misses because of a poor guess, you recover quickly enough to fall down with another air attack, or back

IV. COUNTER HIT → + (M), FORWARD DASH, AIR (M), (H), LAND, CR. (H), → + (H) [CANCEL] FORWARD JUMP, AIR (M), (M), (H), (S) (1~2 HITS), LAND, ST. (M), → + (M), (S) [CANCEL] FORWARD SUPER JUMP, AIR (M), (M), (H) [CANCEL] → ↓ ↘ + (M) [CANCEL] ↓ ↘ → + ATK ATK

(501,500 damage) Use → + (M) to preemptively stop an opponent's attacks when you're at a frame advantage. This goes hand-in-hand her Vector Drain command throw, which is threatening enough to warrant a challenger's attempt to throw or attack it at close ranges. The needles she summons also have a giant area of affect that act as an invulnerable shield to frontal attacks, making it good for preemptively stopping mid range ground attacks. → + (M) causes a heavy stagger when it counter hits an incoming move, leaving you enough time to link into a forward dashing air (M), (H). It also leaves you at a frame advantage when guarded, so have no fear when using it.

ASSISTS

Morrigan's offense consists almost entirely of overheads; having a low-hitting crossover assist is a great recipe for success!

Long ranged assists that provide covering fire make it especially easy to close the gap and start your offense, as well as strengthen your long ranged Soul Fist game.

Dark Harmonizer builds a ton of meter quickly, making Morrigan one of the most useful crossover assists in the game for zoning-based teams.

Morrigan's meter-building Dark Harmonizer assist is often the entire reason why players will place her on a team—she causes your meter gain rate to skyrocket. Using the Dark Harmonizer assist also makes Morrigan a better character as well. Morrigan is one of the most meter-hungry characters in the game, and any meter built from Dark Harmonizer can go toward Astral Vision and Darkness Illusion combos.

If your team absolutely needs a long ranged crossover assist, Soul Fist can fill that role decently well. As always, long ranged assists are a huge benefit to any team. Shadow Blade is difficult to use effectively, because it is simply a fast, non-invincible attack that is difficult to start combos with.

Since Morrigan's offense is comprised of mostly overhead aerial attacks, adding a low-hitting crossover assist into the mix makes her offense extremely deadly. Wesker—β fills this role far better than the other low-hitting crossover assists because it is substantially faster. Wesker—β can also be used to extend corner combos with his OTG-capable gunshot.

Any long ranged crossover assist makes Morrigan a substantially stronger character. Performing Flight-canceled Soul Fist projectiles from across the screen is already a strong zoning tactic, and adding in projectiles from a long ranged crossover assist make it incredibly difficult for an opponent to approach without super jumping! In addition, long ranged projectile assists used as covering fire also make it substantially easier for you to approach your opponent.

ADVANCED TACTICS

SET-UP VERSUS FORWARD KNOCKDOWN RECOVERY

After grabbing your opponent with Vector Drain, punish attempts to knockdown recover past you with a nasty cross-up!

After Vector Drain hits the opposing character, simply hold up forward on the controller. If you see your opponent roll forward, call a crossover assist simultaneously while airdashing backwards. Your foe will initially roll past you, but your backwards airdash will once again place you directly in front of your adversary and force them to guard in the cross-up direction! This also keeps your opponent's back to the corner.

Your assist will also pop out and sandwich your target from the opposite side; this means that any attacks the crossover assist hits with will push your opponent's character towards you instead of away. Use this opportunity to set up a quick airdash mix-up!

If you have Wesker—β on your team, press P1 or P2 simultaneously with the backwards airdash. After airdashing toward your opponent, attack with an air (M), (H) chain. The air (H) will hit simultaneously with Wesker, making the set-up unblockable. This can be avoided if your opponent uses advancing guard on the air (M), but if they are waiting to do that simply omit the air (M) and go straight into air (H). Air (H) is slower, but a challenger expecting air (M) will likely sit there and guard further, allowing your single attack to hit simultaneously with the low-hitting Wesker to start a combo.

COMBO APPENDIX

GENERAL EXECUTION TIPS

After a (S) launcher hits, wait a moment before performing an air chain to ensure that every hit connects.

Hyper canceling →↓↘ + (M) into ↓↘→ + ATK ATK is strangely difficult. Perform the command for the hyper combo much earlier than you think you should; do it during Shadow Blade's first hits.

Requirements (Position, meter, etc.)	Notes	Command Sequence	Damage
Requires 4 hyper combo gauge bars	After the level 3 hyper combo hits, Morrigan lands and recovers before your foe stands, it's difficult, but you can OTG the fallen character with →↓↘ + ATK ATK if done right as she lands	St. (L), st. (M), cr. (M), cr. (H), → + (H) CANCEL▶ forward jump, air (M), (M), (H), (S) (1~2 hits), land, st. (M), → + (M), (S) CANCEL▶ forward super jump, air (M), (M), (H) CANCEL▶ ↓↙← + (S), (L), (M), (H) CANCEL▶ →↓↘ + (M) CANCEL▶ ↓↙← + ATK ATK, land, →↓↘ + ATK ATK	887,200
Requires corner, requires 3 hyper combo gauge bars	After the first aerial ↓↘→ + ATK ATK recovers, watch for Morrigan to recover from the shots, then immediately do another →↓↘ + (M) CANCEL▶ ↓↘→ + ATK ATK again	Counter Hit → + (M), forward dash, air (M), (H), st. (M), cr. (M), cr. (H), → + (H) CANCEL▶ forward jump, air (M), (M), (H), (S) (1~2 hits), land, delayed st. (M), → + (M), (S), CANCEL▶ super jump, air (M), (M), (H) CANCEL▶ →↓↘ + (M) CANCEL▶ ↓↘→ + ATK ATK, →↓↘ + (M) CANCEL▶ ↓↘→ + ATK ATK, →↓↘ + (M) CANCEL▶ ↓↘→ + ATK ATK	701,300
Requires corner, requires 5 hyper combo gauge bars	—	St. (M), cr. (M), cr. (H), → + (H) CANCEL▶ forward jump, air (M), (M), (H), (S) (1~2 hits), land, delayed st. (M), → + (M), (S), CANCEL▶ super jump, air (M), (M), (H) CANCEL▶ →↓↘ + (M) CANCEL▶ ↓↘→ + ATK ATK, →↓↘ + (M) CANCEL▶ ↓↙← + ATK ATK, land, →↓↘ + ATK ATK	1,021,600
Requires level 1 X-Factor, Requires 1 hyper combo gauge bar	—	Cr. (L), st. (M), cr. (M), cr. (H), → + (H) CANCEL▶ forward jump, air (M), (H), (S), land, → + (H) CANCEL▶ forward jump, air (M), (H), (S), land, (S) CANCEL▶ forward super jump, air (M), (M), (H) CANCEL▶ →↓↘ + (H) CANCEL▶ ↓↘→ + ATK ATK	950,200

RYU
"SHOW ME YOUR STRENGTH."
BIO
REAL NAME
RYU
OCCUPATION
FIGHTER
ABILITIES
UTILIZES A UNIQUE FIGHTING STYLE BASED ON ANSATSUKEN, WITH ELEMENTS OF KARATE, JUDO, AND TAEKWONDO BLENDED IN. HE IS ALSO ABLE TO UTILIZE HIS SPIRITUAL ENERGY.
WEAPONS
NONE
PROFILE
RYU'S NAME GAINED GREAT RECOGNITION AMONG MARTIAL ARTISTS AFTER HE DEFEATED THE MUAY THAI KING IN A FIGHT. HOWEVER, INSTEAD OF CLAIMING HIS FAME, RYU BEGAN TO WANDER AROUND THE GLOBE, HOPING TO BECOME A TRUE MARTIAL ARTIST. HE CONTINUES HIS JOURNEY, ENGAGING IN BATTLES WITH FIGHTERS HE MEETS ALONG THE WAY.
FIRST APPEARANCE
STREET FIGHTER (1987)
POWER GRID
4 INTELLIGENCE
6 STRENGTH
5 SPEED
6 STAMINA
7 ENERGY PROJECTION
7 FIGHTING ABILITY
*This is biographical, and does not represent an evaluation of the character's in-game combat potential.
ALTERNATE COSTUMES
PS3: ⊗ Xbox 360: A
PS3: ▢ Xbox 360: X
PS3: △ Xbox 360: Y
PS3: R1 Xbox 360: RB

ATTACK SET

STANDING BASIC ATTACKS

Screen	Command	Hits	Damage	Startup	Active	Recovery	Advantage on Hit	Advantage if Guarded	Notes
1	Standing (L)	1	50,000	5	3	10	+3	+1	—
2	Standing (M)	1	75,000	8	3	21	-3	-5	—
3	Standing (H)	1	90,000	10	3	21	+4	+2	↓↘→ + P1 or P2 snap back
4	(S)	1	100,000	9	5	22	—	-1	Launcher attack, not special or hyper combo cancelable

1

2

3

4

CROUCHING BASIC ATTACKS

Screen	Command	Hits	Damage	Startup	Active	Recovery	Advantage on Hit	Advantage if Guarded	Notes
1	Crouching (L)	1	45,000	5	2	11	+3	+1	Low attack
2	Crouching (M)	1	68,000	8	3	19	-1	-3	Low attack
3	Crouching (H)	1	80,000	10	4	26	—	-4	Low attack, unrecoverable knockdown

1

2

3

AERIAL BASIC ATTACKS

Screen	Command	Hits	Damage	Startup	Active	Recovery	Notes
1	Air (L)	1	55,000	6	13	5	Overhead attack
2	Air (M)	2	108,000	9	4	19	Overhead attack
3	Air (H)	1	90,000	9	4	23	Overhead attack
4	Air (S)	1	95,000	9	8	19	Overhead attack, causes flying screen if used in launcher combo

1

2

3

4

COMMAND ATTACKS

Screen	Command	Hits	Damage	Startup	Active	Recovery	Advantage on Hit	Advantage if Guarded	Notes
1	⇨ + Ⓜ	2	63,000	23	4	22	-3	-5	Overhead attack
2	⇨ + Ⓗ	1	95,000	13	3	21	+4	+2	—

1

2

AS A PARTNER—CROSSOVER ASSISTS

Screen	Type	P1+P2 Crossover Combination Hyper Combo	Description	Hits	Damage	Startup	Active	Recovery (this crossover assist)	Recovery (other partner)	Notes
1	α – Alpha	Shinku Tatsumaki Senpukyaku	Shoryuken H	1	150,000	27	14	132	102	Knocks down opponent
2	β – Beta	Shinku Hadoken	Hadoken L	1	100,000	34	—	128	98	Projectile has 5 low priority durability points
3	γ – Gamma	Shinku Tatsumaki Senpukyaku	Tatsumaki Senpukyaku H	3	135,400	37	17(6)6	115	85	Knocks down opponent

1

2

3

RYU

SPECIAL MOVES

Screen	Name	Command	Hits	Damage	Startup	Active	Recovery	Advantage on Hit	Advantage if Guarded	Notes
1	Hadoken L	↓↘→ + L	1	100,000	10	—	35	-2	-4	Projectile has 5 low priority durability points
	Hadoken M	↓↘→ + M	1	100,000	10	—	39	-6	-8	Projectile has 5 low priority durability points
	Hadoken H	↓↘→ + H	1	100,000	10	—	43	-10	-12	Projectile has 5 low priority durability points
2	Air Hadoken	(in air) ↓↘→ + ATK	1	100,000	14	—	38	—	—	Projectile has 5 low priority durability points
3	Shoryuken L	→↓↘ + L	1	100,000	3	14	25	-18	-13	Invincible from frames 1-2
	Shoryuken M	→↓↘ + M	1	120,000	3	14	33	-21	-21	Invincible from frames 1-5
	Shoryuken H	→↓↘ + H	1	150,000	3	14	47	-30	-35	Invincible from frames 1-9
4	Tatsumaki Senpukyaku L	↓↙← + L	1	90,000	13	6	23	—	-3	Knocks down opponent
	Tatsumaki Senpukyaku M	↓↙← + M	2	114,000	13	7(6)6	21	—	-1	Knocks down opponent
	Tatsumaki Senpukyaku H	↓↙← + H	3	143,500	13	17(6)6	22	—	-2	Knocks down opponent
5	Air Tatsumaki Senpukyaku L	(in air) ↓↙← + L	1	100,000	13	20	Until grounded, 4 frames ground recovery	+25	+23	—
	Air Tatsumaki Senpukyaku M	(in air) ↓↙← + M	4	117,600	13	26(4)6	Until grounded, 1 frame ground recovery	+4	+3	—
	Air Tatsumaki Senpukyaku H	(in air) ↓↙← + H	5	135,800	13	36(4)6	Until grounded, 1 frame ground recovery	+7	+5	—
6	Jodan Sokuto Geri L	←↓↙ + L	1	100,000	14	5	30	—	-9	Wall bounces opponent
	Jodan Sokuto Geri M	←↓↙ + M	1	100,000	16	5	32	—	-11	Wall bounces opponent
	Jodan Sokuto Geri H	←↓↙ + H	1	100,000	18	5	34	—	-13	Wall bounces opponent

1

Hadoken: Much like in his *Street Fighter* incarnations, Ryu's best and most important attack is the Hadoken. The Hadoken has faster startup and significantly faster recovery than most projectile attacks in the game, and the projectile itself is relatively large and remains an active threat on the screen for a long period of time. Each Hadoken deals substantial damage: inflicting 100,000 damage if hit, and 30,000 chip damage if guarded. Hadoken L is the typically the version you'll use the most: it has significantly faster recovery time compared to the other two versions, and usually you'll want your projectiles to occupy the screen for a longer period of time.

The strategy behind using Hadoken is very straight-forward: toss out a Hadoken L and make your opponent deal with it. Anticipate how your opponent will try to avoid the Hadoken and do the proper counter!

2

(in air) Hadoken: Ryu is one of the few characters in *Marvel vs. Capcom 3* with the ability to fire a projectile forward in the air; most characters can only fire projectiles diagonally downward. This allows you to prevent your opponent from maneuvering around your ground projectiles; anticipate the height at which your opponent will attempt to avoid your ground Hadoken, then place an air Hadoken at that height! When attempting to predict and cut off an opponent's route, always use air Hadoken H; Hadoken L likely won't reach your opponent in time to block them off.

Air Hadoken can also be done slightly off of the ground to create a projectile that cannot be crouched under, and is more difficult to jump over. However, the air version of Hadoken has noticeably more recovery time than the grounded versions, giving your opponent much more time to move between projectiles.

Shoryuken: Ryu's Shoryuken is an attack that is invincible from the first frame, an extreme rarity for a special move in *Marvel vs. Capcom 3*. This allows you to blow through any attack patterns that have even the smallest of gaps.

While having a Shoryuken up your sleeve is always a powerful asset that can force any offensive character to change their strategy, it's also a huge risk: Shoryuken is very unsafe if guarded. Even hyper combo-canceling into Shinku Hadoken in the air will not assure safety unless you team hyper combo to another character. Crossover assists can be called immediately before using Shoryuken to make it safer, but this is nearly impossible to do in situations where you only have a tiny window to act.

3

Tatsumaki Senpukaku: Unlike most other games, the ground version of Tatsumaki Senpukyaku cannot be crouched under. However, the attack is still unsafe to throws if guarded, severely limiting its usefulness. Tatsumaki Senpukyaku is at its most useful if you can anticipate when your opponent is going to use advancing guard: simultaneously call a crossover assist while attacking with a normal move, then cancel that normal move into Tatsumaki Senpukyaku. The forward momentum will push you through the advancing guard while the crossover assist keeps you safe after your opponent guards it.

4

IV. AIR THROW, P1 or P2, LAND, DASH, ST. Ⓗ, → + Ⓗ, Ⓢ CANCEL SUPER JUMP, AIR Ⓗ CANCEL ↓ ↘ → + Ⓛ CANCEL ↓ ↘ → + ATK ATK

(490,200 damage, Wesker—β) Air throws are typically Ryu's safest and most reliable anti-air option. Having a quick OTG-capable assist like Wesker—β or Deadpool—β allows you to get major damage after each successful air throw.

It is much easier to hit with the OTG-capable crossover assist if you perform a backwards air throw. Doing backwards air throws also have the benefit of increasing the distance between you and the corner, and allow you to guard unexpected early attacks from your opponent.

V. P1 or P2, FORWARD THROW, ST. Ⓜ, S. Ⓗ, → + Ⓗ, Ⓢ CANCEL SUPER JUMP, AIR Ⓜ (2 HITS), Ⓜ (2 HITS), Ⓗ CANCEL ↓ ↙ ← + Ⓗ (5 HITS) CANCEL ↓ ↘ → + ATK ATK

(463,400 damage) With an OTG-capable assist available Ryu can land full combos after a forward throw on the ground. However, this must be premeditated ahead of time as the P1 or P2 button must be pressed before the throw attempt.

Ryu has a strong mix-up against opponents attempting to throw escape; see the Advanced Tactics section for details.

ADVANCED TACTICS

POST-SHORYUKEN M MIX-UP

Hitting your opponent with Shoryuken M creates a great opportunity to mix up your opponent for more damage.

After hitting your opponent with Shoryuken M your opponent will air recover very high in the air. Most players will unconsciously air recover backwards in this situation. If you dash forward and press → + Ⓗ you can anti-air nearly anything the opponent attacks with after air recovering and then proceed into a full combo.

Once your opponent wises up and begins to guard after air recovering, you can then dash forward and attack with a → + Ⓜ overhead, made more difficult to guard since Ryu is off-screen for most of the startup time. Call a crossover assist to be able to combo after the overhead! Mix up the → + Ⓜ overhead with crouching Ⓜ to hit opponents who aren't guarding low.

If you predict that your adversary will air recover forward, walk backwards after hitting Shoryuken M. This will put you in position to anti-air any attacks out of the air recovery with → + Ⓗ, which eventually will force your challenger to guard after air recovering. Once your opponent begins to guard you can then dash under an opponent at the last second and attack with crouching Ⓛ from the other side, or do a → + Ⓜ overhead from the front side.

THROW MIX-UP

If your opponent attempts to throw escape against you, counter by jumping forward and using air Tatsumaki Senpukyaku L!

Whenever you get near your opponent at a slight frame advantage you should mix up the following options:

Call OTG-capable crossover assist and throw versus guarding opponents.

Air Tatsumaki Senpukyaku L versus opponents attempting to throw escape.

Air throw or crouching Ⓛ versus opponents attempting to jump away.

If you have an OTG-capable crossover assist available, Ryu can easily combo after his forward ground throw. This can often force challengers to attempt to use throw escape when they think a throw is coming. If you jump forward instead of throwing, the opponent will instead get a standing Ⓗ attack when they attempt to throw escape. This allows you to jump over it and hit your opponent from behind with air Tatsumaki Senpukyaku L and go into a full combo!

To prevent getting hit out of the air by your opponent's standing Ⓗ attack, wait until Ryu is near the peak of the jump before performing the Tatsumaki Senpukyaku L. This should cause Ryu to completely clear your opponent's attack and tag them from behind. If your opposition simply waits and guards, the cross-up Tatsumaki Senpukyaku L will still allow you to maintain offensive momentum behind the massive frame advantage.

AIR TATSUMAKI SENPUKYAKU FAKE CROSS-UP

If you jump behind your opponent and perform air Tatsumaki Senpukyaku you'll switch directions and hit your opponent from the front!

Special moves performed in the air will always re-align and face the opposing character. Since air Tatsumaki Senpukyaku L has a small amount of forward and upward movement, this allows you jump behind an opponent, then air Tatsumaki Senpukyaku L back in front of them!

This can be incredibly difficult to guard when used in tandem with a crossover assist: normal jump over the opponent and press the P1 or P2 button at the apex of the jump. When you've cleared your opponent, perform the air Tatsumaki Senpukyaku in the other direction to hop back in front of your target, likely causing them to guard the assist in the wrong direction. Depending on the assist, you can dash forward and continue with a full combo! If your opponent is guarding the fake cross-up, simply land from your jump without performing the air Tatsumaki Senpukyaku to force them to guard in the opposite direction.

COMBO APPENDIX

GENERAL EXECUTION TIPS

To do air Tatsumaki Senpukyaku M or H as low to the ground as possible, slowly input ↓ ↙ ← ↖, then press M or H slightly afterward.

Air Tatsumaki Senpukyaku L offense should be performed by simply jumping forward and inputting the motion as fast as possible.

Requirements (Position, meter, etc.)	Notes	Command Sequence	Damage
Airborne opponent	Anti-air combo at normal jump height. The Shoryuken H is easier to hit the higher your opponent is in relation to Ryu.	Air M (2 hits), H CANCEL ↓ ↙ ← + L, → ↓ ↘ + H	344,200
Corner required	—	Cr. L, st. M, st. H, → + H CANCEL ← ↓ ↙ + L, st. M, st. H, → + H CANCEL ↓ ↙ ← + L, → ↓ ↘ + M CANCEL → ↓ ↘ + ATK ATK, st. M, st. H, → + H, S CANCEL super jump, air H CANCEL ↓ ↙ ← + H (5 hits) CANCEL ↓ ↘ → + ATK ATK	1,058,400
X-Factor level 1	Combo after ↓ + M overhead without using a crossover assist	→ + M (2 hits) CANCEL X-Factor, st. M, cr. H, → + H, S CANCEL super jump, air M (2 hits), M (2 hits), H CANCEL ↓ ↙ ← + H (5 hits) CANCEL ↓ ↘ → + ATK ATK	980,400
—	Do ↓ ↙ ← ↖ + H to do the air Tatsumaki Senpukyaku H as low as possible	Air ↓ ↙ ← + H, land, cr. L, cr. M, cr. H, → + H, S CANCEL super jump, air H CANCEL ↓ ↘ → + L CANCEL ↓ ↘ → + ATK ATK	477,400
—	Combo after hitting opponent with air Tatsumaki Senpukyaku L	Air ↓ ↙ ← + L, land, st. M, cr. H, → + H, S CANCEL super jump, air H CANCEL ↓ ↘ → + L CANCEL ↓ ↘ → + ATK ATK	632,100
—	Combo also works with ground throws but is much more difficult, especially after forward throw. Perform Air Shinku Hadoken with ↓ ↘ → ↗ + ATK ATK	Air throw, ↓ ↘ → + ATK ATK (hold down on controller) OTG	330,000
Corner required	This combo is character-specific; some characters will fly out of the corner after the Shinku Tatsumaki Senpukyaku. Perform the Air Shinku Hadoken by inputting ↓ ↘ → + ATK ATK	Cr. L, st. M, st. H, → + H CANCEL ← ↓ ↙ + L, cr. M, st. H, → + H CANCEL ↓ ↘ → + L CANCEL ↓ ↙ ← + ATK ATK, jump, ↓ ↘ → + ATK ATK (hold down on contoller) OTG	789,000

"I STILL HAVE A LONG JOURNEY BEFORE I AM A TRUE WARRIOR..."

SPENCER

"SOMETIMES I WONDER IF IT'S WORTH FIGHTING AT ALL."

BIO

REAL NAME

NATHAN SPENCER

OCCUPATION

FORMER U.S. GOVERNMENT OPERATIVE (DISHONORABLY DISCHARGED)

ABILITIES

TOGETHER WITH HIS BIONIC ARM ON HIS LEFT SHOULDER, HE IS PROFICIENT WITH VARIOUS FIREARMS.

WEAPONS

IN ADDITION TO HIS BIONIC ARM, HE ALSO UTILIZES HANDGUNS, RIFLES, GRENADE LAUNCHERS, ETC.

PROFILE

ONCE A HERO OF THE WAR AGAINST THE EMPIRE, FOLLOWING THE BIONIC PURGE HE WAS BRANDED A TRAITOR BY THE GOVERNMENT AND SENTENCED TO DEATH. HOWEVER, WITH THE EMERGENCE OF A NEW BIONIC THREAT, HE HAS ANSWERED THE CALL TO RETURN TO THE BATTLEFIELD.

FIRST APPEARANCE

BIONIC COMMANDO (1987)

POWER GRID

4 INTELLIGENCE

5 STRENGTH

4 SPEED

5 STAMINA

1 ENERGY PROJECTION

6 FIGHTING ABILITY

*This is biographical, and does not represent an evaluation of the character's in-game combat potential.

ALTERNATE COSTUMES

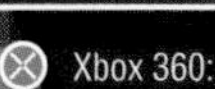

PS3: ⊗ Xbox 360: A | PS3: □ Xbox 360: X | PS3: △ Xbox 360: Y | PS3: R1 Xbox 360: RB

Attack Set

Standing Basic Attacks

Screen	Command	Hits	Damage	Startup	Active	Recovery	Advantage on Hit	Advantage if Guarded	Notes
1	Standing L	1	48,000	6	3	11	0	-1	Rapid fire
2	Standing M	1	67,000	9	3	22	-6	-7	—
3	Standing H	1	88,000	12	3	21	0	-1	↓↙← + P1 or P2 snap back
4	S	1	90,000	10	4	26	—	-7	Launcher, not special or hyper combo cancelable

1

2

3

4

Crouching Basic Attacks

Screen	Command	Hits	Damage	Startup	Active	Recovery	Advantage on Hit	Advantage if Guarded	Notes
1	Crouching L	1	45,000	7	3	10	+1	0	Low attack
2	Crouching M	1	70,000	8	3	21	-5	-6	—
3	Crouching H	1	80,000	13	4	19	—	0	Low attack, knocks down

1

2

3

Aerial Basic Attacks

Screen	Command	Hits	Damage	Startup	Active	Recovery	Notes
1	Air L	1	45,000	6	3	15	Overhead attack
2	Air M	1	63,000	8	5	20	Overhead attack
3	Air H	1	83,000	10	5	21	Overhead attack
4	Air S	1	88,000	10	5	21	Overhead attack

1

2

3

4

COMMAND ATTACKS

Screen	Command	Hits	Damage	Startup	Active	Recovery	Advantage on Hit	Advantage if Guarded	Notes
1	⇨ + Ⓗ	1	90,000	21	3	22	+4	-2	Overhead attack, can be chained from basic attacks, not special or hyper combo cancelable

1

"WITH THIS BIONIC ARM, I HAVE MORE THAN ENOUGH TOOLS TO TAKE DOWN JOKERS LIKE YOU."

AS A PARTNER-CROSSOVER ASSISTS

Screen	Type	P1+P2 Crossover Combination Hyper Combo	Description	Hits	Damage	Startup	Active	Recovery (this crossover assist)	Recovery (other partner)	Notes
1	α – Alpha	Bionic Lancer	Wire Grapple L	1	20,000	34	17	117	87	Causes unrecoverable knockdown
2	β – Beta	Bionic Lancer	Wire Grapple M	1	20,000	34	17	117	87	Pulls foe down to ground
3	γ – Gamma	Bionic Lancer	Armor Piercer	1	130,000	45	4	134	104	Causes wall bounce

1

2

3

SPENCER

SPECIAL MOVES

Screen	Name	Command	Hits	Damage	Startup	Active	Recovery	Advantage on Hit	Advantage if Guarded	Notes
1, 2, 3	Wire Grapple	↓↘→ + (ATK)	1	30,000	10	22	51	-33	-12	Projectile has 5 low priority durability points
4	Reel in Punch	(When Wire Grapple hits) (L)	1	72,000	—	—	—	—	—	Wire Grapple follow-up, unrecoverable knockdown, not hyper combo-cancelable
5	Zip Kick	(When Wire Grapple hits) (M)	1	90,000	—	—	—	—	—	Wire Grapple follow-up, wall bounce
6	Come' ere!	(When Wire Grapple hits) (H)	—	—	—	—	—	+2	—	Wire Grapple follow-up, pulls victim to Spencer with small advantage, not hyper combo-cancelable
7, 8, 9	Air Wire Grapple	↓↘→ + (ATK) (in air)	2	120,000	13		Until landing			Projectile has 5 low priority durability points, causes wall bounce
10	Jaw Breaker	→↓↘ + (ATK)	1	35,000	5	1	31	—	—	Throw attack, unrecoverable knockdown
11	Smash Kick	(During Jaw Breaker M or H) (H)	2	94,500	—	—	—	—	—	Jaw Breaker follow-up, causes wall bounce
11	Critical Smash	(During Jaw Breaker M or H, specific timing) (H)	2	157,500	—	—	—	—	—	Jaw Breaker follow-up, causes wall bounce
12	Armor Piercer	↓↘→ + (S)	1	180,000 / 150,000 / 130,000	4~9 / 21	6(12)4	41	—	-22	Hits on 4th frame if enemy is nearby; 21st frame if not
13	Swing Wire	On ground: Any non-downward direction + (S) + (ATK); in air: any non-upward direction + (S) + (ATK)	1	10,000	11	Until opponent or screen edge hit	—	+9 air / -2 ground	+8 air / -3 ground	Spencer reels himself to wherever the grapple touches, not hyper combo-cancelable
14	Swing Grapple	In air: Any upward direction + (S) + (ATK)	—	—	—	—	—	—	—	Swing can be interrupted after frame 33 with basic attacks and air (S)

Wire Grapple: Spencer's bionic grapple special move on the ground. He fires the grapple on his bionic arm either straight ahead, diagonally up-forward, or straight up, depending on the button used. The grapple itself counts as a low priority projectile with five durability points—it is canceled out by just about any standard projectile, such as Ryu's Hadoken.

If blocked, Wire Grapple is simply retracted. On a successful hit, either (L), (M), or (H) can be input for a follow-up attack. However, many characters can duck under even the straightforward L version of Wire Grapple: Amaterasu, Arthur, Morrigan, Phoenix, Viewtiful Joe, Wolverine, and X-23.

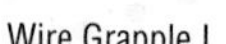
Wire Grapple L

Wire Grapple M

Wire Grapple H

Because of its lengthy time commitment and low durability compared to most projectiles and beams, grounded Wire Grapple's primary purpose is as a combo extender rather than as any sort of ranged poke.

(L) Reel in Punch

(M) Zip Kick

(H) Come'ere!

Reel in Punch, Zip Kick, and Come'ere!: Perform these follow-ups by pressing either (L), (M), or (H) after grounded Wire Grapple hits successfully. (L) or (M) result in either an unrecoverable knockdown (Reel in Punch) or a wall bounce (Zip Kick). Depending on your team, you may be able to combo in various ways after either option. Spencer is almost always capable of continuing a combo without crossover assists, at least until he uses up the one wall bounce possible per combo. After Reel in Punch, you can OTG with air Wire Grapple. After Zip Kick, you'll be in position to land another air Wire Grapple at the least. Near corners, you can score a falling air hit or two after a Zip Kick, before landing and relaunching.

The H version (Come'ere!) pulls the enemy close to Spencer, but it's hard to recommend using. Spencer is left at a frame advantage of only +2 afterward. His fastest move is the close-range Armor Piercer, active in four frames, and his unbreakable command throw is active in five frames. Standing (L) is active in six frames, while crouching (L) is active in seven. In short, going for Come'ere! as a follow-up over the other options sacrifices guaranteed damage for a bad mix-up that opponents can escape simply by jumping backward or by normal-throwing Spencer.

Air Wire Grapple: The air version of grounded Wire Grapple. Spencer fires a grapple out from his body, either straight forward, diagonally down-forward, or straight down. Upon successful contact, air Wire Grapple transitions automatically to Zip Kick, causing a wall bounce (if a wall bounce hasn't already been caused in the same sequence of hits).

Air Wire Grapple is a little more useful than grounded Wire Grapple, primarily because both Air Wire Grapple M and H are OTG-capable attacks. After any throw or flying screen combo, Spencer can either perform Air Wire Grapple M just off the ground, or he can dash forward and perform Air Wire Grapple H. In either case, he hauls opponents off the ground with his grapple and then Zip Kicks them.

Air Wire Grapple L

Air Wire Grapple M

Air Wire Grapple H

Like grounded Wire Grapple, Air Wire Grapple is most useful in combos. As a standalone long-range attack, it leaves something to be desired just like its ground counterpart. If you use Air Wire Grapple and miss, Spencer falls to the ground like a stone, unable to act or guard on the way down. However, there's one way around this: if you perform Swing Wire or Swing Grapple EXACTLY when the Air Wire Grapple hook completely retracts but before Spencer begins to fall, Spencer will cancel his normal freefall into a wire movement in the direction you select! Timing the Grapples manually may be a little difficult, but simply mashing [s] + [a] will generally work every time. Bear in mind that both Air Wire Grapple and Spencer's aerial movement options with Swing Wire and Swing Grapple are considered special moves; only three of these are allowed per airborne period. Thus, you cannot use this to stay airborne indefinitely.

Jawbreaker: Spencer's command throw snags the opponent on the fifth frame. This makes it relatively slow as far as throws are concerned. Normal throws are active in one frame, while many command grabs (such as any of Wesker's, along with the H versions of Thor's and Morrigan's, among others) are active on the first frame after input. Nevertheless, Jawbreaker can be useful for cracking an excessively passive opponent. Even if this command throw is a tad slow, it's slower by only a single-digit number of frames, so it still catches people who expect to guard attacks. The sluggishness simply means that Spencer cannot build effective mix-ups around Jawbreaker alone, although it is still a faster attack than any of his basic attacks.

The L and M versions throw grounded foes, while the H version is actually an air throw—very useful for catching foes either jumping in or trying to jump away from ground tactics. The range on the grounded L and M versions is unexceptional. Like normal throws, you must be more or less flush with the opponent. Like most throws, the anti-air H version can grab for only one frame (the fifth frame after input), but the hitbox on the grab is pretty lenient during that single frame. While Spencer's hand is not invulnerable, the actual area from which he can grab airborne enemies extends in a large circle around it.

All three versions toss enemies straight up into the air. After the M or H versions, you can input H after Spencer throws them into the air but before they stop traveling upward for a Smash Kick follow-up that causes a wall bounce. This follow-up is much stronger with precise timing. Inputting H PRECISELY on the 33rd frame after the grab starts (or the 11th frame after Spencer starts to smack the foe into the air) causes Smash Kick to become Critical Smash. Critical Smash causes 157,500 damage, a great improvement over Smash Kick's 97,500. The resulting wall bounce is also at a much more protracted angle, making it easier for Spencer to score a full combo follow-up.

If you opt not to follow Jawbreaker M or H with Smash Kick/Critical Smash, or after any Jawbreaker L, the enemy can be juggled on the way down. If you opt not to juggle either, the foe lands in an unrecoverable knockdown, which you can easily OTG with Air Wire Grapple H or an OTG-capable assist.

Smash Kick / Critical Smash: The kick follow-up available after Jawbreaker M or H. Smash Kick is easy to get—just press H after Spencer smacks the opponent into the air but before the foe achieves max height. Critical Smash is much more difficult. The window to get Critical Smash is only one frame long, and it occurs 11 frames after Spencer first hits with the upward smack that hurls the opponent skyward. See Advanced Tactics for visual tips on timing Critical Smash.

Armor Piercer: A direct punch attack with Spencer's bionic arm. Depending on the situation, this move has different damage and behavior. Starting on the third frame after input up until the eighth frame after input, an invisible hitbox extends slightly further every two frames, ending about one character width away from Spencer. If the enemy is within this hitbox during any of these frames, Spencer strikes with Armor Piercer on the very next frame. If the opponent is nearby during frames three to four, Armor Piercer deals 180,000 damage, the most damaging single-hit non-hyper combo move in the game! If the enemy is nearby from frames five to six, 150,000 damage is dealt. On frames seven to eight, 130,000 damage is dealt. If the enemy is NOT nearby after eight frames, the move doesn't actually strike until the 21st frame, at which point it deals 130,000 damage. Any version of Armor Piercer causes a wall bounce, which allows for combo follow-ups depending on position.

Up close, Armor Piercer is Spencer's most dangerous attack. It strikes nearby opponents on the fourth frame, which means it can be linked after his ⇨ + H overhead for heavy damage and a wall bounce! However, it's extremely unsafe if guarded, so cover Spencer by calling an assist first if you're using Armor Piercer as a close-range guess.

Swing Wire

Swing Grapple

Swing Wire and Swing Grapple: These are Spencer's options for extra mobility. Swing Wire fires a low-damage grapple in the chosen direction. Once this grapple hits either the ceiling, a screen edge, the ground, or an opponent, Spencer automatically pulls himself to that point. This grapple deals less damage than Wire Grapple and it has no follow ups, but the actual hitbox on the grapple is larger. Only Amaterasu and Morrigan can crouch under Swing Wire on the ground, while most of the small characters can crouch under horizontal Wire Grapple.

Swing Wire is great both for an unconventional approach and to run away when appropriate. You can use Swing Wire to move around in midair or to leave the ground in the first place. Using Swing Wire from the ground to hook the ceiling or walls and go airborne doesn't count against the three special moves possible during each jump. Spencer is also considered to be normal-jumping after using grounded Swing Wire to take to the air, so assist calls are possible between uses of Swing Wire. While in midair, you can also use downward-aimed Swing Wires to return to the ground quickly.

Swing Grapple is possible only while airborne. Spencer affixes his grapple to a diagonal point above the screen and hurls himself forward. Inputting a command for a basic attack halfway through this swing causes him to retract his grapple and fall with momentum, performing the basic attack. In this way, Swing Grapple can be used like an indirect triangle jump in much the same way that Spider-Man uses some of his airborne movement options.

HYPER COMBOS

Screen	Name	Command	Hits	Damage	Startup	Active	Recovery	Advantage on Hit	Advantage if Guarded	Notes
1	Bionic Maneuvers	⇩⇘⇨ + ATK ATK	6	304,500	18+2	22	23	—	-22	Unrecoverable knockdown
2	Bionic Lancer	⇩⇙⇦ + ATK ATK	1	250,000	4+3	10	50	—	-37	Frames 1-11 invulnerable, causes spinning knockdown, unrecoverable knockdown

Bionic Maneuvers: This is the hyper combo most appropriate for Spencer's combos, or as the last stage of a team hyper combo. Because the last hit causes an unrecoverable knockdown, Spencer can OTG the enemy with Air Wire Grapple M. If a wall bounce wasn't previously used in the combo (or THC), Spencer can dish out more punishment from here.

Bionic Lancer: Spencer travels nearly the full length of the screen with a titanic bionic arm punch that sends the enemy spinning upward on a successful hit. Between its speed and invulnerability, Bionic Lancer is an ideal hyper combo to punish the enemy even at great distances. When properly timed, you don't have to worry about projectiles or any onscreen threats, as Spencer is invincible until the very end of this hyper combo. Be aware that this hyper combo doesn't quite travel all the way across the screen, though. If your opponent is truly at full screen distance, Bionic Lancer whiffs harmlessly in front of him. However, if your foe is even one step forward from full screen, it will hit.

In addition to its main use as a move-punisher, Bionic Lancer is also great for starting team hyper combos or X-Factor combos. Bionic Lancer sends enemies into a spinning knockdown straight up in the air, so they're in ideal position to continue the combo by handing off with a THC to the next partner, or by canceling Bionic Lancer just after a hit with X-Factor and continuing the combo with Spencer on his own!

The safest way to get another teammate onscreen is to wait for the opponent to carelessly call an assist, then Bionic Lancer it before using a team hyper combo to the next partner. Not only does this tag-out Spencer safely, but, depending on your next partner, it absolutely fries that assist! Landing Bionic Lancer THC into Storm's Hail Storm, for example, gets Spencer out and Storm in with virtually zero risk while nuking any assist for 80% or more! If you happened to catch their assist AND their point character, well, bonus!

BATTLE PLAN

OVERVIEW

VITALITY: 1,050,000

CHAIN COMBO ARCHETYPE: MARVEL SERIES

X-Factor	Lv.1	Lv.2	Lv.3
Damage	133%	%166	199%
Speed	105%	110%	115%

Spencer is a close-range powerhouse, with some of the game's strongest short-range attacks. Your primary goal with Spencer is to get close to enemies. Your secondary goal is backing them into a corner, and your tertiary goal is building hyper combo gauge.

Why does Spencer want to be near the enemy?

His ranged options are lacking or non-existent. Wire Grapple is easily overpowered by most projectile characters and assists. While he can run away pretty effectively with Swing Wire, he can't actually mount a ranged offense or gain a lead that way.

His Armor Piercer is the strongest non-hyper combo move...but only when pointblank near the enemy.

The Jawbreaker command throw serves as a nice close-range counterpoint to Armor Piercer. Opponents expecting to deal with one will eat the other.

Spencer's combos off of basic attacks deal heavy damage and generate lots of hyper combo gauge even without using any meter.

His Swing Wire and Wire Grapple allow him to close distance to the enemy at odd, indirect angles.

Why does Spencer want the enemy near the corner?

Spencer can capitalize more heavily off of the wall bounce created by many of his moves.

Spencer's ➔ + Ⓗ overhead becomes a wicked counter to advancing guard used against his basic attacks. This command attack can be chained into from any basic attack.

The enemy has fewer routes to escape from Spencer when backed into the corner, and advancing guard is less effective.

Why is Spencer looking to build hyper combo gauge?

His standard combos are very powerful and build lots of bar without using any.

His Bionic Lancer is one of the game's best hyper combos to use *outside* of combos. This incredibly fast, far-reaching punch can heavily damage opponents who think they're harmlessly starting an offense by throwing a projectile or calling an assist from almost full screen! Having this omnipresent deterrent to blow through whatever the opponent does at long range is more valuable than tacking on extra damage to the end of combos (unless, of course, that extra damage will knock out the target).

ON THE GROUND

Your M.O. on the ground is to get close to the enemy. Just about the only real threat Spencer has from far away is Bionic Lancer. That's hardly an empty threat, but limited hyper combo gauge resources mean you have to move in eventually. Luckily, Spencer has built-in tools that keep him from being relegated to trying to wavedash or super-jump forward while covered by an assist. His Swing Wire and Swing Grapple give him unique mobility options. On the ground, Swing Wire can be fired in any non-downward direction. This means Swing Wire can be fired directly *at* the enemy if you prefer an extremely direct approach! Spencer is at a frame disadvantage even on hit with horizontal Swing Wire, but you can cover this gap by calling an appropriate assist first.

Bionic Lancer plows through anything during its active frames.

Start your offense from around the range of ➔ + Ⓗ.

Of course, that isn't the safest approach regardless. You may simply haul yourself into the enemy's assist, or the enemy may throw you immediately or hit you before you fully recover (Spencer is considered airborne even during horizontal Swing Wire). For a slightly safer variation on the theme, call an assist that occupies lots of lateral space, then Swing Wire up or up-forward. From here, depending on what the enemy does, you can choose to Swing Wire or Swing Grapple to a different position, hopefully eventually coming down on your foe with air Ⓢ. Swing Wire used from the ground to take to the air doesn't count against the three special moves per jump you're allowed. Additionally, Spencer is considered to be normal-jumping after using Swing Wire to go airborne. This means that, between using Swing Wire and Swing Grapple to get around, you can continue to call assists! Note that you cannot call an assist *during* Swing Wire or Swing Grapple, as these are considered special moves; you must call the assist between your grappling maneuvers.

Closer up, Spencer has more offensive options. From over half the screen away on the ground, you can threaten with Spencer's ➔ + Ⓗ overhead. This attack must be guarded standing, it has surprising reach, and it can link into either Armor Piercer or standing Ⓛ (for standing Ⓛ to link, you must connect with the last frame of ➔ + Ⓗ). Either way, you get a full combo. If guarded, you're at a -2 frame disadvantage, so watch out for the enemy to throw you afterward. You can avoid this threat by calling a crossover assist that covers a lot of horizontal space just before going for ➔ + Ⓗ. This forces enemies to continue blocking if they guard ➔ + Ⓗ, and will also allow you to easily perform combos afterward! When the enemy is cornered, ➔ + Ⓗ is more potent. In this situation, whenever enemies use advancing guard on your basic attacks, you can react by chaining into ➔ + Ⓗ, which puts you right back in their face with an overhead.

From the range of ➔ + Ⓗ, you're also in position to dash forward and mount a close-range mix-up. You can go low with crouching Ⓛ into a chain combo, or try to snag your foe with Jawbreaker. If enemies avoid your mix-ups by continually jumping away, occasionally dash forward and go for Jawbreaker H, which snags them out of the air. To lessen the risk involved, call an assist for cover just before performing the move.

When foes are putting the pressure on you rather than vice versa, you'll have to rely on universal defensive options and a few moves to stay out of trouble. Spencer doesn't have a fast light attack to interrupt close-range patterns, so if you're after a quick physical attack, Armor Piercer will have to do. This is naturally quite risky, though. If the enemy opts to jump over you rather than to attack from the front, you'll be a sitting duck. Ⓢ launcher and Jawbreaker H are safer options to hold back aggressive opponents, and they become even safer if you first call a defensive assist or at least one that occupies a lot of nearby space. However, these are all gambles to a certain extent, so try to rely on solid blocking and use advancing guard to push the enemy away, and look for a place to regain momentum.

UP IN THE AIR

It's not quite an airdash or Flight, but Spencer can move around the sky deftly enough via Swing Wire and Swing Grapple. If you use Swing Wire to go airborne in the first place, you'll be in a normal jumping state, even at super jump height—this means crossover assist calls are possible.

Use Swing Wire and Swing Grapple to swap sides after positioning assists behind the opponent.

Air Ⓢ makes an excellent cross-up (or fake cross-up) with the right trajectory from Swing Grapple.

The most useful way to apply Swing Wire and Swing Grapple is to use them to get on top of the enemy with advantage. You can do this by either calling an assist that occupies the opponent before super jumping, or by using Swing Wire to leave the ground, then calling an assist, and then using Swing Wire or Swing Grapple to move over the enemy. The most reliable move to use when falling onto the enemy is air Ⓢ. Air Ⓢ hits at a downward arc, and it can cross up the enemy if you happen to fall past his head. This is especially useful after using Swing Grapple to hurl Spencer just past your foe.

To diminish your enemies' expectations that you'll always fall on top of their character or go for a cross-up, drop an assist on one side occasionally. Then use diagonal Swing Wire (or aerial Swing Grapple) to fly clean over their head, and then immediately attack with Air Wire Grapple M. Air Wire Grapple briefly stops Spencer's aerial inertia. If your foe is expecting you to fall directly onto him, he may use an anticipatory anti-air that Air Wire Grapple will cleanly catch. If your opponent blocks both your pinning assist and Air Wire Grapple, you can cancel the very end of Air Wire Grapple's recovery into either Swing Wire backward to safety or an aggressive aerial grapple right back in your foe's face.

When you go air-to-air with adversaries, air Ⓗ is the best from below, and air Ⓢ is the best from above. Spencer's attacks don't have lengthy periods of active frames, so you'll have to be precise with your aerial pokes. Usually, it's best just to go for air throws, which easily translate into OTG combos, or to just remain grounded and go for mix-ups when the opponent is forced to land.

SPENCER

COMBO USAGE

I. CR. Ⓛ, CR. Ⓜ, ST. Ⓗ, Ⓢ CANCEL ➡ SUPER JUMP, AIR Ⓜ, Ⓜ, Ⓗ, Ⓢ, LAND, DASH, ⬇⬊➡⬈ + Ⓗ OTG, AIR ⬇⬊➡ + Ⓜ

(429,400 damage mid screen) Spencer's standard, most basic combo. This can be performed anywhere, but it has quite a few variants.

By opening with far ➡ + Ⓗ as an overhead so that the last active frame of the overhead hits, you allow this combo to link afterward for 453,500 damage. The link is slightly easier (and inflicts a tiny bit more damage) if you follow ➡ + Ⓗ with standing Ⓛ rather than crouching Ⓛ, because standing Ⓛ is one frame faster.

537,200 damage results if Bionic Lancer is used instead of the final Wire Grapple. Depending on how quickly Spencer lands after the first OTG Air Wire Grapple, this may not be possible.

Near corners, Spencer is close enough to capitalize further off of the initial wall bounce caused by the Air Wire Grapple OTG. You can fall from the automatic Zip Kick and juggle with air Ⓢ. You can then land and re-launch with Ⓢ into another air chain to flying screen, and to another OTG Air Wire Grapple. This deals 485,200 damage. Just after the Zip Kick here, if you Swing Wire down-forward and then perform air Ⓢ, you'll cross up your foe into the corner as he gets back up.

II. ➡ + Ⓗ, ⬇⬊➡ + Ⓢ CANCEL ➡ ⬇⬊➡ + ATK ATK

(528,700 damage) This combo starts off of Spencer's ➡ + Ⓗ command attack, which is an overhead with tremendous reach. Standing or crouching Ⓛ will link after the last active frame of the overhead. However, linking Armor Piercer is much easier, as it's faster than Spencer's light attacks up close. Armor Piercer linked after ➡ + Ⓗ causes a wall bounce. Depending on Spencer's position, your ability to add further damage will differ. Far from a corner, the best you can do is hyper combo cancel Armor Piercer late, into Bionic Maneuvers. It's sometimes possible to land Wire Grapple L to pull in your foe instead of Bionic Maneuvers, but the timing is extremely strict.

Near the corner, you can tack on basically the same damage without wasting meter. After Armor Piercer, juggle the wall-bounced foe with standing Ⓛ, crouching Ⓜ, standing Ⓗ, Ⓢ CANCEL ➡ super jump, air Ⓜ, Ⓜ, Ⓗ, Ⓢ, land, ⬇⬊➡⬈ + Ⓜ OTG. This delivers 528,100 damage while building nearly a full bar of hyper combo gauge!

III. ➡⬇⬊ + ATK, Ⓗ (CRITICAL SMASH), JUMP FORWARD, AIR Ⓜ, Ⓗ, Ⓢ, LAND, JUMP FORWARD, AIR Ⓜ, Ⓗ, Ⓢ, LAND, CR. Ⓜ, ST. Ⓗ, Ⓢ CANCEL ➡ SUPER JUMP, AIR Ⓜ, Ⓜ, Ⓗ, Ⓢ, LAND, ⬇⬊➡⬈ + Ⓗ OTG

(435,600 damage, requires Critical Smash) This combo takes advantage of Spencer's precise Critical Smash follow-up to his Jawbreaker throw. Critical Smash kicks the opponent off the wall much more forcibly, both dealing more damage on the kick itself and putting the enemy into a great juggle position even if Spencer is cornered upon landing the throw. For the normal-jumping loop of air Ⓜ, Ⓗ, Ⓢ, perform air Ⓜ, Ⓗ quickly, but wait and perform air Ⓢ just before landing. This allows both the second jumping loop and the eventual ground chain and launcher to link. Once you get to the ground chain and launcher portion, perform everything as quickly as possible. The Critical Smash effect is obvious—you will have enough time to verify you got the "good" version of Jawbreaker's follow-up before going for this combo.

Of course, no one in the world is going to hit the 33rd frame after landing Jawbreaker every single time. When you just get normal Smash Kick, you can still squeeze good damage out of Jawbreaker. You can still perform the same juggle—you just need to dash forward before the first normal jumping air Ⓜ. Getting Smash Kick rather than Critical Smash into this combo results in 372,600 damage. It's a step down, but not an enormous step.

Landing Jawbreaker against a foe near the corner actually makes either version—Smash Kick or Critical Smash—more awkward. The enemy will bounce off the wall.

IV. AIR THROW BACKWARD OR FORWARD, ⬇⬊➡ + Ⓗ OTG, ⬇⬊➡ + Ⓜ

(167,800 damage) This is Spencer's combo off an air throw. The initial Air Wire Grapple H OTG is the only part that's concrete. After that, what you can do depends on screen position. If you're far from a corner, tacking on Air Wire Grapple M finishes the combo. Use Swing Wire immediately afterward to regain the distance you give up with the juggle. Near a corner, as is usually the case with Spencer, you can expand the combo by falling from the OTG grapple with air Ⓢ, then landing and chaining crouching Ⓜ, standing Ⓗ, Ⓢ into an air combo. Near the corner, this combo can deal 247,400 damage or more depending on what you can fit in.

Mid screen, it's very hard to land an Air Wire Grapple OTG after a normal ground throw. If the enemy recovers in either direction, it's basically not possible. In the corners, however, a normal throw easily translates into an OTG opportunity.

ASSISTS

Defensive assists make guessing on moves like Armor Piercer less of a risk.

Long-range pinning or projectile assists allow Spencer to use Swing Wire more freely.

In addition to Armor Piercer, Spencer has two variations of Wire Grapple as his assist. The Wire Grapple assists are less effective, as the grapple itself is a weak projectile that doesn't control space in the way a normal projectile does. The horizontal grapple assist, Spencer—α, creates an unrecoverable knockdown. Certainly, some characters can take advantage of an unrecoverable knockdown on their own, but many characters can't OTG without an assist. And, if you just used Spencer—α for an unrecoverable knockdown, then you definitely don't have another assist reloaded and ready to go for an OTG. Spencer—β is a diagonal grapple assist, which simply pulls the foe to the ground if it hits. If you don't hit your opponent immediately, he or she simply recovers in a standing state. Off of either grapple assist, you can hit the foe before the grapple, which either knocks them down or pulls them to earth. However, many assists perform the functions of horizontal or diagonal space control with much greater effect.

Instead, choose Spencer—γ. This is Armor Piercer. It's one of the only assists that causes a wall bounce, making it useful for many characters who cannot wall bounce on their own. The only deficiency here is that it's strictly the slower 130,000-damage version of Armor Piercer. This still makes it one of the most damaging assists, packing quite a punch into a single hit. This makes Spencer—γ great for combos. It won't add much to damage scaling or hitstun deterioration, and the wall bounce will open up new worlds for characters who can't normally do it.

On point, Spencer benefits greatly from assists that control space from a good distance. This allows him to use the opening to jump or Swing Wire into closer position. Examples include Sentinel—α, Doctor Doom—γ, and just about any good beam or projectile assist. The point is to put something at ground level that the opponent is forced to deal with or block. Spencer can then freely take to the skies and Swing Wire or Swing Grapple into position above the enemy's head.

As is the case for just about everyone, Spencer can also take great advantage of low-hitting assists or OTG-capable ones. You can always OTG on with Spencer's Air Wire Grapple M or H, but if you've already used up the one wall bounce allowed per combo, the opponent will simply be knocked down afterward. If you instead use an assist to OTG (or call an assist that hits the enemy after Spencer OTGs with Air Wire Grapple, but before the enemy hits the ground), you'll have more follow-up options.

ADVANCED TACTICS

JAWBREAKER FOLLOW-UP FRAME

You'll gain more damage and better juggle opportunities after Jawbreaker if you can consistently hit Critical Smash. The timing is a little awkward—it's not right as Spencer hurls your foe aloft, but it's not long after. The exact frame is as Spencer finishes the follow-through on his bionic punch, just as the screen begins to shift upward to follow the pummeled opponent. You cannot mash (H) to get Critical Smash; you must press (H) only once, and it must be on exactly the right frame. As mentioned earlier, this frame is exactly 33 frames after first connecting with Jawbreaker, and 11 frames after Spencer first hits the enemy during the throw. In short, you must press (H) just slightly, imperceptibly more than half a second after you initiate Jawbreaker.

This is the exact frame during which you must press (H) for Critical Smash.

COMBO APPENDIX

GENERAL EXECUTION TIPS

For the most part, Spencer's chains can be performed more slowly than with other characters, whether grounded or airborne. Don't rush.

Requirements (Position, meter, etc.)	Notes	Command Sequence	Damage
1 bar of hyper combo gauge	Cancel to Bionic Maneuvers after the opponent bounces off the wall, but before the foe descends too far	Cr. (L), st. (M), st. (H), → + (H), ↓↘→ + (S) CANCEL ↓↘→ + ATK ATK	575,400
Must be near corner	Score the falling air (S) hit as late as possible in order to follow up with the ground chain afterward; for an easier time, simply launch upon landing	Air (S), land, cr. (L), cr. (M), st. (H), (S) CANCEL super jump, air (M), (M), (H), (S), land, dash, ↓↘→↗ + (H) OTG, falling air (S), land, cr. (M), st. (H), (S) CANCEL super jump, air (M), (M), (H), (S), land, ↓↘→↗ + (H) OTG	512,500
Must be near corner	Combo usually won't work after → + (H) if preceded by a jump-in	Cr. (L), cr. (M), st. (H), → + (H), ↓↘→ + (S), st. (L), cr. (M), st. (H), (S) CANCEL super jump, air (M), (M), (H), (S), land, dash, ↓↘→↗ + (M) OTG	506,000
Must be near corner, 2 bars of hyper combo gauge	During vertical jumping air (M), (H), (S), perform the (S) input much later than normal, this gives you more time after landing to juggle with st. (M), st. (H), omit st. (H) from the combo if you have trouble juggling with it against smaller characters	Cr. (L), cr. (M), st. (H) CANCEL ↓↙← + ATK ATK, ↓↘→↗ + (H), late air (S), land, vertical jump air (M), (H), delayed (S), land, st. (M), st. (H) CANCEL ↓↘→ + ATK ATK, ↓↘→↗ + (H)	826,900
Must be far from corner	A more damaging, yet more difficult version of Spencer's standard meter-less combo. Use the Swing Wire as soon as you recover from the Zip Kick. After the Swing Wire connects, the timing to hit air (S) is later than what is intuitive.	Cr. (L). st. (M), st. (H) CANCEL super jump, air (M), (M), (H), (S), land, ↓↘→↗ + (H) OTG, ↘ + (S)ATK, air (S), land, st. (H), (S) CANCEL super jump, air (M), (M), (H), (S), land, ↓↘→↗ + (H) OTG	486,300
Must be far from corner	Positioning for this combo is rather strict: you can be both too close and too far from the corner for this combo to work! If you're too close several different combo enders can be improvised. If you're too far end the combo with Bionic Lancer instead.	Cr. (L). st. (M), st. (H) CANCEL super jump, air (M), (M), (H), (S), land, ↓↘→↗ + (H) OTG, ↘ + (S)ATK, air (S), land, st. (H) CANCEL ↓↘→ + (S) CANCEL ↓↘→ + ATK ATK	654,800
X-Factor level 1, 2 bars of hyper combo gauge	Perform air (M), (H) quickly, then wait as long as possible before air (S) during normal jumps, cancel ↓↘→ + (S) to Bionic Maneuvers after foe bounces off wall, but before the foe falls too far	↓↙← + ATK ATK X-FACTOR, jump up, air (M), (H), (S), land, jump up, air (M), (H), (S), land, jump up, air (M), (H), (S), land, cr. (M), st. (H) CANCEL ↓↘→ + (S) CANCEL ↓↘→ + ATK ATK	1,258,600

TRISH

"ALL OF THOSE PEOPLE TO FIGHT ONE LADY? AT LEAST YOU DIDN'T UNDERESTIMATE ME."

BIO

REAL NAME

TRISH

OCCUPATION

DEVIL HUNTER

ABILITIES

EXCELLENT AT FIGHTING WITH GUNS AND SWORDS. SHE ALSO WIELDS LIGHTNING-BASED POWERS.

WEAPONS

SHE USES THE GREAT SWORD SPARDA, ONCE WIELDED BY THE LEGENDARY DEVIL KNIGHT OF THE SAME NAME. SHE ALSO HAS DUAL GUNS, LUCE + OMBRA.

PROFILE

ORIGINALLY CREATED BY A DEMON IN ORDER TO LURE DANTE INTO A TRAP, SHE WORKED SIDE BY SIDE WITH HIM AND FELL TO HIS CHARMS AND BETRAYED THE DEMON WORLD. NOW SHE WORKS TOGETHER WITH DANTE AS A PARTNER IN BUSINESS.

FIRST APPEARANCE

DEVIL MAY CRY (2001)

POWER GRID

5	INTELLIGENCE
4	STRENGTH
5	SPEED
4	STAMINA
3	ENERGY PROJECTION
5	FIGHTING ABILITY

*This is biographical, and does not represent an evaluation of the character's in-game combat potential.

ALTERNATE COSTUMES

PS3: ✕ Xbox 360: A

PS3: □ Xbox 360: X

PS3: △ Xbox 360: Y

PS3: R1 Xbox 360: RB

ATTACK SET

STANDING BASIC ATTACKS

Screen	Command	Hits	Damage	Startup Frames	Active Frames	Recovery Frames	Frame Advantage on Hit	Frame Advantage if Guarded	Notes
1	Standing L	1	38,000	5	3	8	+2	+2	Rapid fire
2	Standing M	1	50,000	9	4	17	-4	-4	—
3	Standing H	1	70,000	13	2	24	-3	-3	—
4	S	1	80,000	12	4	23	—	-4	Launcher, not special or hyper combo cancelable

CROUCHING BASIC ATTACKS

Screen	Command	Hits	Damage	Startup Frames	Active Frames	Recovery Frames	Frame Advantage on Hit	Frame Advantage if Guarded	Notes
1	Crouching L	1	40,000	5	3	8	+2	+2	Low attack, rapid fire, chains into standing L
2	Crouching M	1	48,000	10	8	13	-4	-4	Low attack
3	Crouching H	1	68,000	13	4	22	—	-3	Low attack, knocks down

AERIAL BASIC ATTACKS

Screen	Command	Hits	Damage	Startup Frames	Active Frames	Recovery Frames	Frame Advantage on Hit	Frame Advantage if Guarded	Notes
1	Air L	1	42,000	4	3	18	—	—	Overhead attack
2	Air M	1	52,000	8	4	20	—	—	Overhead attack, ⇩ ⇘ ⇨ + P1onP2 snap back
3	Air H	1	75,000	14	3	26	—	—	Overhead attack
4	Air S	1	80,000	11	2	26	—	—	Unrecoverable knockdown when used in air combo after S launcher

COMMAND ATTACKS

Screen	Command	Hits	Damage	Startup Frames	Active Frames	Recovery Frames	Notes
1	(In air) ⇩ + H	1	70,000	13	Until grounded	7	Cancelable into TAC attack; cannot be performed at very low altitude

AS A PARTNER—CROSSOVER ASSISTS

Screen	Type	P1+P2 Crossover Combination Hyper Combo	Description	Hits	Damage	Startup Frames	Active Frames	Recovery Frames (this crossover assist)	Recovery Frames (other partner)	Notes
1	α – Alpha	Round Harvest	Trick "Hopscotch"	1	70,000	44	—	117	87	Trap stays active for 300 frames, projectile has 1 low priority durability point
2	β – Beta	Round Harvest	Trick "Peekaboo"	1	10,000	34	—	127	97	Activates when glyph is touched, opponents can attack the glyph to make it disappear, incapacitates opponent for 53 frames, trap stays active for 300 frames, projectile has 3 low priority durability points
3	γ – Gamma	Maximum Voltage	Low Voltage H	3	121,900	49	—	132	102	Each projectile has 3 low priority durability points

1

2

3

SPECIAL MOVES

Screen	Name	Command	Hits	Damage	Startup Frames	Active Frames	Recovery Frames	Frame Advantage on Hit	Frame Advantage if Guarded	Notes
1	Low Voltage L (in air OK)	⇩⇘⇨ + L	1	70,000	15	—	35	-13	-13	Each projectile has 3 low priority durability points
	Low Voltage M (in air OK)	⇩⇘⇨ + M	2	95,000	20	—	37	-15	-15	Each projectile has 3 low priority durability points
	Low Voltage H (in air OK)	⇩⇘⇨ + H	3	121,900	25	—	40	-18	-18	Each projectile has 3 low priority durability points
2	Trick "Hopscotch" (in air OK)	⇩⇙⇦ + L	1	80,000	20	—	25	-2	-2	Projectile fires when enemy touches or flies over the glyph, it disappears if Trish is hit, trap stays active for 300 frames, projectile has 1 low priority durability point
3	Trick "Peekaboo" (in air OK)	⇩⇙⇦ + M	1	10,000	10	—	35	+19	-13	Activates when glyph is touched, opponents can attack the glyph to make it disappear, Incapacitates opponent for 53 frames, trap stays active for 300 frames, projectile has 3 low priority durability points
4	Round-Trip (in air OK)	⇩⇙⇦ + H	20	133,600	35	—	15	—	—	Blade advances for 40 frames or until durability points are used, then returns to owner, projectile has 5 low priority durability points
5	Switch Sign (in air OK)	⇨⇩⇘ + ATK	—	—	10	—	10	—	—	Causes Round-Trip blade to hold its position momentarily
6	Air Raid (in air OK)	⇩⇙⇦ + S	—	—	31	—	—	—	—	Activates Flight mode, Flight mode lasts for 120 frames

1

Low Voltage: This basic projectile is used to stop ground movement, to attack grounded enemies from hard to reach aerial positions, and to build hyper combo gauge. Both the M and H versions of the attack have horrendous recovery periods, so you should rely on the L version.

2

Trick "Hopscotch": The glyph Trish sets on the ground triggers when an opponent steps near it. Its vertical range is infinite—as long an enemy flies over it, the bolt fires upwards to meet them. Use this to shield Trish from any type of frontal assault, whether foes are in the sky or on the ground. Unfortunately, the glyph disappears if Trish is hit, making it vulnerable to fast projectiles.

3

Trick "Peekaboo": Trish summons an airborne glyph that ensnares foes that approach it. Successfully catching an opponent leaves them vulnerable to follow-up combos. Peekaboo has one major downfall: an opposing character can destroy it with an attack. Cast it in the air where it's more effective, then use the shield to safely fire Low Voltage shots.

4

Round-Trip & Switch Sign: Trish throws her sword across the screen. Once released, the blade boomerangs back to her location while hitting several times along the way. Even though the start up is slow, Round-Trip should be used to cover a lot of horizontal space at one time and to shield Trish during an approach. Throw it after super jumping to minimize the risk in using it. Switch Sign is a secondary command that forces the blade to stay stationary. If you're grounded, use it when the blade makes contact with your challenger to inflict additional guard damage.

5

Air Raid: This allows you to fly for a short period of time, a great tool for staying away from your opponent. Once activated, you can dash any direction as many times as you want. It also increases the amount of special attacks you can do while airborne. Normally you can only use three specials at a time while in the air, but using Air Raid enables you to use two more.

HYPER COMBOS

Screen	Name	Command	Hits	Damage	Startup Frames	Active Frames	Recovery Frames	Frame Advantage on Hit	Frame Advantage if Guarded	Notes
1	Round Harvest	⇩⇙⇦ + ATK ATK	24	244,700	20+19	—	10	—	—	Projectile homes in on opponent for 120 frames, projectile has 1 high priority durability point
2	Maximum Voltage (in air OK)	⇩⇘⇨ + ATK ATK	30	269,300	15+1	116	20	+2	+2	Each projectile has 1 high priority durability point
3	Duet Pain (Level 3 hyper combo)	⇨⇩⇘ + ATK ATK	18	400,000	10+11	4	30	—	-11	Frames 1-22 invincible, causes unrecoverable knockdown, unaffected by damage scaling

Round Harvest: Round Harvest has numerous applications in combat and is one of the more useful hyper combos in *Marvel vs. Capcom 3.*. The thrown blade homes in on an opponent's location and racks up massive guard damage. Trish is free to act shortly after its release, giving you ample time to mount an attack, call assists for backup, or to fire additional projectiles to build hyper combo gauge. Its only weakness is the slow starting period, which must be shielded by some means. To safely throw Round Harvest, cancel into it from ⬇ ⬊ ➡ + Ⓛ or ⬇ ⬋ ⬅ + Ⓛ, or cover yourself with an assist.

Maximum Voltage: Trish fires a stream of bolts at her opponent. Outside of its obvious use in combos, Maximum Voltage is good for countering projectile attacks, punishing mistakes from afar, or using the air version to counter anti-air attempts. This is a perfect supplement to Round Harvest, which is slow and requires a faster secondary option to compensate for its weaknesses.

Duet Pain: Like most level 3 hyper combos, Duet Pain is used in combos when you need to make a comeback. It's unaffected by damage scaling. This means that it guarantees severe damage even when used after long combos. It isn't generally worth the meter to use it otherwise, but since Trish's damage output is low, you may need it if she's the last surviving character on your team.

"I DON'T CARE IF YOU'RE QUEEN, OR COURT JESTER: YOU STILL LOST, AND THAT'S GOTTA HURT!"

BATTLE PLAN

OVERVIEW

VITALITY: 850,000

CHAIN COMBO ARCHETYPE: MARVEL SERIES

X-Factor	Lv.1	Lv.2	Lv.3
Damage	120%	140%	160%
Speed	110%	125%	140%

Despite her flexible mobility options, Trish's low damage output and lackluster vitality rating stop her from being an aggressor. Instead, her mobility should be used to stay away from an opponent. When this mobility is combined with her projectile-heavy move set, it allows her to stay out of trouble while building hyper combo gauge. With that said, your objective with Trish is to keep your distance and obtain meter for her flexible hyper combos.

This plan works because:

- **Trish can stay airborne for long periods of time by using her numerous projectiles, 8-way airdash, and Air Raid ability.**
- **The Trick "Peekaboo" and Trick "Hopscotch" attacks act as traps against foes trying to approach her.**
- **Her Round-Trip projectile boomerangs towards her position after the initial throw, acting as cover when she's moving around.**
- **Obtained meter can be used for the Round Harvest, a flexible hyper combo that supports strong team dynamics.**

This goal is accomplished by:

- **Firing Low Voltage and the "Trick" attacks to control space while staying in the air.**
- **Throwing an aerial Round-Trip when there's a lull in combat.**
- **Using Air Raid to fly to safety when a challenger gets too close.**
- **Firing the Round Harvest hyper combo to shut down your opponent's lines of approach.**

ON THE GROUND

Fortify your position and attack from afar.

Keep your enemy out of the sky with standing (H)!

Push your opponent away so you can take to the air. Low Voltage (↓↘→ + ATK) controls horizontal space, but has terrible recovery and is very vulnerable to jumps. Deter jumps by setting Trick "Hopscotch" (↓↙← + (L)), a ground glyph that fires a vertical projectile when an opponent passes over it. Trick "Peekaboo" is used for the same purpose, but jumping attacks nullify it on contact, making it somewhat risky. With either trap out, fire Low Voltage shots to push your foe away. If they try to match your projectiles with one of their own, cancel into ↓↘→ + ATK ATK to blast through their shot. Canceling into ↓↘→ + ATK ATK also counters low-altitude jumps when you don't have a trap set. In cases where you aren't committed to an attack, standing (H) (**Combo V**) works against obvious attempts to airdash towards you. Its arc completely covers Trish's upper body, shielding her from harm.

The Round Harvest hyper combo has a number of important utilities. Whenever you anticipate a super jump or Flight of some sort, perform ↓↙← + ATK ATK to catch your target. If your vitality is ever low, perform Round Harvest and cancel into a teammate's hyper combo (a THC). This is also a safe way to bring Trish back into play; perform a hyper combo with another character, then THC cancel into Round Harvest. If the enemy's health is low, use it to chip away at their last vitality reserves via guard damage.

Stay in the air!

Attack only when Round-Trip is actively protecting you.

UP IN THE AIR

Your goal is to stay in the air and pester your opponent at a safe distance. Use Trish's 8-way airdash (press any direction plus ATK ATK) to avoid projectiles and attacks aimed at you (like Dormammu's Purification or Dante's Jam Session). To keep foes from attacking from below, place Trick "Hopscotch" sigils early on to cover you. From there you have three options: fire ↓↘→ + (L) to attack grounded enemies at an angle, perform ↓↙← + (H) to cover the horizontal space in front of you, or input ↓↙← + (S) (Air Raid) to enter Flight. You can do up to three special moves during a single jump, all of which slow your falling speed. The only exception to the aerial special move rule is Air Raid, which allows you to do more special moves. This is vital for keeping your offense going. Note that activating Air Raid itself counts as a special move, so you must start Flight before you use the three special moves that you're allotted per airborne period.

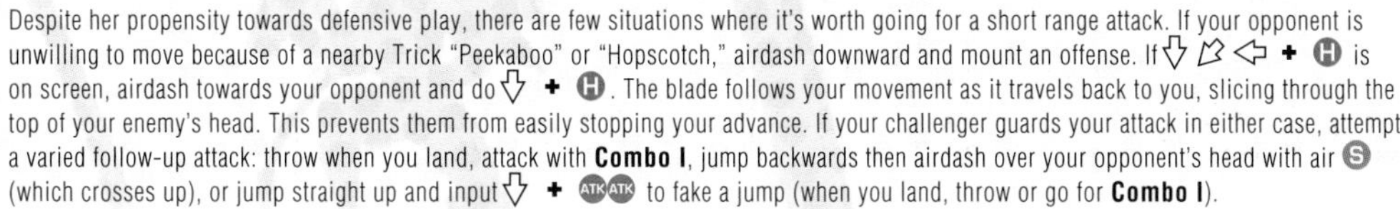

Despite her propensity towards defensive play, there are few situations where it's worth going for a short range attack. If your opponent is unwilling to move because of a nearby Trick "Peekaboo" or "Hopscotch," airdash downward and mount an offense. If ↓↙← + (H) is on screen, airdash towards your opponent and do ↓ + (H). The blade follows your movement as it travels back to you, slicing through the top of your enemy's head. This prevents them from easily stopping your advance. If your challenger guards your attack in either case, attempt a varied follow-up attack: throw when you land, attack with **Combo I**, jump backwards then airdash over your opponent's head with air (S) (which crosses up), or jump straight up and input ↓ + ATK ATK to fake a jump (when you land, throw or go for **Combo I**).

COMBO USAGE

I. CR. (L), CR. (L), CR. (M), CR. (H), (S) CANCEL SUPER JUMP, AIR (M) CANCEL ↓ + (H) CANCEL ↓↙← + (L), (M), (M) CANCEL DOUBLE JUMP FORWARD, (M), (H), ↓ + (H) CANCEL ↓↘→ + (L) CANCEL ↓↘→ + ATK ATK

(545,000 damage) Trish's basic mid screen combo. After the launch, do air (M) CANCEL ↓ + (H) very early during the jump. This ensures that ↓↙← + (L) connects properly. The (M), (M) following that is done as you fall from Trick "Hopscotch".

If crouching (L) x 2 is blocked, dash forward and crouch cancel into a throw (→ →, ↓, → + (H)), or attack with a delayed crouching (L), crouching (M) (shift into **Combo I** if it hits). When crouching (M) is guarded, throw after you recover, or chain into a delayed standing (H) to counterhit attempts to stop the throw. Against advancing guard attempts, stop your attack and airdash forward with air (H), ↓ + (H).

II. AIR THROW, AIRDASH FORWARD, P1 or P2 WESKER—β SAMURAI EDGE, LAND, JUMP FORWARD AIR (M), (M), (H), (S), LAND, ST. (M), (S) CANCEL SUPER JUMP, AIR (M), (M) CANCEL DOUBLE JUMP FORWARD, (M), (M), (H) CANCEL ↓↘→ + (L) CANCEL ↓↘→ + ATK ATK

(509,000 damage) Trish's airthrow recovers fairly quickly, but she throws her challenger too far away to use an assist to OTG them. To compensate, immediately airdash forward after the throw and call the assist just as you start moving. If you use Wesker, he should barely make it in time to OTG your foe. Note that the airdash is not necessary near corners; also note that assists can only be called during normal jumps (air throwing the foe during a super jump prevents this from working).

III. CR. (L), CR. (L), CR. (M), P1 or P2 DANTE—β CRYSTAL, ST. (H) CANCEL ↓↙← + ATK ATK, AIRDASH FORWARD AIR (H), JUST AS THE HYPER COMBO ENDS PRESS (S) CANCEL SUPER JUMP, AIR (M), (M), (H) CANCEL ↓↘→ + (L) CANCEL ↓↘→ + ATK ATK

(666,300 damage) Assists are helpful for performing Round Harvest combos. To ensure that it links after your ground chain, perform cr. (L), cr. (L), then press (M) + P1 or P2 at the same time. Once the Round Harvest is hitting your foe, airdash forward with air (H) to catch up to them, then land and time (S) to hit them just as the hyper combo disappears. Doing it any earlier causes the blade to catch your rising foe, ruining the combo.

IV. ST. (H) CANCEL ↓↙← + (L), ST. (L), ST. (M), ST. (H), (S) CANCEL SUPER JUMP, AIR (M), (M), (H) CANCEL ↓↘→ + ATK ATK

(472,800 damage) This is a basic anti-air combo. Standing (H) must hit as high as possible for ↓↙← + (L) to juggle. You're safe if the attack is defended, though you're left at a slight frame disadvantage.

ASSISTS

First and foremost, Trish needs OTG-capable assists to help with her awful damage output. Dante's—β Crystal, C. Viper's—β Seismic Hammer, Wesker's—β Samurai Edge, Deadpool's—β Katanarama!, etc., all fit the bill. Your second concern is building hyper combo gauge. Trish's Round Harvest is hard to avoid, so it's worth throwing around to keep your opponent stationary. Tossing it at random can become costly, unless you're taking action to obtain meter. Amaterasu's—γ Blossom and Morrigan's—γ Dark Harmonizer gauge-building assists are an answer to this problem. Since Round Harvest leaves you free to perform actions while it's grinding your foe down, call either assist to replenish some of your gauge. You can also fire ↓ ↘ → + (L) as the blade hits to build even more meter. If done correctly, you'll have more gauge to spend on periodic Round Harvests!

Crush your challenger's vitality with OTG assist combos!

ADVANCED TACTICS

ROUND HARVEST TACTICS

Bring in a friend while Round Harvest shields them.

Trish's greatest asset is the homing Round Harvest, which is practically impossible to avoid. Outside of its obvious uses, canceling it into another teammate's hyper combo has a number of interesting possibilities. For example, cancel it into Wolverine's Berserker Charge (↓ ↓ + ATK ATK) to safely put him on the screen. Since the blade is considered a part of Trish, your opponent's attempts to use advancing guard against *it will not push Wolverine away*, leaving him free to attack in his powered up form while the blade locks your challenger down! From there Wolverine can dash in with an air (L) right as he leaves the ground for a quick overhead, or crouching (L). If either option hits, the remainder of Round Harvest combos. This idea works well with other power-up hyper combos, like Felicia's Kitty's Helper, Zero's Sougenmu, Morrigan's Astral Vision, and Dante's Devil Trigger.

ROUND HARVEST CROSSOVER COMBINATION

Trish deals heavy damage whether they guard or not.

As mentioned, the Round Harvest inflicts heavy guard damage while leaving you free to perform actions. The same applies if you use a crossover combination with Trish on point! An interesting tactic is to pick two teammates with hyper combos that deal heavy guard damage (for example, Iron Man with Proton Cannon and Storm with Hail Storm), then activate a crossover combination. With the hyper combos locking your opponent down, move in and attack with an instant air (L) CANCEL → ↓ + (H) (do it just as you leave the ground so that it hits your opponent even if they're crouching), or attack with crouching (L). If either option hits, the remainder of all active hyper combos link afterwards for massive damage. Even if your foe manages to block the attack, the combination of high damage hyper combos inflicts a whopping 30~50% guard damage!

COMBO APPENDIX

GENERAL EXECUTION TIPS

When doing her general air chains, wait a moment after the launcher hits before attacking with (M), (M). If you're starting an air combo with air (M) CANCEL → ↓ + (H), perform the jumping (M) as soon as possible after the launch.

Requirements (Position, meter, etc.)	Notes	Command Sequence	Damage
—	This combo is intended to be the extension of a successful setup. If you manage to make the enemy block ↓ ↙ ← + (H), dash forward and do instant air (L). The kick hits if your opponent blocks low. The blade hits just after air (L) connects, allowing the ↓ + (H) to combo	↓ ↙ ← + (H), as the enemy guards the blade, dash forward and do air (L), ↓ + (H) as soon as you leave the ground, blades hits, then link into cr. (L), cr. (M), cr. (H), (S) CANCEL → super jump, air (M), (M), (H) CANCEL → ↓ ↘ → + (L) CANCEL → ↓ ↘ → + ATK ATK	479,100
—	The alternate variation to the previous combo, this works if the enemy tries to guard high when they're blocking the blade	↓ ↙ ← + (H), as the enemy guards the blade, dash forward and do cr. (L), cr. (M), cr. (H), (S) CANCEL → super jump, air (M), (M), (H) CANCEL → ↓ ↘ → + (L) CANCEL → ↓ ↘ → + ATK ATK	435,600
—	Trick "Peekaboo" must catch the enemy for the remainder of the combo to work	↓ ↙ ← + (M), enemy freezes, st. (H), (S) CANCEL → super jump, air (M) ,(M) CANCEL → double jump, (M), (M), (H) CANCEL → ↓ ↘ → + ATK ATK	445,500
Corner required, Deadpool—β	—	cr. (L), cr. (L), cr. (M), cr. (H), (S) CANCEL → super jump, air (M), ↓ + (H) CANCEL → ↓ ↙ ← + (L), (M), (M) CANCEL → double jump forward, (M), (H), (S), land, P1 or P2, (S) CANCEL → super jump, air (H) CANCEL → ↓ + (H) CANCEL → ↓ ↘ → + (L) CANCEL → ↓ ↘ → + ATK ATK	601,800
Requires level 1 X-factor, requires 1 hyper combo gauge bar	After the first launch, air (H), ↓ + (H) must be done as early as possible to be able to land and juggle with st. (L)	cr. (L), cr. (L), cr. (M), st. (H), X-FACTOR, cr. (M), st. (H), (S) CANCEL → super jump, air (H), ↓ + (H), land, st. (L), st. (M), st. (H), (S), air (M), (M) CANCEL → double jump, (M), (M), (H) CANCEL → ↓ ↘ → + (L) CANCEL → ↓ ↘ → + ATK ATK	898,300
Corner required. Requires 3 hyper combo gauge bars, Wesker—β	—	cr. (L), cr. (L), cr. (M), st. (H), (S) CANCEL → super jump, air (M), ↓ + (H) CANCEL → ↓ ↙ ← + (L), (M), ↓ + (H) CANCEL → ↓ ↙ ← + (L), (M), ↓ + (H) CANCEL → ↓ ↙ ← + (L), (S), land, P1 or P2, → ↓ ↘ + ATK ATK	823,900

TRON

BIO

REAL NAME
TRON BONNE

OCCUPATION
SKY PIRATE

ABILITIES
A MECHANICAL ENGINEERING GENIUS, SHE IS ABLE TO CREATE ANYTHING FROM SMALL ROBOTS, SUCH AS THE SERVBOTS TO LARGE AERIAL BATTLESHIPS. SHE IS ALSO ABLE TO PILOT MECHS.

WEAPONS
UTILIZES THE SERVBOTS AS WELL AS MECHS SHE HAS BUILT. IN THE VS. SERIES, SHE PILOTS A WALKING BATTLE MECH TANK CALLED THE GUSTAFF.

PROFILE
THE ONLY DAUGHTER OF THE BONNE FAMILY OF SKY PIRATES, SHE IS EXTREMELY PRIDEFUL AND IS A SORE LOSER. HOWEVER, SHE CAN BE CHARMINGLY AWKWARD IN FRONT OF SOMEONE SHE HAS A CRUSH ON, AND VALUES HER FAMILY ABOVE ALL ELSE. SHE TRAVELS THE WORLD IN THE HOPES OF GETTING RICH QUICK, BUT HER MISADVENTURES USUALLY ONLY END UP ADDING TO HER DEBT.

FIRST APPEARANCE
MEGA MAN LEGENDS (1997)

"TRON BONNE, QUEEN OF SERVBOTS, AT YOUR SERVICE!"

POWER GRID

7	INTELLIGENCE
5	STRENGTH
4	SPEED
5	STAMINA
1	ENERGY PROJECTION
4	FIGHTING ABILITY

*This is biographical, and does not represent an evaluation of the character's in-game combat potential.

ALTERNATE COSTUMES

PS3: ⨂ Xbox 360: Ⓐ

PS3: ▢ Xbox 360: Ⓧ

PS3: △ Xbox 360: Ⓨ

PS3: R1 Xbox 360: RB

ATTACK SET

STANDING BASIC ATTACKS

Screen	Command	Hits	Damage	Startup	Active	Recovery	Advantage on Hit	Advantage if Guarded	Notes
1	Standing L	1	55,000	7	3	12	+1	-1	—
2	Standing M	4	72,800	9	8	29	-10	-13	—
3	Standing H	1	100,000	15	30	31	—	-38	Knocks down opponent, ↓↘→ + P1 or P2 snap back
4	S	1	100,000	8	5	38	—	-20	Launcher, not special or hyper combo cancelable

CROUCHING BASIC ATTACKS

Screen	Command	Hits	Damage	Startup	Active	Recovery	Advantage on Hit	Advantage if Guarded	Notes
1	Crouching L	6	65,600	8	13	18	-5	-7	Low attack
2	Crouching M	1	75,000	11	5	19	-3	-6	Low attack
3	Crouching H	4	95,500	11	9	16	—	+4	Low attack, knocks down, OTG-capable, can move forward or backward during attack, not special or hyper combo cancelable

AERIAL BASIC ATTACKS

Screen	Command	Hits	Damage	Startup	Active	Recovery	Notes
1	Air L	3	69,300	9	6	21	Overhead attack
2	Air M	1	80,000	9	5	21	Overhead attack
3	Air H	1	100,000	15	Until grounded	3	Overhead attack, knocks down opponent
4	Air S	1	100,000	17	4	30	Overhead attack, ground bounces opponent, not special cancelable, causes flying screen when used in launcher combo

COMMAND ATTACKS

Screen	Command	Hits	Damage	Startup	Active	Recovery	Advantage on Hit	Advantage if Guarded	Notes
1	⇨ + Ⓜ	5	84,000	12	20	17	-3	-6	Not special or hyper combo cancelable, 5th hit is jump cancelable, inflicts chip damage, projectile has 10 medium priority durability points
2	⇨ + Ⓗ	3	165,300	15	5(15)1	21	+4	+1	Not special or hyper combo cancelable, inflicts, chip damage, nullifies low and medium priority projectile and beams during first 5 active frames, rock can be held for 72 frames, projectile has 10 low priority durability points

1

2

TRON

AS A PARTNER-CROSSOVER ASSISTS

Screen	Type	P1+P2 Crossover Combination Hyper Combo	Description	Hits	Damage	Startup	Active	Recovery (this crossover assist)	Recovery (other partner)	Notes
1	α – Alpha	Servbot Surprise	Bonne Strike M	6	117,000	35	14(1)2	112	82	Knocks down opponent
2	β – Beta	Servbot Surprise	Gustav Fire (⇨ + Ⓜ)	5	102,300	38	20	111	81	Projectile has 10 medium priority durability points
3	γ – Gamma	Servbot Surprise	Bandit Boulder (⇨ + Ⓗ)	3	151,600	40	5(16)1	115	85	Nullifies low and medium priority projectile and beams during first 5 active frames, projectile has 10 low priority durability points

1

2

3

SPECIAL MOVES

Screen	Name	Command	Hits	Damage	Startup	Active	Recovery	Advantage on Hit	Advantage if Guarded	Notes
1	Bonne Strike L	← ↓ ↙ + L	4~8	75,900~118,400	9	8~20 (1)2	18	—	-7	Knocks down, can be mashed for extra hits
	Bonne Strike M	← ↓ ↙ + M	6~11	99,400~140,300	9	14~29 (1)2	18	—	-7	Knocks down, can be mashed for extra hits
	Bonne Strike H	← ↓ ↙ + H	8~15	118,400~160,400	9	20~41 (1)2	18	—	-7	Knocks down, can be mashed for extra hits
2	Air Bonne Strike L	(in air) ← ↓ ↙ + L	4~8	75,900~118,400	13	8~20 (1)2	Until grounded, 7 frames ground recovery	—	—	Knocks down, can be mashed for extra hits
	Air Bonne Strike M	(in air) ← ↓ ↙ + M	6~11	99,400~140,300	13	14~29 (1)2	Until grounded, 7 frames ground recovery	—	—	Knocks down, can be mashed for extra hits
	Air Bonne Strike H	(in air) ← ↓ ↙ + H	8~15	118,400~160,400	13	20~41 (1)2	Until grounded, 7 frames ground recovery	—	—	Knocks down, can be mashed for extra hits
3	Beacon Bomb L	↓ ↘ → + L	1	50,000	33	—	17	—	+5	Incapacitates opponent for 82 frames on hit, projectile disappears after 16 frames, projectile has 1 low priority durability point
	Beacon Bomb M	↓ ↘ → + M	1	60,000	43	—	16	—	+6	Incapacitates opponent for 82 frames on hit, projectile has 1 low priority durability point
4	Beacon Bomb H	↓ ↘ → + H	1	70,000	33	—	17	—	+5	Incapacitates opponent for 82 frames on hit, projectile has 1 low priority durability point
5	Servbot Launcher L	→ ↓ ↘ + L	1	70,000	18	—	37	-12	-15	Servbot projectile is in play for 50 frames, projectile has 5 low priority durability points
	Servbot Launcher M	→ ↓ ↘ + M	1	70,000	18	—	37	-12	-15	Servbot projectile is in play for 92 frames, projectile has 5 low priority durability points
	Servbot Launcher H	→ ↓ ↘ + H	1	70,000	18	—	37	-12	-15	Servbot projectile is in play for 68 frames, projectile has 5 low priority durability points
6	Bonne Mixer L	→ ↘ ↓ ↙ ← + L	4	120,000	5	1	41	—	—	Throw attack, unrecoverable knockdown
	Bonne Mixer M	→ ↘ ↓ ↙ ← + M	7	165,000	3	1	43	—	—	Throw attack, unrecoverable knockdown
	Bonne Mixer H	→ ↘ ↓ ↙ ← + H	10	210,000	1	2	44	—	—	Throw attack, unrecoverable knockdown

1

2

Bonne Strike: Bonne Strike is Tron's most combo-friendly attack. If it hits, you can easily link standing M afterward and transition into a full combo. It can actually be used several times in succession for a combo, though its multiple hits will cause severe damage scaling. The most common use of this move should be relatively early in combos to set up for a follow-up link, or as a final move before using a hyper combo.

Don't use Bonne Strike blindly; the attack is very unsafe if guarded! If you want to use Bonne Strike to attack the opponent from a distance, first call a long-ranged crossover assist before performing the attack. Your opponent should be forced to guard the crossover assist's projectile after Bonne Strike has finished hitting, making the attack safe from punishment.

Mashing the same attack button with which you initiate Bonne Strike results in Tron traveling much further and inflicting more hits and damage. Used in tandem with a crossover assist, Bonne Strike H (and mashing!) can cover a lot of horizontal distance quickly.

Bonne Strike's air version is most useful to attack the opponent freely: if performed low enough to the ground, a perfectly executed Air Bonne Strike has a frame advantage of +1 if guarded. Along with airdash attacks, Air Bonne Strike forms the foundation of Tron's midrange offense.

Beacon Bomb: Beacon Bomb is Tron's strange take on projectiles. Beacon Bomb L does not reach all the way across the screen but is substantially faster than the full-screen Beacon Bomb M. Beacon Bomb H attacks at an upward angle, potentially useful to counter opponents harassing you at long range from above.

All versions of Beacon Bomb have much slower startup than most other projectile attacks. They also have only a single low priority durability point, making them essentially worthless in long-range firefights. To make matters worse, most characters can completely crouch under Beacon Bomb L and M!

3

4

Characters who *cannot* crouch under Beacon Bomb:

Captain America	Hulk	M.O.D.O.K.	Tron
Haggar	Iron Man	Sentinel	

With all these disadvantages, why use Beacon Bomb? When you manage to hit opponents, a pair of Servbots jumps onto them and mugs them for some cash! While the cash they bring to you is of no value in this game, the opponent is completely incapacitated for a full 82 frames while the Servbots have their way. This allows for free combos!

Beacon Bombs can actually be linked together indefinitely, resulting in a true infinite combo! However, actually performing the combo is prohibitively difficult; you must hit with the Beacon Bomb projectile on the very last frame before the previous set of Servbots jumps off the opponent. If you hit the projectile even a single frame earlier, the opponent isn't incapacitated at all. If you wait even one frame later, the opponent can guard the Beacon Bomb projectile.

If you hit Beacon Bomb L at pointblank range, the proper timing to hit the subsequent Beacon Bomb L is to input it exactly 34 frames after the previous one recovers. Consult the frame data tables within this guide and see if you can find a timing aid that works for you!

Beacon Bomb's prohibitively long startup time makes it very difficult to use without the cover of a crossover assist. Generally, Tron can combo into Beacon Bomb only using air S to ground-bounce the opponent, or by successfully linking it while the opponent is already incapacitated by another Beacon Bomb! Beacon Bomb's best use is to convert stray crossover assist hits into combos from anywhere on the screen. With a bit of foresight (or just good planning), all of your random assist hits can become much more threatening!

Servbot Launcher: Servbot Launcher fires a Servbot projectile diagonally into the air, which then slowly hovers down to the ground. The Servbot is an active threat the entire time it descends. Servbot Launcher L and H cause the Servbots to drop much faster, while Servbot Launcher M causes them to remain onscreen substantially longer. Each version of Servbot Launcher has progressively longer range.

Performing Servbot Launcher repeatedly can actually be a very effective way to zone out offensive opponents. The M version in particular can be difficult to deal with, as the Servbots stay onscreen for a long time. Timing a wavedash between these Servbots can be very difficult for some opposing characters. If you predict that the opponent will attempt to dash through your Servbots, stop your foe cold in his or her tracks with standing Ⓜ and transition into a combo!

Bonne Mixer: Bonne Mixer is a fairly damaging command throw. It can then be followed up with an OTG-capable attack in the corner to convert into a full combo. With near-perfect wavedashing, you can follow up with an OTG-capable attack anywhere on the screen, but this is very difficult to perform consistently.

Stronger versions of Bonne Mixer are progressively faster and more damaging, with Bonne Mixer H having only a single frame of startup. However, stronger versions also have progressively less range; Bonne Mixer H has almost exactly the same range as a regular ground throw. Normal ground throws also have only one frame of startup and allow much easier combos from midscreen, but they can be escaped.

TRON

"I NEED A NEW ASSISTANT—LOOKING FOR SOME WORK? I DOUBT THERE'S MUCH AVAILABLE FOR WASHED-UP FIGHTERS!"

HYPER COMBOS

Screen	Name	Command	Hits	Damage	Startup	Active	Recovery	Advantage on Hit	Advantage if Guarded	Notes
1	Servbot Takeout	⇩⬂⇨ + ATK ATK	41	251,800	10+6	—	83	—	-61	Frames 1-10 invincible, knocks down opponent, projectile has 1 high priority durability point
2	Servbot Surprise	⇨⇩⬂ + ATK ATK	10	320,700	6+24	—	95	—	+24	Frames 4-7 invincible, knocks down opponent, huge Servbot is active for 10(22)65 frames
3	Shakedown Mixer (Level 3 hyper combo)	⇨⬂⇩⬃⇦ + ATK ATK	18	440,000	6+0	3	43	—	—	Frames 1-9 invincible, throw, unrecoverable knockdown

Servbot Takeout: Servbot Takeout mainly functions as the ender to most of your combos. The projectile has a deceptively large hit box and a decent speed, allowing you to use it in combos fairly easily. At close to medium range, you can also use it on reaction to any opponent using any low or medium priority projectile. Your beacon blows through almost all other projectiles and starts the lunch rush!

Servbot Takeout has some additional defensive utility, as it features 10 frames of invincibility. It's not invincible all the way until the attack occurs, however, so using it against attacks with many active frames is not recommended. If Servbot Takeout is guarded, Tron is incredibly open for punishment, so use it with caution.

Servbot Surprise: While this hyper combo has a lengthy startup period, it results in a ridiculous amount of frame advantage as long as the giant Servbot makes contact with the opponent. However, there is a large window between the hyper combo cutscene and the Servbot growing during which the opponent can easily hit you. However, doing so doesn't prevent the giant Servbot from hitting your foe in return! Try to avoid performing Servbot Surprise too close to your opponent. At that range, your challenger can simply throw you and be invincible from the giant Servbot until the throw finishes.

Tron recovers from Servbot Surprise slightly before the giant Servbot finishes whacking the opponent. This allows you to continue attacking a guarding opponent, or to transition into a full combo if it hits the opponent!

Shakedown Mixer: Unlike Bonne Mixer, you cannot follow up Shakedown Mixer with an OTG-capable attack. However, this level 3 hyper combo is fast and cannot be avoided once the freeze animation begins. Shakedown Mixer is a serious threat to any opponent on the ground within range, so expect your opponents to jump around a lot any time you're near them with three bars to spare. Use air throws in this situation to start combos that deliver more damage than the Shakedown Mixer!

BATTLE PLAN

OVERVIEW

VITALITY: 1,200,000

CHAIN COMBO ARCHETYPE: MARVEL SERIES

X-Factor	Lv.1	Lv.2	Lv.3
Damage	133%	166%	199%
Speed	105%	110%	115%

When playing as Tron, your goal is simply to get close to the opponent. As Tron, you pilot a big, slow robot. Why would you want to be close to your opponent?

Tron can start combos from the Bonne Mixer special throw attack, as well as normal ground throws. She can also threaten with the level 3 Shakedown Mixer.

Opponents attempting to jump away from her throws become susceptible to air throws, which also lead into combos.

Tron has a strong airdash-based offense, with cross-up air (H) and high-priority air (L) and (M).

How do you get close to opponents using Tron?

Perform Air Bonne Strikes as low to the ground as possible. This allows you to travel the screen's entire length, ending up with slight frame advantage.

Use Bonne Strikes followed by a projectile crossover assist.

Use → + (H) at mid range to nullify zoning defenses and force the opponent to come to you.

Use Beacon Bomb to combo from long-ranged crossover assist hits.

Use strong air attacks like air (H) and air (S) to dominate the airspace.

ON THE GROUND

Tron Bonne best fills the role of a battery on your team. Her combos that incorporate multiple hits of Bonne Strike and → + (M) fill a lot of the hyper combo gauge. Even after ending combos with Servbot Takeout, you still end up with a net gain of 40% of one bar! Even if your opponent guards Air Bonne Strike, mashing for extra hits results in a lot of bar and slight frame advantage.

As a meter-user, Tron gains a lot of opportunities to threaten the opponent with Shakedown Mixer, forcing the foe to jump around. However, Shakedown Mixer generally isn't a very efficient use of meter, and it isn't guaranteed to grab the opponent.

Tron's ground-based options for approaching the opponent are very limited. You can call a long-range assist and wavedash behind the projectile, or you can call a long-range assist and Bonne Strike H in front of the projectile. The former approach is much safer, but it quickly falls apart if your opponent can out-produce your crossover assist's total projectile durability points. Getting in front of your crossover assist's projectile with Bonne Strike H will very likely cause you to run into a lot of stray hits, but the projectile following behind you almost ensures that your opponent will be forced to guard eventually. Such an approach allows you start your offense at a price. If you hit your opponent with the Bonne Strike, you can follow with a full combo, making this a medium-risk, high-reward tactic. However, beam-based attacks and most projectile hyper combos shut down this approach completely.

As a more stable alternative, working your way into mid-range allows you to get into a firefight using → + (H). This attack nullifies low and medium priority projectiles and beams during the first five active frames while Tron lifts the boulder. It then has a hefty 10 durability points once thrown. At mid-range, you can actually out-produce almost all zoning characters in terms of durability points! Once you destroy their projectiles with the lift animation, you can counterattack opponents by tossing the rock at them and pinning them in place momentarily. Because → + (H) is not a special move, you can also call a crossover assist anytime during its duration. Use that as your chance to close in on your opponent!

Once you get close to the opponent, your strongest threats are both your normal ground throw and Bonne Mixer. Bonne Mixer is much more difficult to start a combo from mid-screen without an OTG-capable crossover assist. However, it has more range on the lighter versions, and the throw cannot be broken. Failed regular throw attempts result in an accidental standing (H) attack, which is a very bad situation. When you attempt to throw the opponent, always press P1 or P2 immediately afterward. If you throw the opponent, great—the crossover assist won't attack. If you don't throw the opponent and get standing (H), your crossover assist will jump out immediately afterward, giving you time to cancel into a Servbot Launcher for safety.

If your opponent tries to break your normal throw attempts, you gain a great opportunity to land major damage. Counter your opponent's attempts to break your throw by jumping forward and hitting him or her with a cross up air (S)! Your opponent will accidentally get a standing (H) as you jump over and hit from behind with air (S). Transition into a full combo from there!

If the opponent tries to counter your throw attempts by jumping, counter this by jumping up and air-throwing your opponent. Like the ground throw, air throws transition easily into combos from anywhere on the screen, provided you have a crossover assist handy. If your opponent does not jump away, you still jump over your opponent and cross him up with air (H), which is a great way to salvage the situation. If your opponent jumps and attempts to break your air throw attempts, jump slightly later and perform an aerial chain ending with air (S). If your opponent jumps and whiffs his air (H) attack in an attempt to break an air throw, you can punish his whiff with a full combo!

Up close, cancel guarded basic attacks into → + (M). This attack does a bit of chip damage and is jump-cancelable. This allows you to continue attacking your opponent with a large frame advantage. Your opponent is forced to use advancing guard to push you away. Many smaller characters can crouch completely under → + (M) unless it is performed extremely close to them. Against these characters, chain your guarded basic attacks into crouching (H) and hold toward your opponent with the controller. This continues to move you forward and still results in a +4 frame advantage.

→ + (H) is Tron's best zoning tool. It deals a fair amount of chip damage and can be relatively difficult to get around. You can hold the (H) button to fake opponents into jumping forward, and release the rock later to hit them as they fall toward you. Calling an assist in anticipation of the opponent jumping into the rock can often result in a combo or at least a large amount of frame advantage.

When you play a zoning game, you often rely on a long-ranged crossover assist to do most of your dirty work. Normally it would be very difficult to get any sort of meaningful damage at long range using Tron. Using Beacon Bomb L or M in anticipation of a crossover assist hitting the opponent can result in starting combos from all the way across the screen!

Mixing in Servbot Launcher M with your → + (H) attacks is a great way to preemptively prevent opponents from jumping. Repeated use of Servbot Launcher M can actually be fairly difficult to get around without super jumping—the gap to dash between Servbots is fairly small. You still have to use → + (H) every now and then to chip at opponents, which forces them to make a move you can counter.

Like most characters, Tron's best anti-air is a simple air throw. Barring that, → + (M) works great if you perform it ahead of time. It can be jump-canceled for full combos if it hits, and it still leads into offense if it's guarded.

If an opponent doesn't use advancing guard against Bonne Strike, you can threaten with a late cancel into Shakedown Mixer.

Chaining blocked attacks into → + (M) allows you to jump-cancel forward and maintain offensive momentum.

→ + (H) nullifies low and medium priority projectiles and beams during the first five active frames. Counterattack with your own rock projectile while calling a crossover assist!

UP IN THE AIR

Tron Bonne's aerial mobility options are relatively average. She can horizontally airdash in either direction, and she can cover a ton of ground with Air Bonne Strike.

Like all airdashes, Tron's air dash has a height requirement. You can super jump to reach this minimum height more quickly. Doing so allows you to airdash nearly instantly and then use air (H) to start falling. This creates a very fast cross-up situation that can be difficult to guard, especially in tandem with crossover assists.

Tron's air attacks are very threatening at close range. Her air (H) has active frames until she lands, and it can cross up opponents from a huge distance away. This makes air (H) a dominating attack at close range against a grounded opponent—jump and immediately perform air (H) to dominate surrounding airspace. If the opponent tries to jump at the same time, you'll land an easy air throw if you hold ⇨ or ⇦ while pressing (H). On top of that, air (H) sends opponents into a knockdown state, leaving them vulnerable to follow-up combos. You may have to cancel into Air Bonne Strike to start a combo when you're a little farther away from the opponent. Air (S) can also be used to cross up. Simply jump over the opponent without airdashing and press (S). If it hits, air (S) causes a ground bounce, which makes starting a combo afterward very easy.

Use long-range assists with Air Bonne Strike to get in on opponents.

Super Jump into instant airdash (H) up close to cross up opponents or get an air throw if they try to jump.

From farther away, airdashing toward the opponent with air (L) is a great way to begin your offense. Due to its large range, air (L) beats most attempts to anti-air it. It can chain into air (M) before landing to create much more frame advantage. From even farther out, airdashing and using air (H) is your longest-range basic attack.

Using long-range assists with Air Bonne Strike can be an effective means of closing in on the opponent. These also greatly increase your frame advantage if your opponent guards the Air Bonne Strike, allowing you to continue attacking.

Air (M) is an instant overhead on large characters!

Against very large characters, you can press air (M) on the way up from a jump for an instant overhead. You can then chain this into air (S) for a ground bounce, allowing for an easy combo follow-up. Use this to train your opponents to block high, and then start hitting them with low attacks.

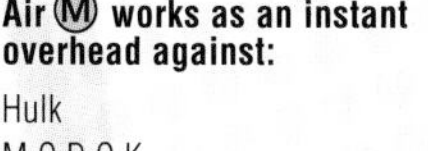

Air (M) works as an instant overhead against:

Hulk
M.O.D.O.K.
Sentinel
Tron

TRON

COMBO USAGE

I. ST. (L), CR. (M), ST. (H) [CANCEL] ← ↓ ↙ + (H) (MASH (H)), ST. (M) (3 HITS), → + (M) [CANCEL] FORWARD JUMP, AIR (M), (H), (S), LAND, ST. (H) [CANCEL] ← ↓ ↙ + (H) (MASH (H)) [CANCEL] ↓ ↘ → + (ATK)(ATK)

(617,800 damage) Tron has difficulty delivering heavy damage from launcher combos without the help of assists. However, Bonne Strike, → + (M), and the ground bounce from air (S) all combine to make a great combo that never requires a launcher. The important parts of this combo are to make sure you hit the air (M) after the → + (M) as soon as possible to allow time for the entire air chain to hit. After standing (H), cancel Bonne Strike as late as possible to get full damage from Bonne Strike. Cancel Bonne Strike's last hit as soon as possible to ensure Servbot Takeout hits. Cancel Bonne Strike slightly early for a little less damage if this gives you trouble.

If this combo's initial two hits are guarded, chain into → + (M) and jump-cancel to maintain your offensive momentum. If your opponent's character can crouch under → + (M) at range, cancel into crouching (H) instead, holding forward to move into your opponent. From there, you are at a +4 frame advantage and can continue your offense!

II. AIR THROW, AIR ← ↓ ↙ + (H), LAND, [P1 or P2], CR. (H), ST. (M) (3 HITS), → + (M) [CANCEL] FORWARD JUMP, AIR (M), (H), (S), LAND, ST. (H) [CANCEL] ← ↓ ↙ + (H) (MASH (H)) [CANCEL] ↓ ↘ → + (ATK)(ATK)

(484,500 damage, Wesker—β) Bonne Strike's forward mobility allows you to close the distance quickly toward your newly grounded opponent. This gives you ample time to OTG with her crouching (H). However, Tron requires an assist to inflict big damage. Several assists will work, but the timing of calling the assist and when to use her crouching (H) varies. An ideal assist keeps the opponent in hit stun long enough for Tron to hit with either standing (M) or with air (M) or (H). Experiment with your favorite assist!

III. → ↘ ↓ ↙ ← + (H), [P1 or P2], CR. (H), → + (H), JUMP, AIR (H), (S), LAND, ST. (H) X ← ↓ ↙ + (H) (MASH (H)) [CANCEL] ↓ ↘ → + (ATK)(ATK)

(551,800 damage, Sentinel—α, corner only) For many characters, Sentinel—α assist drones take too long to assist in an OTG situation. Tron is not one of these characters. Her crouching (H) can be canceled into → + (H) for an extended OTG situation that sets up Sentinel—α drones to hit perfectly after she throws her rock. This sets her up to easily combo for worthwhile damage after her command throw. You can actually pull this off in mid-screen, but doing so requires near-perfect wavedashing to reach the opponent before he or she begins to stand.

IV. ST. (L), CR. (M), ST. (H) [CANCEL] [X-FACTOR], DASH FORWARD, ST. (M), ST. (H) [CANCEL] ← ↓ ↙ + (H) (MASH (H)), ST. (M) (3 HITS), → + (M) [CANCEL] FORWARD JUMP, AIR (M), (H), (S), LAND, ST. (H) [CANCEL] ← ↓ ↙ + (H) (MASH (H)) [CANCEL] ↓ ↘ → + (ATK)(ATK)

(1,378,800, level 1 X-Factor) Tron benefits greatly from the reduced scaling that comes with X-Factor, as she has several multi-hit attacks. This combo, which varies only slightly from **Combo I**, illustrates the point. However, her combo damage *more than doubles* with level 1 X-Factor, allowing a combo that will easily knock out any character.

V. ST. (L), CR. (M), ST. (H), (S) [CANCEL] SUPER JUMP, AIR (M), (H), (S), LAND, [P1 or P2], CR. (H) (3 HITS), → + (H), ↓ ↘ → + (H), JUMP, AIR (H), (S), LAND, ST. (H) X ← ↓ ↙ + (H) (MASH (H)) [CANCEL] ↓ ↘ → + (ATK)(ATK)

(750,700 damage, Sentinel—α) Tron again makes good use of Sentinel—α to OTG after a launcher combo and extend into a highly damaging combo. Against smaller characters, you may have to delay your super jump cancel after (S) to ensure air (H) hits.

ASSISTS

Tron—γ is slightly different from her → + (H) because the boulder is thrown full screen!

Tron can make extensive use of Sentinel—α assist, whether it be for pressure or OTG combos.

Low-hitting assists can be combined with airdash attacks to create difficult-to-block situations.

Like most long-range crossover assists, Tron—γ is useful for nearly any team. The rock's beefy 10 durability points can be used to win firefights against zoning characters. They can also be used as an offensive tool to pin down opponents. Tron—α is a strong "pinning" crossover assist, used similarly to other popular assists, like Chun-Li—γ and Doctor Doom—γ. Use the Bonne Strike assist for locking down an opponent during a gap in your offense. This helps you combat advancing guard and get back in range to resume offense.

Tron benefits most from long-range projectile assists that make Bonne Strike safe or have frame advantage, such as Sentinel—α or Arthur—β. These types of assist also greatly improve her offense and OTG combo capabilities. You can also use them to bolster Tron's surprisingly strong mid-range zoning game!

Tron also benefits from low-hitting assists, such as Wesker—β. These, combined with her airdash attacks, allow you to create situations that are difficult, if not impossible, to guard. Wesker—β also allows you to start combos from Bonne Mixer mid-screen!

ADVANCED TACTICS

INSTANT AIR BONNE STRIKE

Normally, any Bonne Strike is at a frame disadvantage when blocked. However, you can do an Air Bonne Strike the instant you leave the ground by inputting the command a special way. Inputting ← ↓ ↙ ↖ + (ATK) while slightly delaying the attack button executes the Bonne Strike immediately after Tron leaves the ground. If you do this correctly, it leaves you at +1 frame advantage instead of being vulnerable to throws if guarded.

Use the command ← ↓ ↙ ↖ + (ATK) to make Tron's Air Bonne Strike attack instantly off the ground and have frame advantage.

However, Tron's basic attacks are very slow, making the +1 frame advantage a little less meaningful. Most characters can still beat you to the punch with their faster (L) attacks. Bonne Mixer L has only five frames of startup. Performing Bonne Mixer L right when you land grabs on the first frame that the opponent becomes throwable. Throws beat strikes in the event of a trade, so Bonne Mixer L wins out against even a four-frame light attack in this situation. Shakedown Mixer can also be used for essentially the same purpose, but it's easier to use.

If the opponent tries to throw after guarding the instant Air Bonne Strike, he or she will still grab you before you can get the Bonne Mixer out. Counter opposing throw attempts simply by jumping over them and hitting foes from behind with air (H). Your opponents will whiff a standing (H) when trying to throw you, and you can pick up a full combo from their whiffed attacks!

COMBO APPENDIX

GENERAL EXECUTION TIPS

Delay Bonne Strikes after standing (H) to get maximum damage.

Air (H) has a high hitbox, so try to delay super jump-canceling in launcher combos to ensure it hits.

Hyper combo-cancel the final hit of Bonne Strike into Servbot Takeout as fast as possible. The opponent may otherwise air recover due to hitstun deterioration.

Requirements (Position, meter, etc.)	Notes	Command Sequence	Damage
—	Combo from cross-up air (H)	Super jump, airdash, air (H) CANCEL➔ ←↓↙ + (H) (mash (H)), land, st. (M), → + (M) CANCEL➔ jump forward, air (M), (H), (S), land, st. (H) CANCEL➔ ←↓↙ + (H) (mash (H)) CANCEL➔ ↓↘→ + (ATK)(ATK)	558,000
Corner required	—	→↘↓↙← + (H), cr. (H) (4 hits) OTG, → + (H)	261,500
—	Instant overhead on large characters	Air (M), (S), land, st. (H) CANCEL➔ ←↓↙ + (H) (mash (H)), st. (M) (3 hits), st. (H), CANCEL➔ ←↓↙ + (H) (mash (H)) CANCEL➔ ↓↘→ + (ATK)(ATK)	610,300
Corner required	Hyper combo-cancel the final Bonne Strike H before the final hit; the Servbot Takeout will not successfully combo otherwise	St. (L), cr. (M), st. (H) CANCEL➔ ←↓↙ + (M) CANCEL➔ →↓↘ + (ATK)(ATK), → + (M) CANCEL➔ jump forward, air (M), (H), (S), land, ↓↘→ + (L), ←↓↙ + (H) (mash (H)) CANCEL➔ ↓↘→ + (ATK)(ATK)	733,800

WESKER

"A NEW AGE WILL BEGIN, AND IT WILL REQUIRE A GOD."

BIO

REAL NAME

ALBERT WESKER

OCCUPATION

FORMER S.T.A.R.S. CAPTAIN

ABILITIES

HAVING INFECTED HIMSELF WITH A SPECIAL VIRUS, HE GAINED SEVERAL SUPER-HUMAN ABILITIES, INCLUDING BEING ABLE TO DODGE BULLETS. IN ADDITION TO HIS SKILLS WITH FIREARMS, HE IS ALSO VERY KNOWLEDGEABLE ABOUT BIOENGINEERING.

WEAPONS

USES MANY FIREARMS.

PROFILE

A VERY CALCULATING AND DANGEROUS INDIVIDUAL, HE WILL DO ANYTHING TO FURTHER HIS OWN GAINS. HAVING PERFECTED THE UROBOROS VIRUS, HE PLANS TO INFECT THE GLOBAL POPULATION WITH IT, LEAVING ONLY THE CHOSEN ONES SUCH AS HIMSELF TO CREATE A NEW WORLD.

FIRST APPEARANCE

RESIDENT EVIL (1996)

POWER GRID

- 7 INTELLIGENCE
- 6 STRENGTH
- 6 SPEED
- 5 STAMINA
- 1 ENERGY PROJECTION
- 6 FIGHTING ABILITY

*This is biographical, and does not represent an evaluation of the character's in-game combat potential.

ALTERNATE COSTUMES

PS3: ⓧ Xbox 360: Ⓐ

PS3: □ Xbox 360: Ⓧ

PS3: △ Xbox 360: Ⓨ

PS3: R1 Xbox 360: RB

ATTACK SET

STANDING BASIC ATTACKS

Screen	Command	Hits	Damage	Startup	Active	Recovery	Advantage on Hit	Advantage on Guard	Notes
1	Standing L	1	55,000	5	5	8	+2	+1	—
2	Standing M	1	73,000	8	2	22	-4	-6	—
3	Standing H	2	92,500	12	3*5	18	+2	0	—
4	S	1	100,000	10	3	21	—	-1	Launcher attack, not special- or hyper combo-cancelable

CROUCHING BASIC ATTACKS

Screen	Command	Hits	Damage	Startup	Active	Recovery	Advantage on Hit	Advantage on Guard	Notes
1	Crouching L	1	53,000	5	2	11	+2	+1	Low attack
2	Crouching M	1	75,000	8	5	14	+1	-1	Low attack
3	Crouching H	1	80,000	10	3	25	—	-5	Low attack, knocks down

AERIAL BASIC ATTACKS

Screen	Command	Hits	Damage	Startup	Active	Recovery	Advantage on Hit	Advantage on Guard	Notes
1	Air L	1	55,000	5	8	16	—	—	Overhead attack
2	Air M	1	73,000	10	5	15	—	—	Overhead attack
3	Air H	1	88,000	11	7	18	—	—	Overhead attack
4	Air S	1	95,000	10	5	24	—	—	Overhead attack, causes flying screen if hit within a launcher combo

COMMAND ATTACKS

Screen	Command	Hits	Damage	Startup	Active	Recovery	Advantage on Hit	Advantage if Guarded	Notes
1	⇨ + Ⓗ	1	80,000	15	—	31	-6	-8	Not special or hyper combo-cancelable, inflicts chip damage, projectile has 3 low priority durability points, Ⓛ, Ⓜ or Ⓗ all cancel into respective Phantom Moves
2	⬂ + Ⓗ	1	80,000	15	2	24	-1	-3	Low attack, OTG-capable, not special- or hyper combo-cancelable, inflicts chip damage, projectile has 3 low priority durability points, Ⓛ, Ⓜ or Ⓗ all cancel into respective Phantom Moves
3	Air ⇩ + Ⓗ	1	80,000	15	—	Until landing, 1 frame ground recovery	—	—	Not special- or hyper combo-cancelable, inflicts chip damage, projectile has 3 low priority durability points, Ⓛ, Ⓜ or Ⓗ all cancel into respective Phantom Moves

1

2

3

AS A PARTNER-CROSSOVER ASSISTS

Screen	Type	P1+P2 Crossover Combination Hyper Combo	Description	Hits	Damage	Startup	Active	Recovery (this crossover assist)	Recovery (other partner)	Notes
1	α – Alpha	Phantom Dance	Ghost Butterfly	1	120,000	42	3	118	88	Wall bounces opponent
2	β – Beta	Phantom Dance	Samurai Edge (Lower)	1	80,000	39	2	117	87	OTG-capable, low attack , projectile has 3 durability points
3	γ – Gamma	Phantom Dance	Jaguar Dash + Jaguar Kick	3	116,400	49	5(9)4	115	85	Spinning knockdown

1

2

3

SPECIAL MOVES

Screen	Name	Command	Hits	Damage	Startup	Active	Recovery	Advantage on Hit	Advantage on Guard	Notes
1	Cobra Strike	↓↘→ + Ⓛ	1	100,000	10	4	32	—	-13	Unrecoverable knockdown, ↓↘→ + P1 or P2 snap back
2	Ghost Butterfly	↓↘→ + Ⓜ	1	120,000	18	3	25	—	-5	Wall bounces, pressing Ⓛ, Ⓜ or Ⓗ all cancel into respective Phantom Moves
	Phantom Move L	(During Ghost Butterfly or Samurai Edge) Ⓛ	—	—	11	—	20	—	—	—
	Phantom Move M	(During Ghost Butterfly or Samurai Edge) Ⓜ	—	—	11	—	24	—	—	—
	Phantom Move H	(During Ghost Butterfly or Samurai Edge) Ⓗ	—	—	11	—	19	—	—	—
3	Jaguar Dash	↓↘→ + Ⓗ	5	122,600	25	10	27	-4	-6	Can switch sides with opponent on contact, Ⓗ cancels into Jaguar Kick on hit
4	Jaguar Kick	(during Jaguar Dash) Ⓗ	1	50,000	10	4	22	—	-3	Spinning knockdown, can cancel into Cobra Strike
5	Mustang Kick	→↘↓↙← + ATK	2	120,000	1	2	26	—	—	Throw, Ⓜ version causes un-recoverable knockdown, Ⓗ version wall bounces
6	Phantom Move L (in air OK)	→↓↘ + Ⓛ	—	—	11	—	20	—	—	—
7	Phantom Move M (in air OK)	→↓↘ + Ⓜ	—	—	11	—	24	—	—	—
8	Phantom Move H (in air OK)	→↓↘ + Ⓗ	—	—	11	—	19	—	—	—
9	Tiger Uppercut L	←↓↙ + Ⓛ	—	—	5	15	11	—	—	Counters mid/high attacks
	Tiger Uppercut L Follow-Up Attack	—	1	120,000	18	4	27	—	-8	Invincible from frames 1-18, launcher, can travel through opponent, automatically aligns with opponent
10	Tiger Uppercut M	←↓↙ + Ⓜ	—	—	5	15	11	—	—	Counters low attacks
	Tiger Uppercut M Follow-Up Attack	—	1	120,000	21	4	24	—	-5	Invincible from frames 1-20, launcher, can travel through opponent, automatically aligns with opponent
11	Tiger Uppercut H	←↓↙ + Ⓗ	—	—	5	13	13	—	—	Counters projectiles
	Tiger Uppercut H Follow-Up Attack	—	1	120,000	19	4	24	—	-5	Invincible from frames 1-18, wall bounces, can travel through opponent, automatically aligns with opponent

1

Cobra Strike: Cobra Strike is a short ranged punch with no special properties other than the ability to create an unrecoverable knockdown. If used early in a combo, you can dash forward afterwards and OTG with ↘ + Ⓗ, then continue with a combo without help from an assist. Cobra Strike is very unsafe if guarded, so confirm that your attacks are hitting the opponent before canceling into it.

2

Ghost Butterfly: Ghost Butterfly is slower than Cobra Strike, making it slightly more difficult to combo into. As a tradeoff, it wall bounces opponents if it successfully hits. In addition, Ghost Butterfly has the special property of being able to cancel directly into any Phantom Move at the press of a button. Ghost Butterfly is surprisingly difficult to punish if it is guarded due to the distance that it pushes an opponent backwards. You can also cancel into a Phantom Move for additional safety.

3

Jaguar Dash: Jaguar Dash is a long ranged attacking dash with slow start up. It cancels into Jaguar Kick, which creates a spinning knockdown combo opportunity. Jaguar Dash is mainly used as a long ranged punisher for unsafe moves. For general battle purposes, Phantom Move L or H accompanied by a crossover assist is a much better attacking tool. Jaguar Dash isn't punishable by most normal moves if guarded, but is still easily punishable by normal and special throws.

4

Jaguar Kick: Jaguar Kick is a canned follow up to the Jaguar Dash. It puts an opponent in a spinning knockdown state, allowing combos after a successful hit. It is also cancelable into Cobra Strike. Note that many crouching characters will be able to sit clean under a Jaguar Kick, leaving Wesker open for punishment. Jaguar Kick is punishable by throws if it is guarded.

5

Mustang Kick: Mustang Kick is a throw attack that results in a full combo from anywhere on the screen. Best of all, it activates in only 1 frame of start up! The (L) version should be used most, since it has the most range and can lead to a combo from any position. The (M) version has slightly less range and much more recovery, making its usefulness questionable. The (H) version has the least range, but results in a wall bounce if successful. This makes it the easiest version of Mustang Kick to land a combo after, but it also results in less damage because you have already used your one allowed wall bounce in a combo.

In battle situations, throw in a Mustang Kick whenever you think your opponent is waiting for something to guard, attempting to use advancing guard to push you away. Also, you can use the Mustang Kick defensively due to its 1 frame start up speed, grabbing any opponents close enough that leave tiny holes in their offense.

By the same token, you can use Mustang Kick to punish any attacks that are guarded that have a frame disadvantage of least -1, and are within range. Think twice before using advancing guard; you may be passing up on a chance to score a lot of free damage on your opponent!

WESKER

Phantom Move L: Phantom Move L is one of Wesker's most important moves. It quickly teleports Wesker a large distance forward, usually behind an adversary. This not only sets up cross-ups when used in tandem with crossover assists, but it can also be used to go through the projectiles of a zoning opponent. Note that unlike some teleport moves, Wesker's Phantom Move travels to a location relative to Wesker's current position, not the position of your opponent. This means that Phantom Move L will not always be in range to go behind the opposing character.

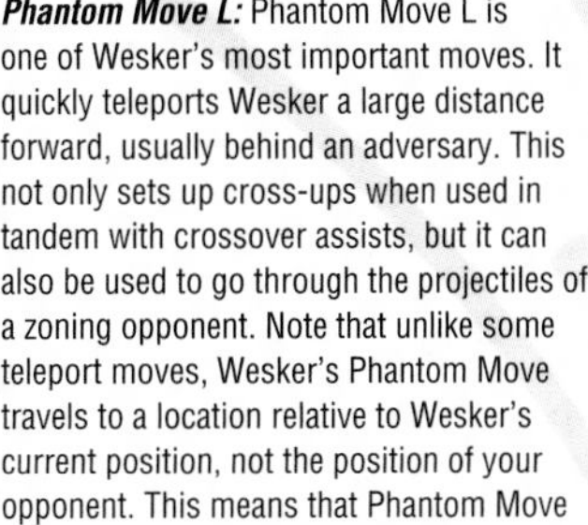

6

The air version of Phantom Move L has very lengthy recovery, and should be used only rarely as a sort of invincible air dash. Wesker does retain the ability to attack or block after emerging from the teleport, however.

Phantom Move M: Phantom Move M teleports Wesker backwards. It has no invulnerable frames, making it difficult to use effectively as anything other than a retreating move.

Use the air version of the Phantom Move M whenever you find yourself in a risky situation while jumping forward. For example, when jumping towards a She-Hulk player that is waiting to anti-air you with Taking out the Trash—use Phantom Move M to get out of danger!

7

8

Phantom Move H: Phantom Move H teleports Wesker diagonally up and forward. Wesker emerges from the teleport in mid-air, aligned to face whichever direction his opponent is, able to attack or guard on the way down. Phantom Move H does not travel as far horizontally as Phantom Move L, so at certain ranges you can set up a situation where Phantom Move H will not cross-up an opponent while Phantom Move L will.

The air version of Phantom Move H is very useful because it teleports Wesker to the ground almost instantly. This is great during super jumps to suddenly get the drop on your opponent, and also to set up resets after a launcher combo.

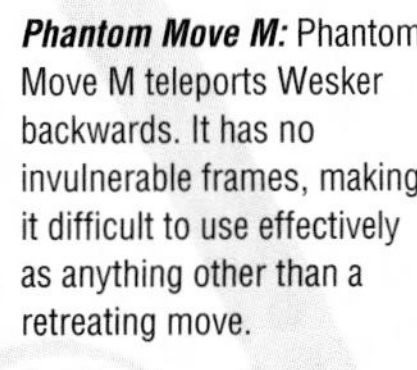

9

Tiger Uppercut L: Tiger Uppercut L is a counter move that will trigger against all high and mid attacks. While it leads to a launcher if hit, be aware that its 5 frame start up isn't particularly fast. In addition, the attack that gets automatically triggered by the counter isn't necessarily guaranteed; it comes out 18 frames after the point of impact, and is punishable by combos if guarded.

With that said, the Tiger Uppercut moves are still an invaluable part of Wesker's arsenal. When the attack is triggered Wesker will quickly teleport behind an adversary before attacking, so any foe not expecting to get countered will almost definitely block the launcher in the wrong direction. Calling a crossover assist before activating Tiger Uppercut can also help mitigate the risk of the attack being guarded, but you also risk getting both Wesker and the assist character hit by a full combo if your counter does not successfully trigger.

10

Tiger Uppercut M: Tiger Uppercut M is identical to the L version, except it triggers against low-hitting attacks.

11

Tiger Uppercut H: Tiger Uppercut H is an interesting move—it's a counter move that triggers versus projectiles! Upon triggering, Wesker will teleport forward about four character widths before performing a shoulder check that wall bounces an opponent. After emerging from the teleport, Wesker will automatically re-align with the opposing character and shoulder check in the proper direction. In other words, whether or not the shoulder check crosses up depends on the distance between Wesker and his adversary when the projectile was countered. This makes the Tiger Uppercut H more effective at closer ranges. If guarded, the shoulder check leaves Wesker at a considerable distance away from his challenger, making Tiger Uppercut H nearly impossible for some characters to punish afterwards. When facing these characters, Tiger Uppercut H against projectiles can be a great method to close the distance!

HYPER COMBOS

Screen	Name	Command	Hits	Damage	Startup	Active	Recovery	Advantage on Hit	Advantage on Guard	Notes
1	Phantom Dance (in air OK)	↓↘→ + ATK ATK	Max 16	299,200	10+1	—	40	—	—	All hits cause spinning knockdown
2	Rhino Charge	↓↙← + ATK ATK	1	250,000	5+0	16	28	—	—	Invincible from frames 1-5, counters high/mid/low attacks, puts the opponent in a crumple stun state where the opponent is still considered grounded, unrecoverable knockdown
3	Lost in Nightmares	→↓↘ + ATK ATK (Level 3 Hyper Combo)	12	450,000	6+8	5	30	—	-12	Invincible from frames 1-16, unrecoverable knockdown

Phantom Dance: While the Phantom Dance is easily used in combos in many situations, it will often miss many of the hits unless an opponent is right in the middle of the screen. This generally makes it an inefficient use of hyper combo gauge. It does have its uses, however. Each hit of the Phantom Dance leaves the opposition in a spinning knockdown state, making it easy to team hyper combo to another character. In addition, its raw speed makes it a good way to punish unsafe moves from across the screen. Note that Phantom Dance has no invulnerability frames at all.

Rhino Charge: The Rhino Charge has great potential: it counters all non-projectile attacks with a guaranteed, single-hit 250,000 damage combo starter! However, it's a little difficult to use. There are five frames of invincible start up before the counter activates. This means that attacks that would have made contact with you will go straight through, not triggering the counter! The simplest way to use Rhino Charge is to just consider it to have a 5 frame non-invincible start up, like his Tiger Uppercuts. This may be a little unintuitive if you have experience from other games with similar moves, but will lead to less frustration down the road.

Unlike Tiger Uppercut, Rhino Charge flashes a huge full-screen warning for your opponent that a counter move is incoming. Combined with the invincible 5 frame start up that potentially makes anticipated close-ranged attacks pass clean through, this makes Rhino Charge best used on reaction to predictable attacks from your opponent.

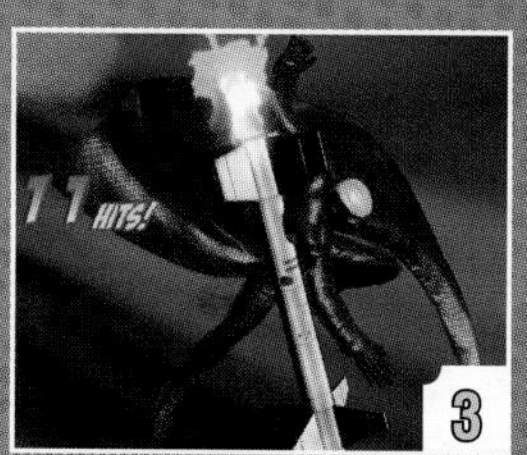

Lost in Nightmares: Wesker's level 3 hyper combo is among the most damaging in the game, at 450,000. Since level 3 hyper combos aren't subject to damage scaling, ending most of Wesker's combos with an OTG ↘ + Ⓗ gunshot with crossover assist, then tacking on Lost in Nightmares will result in 100% damage against many characters.

BATTLE PLAN

OVERVIEW

VITALITY: 1,100,000

CHAIN COMBO ARCHETYPE: MARVEL SERIES

X-Factor	Lv.1	Lv.2	Lv.3
Damage	133%	166%	199%
Speed	110%	120%	130%

Your goal with Wesker is to get into position to cross-up with Phantom Move L or H, with your primary crossover assist still available.

Why?

Wesker can use the crossover assist in tandem with Phantom Move to cross-up an adversary and score a combo.

Even if the cross-up attempt is guarded, you can establish point-blank range with Wesker quickly while your opponent is guarding the assist, then perform a mix-up between crouching Ⓛ and the Mustang Kick throw attack.

If your opponent attempts to guard your cross-up set-ups, you can simply attack from the front, or use that moment of hesitation to dash forward and land a Mustang Kick grab.

All of Wesker's combos can set up an OTG ↘ + Ⓗ, putting a foe in the air. When used in tandem with an assist, you can use Wesker to immediately put his target in another mix-up that your opponent can do little about besides guard in the proper direction.

Wesker does strong damage without requiring hyper combo gauge, and can K.O. most characters with a combo followed by a single successful mix-up.

How do you get Wesker into position to cross-up with Phantom Move?

Go through zoning projectiles using...Phantom Move L or H!

Super jump above the desired location and teleport down using...Phantom Move H!

Advance forward by hitting airborne opponents with → + Ⓗ and canceling into...Phantom Move L!

Counter defensive measures from your opponent by using...Tiger Uppercut L, M or H.

Note that none of these maneuvering tactics involve using a crossover assist for cover. Remember, your goal with Wesker is to get into cross-up Phantom Move range while you keep your primary assist available!

ON THE GROUND

Phantom Moves are used both as an offensive mix-up and as a method of maneuvering around your opponent's defenses.

Jumping opponents are more difficult to pin down, but successfully hitting them with ⇨ + Ⓗ can lead to a full combo.

Creative use of Tiger Uppercut is one of the keys to using Wesker effectively.

As mentioned before, you should be trying to move Wesker into range to cross-up your opponent with Phantom Moves, while still keeping an assist available. How you go about doing that depends on what your opponent is doing.

Against a defending opponent, use the methods outlined above in Wesker's overview. If a grounded foe is not giving you any projectiles to use Phantom Move or Tiger Uppercut, wavedash into the desired range while you look for sudden defensive measures to Tiger Uppercut against.

Opponents that jump around are a little more difficult to pin down. If you can successfully hit them with a ⇨ + Ⓗ gunshot, then you can teleport in with Phantom Move L and land a full juggle combo from the gunshot. However, if they guard the shot, your Phantom Move becomes unsafe, so you need to be careful. Using a long-ranged crossover assist before firing the ⇨ + Ⓗ will help mitigate the risk involved with this tactic. You'll also generally be close to your opponent at frame advantage due to your long-ranged assist. Use this situation to mix-up your opponent with Mustang Kick or crouching Ⓛ!

A safer, less aggressive option is to cancel the gunshot into Phantom Move H to cover a lot of ground, possibly even dropping right on top of your opponent if you were close enough. If your challenger isn't giving you any opportunities to tag them with a gunshot, simply dashing forward and guarding is a good way to push them backwards towards the corner. Keep your opponent honest about throwing defensive moves out by keeping Tiger Uppercut and Rhino Charge at the ready.

Offensive opponents are easier to deal with because they will typically come right into your desired range. There are two main points to remember in dealing with offensive characters: shutting down their ability to approach by air, and gaining enough space to safely call your assist and Phantom Move.

Wesker's anti-air options are fairly solid, but must be mixed up to keep them unpredictable. The typical answer for foes approaching via the air is to air throw them backwards, which leads into a full combo using OTG ⬂ + Ⓗ. Air throws can be throw escaped, so anti-airs should be varied to remain unpredictable. Tiger Uppercut Ⓛ is another strong option that leads into a full combo, but the launching attack typically isn't guaranteed against air attacks. However, most opponents usually won't be ready to block the launcher in the opposite direction. Rhino Charge is guaranteed if triggered and results in major damage if you want to spend the hyper combo gauge bar. Of course, it can be easily baited by opposing players. Crouching Ⓜ is low enough to go under many air attacks and is easily chained into a full combo. Ⓢ performed early enough will anti-air most things cleanly, but your foe is at a very awkward height to continue the launcher combo. Super jumping straight up after the launcher and doing a simple air Ⓜ, Ⓗ, Ⓢ combo is typically the most consistent solution. Against challengers empty jumping toward you to prevent getting hit by anti-airs, call your crossover assist and cross your challenger up with Phantom Move L!

Against a character with a heavy ground-based approach, try to create space for yourself with ⇨ + Ⓗ and air ⇩ + Ⓗ. Making contact with either one of these gunshots will buy you enough time to call a crossover assist and Phantom Move safely. Note that most characters can crouch completely under Wesker's ⇨ + Ⓗ gunshot. The only characters that cannot are M.O.D.O.K., Sentinel and Hulk.

Sporadically using Phantom Move H will allow you to counter attack certain attack patterns as well. Like most other situations, smart use of Phantom Move and Tiger Uppercut should solve most problems you come across. If things get too dicey, super jumping to safety or retreating with Phantom Move M are also strong options.

UP IN THE AIR

Phantom Move H is arguably Wesker's most useful move in the air.

Air ⇩ + Ⓗ is a strong tool for creating time to cross an attacking opponent up with Phantom Move.

Phantom Move M is very useful for emergency last-second maneuvers.

Wesker isn't at his best in the air. He doesn't have any typical aerial movement options, like a double jump or airdash, and he loses access to most of his special moves. The one special move he does have access to, Phantom Move, is severely weakened in the air. As such, his most useful move in the air is typically Phantom Move H, which puts him back on the ground almost instantly.

Wesker can still use Phantom Move L in the air to cross-up foes in a normal jump, but the lengthy recovery time of the air version of Phantom Move L will typically prevent you from landing a combo after the assist hits. In addition, Wesker does not emerge from air Phantom Move L automatically facing his opposition. If you do cross-up your adversary with Phantom Move L you'll have to wait all the way until Wesker lands to be able to attack.

Air ⬂ + Ⓗ is Wesker's most useful air attack, as it controls the space diagonally in front of Wesker very well. It also creates enough time to safely call a crossover assist and Phantom Move. In air-to-air duels, you'll typically want to use Wesker's air Ⓛ most often, since his other air attacks are relatively slow. However, given time and proper range, air Ⓜ and air Ⓗ both do very well at beating other air attacks.

COMBO USAGE

I. (MIDSCREEN ONLY) CR. Ⓛ, CR. Ⓜ, CR. Ⓗ CANCEL ↓↘→ + Ⓛ, DASH, ↘ + Ⓗ OTG, CR. Ⓜ, ST. Ⓗ (2 HITS) CANCEL ↓↘→ + Ⓜ CANCEL (DURING GHOST BUTTERFLY) Ⓗ, AIR Ⓗ, LAND, CR. Ⓗ, Ⓢ CANCEL SUPER JUMP, AIR Ⓜ, Ⓜ, Ⓗ, Ⓢ, DASH, ↘ + Ⓗ OTG

(515,200 damage) Wesker's standard combo does very solid damage without requiring any hyper combo gauge, and also sets up another mix-up. When falling from Phantom Move H, delay the air Ⓗ a bit so that your opponent will be lower, allowing you to squeeze in a bit more damage with Wesker's crouching Ⓗ. The final OTG gunshot leads into a strong mix-up on your opponent—see the Advanced Tactics section for details.

If your challenger is near the corner, canceling the Ghost Butterfly into Phantom Move H can result in some inconsistent situations. When near the corner it's better to sacrifice a little damage and simply do a crouching Ⓜ, crouching Ⓗ, Ⓢ chain instead of canceling into Phantom Move H. The modified combo near the corner does 504,900 damage.

II. →↘↓↙← + Ⓛ, → + Ⓗ, (DURING SAMURAI EDGE) Ⓛ, CR. Ⓜ, ST. Ⓗ (2 HITS) CANCEL ↓↘→ + Ⓜ CANCEL (DURING GHOST BUTTERFLY) Ⓗ, AIR Ⓗ, LAND, CR. Ⓗ, Ⓢ CANCEL SUPER JUMP, AIR Ⓜ, Ⓜ, Ⓗ, Ⓢ, DASH, ↘ + Ⓗ OTG

(371,600 damage) Very good damage for a no-meter, no-assist, midscreen, one-frame throw combo! Landing the initial → + Ⓗ takes a bit of getting used to; Mustang Kick L has practically no recovery at the end of it. Simply time the gunshot like you are canceling the second hit of the throw. Timing the Phantom Move early enough to be able to juggle crouching Ⓜ also may be tricky; if you're having trouble, just do a crouching Ⓛ first.

III. (CORNER REQUIRED) CR. Ⓛ, CR. Ⓜ, CR. Ⓗ CANCEL ↓↘→ + Ⓛ, DASH, ↘ + Ⓗ OTG, CR. Ⓜ, ST. Ⓗ (2 HITS), → + Ⓗ, CR. Ⓜ, CR. Ⓗ CANCEL ↓↘→ + Ⓛ, P1, ↘ + Ⓗ, ↓↘→ + Ⓜ, →↓↘ + ATK ATK

(981,700 damage, Iron Man—α) It's actually a bit harder for Wesker to do combo damage in the corner, due to the difficulty of continuing combos after the Ghost Butterfly wall bounce. The difference is marginal, however. Wesker's Lost in Nightmares is one of the most damaging level 3 hyper combos in the game, so ending any of his combos with it will typically K.O. most characters.

ASSISTS

Iron Man—α is useful in a wide variety of situations, but its many hits causes harsh damage scaling in combos.

Arthur—β significantly increases the damage from your crossover assist-using combos, but gives you a few less tools to work with compared to Iron Man's Unibeam.

She-Hulk—α is a low-hitting attack, allowing for situations where you can make your air Ⓗ out of Phantom Move H nearly impossible to guard.

Wesker's Samurai Edge (Lower Shot) assist is one of the best OTG-capable assists in the game. Its fast startup speed allows characters to OTG in situations that would otherwise be impossible, and is a strong asset to any team. It is also considered to be a low-hitting attack!

Ghost Butterfly is one of the few assist types in the game with the ability to wall bounce an opponent, and it can be used to increase the damage of characters that do not have access to a wall bounce normally. Jaguar Dash leaves your foe in a vulnerable spinning knockdown state, but will generally push a challenger too far away to easily get a combo after it. Its many hits also introduce a large amount of damage scaling into a combo.

Iron Man's UniBeam assist is great for Wesker's Phantom Move cross-ups; if you cancel any up-close move into Phantom Move L Wesker will end up far behind a midscreen opponent, making it difficult to land a combo after most crossover assists that hit. Iron Man's UniBeam pushes your opponent across the screen towards you while still leaving them on the ground, allowing you to perform combos without having to suddenly improvise. In addition, Unibeam creates enough hitstun to allow Wesker to combo after cross ups using the air version of Phantom Move L.

If the UniBeam attack is guarded, it still creates plenty of blockstun for you to dash forward and perform a mix-up between crouching Ⓛ and Mustang Kick, even if the opponent does an advancing guard.

Arthur's Dagger Toss performs largely the same role as the UniBeam assist. However, since Dagger Toss is only three hits, damage scaling doesn't hit Wesker's crossover assist combos as severely; Dagger Toss combos do about 150,000 more damage than Unibeam combos. The tradeoff is that Dagger Toss does not produce as much hitstun and blockstun as UniBeam, making it less well-rounded. For example, it is generally impossible to combo after a Dagger Toss cross up using the air version of Phantom Move L.

She-Hulk's Torpedo is a low attack. Combined with Wesker's Phantom Move H, set-ups can be created that are essentially impossible to guard. Set up properly, this can lead to practically-guaranteed combos in certain situations! See the Advanced Tactics section for details. As an added bonus, the third character on this team will have the option to perform double OTG combos using She-Hulk—α and Wesker—β!

IV. P1, →↓↘ + Ⓛ, CR. Ⓜ, CR. Ⓗ (CANCEL) ↓↘→ + Ⓛ, DASH, ↘ + Ⓗ OTG, CR. Ⓜ, ST. Ⓗ (2 HITS) (CANCEL) ↓↘→ + Ⓜ (CANCEL) (DURING GHOST BUTTERFLY) Ⓗ, AIR Ⓗ, LAND, CR. Ⓗ, Ⓢ (CANCEL) SUPER JUMP, AIR Ⓜ, Ⓜ, Ⓗ, Ⓢ, DASH, ↘ + Ⓗ OTG

(286,100 damage, Iron Man—α) Wesker's standard combo off of a crossover assist and Phantom Move cross-up. Strangely, even though Iron Man's UniBeam is 8 hits, it still doesn't cause much hit stun deterioration at all. This allows you to still do Wesker's full combo involving both Cobra Strike and Ghost Butterfly. Although the damage is scaled fairly severely from the UniBeam's 8 hits, the ease of landing this combo combined with the promise of a strong mix-up after more than makes up for it.

V. FORWARD AIR THROW, DASH, ↘ + Ⓗ OTG, CR. Ⓜ, ST. Ⓗ (2 HITS) (CANCEL) ↓↘→ + Ⓜ, (DURING PHANTOM MOVE) Ⓗ, AIR Ⓗ, LAND, CR. Ⓗ, Ⓢ (CANCEL) SUPER JUMP, AIR Ⓜ, Ⓜ, Ⓗ, Ⓢ, LAND, DASH, ↘ + Ⓗ OTG

(250,400 damage) Wesker can combo after air throws in either direction easily, without help from assists. Unfortunately, hitstun scaling has already deteriorated to the point where you cannot combo after a Cobra Strike without help from an assist, but at the very least you get respectable damage and an opportunity to mix up your opponent.

ADVANCED TACTICS

SET-UP AFTER HITTING ↘ + Ⓗ OTG

After ending a combo with a ↘ + Ⓗ OTG hit, your opponent recovers in the air. This gives you three possibilities to look out for: air recovery backwards, forwards, or not air recovering at all. Correctly guessing which one your opponent will do will give you an opportunity to place them in a very strong mix-up.

The most common reaction from an opponent is to air recover backwards. Midscreen, this allows you to cross-up your opponent by wavedashing twice. Call a crossover assist immediately after the ↘ + Ⓗ has completely finished recovering, then proceed with the wavedashes. The mix-up to this is simple: wavedashing twice at a greater speed reduces the amount of forward distance Wesker travels, allowing you to stay in front of your challenger!

Against a cornered opponent you cannot cross-up by wavedashing under them. Instead, use Phantom Move L or H after calling the crossover assist to get behind your adversary. To mix-up an opponent guarding in the opposite direction, simply dash forward and attack them from the front. In this situation it is nearly impossible to guard Phantom Moves on reaction—the opposing player must commit to guarding in the opposite direction before they even see the Phantom Move activate.

If She-Hulk is on your team, an opponent air recovering backwards puts them in position to get hit by an un-guardable set-up; see the following section for details.

If you correctly guess how your opponent will air recover after a ↘ + Ⓗ OTG hit, you can place your foe in a very strong mix-up!

If your opponent begins to air recover forward your options get a little weaker. In this situation you can crouch as your opponent passes over your head and place them in a mix-up of crouching Ⓛ or Mustang Kick as soon as they land. Air throwing your foe backwards is also an option, allowing you to land a full combo afterwards. Note that some characters can air recover forward and hit you with an air attack that has the ability to cross-up. You can counter this with Tiger Uppercut L or Rhino Charge, or you can dash forward after the ↘ + Ⓗ and anti-air your foe with standing Ⓗ from the opposite side. If it hits, cancel the standing Ⓗ into a Cobra Strike to convert the hit into a full combo.

If your opposition does not air recover at all, you must call your crossover assist simultaneously with the ↘ + Ⓗ shot, then cancel the shot into Phantom Move L or H.

If your foe successfully guards your crossover assist in any of these mix-ups, you can still salvage the situation by placing them in another immediately mix-up of crouching Ⓛ or Mustang Kick.

UN-GUARDABLE SET-UP USING SHE-HULK—α

If your adversary air recovers backwards after a ↘ + Ⓗ OTG shot, you can set up a practically un-guardable situation using a low-hitting crossover assist.

She-Hulk—α is a low-hitting crossover assist that has just the right amount of startup frames to allow you easily use it to hit simultaneously with an attack after Phantom Move H.

This is most easily set up after ending a combo with a ↘ + Ⓗ OTG shot. If your opposition air recovers backwards, it creates the perfect distance and timing to utilize this tactic: wait until the ↘ + Ⓗ attack has completely finished recovering, then press the partner button immediately before inputting the command for Phantom Move H. Drop down with air Ⓗ, then continue to juggle your challenger with a full combo!

Characters that can alter their trajectory in the air can escape this set-up. Almost all escapes can be countered if correctly predicted, but that information is very character-specific and is beyond the scope of this guide.

CROSS-UP SET-UPS USING PHANTOM DANCE

Timed a little early, Wesker's first rebound during Phantom Dance can be used to cross up your opponent!

After finishing a mid-screen combo with a ↘ + Ⓗ OTG hit, manually dash forward. If your opponent air recovers backwards, activate Phantom Dance while they are coming down—the Phantom Dance will strike your opponent in the back as Wesker rebounds off of the wall, crossing them up!

Timing the Phantom Dance activation slightly later (or earlier!) will result in your opponent getting hit in the front. The mix-up is practically impossible to predict for the defender!

The mix-up remains the same if your opposition air recovers forward; simply input the Phantom Dance in the other direction with the same timing. If your opponent guards the Phantom Dance it is almost completely safe; Wesker reappears on the other side of the screen.

Phantom Dance can be used as a cross-up whenever the first hit will miss; crossing opponents up that ground recover or even jump is very possible. However, there needs to be enough room on the screen for Wesker to get behind his adversary.

COMBO APPENDIX

GENERAL EXECUTION TIPS

Dash as far as possible after hitting Cobra Strike to be able to combo after the ⇘ + Ⓗ OTG mid-screen.

When canceling Ghost Butterfly into Phantom Move H, try to hit an opponent with air Ⓗ as late as possible.

Try performing the ⇨ + Ⓗ gunshot after Mustang Kick L before the kick even hits an opponent; you're much more likely to perform the shot too late than too early.

Requirements (Position, meter, etc.)	Notes	Command Sequence	Damage
Corner required	—	⇨⇘⇩⇙⇦ + Ⓛ, cr. Ⓜ, cr. Ⓗ CANCEL▶ ⇩⇘⇨ + Ⓛ, ⇘ + Ⓗ, cr. Ⓜ, st. Ⓗ (2 hits) CANCEL▶ ⇩⇘⇨ + Ⓜ, cr. Ⓜ, cr. Ⓗ, Ⓢ CANCEL▶ super jump, air Ⓜ, Ⓜ, Ⓗ, Ⓢ, land, dash ⇘ + Ⓗ OTG	392,800
She-Hulk—α	—	P1 or P2, ⇨⇩⇘ + Ⓗ, air Ⓗ, land, cr. Ⓜ, cr. Ⓗ CANCEL▶ ⇩⇘⇨ + Ⓛ, dash, ⇘ + Ⓗ OTG, cr. Ⓜ, st. Ⓗ (2 hits), Ⓢ CANCEL▶ super jump, air Ⓜ, Ⓜ, Ⓗ, Ⓢ, land, dash, ⇘ + Ⓗ OTG	503,800
—	Rhino Charge cause a large amount of hitstun deterioration; standard Cobra Strike combos involving a ⇘ + Ⓗ OTG will not work	⇩⇙⇦ + ATK ATK, cr. Ⓜ, cr. Ⓗ CANCEL▶ ⇩⇘⇨ + Ⓜ, (during Ghost Butterfly) Ⓗ, air Ⓗ, land, cr. Ⓗ, Ⓢ CANCEL▶ super jump, air Ⓜ, Ⓜ, Ⓗ, Ⓢ, land, dash, ⇘ + Ⓗ OTG	681,200
Against airborne opponent	—	⇨ + Ⓗ, (during Samurai Edge) Ⓛ, cr. Ⓜ, cr. Ⓗ CANCEL▶ ⇩⇘⇨ + Ⓛ, dash, ⇘ + Ⓗ OTG, cr. Ⓜ, st. Ⓗ (2 hits), Ⓢ CANCEL▶ super jump, air Ⓜ, Ⓜ, Ⓗ, Ⓢ, land, dash, ⇘ + Ⓗ OTG	491,300
—	—	⇦⇩⇙ + Ⓛ or Ⓜ CANCEL▶ super jump, air Ⓜ, Ⓜ, Ⓗ, Ⓢ, land, dash ⇘ + Ⓗ OTG	375,800
—	Tiger Uppercut H causes too much hitstun deterioration to use Cobra Strike	⇦⇩⇙ + Ⓗ, ⇨ + Ⓗ CANCEL▶ (during Samurai Edge) Ⓛ, cr. Ⓜ, cr. Ⓗ, Ⓢ CANCEL▶ super jump, air Ⓜ, Ⓜ, Ⓗ, Ⓢ, land, dash, ⇘ + Ⓗ OTG	482,600
Level 1 X-Factor	—	Cr. Ⓛ, cr. Ⓜ, cr. Ⓗ CANCEL▶ ⇩⇘⇨ + Ⓛ, dash, ⇘ + Ⓗ, cr. Ⓜ, st. Ⓗ (2 hits) CANCEL▶ ⇩⇘⇨ + Ⓜ, (During Ghost Butterfly) Ⓗ, air Ⓗ, land, cr. Ⓗ, Ⓢ CANCEL▶ super jump, air Ⓜ, Ⓜ, Ⓗ, Ⓢ, dash, OTG ⇘ + Ⓗ CANCEL▶ X-FACTOR, ⇨⇩⇘ + ATK ATK	1,113,700

"EVERYTHING IS ACCORDING TO PLAN.
I WILL BE A GOD."

Viewtiful Joe

BIO

REAL NAME

JOE

OCCUPATION

HIGH SCHOOL STUDENT, YOUNG HERO

ABILITIES

HIS VFX POWER GIVES HIM ABILITIES SIMILAR TO CAMERA EFFECTS SEEN IN MOVIES, SUCH AS THE ABILITY TO SLOW EVERYTHING DOWN ON SCREEN.

WEAPONS

UTILIZES VARIOUS WEAPONS, INCLUDING HIS VOOMERANG AND SHOCKING PINK BOMBS. WITH HIS BELOVED SIX MACHINE, AN AIRCRAFT CAPABLE OF TRANSFORMING INTO A ROBOT OR A CANNON, HE IS READY FOR ANY BATTLE.

PROFILE

BEFORE BECOMING VIEWTIFUL JOE, HE WAS JUST A 17-YEAR-OLD WHO LOVED THE MOVIES. HIS GIRLFRIEND SILVIA OFTEN BECAME ANGRY OVER HIS IMMATURE WAYS.

FIRST APPEARANCE

VIEWTIFUL JOE (2003)

"OH, CRAP! I'M LATE FOR MY DATE WITH SYLVIA! SHE'S GONNA KILL ME!"

POWER GRID

3	INTELLIGENCE
4	STRENGTH
5	SPEED
4	STAMINA
1	ENERGY PROJECTION
5	FIGHTING ABILITY

*This is biographical, and does not represent an evaluation of the character's in-game combat potential.

ALTERNATE COSTUMES

PS3: ⓧ Xbox 360: Ⓐ

PS3: ◻ Xbox 360: Ⓧ

PS3: △ Xbox 360: Ⓨ

PS3: R1 Xbox 360: RB

ATTACK SET

STANDING BASIC ATTACKS

Screen	Command	Hits	Damage	Startup	Active	Recovery	Advantage on Hit	Advantage if Guarded	Notes
1	Standing L	1	38,000	4	3	11	-2	-3	Rapid fire, chains into standing L
2	Standing M	1	50,000	7	3	17	-3	-4	—
3	Standing H	1	65,000	9	3	21	-1	-3	⇩ ⬃ ⇨ + P1 or P2 snap back
4	S	1	70,000	8	3	23	—	-5	Launcher, not special or hyper combo cancelable

CROUCHING BASIC ATTACKS

Screen	Command	Hits	Damage	Startup	Active	Recovery	Advantage on Hit	Advantage if Guarded	Notes
1	Crouching L	1	35,000	5	3	10	-1	-2	Low attack, rapid fire
2	Crouching M	1	48,000	8	3	17	-3	-4	Low attack, chains into standing M
3	Crouching H	1	60,000	9	13	21	—	-13	Low attack, knocks down

AERIAL BASIC ATTACKS

Screen	Command	Hits	Damage	Startup	Active	Recovery	Notes
1	Air L	1	38,000	5	3	15	—
2	Air M	1	50,000	7	3	20	—
3	Air H	1	65,000	8	4	24	—
4	Air S	3	64,200	9	8	24	Unrecoverable knockdown when used in air combo after S launcher

ZERO

"I'M NOT ARROGANT, BUT I DON'T MAKE MISTAKES. I JUST CUT DOWN MY ENEMIES."

BIO

REAL NAME

ZERO

OCCUPATION

MAVERICK HUNTER

ABILITIES

HAS GREAT PHYSICAL ABILITY AS WELL AS EXCELLENT SKILLS WITH A VARIETY OF WEAPONS. HE IS ABLE TO LEARN THE ABILITIES OF THE ENEMIES HE DEFEATS AND ADDS THEM TO HIS EXISTING ARSENAL, MAKING HIM EVEN STRONGER THAN BEFORE.

WEAPONS

HIS PRIMARY WEAPONS ARE THE Z-SABER, AN ENERGY SWORD, AND HIS ZERO BUSTER, A WEAPON CAPABLE OF FIRING ENERGY SHOTS.

PROFILE

EVER SINCE BEING FOUND IN A CAVE BY SIGMA, HE HAS WORKED TIRELESSLY AS A MAVERICK HUNTER. BENEATH HIS COOL EXTERIOR LIES AN EXTREME INTOLERANCE FOR EVIL; ONCE HE GETS INTO A FIGHT WITH A MAVERICK, HE WON'T STOP UNTIL HIS ENEMY HAS BEEN MERCILESSLY CUT DOWN. HE IS BEST FRIENDS WITH X OF THE MAVERICK HUNTERS' 17TH ELITE UNIT.

FIRST APPEARANCE

MEGA MAN X (1993)

POWER GRID

5	INTELLIGENCE
5	STRENGTH
5	SPEED
3	STAMINA
5	ENERGY PROJECTION
7	FIGHTING ABILITY

*This is biographical, and does not represent an evaluation of the character's in-game combat potential.

ALTERNATE COSTUMES

PS3: ⨂ Xbox 360: Ⓐ

PS3: ▢ Xbox 360: Ⓧ

PS3: △ Xbox 360: Ⓨ

PS3: R1 Xbox 360: RB

ATTACK SET

STANDING BASIC ATTACKS

Screen	Command	Hits	Damage	Startup	Active	Recovery	Advantage on Hit	Advantage if Guarded	Notes
1	Standing Ⓛ	1	35,000	5	3	12	-2	-3	—
2	Standing Ⓜ	2	53,000	7	3	19	-4	-5	—
3	Standing Ⓗ	3	64,200	11	10	16	+1	0	—
4	Ⓢ	1	80,000	9	5	22	—	-5	Launcher attack, not special or hyper combo cancelable

CROUCHING BASIC ATTACKS

Screen	Command	Hits	Damage	Startup	Active	Recovery	Advantage on Hit	Advantage if Guarded	Notes
1	Crouching Ⓛ	1	30,000	4	2	11	0	-1	Low attack
2	Crouching Ⓜ	1	56,000	8	3	20	-5	-6	Low attack
3	Crouching Ⓗ	1	70,000	13	5	18	+3	-1	Knocks down

AERIAL BASIC ATTACKS

Screen	Command	Hits	Damage	Startup	Active	Recovery	Notes
1	Air Ⓛ	1	33,000	5	3	12	Overhead attack
2	Air Ⓜ	1	55,000	8	3	19	Overhead attack
3	Air Ⓗ	3	64,200	10	18	15	Overhead attack, can only chain into air Ⓢ
4	Air Ⓢ	1	75,000	13	9	17	Overhead attack , causes flying screen if used in launcher combo

COMMAND ATTACKS

Screen	Command	Hits	Damage	Startup	Active	Recovery	Advantage on Hit	Advantage if Guarded	Notes
1	⇨ + Ⓗ	3	77,100	14	7	17	+5	+4	Chains from any basic attack, ⇩ ⬃ ⇨ + P1orP2 snap back
2	(in air) ⇩ + Ⓗ	3	64,200	9	18	9	—	—	Reverses the direction Zero spins, , can only chain into air Ⓢ

1

2

AS A PARTNER-CROSSOVER ASSISTS

Screen	Type	P1+P2 Crossover Combination Hyper Combo	Description	Hits	Damage	Startup	Active	Recovery (this crossover assist)	Recovery (other partner)	Notes
1	α – Alpha	Rekkoha	Ryuenjin H	5	102,300	29	25	117	87	Knocks down
2	β – Beta	Rekkoha	Hadangeki M	1	70,000	32	—	127	97	Projectile has 3 low priority durability points
3	γ – Gamma	Rekkoha	Shippuga (⇨ + Ⓗ)	3	81,200	37	7	110	80	—

1

2

3

ZERO

SPECIAL MOVES

Screen	Name	Command	Hits	Damage	Startup	Active	Recovery	Advantage on Hit	Advantage if Guarded	Notes
1	Hadangeki L	↓↘→ + L	1	70,000	17	—	25	-1	-2	Projectile has 3 low priority durability points
	Hadangeki M	↓↘→ + M	1	70,000	8	—	34	-7	-8	Projectile has 3 low priority durability points
2	Hadangeki H	↓↘→ + H	2	104,500	13	—	34	-7	-8	Each projectile has 3 low priority durability points
3	Ryuenjin L	→↓↘ + L	1	70,000	5	9	24	-9	-11	Knocks down
	Ryuenjin M	→↓↘ + M	3	81,200	5	15	21	-4	-10	Knocks down
	Ryuenjin H	→↓↘ + H	5	102,300	5	25	21	-6	-20	Knocks down
4, 5, 6	Raikousen	(in air) →↓↘ + ATK	5	102,300	30	15	8~until grounded, 1 frame ground recovery	—	—	Knocks down airborne opponents, can pass through opponent
7	Hienkyaku L	↓↙← + L	—	—	29	—	—	—	—	Can pass through opponents
8	Hienkyaku M	↓↙← + M	—	—	39	—	—	—	—	Can pass through opponents
9	Hienkyaku H	↓↙← + H	—	—	27	—	—	—	—	Can pass through opponents
10	Air Hienkyaku L	(in air) ↓↙← + L	—	—	Until grounded	—	1	—	—	Can pass through opponents
11	Air Hienkyaku M	(in air) ↓↙← + M	—	—	25	—	—	—	—	Can pass through opponents
12	Air Hienkyaku H	(in air) ↓↙← + H	—	—	26	—	—	—	—	Can pass through opponents
13	Sentsuizan L	(in air) ↓↘→ + L	—	—	16	—	—	—	—	—
14	Sentsuizan M	(in air) ↓↘→ + M	1	60,000	13	Until grounded	8	+12 or less	+11 or less	OTG-capable
	Sentsuizan H	(in air) ↓↘→ + H	1	80,000	18	Until grounded	8	+12 or less	+11 or less	OTG-capable
15, 16, 17, 18, 19, 20	Hyper Zero Blaster (can be charged, in air OK)	ATK (hold down)	1/1/3	40,000/ 70,000/ 108,300	5	—	23	-6/-4/—	-7/-5/+2	Levels 1/2/3 must be charged for 30/70/150 frames respectively, level 3 gains beam properties, Level 3 unrecoverable knockdown, projectile has 2/4 low priority durability points, beam durability: 3 frames x 3 low priority durability points

Hadangeki L/M

Hadangeki H

Hadangeki: Hadangeki is one of two projectiles in Zero's arsenal. The most useful version is Hadangeki L which has the slowest traveling speed and the best recovery. Zero can actually dash behind his Hadangeki L and use it to start a combo if his opponent is far enough away when he starts. Against foes with poor zoning tools, this can force them into the air, where Zero has strong options to deal with them.

Hadangeki can also be used to zone to a limited degree. Repeated Hadangeki L usage can be difficult for some opponents to deal with. There is little gap between the projectiles, so it will likely force most opposing characters into the air.

Ryuenjin: Ryuenjin lacks the invincibility frames of similar moves such as Shoryuken to be used to stop an opponent's offensive pressure. Ryuenjin does have a fairly fast startup at 5 frames, so it can be a last resort in a defensive situation, if you use an assist that can cover your recovery time beforehand. Even so, Ryuenjin will see little use outside of a few combos. This attack is very unsafe when blocked and does not provide enough benefit when it does hit to be worth the risk.

Raikousen L

Raikousen M

Raikousen H

Raikousen: Raikousen L will be a staple in your launcher combos when you have time to charge Hyper Zero Blaster to level 3. When used after a fully charged Hyper Zero Blaster in the air, it will cause an opponent to fall to the ground, providing an opportunity to go into another launcher combo. Outside of combos, Raikousen L can be used if you expect an anti-air from your opponent and can lead into a combo. However, it has slow startup, making it risky if your foe decides to attack you in the air. Raikousen M and H are completely vulnerable until landing, making them even more dangerous to use.

Hienkyaku L

Hienkyaku M

Hienkyaku H

Air Hienkyaku L

Air Hienkyaku M

Air Hienkyaku H

Hienkyaku: Hienkyaku is a key element to Zero's offense. It is his primary means of countering advancing guard and creating difficult to block situations for opponents. However, it lacks any invincibility frames and Zero requires a good assist to cover him during the teleport. For Hienkyaku L & M, look for assists that can keep an opposing character from attacking you safely while you teleport. For Hienkyaku H, an assist that has a low attack can make for a difficult to block situation. In the air, Hienkyaku L can be used to quickly get to the ground and Hienkyaku H can be used to further extend your time in the air.

Sentsuizan L *Sentsuizan M & H*

Sentsuizan: Sentsuizan is Zero's main OTG special, even though he will need an assist to extend the combo. Sentsuizan M has faster startup, but causes less damage than Sentsuizan H. The version that you need to use will depend on how much time you have to connect with an OTG and when your assist will hit. Practicing Sentsuizan with any assists you plan to use will be crucial for combo mastery with Zero.

Sentsuizan L is a feint that mimics the start up of Sentsuizan M & H, but it does not have an actual attack and it recovers quickly. You can cancel air Ⓛ and Ⓜ with Sentsuizan L to stay airborne slightly longer to possibly create mix-up situations.

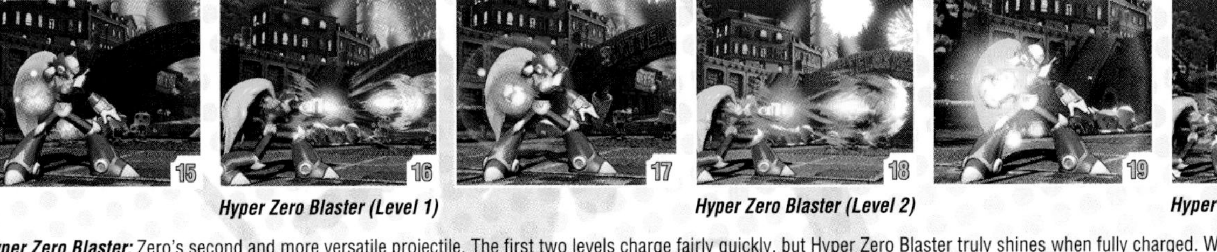

Hyper Zero Blaster (Level 1) *Hyper Zero Blaster (Level 2)* *Hyper Zero Blaster (Level 3)*

Hyper Zero Blaster: Zero's second and more versatile projectile. The first two levels charge fairly quickly, but Hyper Zero Blaster truly shines when fully charged. When fully charged, it causes a much sought after unrecoverable knockdown. This is useful in long combos where hitsun deterioration becomes an issue. Zero should have little problem reaching a full charge during a combo as long as he has 1 assist that can either extend his ground chain or allow a second launcher after Zero's OTG. When using Hyper Zero Blaster in a launcher combo, the combo can be extended with a Raikousen L anywhere on the screen, and can be followed up by a Hienkyaku L only in the corner.

While any ATK button can be held down to charge his Hyper Zero Blaster, Ⓛ is the ideal button to use to charge during combos. The Hyper Zero Blaster will remain charging as long as at least one ATK button is held down, so it is possible to alternate holding down different ATK buttons during combos!

HYPER COMBOS

Screen	Name	Command	Hits	Damage	Startup	Active	Recovery	Advantage on Hit	Advantage if Guarded	Notes
1	Rekkoha	⇩⇘⇨ + ATK ATK	30	269,300	16+21	69	29	+2	-13	OTG-capable, knocks down, beam durability: 30 frames x 1 high priority durability points
2	Sougenmu	⇩⇙⇦ + ATK ATK	—	—	10+0	—	3	—	—	Frames 9-10 invincible, creates a shadow of Zero that mimics Zero 16 frames later, shadow lasts 300 frames, using any hyper combo will cause the shadow to disappear
3	Genmu Zero (Level 3 hyper combo)	⇨⇩⇘ + ATK ATK	1	350,000	10+1	—	66	—	-36	Frames 1-24 invincible, unrecoverable knockdown, projectile has 100 high priority durability points

Rekkoha: Rekkoha should primarily be used as an OTG finishing hyper combo. The lack of invincibility frames, as well as the long startup and recovery, make it impractical for most other uses. Rekkoha can be used in nearly any OTG situation provided that you have ample time to execute it. The most common usage is after a launcher combo that ends with flying screen. Grounded or airborne opponents who are hit by Rekkoha will slowly be lifted upwards during the beam.

Even though Rekkoha has a long startup, the beam remains active for a long time regardless of Zero's state. You can then chain a team hyper combo or cancel the move with X-Factor almost immediately after the startup animation. One example would be to use Rekkoha on a grounded opponent and X-Factor cancel as soon you see the beam, then link into Genmu Zero while Rekkoha's beam is hitting the opposing character and lifting them up.

Sougenmu: Sougenmu is a great tool for creating extra pressure on your opponent. It can be used as a makeshift replacement for an assist in covering Zero's Hienkyaku (though not as effective as a proper assist), or used to create difficult to block situations through jumping attacks, likely air Ⓢ, followed by an immediate low attacks. This causes the shadow's attacks to hit as an overhead, while Zero hits with a crouching Ⓛ that hits low at the same time. The additional attacks also create new and interesting combo opportunities!

Sougenmu is also a fairly safe hyper combo to chain into, if a teammate's unsafe hyper combo is blocked. Zero also retains his Sougenmu power up if a new character becomes the point character while Sougenmu is still active.

Genmu Zero: Genmu Zero is Zero's only attack with significant invincibility frames. It costs 3 hyper combo gauges and is not subject to damage scaling. However, it has a lengthy recovery, so it is only a last resort defensive measure. It is not too difficult to land in a combo, because it is fairly quick. The most common uses in a combo will be after an X-Factor cancel from Rekkoha, or on an opponent who is falling to the ground.

Genmu Zero actually fires one of the strongest projectiles in *Marvel vs. Capcom 3*. Combined with invincibility frames, it will defeat nearly any projectile or beam attack in the game, even hyper combos! If another character ever uses a beam or projectile hyper combo against you on the ground and outside of a combo, input Genmu Zero's command during the hyper combo animation and chances will be good that you just scored 350,000 damage.

BATTLE PLAN

OVERVIEW

VITALITY: 800,000

CHAIN COMBO ARCHETYPE: MARVEL

X-Factor	Lv.1	Lv.2	Lv.3
Damage	125%	150%	175%
Speed	111%	122%	133%

Your goal with Zero is to apply pressure to your opponent at close range as much as possible. If possible, you should pressure your opponent all the way into the corner.

Why should a Zero player attempt to constantly pressure an opponent?

Zero has many mix-up options that can lead to an opponent not blocking correctly. Hienkyaku L and M can be used with cover from assists to ambiguously cross up a foe or regain lost ground from advancing guard. Hienkyaku H can be used in tandem with low hitting assists to create near impossible to block situations. Sougenmu's shadow can be used to also create difficult to block situations.

Zero has excellent combo options from anywhere on the screen. However, a cornered opponent will have an even harder time stopping Zero's offense.

Zero's zoning tools are not strong enough to warrant a zoning game.

Zero has relatively low vitality and weak defensive options. It is important to play this character offensively to offset this disadvantage.

How does Zero get and stay within range to apply constant pressure?

Follow Hadangeki L as a relatively safe way to being pressure or to force your opponent into the air.

Use Zero's airdash and excellent air basic attacks to gain air superiority to force your opponent to stay on the ground.

Once you are within range, use Hienkyaku with assists or Sougenmu to create mix-up opportunities.

If an opponent uses advancing guard against you, use Hienkyaku L and M with assist coverage to regain lost ground and continue pressure.

Zero's natural forward momentum during his combos will ensure his opponents quickly reach the corner during combos.

ON THE GROUND

Hadangeki L is great to lead the way. Zero's dash moves very fast and covers a large distance, making it great to follow the slow Hadangeki L.

Many of Zero's ground basic attacks are fairly quick, have many active frames, occupy large amounts of space, and his primary ground ender (⇨ + Ⓗ) has frame advantage even when blocked.

Hienkyaku is a key part of Zero's sustained offense. Intelligent use of his Hienkyaku will make it difficult for opponents to get out of a defensive position and mount an effective offense against Zero.

Zero's role on a team is very versatile. He is an excellent point character for players who want to play an aggressive, rushdown style right from the beginning. Zero can fill either the role of meter-builder or meter-user. He can also be used to mount an effective offense with little meter usage, but meter can be used to increase his damage, or compound the pressure that you can create with his mix-up offense. Furthermore, Zero can make an excellent assist for any team by activating his Sougenmu attack and finding a way to safely tag in your desired character. Zero's assists become incredibly powerful with Sougenmu active; namely Shippuga to shore up gaps in other team members' offenses and Hadengeki to assist zoning characters. Zero will retain his power-up state indefinitely until he becomes the point character again. At that point the power-up timer will continue to tick down as normal.

You should maintain a constant offense with Zero because of his low vitality and his decreased zoning ability. Zero has a tough time dealing with zoning characters. His projectiles are too slow and too weak to effectively counter a dedicated zoning opponent. Against zoning characters, you need to either rely on a very strong projectile assist, or take to the air to get Zero close to an opponent.

Against non-zoning characters with a poor air offense, Hadangeki L can be used from full screen as an effective method of creating an opening to begin an offense. Zero can follow his projectile in and even begin a combo if the projectile hits. Be careful about using this attack too often against opponents with excellent air mobility options, because the startup and recovery on Hadangeki is somewhat lengthy.

At close to mid range, Zero's attacks will dominate the space in front of him. All of his Z-Saber basic attacks extend past Zero's body, making it risky for opponents to attack and leaving him relatively safe. Any landed attack can easily be hit-confirmed and converted into a highly damaging combo. If Zero's attacks are blocked, you can use assists with his Hienkyaku to continue pressure, counter advancing guard, or create mix-up opportunities. Hienkyaku can be used to get behind opponents while being covered by an assist, or create high/low mix-up with low hitting assists. Once you are on offense, you will want to maintain that momentum as long as possible.

Against airborne opponents, Zero's options are limited on the ground. Standing Ⓗ can be used early if your opponent is attacking from a shallow angle, but has almost no coverage for foes who can attack from steeper angles or who can airdash or double jump behind him. If you see your opponent make an attempt to get behind Zero during his attack, you can attempt to immediately cancel into a Hienkyaku L or M to regain a better position. Zero is better used by taking him to the air to fight against airborne opponents. His basic attacks dominate most opponents in the air.

If you are put on defense by another aggressive character, your best option a majority of the time is to use advancing guard to push your opponent away from you and attempt to use Zero's and high priority attacks to regain the offensive momentum. If you become really desperate, you can attempt Genmu Zero, but be aware that you will be vulnerable if your foe avoids or blocks your attack.

UP IN THE AIR

Zero's air H and air ↓ + H are amazing air attacks that can attack in all directions, making it both a strong air-to-air and air-to-ground attack.

Zero's airdash gives him excellent mobility and is a great tool to close in on zoning characters on the ground.

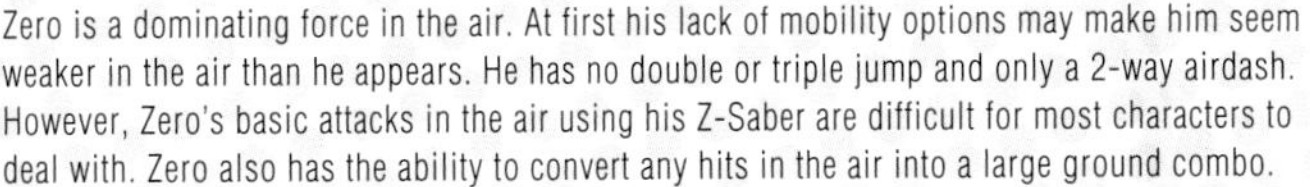

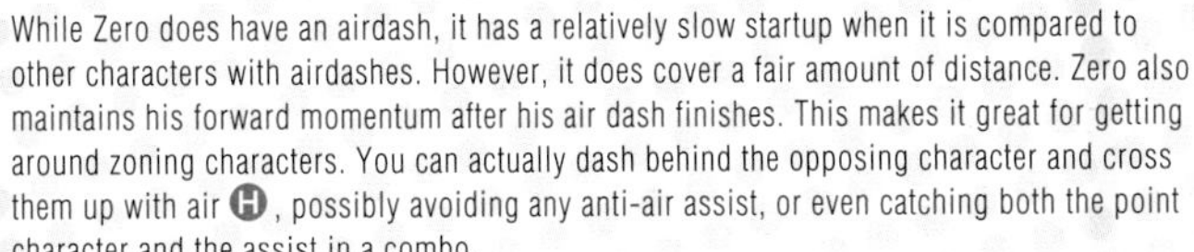

Zero is a dominating force in the air. At first his lack of mobility options may make him seem weaker in the air than he appears. He has no double or triple jump and only a 2-way airdash. However, Zero's basic attacks in the air using his Z-Saber are difficult for most characters to deal with. Zero also has the ability to convert any hits in the air into a large ground combo.

While Zero does have an airdash, it has a relatively slow startup when it is compared to other characters with airdashes. However, it does cover a fair amount of distance. Zero also maintains his forward momentum after his air dash finishes. This makes it great for getting around zoning characters. You can actually dash behind the opposing character and cross them up with air H, possibly avoiding any anti-air assist, or even catching both the point character and the assist in a combo.

Zero's air throw leads to fairly easy and damaging combo opportunities when used with proper assists.

All of Zero's air basic attacks are fairly good, but two stand out in particular. Air H and air ↓ + H cause Zero to spin with his Z-Saber extended, causing the attack to hit in all directions in a small circle around him. While these are not the fastest basic attacks in the game, they are both fairly fast for an air H attack, and both stay active for 18 frames! This means that you can use this move early in anticipation of air-to-air or air-to-ground situations and win a majority of the time. Against airborne opponents, these attacks can easily be hit confirmed because of the large amount of active frames and the fact that they have multiple hits. Either of these attacks can be chained into an air S in any non-launcher, air combo to keep your opponent in airborne hitsun slightly longer, giving him time to land and continue the combo on the ground.

Zero's air H has added effectiveness because you can hold → or ← while pressing H in the air. If your foe attempts to meet you in the air, you may end up throwing them. If it is during a normal jump, you can airdash (if it has not been used already), call an assist and use Sentsuizan M or H to OTG your opponent into your assist and continue the combo. If you throw during a super jump, things become more difficult. You'll have to Hienkyaku L to land quickly and call an assist while dashing immediately and doing an OTG. She-Hulk—α makes a great assist for Zero because she will OTG with her assist at just the right time, making it easier to convert throws into combos.

COMBO USAGE

I. CR. Ⓛ(HOLD Ⓛ), CR. Ⓜ, CR. Ⓗ, → + Ⓗ(RELEASE Ⓛ, HOLD Ⓗ), ST. Ⓛ(RELEASE Ⓗ, HOLD Ⓛ), ST. Ⓜ, ST. Ⓗ (3 HITS), → + Ⓗ (3 HITS), Ⓢ CANCEL SUPER JUMP, AIR Ⓜ, Ⓜ, RELEASE Ⓛ, → ↓ ↘ + Ⓛ, LAND, Ⓢ CANCEL SUPER JUMP, AIR Ⓜ, Ⓜ, Ⓗ (3 HITS), Ⓢ, LAND, ↓ ↘ → + ATK ATK

(588,000 damage) Zero's → + Ⓗ has increased frame advantage against airborne opponents, allowing you to link standing Ⓛ afterwards. In this combo, crouching Ⓗ is used to put an opponent in an airborne state. The tricky part is that you need to both charge and use all three ATK buttons in the combo, so you can't just hold one button down through the whole combo. The secret to doing this is holding each button down at points indicated when you make the attack, but do not release the button as you normally would. As you hold a new ATK button down, you can release the other button right after it. It may seem difficult at first, but with practice it should become fairly easy. If you still have difficulty with this method of charging, you can simply charge with Ⓛ and use an assist to extend the early part of the ground combo. The timing will depend on the assist, but usually you will either have to call it right before or right after you start the first → + Ⓗ, then continue with Ⓜ, Ⓗ, Ⓢ. You'll need to be patient and make sure all three hits of Ⓗ hit before chaining to → + Ⓗ.

After the first Ⓢ launcher, delay your first air Ⓜ slightly so you are high enough with all three hits of Hyper Zero Blaster. Use Raikousen L as soon as possible after Hyper Zero Blaster to give yourself the most possible time to relaunch. After the second launcher combo use Rekkoha as soon as you land or else you will miss your OTG window.

While the above combo can be modified any number of ways, it contains the core of Zero's combo system. Zero's multi-hitting moves and the large frame advantage given by → + Ⓗ give you time to easily hit confirm combos, charge Zero's Hyper Zero Blaster, and create extended ground combos. Hyper Zero Blaster allows for an unrecoverable knockdown state which allows Raikousen with its lengthy startup to juggle. Raikousen will keep an opponent in the air longer and guarantee they will continue to fall until grounded. It also moves Zero closer to both the ground and his opponent, ensuring that he is in position to continue the combo with another launcher. This Hyper Zero Blaster, Raikousen link decreases Zero's reliance on assists to create extended combos, allowing you to choose assists that improve his pressure offense against blocking opponents.

You can X-Factor cancel Rakkoha as soon as the beam forms and link Genmu Zero for 1,081,600 damage.

II. JUMP, AIR THROW (HOLD Ⓛ), P1 or P2, LAND, DASH, JUMP, AIR Ⓜ, Ⓗ (2 HITS), Ⓢ, LAND, ST. Ⓜ, ST. Ⓗ (3 HITS), → + Ⓗ (3 HITS), Ⓢ CANCEL SUPER JUMP, AIR Ⓜ, Ⓜ, RELEASE Ⓛ, → ↓ ↘ + Ⓛ, LAND, Ⓢ CANCEL SUPER JUMP, AIR Ⓜ, Ⓜ, Ⓗ (3 HITS), Ⓢ, LAND, ↓ ↘ → + ATK ATK

(542,900~584,00, She-Hulk—α) Zero's air throws are fairly easy to convert into full combos for good damage. She-Hulk—α is an ideal assist to OTG after Zero's air throws, since you can press it immediately after the throw and her low attack will OTG at the perfect time. Many assists will work, but most will require the use of Sentsuizan M or H after the dash to OTG so the assist can hit. Certain assists may not allow for the air Ⓜ, Ⓗ, Ⓢ chain after the assist hits. In those cases, simply omit that part of the combo. You should still have enough time to fully charge Hyper Zero Blaster by the time you need it.

ASSISTS

Low hitting assists like She-Hulk—α can be used with Zero's Hienkyaku H to create nearly unblockable setups.

Multi-hit projectile assists such as Arthur—β help to protect Zero during his Hienkyaku L and M, allowing him to maintain constant pressure on his opponents.

Zero powered up with Sougenmu makes an incredibly powerful assist for nearly any teammate.

All of Zero's assists can be useful, but β Hadangeki and γ Shippuga are arguably his two best assists, especially when powered up with Sougenmu.

β Hadangeki is a decent projectile assist for zoning characters such as Arthur. By itself, it is somewhat lackluster. If you can manage to power up with Sougenmu and safely switch out with another zoning character, you suddenly have a powerful multi-hit projectile assist.

γ Shippuga will find better use on a team with aggressive partners who need help stopping up gaps in their offense, or to help lock an opponent down. Again, once powered up with Sougenmu, this move becomes much stronger, adding several active frames to the assist, and allowing for more gaps in your block strings.

Zero does not necessarily need an assist to provide OTG opportunities, but they certainly don't hurt. More importantly, Zero needs an assist that causes enough hitsun for you to continue his combos after an OTG and come out quick enough to hit after his OTG. Several characters in the cast can fill this role with their assists. So, many assists that can help out other aspects of Zero's game can be used in this regard.

Since Zero relies so heavily on maintaining momentum, you should choose assists that can shore up gaps in his offense and protect his Hienkyaku L and H. Beam and multi-hit projectile assists work particularly well, such as Iron Man—α or Arthur—β. Multi-hitting assists with forward momentum can work well too. These assists should be timed to be active during Hienkyaku, since this is when Zero is the most vulnerable.

Low hitting assists in combination with Hienkyaku H, canceled from a series of blocked attacks, can be used to make nearly impossible to block situations. She-Hulk—α is a prime example of this because the slow startup gives Zero's Hienkayku H time to finish, and allows for nearly simultaneous low and high attacks.

III. ↓↙← + ATK ATK, AIR Ⓗ (3 HITS), CR. Ⓛ(HOLD Ⓛ), CR. Ⓜ, ST. Ⓗ (3 HITS), → + Ⓗ, ST. Ⓜ, ST. Ⓗ (3 HITS), → + Ⓗ, ST. Ⓜ, ST. Ⓗ (3 HITS), → + Ⓗ (3 HITS), Ⓢ CANCEL SUPER JUMP, AIR Ⓜ, Ⓜ, RELEASE Ⓛ, →↓↘ + Ⓛ, LAND, Ⓢ CANCEL SUPER JUMP, AIR Ⓜ, Ⓜ, Ⓗ (3 HITS), Ⓢ, LAND, ↓↘→ + ATK ATK

(756,100 damage) A combo after a Sougenmu high/low mix-up, Zero hits low while the shadow is still attacking with an overhead, making it very difficult to block. The combo can easily be hit confirmed and converted into a high damage combo. The timing on this combo is fairly tight, especially while your foe is still on the ground. The → + Ⓗ, Ⓜ, Ⓗ link requires particularly strict timing. You'll have to press the buttons quickly to get your combo.

If you have difficulty with linking the ground chains, one repetition can be removed for about 100,000 less damage. This combo does become **much** easier in the corner because your shadow will get more hits, create more hitsun, and making your links easier to pull off.

IV. AIR Ⓗ (3 HITS), Ⓢ, LAND, ST. Ⓛ(HOLD Ⓛ), ST. Ⓜ, ST. Ⓗ (3 HITS), → + Ⓗ(RELEASE Ⓛ, HOLD Ⓗ), ST. Ⓛ(RELEASE Ⓗ, HOLD Ⓛ), ST. Ⓜ, ST. Ⓗ (3 HITS), → + Ⓗ (3 HITS), Ⓢ CANCEL SUPER JUMP, AIR Ⓜ, Ⓜ, RELEASE Ⓛ, →↓↘ + Ⓛ, LAND, Ⓢ CANCEL SUPER JUMP, AIR Ⓜ, Ⓜ, Ⓗ (3 HITS), Ⓢ, LAND, ↓↘→ + ATK ATK

(591,700 damage, airborne opponent) You can convert Zero's air hits into full combos—in non-launcher combos. This combo works better the closer your opponent is to the ground, but it works in most situations. You want your foe to be slightly above Zero when you hit with Ⓢ. When you land, you want Ⓛ to hit when the opposing character is as low as possible to ensure full damage from Ⓗ and → + Ⓗ. Again, you can use an assist if the button swapping for charging Hyper Zero Blaster is difficult, or just skip the Hyper Zero Blaster part of the combo.

V. CR. Ⓛ, CR. Ⓜ, CR. Ⓗ, → + Ⓗ (3 HITS) CANCEL X-FACTOR (HOLD L), ST. Ⓜ, ST. Ⓗ (3 HITS), → + ST. Ⓗ (3 HITS), ST. Ⓜ, Ⓗ, → + Ⓗ, Ⓢ CANCEL SUPER JUMP, AIR Ⓜ, Ⓜ, RELEASE Ⓛ, →↓↘ + Ⓛ, LAND, Ⓢ CANCEL SUPER JUMP, AIR Ⓜ, Ⓜ, Ⓗ (3 HITS), Ⓢ, LAND, ↓↘→ + ATK ATK

(1,207,400 damage, level 1 X-Factor) X-Factor is a huge boon to Zero, since he has many multi-hit basic attacks. This has the drawback of scaling damage on combos back quite a bit. With X-Factor's damage boost and lessened damage scaling, this makes Zero's combos pack a much bigger punch!

With the increased speed from X-Factor, new combo potential is unlocked. This combo is remarkably similar to **Combo I**, but you'll notice that you can use standing Ⓜ now to link after → + Ⓗ. This, on top for the speed increase, allows more Ⓜ, Ⓗ, → + Ⓗ repetitions before the launcher without making the relaunch combo impossible.

It is worth noting that level 2 and 3 X-Factor cause → + Ⓗ to only hit twice instead of three times. This is not an issue because of the increased speed, but you'll have to be aware of that and follow up with attacks slightly faster after → + Ⓗ.

ADVANCED TACTICS

BAITING ADVANCING GUARD

Opponents will try to constantly use advancing guard against Zero.

If you notice an excessive use of advancing guard, you can use that to land a counterhit and start a combo!

Playing Zero is a constant struggle to maintain offensive momentum. Advancing guard will be one of your biggest obstacles to this goal. However, it can be used to your advantage. Opponents who excessively use advancing guard against you can be tricked into leaving themselves open. If you watch for players who abuse this mechanic with abandon, you can adjust your offense slightly to account for this.

Most players will be used to Zero's multi-hitting Ⓗ attacks and attempt to use advancing guard against them. If you notice that your opponent uses advancing guard a lot during these times, you should call your assists earlier so that they would normally hit during your standing Ⓗ. Instead of using Ⓗ, cancel an attack like Ⓜ into a Hienkyaku. Watch as your opponent tries to advancing guard against this maneuver. When this happens their character attacks and leaves them vulnerable to Zero who is either above or behind their character.

Another option is to simply stop attacking in the middle of your blocked chain when you are far enough out of risk of being attacked by a normal attack. Wait for a moment then use standing Ⓗ— you may get a counterhit and free combo!

COMBO APPENDIX

GENERAL EXECUTION TIPS

To ensure maximum damage, allow standing (H) and → + (H) to land all hits before chaining to the next move unless otherwise specified.

Whenever you are charging Hyper Zero Blaster, hold down the button specified as you push the corresponding attack instead of releasing it.

You will want to use Rekkoha as soon as possible in OTG situations.

Requirements (Position, meter, etc.)	Notes	Command Sequence	Damage
—	Similar to Combo I in Combo Usage section, but with no Hyper Zero Blaster	Cr. (L), cr. (M), cr. (H), → + (H), st. (L), st. (M), cr. (H), → + (H), st. (L), st. (M), st. (H) (3 hits), → + (H) (3 hits), (S) CANCEL → super jump, air (M), (M), (H) (3 hits), (S), land, ↓ ↘ → + ATK ATK	(527,200 damage)
Arthur—β	Similar to **Combo I**, but uses a crossover assist to allow one button charge	cr. (L) (hold (L)), cr. (M), st. (H) (3 hits), P1 or P2, → + (H), st. (M), st. (H) (3 hits), → + (H) (3 hits), (S) CANCEL → super jump, air (M), (M), release (L), → ↓ ↘ + (L), land, st. (M), st. (H) (3 hits), → + (H) (3 hits), (S) CANCEL → super jump, air (M), (M), (H), (S), land, ↓ ↘ → + ATK ATK	648,500
Level 3 X-Factor	Slightly modified X-Factor combo to take advantage of added speed and make less use of the weakened → + (H)	Cr. (L), cr. (M), cr. (H), → + (H) (3 hits) CANCEL → X-FACTOR (hold l), jump, air (M), (H) (3 hits), (S), land, st. (M), st. (H) (3 hits), → + (H) (3 hits), (S) CANCEL → super jump, air (M), (M), release (L), → ↓ ↘ + (L), land, st. (M), (S) CANCEL → super jump, air (M), (M), (H) (3 hits), (S), land, ↓ ↘ → + ATK ATK	1,711,200
Level 1 X-Factor, 4 hyper combo gauges	Flashy looking combo that uses both Sougenmu and X-Factor, and a level 3 hyper combo.	Cr. (L), cr. (M), cr. (H), → + (H) (3 hits) CANCEL → ↓ ↙ ← + ATK ATK, st. (L), st. (M), st. (H) (3 hits), → + (H) CANCEL → X-FACTOR, jump, air (M), (H) (2 hits), (S), land, jump, air (M), (H) (2 hits), (S), land, jump, air (M), (H) (2 hits), (S), land, st. (M), (S) CANCEL → super jump, air (M), (M), release (L), → ↓ ↘ + (L), land, → ↓ ↘ + ATK ATK	1,444,600

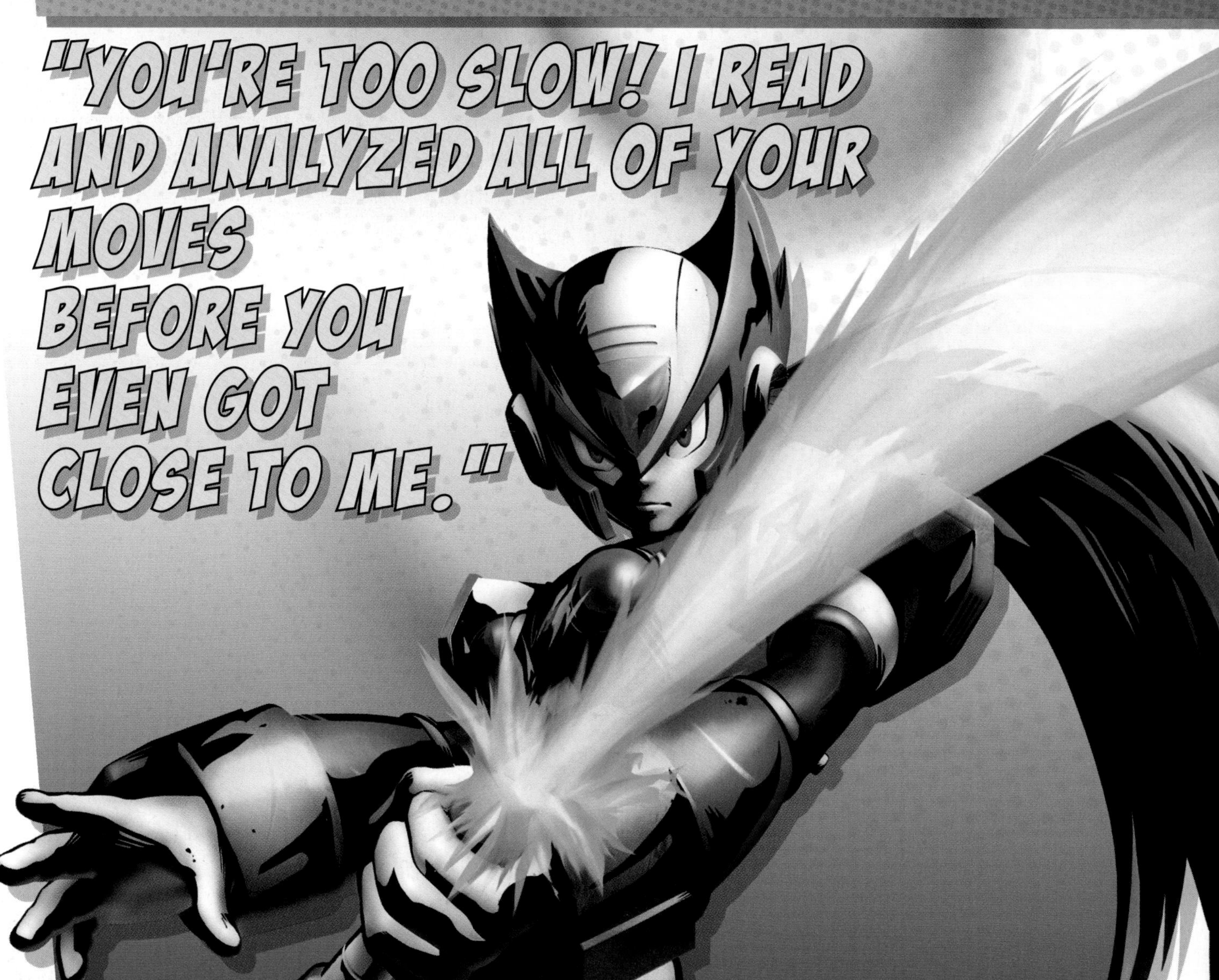

"YOU'RE TOO SLOW! I READ AND ANALYZED ALL OF YOUR MOVES BEFORE YOU EVEN GOT CLOSE TO ME."

SENTINEL

BIO

REAL NAME

SENTINEL

OCCUPATION

MUTANT HUNTER

ABILITIES

THE SENTINEL'S STRONG, GIANT METAL BODY BOASTS INCREDIBLE POWER. IT ALSO HAS THE ABILITY TO FLY AND TRACK DOWN MUTANTS.

WEAPONS

ITS PRIMARY WEAPONS ARE THE LASER BLASTS (A SPECIAL GENE SCRAMBLER) IT CAN FIRE FROM BOTH HIS PALMS, AS WELL AS ITS FINGERTIPS. IT CAN ALSO RELEASE KNOCKOUT GASES.

PROFILE

A ROBOT MUTANT HUNTER DEVELOPED BY BOLIVER TRASK, A SCIENTIST WHO FELT THAT MUTANTS WERE BECOMING A THREAT TO MANKIND. WITHOUT DEVELOPING THEIR OWN ARTIFICIAL INTELLIGENCE, THEY DUTIFULLY OBEY THEIR ORDERS, NO MATTER WHO GIVES THEM.

FIRST APPEARANCE

THE X-MEN #14 (1965)

"RESISTANCE IS FUTILE. ACCEPT YOUR EXTERMINATION."

POWER GRID

1	INTELLIGENCE
6	STRENGTH
3	SPEED
6	STAMINA
6	ENERGY PROJECTION
4	FIGHTING ABILITY

*This is biographical, and does not represent an evaluation of the character's in-game combat potential.

ALTERNATE COSTUMES

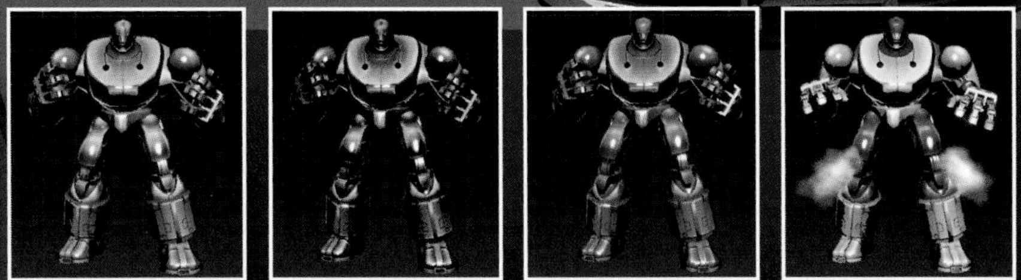

PS3: ⨂ Xbox 360: (A)

PS3: ▢ Xbox 360: (X)

PS3: △ Xbox 360: (Y)

PS3: R1 Xbox 360: RB

ATTACK SET

STANDING BASIC ATTACKS

Screen	Command	Hits	Damage	Startup	Active	Recovery	Advantage on Hit	Advantage if Guarded	Notes
1	Standing Ⓛ	1	70,000	7	3	28	-12	-15	Nullifies low priority projectiles during active frames
2	Standing Ⓜ	1	70,000	14	3	32	-11	-15	Super armor from frames 6-15, nullifies medium priority projectiles during active frames, ⇩ ⇘ ⇨ + P1⇔P2 snap back
3	Standing Ⓗ	5	102,300	20	20	17	+6	-11	Hits full-screen in 26 frames, chains to crouching Ⓗ, deals chip damage, beam durability: 5 frames x 2 low priority durability points
4	Ⓢ	1	120,000	16	8	26	—	-8	Launcher, not super or hyper combo cancelable, hyper armor from frames 12-21, nullifies medium priority projectiles during active frames

1

2

3

4

CROUCHING BASIC ATTACKS

Screen	Command	Hits	Damage	Startup	Active	Recovery	Advantage on Hit	Advantage if Guarded	Notes
1	Crouching Ⓛ	1	70,000	9	3	25	-9	-12	Nullifies low priority projectiles during active frames
2	Crouching Ⓜ	3	97,600	13	3(1)4(1)4	30	—	-14	Low attack, super armor from frames 6-15, hits close range at 13 frames, mid range at 17 frames, nullifies medium priority projectiles during active frames
3	Crouching Ⓗ	5	103,600	20	19	17	+6	-11	Hits full-screen in 26 frames, deals chip damage, beam durability: 5 frames x 2 low priority durability points

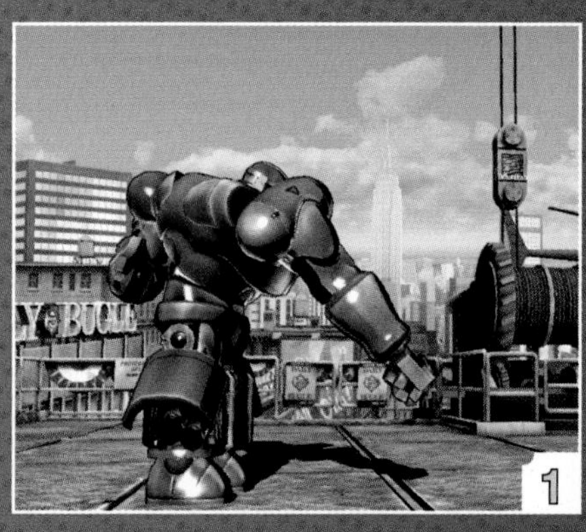
1

2

3

AERIAL BASIC ATTACKS

Screen	Command	Hits	Damage	Startup	Active	Recovery	Notes
1	Air Ⓛ	1	75,000	8	6	22	Overhead attack, double jump cancelable, nullifies low priority projectiles during active frames
2	Air Ⓜ	1	100,000	12	4	32	Overhead attack, double jump cancelable, nullifies medium priority projectiles during active frames
3	Air Ⓗ	1	110,000	17	4	28	Overhead attack, nullifies medium priority projectiles during active frames
4	Air Ⓢ	1	120,000	18	5	23	Overhead attack, ground bounces opponent, , nullifies medium priority projectiles during active frames, causes flying screen when used in launcher combo

1

2

3

4

AS A PARTNER-CROSSOVER ASSISTS

Screen	Type	P1+P2 Crossover Combination Hyper Combo	Description	Hits	Damage	Startup	Active	Recovery (this crossover assist)	Recovery (other partner)	Notes
1	α – Alpha	Hyper Sentinel Force	Sentinel Force L	3	135,000	45	—	147	117	Launches 3 projectile drones with 4 low priority durability points each, drones disappear if Sentinel is hit
2	β – Beta	Hyper Sentinel Force	Sentinel Force H	3~10	67,700~162,400	79	—	113	83	OTG-capable, 3 drones drop 5 bombs each, each projectile has 1 low priority durability point
3	γ – Gamma	Plasma Storm	Rocket Punch L	1	130,000	42	8	131	101	Knocks down, OTG-capable, nullifies medium priority projectiles during active frames

1

2

3

SPECIAL MOVES

Screen	Name	Command	Hits	Damage	Startup	Active	Recovery	Advantage on Hit	Advantage if Guarded	Notes
1	Rocket Punch L	↓↘→ + L	1	150,000	18	8	38	—	-20	Knocks down, OTG-capable, nullifies medium priority projectiles during active frames
2	Rocket Punch M	↓↘→ + M	1	150,000	18	8	38	—	-20	Knocks down, nullifies medium priority projectiles during active frames
3	Rocket Punch H	↓↘→ + H	1	150,000	18	8	38	—	-20	Knocks down, nullifies medium priority projectiles during active frames
1	Air Rocket Punch L	↓↘→ + L	1	150,000	16	8	32	—	-14	Knocks down, OTG-capable, nullifies medium priority projectiles during active frames
2	Air Rocket Punch M	↓↘→ + M	1	150,000	18	8	32	—	-14	Knocks down, nullifies medium priority projectiles during active frames
3	Air Rocket Punch H	↓↘→ + H	1	150,000	18	8	32	—	-14	Knocks down, nullifies medium priority projectiles during active frames
4	Sentinel Force L	↓↙← + L	3	135,400	21	—	54	33	+26	Launches 3 projectile drones with 4 low priority durability points each, drones disappear if Sentinel is hit
5	Sentinel Force M	↓↙← + M	3	135,400	21	—	54	+30	+27	Launches 3 projectile drones with 4 low priority durability points each, drones disappear if Sentinel is hit
6	Sentinel Force H	↓↙← + H	1~15	25,000 per bomb	55	—	31	+30	+25	OTG-capable, 3 drones drop 5 bombs each, each projectile has 1 low priority durability point
7	Human Catapult L	→↓↘ + L	1	120,000	2	1	43	—	—	Throw attack, causes unrecoverable knockdown
7	Human Catapult M	→↓↘ + M	1	140,000	6	1	39	—	—	Throw attack, causes unrecoverable knockdown
7	Human Catapult H	→↓↘ + H	1	160,000	10	1	35	—	—	Throw attack, causes unrecoverable knockdown
8	Flight (in air OK)	↓↙← + S	—	—	16	—	—	—	—	Enters or exits Flight mode, Flight lasts 104 frames

1
Rocket Punch L

2
Rocket Punch M

3
Rocket Punch H

Rocket Punch: Sentinel's signature attack can be performed both on the ground and in the air. Sentinel's fist propels violently out from its arm, at one of three angles—diagonally downward, straight forward, or diagonally upward, depending on the button used. The range is slightly further than half-screen distance, and longer for the straight-ahead M version than the diagonal versions. Rocket Punch will be interrupted if Sentinel is struck during the attack, but both the fist, and the piston on which it extends, have no vulnerable hitboxes! Additionally, Rocket Punch will destroy any low priority projectiles it touches during active frames (with the notable exception of Chris's Grenade Toss M and H). If Rocket Punch strikes a medium priority projectile, like Arthur's Golden Lance, the hitbox on both Rocket Punch and the other medium priority attack will be mutually negated.

The primary application of Rocket Punch is to use the L version, whether on the ground or in the air, to OTG foes after unrecoverable knockdowns. Sentinel can score unrecoverable knockdowns by causing flying screen with air S during a launcher combo, after Human Catapult or normal throw, or after hitting with an assist like Haggar—α. Rocket Punch on the ground is also great for extending combos from successful mid range H mouth lasers. Nearly any hit Sentinel lands can lead to a Rocket Punch, which can then be canceled into one of Sentinel's hyper combos for additional damage. If you land close range hits, however, it's better to chain into S launcher rather than using a Rocket Punch—air combos end up building more hyper combo gauge while dealing more damage, and you'll end up fitting Rocket Punch L into the combo later anyway, to OTG after flying screen!

As an exception to this, you can usually link Rocket Punch M or H after landing either Hard Drive or Hyper Sentinel Force in a corner. Of course, from a Rocket Punch that links after a hyper combo, you can cancel into yet another hyper combo. Plasma Storm works best in this situation, as Hyper Sentinel Force may not combo, or only the top layer of drones may hit.

You may be tempted to use Rocket Punches as pokes, or to end blocked chains, but this is not a great idea—when guarded, all versions of Rocket Punch are unsafe. If your opponent uses advancing guard to push you away, you're probably OK. However, smart foes will know that most of Sentinel's close range offense is punishable when blocked, and will probably opt ***not*** to advancing guard, so they can take advantage. Against an attentive opponent, hyper combo cancel to Hyper Sentinel Force from blocked ground Rocket Punches to make them safe. Better yet, don't rely on Rocket Punches as close range pokes or blocked chain finishers to begin with.

Air Rocket Punch L is a little safer as a poke than ground Rocket Punches, especially when backed by a crossover assist. Call an assist that takes up much of the screen at ground level, then input ↓↘→↗ + L to perform air Rocket Punch L just off the ground. If the Rocket Punch hits your foe, especially if it hits an assist, hyper combo cancel into Hard Drive for severe damage. If you anticipate that your opponent may start super jumping out of the way, expecting your "tiger knee" Rocket Punch L, use the H version to intercept their escape path.

Sentinel Force L

Sentinel Force M

Sentinel Force L & M: Sentinel summons three smaller Sentinel drones, which travel across the screen. The difference between Ⓛ and Ⓜ versions is strictly in the angle of attack. Sentinel Force L directs the drones to start at Sentinel's shoulders and travel downward, eventually striking the ground. Sentinel Force M directs the drones to start from the ground, before traveling slightly upward on a diagonal path.

Sentinel Force L and M behave uniquely for projectile attacks. The drones are individual threats that are separate from Sentinel; in this respect they resemble other standard projectiles, like Ryu's Hadoken. Yet the drones all disappear instantly if Sentinel is hit while the drones are onscreen—even if Sentinel has fully recovered from summoning the drones and is free to move! In this way the drones behave like a beam. No other projectile behaves quite this way. This restriction applies to the version of Sentinel Force M used during Sentinel—α, as well—if partner Sentinel is hit after drones are summoned but before he leaps off-screen, the drones will simply vanish.

In spite of the disappearing act that happens if Sentinel is struck, Sentinel Force L/M is Sentinel's most important ranged attack. Sentinel is free to move 75 frames after the command for Sentinel Force is completed, and the drones occupy a huge horizontal area of the screen for a very long time. If you can successfully get drones onscreen without Sentinel being interrupted, you create a huge opportunity. Your opponent will be forced to deal with the drones and Sentinel! Against passive foes you can use the drones as cover, wavedashing forward alongside the drones to start your offense.

If your foe tries to nullify Sentinel Force drones with their own ranged attacks, you can deal with this by backing the drones up with more ranged threats of your own. For example, you can perform Ⓗ mouth laser (either standing, or crouching, or even standing chained to crouching if your foe blocks) while calling a long range crossover assist like Iron Man—α, then simply cancel lasers into calling yet more drones—there is no restriction on calling more drones while a previous instance of Sentinel Force remains on screen! While some characters can deal with this backed with their own crossover assists, like Arthur, Dormammu, Doctor Doom, or Iron Man, most characters will simply be overwhelmed. The recourse for most characters will be to take to the skies, avoiding the drones entirely, but Sentinel is hardly uncomfortable taking the battle to the air. If you don't feel like leaving the ground, you can reposition while your opponent is airborne and use Sentinel Force to summon more drones for them to land on wherever they're eventually forced to return to the ground.

The angle of Sentinel Force M (and the Sentinel—α assist) means that an opponent at full screen can simply crouch under the drones, avoiding the issue entirely. This can backfire on them if you use the opportunity to wavedash forward and throw them, either with a normal throw or Sentinel's Human Catapult. As a mix-up, you can also opt to wavedash forward, then jump and go for overhead air Ⓗ, Ⓢ. This is kind of a sluggish overhead, but the nature of Sentinel's air Ⓗ (it has no vulnerable hitbox on Sentinel's foot) means that assists your opponent calls to protect their character will be snuffed. Air Ⓗ, Ⓢ on hit leads to a huge combo, and although this overhead isn't fast, your foe must respect it—meaning that if you wavedash forward and use crouching Ⓜ to hit low behind the drones, you may catch them unaware!

The deficiency of both Sentinel Force L and M is simply that they take a bit of time to summon. In a long range firefight, characters such as Iron Man and Doctor Doom can easily outgun Sentinel and either destroy all the drones outright, or hit Sentinel with their beams before the drones even become a threat to them. As a result, you should not summon Sentinel Force on its own, without cover. Ideally, you should precede Sentinel Force by insuring that your foe is forced to guard standing or crouching Ⓗ while you also call a long range crossover assist to provide even more protection. This helps insure that when you use Sentinel Force, you'll actually summon drones successfully. Of course, if you are seeking to use Sentinel Force to greet an airborne opponent you know will be forced to land soon, simply perform the move on its own.

Sentinel Force H: This variation of Sentinel Force summons three drones that fly across the screen quickly at around the level of Sentinel's head. Each drone releases five small bombs, essentially carpet-bombing the center of the playing field. The advantages of Sentinel Force H over the other versions are that the bombing drones themselves cannot be destroyed, and the attack is not interrupted if Sentinel takes a hit. The disadvantages are that Sentinel Force H takes twice as long as Sentinel L or M to create active onscreen threats, and the damage is likely to be lower with successful hits, since landing even half of the 15 bombs is very unlikely. Also, since Sentinel Force H only saturates the center of the screen, it doesn't threaten full screen foes. If a nearby opponent is hit by Sentinel Force H, however, Sentinel recovers and is free to act fast enough for you to combo with Ⓢ launcher at close range, or Rocket Punch at mid range.

Human Catapult: Sentinel's command throw. The higher the strength, the farther an opponent is hurled, and the damage is increased by the throw. Higher strengths have a much longer startup, however; while Human Catapult L is active in 2 frames, same as a normal throw, Human Catapult H takes 10 frames to grab, a veritable eternity for a grab.

Human Catapult L can essentially replace your use of normal throws on the ground; all versions of Human Catapult have significantly longer range than a normal throw, and command throws are inescapable. The only caveat is that Human Catapult L tosses a foe too far away at mid-screen to guarantee a follow-up; with normal throws, whether forward or backward, you can at least dash and OTG with Rocket Punch L. You can get around this by calling certain crossover assists just as you attempt Human Catapult L. For example, if you call Iron Man—β just before the command grab, Sentinel will hurl an opponent as normal, but they'll immediately be caught in Iron Man's Repulsor Blast, allowing you to continue with the combo of your choice. Even if you don't use a preemptive assist call to combo after mid-screen Human Catapult, it's not sour grapes—your opponent is hurled a huge distance toward the corner, and meanwhile you're assured a risk-free summon of Sentinel Force L or M.

Near corners, the story changes considerably. Rocket Punch L easily OTGs after Human Catapult L into the corner, and Human Catapult M and H get a lot more interesting. Sentinel tosses his foe so high into the air for either Ⓜ or Ⓗ versions that you can follow-up with a full combo, unassisted! After Human Catapult M, standing Ⓜ can juggle the target, which can then chain into Ⓢ launcher, and then an air combo. After Human Catapult H, possibilities are much more open. Visit the Combo Usage section for details.

It might seem like Human Catapult H has far too long a startup period to use successfully, and on its own that's true. You can make this lengthy startup work, however, by canceling into Human Catapult H late from close range basic attacks! Characters stuck in guardstun or hitstun cannot be thrown, so you don't want to cancel into Human Catapult H from close range attacks right away—instead, wait a few beats before canceling. With proper timing, Human Catapult H can arrive at its active, grabbing frame just as your foe leaves hitstun or guardstun, and can be thrown. Mid-screen, the only follow-up you're guaranteed after Human Catapult H is a standing Ⓗ laser, but in the corner you can follow the hefty toss with combos that exceed 500,000 damage without using any hyper combo gauge, or surpassing 800,000 if you're willing to burn some meter!

Flight: Sentinel's yellow rocket jets turn blue, and Sentinel can maneuver freely in mid air. With the possible exceptions of Iron Man and M.O.D.O.K., Sentinel has the most important Flight mode to its general gameplan. Sentinel moves very quickly during Flight, and is actually a smaller target than it is while standing, since Sentinel's legs retract into its body. While blocking isn't possible during Flight, Sentinel also has the largest vitality pool of the cast, making it a lot more reasonable for Sentinel to take aggressive risks while flying than, say, Phoenix. Basic attacks, including Ⓗ lasers, can be canceled into Flight for both offensive and defensive purposes. Canceling basic attacks with both Flight activation and deactivation can be used to extend air combos greatly. Finally, Sentinel's air basic attacks are invulnerable on the hitting portions that project away from Sentinel's body, making it very difficult, or impossible, for other characters to successfully win air-to-air or ground-to-air exchanges against Sentinel's limbs.

HYPER COMBOS

Screen	Name	Command	Hits	Damage	Startup	Active	Recovery	Advantage on Hit	Advantage if Guarded	Notes
1	Plasma Storm	↓↘→ + ATK ATK	20	282,000	10+1	81	26	—	-8	Knocks down opponent, beam durability: 20 frames x 3 high priority durability points
2	Hard Drive	↓↘→ + ATK ATK (in air)	12	275,400	10+2	42(1)13	In recovery until landing	—	—	Frames 1-70 invincible, last hit causes spinning knockdown that ignores hitstun deterioration
3	Hyper Sentinel Force	↓↙← + ATK ATK	9	306,000	10+4	—	83	—	+13	Frame 8-14 invincible, knocks down opponent, 9 projectiles with 3 high priority durability points each

Plasma Storm: Plasma Storm is intended as a combo finisher, primarily after using a grounded Rocket Punch L to OTG a floored foe. It's also generally the best hyper combo to team hyper combo to Sentinel from a teammate, if you've landed a hyper combo with a teammate that puts your opponent in a place that Plasma Storm will reach—it also tends to be the best hyper combo to use to start THCs with Sentinel, since the opposing character will be positioned in the center of the screen, perfect for handing off a team hyper combo to most partners. Plasma Storm can also be linked in the corner after both of Sentinel's other hyper combos! (You can simply link into Plasma Storm on its own, or link into Rocket Punch M or H first, then cancel to Plasma Storm for extra oomph.) These are the best uses of Plasma Storm. There are generally stronger options for solo Sentinel combos mid-screen or post-OTG. Plasma Storm is also not safe if guarded; use Hyper Sentinel Force if you need to use a hyper combo for chip damage or safety.

Hard Drive (in air): Hard Drive is Sentinel's most threatening attack, and you should look for opportunities to land it whenever possible. It has a lengthy laundry list of gross advantages. It's invulnerable during active frames, it travels so fast and so far that it can cross from one corner all the way to the other, it does solid damage, and the last hit causes a spinning knockdown. These factors come together to insure that almost any time you land Hard Drive fully you will corner your foe, with the ability to tack on more damage!

The most common (and useful) situation in which you can land Hard Drive is either after an air Rocket Punch in an air combo, or after an unrecoverable knockdown. Remember that air Rocket Punch L OTGs, just like the ground version—dash (or wavedash, if far away) forward after flying screen (or a throw, with the right positioning), perform air Rocket Punch L just off the ground with the "tiger knee" motion (↓↘→↗ + Ⓛ), then hyper combo cancel into Hard Drive! Mid-screen you'll want to cancel from air Rocket Punch L to Hard Drive immediately; in the corner it's better to wait a split second. The reason for this is that the only issue with Hard Drive is that sometimes, due to Sentinel's extreme velocity (and various character sizes and possible positions when the hyper combo actually starts hitting), opposing characters may fall out of Hard Drive before the last hit. By either canceling immediately after the OTG from mid-screen, or pausing slightly in the corner before canceling, you'll get more consistent results. It's also generally better for Hard Drive to strike characters lower in altitude rather than higher up.

The spinning knockdown produced by Hard Drive ignores hitstun deterioration. After carrying your opponent into the corner with an initial Hard Drive, it's actually possible to continue linking "tiger knee" (↓↘→↗) Hard Drives over and over again until you either run out of hyper combo gauge, the opposing character is knocked out, or the last hit of a given Hard Drive misses! You can also capitalize on the Hard Drive spinning knockdown by linking Rocket Punch M or H canceled into Plasma Storm. Ⓢ launcher will link as well, but hitstun deterioration means that worthwhile, basic attack, air combo follow-ups are close to impossible.

Hyper Sentinel Force: This is Sentinel's safest hyper combo; cancel into it off of blocked Rocket Punches to chip your foe and prevent them from punishing you. It's also the best hyper combo to use to THC Sentinel in safely from a partner whose hyper combo was guarded.

Hyper Sentinel Force also works well in combos—just like Plasma Storm, Hyper Sentinel Force easily combos after grounded Rocket Punch L, whether in a normal combo or after an OTG. Land Hyper Sentinel Force mid-screen, and you can often tack on standing Ⓗ for good measure. Land Hyper Sentinel Force in the corner and you can immediately either launch with Ⓢ, link into Rocket Punch M or H canceled to Plasma Storm, or link into "tiger knee" Hard Drive!

Hyper Sentinel Force is also an incredible assist killer. Opponents who are guarding Hyper Sentinel Force, but who have called an assist into the fray, will virtually guarantee that their partner takes at least 60% red damage, since damage against partners is not affected by damage scaling when the point character who called them is blocking! The assist character is basically eating nine separate drones, without damage scaling! Against many assists, you can simply activate Hyper Sentinel Force on reaction when you see the assist come on screen.

Finally, any combo that leads into Hyper Sentinel Force can become a knockout blow with X-Factor, even at outlandish range. Immediately after starting Hyper Sentinel Force, cancel with X-Factor, then immediately activate Flight. Fly forward, and as the last wave of drones hits your foe, combo air Ⓗ, Ⓢ. Air Ⓢ will both cause a ground bounce, and force Sentinel to land. From here, launch your target with Ⓢ and finish them off with an air combo.

"ALL THREATS TO HUMANITY HAVE BEEN TERMINATED."

BATTLE PLAN

OVERVIEW

VITALITY: 1,300,000

CHAIN COMBO ARCHETYPE: 2-HITS LIMITED

X-Factor	Lv.1	Lv.2	Lv.3
Damage	150%	180%	220%
Speed	110%	120%	130%

Sentinel reprises much of the unique design that allowed it to dominate *MvC2*. Your plan with Sentinel is to use this mutant-killing robot's formidable set of zoning and positioning tools to coax mistakes from your opponent, while pushing them toward the corner. As a secondary goal, you should look for opportunities to fry crossover assists.

Why do you want your opponent backed into a corner with Sentinel?

Sentinel's combo potential near the corner, especially with hyper combos (and the aforementioned Human Catapult), increases greatly. Essentially, you can continue corner combos with Sentinel until you run out of hyper combo gauge, or your opponent is defeated.

Your foe will end up in the corner anyway—successfully landing Sentinel's Hard Drive hyper combo almost always takes the opposing character all the way to the corner. In a sense, Sentinel's primary goals in general boil down to: "land Hard Drive!"

Sentinel's inescapable Human Catapult command throw becomes much more valuable close to the corner.

How do you push your opponent into the corner with Sentinel? In order of effectiveness:

Landing Hard Drive, whether during a combo or on reaction to an opponent's attack that Hard Drive can blow through in time.

Using Ⓗ mouth lasers, ranged crossover assists, and variations of Sentinel Force to force your foe backward, or into the air.

Responding to your opponent's hesitance, or their desperate escape to the air, by activating Flight and becoming a direct aggressor.

Finally, what makes Sentinel an effective anti-assist character?

Standing and crouching Ⓗ mouth lasers, as well as Hyper Sentinel Force, have infinite range, and will cut through guarding point characters to deal heavy unscaled damage to their assists.

Many of Sentinel's moves do not have vulnerable hitboxes on the striking portions, allowing Sentinel to attack with impunity without worrying about being countered by opposing assist calls. Instead, attacks can frequently catch both the opposing point character and their assist together.

In the instance that a Sentinel player realizes they've caught two characters simultaneously, there is ample time to X-Factor cancel and perform combos that K.O. any two characters in the game at once, from virtually any screen position, even with both of Sentinel's partners still available, thus using "only" level 1 X-Factor.

It's worth noting that a Sentinel player should look for opportunities to make use of the hyper combo gauge; all of Sentinel's hyper combos have excellent applications, hyper combos can often be strung together without any help from X-Factor, THCs, or crossover assists, and while Sentinel builds hyper combo gauge adequately well for its own use with extended air combos and constant laser and Sentinel Drone assaults, it's far from the giant piles of meter that a character like Chun-Li builds. This puts Sentinel slightly at odds with teaming up with other meter-hungry characters, like Phoenix or Ryu—it also places a premium on scoring down or side-angled team aerial combos when you get a chance, to bolster the gauge reserves of your team.

ON THE GROUND

Sentinel's standing or crouching Ⓗ "mouth lasers" are the foundation of ground efforts. What makes these attacks so important?

Both standing and crouching Ⓗ have infinite range, reaching all the way across the screen after about 26 frames, and standing Ⓗ can actually be chained into crouching Ⓗ.

Sentinel commits no part of its body to the attack—these are full-screen lasers with no hitbox.

As basic attacks, crouching and standing Ⓗ can be used while pressing P1 or P2 to call partners for crossover assists. This also means these lasers are cancelable into special moves and hyper combos, but more importantly into Flight as well—this makes Sentinel more dynamic than it might appear at first glance.

Mouth lasers alone give Sentinel the advantage on the ground against anyone who doesn't have a beam or projectile that can overpower the lasers.

Sentinel Force takes a while to get on screen, but it's worth finding the time. Cover yourself by forcing non-projectile characters to block lasers first, or call a crossover assist for cover.

Sentinel's long range and high damage in general grant outsized rewards for even glancing hits with these lasers, especially against opposing assists, and especially if Sentinel is teamed with partners possessing long range crossover assists.

A little further than mid range is the ideal distance to poke the opposing character with standing or crouching Ⓗ—ideally from the tip of the range of Rocket Punch L or M. Closer up isn't safe, and further out has no guaranteed follow-up options. When attacking with a foundation of ranged lasers, you'll have varied options to follow-up (depending on the partners you've teamed with Sentinel and the opponent's response). Against opposing characters that lack strong ranged threats (and therefore cannot keep up with or outpace Sentinel's laser offense), you can simply harangue them with lasers, assists, and Sentinel Force drones. If they don't take evasive action, that's fine—every moment they remain stymied on the ground is another moment you're dealing chip damage to them, building hyper combo gauge, and inciting them to do something foolish like call an assist into a wave of drones and lasers.

More likely, your foe will super jump out of the way of your ground projectile threats, and take to the skies. If you can get far out from under wherever they'll land, you can simply call more Sentinel Force drones to greet them, then continue your pressure. If they land near you, you can opt to attempt to anti-air them with Ⓢ. Sentinel's Ⓢ launcher is unique among basic and special attacks because it has innate hyper armor during a portion of it. Couple that with the huge swath it cuts in front of Sentinel, and the high number of active frames, and you have a terrific attack to keep foes honest. It's technically unsafe if guarded, but your foe is pushed back so far on block that it's awkward for them to punish Sentinel cleanly.

The usefulness of an offense based on mouth lasers is related to your current opponent. Some larger characters can't even crouch under standing Ⓗ laser, forcing them to shoot back or take to the air if they want to be proactive dealing with Sentinel's ranged offense. However, some characters can avoid even the crouching Ⓗ laser by crouching.

HEROES WHO CAN'T CROUCH UNDER STANDING Ⓗ LASER

Captain America
Hulk
Iron Man
M.O.D.O.K.
Sentinel
Tron

HEROES WHO CAN CROUCH UNDER CROUCHING Ⓗ LASER

Amaterasu
Arthur
Felicia*
Morrigan
Phoenix
Viewtiful Joe
Wolverine

*Depending on Felicia's exact position during her crouching animation, crouching Ⓗ will occasionally hit her.

Against characters who can duck under either laser, you'll want to amend your strategy a bit. Either use crossover assists to lay down cover for Sentinel Drones and omit the lasers entirely (unless you expect a well-placed laser may keep them from jumping forward), or be more aggressive and take to the fight to them with crossover assists and Sentinel's super armor basic attacks (standing and crouching Ⓜ, and Ⓢ), or Flight-based overhead attacks.

Some characters, most notably Arthur, Doctor Doom, Dormammu, and Iron Man (also Akuma and Ryu, when they are loaded with hyper combo gauge), can keep up easily with Sentinel's barrage of lasers and drones with their own strong projectiles. Just like small characters, these foes force you into the role of aggressor. That's not a tall order —Sentinel's wavedash is extremely fast, and both standing and crouching Ⓜ have good range, no vulnerable hitboxes away from Sentinel's body, super armor that absorbs one incoming attack, and lead to combos on a successful hit. Between the two, favor dashing forward with crouching Ⓜ, since this is Sentinel's only low attack, and the only way you can encourage your enemies to block low occasionally, paving the way for them to eat flying and jumping air overheads later.

Characters that can teleport around Sentinel's attacks also encourage you to take on the mantle of an aggressor. Lasers and Sentinel Force summons are unwise time commitments against foes that can flicker across the screen in an instant and potentially punish you from full screen. Take the fight to them instead.

UP IN THE AIR

Sentinel can transition from ground offense to aerial combat at just about any time, by canceling basic attacks into Flight. Sentinel is the most nimble flier, and while relatively slow, aerial attacks are second to none. None of Sentinel's air basic attacks have vulnerable hitboxes on the striking portions. This means that Sentinel will win any aerial exchange outright against any other move that isn't invulnerable.

Air Ⓛ is a fast stab that strikes straight downward. At low altitudes this is useful for attacking grounded opponents underneath you. While super jumping or flying at great height, air Ⓛ can be used as an inquisitive poke, when you feel that your foe will super jump or fly up to meet you. A hit against either a grounded or airborne opponent can lead to a full combo by chaining into air Ⓗ, Ⓢ, which forces Sentinel to land while causing a ground bounce.

If it's airborne and above, air Ⓜ will hit it. Chain into another air Ⓜ, then double jump cancel to continue the air chain.

Air Ⓜ is a bit slower, but strikes at a tremendous diagonal, up-forward range. You can use this to rise to meet other super jumping or flying characters, at a range no other character can match with direct air basic attacks. As with air Ⓛ, a successful hit grants you the opportunity to chain into air Ⓢ, ground bouncing your opponent and scoring a full combo even from the very top of the playing field. The only issue with air Ⓜ is that its upward angle can make sticking it into traditional air combos tricky. For this reason, Sentinel is one of the few characters where it isn't beneficial to open air combos with air Ⓛ, Ⓛ. The downward stabs drag victims slightly upward, allowing air Ⓜ to connect and continue the air chain.

Air Ⓗ and Ⓢ should be used for attacking grounded opponents. Air Ⓢ can be used to fall with the famous "frying pan," (returning from *MvC2*) this attack will cause a ground bounce on any hit, leading to huge damage. Use it when you want to return to the ground while also attacking. Air Ⓗ can be used as a general overhead attack while jumping, or as a "stomp" on an opposing character's face while flying. As with other Sentinel basic attacks, the tip of this move simply does not lose to other attacks. If the opposing point character attempts an anti-air while summoning an assist as you initiate air Ⓗ, you'll probably stomp on both characters, allowing you to chain into air Ⓢ, land, and annihilate two characters at once!

Similarly, air Ⓗ will crush anything diagonally below. Chain into air Ⓢ, then a full ground combo!

When going air-to-air, or air-to-ground, against opponents who are further out than the range of air Ⓜ or air Ⓗ, Rocket Punches can be used as long range pokes. These pokes have the same problems that naked Rocket Punches have: Sentinel is committed to the attack for a while, the attacks are not technically safe if guarded, and teleport-capable characters may make you regret sticking out a Rocket Punch. However, these issues are diminished simply by being in the air; as long as you're not performing air Rocket Punches all the time, or particularly close to your opposition, you'll get away with it more often than not. Depending on positioning and proximity, successful air Rocket Punches can be hyper combo canceled into Hard Drive.

While airborne, always be mindful that you have Hard Drive at your disposal, provided you have spare hyper combo gauge. Near the ground, it can be performed while flying or jumping so low that it will even hit crouching opponents! Higher up, it can be used on reaction to blow through anything your opponent performs in mid-air. Even hyper combo beams are powerless to stop the approach of Hard Drive.

Sentinel's quick Flight speed makes it very useful to stay in normal jump Flight when possible, started either from a grounded or normal jumping state. This allows you to call crossover assists while flying, while still fishing for air-to-air or air-to-ground hits with basic attacks, and Rocket Punches as described above. This is particularly useful for dropping an assist on one side of your foe, as you fly over their head to the other side. This provides you a moment to stomp with impunity while they're forced to block the crossover assist at their back; you can even set up virtually unblockable situations by calling low-hitting assists while flying and attacking!

COMBO USAGE

I. ST. Ⓗ, CR. Ⓗ [CANCEL] ↓↘→ + Ⓜ [CANCEL] ↓↙← + [ATK ATK], STANDING Ⓗ

(369,900~407,900 damage; or 100% on two characters with possible X-Factor follow-up) Sentinel's standing and crouching Ⓗ mouth lasers are a vital part of ranged offense, and you are bound to occasionally score clean hits against grounded opponents at mid to long range when you employ them. There's plenty of time to verify whether standing to crouching Ⓗ laser hits before committing to the Rocket Punch. Rocket Punch M has slightly more range, but Rocket Punch L will result in more damage, because it leaves your opponent lower in altitude and allows more of the Hyper Sentinel Force drones to hit.

If lasers are guarded by a character without a quick long range threat, cancel into Sentinel Force L or M, then use the cover provided by the drones to either transition to offense, or call a long range crossover assist and go back to firing mouth lasers. Against characters like Doctor Doom or Iron Man, who can outclass Sentinel's beams if any gaps are left at all, cancel the lasers into Flight and wait to see what action your opponent takes before looking for a place to go back to fishing for laser hits.

If you realize you've caught both the enemy point character and their assist with Rocket Punch after the lasers, cancel to Hyper Sentinel Force as normal, then *immediately* activate X-Factor to cancel the hyper combo and regain control of Sentinel early. Unlike most hyper combos, Hyper Sentinel Force will still play out fully when interrupted with X-Factor! After activating X-Factor, immediately activate Flight and fly forward. Just as the third wave of drones strikes both opposing characters, perform: air Ⓗ, Ⓢ, land, Ⓢ [CANCEL] super jump, air Ⓜ, Ⓗ, Ⓢ, land, ↓↘→ + Ⓛ. You could tack on another hyper combo here in theory, but you won't need to—at this point *any* two characters are knocked out, even from full vitality!

II. ST. Ⓛ, CR. Ⓜ, Ⓢ [CANCEL] SUPER JUMP, AIR Ⓗ [CANCEL] ↓↙← + Ⓢ, AIR Ⓛ, Ⓛ, Ⓜ, Ⓗ [CANCEL] ↓↙← + Ⓢ, AIR Ⓜ [CANCEL] DOUBLE JUMP, AIR Ⓜ, Ⓢ, LAND, WAVEDASH, ↓↘→↗ + Ⓛ OTG [CANCEL] ↓↘→ + [ATK ATK]

(542,800 damage) Sentinel's basic close-range combo suggests itself naturally—standing Ⓛ is Sentinel's fastest attack, and crouching Ⓜ is the *only* available low attack (without employing a low-hitting crossover assist). Crouching Ⓜ strikes three times with brief inactive periods in between hits, giving you plenty of time to verify whether your initial attacks are guarded or not. As a bonus, this also gives your opponent time to leave crouching guard too early, which will cause the end of crouching Ⓜ to hit. If crouching Ⓜ hits, launch with Ⓢ and proceed into the air combo. Of course, this same combo can start off of just crouching Ⓜ, which has the advantage of going low from the first hit, while backed with super armor.

This air combo uses both Flight activation and cancelation to interrupt basic attacks. After air Ⓗ, cancel into Flight immediately, but you don't need to rush the air Ⓛ follow-up link—you have more time than you think. Two air Ⓛ attacks are notated here—this is to drag your target a little higher up so air Ⓜ will also connect. On bigger opponents, or with the right positioning, you can omit one of the air Ⓛ attacks. After chaining to air Ⓜ, Ⓗ, input ↓↙← + Ⓢ again to "unfly." Sentinel will start falling, and commands can be input immediately. This is how you can land falling air Ⓜ, double jump canceled into another air Ⓜ, then air Ⓢ for flying screen. With longer combos, especially any that start with standing to crouching Ⓗ lasers, the final air Ⓢ will whiff because of hitstun deterioration, but for the purposes of most combos the entire air sequence is consistent.

After flying screen, wavedash forward and "tiger knee" (↓↘→↗) the Rocket Punch to get instant air Rocket Punch L just off the ground. This will OTG your foe, allow Hard Drive to combo, and carry them all the way to the corner! (If you just dash rather than wavedash, Hard Drive will sometimes drop your target.) One bonus of this combo is that it builds all the hyper combo gauge needed for Hard Drive within the combo—no extra resources required, you can always tack on Hard Drive (or Hyper Sentinel Force or Plasma Storm, if you prefer; this is considerably easier, and roughly the same damage, but doesn't instantly put your opponent into the corner). If Hard Drive hits properly, the last hit will cause a spinning knockdown. Here, you can link Rocket Punch to Plasma Storm, or another Hard Drive with the ↓↘→↗ "tiger knee" method! Adding at least another hyper combo in the corner easily pushes this combo into 800,000+ damage territory; if you have the gauge to spare, adding multiple corner hyper combos (such as one or two "tiger knee" Hard Drives before a Rocket Punch to Plasma Storm finisher) can break one million damage easily.

If you find the Flight cancel version of this combo (followed by a wavedash after flying screen) too difficult, you can simplify matters greatly by performing a chain of air Ⓜ, Ⓗ, Ⓢ in mid-air, then just a forward dash before the air Rocket Punch L canceled into Hard Drive. This version of the combo isn't self-sufficient in terms of meter. It does accomplish the same goal of cornering the foe, however, and is far easier to perform.

If crouching Ⓜ at the beginning is guarded, you have several options. As is usually the case, you can cancel into Flight and either go for overhead attacks, or hang back in mid-air to bait a reaction. If your opponent pushed your initial chain attempt out with advancing guard, you can use the opportunity to naturally transition back to chipping from afar with lasers, crossover assists, and Sentinel Force drones, or you can activate Flight and decide if an aggressive flight path to the foe exists.

III. AIR-TO-AIR: SUPER JUMP, AIR Ⓛ, Ⓛ (OR AIR Ⓜ, Ⓜ) [CANCEL] DOUBLE JUMP, AIR Ⓛ, Ⓛ, Ⓗ [CANCEL] ↓↙← + Ⓢ, AIR Ⓛ, Ⓜ, Ⓗ, Ⓢ, LAND, Ⓢ [CANCEL] SUPER JUMP, AIR Ⓜ, Ⓜ, Ⓗ, Ⓢ, LAND, DASH, ↓↘→↗ + Ⓛ OTG [CANCEL] ↓↘→ + [ATK ATK]

(617,000~677,800 damage with double jump and Flight; 724,000~749,000 with 3-hit chain opening) Sentinel can score huge damage off even a glancing blow in mid-air, from just about any aerial state. When attacking foes next to or below Sentinel in mid-air, begin air chain combos with air Ⓛ. When attacking foes diagonally up and above, open chains with air Ⓜ. If you're super jumping, or flying from a super jump, you can perform full aerial chains. If you caught a mid-air blow off a normal jump, or flight starting from a normal jump or from the ground, you can only do 3-hit air chains.

Your options will also vary depending on whether you've used up Flight and/or your double jump already when you score the first hit. The simplest air chain to use air-to-air to score a ground bounce is thus either air Ⓛ, Ⓗ, Ⓢ, or air Ⓜ, Ⓗ, Ⓢ. Open with either air Ⓛ or Ⓜ as appropriate, depending on where your foe is positioned. Neither chain requires a super jump state, a double jump, or Flight (even though both chains work well during Flight), so they're always possible. Without aerial mobility options, you won't be able to finely position off the first hit, so Ⓗ, Ⓢ may sometimes whiff.

Because of damage scaling, this combo deals more damage with the simpler, three hit chain opening. With both versions, either including a double jump and Flight or not, the combo is self-sufficient in terms of hyper combo gauge; the more complex version builds almost another full bar too —useful for tacking on another Hard Drive or a Plasma Storm in the corner—and is considerably flashier!

IV. AGAINST A GROUNDED OPPONENT: [X-Factor] WHILE FLYING, AIR Ⓛ, Ⓛ, Ⓢ, LAND, ST. Ⓗ, CR. Ⓗ, Ⓢ [CANCEL] SUPER JUMP, AIR Ⓗ [CANCEL] ↓↙← + Ⓢ, AIR Ⓛ, Ⓛ, Ⓜ, Ⓜ, Ⓗ, Ⓢ, LAND, DASH, ↓↘→ + Ⓛ OTG [CANCEL] ↓↙← + [ATK ATK], STANDING Ⓗ

(1,774,100 damage with X-Factor level 1) This combo really shines a spotlight on the strength of X-Factor. To begin, air Ⓛ, Ⓢ doesn't normally link against a standing foe—but it does during X-Factor (to reproduce this combo without X-Factor, begin with either air Ⓛ, Ⓗ, Ⓢ or air Ⓗ, Ⓢ). Reduced damage scaling on combos during X-Factor means that using multi-hit moves (like the standing and crouching Ⓗ lasers, or Hyper Sentinel Force) *boosts* damage, rather than scaling it heavily. Roughly the same combo performed without X-Factor scores about 675,000 damage, almost three times *less*...

V. FORWARD OR BACKWARD THROW, DASH, ↓↘→ + Ⓛ OTG CANCEL ↓↙← + ATK ATK X ↓↙← + Ⓢ, FLY FORWARD, AIR Ⓗ, AIR Ⓢ, LAND, Ⓢ CANCEL SUPER JUMP, AIR Ⓜ, Ⓗ, Ⓢ, LAND, DASH, ↓↘→ + Ⓛ OTG CANCEL ↓↙← + ATK ATK

(Requires X-Factor, 1,356,000–1,468,500 damage with X-Factor level 1) Sentinel can score a Rocket Punch L OTG after either direction of normal throw. On some characters no forward dash is necessary before the Rocket Punch L OTG, but on others the Rocket Punch won't reach unless you dash first. To be safe, just dash unless you're certain it's unnecessary (to generalize, you'll have to dash first against hefty characters, but not against small ones). The Rocket Punch can be hyper combo canceled into Hyper Sentinel Force, and then the enemy can be juggled with standing Ⓗ for a very respectable total of 414,300 damage off the throw. With X-Factor handy, a normal throw can become a knock out against any character.

VI. (NEAR CORNER) →↓↘ + Ⓗ, IMMEDIATE NORMAL JUMP FORWARD, AIR Ⓜ, Ⓜ CANCEL DOUBLE JUMP FORWARD, AIR Ⓜ, Ⓗ, Ⓢ, LAND, Ⓢ CANCEL SUPER JUMP, AIR Ⓜ, Ⓗ CANCEL ↓↙← + Ⓢ, AIR Ⓛ, Ⓜ, Ⓗ, Ⓢ, LAND, ↓↘→ + Ⓛ OTG CANCEL ↓↙← + ATK ATK, ↓↘→ + Ⓜ CANCEL ↓↘→ + ATK ATK

(813,100–833,100 damage) Sentinel can score tremendous damage with flashy combos off of Human Catapult M or H near a corner. Off of Human Catapult M, you have time to link standing Ⓜ Ⓢ and proceed to an air combo, but off of Human Catapult H you have time for far more, as notated here. As is usually the case, you can mix and match hyper combos into each other as you desire at the end, but this is generally the most damaging combination for using just two bars. Sentinel combos in general can utilize hyper combos interchangeably, but to generalize: Plasma Storm tends to give you the best direct damage and THC potential; Hyper Sentinel Force deals heavier damage if you can put the opponent into position for most of the drones to hit (rather than just skipping across the top), and Hard Drive drive does less damage but has the benefit of nearly always cornering the enemy, being the safest to use, and the best to land against opposing assists. Both Hyper Sentinel Force and Hard Drive offer excellent follow-up opportunites in the corner.

ASSISTS

Beam-based crossover assists bolster Sentinel's ranged game considerably, and also allow hit-confirm combos into Hyper Sentinel Force from an outrageous distance.

Assists that take up a lot of screen space near Sentinel can be useful for preemptively keeping teleporting characters off of Sentinel's back, literally!

Each of Sentinel's crossover assist types has some appeal. The best is dependent on the makeup of your team. Sentinel—α is a great all-purpose assist, granting enhanced space control and forward movement to any character. Since this assist is the Ⓜ version of Sentinel Force, it can also be used deviously to go for throws or overheads on opponents who attempt to crouch under the drones. The only disadvantage is that it can't be used defensively; the angle isn't right to stop opponents jumping in, and aggressive characters who hit Sentinel will simply make the drones disappear. Sentinel—β, on the other hand, will always bomb the playing field once the drones are onscreen, even if Sentinel is struck while summoning them. It's almost never as damaging as Sentinel—α, but is more valuable in a defensive or close to mid range zoning capacity for this reason. Sentinel—β can be used for particular zoning patterns at mid range, or delayed OTGs and specialized combos. It's harder to recommend Sentinel—γ over the other two types; while the Rocket Punch assist is OTG-capable, which is never a bad thing, this is hardly a unique ability. Sentinel's assists that take up lots of screen real estate are more useful, so try to fulfill your OTG needs elsewhere.

As is the case with just about any character in *Marvel vs. Capcom 3*, beam crossover assists are never a bad choice. Selections like Iron Man—α and Doctor Doom—α enhance Sentinel's laser game a great deal. With some beam assists, standing Ⓗ + P1 or P2 can hit-confirm into Hyper Sentinel Force on a point character or assist from all the way across the playing field!

Beam assists also help you keep the pressure on after opponents use ground or air recovery to roll away from corner combos, and help you achieve cross-ups with Sentinel by flying over the opposing character's head while a beam assist is about to shoot them in the back.

Sentinel's biggest weakness is the lack of great options for getting away from aggressive characters, or avoiding teleports. Basic attacks are slower than average, and while super armor Ⓜ attacks help out somewhat, using them defensively is still a guess with potentially heavy consequences. Sentinel is absolutely huge compared to anyone else, and makes a gigantic target for a foe to strike with rushing ground and air chains. Many characters can virtually climb up and down standing Sentinel's tall body with normal jumping air attacks, especially if they get around Sentinel's high time commitment ranged moves. You can shore up these gaps by selecting a solid defensive assist, preferably one that strikes on both sides. Good examples include Haggar—α and Iron Man—β. If you call these assists preemptively when you expect a teleport-capable character to attempt to warp around your laser and drone offense, they'll almost certainly simply run into the assist. At the very least, they will not have a clear path to Sentinel, which is the solution you're looking for. Call the assist slightly before performing lasers, not during or after. This will make it much less likely that the enemy just ends up hitting Sentinel and the assist simultaneously. These two assists in particular have other bonuses—Haggar is invincible, which also makes him a great crossover counter, and Iron Man's Repulsor Blast is technically considered a beam itself; this means that Iron Man—β can not only help keep aggressors off of Sentinel, but also help Sentinel stay even in firefights against other beamers. Iron Man—β doesn't directly attack the opponent from far away, but it can intercept their beams before they make it to Sentinel, giving you precious time to actually fire off lasers and drones.

Another weakness is that Sentinel's only low attack is crouching Ⓜ. Assists can make up for this deficiency as well. Using an assist like She-Hulk—α or Wesker—β opens the way for potentially unblockable attacks if you call these assists out just before stomping with air Ⓗ from a jump or during Flight. These assists also expand Sentinel's combo repertoire a little bit—while Sentinel doesn't have problems landing OTG hits by itself, hyper combo gauge is needed to continue combos solo after Rocket Punch L OTG. With an OTG-capable assist, you can score another launcher combo without using any hyper combo gauge.

ADVANCED TACTICS

FLIGHT AND DOUBLE JUMP CANCELING

To use Sentinel to full potential, you'll have to get comfortable with Flight and double jump air mobility options.

The first thing to understand is that Flight can be deactivated in mid-air. That's pretty obvious, and important for doing things like "unflying" to block if your opponent is winding up a big attack—after all, you can't guard while flying. However, the less obvious use is to use Flight activation and deactivation to cancel basic attack recovery. After Flight activation, you must wait 16 frames before inputting an attack, but you have plenty of time after landing air (H) early in an air combo, long before hitstun deterioration makes that a prohibitive time to wait. After Flight deactivation, however, you can input commands immediately!

By comboing into Flight, then continuing the combo, you can eventually use "unfly," or Flight deactivation, to cancel an air basic attack instantly...

...so you can land another hit immediately while falling! From here, you can cancel this hit into a double jump, and attack instantly again!

Additionally, double jumps can be used to interrupt air (L) and (M). As with Flight deactivation, you can input commands instantly after double jump canceling.

Using Flight activation, "unflying," and double jump canceling is what makes Sentinel's launcher combo possible: (S) CANCEL→ super jump, air (H) CANCEL→ ↓↙← + (S), air (L), (M), (H) CANCEL→ ↓↙← + (S), air (M) CANCEL→ double jump, air (M), (S).

Be careful with your inputs anytime you're canceling into or from Flight in mid-air, or anytime you're double-jumping into air (M), then (S) for flying screen... imprecise (S) inputs may be interpreted by the game as team aerial combo starts, giving you unexpected results.

COMBO APPENDIX

GENERAL EXECUTION TIPS

Pause slightly before canceling (S) launchers into super jumps for air combos. You want to catch the enemy as they level off, not right away as they ascend.

Chain air attacks quickly after canceling to Flight in air combos, after canceling flight, and after double jump canceling.

For easier, closer range OTG opportunities mid screen after air combos, perform air (M), (H), (S) very slowly.

Requirements (Position, meter, etc.)	Notes	Command Sequence	Damage
Requires 1 bar of hyper combo gauge	Low combo	Cr. (M), (S) CANCEL→ super jump, air (M), (M), (H), (S), land, dash, ↓↘→ + (L) OTG CANCEL→ ↓↘→ + ATK ATK	600,800
Requires 1 bar of hyper combo gauge	Overhead combo	Flying air (L), (H), (S), land, st. (M), (S) CANCEL→ super jump, air (M), (H) CANCEL→ ↓↙← + (S), air (L), (M), (H) CANCEL→ ↓↙← + (S), air (M) CANCEL→ double jump, air (M), (S), land, dash, ↓↘→ + (L) OTG CANCEL→ ↓↘→ + ATK ATK	766,600
Requires Trish—β and Dante—α, 1 bar of hyper combo gauge		St. (L), cr. (M) + P1 or P2 Trish CANCEL→ ↓↙← + (S), air (H), (S) ground bounce, land, (S) CANCEL→ super jump, air (M), (H), (S), land, dash, P1 or P2 Dante, ↓↘→ + ATK ATK OTG CANCEL→ ↓↙← + ATK ATK	577,100
Requires Iron Man—α, 1 bar of hyper combo gauge	Possible from full screen!	St. or cr. (H) + P1 or P2 Iron Man CANCEL→ ↓↙← + ATK ATK, st. (H)	331,500~ 350,600
If you want to combo side or down TAC instead, use → + (S) or ↓ + (S) to finish Flight.	Team aerial combo starter	(S) CANCEL→ super jump, air (H) CANCEL→ ↓↙← + (S), air (L), (L), (M), (H) CANCEL→ ↓↙← + (S), air (M) CANCEL→ double jump up, air (M) CANCEL→ ↑ + (S)	469,100
From team aerial combo starter. Can end with (S) for flying screen, or direction + (S) for another TAC (up to twice in one combo)	Team aerial combo follow-up. Go through the first 2 (L) attacks and into the double jump as fast as possible to stop lateral momentum.	Air (L), (L) CANCEL→ double jump, air (L), (L), (H) ↓↙← + (S), air (L), (H) CANCEL→ ↓↙← + (S), air (M) CANCEL→ double jump air (M), (H), (direction + (S) or (S))	372,200+
Requires corner, 2 bars of hyper combo gauge	Command throw combo	→↓↘ + (M), st. (M), (S) CANCEL→ super jump, air (M), (H) CANCEL→ ↓↙← + (S), air (L), (L), (M), (H) CANCEL→ ↓↙← + (S), air (M) CANCEL→ double jump, air (M), (S), land, ↓↘→↗ + (L) OTG CANCEL→ ↓↘→ + ATK ATK, ↓↘→ + (M) CANCEL→ ↓↘→ + ATK ATK	804,400
Requires corner, 5 bars of hyper combo gauge, and a bit of luck scoring the last hit of each Hard Drive	Command throw combo	→↓↘ + (H), jump forward, air (M), (H) CANCEL→ ↓↙← + (S), air (L), (M), (S), land, (S) CANCEL→ super jump, air (M), (M), (H), (S), land, ↓↘→ + (L) OTG CANCEL→ ↓↙← + ATK ATK, ↓↘→↗ + ATK ATK, ↓↘→↗ + ATK ATK, ↓↘→↗ + ATK ATK, ↓↘→ + ATK ATK	1,181,300
Requires X-Factor, 2 levels of hyper combo gauge		St. (L), cr. (M) CANCEL→ ↓↘→ + (L) CANCEL→ ↓↙← + ATK ATK X-FACTOR ↓↙← + (S), fly forward, air (H), (S), land, (S) CANCEL→ super jump, air (H) CANCEL→ ↓↙← + (S), air (L), (M), (H), (S), land, ATK ATK command dash, ↓↘→ + (L) CANCEL→ ↓↙← + ATK ATK, st. (H)	1,672,600

TASKMASTER

"YOU FIGHT LIKE A LOSER! I'M NOT EVEN GONNA BOTHER STEALING YOUR MOVES."

BIO

REAL NAME

UNREVEALED

OCCUPATION

PROFESSIONAL CRIMINAL, COMBAT INSTRUCTOR

ABILITIES

TASKMASTER POSSESSES PHOTOGRAPHIC REFLEXES, WHICH ENABLE HIM TO WATCH ANOTHER PERSON'S PHYSICAL MOVEMENTS AND DUPLICATE THEM WITHOUT PRACTICE, NO MATTER HOW COMPLEX.

WEAPONS

TASKMASTER PERFECTLY COPIES THE WEAPON-FIGHTING STYLES OF SUPER HEROES, SUCH AS CAPTAIN AMERICA'S SHIELD, HAWKEYE'S BOW, AND SPIDER-MAN'S WEB-SHOOTERS.

PROFILE

HE LEARNED MANY MOVES BY WATCHING VIDEOS OF HEROES IN ACTION, AND USED HIS PHOTOGRAPHIC REFLEXES TO COPY THEM AND MAKE THEM HIS OWN. CONSIDERING HIMSELF A BUSINESSMAN, TASKMASTER OPENED A MERCENARY SCHOOL FOR TRAINING CRIMINALS IN THE FIGHTING ARTS.

FIRST APPEARANCE

THE AVENGERS #195 (1980)

POWER GRID

- 4 INTELLIGENCE
- 3 STRENGTH
- 3 SPEED
- 2 STAMINA
- 1 ENERGY PROJECTION
- 7 FIGHTING ABILITY

*This is biographical, and does not represent an evaluation of the character's in-game combat potential.

ALTERNATE COSTUMES

PS3: ⓧ Xbox 360: Ⓐ

PS3: ▢ Xbox 360: Ⓧ

PS3: △ Xbox 360: Ⓨ

PS3: R1 Xbox 360: RB

ATTACK SET

STANDING BASIC ATTACKS

Screen	Command	Hits	Damage	Startup	Active	Recovery	Advantage on Hit	Advantage if Guarded	Notes
1	Standing L	1	48,000	5	3	10	+2	+1	—
2	Standing M	2	72,000	8	2(1)3	17	0	-2	—
3	Standing H	1	90,000	11	3	20	+2	0	↓↘→ + P1⇔P2 snap back
4	S	1	90,000	9	5	30	—	12	Launcher, not special or hyper combo cancelable

1

2

3

4

CROUCHING BASIC ATTACKS

Screen	Command	Hits	Damage	Startup	Active	Recovery	Advantage on Hit	Advantage if Guarded	Notes
1	Crouching L	1	45,000	5	3	14	-2	-3	Low attack
2	Crouching M	1	65,000	8	3	19	-2	-4	Low attack
3	Crouching H	1	80,000	10	3	23	-2	-3	Knocks down opponent

1

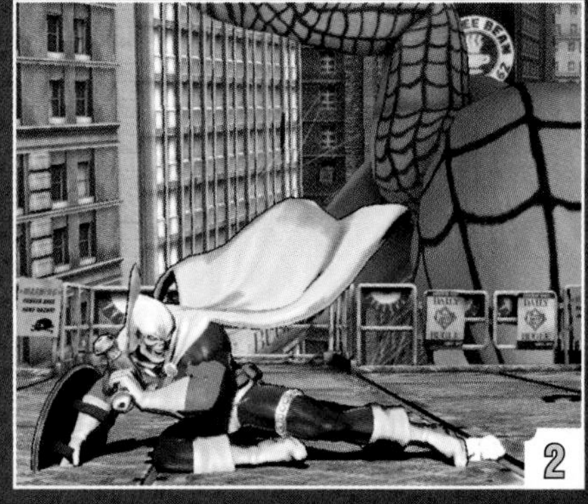
2

3

AERIAL BASIC ATTACKS

Screen	Command	Hits	Damage	Startup	Active	Recovery	Notes
1	Air L	1	50,000	5	3	15	Overhead attack
2	Air M	1	68,000	7	4	17	Overhead attack
3	Air H	2	92,500	11	4	21	Overhead attack
4	Air S	1	90,000	11	3	27	Overhead attack, unrecoverable knockdown when used in air combo after S launcher

1

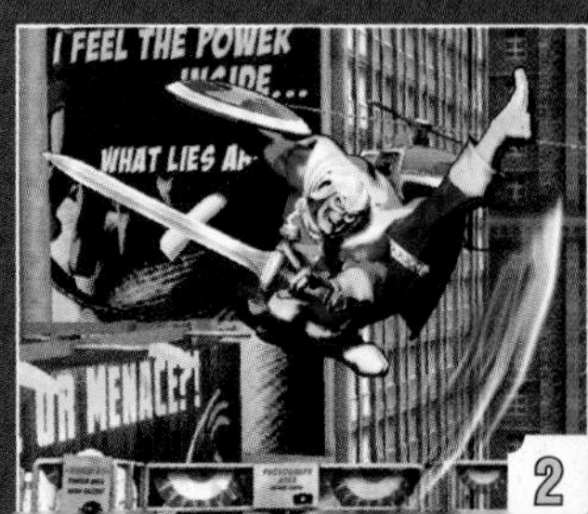

2

3

4

COMMAND ATTACKS

Screen	Command	Hits	Damage	Startup	Active	Recovery	Advantage on Hit	Advantage if Guarded	Notes
1	⇨ + Ⓗ (in air OK)	1	80,000	11	13	16	+7	-6	Knockdown, recovers in air neutral state, can only be performed one time while in the air
2	⇦ + Ⓗ	1	95,000	6	9	29	—	-15	Immune to low and medium priority projectile and beams during frames 4-18, knocks down, may be chained into Ⓢ

1

2

TASKMASTER

AS A PARTNER-CROSSOVER ASSISTS

Screen	Type	P1+P2 Crossover Combination Hyper Combo	Description	Hits	Damage	Startup	Active	Recovery (this crossover assist)	Recovery (other partner)	Notes
1	α – Alpha	Legion Arrow L+M	Aim Master L	3	162,500	45	9	121	91	Each projectile has 3 low priority durability points
2	β – Beta	Legion Arrow L+H	Aim Master M	3	162,500	45	9	126	96	Each projectile has 3 low priority durability points
3	γ – Gamma	Legion Arrow M+H	Aim Master H	3	162,500	45	9	131	101	OTG-capable, each projectile has 3 low priority durability points

1

2

3

SPECIAL MOVES

Screen	Name	Command	Hits	Damage	Startup	Active	Recovery	Advantage on Hit	Advantage if Guarded	Notes
1	Aim Master L (can be charged, in air OK)	↓↘→ + L	1~3	60,000~162,500	13~21	1~9	37~21	-13~+3	-15~+1	Each projectile has 3 low priority durability points
2	Aim Master M (can be charged, in air OK)	↓↘→ + M	1~3	60,000~162,500	13~21	1~9	42~26	-18~-2	-20~-4	OTG-capable, each projectile has 3 low priority durability points
3	Aim Master H (can be charged, in air OK)	↓↘→ + H	1~3	60,000~162,500	13~21	1~9	47~31	-23~-7	-25~-9	OTG-capable, each projectile has 3 low priority durability points
4	Guard Master L	↓↙← + L	2	100,000	5	20	20	—	—	Counter attack, counters mid and high attacks, unrecoverable knockdown
	Guard Master M	↓↙← + M	2	100,000	5	20	20	—	—	Counter attack, counters low and mid attacks, unrecoverable knockdown
	Guard Master H	↓↙← + H	1	40,000	5	20	20	-20	-24	Counter attack, rlow and medium priority projectiles
5	Sword Master L	→↓↘ + L	1	50,000	31	5	22	—	-4	Knocks down
	Head Butt	(When Sword Master L is blocked) H	1	30,000	24	5	16	+4	—	Unblockable
	Lights Out	(During Head Butt) ↓↘→ + H	2	60,000	15	5	1	—	—	Unblockable, unrecoverable knockdown
	Sword Master M	→↓↘ + M	1	50,000	44	5	22	—	-4	Knocks down
	Head Butt	(When Sword Master M is blocked) H	1	30,000	24	5	16	+4	—	Unblockable
	Below the Belt	(During Head Butt) M	1	28,000	13	5	21	-1	-3	—
	Low Kick	(During Below the Belt) H	1	30,000	20	5	16	+4	+2	Low attack
	Lights Out	(During Low Kick) ↓↘→ + H	2	70,000	15	5	1	—	—	Unblockable, unrecoverable knockdown
	Sword Master H	→↓↘ + H	1	50,000	57	5	22	—	-4	Knocks down
6	Head Butt	(When Sword Master H is blocked) H	1	30,000	24	3	18	+4	—	Unblockable
7	Below the Belt	(During Head Butt) M	1	28,000	13	3	23	-1	-3	—
8	Low Kick	(During Below the Belt) H	1	30,000	20	4	17	+4	+2	Low attack
9	Shield Bash	(During Low Kick) H	1	25,000	21	3	22	0	-2	—
10	Knee Kick	(During Shield Bash) M	1	31,000	18	4	17	+4	+2	—
11	Lights Out	(During Knee Kick) ↓↘→ + H	2	80,000	15	5	1	—	—	Unblockable, unrecoverable knockdown

1

2

3

Aim Master. The perfect supplement to Taskmaster's defensive goal, Aim Master is a chargeable projectile attack with variable directions of fire. ↓↘→ + L is used to combat ground movement, while M and H are used against aerial foes. The charged shot has a slower startup period than normal, but increases the amount of arrows fired and reduces the overall recovery time. Charged shots are used for controlling positions when you are uncertain where your opposition will move, while the faster, regular shot is used to preemptively stop your opponent's actions after they've blocked a charged shot. For example, if you force your opponent to guard a charged ↓↘→ + L and expect them to super jump right as they leave guardstun, doing an immediate charged ↓↘→ + M will miss them as they fly into the air. However, doing the regular version of ↓↘→ + M will catch their jump or super jump attempt.

4

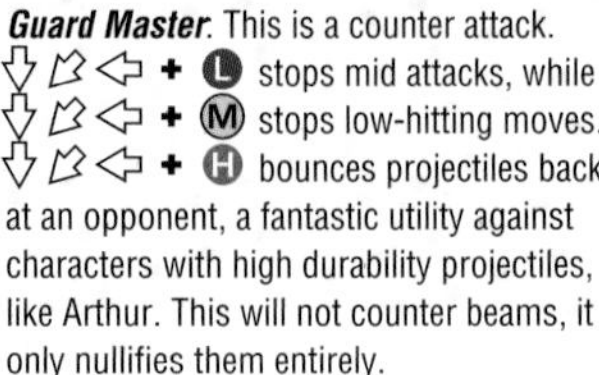

Guard Master. This is a counter attack. ↓↙← + L stops mid attacks, while ↓↙← + M stops low-hitting moves. ↓↙← + H bounces projectiles back at an opponent, a fantastic utility against characters with high durability projectiles, like Arthur. This will not counter beams, it only nullifies them entirely.

5

6

7

8

9

10

11

Sword Master. This odd, leaping slash has numerous attack extensions that are only available if a character guards it. These extensions are unblockable and lead to an unrecoverable knockdown or hyper cancelable hits. The L version is the hardest version for foes to avoid because of its speed, but it has a much smaller and less damaging attack extensions. The H version is the slowest but has the longest follow-up. Unfortunately, an opponent can use advancing guard against the opening hit to force the unguardable attacks to miss. This problem is bypassed only through assists, which can lock a foe in guardstun without advancing guard taking affect.

HSIEN-KO

"WHY ARE ALL THESE COMIC BOOK HEROES ATTACKING US? DID WE DO SOMETHING WRONG?"

BIO

REAL NAME

HSIEN-KO

OCCUPATION

PRIEST (HOUSE OF SENJUTSU)

ABILITIES

A UNIQUE STYLE OF CHINESE MARTIAL ARTS BLENDING TECHNIQUES PASSED DOWN THROUGH SENJUTSU, AS WELL AS HIDDEN WEAPONRY.

WEAPONS

USES LARGE STEEL TALONS, A GONG, AND OTHER VARIOUS WEAPONS. SHE ALSO USES MANY ASSORTED ITEMS SUCH AS AN AKUMA DOLL, VEGA'S CLAW, CHUN-LI'S BRACELETS, ETC.

PROFILE

HSIEN-KO AND MEI-LING ARE TWIN SISTERS WHO TRANSFORMED INTO A JIANGSHI USING IGYO TENSHIN-NO-JUTSU. THEY FIGHT TO SAVE THEIR MOTHER'S SOUL FROM THE DARKNESS. HSIEN-KO DOES THE FIGHTING, WHILE MEI-LING TRANSFORMED INTO THE CHARM ON HER HAT IN ORDER TO KEEP HSIEN-KO'S POWERS UNDER CONTROL.

FIRST APPEARANCE

NIGHT WARRIORS (1995)

POWER GRID

4 INTELLIGENCE

4 STRENGTH

5 SPEED

5 STAMINA

1 ENERGY PROJECTION

5 FIGHTING ABILITY

*This is biographical, and does not represent an evaluation of the character's in-game combat potential.

ALTERNATE COSTUMES

PS3: ⓧ Xbox 360: Ⓐ

PS3: □ Xbox 360: Ⓧ

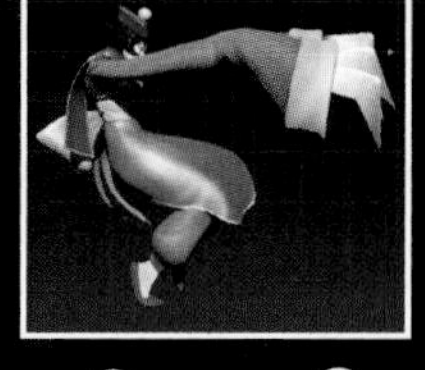
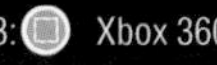
PS3: △ Xbox 360: Ⓨ

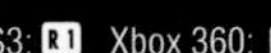
PS3: R1 Xbox 360: RB

ATTACK SET

STANDING BASIC ATTACKS

Screen	Command	Hits	Damage	Startup	Active	Recovery	Advantage on Hit	Advantage if Guarded	Notes
1	Standing L	1	40,000	5	3	10	0	0	—
2	Standing M	1	60,000	7	5	20	-2	-2	—
3	Standing H	3	84,800	10	7	21	-1	-1	—
4	S	1	75,000	11	5	30	—	-12	Launcher attack, not special or hyper combo cancelable

1

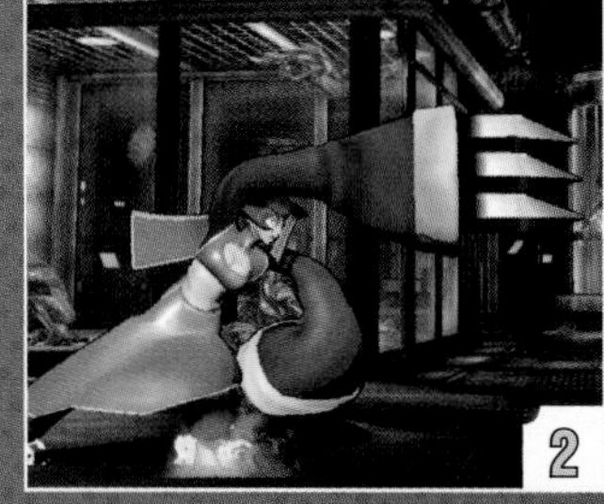
2

3

4

CROUCHING BASIC ATTACKS

Screen	Command	Hits	Damage	Startup	Active	Recovery	Advantage on Hit	Advantage if Guarded	Notes
1	Crouching L	1	40,000	5	3	12	-2	-2	Low attack
2	Crouching M	1	60,000	10	7	18	-7	-7	—
3	Crouching H	1	70,000	12	20	8	—	-5	Low attack, knocks down

1

2

3

AERIAL BASIC ATTACKS

Screen	Command	Hits	Damage	Startup	Active	Recovery	Notes
1	Air L	1	42,000	6	6	18	Overhead attack
2	Air M	1	63,000	8	6	31	Overhead attack
3	Air H	3	84,800	13	12	26	Overhead attack
4	Air S	1	70,000	9	6	31	Overhead attack, causes flying screen if used in launcher combo

1

2

3

4

SHUMA-GORATH

DLC

"HOW DO YOU EXPECT TO WIN A FIGHT WITH ONLY TWO ARMS?"

BIO

REAL NAME

SHUMA-GORATH

OCCUPATION

LORD OF CHAOS, MASTER OF THE GREAT OLD ONES, RULER OF A HUNDRED DIMENSIONS

ABILITIES

SHUMA-GORATH GENERATES HIS OWN MYSTICAL POWER, BUT ALSO DRAWS ENERGY, MYSTICAL OR OTHERWISE, FROM OTHERS. SHUMA-GORATH CAN RELEASE DESTRUCTIVE BLASTS AND CAN MANIPULATE MAGICAL ENERGY ON A PLANETARY SCALE. HE CAN COMMUNICATE TELEPATHICALLY AND CONTROL OTHERS, EVEN ACROSS DIMENSIONS.

WEAPONS

NONE

PROFILE

GOD OF ANOTHER DIMENSION. AS HE WILL ASSUME THE FORM OF WHATEVER IT IS THAT PEOPLE FEAR, HE HAS NO TRUE FORM. HAVING TAKEN A LIKING TO EARTH, HE HAS TRIED TO RULE OVER THE PLANET MANY TIMES SINCE THE PREHISTORIC AGE, BUT HAS USUALLY BEEN THWARTED BY A SHAMAN OR MAGIC USER, SUCH AS DOCTOR STRANGE.

FIRST APPEARANCE

MARVEL PREMIERE #5 (1972)

POWER GRID

3	INTELLIGENCE
7	STRENGTH
7	SPEED
7	STAMINA
6	ENERGY PROJECTION
2	FIGHTING ABILITY

*This is biographical, and does not represent an evaluation of the character's in-game combat potential.

ALTERNATE COSTUMES

PS3: ✕ Xbox 360: A

PS3: ☐ Xbox 360: X

PS3: △ Xbox 360: Y

PS3: R1 Xbox 360:  RB

ATTACK SET

STANDING BASIC ATTACKS

Screen	Command	Hits	Damage	Startup	Active	Recovery	Advantage on Hit	Advantage if Guarded	Notes
1	Standing Ⓛ	1	33,000	4	3	11	0	0	Rapid fire
2	Standing Ⓜ	2	62,000	5	2 (2) 3	19	-3	-3	—
3	Standing Ⓗ	6	82,800	9	2 (2) 2 (2) 2 (2) 2 (2) 2 (2) 2	10	+12	+12	—
4	Ⓢ	1	75,000	7	4	28	—	-8	Launcher attack, not special or hyper combo cancelable

CROUCHING BASIC ATTACKS

Screen	Command	Hits	Damage	Startup	Active	Recovery	Advantage on Hit	Advantage if Guarded	Notes
1	Crouching Ⓛ	1	33,000	5	3	13	-2	-2	Low attack, rapid fire
2	Crouching Ⓜ	2	63,000	6	3(1)4	15	—	0	Low attack, knocks down opponent
3	Crouching Ⓗ	1	70,000	10	4	20	+7	0	Knocks down opponent, jump cancelable

AERIAL BASIC ATTACKS

Screen	Command	Hits	Damage	Startup	Active	Recovery	Notes
1	Air Ⓛ	1	38,000	4	3	16	Overhead attack
2	Air Ⓜ	2	54,000	6	7	18	Overhead attack
3	Air Ⓗ	1	75,000	11	4	21	Overhead attack
4	Air Ⓢ	1	80,000	8	Until grounded	22	Overhead attack, knocks down opponent, OTG-capable, not special or hyper combo cancelable, causes flying screen if used in launcher combo

COMMAND ATTACKS

Screen	Command	Hits	Damage	Startup	Active	Recovery	Advantage on Hit	Advantage if Guarded	Notes
1	⇨ + Ⓗ	1	75,000	15	6	15	—	+3	Knocks down opponent
2	(in air) ⇧ + Ⓗ	1	75,000	11	4	21	—	—	Knocks down opponent

1

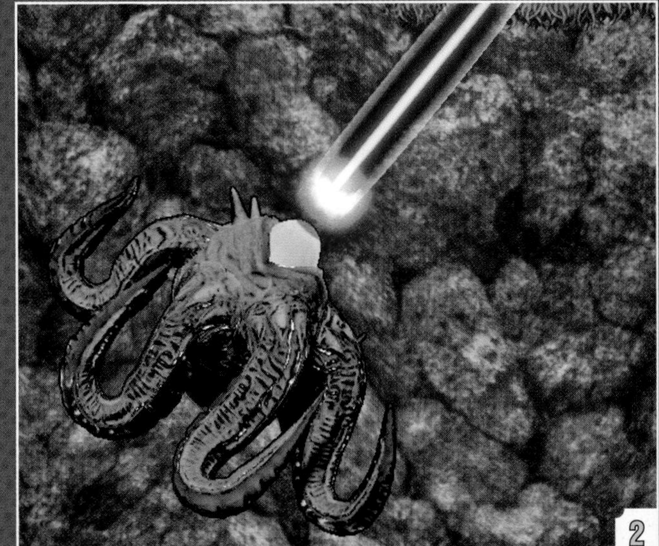
2

SHUMA-GORATH

DLC

AS A PARTNER-CROSSOVER ASSISTS

Screen	Type	P1+P2 Crossover Combination Hyper Combo	Description	Hits	Damage	Startup	Active	Recovery (this crossover assist)	Recovery (other partner)	Notes
1	α – Alpha	Hyper Mystic Ray	Mystic Ray H	10	129,900	52	30	95	65	OTG-capable, knocks down opponent, beam durability: 10 frames x 1 low priority durability points
2	β – Beta	Hyper Mystic Smash	Mystic Stare L	12	105,200	46	—	120	90	Projectiles disappear after 29 frames, beam durability: 6 frames x 1 low priority durability points
3	γ – Gamma	Hyper Mystic Smash	Mystic Smash L	8	113,600	37	32	110	80	—

1

2

3

SPECIAL MOVES

Screen	Name	Command	Hits	Damage	Startup	Active	Recovery	Advantage on Hit	Advantage if Guarded	Notes
1	Mystic Stare L	← (charge), → + Ⓛ	6/6	46,600/ 117,000	22	—	23	+10	+10	Projectiles disappear after 29 frames, on hit projectiles attach to opponent, explode 180 frames later, Mystic Stare cannot be used while projectiles are attached to opponent, exploding projectiles are OTG-capable, attached projectiles disappear if Shuma-Gorath is hit, beam durability: 6 frames x 1 low priority durability points
	Mystic Stare M	← (charge), → + Ⓜ	6/6	46,600/ 117,000	22	—	28	+5	+5	Projectiles disappear after 29 frames, on hit projectiles attach to opponent, explode 180 frames later, Mystic Stare cannot be used while projectiles are attached to opponent, exploding projectiles are OTG-capable, attached projectiles disappear if Shuma-Gorath is hit, beam durability: 6 frames x 1 low priority durability points
	Mystic Stare H	← (charge), → + Ⓗ	6/6	46,600/ 117,000	22	—	33	0	0	Projectiles disappear after 29 frames, on hit projectiles attach to opponent, explode 180 frames later, Mystic Stare cannot be used while projectiles are attached to opponent, exploding projectiles are OTG-capable, attached projectiles disappear if Shuma-Gorath is hit, beam durability: 6 frames x 1 low priority durability points
2	Mystic Smash L	↓↘→ + Ⓛ	8	113,600	13	32	18	+2	+2	—
	Mystic Smash M	↓↘→ + Ⓜ	9	122,200	15	36	18	+2	+2	—
	Mystic Smash H	↓↘→ + Ⓗ	10	129,900	18	40	18	+2	+2	—
3	Air Mystic Smash L	(in air) ↓↘→ + Ⓛ	6	117,000	12	Until grounded	13	+7~10	+7~10	—
	Air Mystic Smash M	(in air) ↓↘→ + Ⓜ	7	130,200	15	Until grounded	13	+7~10	+7~10	—
	Air Mystic Smash H	(in air) ↓↘→ + Ⓗ	8	142,100	18	Until grounded	13	+7~10	+7~10	—
4	Devitalization L	→↘↓↙← + Ⓛ	2	110,000	5	1	44	—	—	Throw, unrecoverable knockdown
	Devitalization M	→↘↓↙← + Ⓜ	2	140,000	3	1	46	—	—	Throw, unrecoverable knockdown
	Devitalization H	→↘↓↙← + Ⓗ	2	170,000	1	2	47	—	—	Throw, unrecoverable knockdown
5	Mystic Ray L	↓ (charge), ↑ + Ⓛ	6	93,500	22	30	9	-10	-10	Knocks down opponent, OTG-capable, beam durability: 6 frames x 1 low priority durability points
6	Mystic Ray M	↓ (charge), ↑ + Ⓜ	8	113,600	25	30	6	+12	+9	Knocks down opponent, OTG-capable, beam durability: 8 frames x 1 low priority durability points
7	Mystic Ray H	↓ (charge), ↑ + Ⓗ	10	129,900	28	30	3	+11	+9	Knocks down opponent, OTG-capable, beam durability: 10 frames x 1 low priority durability points

Mystic Stare: Mystic Stare fires a set of six eyeballs at the opponent. Every eyeball that hits the opponent attaches itself to their body, exploding 180 frames later. This explosion is treated like any other attack and can be guarded. If the opponent manages to hit you while having eyeballs attached, all eyeballs disappear without exploding. Mystic Stare also cannot be used at all while the opponent already has eyeballs stuck to them.

All versions of Mystic Stare fire projectiles that eventually disappear, similar to Chun-Li's Kikosho projectiles. Mystic Stare L recovers much more quickly than the other versions, but only travels 30% of the length of the screen. Mystic Stare M travels 60%, while Mystic Stare H can just barely hit an opponent all the way across the screen with a couple eyeballs.

Hitting your opponent with Mystic Stare puts you in a great situation: it's almost like insurance that your opponent will not do anything after a certain period of time, lest they risk getting hit by the explosion! This allows you to attack your opponent a little more freely.

Mystic Stare is an important component of corner combos, as the attached eyeball explosions are OTG-capable. You can combo into Mystic Stare, link further hits and cause a flying screen state, then combo from the eyeball explosion! See the Combo Usage section for details.

Mystic Smash: Mystic Smash is a great tool that allows you to safely advance while attacking. It always results in at least a slight frame advantage when guarded, and sometimes allows combos afterwards if it hits.

Mystic Smash can pass through to the other side of opponents while hitting them. Though you can't do much that's particularly tricky here due to the opponent being stuck in hitstun or guardstun, it's a great way to sandwich the opponent between yourself and a crossover assist!

Mystic Smash L travels a short distance, making it useful for the aforementioned crossover assist sandwich tactic. This is effective when set up from guarded basic attacks, but be wary of opponents that use advancing guard: you'll often get pushed out of range and your Mystic Smash L will whiff completely.

Mystic Smash M travels about the same distance as Mystic Smash L, but reaches a much greater height first. This can be used to avoid attacks from your opponent, but it is much more commonly used as a sneaky way to cross your opponent up at certain ranges. If Mystic Smash M hits the opponent, you can usually link standing Ⓛ afterwards to start a combo! Mystic Smash M cross-ups become much more effective when used in tandem with a crossover assist.

Mystic Smash H travels almost the entire length of the screen, making it great for going over projectiles while attacking the opponent. It's also strong when used in anticipation of the opponent using advancing guard: call a crossover assist, then cancel your guarded basic attacks into Mystic Smash H to get back into your opponent's face!

Air Mystic Smash: Air Mystic Smash is just as useful as the ground version of the attack: they all result in frame advantage if guarded and will almost always allow you to link standing Ⓛ afterwards if hit, making it a very versatile combo-starter.

Air Mystic Smash L drops you down sharply at a roughly 60-degree angle. This is mostly useful at mid-range, or as a mix-up to cross-up airdash Ⓜ. Air Mystic Smash M travels quite a bit farther, and allows you to attack the opponent from much farther away. Against an opponent that is quick to use advancing guard, use a jump-canceled crouching Ⓗ into Air Mystic Smash M to continue attacking! Air Mystic Smash H travels upward a bit before dropping down, making it great for surprise cross-ups.

Devitalization: Like most command throws, Devitalization offers progressively more damage and speed at higher strengths, at the expense of range. Devitalization L doesn't have substantially more range than the H version, however, which also happens to only have a single frame of startup. While Devitalization leaves the opponent in an unrecoverable knockdown state, it is nearly impossible to start a combo afterwards in most situations. This makes Shuma-Gorath's ground throw a much deadlier option, even though it's escapable.

Mystic Ray L

Mystic Ray M

Mystic Ray H

Mystic Ray: All versions of Mystic Ray first aim straight down before sweeping upward. Mystic Ray L ends aiming straight forward, the M version swings around to a 45-degree angle, and the H version ends up pointing straight up. It's almost impossible to completely avoid Mystic Ray H, making it a strong option for zoning opponents when used in tandem with a long-ranged crossover assist. Mystic Ray M is great for attacking opponents that are trying to use projectiles from the air, and Mystic Ray L is a more effective full-screen attack than Mystic Stare H.

Mystic Ray is also OTG-capable, though you can usually get more damage by using Hyper Mystic Smash or Hyper Mystic Ray by themselves.

"CHAOS IS EVERYTHING, AND SHUMA-GORATH IS A FRACTAL OF CHAOS."

HYPER COMBOS

Screen	Name	Command	Hits	Damage	Startup	Active	Recovery	Advantage on Hit	Advantage if Guarded	Notes
1	Hyper Mystic Smash	→ ↓ ↘ + ATK ATK	30	298,000	18+10	73	69	—	-42	Frames 16-41 invincible, OTG-capable, unrecoverable knockdown, each projectile has 3 frames x 1 high priority durability points
2	Hyper Mystic Ray	↓ ↙ ← + ATK ATK	20	279,700	20+4	30(29)12	100	—	-88	Frames 1-18 invincible, OTG-capable, unrecoverable knockdown, 2 beams, beam durability: 20 frames x 1 high priority durability points
3	Chaos Dimension (Level 3 hyper combo)	↓ ↘ → + ATK ATK, Ⓗ	1	50,000	10+1	5	20	—	-1	Frames 1-15 invincible, knocks down opponent, enters Chaos Dimension state, Chaos Dimension state lasts for 300 frames
4,5	Chaos Dimension Attack (in air OK)	(during Chaos Dimension state) Ⓗ	2	350,000	4	3	11	—	—	Unguardable, causes unrecoverable knockdown

Hyper Mystic Smash: Hyper Mystic Smash fires a ton of bouncing spiked balls (Shuma-balls!) across the screen. Each Shuma-ball is fired at a completely random angle; sometimes you'll luck out and fire a few that bounce almost completely vertically and stay in play for a long time. Hyper Mystic Smash is OTG-capable, and is Shuma-Gorath's most damaging follow-up to a normal, mid screen throw.

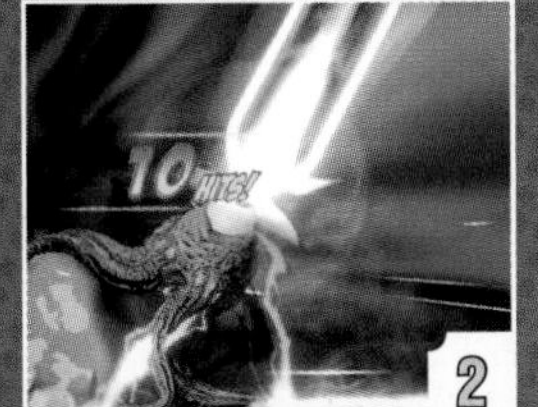

Hyper Mystic Ray: Hyper Mystic Ray is essentially two consecutive Mystic Ray H beams. Hyper Mystic Ray has a lot of invincibility frames, which unfortunately do not last until Shuma-Gorath begins firing. Regardless, it is still a useful defensive tool to stop opponents from attacking. Also OTG-capable, Hyper Mystic Ray is Shuma-Gorath's most damaging combo-ender in the corner—Hyper Mystic Smash generally tosses a bunch of Shuma-balls over the opponent in corners.

Chaos Dimension: Chaos Dimension is a level 3 hyper combo that begins with a quick invincible attack that knocks the opponent into the air. Once in Chaos Dimension state, all Ⓗ attacks become a quick unguardable attack that triggers a cutscene for major damage. This is relatively easy to hit the opponent with; all you have to do is get near them and just grab while they're in guardstun.

If the initial attack hits the opponent you can easily juggle a launcher afterwards, which lets you add a few more hits before hitting your opponent with Ⓗ for major damage. The invincible activation of Chaos Dimension can be used defensively to great effect: if your opponent guards it, you can still threaten with the unblockable Ⓗ attack.

BATTLE PLAN

OVERVIEW

Please note Shuma-Gorath is a downloadable character not available at game launch, who may change before actually being released one month later.

VITALITY: 950,000

CHAIN COMBO ARCHETYPE: HUNTER SERIES

X-Factor	Lv.1	Lv.2	Lv.3
Damage	130%	160%	190%
Speed	112.5%	125%	137.5%

Your goal with Shuma-Gorath is to get within range to cross your opponent up with airdash air Ⓜ. Why is that a good range to be in?

Airdash air Ⓜ is a quick, difficult to guard cross-up that leads into combos.

If your opponent guards the air Ⓜ, you can mix up a delayed air Ⓜ with a low attack.

If your opponent guards all air Ⓜ attacks, you can still threaten with a ground throw into combo.

Mystic Smash L and M, along with Air Mystic Smash, are all very strong at this range.

How do you get into cross-up range with Shuma-Gorath?

Using Mystic Smash H and Air Mystic Smash M to go around zoning tactics.

Super jumping and dropping down with Air Mystic Smash L.

Beating your opponent at long range with Mystic Ray and crossover assists, forcing them to come to you.

COMBO APPENDIX

GENERAL EXECUTION TIPS

Super jump to reach the minimum height requirement to airdash much more quickly.

During combos that involve jump canceled crouching Ⓗ, delay the air Ⓗ and ⇧ + Ⓗ attacks as much as you can to keep the opponent low to the ground.

During launcher combos, don't start charging down until immediately after air Ⓢ hits the opponent.

Requirements (Position, meter, etc.)	Notes	Command Sequence	Damage
—	Mid screen combo with meter	Cr. Ⓛ, cr. Ⓗ (CANCEL) jump forward, air Ⓜ (2 hits), Ⓗ, ⇧ + Ⓗ, land, jump forward, air Ⓜ (2 hits), Ⓗ, ⇧ + Ⓗ, land, jump forward, air Ⓜ (2 hits), air Ⓜ (2 hits), Ⓗ (CANCEL) ⇩ ⬂ ⇨ + Ⓜ, ⇩ ⬂ ⇨ + ATK ATK, st. Ⓜ (2 hits), cr. Ⓜ (2 hits), Ⓢ (CANCEL) super jump, air Ⓜ (2 hits), Ⓜ (2 hits), Ⓗ	817,000
—	Mid screen combo with no meter	Cr. Ⓛ, cr. Ⓗ (CANCEL) jump forward, air Ⓜ (2 hits), Ⓗ, ⇧ + Ⓗ, land, cr. Ⓗ (CANCEL) jump forward, air Ⓜ (2 hits), Ⓗ, ⇧ + Ⓗ (CANCEL) ⇩ ⬂ ⇨ + Ⓜ, cr. Ⓜ (2 hits), Ⓢ (CANCEL) super jump, Ⓜ (2 hits), Ⓜ (2 hits), Ⓗ, ⇧ + Ⓗ (CANCEL) ⇩ ⬂ ⇨ + Ⓜ	448,000
Corner required	—	Cr. Ⓛ, cr. Ⓗ (CANCEL) jump forward, air Ⓜ (2 hits), Ⓗ, ⇧ + Ⓗ, land, cr. Ⓗ (CANCEL) jump forward, air Ⓜ (2 hits), Ⓗ, ⇧ + Ⓗ, land, cr. Ⓗ (CANCEL) ⇦ (charge), ⇨ + Ⓜ, cr. Ⓜ (1 hit), Ⓢ (CANCEL) super jump, air Ⓜ (2 hits), Ⓜ (2 hits), Ⓗ, Ⓢ, land, Ⓢ (CANCEL) super jump, air Ⓗ, Ⓢ, land, ⇩ ⬃ ⇦ + ATK ATK OTG	666,900
Corner required	—	Cr. Ⓛ, cr. Ⓗ (CANCEL) jump forward, air Ⓜ (2 hits), Ⓗ, ⇧ + Ⓗ, land, cr. Ⓗ (CANCEL) jump forward, air Ⓜ (2 hits), Ⓗ, ⇧ + Ⓗ, land, cr. Ⓗ (CANCEL) ⇦ (charge), ⇨ + Ⓜ, cr. Ⓜ (1 hit), Ⓢ (CANCEL) super jump, air Ⓜ (2 hits), Ⓜ (2 hits), Ⓗ, Ⓢ, land, ⇩ ⬂ ⇨ + ATK ATK, Ⓢ (CANCEL) super jump, air Ⓜ (2 hits), Ⓗ	877,900
—	Works for both air and ground throws	Throw, ⇩ ⬃ ⇦ + ATK ATK OTG	261,100
—	Works after a throw in either direction, fairly difficult to time, works for both air and ground throws	Throw, ⇨ ⇩ ⬂ + ATK ATK OTG	343,800
—	Works for both air and ground throws	Throw, ⇩ (charge), ⇧ + Ⓜ (8 hits) OTG (CANCEL) ⇩ ⬂ ⇨ + ATK ATK, dash, st. Ⓜ (1 hit), cr. Ⓜ (2 hits), Ⓢ (CANCEL) super jump, air Ⓛ, Ⓛ, Ⓜ (2 hits), Ⓜ (2 hits), Ⓗ	617,800
—	Forward air throw only	Air throw, air Ⓜ (2 hits), Ⓜ (2 hit), land, jump forward, air Ⓜ (2 hits), Ⓗ, ⇧ + Ⓗ, land, jump forward, air Ⓜ (2 hits), Ⓗ, ⇧ + Ⓗ, land, jump forward, air Ⓜ (2 hits), air Ⓜ (2 hits), Ⓗ (CANCEL) ⇩ ⬂ ⇨ + Ⓜ, ⇩ ⬂ ⇨ + ATK ATK, st. Ⓜ, cr. Ⓜ, Ⓢ (CANCEL) super jump, air Ⓜ (2 hits), Ⓜ (2 hits), Ⓢ	778,100

JILL

DLC

BIO

REAL NAME

JILL VALENTINE

OCCUPATION

BSAA OPERATIVE

ABILITIES

VARIOUS ABILITIES INCLUDING MASTERFUL UNLOCKING ABILITIES, BOMB DISPOSAL, HAND-TO-HAND COMBAT, AND GUN SKILLS LEARNED DURING AMERICAN MILITARY TRAINING.

WEAPONS

MANY DIFFERENT FIREARMS SUCH AS HANDGUNS, SUB-MACHINE GUNS, SHOTGUNS, ROCKET LAUNCHERS, ETC. SHE IS ALSO ABLE TO USE MILITARY-ISSUE KNIVES.

PROFILE

TO SAVE CHRIS DURING A FIGHT, SHE THREW HERSELF OFF A CLIFF ALONG WITH WESKER. HER BODY WAS NEVER FOUND AND SHE WAS PRESUMED DEAD; HOWEVER, SHE SURVIVED THE FALL, AND WAS TAKEN BY WESKER TO BE ONE OF HIS EXPERIMENTS. AFTER BEING SUBJECTED TO UROBOROS TESTS, SHE WAS OUTFITTED WITH A MIND CONTROL DEVICE, MAKING HER INTO A PUPPET SOLDIER.

FIRST APPEARANCE

RESIDENT EVIL (1996)

POWER GRID

2	INTELLIGENCE
5	STRENGTH
6	SPEED
5	STAMINA
1	ENERGY PROJECTION
6	FIGHTING ABILITY

*This is biographical, and does not represent an evaluation of the character's in-game combat potential.

ALTERNATE COSTUMES

PS3: ⓧ Xbox 360: Ⓐ

PS3: ◻ Xbox 360: Ⓧ

PS3: △ Xbox 360: Ⓨ

PS3: R1 Xbox 360: RB

ATTACK SET

STANDING BASIC ATTACKS

Screen	Command	Hits	Damage	Startup	Active	Recovery	Advantage on Hit	Advantage if Guarded	Notes
1	Standing Ⓛ	1	33,000	4	2	12	0	-1	Rapid fire
2	Standing Ⓜ	1	45,000	7	3	20	-4	-6	—
3	Standing Ⓗ	1	63,000	9	3	21	0	-2	⇩⇙⇨ + P1 or P2 snap back
4	Ⓢ	1	70,000	8	3	24	—	-5	Launcher, not special or hyper combo cancelable

CROUCHING BASIC ATTACKS

Screen	Command	Hits	Damage	Startup	Active	Recovery	Advantage on Hit	Advantage if Guarded	Notes
1	Crouching Ⓛ	1	30,000	5	2	11	+2	0	Low attack, rapid fire, chains into standing Ⓛ
2	Crouching Ⓜ	1	43,000	8	12	16	-9	-11	Low attack, chains into standing Ⓜ
3	Crouching Ⓗ	1	60,000	9	3	26	—	-7	Low attack, knocks down

AERIAL BASIC ATTACKS

Screen	Command	Hits	Damage	Startup	Active	Recovery	Notes
1	Air Ⓛ	1	35,000	5	7	6	Overhead attack
2	Air Ⓜ	1	50,000	8	3	20	Overhead attack
3	Air Ⓗ	1	65,000	9	4	21	Overhead attack
4	Air Ⓢ	1	68,000	9	6	21	Overhead attack, unrecoverable knockdown when used in air combo after Ⓢ launcher

COMMAND ATTACKS

Screen	Command	Hits	Damage	Startup	Active	Recovery	Advantage on Hit	Advantage if Guarded	Notes
1	⇦ + Ⓗ	1	63,000	11	4	21	-1	-3	Chains from any basic attack
2	⇨ + Ⓗ	1	65,000	23	3	12	+9	+7	Overhead, recovers in Feral Crouch

"GYAH...I DON'T KNOW...ANY CHRIS"

AS A PARTNER-CROSSOVER ASSISTS

Screen	Type	P1+P2 Crossover Combination Hyper Combo	Description	Hits	Damage	Startup	Active	Recovery (this crossover assist)	Recovery (other partner)	Notes
1	α – Alpha	Machine Gun Spray	Cartwheel Kick	1	80,000	39	10	117	87	Ground bounces opponent
2	β – Beta	Machine Gun Spray	Arrow Kick	1	100,000	44	9	120	90	Wall bounces opponent, unrecoverable knockdown
3	γ – Gamma	Machine Gun Spray	Somersault Kick	1	90,000	34	10	134	104	Knocks down opponent

JILL

DLC

SPECIAL MOVES

Screen	Name	Command	Hits	Damage	Startup	Active	Recovery	Advantage on Hit	Advantage if Guarded	Notes
1	Flip Kick	↓↘→ + (L)	1	70,000	13	10	13	—	-1	Knocks down opponent, recovers in Feral Crouch, cancels into Feral Crouch
2	Cartwheel Kick	↓↘→ + (M)	1	80,000	15	10	21	—	-7	Ground bounces opponent, recovers in Feral Crouch, cancels into Feral Crouch
3	Arrow Kick	↓↘→ + (H)	1	100,000	20	9	27	—	-11	Wall bounces opponent, unrecoverable knockdown, cancels into Feral Crouch
4	Double Knee Drop L	(in air) ↓↘→ + (L)	1	70,000	18	Until grounded	11	+10	+8	Unrecoverable knockdown against airborne opponents
4	Double Knee Drop M	(in air) ↓↘→ + (M)	1	80,000	23	Until grounded	11	+15	+13	Ground bounces airborne opponents, unrecoverable knockdown against airborne opponents
4	Double Knee Drop H	(in air) ↓↘→ + (H)	1	90,000	30	Until grounded	14	+34	+5	Staggers grounded opponents, ground bounces airborne opponents, unrecoverable knockdown against airborne opponents
5	Fallen Prey	→↓↘ + (L)	2	98,000	8	2	31	—	-11	Low attack, unrecoverable knockdown, OTG-capable
6	Ensnarement	→↓↘ + (M)	2	98,000	10	3	28	—	-9	Unrecoverable knockdown
7	Position Exchange	→↓↘ + (H)	1	—	10	1	25	+4	—	Throw, switches sides with opponent
8	Feral Crouch	↓↓ + (S)	—	—	10	—	—	—	—	Cannot block while in Feral Crouch, press (S) again to cancel, cancelling Feral Crouch takes 5 frames to complete
9	Low Sweep	(During Feral Crouch) (L)	1	45,000	8	5	26	-7	-9	Low attack, recovers in Feral Crouch, cancelable, not affected by hitstun deterioration
10	Jumping Roundhouse	(During Feral Crouch) (M)	1	85,000	20	3	23	—	-4	Wall bounces opponent, cancelable into Feral Crouch
11	Somersault Kick	(During Feral Crouch) (H)	1	90,000	10	10	41	-15	-29	Frames 1-14 invincible, knocks down opponent, jump cancelable, cancelable into Feral Crouch
12	Teleport	(During Feral Crouch) ←, ↖, ↑, ↗, or → / (During Mad Beast) input any direction	—	—	9	—	7	—	—	Frames 9-14 invincible, can pass through opponents, automatically re-aligns to face the opponent, teleport is cancelable into special moves and hyper combos at any time

Flip Kick: Jill flips backwards, knocking the enemy into the air and leaving them open to an air combo. Jill is left at -1 afterwards, but is usually too far away to be punished by one frame throws. If you think your opponent will attack afterwards, beat out their attack with the safe, jump-cancelable Somersault Kick! If you predict your foe will try to guard, then Teleport behind them and continue your offense.

Cartwheel: This is Jill's only means of inducing a ground bounce. It shifts into Feral Crouch automatically when it recovers, but Feral Crouch options cannot be used to defend against Cartwheel's punishable guard disadvantage. To help mitigate this, cancel Cartwheel Kick into Feral Crouch manually to leave yourself at frame advantage!

Arrow Kick: A jumping kick that flies across the screen, causing a wall bounce on hit. Cancel Arrow Kick into Feral Crouch to leave yourself at frame advantage, and also to enable mid-screen combos afterwards!

Double Knee Drop: The main use of Double Knee Drop is as a quick overhead; it's very difficult to react to if performed very close to the ground by inputting ↓↘→↗ + (L). It can also be canceled into from aerial attacks to trick your opponent's guarding habits. If, for instance, the opponent is conditioned to guard low after Jill's → + (H) overhead (due to its shift into Feral Crouch and the common use of its Low Sweep extension), cancel into air ↓↘→ + (L) to hit their crouching guard. It's also used to change the trajectory of your jumps. If you're in range to go for cross-up air (S), which your foe is expecting, perform air ↓↘→ + (L) before you pass over the opponent's head to hit them from the front.

The (H) version of the Double Knee Drop causes a stagger. This allows for a very difficult infinite corner combo. Perform ↓↘→↗ + (H) directly next to the opponent, then, as you recover, do the same command again, ensuring that the final (H) input is performed at the exact moment Jill leaves the ground. If done correctly, the second knee drop will link after the first. Do this repeatedly to keep the combo going.

Fallen Prey: This basic low kick is OTG-capable and grants opportunities to score extra damage off of Jill's throws and unrecoverable knockdowns. It's extremely open to punishment when guarded, so use it only in combos.

Ensnarement: Jill kicks and flings the opponent behind her, swapping positions with them. They're left in an unrecoverable knockdown state upon recovery, allowing you to dash forward and strike with Fallen Prey or Machine Gun Spray. You can also juggle the enemy before they land if your back is flush against the corner. This is valuable for regaining a positional advantage after a risky setup. For example, if the enemy is cornered and you use Teleport to pass behind and confuse them, perform a combo into Ensnarement and then juggle after it to keep the opposition cornered.

Position Change: A command throw that leaves the opponent vulnerable to a combo. The advantage gained when the throw recovers is + 4, which can be linked after with Jill's only 4 frame startup move, standing (L). Use Position Change when your foe is less prone to jump or attack.

8

9

10

11

12

Feral Crouch: This stance eliminates your ability to guard, but grants access to 4 unique moves. Outside of its usefulness in combos, Feral Crouch can be canceled into from blocked attacks to mount a secondary offensive behind frame advantage; canceling into it off of Ⓗ attacks grants a +10 advantage, enough to ensure a follow-up Feral Crouch offense works. Upon activation, press Ⓛ to perform Low Sweep, which is cancelable into special moves. Low Sweep's 8 frame start-up makes it perfect for preemptively stopping incoming attacks. Variation Ⓜ does a leaping kick—Jumping Roundhouse—which causes a wall bounce, though Jumping Roundhouse is extremely unsafe if blocked, cancel it into Feral Crouch to maintain frame advantage! Version Ⓗ initiates an invulnerable Somersault Kick used to stop any and all incoming attacks. Somersault Kick is cancelable into a jump when it connects, making it safe on guard while allowing for follow-up juggle combos. Use this to compensate for the inability to guard while in Feral Crouch.

The cream of the crop is the Teleport, a lightning-fast movement that can be done in 1 of 5 directions: ⇦, ⇖, ⇧, ⇗ or ⇨. The middle period of all Teleport versions is invulnerable, allowing it to pass through some attacks if timed properly. The ⇨ version should be used to move next to an opponent after they push you away with advancing guard, or to pass behind the enemy at close distances for a tricky side switch. ⇗ launches you upwards at an angle, causing you to pass over the opponent's head in position for a cross-up air Ⓢ or Ⓗ. The ⇧, ⇖, and ⇦ versions offer safe ways to retreat.

All versions of Teleport can be canceled into special moves and hyper combos at any time! This makes for interesting offensive tactics. For example, perform standing Ⓗ CANCEL ⇩⇩ + Ⓢ CANCEL ⇨, then as the teleport reaches its mid period, do ⇨⇩⇘ + Ⓗ to cancel into the Position Change command throw. When using the ⇗ Teleport to go for a cross-up, occasionally cancel it into air ⇩⇘⇨ + Ⓛ before you pass over the opponent's head. This changes the trajectory of your attack, hitting them from the front.

HYPER COMBOS

Screen	Name	Command	Hits	Damage	Startup	Active	Recovery	Advantage on Hit	Advantage if Guarded	Notes
1	Machine Gun Spray	⇩⇘⇨ + ATK ATK	—	11,000 per bullet	10+9	38	23	0	-7	Frames 1-20 invincible, OTG-capable, each projectile has 3 high priority durability points
2	Raven Spike	⇨⇩⇘ + ATK ATK	7	290,800	8+1	5	36	—	-19	Unrecoverable knockdown
3	Mad Beast (Level 3 hyper combo)	⇩⇙⇦ + ATK ATK	—	—	10+1	—	1	—	—	Frames 1-10 invincible, lasts 600 frames, in Feral Crouch during the duration but without its signature attacks, Flip Kick and Carthwheel kick become cancelable into Teleport on hit or guard, able to crouch block only, able to perform up to 2 teleports in air

1

Machine Gun Spray: Jill spirals into the air with machine gun fire. This is an all-purpose reversal that sports a long window of invulnerability, making it usable as anti-air, to beat projectiles, or to stop incoming close-range attacks. It's also OTG-capable for scoring additional damage off of throws and other unrecoverable knockdowns. Unfortunately, its odd firing pattern causes it to frequently miss shots, and stops it from fully linking together. Use it when the enemy is at the peak of their jump to ensure it fully connects.

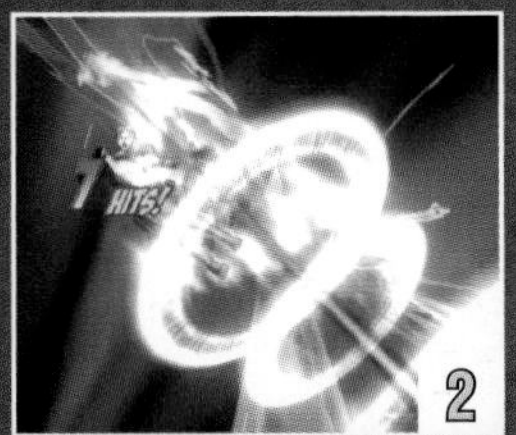
2

Raven Spike: This is used only in combos. It inflicts relatively high damage and is fast enough to combo if canceled into off of light attacks. It's completely punishable when guarded and has no invulnerability. Avoid it unless you're nailing the enemy with a verifiable combo opening.

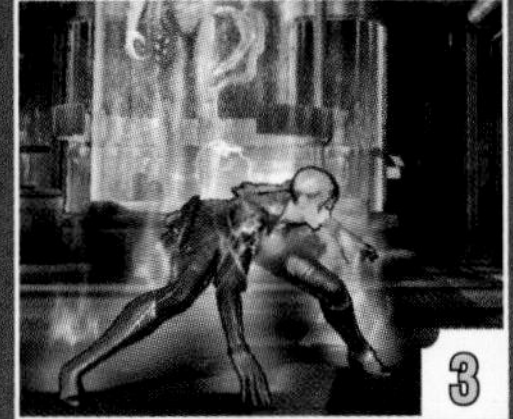
3

Mad Beast: Her level 3 hyper combo shifts her into a permanent Feral Crouch state; she cannot guard high and cannot jump or dash normally. Instead, inputting ←, ↖, ↑, ↗, or → causes her to teleport in that direction. The same thing occurs when she's in the air, except she can teleport in any direction needed, including ↙, ↓, and ↘. Certain special moves can also be canceled into each other, which is the most important aspect of this mode: you can cancel ↓↘→ + Ⓛ CANCEL ↓↘→ + Ⓜ repeatedly until the Mad Beast timer runs out for massive damage. This is far more important than the crazy mobility options available in this mode, as the inability to guard high attacks makes it far too risky to use strictly for movement. Combo into Mad Beast off of basic ground chains to obliterate the opponent's vitality.

BATTLE PLAN

OVERVIEW

Please note Jill is a downloadable character not available at game launch, who may change before actually being released one month later.

VITALITY: 850,000

CHAIN COMBO ARCHETYPE: HUNTER SERIES

X-Factor	Lv.1	Lv.2	Lv.3
Damage	125%	150%	175%
Speed	115%	130%	145%

Jill's objective is to establish close range and stage a varied attack. She has access to a practical infinite combo (see the third from the last combo in the Combo Appendix). This combo works off of all of her strongest attack openings. This means any stray mix-up hit can lead to a knock out!

A close-range strategy is effective because:

- **Jill has access to every attack needed to stage a threatening offense: a fast overhead that leads to a combo, a command throw that also transitions to a combo, and fast, flexible low-hitting combos.**
- **Her Feral Crouch maneuvers, particularly her Teleport, allow her to attack from multiple angles while also giving her ways to compensate for advancing guard.**
- **A single hit can potentially transition into her infinite combo.**

This goal is accomplished by:

- **Using ↗ Teleport to pass over a projectile or ground attack.**
- **Calling a projectile assist to over her as she moves in with → Teleport.**
- **Attacking the enemy from mid range with crouching Ⓜ, then canceling into Feral Crouch to stage an offense.**
- **Using the invulnerability from a → Teleport to pass through a projectile or ground attack.**

COMBO APPENDIX

GENERAL EXECUTION TIPS

When performing ↓↘→ + Ⓛ CANCEL Feral Crouch Ⓛ loops, wait a moment after shifting to Feral Crouch before performing Ⓛ. This ensures the enemy doesn't get popped too high for additional hits.

Linking after Position Change requires you to perform a 1 frame link into standing Ⓛ. To help with executing this, compensate for human error by brushing your index and middle fingers across Ⓛ twice in succession.

Requirements (Position, meter, etc.)	Notes	Command Sequence	Damage
—	After hitting with Feral Ⓗ, cancel into a forward jump and wait until you begin to fall before doing air Ⓗ, Ⓢ	Cr. Ⓜ, cr. Ⓗ, ← + Ⓗ CANCEL ↓↘→ + Ⓜ, Feral Ⓗ CANCEL forward jump, late air Ⓗ, Ⓢ, land, st. Ⓜ, Ⓢ CANCEL super jump, air Ⓜ, Ⓜ, Ⓗ, Ⓢ	408,400
—	→ + Ⓗ is canceled before it lands into air ↓↘→ + Ⓛ	→ + Ⓗ CANCEL air ↓↘→ + Ⓛ, cr. Ⓜ, cr. Ⓗ, ← + Ⓗ, ↓↘→ + Ⓜ, Feral Ⓗ CANCEL forward jump, late air Ⓗ, Ⓢ, land, st. Ⓜ, Ⓢ CANCEL super jump, air Ⓜ, Ⓜ, Ⓗ, Ⓢ	429,400
—	—	Forward, back, or air throw, forward dash, →↓↘ + Ⓛ	145,100
—	—	→↓↘ + Ⓗ, st. Ⓛ, st. Ⓜ, cr. Ⓗ, ← + Ⓗ, ↓↘→ + Ⓜ, Feral Ⓗ CANCEL forward jump, late air Ⓗ, Ⓢ, land, st. Ⓜ, Ⓢ CANCEL super jump, air Ⓜ, Ⓜ, Ⓗ, Ⓢ	286,300
Requires 1 hyper combo gauge bar	—	Against aerial enemy, st. Ⓜ CANCEL ↓↘→ + Ⓛ, Feral Ⓛ CANCEL ↓↘→ + Ⓛ, Feral Ⓛ CANCEL ↓↘→ + Ⓜ, Feral Ⓛ CANCEL Ⓢ CANCEL super jump, air Ⓜ, Ⓜ, Ⓗ, Ⓢ, land, ↓↘→ + ATK ATK	481,600
—	Does not work against the following characters mid screen: Chun-li, Felicia, Jill, Morrigan, Super-Skrull, X-23	Cr. Ⓜ, st. Ⓜ, st. Ⓗ, cr. Ⓗ, ← + Ⓗ CANCEL ↓↘→ + Ⓛ, Feral Ⓛ CANCEL ↓↘→ + Ⓛ, Feral Ⓛ CANCEL ↓↘→ + Ⓜ, Feral Ⓛ CANCEL Ⓢ CANCEL super jump, air Ⓜ, Ⓜ, Ⓗ, Ⓢ, land, forward dash, →↓↘ + Ⓛ	450,000
—	Does not work against the following characters mid screen: Chun-li, Felicia, Jill, Morrigan, Super-Skrull, X-23	→ + Ⓗ CANCEL air ↓↘→ + Ⓛ, land, cr. Ⓜ, st. Ⓜ, st. Ⓗ, cr. Ⓗ, ← + Ⓗ CANCEL ↓↘→ + Ⓛ, Feral Ⓛ CANCEL ↓↘→ + Ⓛ, Feral Ⓛ CANCEL ↓↘→ + Ⓜ, Feral Ⓛ CANCEL Ⓢ CANCEL super jump, air Ⓜ, Ⓜ, Ⓗ, Ⓢ, land, forward dash, →↓↘ + Ⓛ	486,100
Requires corner, requires 1 hyper combo gauge bar	Each Feral Ⓛ CANCEL ↓↘→ + Ⓛ input should be delayed slightly to ensure all 3 repetitions of the sequence will hit, otherwise the enemy is bumped too high	Cr. Ⓜ, st. Ⓜ, st. Ⓗ, ← + Ⓗ CANCEL ↓↓ + Ⓢ, Feral Ⓛ CANCEL ↓↘→ + Ⓛ, Feral Ⓛ CANCEL ↓↘→ + Ⓛ, Feral Ⓛ CANCEL ↓↘→ + Ⓛ, Feral Ⓛ CANCEL ↓↘→ + Ⓗ, air ↓↘→ + Ⓗ, land, st. Ⓗ, ← + Ⓗ CANCEL →↓↘ + ATK ATK	570,100
—	This sequence can be done indefinitely after the first hit, can be canceled and linked into off of any chain that ends with standing Ⓗ or ← + Ⓗ	↓↓ + Ⓢ, Feral Ⓛ CANCEL ↓↓ + Ⓢ, Feral Ⓛ CANCEL ↓↓ + Ⓢ, Feral Ⓛ CANCEL ↓↓ + Ⓢ, Feral Ⓛ CANCEL ↓↓ + Ⓢ, Feral Ⓛ CANCEL ↓↓ + Ⓢ...	100%
—	When canceling into each consecutive ↓↘→ + Ⓛ CANCEL ↓↘→ + Ⓜ, delay the button input to ensure the special move comes out and not the Teleport; you're not actually canceling special moves into each other, you're canceling the teleport into a special move, delaying the button input causes the teleport to come out for a frame or two	Cr. Ⓜ, st. Ⓜ, st. Ⓗ, cr. Ⓗ, CANCEL ← + Ⓗ CANCEL ↓↘→ + Ⓜ CANCEL ↓↙← + ATK ATK, ↓↘→ + Ⓛ CANCEL ↓↘→ + Ⓜ CANCEL ↓↘→ + Ⓛ CANCEL ↓↘→ + Ⓜ CANCEL ↓↘→ + Ⓛ CANCEL ↓↘→ + Ⓜ CANCEL ↓↘→ + Ⓛ CANCEL ↓↘→ + Ⓜ CANCEL ↓↘→ + Ⓛ CANCEL ↓↘→ + Ⓜ CANCEL ↓↘→ + Ⓛ CANCEL ↓↘→ + Ⓜ CANCEL ↓↘→ + Ⓛ CANCEL ↓↘→ + Ⓜ CANCEL ↓↘→ + Ⓛ CANCEL ↓↘→ + Ⓜ CANCEL ↓↘→ + Ⓛ CANCEL ↓↘→ + ATK ATK	783,400
Requires corner	This sequence can be done indefinitely after the first hit, Ⓗ must be pressed after the ↓↘→↗ on the exact frame Jill leaves the ground for the jump, or else each knee will not combo together, does not work against Dormammu or Sentinel	↓↘→↗ + Ⓗ, ↓↘→↗ + Ⓗ, ↓↘→↗ + Ⓗ, ↓↘→↗ + Ⓗ...	100%

Trophies, Achievements, Icons, & Titles

Trophies & Achievements

Most trophies and achievements in *Marvel vs. Capcom 3* are self-explanatory. Use a certain number of moves, or win a certain number of matches, or play the game online in ranked mode. The most interesting unlocks require that you play as particular characters or matchups.

Trophies & Achivements

Name	Description	Mode	Gamerscore	Trophy
Master of Fate	Unlock all achievements.	—	50	Platinum
I Buy the Issues	View one ending in Arcade mode.	Arcade	10	Bronze
Waiting for the Trade	View all endings in Arcade mode.	Arcade	50	Gold
Herculean Task	Beat Arcade mode on the hardest difficulty.	Arcade	30	Silver
Saving My Quarters	Beat Arcade mode without using any continues.	Arcade	20	Bronze
World Warrior	Earn 5,000 Player Points (PP).	All	10	Bronze
Champion Edition Hero	Earn 30,000 Player Points (PP).	All	30	Silver
Super Turbo Brawler	Earn 100,000 Player Points (PP).	All	50	Silver
Average Joe	Land a Viewtiful Combo. (31+ hits, Arcade/online only)	All	10	Bronze
Brusin' Bruce	Land an Incredible Combo. (65+_hits, Arcade/online only)	All	20	Bronze
Charles in Charge	Land an Uncanny Combo. (91+ hits, Arcade/online only)	All	30	Silver
Playtime Is Over	Surpass the rank of Amateur.	Ranked Match	10	Bronze
Leading the Charge	Surpass the rank of Fighter.	Ranked Match	30	Silver
Combat Specialist	Surpass the "1st" class rank, or fight someone who has.	Online battle	30	Silver
Welcome to Avengers Academy!	Clear 80 missions in Mission mode.	Mission	10	Bronze
Passed the Field Test	Clear 160 missions in Mission mode.	Mission	20	Bronze
A New Avenger	Clear 320 missions in Mission mode.	Mission	40	Silver
Comic Collector	Unlock all items in the Gallery.	All	50	Gold
Mega Buster	Use 1,000 Hyper Combo Gauge bars. (Arcade/online only)	Arcade & Online battle	20	Bronze
Ultimate Nullifier	Perform 30 successful Advancing Guards. (Arcade/online only)	Arcade & Online battle	10	Bronze
Be Gone!	Perform 10 Snap Backs. (Arcade/online only)	Arcade & Online battle	10	Bronze
Back at 'Cha!	Perform 10 successful Crossover Counters. (Arcade/online only)	Arcade & Online battle	10	Bronze
Excelsior!	Perform 10 Team Air Combos. (Arcade/online only)	Arcade & Online battle	10	Bronze
Big Bang Theory	Perform 30 Hyper Combo Finishes. (Arcade/online only)	Arcade & Online battle	30	Silver

TROPHIES & ACHIVEMENTS

Name	Description	Mode	Gamerscore	Trophy
Galactic Smasher	Perform 30 Crossover Combination Finishes. (Arcade/online only)	Arcade & Online battle	40	Silver
Wreak "Havok"	Use X-Factor in a match.	Arcade & Online battle	10	Bronze
Turn the Tables	Land a Team Air Counter in a match.	Arcade & Online battle	10	Bronze
One Step Ahead	Land 50 First Attacks in a match.	Arcade & Online battle	30	Silver
Avengers Assemble!	Make a team composed of Captain America, Iron Man, and Thor, and win a match.	Arcade & Online battle	15	Bronze
Badds to the Bone	Make a team composed of Spencer, Iron Man, and M.O.D.O.K., and win a match.	Arcade & Online battle	15	Bronze
Darkstalkers	Make a team composed of Felicia, Hsien-Ko, and Morrigan, and win a match.	Arcade & Online battle	15	Bronze
Weapon X	Make a team composed of Deadpool, Wolverine, and X-23, and win a match.	Arcade & Online battle	15	Bronze
Female Flyers	Make a team composed of any three of Storm, Phoenix, Morrigan, and Trish, and win a match.	Arcade & Online battle	15	Bronze
Whose Side Are You On?	Bring about an end to the Civil War in an online match—unlocked when a team which includes Captain America is fighting against a team which includes Iron Man online.	Online battle	20	Bronze
Fate of Two Worlds	Make a match between the marquee characters for this game a reality in an online match—unlocked when a team which includes Ryu is fighting against a team which includes Wolverine online.	Online battle	20	Bronze
Duty and Deus Ex Machina	Make a match between a national hero and a killing machine a reality in an online match—unlocked when a team which includes Captain America is fighting against a team which includes M.O.D.O.K. online.	Online battle	20	Bronze
Copy This!	Put an end to this game of spider and fly in an online match—unlocked when a team which includes Spider-Man is fighting against a team which includes Taskmaster online.	Online battle	20	Bronze
Raccoon City Incident	Settle things between former S.T.A.R.S members in an online match—unlocked when a team which includes Chris is fighting against a team which includes Wesker online.	Online battle	20	Bronze
Fate of the Satsui no Hadou	Decide who is the true master of the fist in an online match—unlocked when a team which includes Ryu is fighting against a team which includes Akuma online.	Online battle	20	Bronze
Brave New World	Participate in any mode online.	Online battle	10	Bronze
Steel Battalion	Block 100 times. (Arcade/online only)	Arcade & Online battle	20	Bronze
Passport to Beatdown Country	Fight in all of the stages.	Arcade & Online battle	10	Bronze
Full Roster	Battle against all characters online.	Online battle	40	Silver
Who Will Answer the Call?	Participate in an 8 player Lobby online.	Lobby	10	Bronze
A Hero Stands Alone	Win a match without calling your partners or switching out. (Arcade/online only)	Arcade & Online battle	10	Bronze
Need a Healing Factor	Win a match without blocking. (Arcade/online only)	Arcade & Online battle	10	Bronze
School for the Gifted	Get a 5 game win streak in Ranked Match.	Ranked Match	15	Bronze

ICONS & TITLES

LIKE ACHIEVEMENTS AND TROPHIES, ICONS AND TITLES FOR YOUR LICENSE CARD ARE EARNED IN VARIOUS WAYS. MOST OF THESE ARE ALSO STRAIGHTFORWARD, AND TITLE REQUIREMENTS ARE EVEN OFFERED BY THE GAME ITSELF RIGHT FROM THE GET-GO, BUT SOME OF THESE AESTHETIC REWARDS ARE UNAVAILABLE UNTIL ONLINE EVENTS OCCUR. THESE EVENTS WERE UNKNOWN AT THE TIME WHEN THIS STRATEGY WAS WRITTEN.

LICENSE CARD ICONS

LICENSE CARD TITLES

	Unlock	Condition
The True Warrior	The True Warrior	Clear Arcade mode with Ryu on any difficulty.
One with Nature	One with Nature	Clear Arcade mode with Ryu on Very Hard.
Street Fighter	Street Fighter	Complete five Missions with Ryu.
Training Everyday	Training Everyday	Complete all Missions with Ryu.
Fair & Square	Fair & Square	Use Ryu 30 times.

	Unlock	Condition
Miss Princess	Miss Princess	Clear Arcade mode with Morrigan on any difficulty.
Heir to the Makai	Heir to the Makai	Clear Arcade mode with Morrigan on Very Hard.
Succubus	Succubus	Complete five Missions with Morrigan.
Darkstalker	Darkstalker	Complete all Missions with Morrigan.
Too Hot to Handle	Too Hot to Handle	Use Morrigan 30 times.

	Unlock	Condition
Original 11	Original 11	Clear Arcade mode with Chris on any difficulty.
Tough Guy	Tough Guy	Clear Arcade mode with Chris on Very Hard.
Investigating	Investigating	Complete five Missions with Chris.
S.T.A.R.S.	S.T.A.R.S.	Complete all Missions with Chris.
Big Bro	Big Bro	Use Chris 30 times.

	Unlock	Condition
Jack of All Trades	Jack of All Trades	Clear Arcade mode once with Dante on any difficulty.
Devil May Cry	Devil May Cry	Clear Arcade mode once with Dante on Very Hard.
Devil Hunter	Devil Hunter	Complete five Missions with Dante.
Devil Arms	Devil Arms	Complete all Missions with Dante.
Jackpot!	Jackpot!	Use Dante 30 times.

	Unlock	Condition
Singing and Dancing	Singing and Dancing	Clear Arcade mode once with Felicia on any difficulty.
Musical Star	Musical Star	Clear Arcade mode once with Felicia on Very Hard.
Cat Woman	Cat Woman	Complete five Missions with Felicia.
Performer	Performer	Complete all Missions with Felicia.
Thank You, Everyone!	Thank You, Everyone!	Use Felicia 30 times.

	Unlock	Condition
Dangerous Thigh Line	Dangerous Thigh Line	Clear Arcade mode once with Chun-Li on any difficulty.
Interpol	Interpol	Clear Arcade mode once with Chun-Li on Very Hard.
Gomen ne!	Gomen ne!	Complete five Missions with Chun-Li.
The Chun-Li Dynasty	The Chun-Li Dynasty	Complete all Missions with Chun-Li.
Just a Normal Girl	Just a Normal Girl	Use Chun-Li 30 times.

	Unlock	Condition
Moody	Moody	Clear Arcade mode once with Trish on any difficulty.
Filled with Light	Filled with Light	Clear Arcade mode once with Trish on Very Hard.
Safe Driver	Safe Driver	Complete five Missions with Trish.
Seize the Day	Seize the Day	Complete all Missions with Trish.
Numb All Over	Numb All Over	Use Trish 30 times.

	Unlock	Condition
Little Doggie	Little Doggie	Clear Arcade mode once with Amaterasu on any difficulty.
Okami	Okami	Clear Arcade mode once with Amaterasu on Very Hard.
No Problem	No Problem	Complete five Missions with Amaterasu.
Shiranui	Shiranui	Complete all Missions with Amaterasu.
Sun God	Sun God	Use Amaterasu 30 times.

	Unlock	Condition
Viewtiful!	Viewtiful!	Clear Arcade mode once with Viewtiful Joe on any difficulty.
Revenge of the Nerd!	Revenge of the Nerd!	Clear Arcade mode once with Viewtiful Joe on Very Hard.
Student	Student	Complete five Missions with Viewtiful Joe.
Full of Heroic Powers	Full of Heroic Powers	Complete all Missions with Viewtiful Joe.
Heroic Comeback	Heroic Comeback	Use Viewtiful Joe 30 times.

	Unlock	Condition
The Bonne Family	The Bonne Family	Clear Arcade mode once with Tron on any difficulty.
Sky Pirate	Sky Pirate	Clear Arcade mode once with Tron on Very Hard.
Get Rich Quick	Get Rich Quick	Complete five Missions with Tron.
Debt Ridden	Debt Ridden	Complete all Missions with Tron.
Prone to Mood Swings	Prone to Mood Swings	Use Tron 30 times.

	Unlock	Condition
Bad to the Bone	Bad to the Bone	Clear Arcade mode once with Wesker on any difficulty.
Virus Carrier	Virus Carrier	Clear Arcade mode once with Wesker on Very Hard.
Secret Maneuvers	Secret Maneuvers	Complete five Missions with Wesker.
Uroboros	Uroboros	Complete all Missions with Wesker.
Original Squad Leader	Original Squad Leader	Use Wesker 30 times.

	Unlock	Condition
Chivalrous Heart	Chivalrous Heart	Clear Arcade mode once with Arthur on any difficulty.
Knight of the Court	Knight of the Court	Clear Arcade mode once with Arthur on Very Hard.
Reckless	Reckless	Complete five Missions with Arthur.
Daring and Courageous	Daring and Courageous	Complete all Missions with Arthur.
Middle-Aged	Middle-Aged	Use Arthur 30 times.

	Unlock	Condition
Special Forces	Special Forces	Clear Arcade mode once with Spencer on any difficulty.
Hero Revived	Hero Revived	Clear Arcade mode once with Spencer on Very Hard.
Captain	Captain	Complete five Missions with Spencer.
Rugged Veteran	Rugged Veteran	Complete all Missions with Spencer.
Hard Boiled	Hard Boiled	Use Spencer 30 times.

	Unlock	Condition
Reploid	Reploid	Clear Arcade mode once with Zero on any difficulty.
A-Rank Hunter	A-Rank Hunter	Clear Arcade mode once with Zero on Very Hard.
Maverick Hunter	Maverick Hunter	Complete five Missions with Zero.
Special Zero Unit	Special Zero Unit	Complete all Missions with Zero.
Level Headed	Level Headed	Use Zero 30 times.

	Unlock	Condition
Spy	Spy	Clear Arcade mode once with C. Viper on any difficulty.
Secret Agent	Secret Agent	Clear Arcade mode once with C. Viper on Very Hard.
Infiltrating S.I.N.	Infiltrating S.I.N.	Complete five Missions with C. Viper.
Perfect at Work	Perfect at Work	Complete all Missions with C. Viper.
No Overtime	No Overtime	Use C. Viper 30 times.

	Unlock	Condition
Public Servant	Public Servant	Clear Arcade mode once with Haggar on any difficulty.
I'm the Mayor	I'm the Mayor	Clear Arcade mode once with Haggar on Very Hard.
Filled with Power	Filled with Power	Complete five Missions with Haggar.
Muscled Man	Muscled Man	Complete all Missions with Haggar.
Macho	Macho	Use Haggar 30 times.

	Unlock	Condition
Battle to the Death	Battle to the Death	Clear Arcade mode once with Akuma on any difficulty.
Need Strong Foes	Need Strong Foes	Clear Arcade mode once with Akuma on Very Hard.
True Warrior	True Warrior	Complete five Missions with Akuma.
Annihilation	Annihilation	Complete all Missions with Akuma.
Speak With My Fist	Speak With My Fist	Use Akuma 30 times.

	Unlock	Condition
Jiang Shi	Jiang Shi	Clear Arcade mode once with Hsien-Ko on any difficulty.
Chinese Ghost	Chinese Ghost	Clear Arcade mode once with Hsien-Ko on Very Hard.
Looking for Work	Looking for Work	Complete five Missions with Hsien-Ko.
Cute Corpse	Cute Corpse	Complete all Missions with Hsien-Ko.
Upstanding Values	Upstanding Values	Use Hsien-Ko 30 times.

	Unlock	Condition
I Win My Fights	I Win My Fights	Clear Arcade mode once with Wolverine on any difficulty.
Man without a Past	Man without a Past	Clear Arcade mode once with Wolverine on Very Hard.
Berserker	Berserker	Complete five Missions with Wolverine.
Professional	Professional	Complete all Missions with Wolverine.
Adamantium Powered	Adamantium Powered	Use Wolverine 30 times.

	Unlock	Condition
Scientist at Heart	Scientist at Heart	Clear Arcade mode once with Hulk on any difficulty.
Unparalleled Strength	Unparalleled Strength	Clear Arcade mode once with Hulk on Very Hard.
Bring It On!	Bring It On!	Complete five Missions with Hulk.
Power Fighter	Power Fighter	Complete all Missions with Hulk.
Man Among Boys	Man Among Boys	Use Hulk 30 times.

	Unlock	Condition
Steel Soldier	Steel Soldier	Clear Arcade mode once with Iron Man on any difficulty.
Shell Head	Shell Head	Clear Arcade mode once with Iron Man on Very Hard.
Peace Keeper	Peace Keeper	Complete five Missions with Iron Man.
Genius Inventor	Genius Inventor	Complete all Missions with Iron Man.
C.E.O.	C.E.O.	Use Iron Man 30 times.

	Unlock	Condition
Super Soldier	Super Soldier	Clear Arcade mode once with Captain America on any difficulty.
Living Legend	Living Legend	Clear Arcade mode once with Captain America on Very Hard.
No Ordinary Man	No Ordinary Man	Complete five Missions with Captain America.
Avengers Assemble!	Avengers Assemble!	Complete all Missions with Captain America.
Keeper of Freedom	Keeper of Freedom	Use Captain America 30 times.

	Unlock	Condition
Rules? What Rules?	Rules? What Rules?	Clear Arcade mode once with Deadpool on any difficulty.
Dude, I'm a NINJA!	Dude, I'm a NINJA!	Clear Arcade mode once with Deadpool on Very Hard.
Merc with a Mouth	Merc with a Mouth	Complete five Missions with Deadpool.
Gotta Have the Bling!	Gotta Have the Bling!	Complete all Missions with Deadpool.
Trigger Happy!	Trigger Happy!	Use Deadpool 30 times.

	Unlock	Condition
Created by A.I.M.	Created by A.I.M.	Clear Arcade mode once with M.O.D.O.K. on any difficulty.
Superior Smarts	Superior Smarts	Clear Arcade mode once with M.O.D.O.K. on Very Hard.
Big Headed	Big Headed	Complete five Missions with M.O.D.O.K..
Battle of Wits	Battle of Wits	Complete all Missions with M.O.D.O.K..
Artificial Human	Artificial Human	Use M.O.D.O.K. 30 times.

	Unlock	Condition
Iron Mask	Iron Mask	Clear Arcade mode once with Doctor Doom on any difficulty.
Ruler of My Own Fate	Ruler of My Own Fate	Clear Arcade mode once with Doctor Doom on Very Hard.
Perfectionist	Perfectionist	Complete five Missions with Doctor Doom.
World Conquest	World Conquest	Complete all Missions with Doctor Doom.
Dictator	Dictator	Use Doctor Doom 30 times.

	Unlock	Condition
I've Read Your Mind	I've Read Your Mind	Clear Arcade mode once with Phoenix on any difficulty.
Godlike Powers	Godlike Powers	Clear Arcade mode once with Phoenix on Very Hard.
Space Voyager	Space Voyager	Complete five Missions with Phoenix.
Marvel Girl	Marvel Girl	Complete all Missions with Phoenix.
From the Ashes	From the Ashes	Use Phoenix 30 times.

	Unlock	Condition
For Dorrek VII!	For Dorrek VII!	Clear Arcade mode once with Super-Skrull on any difficulty.
Hello Earth!	Hello Earth!	Clear Arcade mode once with Super-Skrull on Very Hard.
Check Out My Chin	Check Out My Chin	Complete five Missions with Super-Skrull.
Shapeshifter	Shapeshifter	Complete all Missions with Super-Skrull.
Elite Warrior	Elite Warrior	Use Super-Skrull 30 times.

	Unlock	Condition
Mutant Savior	Mutant Savior	Clear Arcade mode once with Magneto on any difficulty.
Charismatic Leader	Charismatic Leader	Clear Arcade mode once with Magneto on Very Hard.
Playtime Is Over	Playtime Is Over	Complete five Missions with Magneto.
By Any Means	By Any Means	Complete all Missions with Magneto.
Master of Magnetism	Master of Magnetism	Use Magneto 30 times.

	Unlock	Condition
The Power of Asgard	The Power of Asgard	Clear Arcade mode once with Thor on any difficulty.
Thunder God	Thunder God	Clear Arcade mode once with Thor on Very Hard.
Thunderstrike	Thunderstrike	Complete five Missions with Thor.
Hammer of Justice	Hammer of Justice	Complete all Missions with Thor.
Mjolnir	Mjolnir	Use Thor 30 times.

	Unlock	Condition
Rides the Wind	Rides the Wind	Clear Arcade mode once with Storm on any difficulty.
Electrifying Attacks	Electrifying Attacks	Clear Arcade mode once with Storm on Very Hard.
Heart of a Leader	Heart of a Leader	Complete five Missions with Storm.
Queen of Wakanda	Queen of Wakanda	Complete all Missions with Storm.
X-Men	X-Men	Use Storm 30 times.

	Unlock	Condition
Lawyer at Heart	Lawyer at Heart	Clear Arcade mode once with She-Hulk on any difficulty.
Career Woman	Career Woman	Clear Arcade mode once with She-Hulk on Very Hard.
Brainy Brawler	Brainy Brawler	Complete five Missions with She-Hulk.
Shapely Beauty	Shapely Beauty	Complete all Missions with She-Hulk.
Talk of the Town	Talk of the Town	Use She-Hulk 30 times.

	Unlock	Condition
Soul Eater	Soul Eater	Clear Arcade mode once with Dormammu on any difficulty.
Dark Dimension Ruler	Dark Dimension Ruler	Clear Arcade mode once with Dormammu on Very Hard.
Phantasmagoric	Phantasmagoric	Complete five Missions with Dormammu.
True Conqueror	True Conqueror	Complete all Missions with Dormammu.
Lord of Darkness	Lord of Darkness	Use Dormammu 30 times.

	Unlock	Condition
Amazing Spider-Man!	Amazing Spider-Man!	Clear Arcade mode once with Spider-Man on any difficulty.
Web Slinger	Web Slinger	Clear Arcade mode once with Spider-Man on Very Hard.
Great Power	Great Power	Complete five Missions with Spider-Man.
Great Responsibility	Great Responsibility	Complete all Missions with Spider-Man.
Spider Sense, Tingling!	Spider Sense, Tingling!	Use Spider-Man 30 times.

	Unlock	Condition
Expert	Expert	Clear Arcade mode once with Taskmaster on any difficulty.
Super Elite	Super Elite	Clear Arcade mode once with Taskmaster on Very Hard.
The Teacher	The Teacher	Complete five Missions with Taskmaster.
Mentor to Many	Mentor to Many	Complete all Missions with Taskmaster.
Master of 1000 Moves	Master of 1000 Moves	Use Taskmaster 30 times.

	Unlock	Condition
Pretty Assassin	Pretty Assassin	Clear Arcade mode once with X-23 on any difficulty.
Pedigree of Justice	Pedigree of Justice	Clear Arcade mode once with X-23 on Very Hard.
On the Run	On the Run	Complete five Missions with X-23.
Clone	Clone	Complete all Missions with X-23.
Beautiful Beast	Beautiful Beast	Use X-23 30 times.

	Unlock	Condition
Mass Production Model	Mass Production Model	Clear Arcade mode once with Sentinel on any difficulty.
Super Sized Weapon	Super Sized Weapon	Clear Arcade mode once with Sentinel on Very Hard.
Mutant Hunter	Mutant Hunter	Complete five Missions with Sentinel.
Search & Destroy	Search & Destroy	Complete all Missions with Sentinel.
Cold, Killing Machine	Cold, Killing Machine	Use Sentinel 30 times.

	Unlock	Condition
Burnin' Up!	Burnin' Up!	Win 50 times with a Hyper Combo.
Cooling Down	Cooling Down	Win once via block damage.
Schemer	Schemer	Win 10 times via block damage.
Just As Planned	Just As Planned	Win 10 times via judgment.
First Hit Wins	First Hit Wins	Get a First Attack bonus 50 times.
Reading Your Mind	Reading Your Mind	Perform a team air combo.
Win with Experience	Win with Experience	Perform a team air counter.
Bring It On!	Bring It On!	Land 30 counterhits.
Airborne Fighter	Airborne Fighter	Perform an air combo.
I Ain't Done Yet!	I Ain't Done Yet!	Win with X-Factor activated.

	Unlock	Condition
Just Started	Just Started	Win 1 match online.
Rookie	Rookie	Win 5 matches online.
Average Joe	Average Joe	Win 10 matches online.
Just You and Me	Just You and Me	Win 15 matches online.
Seeking Apprentices	Seeking Apprentices	Win 20 matches online.
Team Captain	Team Captain	Win 25 matches online.
Wise Beyond My Years	Wise Beyond My Years	Win 50 matches online.
Poetry in Motion	Poetry in Motion	Win 75 matches online.
Savvy Warrior	Savvy Warrior	Win 100 matches online.
Legend in My Mind	Legend in My Mind	Win 200 matches online.

	Unlock	Condition
Opportunist	Opportunist	Defeat an opponent who has this title.
Well Travelled	Well Travelled	Defeat an opponent who has this title.
Survivor	Survivor	Defeat an opponent who has this title.
Rebel With A Cause	Rebel With A Cause	Defeat an opponent who has this title.
Class Clown	Class Clown	Defeat an opponent who has this title.
World's Strongest	World's Strongest	Defeat an opponent who has this title.
My Stock is Rising!	My Stock is Rising!	Defeat an opponent who has this title.
Orbital	Orbital	Defeat an opponent who has this title.
Lucky Star	Lucky Star	Defeat an opponent who has this title.
Unpredictable	Unpredictable	Defeat an opponent who has this title.
My Destiny	My Destiny	Defeat an opponent who has this title.
Princess	Princess	Defeat an opponent who has this title.
Assassin	Assassin	Defeat an opponent who has this title.
I'm Invincible!	I'm Invincible!	Defeat an opponent who has this title.
Go-Getter	Go-Getter	Defeat an opponent who has this title.
Technician	Technician	Defeat an opponent who has this title.
The Last Hope	The Last Hope	Defeat an opponent who has this title.
Ninja	Ninja	Defeat an opponent who has this title.
Hybrid	Hybrid	Defeat an opponent who has this title.
Indestructible	Indestructible	Defeat an opponent who has this title.
Dare to be Stupid	Dare to be Stupid	Defeat an opponent who has this title.
The Promised Land	The Promised Land	Defeat an opponent who has this title.
Honorable	Honorable	Defeat an opponent who has this title.
I'm Famous!	I'm Famous!	Defeat an opponent who has this title.
Love of the Game	Love of the Game	Defeat an opponent who has this title.
Man, Myth, Legend	Man, Myth, Legend	Defeat an opponent who has this title.
Eastern Discipline	Eastern Discipline	Defeat an opponent who has this title.
I Need a Hug	I Need a Hug	Defeat an opponent who has this title.
Gone Too Soon	Gone Too Soon	Defeat an opponent who has this title.
Pros and Cons	Pros and Cons	Defeat an opponent who has this title.

	Unlock	Condition
Freshman	Freshman	Complete Event #1
Fundamentally Sound	Fundamentally Sound	Complete Event #2
Roll with the Punches	Roll with the Punches	Complete Event #3
Fight Like Gentlemen!	Fight Like Gentlemen!	Complete Event #4
Take You for a Ride	Take You for a Ride	Complete Event #5
Adept at Adapting	Adept at Adapting	Complete Event #6
Best at What I Do	Best at What I Do	Complete Event #7
All According to Plan	All According to Plan	Complete Event #8
Ready for War!	Ready for War!	Complete Event #9
Ready for Action!	Ready for Action!	Complete Event #10
I'm Too Good	I'm Too Good	Complete Event #11
The Graduate	The Graduate	Complete Event #12
Second-Rate Fighter	Second-Rate Fighter	Complete Event #13
Precocious	Precocious	Complete Event #14
Perfection Takes Time	Perfection Takes Time	Complete Event #15
Cool & Calm	Cool & Calm	Complete Event #16
Genius	Genius	Complete Event #17
Unleash the Beast	Unleash the Beast	Complete Event #18
Go Easy on Me	Go Easy on Me	Complete Event #19
Looking to Spar!	Looking to Spar!	Complete Event #20
Looking for Love!	Looking for Love!	Complete Event #21
Attention to Detail	Attention to Detail	Complete Event #22
Amateur	Amateur	Complete Event #23
Hardened Warrior	Hardened Warrior	Complete Event #24
Playing to Win	Playing to Win	Complete Event #25
Act on Instinct	Act on Instinct	Complete Event #26
It's Flowchart Time!	It's Flowchart Time!	Complete Event #27
Rush Down!	Rush Down!	Complete Event #28
Tough Nut to Crack	Tough Nut to Crack	Complete Event #29
Cucumber Cool	Cucumber Cool	Complete Event #30
Doing My Part	Doing My Part	Complete Event #31
Employee of the Month	Employee of the Month	Complete Event #32
Specialist	Specialist	Complete Event #33
Don't Blink	Don't Blink	Complete Event #34
It's Already Over	It's Already Over	Complete Event #35
Steel Defense	Steel Defense	Complete Event #36
Show Me Your Best!	Show Me Your Best!	Complete Event #37
Fear the Mix-Up!	Fear the Mix-Up!	Complete Event #38
One Way Street	One Way Street	Complete Event #39
You've Already Lost	You've Already Lost	Complete Event #40
Final Round!	Final Round!	Complete Event #41
Head of the Class	Head of the Class	Complete Event #42

	Unlock	Condition
Still Learning	Still Learning	Complete Event #43
Services for Sale	Services for Sale	Complete Event #44
One Hit Kill	One Hit Kill	Complete Event #45
Eternal Challenger	Eternal Challenger	Complete Event #46
Cunning Old Fox	Cunning Old Fox	Complete Event #47
Carpe Diem!	Carpe Diem!	Complete Event #48
Striker	Striker	Complete Event #49
Grappler	Grappler	Complete Event #50

	Unlock	Condition
Well Rounded	Well Rounded	Acquire 10,000 player points.
I Got Next!	I Got Next!	Acquire 20,000 player points.
Sharpshooter	Sharpshooter	Acquire 30,000 player points.
Rage Inducing	Rage Inducing	Acquire 40,000 player points.
Nice Guy	Nice Guy	Acquire 50,000 player points.
King of Kings	King of Kings	Acquire 60,000 player points.
I'll Take My Chances	I'll Take My Chances	Acquire 70,000 player points.
All or Nothing!	All or Nothing!	Acquire 80,000 player points.
This One's for Me!	This One's for Me!	Acquire 100,000 player points.

OFFICIAL STRATEGY GUIDE

By Joe Epstein, Adam Deats, Campbell Tran, and Ian Rogers

DK/BradyGAMES, a division of Penguin Group (USA) Inc.
800 East 96th Street, 3rd Floor
Indianapolis, IN 46240

ISBN: 978-07440-1287-3

Printing Code: The rightmost double-digit number is the year of the book's printing; the rightmost single-digit number is the number of the book's printing. For example, 11-1 shows that the first printing of the book occurred in 2011.

14 13 12 11 4 3 2 1

Printed in the USA.

BRADYGAMES STAFF

Global Strategy Guide Publisher
Mike Degler

Editor-In-Chief
H. Leigh Davis

Digital and Trade Category Publisher
Brian Saliba

Operations Manager
Stacey Beheler

CREDITS

Sr. Development Editor
Chris Hausermann

Book Designer
Brent Gann

Production Designer
Areva

ACKNOWLEDGMENTS

BradyGAMES sincerely thanks Capcom and Marvel for their incredible support throughout this entire project, and for a game that does justice to all of its characters. Very special thanks to Brian Oliveira, Steve Lee, Joshua Izzo, Seth Killian, and Rey Jimenez—without your tireless effort and gracious assistance, this guide would not be possible—thank you! And special thanks to everyone at Marvel for saving the day during reviews and approvals—your help was invaluable, and we're truly grateful!

Joe Epstein: My friend Daniel Maniago, a pillar of the fighting game scene, once told me that playing competitive *MvC2* made him better at thinking about life. Wait, come back—that's not as silly as you might think. Competitive games teach you to strategize, to analyze without bias, to persevere. I can't disagree with him and, in that sense, this book is a decade in the making rather than just a month. Thus, despite my passion for *MvC* and competitive fighting games, there's no way I could do it alone—not in a month, nor in ten months or ten years. I'm indebted to my co-authors Adam, Campbell, and Ian for their indispensable and tireless assistance; our editor Chris for his unerring guidance; Areva and Brent for working design miracles with giant, unwieldy blocks of jargon-filled text; and Tim and Christian for filling in for Chris at the end. I must also thank our publisher Mike and editor-in-chief Leigh for the unexpected privilege of working on the sequel to my favorite game. It was an honor. Thanks to Capcom and Marvel in general for giving us what we waited a decade for; to Josh Izzo and Steve Lee for a great kick-off meeting; and to Brian Oliveira and Seth Killian for their continued assistance throughout. Last but not least, thanks to Mia, who probably forgot she had a partner for the last month, because she kind of didn't. In my defense, it was for a good cause!

Adam Deats: I started working for BradyGAMES in 2005, a period when good American-made fighting game books were nonexistent. Five years later, after 28 books, 11 of them being fighters, I can say with certainty that we improved the quality of fighting game books in a big way. This is all thanks to Leigh Davis, Chris Hausermann, Christian Sumner, Tim Fitzpatrick, Brent Gann, Areva, and the numerous other souls at BradyGAMES who gave us the means to do this. Knowing that I won't be able to do books with you very often anymore, I want you all to know that I appreciate the opportunity you granted me and the effort you showed to make our obsessive gaming ideas come to fruition. I'll never forget it.

My fellow writers also deserve thanks. Campbell, I'm glad I pulled for you on this project. You did an outstanding job, you blew us all away. Joe, we are friends, thanks for writing another intro section that says the same thing every other fighting game book has, but bigger and better. Ian, thank you for slaving over frame data, the most mundane of all jobs. I'm also sorry to hear about the death in your girlfriend's family. I wish you both the best.

Finally, thanks goes to my family and friends, those who kept me sane during heavy work hours. Others have bailed on me when I needed them most, but you stuck around regardless and I'll always remember that.

Ian Rogers: First and foremost, I'd like to thank Michelle for being so supportive and patient while writing this guide. You helped keep me sane while working through the holidays. You're the most wonderful woman in the world. I'd also like to thank all my fellow authors for working so hard on this guide. I'd like to especially thank Joe for taking a chance on me to help author some of these guides. If you ever come to visit, I have a place to take you that has top-tier burgers and fries! Finally, shout outs to the Memphis players for getting me back into the fighting game scene. Fight nights and post-match analysis are epic!

Campbell Tran: Thanks to all my friends and family for not being jerks when I suddenly disappeared from everybody's life to work on this project. Thanks to TWG Arthur for (unknowingly) doing the math to figure out the damage scaling formula. Thanks to Seth Killian for willingly sticking around for me to bounce my wacky ideas off him. Thanks to coffee and beer for making all of this possible, and thanks to everybody else on this project for all their hard work!